The Almanac of New York City

The
Almanac
of Edited by **Kenneth T. Jackson** & **Fred Kameny**
New York City

Columbia University Press

New York

Columbia University Press
Publishers Since 1893
New York & Chichester, West Sussex
Copyright © 2008 Kenneth T. Jackson and Fred Kameny

Library of Congress Cataloging-in-Publication Data
The almanac of New York City / edited by Kenneth T.
Jackson and Fred Kameny.
p. cm.
ISBN 978-0-231-14062-1 (alk. paper) —
ISBN 978-0-231-14063-8 (pbk. : alk. paper)
1. New York (N.Y.)—Miscellanea.   2. New York
(N.Y.)—Statistics.   3. Almanacs, American—New
York (State)—New York.   I. Jackson, Kenneth T.
II. Kameny, Fred.   III. Title.
F128.3.A455   2009
974.7'1044021—dc22   2008022015
∞
Columbia University Press books are printed on
permanent and durable acid-free paper.
This book is printed on paper with recycled content.

Printed in the United States of America

C 10 9 8 7 6 5 4 3 2 1
P 10 9 8 7 6 5 4 3 2 1

References to Internet Web sites (URLs) were accurate
at the time of writing. Neither the author nor Columbia
University Press is responsible for URLs that may have
expired or changed since the manuscript was prepared.

Contents

Foreword *xiii*

Preface *xv*

1. Population

Population by Race, Citywide *3*

Population by Race and Borough, 2000 *3*

Population by Race, Hispanic Origin, and Sex, 2000 *4*

Population by Sex and Age, Citywide *5*

Selected Asian Subgroups, Citywide *6*

Selected Hispanic Subgroups, Citywide *7*

Selected Asian Subgroups by Borough, 2000 *8*

Selected Hispanic Subgroups by Borough, 2000 *9*

Population Estimates since 2000 Census by Borough (as of 1 July of Each Year) *10*

Change in Population, Census Bureau and Department of City Planning Estimates, 2000–2006 *10*

Nativity and Place of Birth, Citywide *11*

Nativity and Place of Birth by Borough, 2000 *12*

Language Spoken at Home, Citywide *13*

Language Spoken at Home by Borough, 2000 *14*

Ancestry, Citywide *15*

Ancestry by Borough, 2000 *16*

Residence Five Years before the 2000 Census *17*

Migration into the Five Boroughs between 2004 and 2005, by Previous Place of Residence *18*

Migration out of the Five Boroughs between 2004 and 2005, by Subsequent Place of Residence *20*

Population Rank of New York City and Four Largest Boroughs among Largest Cities in United States, 2000 *24*

Most Popular Baby Names in New York City and United States, 1898–2005 *24*

Population Estimates for New York–Northern New Jersey–Long Island Metropolitan Statistical Area, 2000 and 2005 *29*

Projected Population for 2010, 2020, and 2030 Compared with 2000 *30*

Estimated Population of the Planning Zone of the Regional Plan Association, 1 July 2006 *30*

2. Public Health and Safety

Population, Births, Marriages, Deaths, and Infant Mortality, 1898–2005 *33*

Leading Causes of Death, by Sex, 2004 *35*

Causes of Death, by Borough of Residence, 2005 *35*

Selected Characteristics of Deaths Due to Fatal Occupational Injuries, 2005 *41*

Life Expectancy at Selected Ages, New York City and United States, 2003 *42*

Life Expectancy by Borough, 1999 *42*

Live Births by Mother's Ethnic Group, 1989–2005 *43*

Infant Mortality Rate by Mother's Ethnic Group, 1989–2005 (per Thousand Live Births) *44*
Live Births by Mother's Birthplace and Borough of Residence, 2005 *45*
Live Births by Mother's Birthplace and Age of Mother, 2005 *46*
Marriages, Births, Deaths, and Infant Deaths by Month and Average per Day, 2005 *47*
Incidence of AIDS by Sex and Year of Diagnosis, 1980–2005 *47*
Deaths from AIDS and HIV by Sex, Borough, and Race, 2002–2005 *48*
Selected Cases of Reportable Diseases, 1940–2005 *48*
Obesity by Sex, Borough, and Age, 2003 (in Percent) *51*
Hospitals by Borough, with Number of Beds *52*
Fires and EMS Incidents, 2001–2006 *54*

3. Housing and Real Estate

Area of the City, Park Acreage, and Miles of Streets Laid Out *57*
Parks of Ten Acres or More (in Descending Order) *57*
One Hundred Tallest Buildings *60*
Historic Districts on the National Register of Historic Places *63*
Full Market and Assessed Actual Value of Real Property, Fiscal Year 2008 (Tentative Figures, in Millions) *65*
Housing Inventory, 2002 and 2005 *66*
Rental Housing Inventory by Rent Regulation Status, 2002 and 2005 *66*
Number of Owner-Occupied Units and Ownership Rate by Borough, 2002 and 2005 *67*
Vacant Units Available for Rent by Borough, 2002 and 2005 *67*
Rental Prices for Apartments in Manhattan, December 2005 *68*
Average Monthly Gross Apartment Rent for New York and Selected International Cities, 2006 *69*
Apartment Rents in New York and Selected International Cities, 2006 *70*
Prices of Cooperatives and Condominiums Citywide, July–December 2005 *71*
Prices of Cooperatives and Condominiums in Manhattan, 1997–2006 *72*
Average Cost per Square Foot of Cooperatives and Condominiums in Manhattan, 1997–2006 *74*
Highest Sale Prices for Residential Properties in Each Borough, 2006 (in Millions) *75*
Vacancy Rates and Asking Rental Rates for Commercial Office Space in Manhattan, September 2005 to
    February 2007 *76*
Housing Starts by Department of Housing and Preservation Development, Fiscal Years 1994–2003 *77*
Number of Units, New Privately Owned Residential Building Permits, 2000–2006 *78*
Public Housing Developments in Full Operation *79*

4. Crime and Justice

Police Commissioners of the City of New York *101*
District Attorneys of the Five Counties *102*
Incidence of Major Crimes, 2001–2005 *106*
Crime Complaints by Borough, Selected Years, 1990–2006 *107*
Crime Rates per 100,000 People, New York City and United States, 2002–2005 *108*
Incidence of Crimes per 100,000 People, New York City and United States, 2002–2005 *19*

Selected Inmate Statistics, Fiscal Years 2003–2006 *109*

Supreme Court Civil, Filings and Dispositions, 2005 *110*

Supreme Criminal and County Court, Felony Cases, 2005 *110*

Family Court and Supreme Integrated Domestic Violence Court Filings and Dispositions by Type of Petition, 2005 *111*

Civil Court Filings and Dispositions by Case Type and County, 2005 *112*

Criminal Court Filings and Dispositions by Case Type and County, 2005 *112*

Executions within the Present Boundaries of New York City, 1639–1890 *113*

5. Business, Economy, and Labor

Largest Employers by Number of Employees in New York City, 2005 *117*

Top Ten Industrial Firms in the Fortune 500 Based in New York City *117*

Largest Law Firms by Number of Lawyers in Metropolitan Area, 2006 *120*

Largest Architectural Firms by Number of Architects in New York Area, 2006 *120*

Largest Foundations by Market Value of Assets, 2007 *121*

Total Pay of Most Highly Compensated Chief Executives in New York Area, 2005 (in Millions) *122*

Busiest Trading Days, Weeks, Months, and Years by Volume of Shares Traded, New York Stock Exchange *124*

Range of Prices of a Seat on the New York Stock Exchange, 1869–2005 *125*

Occupation of Employed Civilians, Citywide *126*

Occupation of Employed Civilians, by Borough, 2000 *127*

Employees on Nonfarm Payrolls, September 2006 (in Thousands) *127*

Industry of Employed Civilians, Citywide *128*

Industry of Employed Civilians, by Borough, 2000 *129*

Employment and Wages in Selected Sectors, by Borough, 2002 *130*

Employment in Selected Manufacturing Sectors, by Borough, 2002 *134*

Employment in Selected Wholesale Trade Sectors, by Borough, 2002 *143*

Employment in Selected Retail Trade Sectors, by Borough, 2002 *154*

Employment in Selected Information Services, by Borough, 2002 *166*

Employment in Selected Real Estate Sectors and Rental and Leasing Sectors, by Borough, 2002 *167*

Employment in Selected Professional, Scientific, and Technical Services, by Borough, 2002 *172*

Employment in Selected Administrative and Support Services and Waste Management and Remediation Services, by Borough, 2002 *180*

Employment in Selected Educational Services, by Borough, 2002 *185*

Employment in Selected Health Care and Social Assistance Services, by Borough, 2002 *186*

Employment in Selected Arts, Entertainment, and Recreation Sectors, by Borough, 2002 *192*

Employment in Selected Accommodation and Food Services, by Borough, 2002 *195*

Employment in Selected Miscellaneous Services, by Borough, 2002 *198*

Unemployment Rate by Borough, 1994–2006 *205*

Labor Union Locals with at Least One Hundred Members, 2007 *205*

Electricity and Gas Sold and Delivered by Con Edison, 2002–2006 *209*

Gross City Product and Gross Domestic Product, 1993–2005 (in Billions of 2000 Dollars) *210*

Household Income by Borough, 1999 *210*

Median Household Income by Borough, 1999 and 2004 *211*

Family Income by Borough, 1999 *211*

Per Capita Income by Borough, 1989 and 1999 *212*

Poverty Status, Citywide *212*

Poverty Status by Borough, 2000 *213*

Average Quarter-Hour Persons Share of Radio Stations, Listeners 12 Years Old and Above, Monday–Sunday,
6 A.M.–Midnight *214*

Top Countries for International Visitors to New York City, 2005 *215*

Oldest Businesses and Organizations by Year of Founding (Selective List) *215*

Visitors to New York City (in Millions) and Spending by Visitors, 1998–2006 *217*

Largest Hotels, 2006 *218*

Oldest Restaurants in Continuous Operation *219*

Most Expensive Restaurants, 2007 (Average per Person, Including Beverage, Tax, and Tip) *220*

Consumer Expenditures, United States and New York City, 1901 to 2002–2003 *220*

Consumer Price Index for All Urban Consumers, New York–Northeastern New Jersey–Long Island Metropolitan
Statistical Area and United States, 1965–2006 *224*

Detailed Consumer Price Index for All Urban Consumers, New York–Northeastern New Jersey–Long Island
Metropolitan Statistical Area and United States, March 2007 *225*

Cost of Living in New York as Percentage of U.S. Average, 1995–2003 *227*

Average Paid Circulation of Major Newspapers, 2007 *228*

Personal Income Tax Burden and Sales Tax Burden as Percentage of Income, Tax Year 2003 *229*

Total Tax Burden for Family of Three at Selected Income Levels, New York City and United States, 2005 *230*

6. Arts and Letters

Broadway Theater Box Office and Attendance, 2001–2002 to 2005–2006 *233*

Broadway Theaters, with Number of Seats and Affiliation *234*

Longest-Running Broadway Shows *235*

Major Tony Awards, 1947–2007 *236*

Attendance at Cultural Institutions, Fiscal Years 2001–2003 *241*

Most Frequently Performed Works at the Metropolitan Opera *243*

Best-Selling Books in Metropolitan Area by Number of Copies Sold, 2006 *247*

Library Statistics, Fiscal Years 2004–2006 (in Thousands) *249*

7. Sports

New York Yankees Season Records, 1903–2007 *253*

Managers of the New York Yankees *256*

New York Yankees Team Records *257*

New York Mets Season Records, 1962–2007 *265*

Managers of the New York Mets *267*

New York Mets Team Records *268*

Season Home Attendance of Mets and Yankees, 1962–2006 *276*
New York (Baseball) Giants Season Records, 1883–1957 *276*
Brooklyn Dodgers Season Records, 1884–1957 *279*
Postseason Records of New York Baseball Teams *281*
New York (Football) Giants Season Records, 1925–2007 *284*
Head Coaches of the New York (Football) Giants *286*
New York (Football) Giants Team Records *287*
New York Jets Season Records, 1960–2007 *296*
Head Coaches of the New York Jets *298*
New York Jets Team Records *298*
New York Knicks Season Records, 1946–1947 to 2007–2008 *304*
Head Coaches of the New York Knicks *306*
New York Knicks Team Records *307*
New York Rangers Season Records, 1926–1927 to 2007–2008 *312*
Head Coaches of the New York Rangers *314*
New York Rangers Team Records *316*
Venues in New York City of Professional Sports Teams *319*
Payrolls of Professional Teams, 1988–2007 *321*
World Heavyweight Boxing Title Fights *322*
Men's and Women's Singles Winners of the U.S. Tennis Open *324*
Winners of the New York Marathon, 1970–2007 *327*
Median Finishing Times in the New York Marathon, 1970–2006 *330*
Winners of the Wanamaker Mile, Millrose Games *331*
Meet Records at the Millrose Games *332*

8. Government and Politics
Mayors of the City of New York *337*
Mayors of the City of Brooklyn *339*
Presidents of the Board of Aldermen (1898–1937) and City Council (1938–1993) *339*
Comptrollers of the City of New York *340*
Public Advocates of the City of New York *340*
Salaries of Elected and Appointed City Officials, 2007 *341*
Presidents of the Five Boroughs *343*
Results of Mayoral Elections, 1834–1894 *346*
Results of Mayoral Elections by Borough, 1897–2005 *350*
Presidential Election Results for New York City, 1836–2004 (by County 1836–1896, Including Kings,
   Queens, Richmond, and Westchester; by Borough 1900–2004) *366*
Number of Authorized Positions in Major City Agencies, 30 June 2004 *380*
Party Enrollment by Borough, 2007 *381*
Participation Rate by Borough of Registered Voters in General Elections, 1996–2006 *381*

City Revenues, Fiscal Year 2007 *383*
City Expenditures, Fiscal Year 2007 *385*
Salaries of Police Officers, Firefighters, and Teachers *388*
Government Employment by Borough, 2000 *389*

9. Transportation
Principal Bridges over Water *393*
Means of Commuting to Work by Borough, 2000 *395*
New York City Transit Statistics, 2001–2005 *385*
Transit Fare, 1913–2007 *396*
Average Weekday Ridership on Public Transportation, 2001–2005 (in Thousands) *396*
Average Weekday Traffic Volume, Bridges and Tunnels, 2000–2005 *397*
Number of Licensed Drivers and Registered Motor Vehicles, 2005 *398*
Vehicular Accidents, 2005 *399*
Factors Contributing to Vehicular Accidents, 2005 *400*
Most Dangerous Intersections for Pedestrians, 1995–2001 *402*
Average Daily Traffic Volumes into and out of New York City, Selected Years, 1963–2005 *404*
Average Cost of a Taxi Medallion, 1947–2004 *405*
Cost of a Three-Mile Taxi Ride in New York and Selected International Cities, Including Gratuity *406*
Major Airport Activity, 2001–2005 *407*
Oceanborne Cargo Tonnage, Port of New York and New Jersey, 2001–2006 (in Metric Tons) *409*

10. Education
Superintendents of the Board of Education and Schools Chancellors since Consolidation *413*
Educational Attainment by Borough, 2000 *413*
Educational Attainment Citywide, Population 25 Years and Over *414*
Percentage of Public School Students at Selected Proficiency Levels, New York City, Other Large Cities,
    and New York State, 2003 *415*
Number of Eligible Immigrant Children in New York City Public Schools from Fifteen Largest National Sources,
    March 2000 to March 2006 *415*
Public School Statistics, Fiscal Years 1999–2003 *416*
Selected Independent Schools *417*
Four-Year Outcomes for the Classes of 1991–2002, including August Graduates *420*
Nonpublic School Enrollment, 1998–1999 to 2002–2003 *421*
Enrollment at Institutions of Higher Education, 1999–2006 *421*
College and University Campuses, with Fall 2006 Enrollment *422*
Endowments of Colleges and Universities, Fiscal Year 2006 *425*

11. Environment, Flora and Fauna
Selected Weather Records *429*
Monthly Weather Averages *429*

Primary Land Use by Borough (in Acres), 2002 *436*
Resident and Nonresident Hunting, Fishing, and Trapping Licenses, Year Ended 30 September 2000 *437*
Air Quality Measurements by Monitoring Site, 1991–2006 *439*
Quality of Drinking Water, 2006 Test Results *444*
Average Daily Demand and Supply, City and Upstate, for New York City Water Supplies, 1998–2002
    (in Millions of Gallons) *453*
Sanitation Statistics, Fiscal Years 2004–2006 *454*
Percentage of Streets Acceptably Clean, Fiscal Years 1975–2006 *454*
Neighborhoods with Greatest Concentration of Selected Dog Breeds *455*
Winners of Best in Show Award, Westminster Kennel Club, 1907–2008 *456*
Top 20 Species of Trees in Central Park, 2007 *459*
Results of Christmas Bird Count in Central Park, 2004–2007 *459*

12. Religion
Number of Adherents of Major Religious Bodies, 2000 *465*
Number of Congregations of Major Religious Bodies, 2000 *468*
Percentage of Population in Each Borough Belonging to Major Religious Groups, 2000 *472*

13. Social Services
Public Assistance and Related Services, 2001–2006 *475*
Public Assistance Recipients by Borough, January 2007 *476*
Children's Services, Fiscal Years 2001–2006 *477*
Number of Homeless Persons and Families, 1980–2005 *482*

14. Memorials and Monuments
Victims of the World Trade Center Attacks by Ethnicity, Residence, and Employer *485*
Sculptures and Monuments of Central Park *486*
Gravesites of Celebrated Persons *488*

Foreword Sam Roberts

New York is a city of superlatives.

It's been the most populous city in America since 1810. It's still growing, surpassing 8 million people in 2000 for the first time and setting new population peaks every year since. (It also swells in size every workday by more than 500,000 commuters.) Twice as many people live in New York City as in the nation's second biggest city, Los Angeles. New York claims more residents than the next four most populous cities—Chicago, Houston, Philadelphia and Phoenix—combined.

New York is, as Theodore Dreiser once wrote, "so preponderantly large." It has more lawyers, doctors, teachers, security guards, hard hats, firefighters, factory workers, and more people employed in arts and entertainment than any other city. (It does not lead in agriculture, but ranks a respectable tenth nationwide in the number of residents who describe their occupation as farming, fishing, or forestry.)

More people who do not own a car, more who work at home, and more who commute to their jobs by public transportation, car-pooling, bicycle (San Francisco edges New York in motorcycle commuters), and foot. (Manhattan has more sneaker stores than gas stations.)

More who live in college dorms (the city is home to the nation's largest public and private universities, the City University of New York and New York University), nursing homes, jails, mental wards, and religious quarters than any other city in America.

In *The Almanac of New York City* Kenneth T. Jackson and Fred Kameny capture New York-by-the-numbers in a crisp, colorful, panoramic snapshot of a city founded nearly four centuries ago and forever in flux. They even answer questions you might never have thought to ask: Which opera has been performed most frequently at the Met? (*La Bohème*.) How much garbage is collected in the city on an average day? (Nearly 12,000 tons, plus another 5,400 that are recycled.) Who is the largest private

employer? (New York-Presbyterian Healthcare System, with about 25,000.) When was the longest Yankee home game? (A twenty-inning slugfest against Boston in 1967.) How many New Yorkers typically apply for state big-game hunting licenses? (More than 5,000.)

The *Almanac* reminds readers in its section on politics just how close the publisher William Randolph Hearst came to being elected mayor (he got 224,929 votes to 228,397 for George McClellan, son of the Civil War general), and it informs us that although Abraham Lincoln virtually launched his presidential campaign in New York, he resoundingly lost the city in both the 1860 and 1864 elections.

Nobody knows for sure, but dead people buried in New York over four centuries (a universe that ranges from political figures like Alexander Hamilton to President Ulysses Grant, from the saloon keeper Texas Guinan to the photographer Robert Mapplethorpe) probably outnumber all those living ones. Still, twice as many births are recorded in New York as deaths each year (more people die from falls than from firearms). Except among men in their 30s, New Yorkers have a higher life expectancy than the national average. More people get married each year than die. (The most marriages take place in August, as do the most births; the most deaths, in January.) In the last decade alone, the number of Mexican-born New Yorkers has more than tripled. (Children born to Mexican mothers now outnumber those born to Dominicans.)

In New York, change has been the only constant.

If any single number exemplifies New York it has been No. 1. Also, 24. That's the number of hours that New York is open every day, which is why it's celebrated as the city that never sleeps. (Seven, as in 24/7, might also symbolize the city, except that, as former Mayor Jimmy Walker used to say, New York is a "nine-day town.") Twenty-four is also how many dollars (or their equivalent in the iconic 60 guilders' worth of beaver pelts, tools, and other goods) that Peter Minuit paid in 1626 for Manhattan. (Don't feel too sorry for the Indians. The Lenapes, who sold it to Minuit, were from Canarsie, in what would become Brooklyn, and didn't really own the island either.)

Not every factoid about New York is quantifiable, of course. In junior high school I remember being tortured by a math teacher who challenged our algebra class to find the next number in a sequence that began 14, 23, 28, 33, 42. After a few agonizing minutes, he let us in on the joke: They are stops on the Lexington Avenue local subway line on Manhattan's East Side.

Some intangibles cannot be reduced to a number, even if, however hyperbolized, they become elevated to incontrovertible and eternal truths. Like the notorious New York attitude. In 2004, when the Democratic presidential candidates were debating in a Manhattan television studio, John Kerry got so frustrated after repeated interruptions from the panel of questioners that he finally exploded: "Let us finish answering a question!" One of the panelists politely delivered a reality check. "You're in New York," she reminded.

Sometimes numbers can convey a false precision, as Mayor Michael R. Bloomberg discovered when he sought to revoke some of the 70,000 or so parking permits that city officials believed were in circulation. He found out within a few months that, in fact, more than 142,000 had been issued.

Walter B. Wriston, the former chairman of Citicorp, recalled his baptism by municipal bureaucracy during New York's brush with bankruptcy in 1975. Frustrated by official obfuscation, he confronted Deputy Mayor James A. Cavanagh and demanded to know precisely how many employees were on the city payroll. Cavanagh fished a slip of paper out of his pocket, fumbled with it, and finally confided the figure: 397,402. But a Citicorp economist sitting next to him noticed that the paper was completely blank. "That's when I knew we were in trouble," Wriston remembered.

Also, numbers are relative. All the deserved self-congratulation that reported crime in New York has sunk to the lowest levels in nearly 50 years neglects the fact that in the 1950s and 1960s New Yorkers were hardly sanguine about going outside after dark.

Not everything that defines New York is precisely or, for that matter, eternally fixed.

With 67,000 people per square mile, Manhattan has the highest population density of any county in the country. But neither the population nor the space into which it is crammed can be measured with absolute precision. Every year the federal government revises its official population count after city planners find tens of thousands of New Yorkers whom the Census Bureau overlooked. Where do they all fit? The census states that the city covers 303 square miles. For years, the Green Book, the city's official directory, said the land area was nearly 322 square miles. (The difference, at Manhattan's current density, would accommodate another 1.2 million people.) The Department of City Planning, after synchronizing satellite images with aerial photographs, now says the correct figure is 304.8 (which includes about a square half mile of small lakes, ponds, and reservoirs, but not waterways wider than 50 feet, like the Gowanus Canal and Bronx River).

For a long time the city seal, which is festooned with beavers and windmill sails, symbols of trade and the supposed transaction between the Indians and Peter Minuit, proclaimed the city's date of birth as 1664, when the English conquered New Amsterdam and renamed it New York. That formal interpretation stood until 1975, when City Council President Paul O'Dwyer galvanized New York's Anglophobic and politically potent Gaelic community (New Yorkers who claim Irish ancestry outnumber Dutch descendants by about 20 to 1) to legally amend the date on the seal to 1625, when New Amsterdam became the seat of government of New Netherland.

But in New York, diversity is not celebrated merely as a matter of symbolism. To the delight of earlier immigrants, newcomers have been so successful in asserting their political clout over the last few decades that in addition to all the Christian, Jewish, and National holidays, no New Yorker, regardless of race, religion, or ethnicity, has to move his car to comply with alternate-side-of-the-street parking rules on the Asian lunar new year, six Muslim holy days, and the Hindu festival of lights.

A century ago, after debuting in Washington, *The Melting Pot* opened in New York. In Israel Zangwill's play the protagonist, David Quixano, a Russian Jewish immigrant, becomes smitten with the aristocratic daughter of a Russian nobleman. From the rooftop of a Lower East Side settlement house, Quixano proclaims: "America is God's Crucible, the great Melting Pot where all the races of Europe are melting and reforming!" The play ran for four months at Shuberts' Comedy Theatre in 1909. The metaphor, however flawed, would endure long after.

Today New York City is home to a record number of foreign-born—more than 3 million. Their share of the population is inching toward the historic high of about 40 percent a century ago. Hudson's violent encounters with the natives notwithstanding, New York today is home to more American Indians than any other city. Also, more people who speak Yiddish. (They outnumber the American Indians. Yiddish speakers are declining, but the number who speak Hebrew is increasing.) Spanish, Urdu, Arabic, Chinese, Japanese, and English. More who identify their heritage as Italian, German, Scottish, Nigerian, and Swiss. More Hispanic residents than any other city in the United States. More who claim Irish ancestry than any city in the world — even Dublin, by one count. More West Indians than any city outside the West Indies. More Chinese than any city outside Asia. More Puerto Ricans than any city anywhere. More people born in Pakistan, France, Greece, Israel, Lebanon, Ghana, New Zealand, the Dominican Republic—in virtually every country except for Cuba, Mexico, and a few others. Even more people who say they were born at sea.

At 7:46 a.m. Eastern time on October 17, 2006, at the exact moment that the Census Bureau estimated the 300 millionth American would be born, Emanuel Plata weighed in at 6 pounds, 15 ounces at Elmhurst Hospital Center in Queens. His parents, Mexican immigrants, lived in Brooklyn. His father worked as a cook in one of the city's 10,000 restaurants. One of the attending doctors

was from Argentina. They were assisted by a nurse from Russia and another from India. The anesthesiologist was from Bulgaria.

For all the recurring angst about the mongrelization of America, the fears that foreigners are less bent on assimilating, what are the most common baby names in the most diverse big city on Earth? Ashley and Michael (among Asians, Emily and Ryan).

Like the dots that hint at the outlines of a paint-by-numbers matrix, raw numbers can suggest dimensions, broad outlines, the degree of change over time and the distance between two points. New York grew enormously in land area in 1898, when what are now the boroughs of Brooklyn, Queens, the Bronx, and Staten Island were incorporated with Manhattan to create Greater New York. Later, in the twentieth century, newer cities in the more sparsely settled South and West expanded by voraciously annexing adjacent territory. (Los Angeles, Houston, Phoenix, San Antonio, even Jacksonville encompass more square miles than New York.)

Apart from its more or less collaborative consolidation a century ago, though, New York has grown largely not by exercising political muscle over its neighbors, but by flexing its physical profile—bulging its borders by gradually filling in the shorelines that flank all five boroughs (which explains why streets with nautically inspired names like Beach or Water are essentially landlocked). Since Henry Hudson navigated what would become his eponymous river in 1609 (it was also known as the North River, to distinguish it from the Delaware to the south), Manhattan alone has reclaimed more than 1,200 acres from the Hudson, from the Harlem and East Rivers, and from the upper bay—enough land to accommodate another incarnation of Central Park, with hundreds of acres to spare. (How that space is allotted varies enormously, even within each borough: The Bronx, emblematic of urban America, has a higher proportion of parkland than the other four boroughs; in Manhattan, parking lots and garages account for a bigger footprint than one- and two-family homes.)

For all its superlatives, New York is also a city of

contradictions. It sprawls over 300-odd square miles, but even with the proliferation of homogenizing drugstores and bank branches and coffee bars, New York remains a composite of tiny neighborhoods. "Many a New Yorker spends a lifetime within the confines of an area smaller than a country village," E. B. White wrote a half century ago in a lyrical ode to his adoptive city.

Some of the very strengths that distinguish it have also threatened its survival. In Manhattan the disparity between rich and poor is greater than in any other county in the country. (The top fifth of earners make fifty-two times what the lowest fifth make, $365,826, compared with $7,047—a disparity comparable to the differential in Namibia. The highest- and lowest-earning census tracts, Trump Tower on Fifth Avenue and the Wagner Houses in Harlem, are only sixty blocks apart.) Manhattan's white toddlers are being raised by parents whose median income in 2005 was $284,000. Just across the Harlem River, 54 percent of children in the South Bronx are barely subsisting below the poverty rate. Black New Yorkers have twice the infant mortality rate of whites.

"It is," E. B. White wrote, "a miracle that New York works at all." But for all the Cassandras who—in horror or in resentment—have prematurely predicted the city's demise, who saw the seeds of its destruction in the shift of population and political power to the South and the West, in globalization, or in technology that might seem to render the very rationale for cities obsolete, New York has rebounded. Today it is home to one in thirty-six Americans, to more people than live in thirty-nine states. People leave and they continue to come (a decisive majority of the city's residents were born someplace else), because, White wrote, "the city makes up for its hazards and deficiencies by supplying its citizens with massive doses of a supplementary vitamin—the sense of belonging to something unique, cosmopolitan, mighty, and unparalleled."

New York's legendary power broker, Robert Moses, would tell the story of the out-of-town congressman who brought his family to visit the 1939 World's Fair. His son, enraptured by the vista from the Empire State Building, declared: "Dad, this is the most beautiful thing in the country!" To which the congressman replied: "Son, this isn't even part of the United States!"

But if Rudolph Giuliani was lionized as America's Mayor, it was because he was mayor—like John Lindsay and Edward I. Koch before him—of America's City, a city that, as the whole country becomes more diverse, is today, arguably, more American than ever before. In 2008 at least two New York candidates were, for the first time in decades, considered serious contenders for their party's presidential nomination.

New York was the nation's first capital. As Robert Moses once reminded us, it was where Stephen Foster conceived his nostalgic ballads of the South (before being committed to the psychiatric ward at Bellevue Hospital); where Paul Dresser was credited with writing "The Banks of the Wabash," which became Indiana's anthem; where George M. Cohan composed what would become the nation's World War I rallying cries, "I'm a Yankee Doodle Dandy" and "Over There"; and where Irving Berlin wrote the quintessential national hymn, "God Bless America."

With all due respect to Plymouth and St. Augustine, to Santa Fe and even to Jamestown, the Dutch colony founded after Henry Hudson's voyage 400 years ago was very different on at least two counts. Its agenda was the furtherance of free trade and to accomplish that goal it tolerated, even encouraged, tolerance. And it endured. It evolved. It thrived. Unlike, say, Jamestown, which celebrated its quatracentennial in 2007 as America's birthplace. (The lead ship in Terence Malik's movie about Jamestown, *The New World,* was actually played by a replica of Hudson's Half Moon.)

Kenneth T. Jackson, the coeditor of *The Almanac of New York City,* didn't begrudge Jamestown its celebration. He merely put it in perspective: "In Jamestown, they discover a town that disappears into the mud," he said. "New York becomes the greatest city in the world."

What all the numbers add up to, as Professor Jackson likes to say, is that, "America begins in New York."

Preface

In the 1960s the real estate developer Seymour Durst began assembling a library of books and memorabilia about New York City. By the time of his death in 1995, his collection consisted of more than 13,000 volumes. He divided them topically—journalism, sports, neighborhoods, crime, politics, and the like—and his townhouse came to be engulfed and defined by this trove of information about the nation's greatest city. At his death the Old York Library passed into the hands of the City University of New York. It now informs the work of many dozens of scholars who take New York City as their subject.

Even Durst's huge collection was incomplete, because some articles, books, dissertations, and reports about the city eluded his grasp. Moreover, in excess of 1,000 new books about the city have been published in the years since Durst died. Gotham continues to capture the imagination and interest of more authors and scholars than any other place in the United States. Indeed, only London, Paris, and Tokyo come close to engendering books on the scale of those dealing with New York.

Our many thousands of predecessors constitute a distinguished group. Their work includes studies of the city's geography and natural environment, its art and architecture, its extensive transportation system, and its 475 neighborhoods and 1,500 suburbs, not to mention guidebooks of every description, anthologies of prose and poetry, and even an encyclopedia (on which both editors of the *Almanac* worked). But no book has done what *The Almanac of New York City* does: capture in tables, lists, and graphs—and in these alone—one of the most important metropolises of the world.

Why a book like the *Almanac* has never been attempted is a mystery. The city may simply be too big and have too much information available about it. Moreover, three of the fields that predominate in New York City—business, politics, and sports—are inherently statistical and quantitative. A book about the city focused on just one of those topics is potentially limitless.

Because so much information exists, judgments must be made when compiling an almanac about the city. Should it emphasize the city as a whole or its boroughs and neighborhoods? Which topics are worthy of inclusion? How should the book be organized? Which sources can be trusted? Data may be objective, but selecting data and deciding how to present them are always subjective.

We have attempted to strike a balance between the contemporary and the historical, and between the citywide and the local. In the chapter on government and politics, for example, we show the results of presidential and mayoral elections, by borough, as far back as they are available. But the results are not broken down to the precinct level: if they were, many other topics would need to be sacrificed. Although the section on weather records shows the hottest and coldest temperatures ever recorded in the city, it does not record the hottest and coldest temperatures for every day on the calendar. Such data are available, but they are voluminous, and not likely to be of interest to most readers. The same desire for balance informs our approach to Web sites and other electronic sources. Because they are inherently ephemeral and less stable than printed works, we have used electronic sources sparingly. However, to have excluded them completely would have deprived the reader of much useful information.

The *Almanac* is designed to be accurate, useful, and comprehensive—and entertaining. We make no claims that this is a definitive work. If readers do not agree with our choices, we hope they will share with us both their criticisms and their suggestions for subsequent editions by writing to us at nycalmanac@yahoo.com.

This book could not have been compiled without the

help of many scholars, librarians, and colleagues in academia and publishing. We wish to single out our editor at Columbia University Press, Karen Casey; our agent, Sam Stoloff; Gladys Topkis, who provided indispensable advice when the *Almanac* was in its early stages; and Perry Gartner, Vin Montuori, and Bob Near for their research assistance.

1 Population

Population by Race, Citywide

	1990 Number	Percent	2000 Number	Percent
White non-Hispanic	3,163,125	43.2	2,801,267	35.0
Black or African American non-Hispanic	1,847,049	25.2	1,962,154	24.5
Asian and Pacific Islander non-Hispanic	489,851	6.7	783,058	9.8
American Indian and Alaska Native non-Hispanic	17,871	0.2	17,321	0.2
Other non-Hispanic	21,157	0.3	58,775	0.7
Non-Hispanic, two or more races	—	—	225,149	2.8
Hispanic origin	1,783,511	24.4	2,160,554	27.0
Total	7,322,564	100.0	8,008,278	100.0

Source: U.S. Bureau of the Census.

Population by Race and Borough, 2000

	Manhattan	Bronx	Brooklyn	Queens	Staten Island	Total
White non-Hispanic	703,873	193,651	854,532	732,895	316,316	2,801,267
Black or African American non-Hispanic	234,698	416,338	848,583	422,831	39,704	1,962,154
Asian and Pacific Islander non-Hispanic	143,863	39,032	185,094	390,164	24,905	783,058
American Indian and Alaska Native non-Hispanic	2,465	3,488	4,494	6,275	599	17,321
Other non-Hispanic	5,536	8,227	16,057	28,098	857	58,775
Non-Hispanic, two or more races	28,944	27,209	68,688	92,511	7,797	225,149
Hispanic origin	417,816	644,705	487,878	556,605	53,550	2,160,554
Total	1,537,195	1,332,650	2,465,326	2,229,379	443,728	8,008,278

Source: U.S. Bureau of the Census.

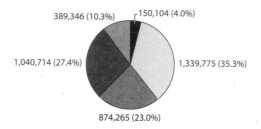

Population by Race, Hispanic Origin, and Sex, 2000
Men

389,346 (10.3%)   ┌150,104 (4.0%)

1,040,714 (27.4%)   1,339,775 (35.3%)

874,265 (23.0%)

☐ Non-Hispanic white   ▦ Non-Hispanic black   ■ Hispanic
▨ Asian and Pacific Islander   ■ Other and multiple race

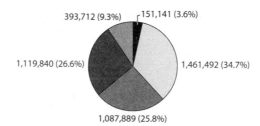

Population by Race, Hispanic Origin, and Sex, 2000
Women

393,712 (9.3%)   ┌151,141 (3.6%)

1,119,840 (26.6%)   1,461,492 (34.7%)

1,087,889 (25.8%)

☐ Non-Hispanic white   ▦ Non-Hispanic black   ■ Hispanic
▨ Asian and Pacific Islander   ■ Other and multiple race

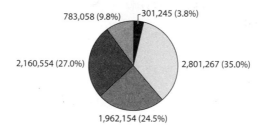

Population by Race, Hispanic Origin, and Sex, 2000
Total

783,058 (9.8%)   ┌301,245 (3.8%)

2,160,554 (27.0%)   2,801,267 (35.0%)

1,962,154 (24.5%)

☐ Non-Hispanic white   ▦ Non-Hispanic black   ■ Hispanic
▨ Asian and Pacific Islander   ■ Other and multiple race

Source: U.S. Bureau of the Census.

Population by Sex and Age, Citywide

	1990		2000		1990–2000	
	Number	Percent	Number	Percent	Number	Percent Change
Female	3,884,877	53.1	4,214,074	52.6	329,197	8.5
Male	3,437,687	46.9	3,794,204	47.4	356,517	10.7
Total	7,322,564	100.0	8,008,278	100.0	685,714	9.4
Under 5 years	509,740	7.0	540,878	6.8	31,138	6.1
5 to 9 years	457,477	6.2	561,115	7.0	103,638	22.7
10 to 14 years	450,072	6.1	530,816	6.6	80,744	17.9
15 to 19 years	470,786	6.4	520,641	6.5	49,855	10.6
20 to 24 years	576,581	7.9	589,831	7.4	13,250	2.3
25 to 29 years	695,687	9.5	680,659	8.5	−15,028	−2.6
30 to 34 years	673,723	9.2	687,362	8.6	13,639	2.0
35 to 39 years	592,364	8.1	660,901	8.3	68,537	11.6
40 to 44 years	524,246	7.2	602,379	7.5	78,133	14.9
45 to 49 years	414,989	5.7	531,118	6.6	116,129	28.0
50 to 54 years	358,853	4.9	481,267	6.0	122,414	34.1
55 to 59 years	319,941	4.4	369,105	4.6	49,164	15.4
60 to 64 years	324,788	4.4	314,349	3.9	−10,439	−3.2
65 to 69 years	298,096	4.1	259,167	3.2	−38,929	−13.1
70 to 74 years	233,635	3.2	235,627	2.9	1,992	0.9
75 to 79 years	190,692	2.6	193,221	2.4	2,529	1.3
80 to 84 years	128,340	1.8	128,139	1.6	−201	0.2
85 years and over	102,554	1.4	121,703	1.5	19,149	18.7
Median age (years)	33.7		34.2		1.5	
18 years and over	5,635,846	77.0	6,068,009	75.8	432,163	7.7
21 years and over	5,322,707	72.7	5,744,033	71.7	421,326	7.9
62 years and over	1,143,559	15.6	1,117,793	14.0	−25,766	−2.3
65 years and over	953,317	13.0	937,857	11.7	−15,460	−1.6

Source: U.S. Bureau of the Census.

Selected Asian Subgroups, Citywide

	1990 Number	Percent	2000 Number	Percent
Bangladeshi	4,955	1.0	19,148	2.2
Cambodian	2,565	0.5	1,771	0.2
Chinese	238,919	46.9	361,531	41.4
Filipino	43,229	8.5	54,993	6.3
Indian	94,590	18.5	170,899	19.6
Indonesian	1,443	0.3	2,263	0.3
Japanese	16,828	3.3	22,636	2.6
Korean	69,718	13.7	86,473	9.9
Malaysian	845	0.2	1,368	0.2
Pakistani	13,501	2.6	24,099	2.8
Sri Lankan	811	0.2	2,033	0.2
Thai	3,944	0.8	4,169	0.5
Vietnamese	8,400	1.6	11,334	1.3
Other Asian and two or more Asian categories[1]	10,207	2.0	24,330	2.8
Asian in combination with another race	—	—	85,730	9.8
Total Asian, alone or in combination	509,955	100.0	872,777	100.0

[1] For 1990 this category includes only those persons in Asian subgroups not listed in the table.
Source: U.S. Bureau of the Census.

Selected Hispanic Subgroups, Citywide

	1990 Number	Percent	2000 Number	Percent
Mexican	61,722	3.5	186,872	8.6
Puerto Rican	896,763	50.3	789,172	36.5
Cuban	56,041	3.1	41,123	1.9
Dominican	332,713	18.7	406,806	18.8
Costa Rican	6,482	0.4	4,939	0.2
Guatemalan	15,873	0.9	15,212	0.7
Honduran	22,167	1.2	25,600	1.2
Nicaraguan	9,372	0.5	6,451	0.3
Panamanian	22,707	1.3	16,847	0.8
Salvadoran	23,926	1.3	24,516	1.1
Other Central American	695	*	5,534	0.3
Argentinean	12,983	0.7	9,578	0.4
Bolivian	3,733	0.2	2,942	0.1
Chilean	6,032	0.3	5,014	0.2
Colombian	84,454	4.7	77,154	3.6
Ecuadorian	78,444	4.4	101,005	4.7
Paraguayan	1,394	0.1	1,658	0.1
Peruvian	23,257	1.3	23,567	1.1
Uruguayan	3,560	0.2	1,907	0.1
Venezuelan	4,752	0.3	6,713	0.3
Other South American	900	0.1	6,836	0.3
Other Hispanic	70,792	4.0	401,108	18.6
Unspecified Hispanic	44,749	2.5	—	—
Total Hispanic	1,783,511	100.0	2,160,554	100.0

* Less than 0.05 percent.
Source: U.S. Bureau of the Census.

Selected Asian Subgroups by Borough, 2000

	Manhattan	Bronx	Brooklyn	Queens	Staten Island	Total
Bangladeshi	819	1,691	3,795	12,786	57	19,148
Cambodian	67	1,082	494	97	31	1,771
Chinese	86,974	6,585	120,662	139,820	7,490	361,531
Filipino	8,654	4,695	6,534	30,520	4,590	54,993
Indian	14,630	15,258	25,404	109,114	6,493	170,899
Indonesian	297	40	220	1,682	24	2,263
Japanese	14,325	580	2,355	5,103	273	22,636
Korean	10,848	3,845	6,210	62,130	3,440	86,473
Malaysian	448	10	227	660	23	1,368
Pakistani	952	1,042	9,903	11,210	992	24,099
Sri Lankan	276	122	141	811	683	2,033
Thai	828	353	361	2,491	136	4,169
Vietnamese	1,370	3,044	3,410	3,268	242	11,334
Other Asian and two or more Asian categories	4,050	1,773	6,102	11,808	597	24,330
Asian in combination with another race	12,172	8,382	20,454	42,053	2,669	85,730
Total Asian, alone or in combination	156,710	48,502	206,272	433,553	27,740	872,777

Source: U.S. Bureau of the Census.

Selected Hispanic Subgroups by Borough, 2000

	Manhattan	Bronx	Brooklyn	Queens	Staten Island	Total
Mexican	30,391	34,377	58,825	55,481	7,798	186,872
Puerto Rican	119,718	319,240	213,025	108,661	28,528	789,172
Cuban	11,950	8,233	6,755	12,793	1,392	41,123
Dominican	136,283	133,087	65,694	69,875	1,867	406,806
Costa Rican	663	846	1,847	1,366	217	4,939
Guatemalan	1,146	2,403	4,037	7,379	247	15,212
Honduran	2,726	10,206	6,837	5,020	811	25,600
Nicaraguan	1,038	1,656	2,023	1,656	78	6,451
Panamanian	1,120	1,585	10,616	3,201	325	16,847
Salvadoran	2,173	3,274	5,082	13,798	189	24,516
Other Central American	567	1,438	1,669	1,763	97	5,534
Argentinean	2,585	641	1,478	4,531	343	9,578
Bolivian	250	83	183	2,318	108	2,942
Chilean	1,154	494	602	2,551	213	5,014
Colombian	5,368	3,050	6,969	60,298	1,469	77,154
Ecuadorian	10,291	12,888	18,951	57,716	1,159	101,005
Paraguayan	123	111	105	1,308	11	1,658
Peruvian	2,486	1,831	2,696	15,957	597	23,567
Uruguayan	276	98	245	1,255	33	1,907
Venezuelan	1,649	865	1,185	2,924	90	6,713
Other South American	1,011	721	1,037	3,838	229	6,836
Other Hispanic	84,848	107,578	78,017	122,916	7,749	401,108
Total Hispanic	417,816	644,705	487,878	556,605	53,550	2,160,554

Source: U.S. Bureau of the Census.

Population Estimates since 2000 Census by Borough (as of 1 July of Each Year)

	2001	2002	2003	2004	2005	2006
Manhattan	1,539,558	1,560,012	1,565,190	1,578,386	1,590,911	1,593,200
Bronx	1,334,801	1,346,550	1,358,895	1,363,875	1,362,523	1,357,589
Brooklyn	2,466,784	2,474,347	2,479,338	2,483,164	2,497,859	2,486,235
Queens	2,231,312	2,244,077	2,248,293	2,244,238	2,250,718	2,241,600
Staten Island	445,525	450,600	455,712	460,333	462,695	464,573
Total	8,017,980	8,075,586	8,107,428	8,129,996	8,164,706	8,143,197

Source: U.S. Bureau of the Census.

Change in Population, Census Bureau and Department of City Planning Estimates, 2000–2006

	U.S. Bureau of the Census, April 2000	Census Bureau Estimates, 2006	Department of City Planning Estimates, 2006
Manhattan	1,537,195	1,611,581	1,612,630
Bronx	1,332,650	1,361,473	1,371,353
Brooklyn	2,465,326	2,508,820	2,523,047
Queens	2,229,379	2,255,175	2,264,661
Staten Island	443,728	477,377	478,876
Total	8,008,278	8,214,426	8,250,567

Source: New York City Department of City Planning.

Nativity and Place of Birth, Citywide

	1990 Number	Percent	2000 Number	Percent
Born in New York State	3,887,681	53.0	3,964,551	49.5
Born in other states	875,594	11.9	798,565	10.0
Native-born, outside United States	476,358	6.5	374,130	4.7
Foreign-born				
Italy	98,868	1.3	72,481	0.9
Poland	61,265	0.8	65,999	0.8
Soviet Union	80,815	1.1	—	—
Russia	—	—	81,408	1.0
Ukraine	—	—	69,727	0.9
Other Europe	254,837	3.5	267,877	3.3
Mainland China, Hong Kong, and Taiwan	160,399	2.2	261,551	3.3
Korea	56,949	0.8	70,990	0.9
Bangladesh	8,695	0.1	42,865	0.5
India	40,419	0.6	68,263	0.9
Pakistan	14,911	0.2	39,165	0.5
Philippines	36,463	0.5	49,644	0.6
Other Asia	93,861	1.3	154,121	1.9
Egypt	10,304	0.1	15,231	0.2
Ghana	5,634	0.1	14,915	0.2
Nigeria	5,676	0.1	15,689	0.2
Other Africa	20,867	0.3	46,600	0.6
Oceania	2,819	*	4,982	0.1
Dominican Republic	225,017	3.1	369,186	4.6
Haiti	71,892	1.0	95,580	1.2
Jamaica	116,128	1.6	178,922	2.2
Trinidad and Tobago	56,478	0.8	88,794	1.1
Mexico	32,689	0.4	122,550	1.5
Honduras	17,890	0.2	32,358	0.4
Colombia	65,731	0.9	84,404	1.1
Ecuador	60,451	0.8	114,944	1.4
Guyana	76,150	1.0	130,647	1.6
Other Latin America	262,257	3.6	294,034	3.7
North America	14,584	0.2	18,066	0.2
Not reported or born at sea	130,882	1.8		
Born at sea	—		39	*
Total	7,322,564	100.0	8,008,278	100.0

* Less than 0.05 percent.
Source: U.S. Bureau of the Census.

Nativity and Place of Birth by Borough, 2000

	Manhattan	Bronx	Brooklyn	Queens	Staten Island	Total
Born in New York State	673,538	713,090	1,227,839	1,014,682	335,402	3,964,551
Born in other states	341,295	95,150	200,277	135,300	26,543	798,565
Native-born, outside						
United States	69,922	138,583	105,441	51,058	9,126	374,130
Foreign-born						
Italy	5,984	9,142	24,719	24,391	8,245	72,481
Poland	5,221	2,133	35,382	21,205	2,058	65,999
Russia	5,832	3,111	51,781	17,232	3,452	81,408
Ukraine	3,194	1,746	55,573	6,994	2,220	69,727
Other Europe	63,096	24,445	70,928	99,192	10,216	267,877
Mainland China, Hong						
Kong, and Taiwan	63,891	4,363	86,064	102,902	4,331	261,551
Korea	8,209	2,955	5,560	51,556	2,710	70,990
Bangladesh	2,252	3,990	9,756	26,589	278	42,865
India	6,354	3,440	6,838	48,132	3,499	68,263
Pakistan	1,780	1,874	16,872	17,314	1,325	39,165
Philippines	7,319	4,129	6,769	27,628	3,799	49,644
Other Asia	32,612	7,905	52,050	57,202	4,352	154,121
Egypt	1,489	505	5,942	5,314	1,981	15,231
Ghana	1,236	9,275	2,481	1,323	600	14,915
Nigeria	869	4,299	5,492	3,596	1,433	15,689
Other Africa	12,244	11,668	9,673	9,915	3,100	46,600
Oceania	3,305	97	829	599	152	4,982
Dominican Republic	125,063	124,032	59,362	59,444	1,285	369,186
Haiti	5,083	1,643	61,267	27,212	375	95,580
Jamaica	5,886	51,120	73,580	47,145	1,191	178,922
Trinidad and Tobago	2,852	6,145	52,256	26,255	1,286	88,794
Mexico	19,426	20,962	39,605	37,667	4,890	122,550
Honduras	3,426	12,774	9,117	6,019	1,022	32,358
Colombia	5,927	3,322	7,597	66,192	1,366	84,404
Ecuador	12,217	14,800	20,256	66,643	1,028	114,944
Guyana	1,727	14,868	46,425	66,918	709	130,647
Other Latin America	37,188	40,073	111,055	100,517	5,201	294,034
North America	8,758	1,011	4,535	3,216	546	18,066
Born at sea	—	—	5	27	7	39
Total	1,537,195	1,332,650	2,465,326	2,229,379	443,728	8,008,278

Source: U.S. Bureau of the Census.

Language Spoken at Home, Citywide

	1990 Number	Percent	2000 Number	Percent
English only	4,026,683	59.0	3,920,797	52.4
Spanish/Spanish Creole	1,498,548	22.0	1,832,402	24.5
Chinese	210,979	3.1	323,517	4.3
French/French Creole	151,200	2.2	195,079	2.6
Russian	67,334	1.0	194,696	2.6
Indic language	60,353	0.9	152,158	2.0
Italian	203,935	3.0	139,698	3.9
Yiddish	91,598	1.3	82,870	2.3
Korean	63,267	0.9	77,172	2.2
Polish	47,510	0.7	60,772	1.7
Greek	59,440	0.9	58,476	1.6
Hebrew	40,044	0.6	50,372	1.4
Arabic	29,910	1.1	49,080	1.4
Tagalog	34,191	1.2	45,861	1.3
African language	15,877	0.6	45,026	1.3
Other language	219,587	3.2	247,626	3.3
Total population over 5 years	6,820,456	100.0	7,475,602	100.0

Source: U.S. Bureau of the Census.

Language Spoken at Home by Borough, 2000

	Manhattan	Bronx	Brooklyn	Queens	Staten Island	Total
English only	849,603	578,996	1,217,121	968,415	306,662	3,920,797
Spanish/Spanish Creole	364,141	534,660	411,346	485,046	37,209	1,832,402
Chinese	75,876	5,848	108,614	126,904	6,275	323,517
French/French Creole	35,735	12,670	97,862	46,730	2,082	195,079
Russian	9,144	5,396	135,980	36,517	7,659	194,696
Indic language	10,237	9,092	33,054	95,484	4,291	152,158
Italian	12,319	16,701	48,076	44,411	18,191	139,698
Yiddish	3,370	2,622	70,858	5,472	548	82,870
Korean	7,816	3,149	5,740	57,447	3,020	77,172
Polish	3,806	1,099	32,509	20,883	2,475	60,772
Greek	4,705	2,945	9,630	39,418	1,778	58,476
Hebrew	10,077	1,531	25,980	10,560	2,224	50,372
Arabic	5,342	2,655	24,968	12,504	3,611	49,080
Tagalog	5,795	3,981	5,700	26,436	3,949	45,861
African language	5,695	19,053	10,397	7,026	2,855	45,026
Other language	58,354	24,694	47,388	105,617	11,573	247,626
Total population over 5 years	1,462,015	1,225,092	2,285,223	2,088,870	414,402	7,475,602

Source: U.S. Bureau of the Census.

Ancestry, Citywide

	1990	2000	Percent Change
Albanian	6,703	24,577	266.7
Egyptian	10,625	17,223	62.1
Lebanese	10,462	11,419	9.1
Other Arab	30,490	42,323	38.8
Austrian	69,427	33,605	−51.6
Brazilian	6,975	12,176	74.6
English	172,709	124,821	−27.7
French	63,539	52,907	−16.7
German	395,230	255,536	−35.3
Greek	82,690	80,145	−3.1
Guyanese	53,028	99,537	87.7
Hungarian	75,721	48,879	−35.4
Irish	535,128	420,810	−21.4
Israeli	17,150	20,946	22.1
Italian	838,780	692,739	−17.4
Norwegian	25,415	23,849	−6.2
Polish	296,809	213,447	−28.1
Romanian	38,858	30,360	−21.9
Russian	298,936	243,015	−18.7
Scotch-Irish	26,751	21,951	−17.9
Scottish	39,824	32,024	−19.6
Nigerian	7,541	17,928	137.7
Other Sub-Saharan African	46,169	104,497	263.4
Swedish	25,008	20,644	−17.5
Ukrainian	31,861	62,695	96.8
Haitian	85,592	118,769	38.8
Jamaican	145,251	212,972	36.6
Trinidadian and Tobagonian	38,919	75,584	94.2
Other non-Hispanic West Indian	121,982	142,339	16.7

Note: Respondents may report more than one ancestry.
Source: U.S. Bureau of the Census.

Ancestry by Borough, 2000

	Manhattan	Bronx	Brooklyn	Queens	Staten Island	Total
Albanian	1,705	7,101	6,121	5,347	4,303	24,577
Egyptian	1,654	475	6,572	5,867	2,655	17,223
Lebanese	2,622	332	5,650	1,851	964	11,419
Other Arab	6,343	2,298	23,517	8,447	1,718	42,323
Austrian	14,156	2,196	6,089	9,741	1,423	33,605
Brazilian	3,818	496	1,098	6,342	422	12,176
English	66,681	5,245	23,018	20,115	9,762	124,821
French	25,728	3,386	9,296	10,720	3,777	52,907
German	91,492	17,620	39,647	79,013	27,764	255,536
Greek	12,162	4,385	13,639	45,257	4,702	80,145
Guyanese	1,482	9,852	38,519	48,970	714	99,537
Hungarian	15,092	2,967	16,763	11,750	2,307	48,879
Irish	104,849	42,051	80,929	121,917	71,064	420,810
Israeli	5,657	688	8,245	5,273	1,083	20,946
Italian	84,956	69,289	183,868	187,540	167,086	692,739
Norwegian	6,901	862	7,345	2,199	6,542	23,849
Polish	53,662	9,346	71,842	60,192	18,405	213,447
Romanian	7,372	1,372	6,661	14,120	835	30,360
Russian	75,885	9,764	93,742	51,192	12,432	243,015
Scotch-Irish	9,814	974	4,252	4,161	2,750	21,951
Scottish	16,898	1,394	6,257	4,908	2,567	32,024
Nigerian	990	4,559	6,260	4,477	1,642	17,928
Other Sub-Saharan African	17,998	31,702	32,103	17,473	5,221	104,497
Swedish	10,328	828	4,376	3,079	2,033	20,644
Ukrainian	9,343	2,297	37,771	10,306	2,978	62,695
Haitian	6,493	2,845	74,152	34,699	580	118,769
Jamaican	8,494	61,081	86,785	54,421	2,191	212,972
Trinidadian and Tobagonian	2,523	4,700	47,389	19,782	1,190	75,584
Other non-Hispanic West Indian	9,677	27,181	75,423	27,726	2,332	142,339

Note: Respondents may report more than one ancestry.
Source: U.S. Bureau of the Census.

Residence Five Years before the 2000 Census

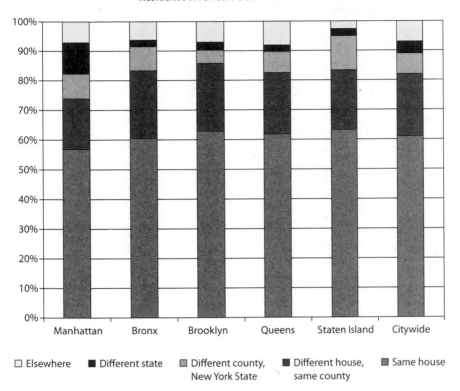

Elsewhere ■ Different state ■ Different county, New York State ■ Different house, same county ■ Same house

Source: U.S. Bureau of the Census.

Migration into the Five Boroughs between 2004 and 2005, by Previous Place of Residence

	Bronx	Brooklyn	Manhattan	Queens	Staten Island	Total
Bronx	—	2,200	5,205	2,603	244	10,252
Brooklyn	2,416	—	6,935	10,700	4,110	24,161
Manhattan	7,071	8,717		5,584	463	21,835
Queens	2,319	7,524	5,276	—	706	15,825
Staten Island	196	1,315	596	430	—	2,537
New York State						
Albany County	56	111	160	110	15	452
Dutchess County	103	116	193	102	14	528
Erie County	41	120	152	120	11	444
Nassau County	280	1,163	2,236	4,047	121	7,847
Orange County	203	152	188	139	25	707
Rockland County	172	158	421	139	10	900
Suffolk County	224	876	1,348	1,695	95	4,238
Ulster County	35	88	119	60	17	319
Westchester County	1,925	495	1,999	576	42	5,037
Other	24	772	1,200	641	81	2,718
New Jersey						
Bergen County	232	288	1,267	448	44	2,279
Burlington County	26	43	83	32	17	201
Essex County	187	313	632	199	43	1,374
Hudson County	283	567	1,811	571	101	3,333
Mercer County	20	86	268	55	11	440
Middlesex County	106	268	506	290	168	1,338
Monmouth County	26	194	450	118	129	917
Morris County	35	101	422	98	26	682
Ocean County	28	92	80	44	73	317
Passaic County	167	97	245	96	15	620
Somerset County	23	77	191	50	18	359
Union County	89	166	290	126	51	722
Connecticut						
New Haven County	96	163	440	133	18	850
Arizona						
Maricopa County	17	90	213	83	10	413

Migration into the Five Boroughs between 2004 and 2005, by Previous Place of Residence (continued)

	Bronx	Brooklyn	Manhattan	Queens	Staten Island	Total
California						
Los Angeles County	57	476	1,569	327	34	2,463
San Diego County	34	125	326	90	18	593
Florida						
Brevard County	11	33	28	24	13	109
Broward County	108	268	296	284	47	1,003
Hillsborough County	52	85	129	86	13	365
Miami-Dade County	172	256	536	292	21	1,277
Orange County	124	133	135	172	14	578
Palm Beach County	53	130	285	127	39	634
Pinellas County	22	44	91	52	14	223
Hawaii						
Honolulu County	18	43	73	56	17	207
Illinois						
Cook County	46	376	1,111	190	21	1,744
Massachusetts						
Middlesex County	50	324	1,058	153	15	1,600
Nevada						
Clark County	18	47	95	52	23	235
North Carolina						
Cumberland County	24	47	23	23	13	130
Pennsylvania						
Monroe County	64	90	55	69	26	304
Philadelphia County	125	299	682	157	14	1,277
Pike County	10	28	21	22	14	95
Virginia						
Fairfax County	19	98	297	64	11	489
Other Northeast	1,287	2,441	6,033	1,681	209	11,651
Other Midwest	368	1,570	3,206	982	97	6,223
Other South	1,472	3,980	7,078	2,779	344	15,653
Other West	240	1,672	4,009	832	107	6,860
Foreign	655	1,031	6,192	1,157	102	9,137
Totals	21,429	39,948	66,254	38,960	7,904	174,495

Note: Figures based on records for individual income tax forms 1040, 1040A, and 1040EZ (foreign category also includes forms 1040NR, 1040PR, 1040VI, and 1040SS) processed through the 39th week in the IRS's processing year.
Source: Internal Revenue Service.

Migration out of the Five Boroughs between 2004 and 2005, by Subsequent Place of Residence

	Bronx	Brooklyn	Manhattan	Queens	Staten Island	Total
Bronx	—	2,416	7,071	2,319	196	12,002
Brooklyn	2,200	—	8,717	7,524	1,315	19,756
Manhattan	5,205	6,935	—	5,276	596	18,012
Queens	2,603	10,700	5,584	—	430	19,317
Staten Island	244	4,110	463	706	—	5,523
New York State						
Albany County	87	146	121	118	15	487
Delaware County	19	31	45	39	13	147
Dutchess County	291	151	238	186	29	895
Erie County	53	103	93	91	14	354
Greene County	15	46	40	66	12	179
Monroe County	45	87	111	77	11	331
Nassau County	457	2,072	1,470	7,770	154	11,923
Orange County	738	367	310	390	101	1,906
Rockland County	426	287	345	242	29	1,329
Saratoga County	14	24	36	43	13	130
Suffolk County	428	1,314	1,081	2,983	120	5,926
Sullivan County	78	104	88	104	20	394
Ulster County	59	144	161	92	22	478
Westchester County	3,631	757	2,309	1,006	69	7,772
Other	506	590	607	670	81	2,454
New Jersey						
Atlantic County	43	61	48	60	18	230
Bergen County	600	572	1,501	992	115	3,780
Burlington County	34	117	59	95	42	347
Camden County	57	101	86	67	17	328
Essex County	359	671	846	483	107	2,466
Hudson County	471	929	2,422	1,014	189	5,025
Mercer County	42	123	194	126	49	534
Middlesex County	235	856	420	794	638	2,943
Monmouth County	52	621	365	240	703	1,981
Morris County	48	133	301	188	60	730
Ocean County	51	286	80	106	368	891
Passaic County	243	177	277	244	24	965
Somerset County	44	149	155	132	100	580

Migration out of the Five Boroughs between 2004 and 2005, by Subsequent Place of Residence (continued)

	Bronx	Brooklyn	Manhattan	Queens	Staten Island	Total
New Jersey (continued)						
Sussex County	17	27	41	31	18	134
Union County	177	384	363	348	109	1,381
Connecticut						
Fairfield County	454	295	1,178	423	31	2,381
Hartford County	115	144	133	162	12	566
New Haven County	294	248	341	213	22	1,118
Arizona						
Maricopa County	72	157	178	235	58	700
California						
Los Angeles County	102	679	2,039	536	60	3,416
Orange County	14	76	204	105	12	411
San Diego County	60	134	308	130	24	656
San Francisco County	21	230	756	101	11	1,119
Delaware						
New Castle County	63	133	158	113	21	488
District of Columbia						
Washington	47	187	591	96	10	931
Florida						
Brevard County	59	107	35	110	25	336
Broward County	419	839	493	1,140	138	3,029
Collier County	23	34	50	66	32	205
Duval County	69	101	70	102	18	360
Flagler County	26	72	11	42	20	171
Hillsborough County	289	334	171	392	74	1,260
Lake County	81	68	13	196	27	385
Lee County	65	105	65	134	57	426
Manatee County	15	24	28	37	16	120
Marion County	75	69	31	130	15	320
Miami-Dade County	374	524	826	713	58	2,495
Orange County	585	536	241	883	64	2,309
Osceola County	278	259	85	349	35	1,006
Palm Beach County	218	448	433	696	160	1,955
Pasco County	59	97	27	146	62	391
Pinellas County	78	118	79	168	56	499

Migration out of the Five Boroughs between 2004 and 2005, by Subsequent Place of Residence (continued)

	Bronx	Brooklyn	Manhattan	Queens	Staten Island	Total
Florida (continued)						
Polk County	87	76	27	146	27	363
St. Lucie County	69	85	28	140	43	365
Sarasota County	18	63	72	79	18	250
Seminole County	126	108	38	157	34	463
Volusia County	84	88	33	116	39	360
Georgia						
De Kalb County	121	265	147	197	17	747
Fulton County	80	162	232	136	15	625
Gwinnett County	142	202	64	315	26	749
Illinois						
Cook County	85	287	788	191	24	1,375
Maryland						
Anne Arundel County	17	44	31	47	11	150
Baltimore County	66	147	90	129	15	447
Montgomery County	71	168	267	154	13	673
Prince George's County	109	156	77	138	17	497
Massachusetts						
Middlesex County	56	205	494	139	19	913
Suffolk County	91	187	590	120	10	998
Worcester County	99	56	78	40	10	283
Nevada						
Clark County	84	162	163	296	59	764
North Carolina						
Mecklenburg County	132	225	177	276	31	841
New Hanover County	28	22	17	15	11	93
Onslow County	13	46	12	41	13	125
Wake County	79	157	116	119	19	490
Ohio						
Cuyahoga County	32	90	96	39	10	267
Pennsylvania						
Berks County	139	166	82	117	13	517
Bucks County	20	78	92	80	33	303
Lehigh County	158	255	129	167	37	746
Monroe County	271	355	120	356	144	1,246

Migration out of the Five Boroughs between 2004 and 2005, by Subsequent Place of Residence (continued)

	Bronx	Brooklyn	Manhattan	Queens	Staten Island	Total
Pennsylvania (continued)						
Montgomery County	23	79	149	91	17	359
Northampton County	43	111	39	77	63	333
Philadelphia County	196	556	634	298	47	1,731
Pike County	61	97	54	93	55	360
Wayne County	12	44	16	32	22	126
Texas						
Harris County	99	142	232	189	17	679
Virginia						
Chesterfield County	25	46	24	57	14	166
Fairfax County	60	131	146	167	20	524
Henrico County	47	72	37	73	10	239
Virginia Beach	62	77	49	76	23	287
Washington						
King County	33	126	250	90	10	509
Foreign						
Puerto Rico	470	173	161	103	18	925
Other	185	635	2,396	537	53	3,806
Other Northeast	963	1,566	2,200	1,250	248	6,227
Other Midwest	552	1,125	1,546	816	114	4,153
Other South	1,888	3,499	3,282	3,207	551	12,427
Other West	286	1,004	1,842	933	156	4,221
Totals	30,809	54,947	61,709	53,879	9,061	210,405

Note: Figures based on records for individual income tax forms 1040, 1040A, and 1040EZ (foreign category also includes forms 1040NR, 1040PR, 1040VI, and 1040SS) processed through the 39th week in the IRS's processing year.
Source: Internal Revenue Service.

Population Rank of New York City and Four Largest Boroughs among Largest Cities in United States, 2000

1. New York	8,008,278		Manhattan	1,537,195
2. Los Angeles	3,694,820		5. Philadelphia	1,517,550
3. Chicago	2,896,016		Bronx	1,332,650
Brooklyn	2,465,326		6. Phoenix	1,321,045
Queens	2,229,379			
4. Houston	1,953,631		Source: U.S. Bureau of the Census.	

Most Popular Baby Names in New York City and United States, 1898–2005

	Boys New York City	Boys U.S.	Girls New York City	Girls U.S.
1898	John	John	Mary	Mary
	William	William	Catherine	Anna
	Charles	George	Margaret	Helen
	George	James	Annie	Margaret
	Joseph	Joseph	Rose	Ruth
	Edward	Charles	Marie	Elizabeth
	James	Frank	Esther	Florence
	Louis	Edward	Sarah	Rose
	Francis	Robert	Frances	Lillian
	Samuel	Henry	Ida	Ethel, Marie (tie)
1928	John	Robert	Mary	Mary
	William	John	Marie	Betty
	Joseph	James	Annie	Dorothy
	James	William	Margaret	Helen
	Richard	Charles	Catherine	Margaret
	Edward	Richard	Gloria	Ruth
	Robert	Donald	Helen	Barbara
	Thomas	George	Teresa	Doris
	George	Joseph	Joan	Maria
	Louis	Edward	Barbara	Patricia
1948	Robert	Robert	Linda	Linda
	John	James	Mary	Mary
	James	John	Barbara	Patricia
	Michael	William	Patricia	Barbara

Most Popular Baby Names in New York City and United States, 1898–2005 (continued)

	Boys		Girls	
	New York City	U.S.	New York City	U.S.
1948 (continued)	William	David	Susan	Susan
	Richard	Richard	Kathleen	Maria
	Joseph	Michael	Carol	Carol
	Thomas	Thomas	Nancy	Nancy, Sandra (tie)
	Stephen	Charles	Margaret	
	David	Donald	Diane	Sharon
1980	Michael	Michael	Jennifer	Jennifer
	David	Jason	Jessica	Jessica
	Jason	Christopher	Melissa	Amanda
	Joseph	David	Nicole	Melissa
	Christopher	James	Michelle	Sarah
	Anthony	Matthew	Elizabeth	Nicole
	John	John	Lisa	Heather
	Daniel	Joshua	Christina	Amy
	Robert	Robert	Tiffany	Michelle
	James	Daniel	Maria	Elizabeth
1985	Michael	Michael	Jennifer	Jessica
	Christopher	Christopher	Jessica	Ashley
	Daniel	Matthew	Christina	Jennifer
	David	Joshua	Stephanie	Amanda
	Anthony	David	Melissa	Nicole
	Joseph	Daniel	Nicole	Sarah
	Jonathan	James	Elizabeth	Stephanie
	Jason	Joseph	Amanda	Heather
	John	Robert	Danielle	Melissa
	Robert	John	Lauren	Elizabeth
1990	Michael	Michael	Stephanie	Jessica
	Christopher	Christopher	Jessica	Ashley
	Jonathan	Joshua	Ashley	Brittany
	Anthony	Matthew	Jennifer	Amanda
	David	David	Amanda	Stephanie
	Daniel	Daniel	Samantha	Jennifer
	Joseph	Andrew	Nicole	Samantha
	Matthew	Joseph	Christina	Sarah

Most Popular Baby Names in New York City and United States, 1898–2005 (continued)

	Boys		Girls	
	New York City	U.S.	New York City	U.S.
1990 (continued)	John	Justin	Melissa	Megan
	Andrew	James	Michelle	Lauren
1995	Michael	Michael	Ashley	Emily
	Christopher	Jacob	Jessica	Ashley
	Kevin	Matthew	Amanda	Jessica
	Daniel	Joshua	Samantha	Sarah
	Jonathan	Christopher	Stephanie	Samantha
	Joseph	Daniel	Jennifer	Taylor
	Anthony	Nicholas	Nicole	Amanda
	Matthew	Tyler	Sarah	Brittany
	David	Brandon	Michelle	Elizabeth
	Justin	Austin	Emily	Rachel
1997	Michael	Michael	Ashley	Emily
	Christopher	Jacob	Samantha	Sarah
	Joseph	Matthew	Jessica	Taylor
	Matthew	Christopher	Nicole	Jessica
	Justin	Nicholas	Amanda	Ashley
	Daniel	Austin	Sarah	Samantha
	Anthony, Brandon	Joshua	Stephanie	Madison
	(tie)	Andrew	Jennifer	Hannah
	David	Joseph	Emily	Kayla
	Jonathan	Brandon	Brianna	Alexis
1998	Michael	Michael	Ashley	Emily
	Christopher	Jacob	Samantha	Hannah
	Justin	Matthew	Jessica	Samantha
	Joseph	Joshua	Amanda	Ashley
	Matthew	Christopher	Nicole	Sarah
	Anthony	Nicholas	Emily	Alexis
	Daniel	Brandon	Jennifer	Taylor
	Brandon	Tyler	Sarah	Jessica
	Nicholas	Andrew	Brianna	Madison
	David	Austin	Stephanie	Elizabeth
1999	Michael	Jacob	Ashley	Emily
	Justin	Michael	Samantha	Hannah
	Matthew	Matthew	Emily	Alexis

Most Popular Baby Names in New York City and United States, 1898–2005 (continued)

	Boys		Girls	
	New York City	U.S.	New York City	U.S.
1999 (continued)	Christopher	Joshua	Sarah	Samantha
	Joseph	Christopher	Nicole	Sarah
	Daniel	Nicholas	Kayla	Ashley
	Anthony	Andrew	Jessica	Madison
	David	Joseph	Brianna	Taylor
	Kevin	Daniel	Amanda	Jessica
	Joshua	Tyler	Jennifer	Elizabeth
2000	Michael	Jacob	Ashley	Emily
	Justin	Michael	Samantha	Hannah
	Christopher	Matthew	Kayla	Madison
	Matthew	Joshua	Emily	Ashley
	Daniel	Christopher	Brianna	Sarah
	Anthony	Nicholas	Sarah	Alexis
	Joshua	Andrew	Jessica	Samantha
	David	Joseph	Nicole	Jessica
	Joseph	Daniel	Michelle	Taylor
	Kevin	Tyler	Amanda	Elizabeth
2001	Michael	Jacob	Ashley	Emily
	Justin	Michael	Kayla	Madison
	Christopher	Matthew	Samantha	Hannah
	Daniel	Joshua	Emily	Ashley
	Matthew	Christopher	Jessica	Alexis
	Joseph	Nicholas	Brianna	Samantha
	Anthony	Andrew	Nicole	Sarah
	David	Joseph	Sarah	Abigail
	Joshua	Daniel	Destiny	Elizabeth
	Kevin	William	Michelle	Jessica
2002	Michael	Jacob	Ashley	Emily
	Justin	Michael	Emily	Madison
	Daniel	Joshua	Kayla	Hannah
	Matthew	Matthew	Brianna	Emma
	Christopher	Ethan	Samantha	Alexis
	Joseph	Andrew	Sarah	Ashley
	Anthony	Joseph	Nicole	Abigail
	Joshua	Christopher	Jessica	Sarah

Most Popular Baby Names in New York City and United States, 1898–2005 (continued)

	Boys		Girls	
	New York City	U.S.	New York City	U.S.
2002 (continued)	Nicholas	Nicholas	Michelle	Samantha
	David	Daniel	Isabella	Olivia
2003	Michael	Jacob	Emily	Emily
	Justin	Michael	Ashley	Emma
	Daniel	Joshua	Kayla	Madison
	Matthew	Matthew	Sarah	Hannah
	Christopher	Andrew	Samantha	Olivia
	Anthony	Ethan	Brianna	Abigail
	David	Joseph	Isabella	Alexis
	Joshua	Daniel	Nicole	Ashley
	Joseph	Christopher	Rachel	Elizabeth
	Kevin	Anthony	Jessica	Samantha
2004	Michael	Jacob	Emily	Emily
	Daniel	Michael	Ashley	Emma
	Matthew	Joshua	Kayla	Madison
	Justin	Matthew	Sarah	Olivia
	Joshua	Ethan	Samantha	Hannah
	David	Andrew	Isabella	Abigail
	Anthony	Daniel	Brianna	Isabella
	Christopher, Joseph	William	Sophia	Ashley
	(tie)	Joseph	Nicole	Samantha
	Ryan	Christopher	Olivia	Elizabeth
2005	Michael	Jacob	Emily	Emily
	Daniel	Michael	Ashley	Emma
	Joshua	Joshua	Kayla	Madison
	David	Matthew	Sarah	Abigail
	Justin	Ethan	Isabella	Olivia
	Matthew	Andrew	Samantha	Isabella
	Anthony	Daniel	Sophia	Hannah
	Christopher	Anthony	Nicole	Samantha
	Joseph	Christopher	Olivia	Ava
	Nicholas	Joseph	Rachel	Ashley

Sources: U.S. Social Security Administration; New York City Department of Health and Mental Hygiene, Bureau of Vital Statistics, *Summary of Vital Statistics 2004*.

Population Estimates for New York–Northern New Jersey–Long Island Metropolitan Statistical Area, 2000 and 2005

	1 April 2000	Percentage of Total Population	1 July 2005	Percentage of Total Population
Edison, N.J., metropolitan division				
Middlesex County, N.J.	750,162	4.1	786,971	4.2
Monmouth County, N.J.	615,301	3.4	635,285	3.4
Ocean County, N.J.	510,916	2.8	562,335	3.0
Somerset County, N.J.	297,490	1.6	324,186	1.7
Total	2,173,869	11.9	2,308,777	12.3
Nassau-Suffolk, N.Y., metropolitan division				
Nassau County, N.Y.	1,334,544	7.3	1,325,662	7.0
Suffolk County, N.Y.	1,419,369	7.7	1,469,715	7.8
Total	2,753,913	15.0	2,795,377	14.9
Newark-Union, N.J.–Pa., metropolitan division				
Essex County, N.J.	792,305	4.3	786,147	4.2
Hunterdon County, N.J.	121,989	0.7	130,783	0.7
Morris County, N.J.	470,212	2.6	493,160	2.6
Sussex County, N.J.	144,170	0.8	153,384	0.8
Union County, N.J.	522,541	2.9	531,088	2.8
Pike County, Pa.	46,302	0.3	58,195	0.3
Total	2,097,519	11.4	2,152,757	11.4
New York–White Plains–Wayne, N.Y.–N.J., metropolitan division				
Bergen County, N.J.	884,118	4.8	904,037	4.8
Hudson County, N.J.	608,975	3.3	601,146	3.2
Passaic County, N.J.	490,377	2.7	497,093	2.6
Bronx County, N.Y.	1,332,650	7.3	1,361,473	7.2
Kings County, N.Y.	2,465,525	13.5	2,508,820	13.3
New York County, N.Y.	1,537,372	8.4	1,611,581	8.6
Putnam County, N.Y.	95,843	0.5	100,603	0.5
Queens County, N.Y.	2,229,379	12.2	2,255,175	12.0
Richmond County, N.Y.	443,728	2.4	477,377	2.5
Rockland County, N.Y.	286,753	1.6	294,965	1.6
Westchester County, N.Y.	923,361	5.0	949,355	5.0
Total	11,298,081	61.7	11,561,625	61.4
Total, metropolitan area	18,323,382	100.0	18,818,536	100.0

Source: U.S. Bureau of the Census.

Projected Population for 2010, 2020, and 2030 Compared with 2000

	2000	2010	2020	2030	Change, 2000–2010		Change, 2000–2030	
					Number	Percent	Number	Percent
Manhattan	1,537,195	1,662,701	1,729,530	1,826,547	125,506	8.2	289,352	18.8
Bronx	1,332,650	1,401,194	1,420,277	1,457,039	68,544	5.1	124,389	9.3
Brooklyn	2,465,326	2,566,836	2,628,211	2,718,967	101,510	4.1	253,641	10.3
Queens	2,229,379	2,279,674	2,396,949	2,565,352	50,295	2.3	335,973	15.1
Staten Island	443,728	491,808	517,597	551,906	48,080	10.8	108,178	24.4
Total	8,008,278	8,402,213	8,692,564	9,119,811	393,935	4.9	1,111,533	13.9

Source: New York City Department of City Planning.

Estimated Population of the Planning Zone of the Regional Plan Association, 1 July 2006

Counties in New York State

Bronx	1,361,473	Dutchess	295,146
Kings	2,508,820	Nassau	1,325,662
New York	1,611,581	Orange	376,392
Putnam	100,603	Queens	2,255,175
Richmond	477,377	Rockland	294,965
Suffolk	1,469,715	Sullivan	76,588
Ulster	182,742	Westchester	949,355
Total	13,285,594		

Counties in New Jersey

Bergen	904,037	Essex	786,147
Hudson	601,146	Hunterdon	130,783
Mercer	367,605	Middlesex	786,971
Monmouth	635,285	Morris	493,160
Ocean	562,335	Passaic	497,093
Somerset	324,186	Sussex	153,384
Union	531,088	Warren	110,919
Total	6,884,139		

Counties in Connecticut

Fairfield	900,440	Litchfield	190,119
New Haven	845,244		
Total	1,935,803		

Total, Planning Zone	22,105,536

Source: Regional Plan Association; U.S. Bureau of the Census.

2 Public Health and Safety

Population, Births, Marriages, Deaths, and Infant Mortality, 1898–2005

| | Population | Live Births | | Marriages | | Deaths | | Infant Mortality | |
	as of April 1	Total Reported[1]	Rate per 1,000 Population	Total Reported[1]	Rate per 1,000 Population	Total Reported[1]	Rate per 1,000 Population	Total Reported[1]	Rate per 1,000 Live Births
1898–1900	3,358,000	119,000	35.4	30,535	9.1	67,503	20.1	16,264	136.7
1901–1905	3,786,000	129,000	34.1	37,988	10.0	71,689	18.9	15,611	121.0
1906–1910	4,473,000	144,000	32.2	44,966	10.1	75,865	17.0	16,609	115.3
1911–1915	5,049,000	140,581	27.8	51,157	10.1	74,666	14.8	14,060	100.0
1916–1920	5,492,000	136,101	24.8	59,081	10.8	80,435	14.6	12,004	88.2
1921–1925	6,175,000	130,462	21.1	62,710	10.2	69,303	11.2	8,985	68.9
1926–1930	6,703,000	125,590	18.7	62,278	9.3	75,395	11.2	7,662	61.0
1931–1935	7,101,000	106,179	15.0	63,273	8.9	75,561	10.6	5,521	52.0
1936–1940	7,363,000	102,418	13.9	69,184	9.4	76,065	10.3	4,079	39.8
1941–1945	7,597,000	126,495	16.7	76,086	10.0	78,382	10.3	3,525	27.9
1946–1950	7,815,000	158,926	20.3	90,914	11.6	79,708	10.2	4,139	26.0
1951–1955	7,867,000	163,526	20.8	71,689	9.1	80,583	10.2	3,986	24.4
1956	7,831,000	165,553	21.1	70,291	9.0	81,118	10.4	4,052	24.5
1957	7,818,000	166,977	21.4	69,498	8.9	84,141	10.8	4,176	25.0
1958	7,806,000	167,775	21.5	67,594	8.7	84,586	10.8	4,435	26.4
1959	7,794,000	168,138	21.6	66,887	8.6	85,352	11.0	4,458	26.5
1960	7,781,984	166,300	21.4	67,133	8.6	86,252	11.1	4,328	26.0
1961	7,793,000	168,383	21.6	66,258	8.5	86,855	11.1	4,307	25.6
1962	7,805,000	165,244	21.2	65,512	8.4	87,089	11.2	4,510	27.3
1963	7,816,000	167,848	21.5	67,886	8.7	88,621	11.3	4,334	25.8
1964	7,828,000	165,695	21.2	70,053	8.9	88,026	11.2	4,438	26.8
1965	7,839,000	158,815	20.3	71,880	9.2	87,395	11.1	4,076	25.7
1966	7,850,000	153,335	19.5	66,689	8.5	88,418	11.3	3,819	24.9
1967	7,862,000	145,802	18.5	68,876	8.8	87,610	11.1	3,489	23.9
1968	7,873,000	141,920	18.0	73,307	9.3	91,169	11.6	3,282	23.1
1969	7,885,000	146,221	18.5	75,220	9.5	88,535	11.2	3,563	24.4
1970	7,894,862	149,192	18.9	74,174	9.4	88,161	11.2	3,230	21.6
1971	7,832,000	131,920	16.8	73,810	9.4	86,724	11.1	2,751	20.9
1972	7,731,000	117,088	15.1	73,253	9.5	85,363	11.0	2,321	19.8
1973	7,648,000	110,639	14.5	70,104	9.2	82,319	10.8	2,206	19.9
1974	7,566,000	110,642	14.6	61,925	8.2	79,846	10.6	2,175	19.7
1975	7,484,000	109,418	14.6	59,591	8.0	76,312	10.2	2,110	19.3
1976	7,401,000	109,995	14.9	55,829	7.5	77,538	10.5	2,092	19.0

Population, Births, Marriages, Deaths, and Infant Mortality, 1898–2005 (continued)

| | Population | Live Births | | Marriages | | Deaths | | Infant Mortality | |
	as of April 1	Total Reported[1]	Rate per 1,000 Population	Total Reported[1]	Rate per 1,000 Population	Total Reported[1]	Rate per 1,000 Population	Total Reported[1]	Rate per 1,000 Live Births
1977	7,318,000	110,486	15.1	52,804	7.2	75,011	10.3	1,971	17.8
1978	7,236,000	106,720	14.7	54,247	7.5	73,081	10.1	1,827	17.1
1979	7,154,000	106,021	14.8	58,532	8.2	72,079	10.1	1,767	16.7
1980	7,071,639	107,066	15.1	58,637	8.3	76,625	10.8	1,719	16.1
1981	7,097,000	108,547	15.3	61,775	8.7	73,329	10.3	1,678	15.5
1982	7,122,000	111,487	15.7	66,619	9.4	73,083	10.3	1,706	15.3
1983	7,147,000	112,353	15.7	68,164	9.5	73,544	10.3	1,603	14.3
1984	7,172,000	113,332	15.8	76,336	10.6	74,278	10.4	1,540	13.6
1985	7,197,000	118,542	16.5	77,897	10.8	74,852	10.4	1,591	13.4
1986	7,222,000	122,108	16.9	82,199	11.4	75,702	10.5	1,566	12.8
1987	7,247,000	127,386	17.6	76,194	10.5	76,448	10.5	1,673	13.1
1988	7,272,000	132,226	18.2	74,137	10.2	77,817	10.7	1,770	13.4
1989	7,297,000	137,673	18.9	69,758	9.6	75,957	10.4	1,827	13.3
1990	7,322,564	139,630	19.1	71,301	9.7	73,875	10.1	1,620	11.6
1991	7,388,000	138,148	18.7	69,314	9.4	72,421	9.8	1,575	11.4
1992	7,455,000	136,002	18.2	71,947	9.7	71,001	9.5	1,390	10.2
1993	7,522,000	133,583	17.8	72,490	9.6	73,408	9.8	1,366	10.2
1994	7,590,000	133,662	17.6	70,438	9.3	71,038	9.4	1,207	9.0
1995	7,658,000	131,009	17.1	71,507	9.3	70,769	9.2	1,155	8.8
1996	7,727,000	126,901	16.4	79,361	10.3	66,784	8.6	992	7.8
1997	7,796,000	123,313	15.8	80,027	10.3	62,506	8.0	881	7.1
1998	7,866,000	124,252	15.8	53,661	6.8	61,010	7.8	843	6.8
1999	7,937,000	123,739	15.6	55,075	6.9	62,470	7.9	848	6.9
2000	8,008,278	125,563	15.7	58,291	7.3	60,839	7.6	839	6.7
2001	8,075,586	124,023	15.4	72,587	9.0	62,964	7.8	760	6.1
						60,218[2]	7.5[2]		
2002	8,107,428	122,937	15.2	65,490	8.1	59,651	7.4	742	6.0
2003	8,129,996	124,345	15.3	61,101	7.5	59,213	7.3	807	6.5
2004	8,164,706	124,099	15.4	62,057	7.6	57,466	7.0	760	6.1
2005	8,143,197	122,725	15.1	66,348	8.1	57,068	7.0	732	6.0

[1] Figures before 1956 are averages across the years presented. Figures for births from 1898 to 1913 are estimated.
[2] Excluding World Trade Center deaths.
Source: New York City Department of Health and Mental Hygiene, Bureau of Vital Statistics.

Leading Causes of Death, by Sex, 2004

	Male Number	Percent	Female Number	Percent	Total Number	Percent
Diseases of heart	9,922	36.3	12,697	42.7	22,619	39.6
Malignant neoplasms	6,469	23.7	6,897	23.2	13,366	23.4
Influenza and pneumonia	1,323	4.8	1,598	5.4	2,921	5.1
Diabetes mellitus	833	3.0	980	3.3	1,813	3.2
Cerebrovascular diseases	671	2.5	976	3.3	1,647	2.9
Chronic lower respiratory diseases	694	2.5	886	3.0	1,580	2.8
Human immunodeficiency virus (HIV) disease	949	3.5	470	1.6	1,419	2.5
Accidents except poisoning by psychoactive substance	730	2.7	429	1.4	1,159	2.0
Use of or poisoning by psychoactive substance	685	2.5	221	0.7	906	1.6
Essential hypertension and renal diseases	314	1.1	447	1.5	761	1.3
All other causes	4,762	17.4	4,115	13.8	8,877	15.6
Total	27,352	100.0	29,716	100.0	57,068	100.0

Source: New York City Department of Health and Mental Hygiene, Bureau of Vital Statistics, *Summary of Vital Statistics 2005.*

Causes of Death, by Borough of Residence, 2005

	Manhattan	Bronx	Brooklyn	Queens	Staten Island	Non-resident	Residence Unknown	Total
Natural causes								
Tuberculosis								
Respiratory	3	2	7	3	—	—	2	17
Nonrespiratory	—	1	1	2	—	—	—	4
Total tuberculosis	3	3	8	5	—	—	2	21
Septicemia	56	82	134	61	8	23	1	365
Viral hepatitis	74	98	88	60	14	46	5	385
Human immunodeficiency virus (HIV) disease	321	419	415	148	46	58	12	1,419

Causes of Death, by Borough of Residence, 2005 (continued)

	Manhattan	Bronx	Brooklyn	Queens	Staten Island	Non-resident	Residence Unknown	Total
All other infective and parasitic diseases	28	33	51	49	8	17	1	187
Malignant neoplasms								
Lip, oral cavity, and pharynx	40	37	66	38	10	23	—	214
Esophagus	77	56	63	59	28	42	1	326
Stomach	96	76	148	135	29	42	—	526
Colon, rectum, and anus	252	199	434	331	82	124	5	1,427
Liver and intrahepatic bile ducts	111	107	146	140	29	70	—	603
Pancreas	176	123	193	191	56	76	2	817
Larynx	26	24	32	19	2	16	1	120
Trachea, bronchus, lung	636	439	752	650	232	264	10	2,983
Melanoma of skin	21	10	28	28	11	36	1	135
Mesothelioma	4	2	9	10	3	10	—	38
Breast	241	169	366	276	73	134	4	1,263
Cervix uteri	24	35	45	26	11	16	—	157
Corpus uteri and uterus, part unspecified	43	42	89	60	16	27	1	278
Ovary	65	43	107	90	20	58	—	383
Prostate	153	116	213	140	36	63	3	724
Kidney and renal pelvis	36	34	52	44	12	38	1	217
Bladder	65	45	66	79	25	27	—	307
Meninges, brain, and other parts of central nervous system	53	32	68	56	17	47	—	273
Hodgkin's disease	7	5	3	11	3	9	—	38
Non-Hodgkin's lymphoma	112	60	135	98	38	90	—	533
Multiple myeloma and immunoproliferative neoplasms	49	48	67	50	8	24	1	247
Leukemia	114	71	121	101	30	123	1	561

Causes of Death, by Borough of Residence, 2005 (continued)

	Manhattan	Bronx	Brooklyn	Queens	Staten Island	Non-resident	Residence Unknown	Total
Other malignant neoplasms	246	184	317	241	42	162	4	1,196
All malignant neoplasms	2,647	1,957	3,520	2,873	813	1,521	35	13,366
In situ or benign neoplasms and neoplasms of uncertain or unknown behavior	42	38	62	61	9	33	—	245
Anemias	11	17	31	21	1	6	—	87
Diabetes mellitus	341	396	562	359	78	69	8	1,813
Mental and behavioral disorders due to use of alcohol	46	45	86	64	9	6	23	279
Mental and behavioral disorders due to use of psychoactive substance excluding alcohol and tobacco	179	187	210	131	41	71	24	843
Diseases of nervous system								
Meningitis	2	4	6	5	—	—	—	17
Parkinson's disease	65	20	19	26	4	6	—	140
Alzheimer's disease	113	41	31	72	8	3	1	269
Other diseases of nervous system	57	61	66	51	16	25	1	277
All diseases of nervous system	237	126	122	154	28	34	2	703
Diseases of heart								
Acute rheumatic fever and chronic rheumatic heart diseases	5	7	11	8	3	13	—	47
Hypertensive heart disease	348	316	494	272	28	56	8	1,522

Causes of Death, by Borough of Residence, 2005 (continued)

	Manhattan	Bronx	Brooklyn	Queens	Staten Island	Non-resident	Residence Unknown	Total
Hypertensive heart and renal disease	22	37	28	17	1	6	1	112
Chronic ischemic heart disease	2,210	2,006	5,159	4,779	1,139	647	55	15,995
Acute myocardial infarction	511	566	1,171	784	308	138	7	3,485
Cardiomyopathy	31	17	52	39	4	28	—	171
Heart failure	144	99	168	107	28	22	1	569
Other diseases of heart	164	131	185	142	31	62	3	718
All diseases of heart	3,435	3,179	7,268	6,148	1,542	972	75	22,619
Essential hypertension and hypertensive renal disease	164	185	227	125	29	28	3	761
Cerebrovascular diseases	365	270	425	398	66	119	4	1,647
Atherosclerosis	31	51	39	37	2	13	1	174
Aortic aneurysm and dissection	56	31	69	72	8	36	3	275
Other cardiovascular diseases	28	29	29	20	2	7	1	116
All major cardiovascular diseases	4,079	3,745	8,057	6,800	1,649	1,175	87	25,592
Influenza and pneumonia	659	399	860	576	298	117	12	2,921
Chronic lower respiratory diseases								
Emphysema	37	14	39	26	11	2	1	130
Asthma	38	46	53	28	10	1	1	177
Other chronic lower respiratory diseases	273	235	312	306	99	42	6	1,273
Total chronic lower respiratory diseases	348	295	404	360	120	45	8	1,580
Pneumoconiosis due to asbestos and other mineral fibers	—	2	4	3	1	—	—	10

Causes of Death, by Borough of Residence, 2005 (continued)

	Manhattan	Bronx	Brooklyn	Queens	Staten Island	Non-resident	Residence Unknown	Total
Pneumonitis due to solids and liquids	15	14	9	5	3	2	—	48
Peptic ulcer	16	12	31	28	4	5	—	96
Chronic liver disease and cirrhosis								
Alcoholic liver disease	58	58	89	57	21	26	2	311
Other chronic liver disease and cirrhosis	22	33	54	24	7	16	2	158
All chronic liver disease and cirrhosis	80	91	143	81	28	42	4	469
Cholelithiasis and other disorders of gallbladder	13	8	13	23	4	3	—	64
Nephritis, nephrotic syndrome, and nephrosis	94	95	167	116	25	23	1	521
Pregnancy, childbirth and the puerperium[1]	1	7	11	4	1	2	—	26
Certain conditions originating in the perinatal period	54	84	139	83	20	47	1	428
Congenital malformations, deformations, and chromosomal abnormalities	37	39	69	48	11	73	—	277
Symptoms, signs, and abnormal findings, not elsewhere classified	84	34	42	45	3	12	4	224
Sudden infant death syndrome	1	3	3	2	1	—	—	10
All other natural causes	483	497	696	536	97	170	11	2,490
All natural causes	9,953	8,727	15,940	12,698	3,320	3,600	241	54,479

Causes of Death, by Borough of Residence, 2005 (continued)

	Manhattan	Bronx	Brooklyn	Queens	Staten Island	Non-resident	Residence Unknown	Total
External causes								
Injury by firearms	48	84	153	82	21	24	1	413
Accidents								
Accidental poisoning by psychoactive substances, excluding alcohol and tobacco	19	5	18	12	3	5	1	63
Motor vehicle accidents	47	46	116	93	26	41	11	380
Accidental falls	76	77	116	145	19	33	4	470
Other accidents	50	36	81	82	20	27	13	309
Total accidents	192	164	331	332	68	106	29	1,222
Intentional self-harm (suicide)	113	65	112	116	32	36	7	481
Assault (homicide)	79	135	205	95	20	36	9	579
Legal intervention	1	1	2	—	—	—	1	5
Events of undetermined intent	34	28	100	54	11	21	21	269
Complications of medical and surgical care	5	4	10	3	4	6	—	32
Total external causes	424	397	761	600	135	205	67	2,589
Total deaths	10,377	9,124	16,701	13,298	3,455	3,805	308	57,068

[1] Maternal deaths exclude deaths occurring more than forty-two days after the termination of pregnancy, and include obstetrical tetanus.
Source: New York City Department of Health and Mental Hygiene, Bureau of Vital Statistics, *Summary of Vital Statistics 2005*.

Selected Characteristics of Deaths Due to Fatal Occupational Injuries, 2005

	Sex		Age Under 25	25–34	35–44	45–54	55 and Above	Total
	Male	Female						
Transportation incident	17	1	1	5	2	6	4	18
Assaults and violent acts	24	5	5	5	7	6	6	29
Homicide	15	4	5	2	4	5	3	19
Shooting	12	1	3	2	4	3	1	13
Falls	17	—	3	4	5	1	4	17
Construction	23	—	4	8	7	3	1	23
Taxicabs	4	—	—	—	—	2	2	4
Grocery stores	1	1	2	—	—	—	—	2
Eating and drinking places	3	—	—	1	—	2	—	3
Police and fire protection	5	—	—	1	3	1	—	5
White	32	2	1	6	9	11	7	34
Black	16	3	4	4	6	4	1	19
Hispanic	21	1	4	8	4	3	3	22
Asian	13	—	1	1	1	5	5	13
Total	82	6	10	19	20	23	16	88

Note: Categories other than sex, age, and race are nonexclusive.
Source: New York City Department of Health and Mental Hygiene, Bureau of Vital Statistics, *Summary of Vital Statistics 2005*.

Life Expectancy at Selected Ages, New York City and United States, 2003

Age	New York City Males	New York City Females	United States Males	United States Females	Age	New York City Males	New York City Females	United States Males	United States Females
0	75.1	80.7	74.8	80.1	45	32.8	37.5	32.8	37.0
1	74.6	80.2	74.3	79.6	50	28.6	33.0	28.5	32.4
5	70.7	76.3	70.4	75.7	55	24.7	28.6	24.4	28.0
10	65.7	71.3	65.5	70.7	60	20.9	24.4	20.4	23.8
15	60.8	66.4	60.6	65.8	65	17.4	20.5	16.8	19.8
20	56.0	61.5	55.8	60.9	70	14.0	16.7	13.5	16.0
25	51.2	56.5	51.2	56.0	75	10.9	13.1	10.5	12.6
30	46.5	51.6	46.5	51.2	80	8.3	9.8	8.0	9.6
35	41.8	46.8	41.9	46.4	85	6.2	7.1	6.0	7.2
40	37.2	42.1	37.3	41.6					

Sources: New York City Department of Health and Mental Hygiene, Bureau of Vital Statistics, *Summary of Vital Statistics 2004*; U.S. Department of Health and Human Services, Centers for Disease Control and Prevention, *National Vital Statistics Reports*, vol. 54, no. 14, *United States Life Tables, 2003* (14 April 2006).

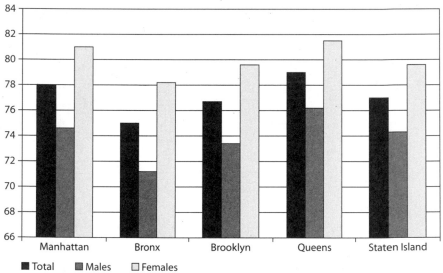

Life Expectancy by Borough, 1999

Source: Harvard Initiative for Global Health.

Live Births by Mother's Ethnic Group, 1989–2005

	Puerto Rican	Other Hispanic	Asian and Pacific Islander	Other White	Other Black	Other and Unknown	Total
1989	19,248	23,013	12,051	39,362	43,069	930	137,673
1990	19,327	24,912	12,394	38,906	42,844	1,247	139,630
1991	18,851	25,564	12,602	37,464	41,486	2,181	138,148
1992	17,856	25,556	12,688	37,102	40,662	2,138	136,002
1993	16,568	26,571	10,742	38,403	39,768	1,531	133,583
1994	15,182	28,298	11,268	38,203	39,195	1,516	133,662
1995	13,895	29,717	11,647	36,711	37,217	1,822	131,009
1996	12,925	28,114	12,782	37,215	34,798	1,067	126,901
1997	12,947	26,108	13,226	37,006	33,500	526	123,313
1998	13,056	26,793	13,132	36,957	33,675	639	124,252
1999	12,184	27,887	13,768	36,369	32,960	571	123,739
2000	11,615	28,695	15,106	36,752	32,879	516	125,563
2001	10,846	29,310	14,662	36,581	32,123	501	124,023
2002	10,678	29,229	15,396	36,445	30,690	499	122,937
2003	10,172	29,587	16,577	38,018	29,646	345	124,345
2004	10,140	29,658	16,736	37,659	29,449	457	124,099
2005	9,922	29,619	16,407	37,340	28,935	502	122,725

Source: New York City Department of Health and Mental Hygiene, Bureau of Vital Statistics, *Summary of Vital Statistics 2005*.

Infant Mortality Rate by Mother's Ethnic Group, 1989–2005
(per Thousand Live Births)

	Puerto Rican	Other Hispanic	Asian and Pacific Islander	Other White	Other Black	Total
1989	13.4	9.5	7.7	8.2	21.2	13.3
1990	12.3	7.8	5.4	7.7	18.6	11.6
1991	11.2	7.3	6.0	7.4	18.7	11.4
1992	10.9	6.7	5.8	6.1	16.6	10.2
1993	10.7	7.4	5.7	6.4	16.2	10.2
1994	7.9	6.1	5.1	5.8	15.3	9.0
1995	10.5	6.6	4.9	5.6	14.0	8.8
1996	8.7	5.8	4.4	5.3	12.9	7.8
1997	7.4	5.4	3.9	5.1	11.5	7.1
1998	6.5	4.8	3.7	5.4	10.8	6.8
1999	7.8	5.6	4.0	4.6	10.6	6.9
2000	8.4	4.9	3.9	4.5	11.1	6.7
2001	6.8	5.2	3.1	4.2	10.0	6.1
2002	7.8	5.1	2.5	4.1	10.1	6.0
2003	8.0	5.5	3.5	3.8	11.3	6.5
2004	7.5	4.5	4.1	3.5	11.6	6.1
2005	6.7	4.6	3.7	4.8	9.7	6.0

Source: New York City Department of Health and Mental Hygiene, Bureau of Vital Statistics, *Summary of Vital Statistics 2005*.

Live Births by Mother's Birthplace and Borough of Residence, 2005

	Manhattan	Bronx	Brooklyn	Queens	Staten Island	Non-resident	Residence Unknown	Total
Bangladesh	47	209	377	890	6	26	—	1,555
China	1,504	93	2,498	1,725	69	211	—	6,100
Colombia	79	54	99	799	26	74	—	1,131
Cuba	12	11	12	15	2	12	—	64
Dominican Republic	2,061	3,341	1,210	1,050	41	200	—	7,903
Ecuador	233	377	599	1,886	34	57	—	3,186
El Salvador	52	89	150	429	9	75	—	804
Germany	114	15	73	28	9	35	—	274
Guyana	29	228	784	1,139	13	82	—	2,275
Haiti	57	48	1,046	349	13	120	—	1,633
Honduras	59	346	182	163	20	24	—	794
India	179	58	136	926	49	251	—	1,599
Ireland	45	18	18	117	5	43	—	246
Israel	226	28	626	186	47	115	—	1,228
Italy	70	11	69	37	26	32	—	245
Jamaica	69	885	1,293	745	27	170	—	3,189
Korea	171	18	79	490	19	119	—	896
Mexico	978	1,676	2,431	2,295	520	46	—	7,946
Pakistan	44	78	488	416	36	72	—	1,134
Philippines	97	50	80	369	50	122	—	768
Poland	48	14	313	340	56	45	—	816
Puerto Rico	204	846	368	197	54	76	—	1,745
Russia	84	11	420	174	65	96	—	850
Trinidad and Tobago	51	99	1,018	568	31	57	—	1,824
Ukraine	63	16	458	40	86	55	—	718
United States	10,672	9,059	18,695	7,589	3,522	6,855	3	56,395
Other and not stated	2,769	3,088	5,504	4,088	740	1,213	5	17,407
Total	20,017	20,766	39,026	27,050	5,575	10,283	8	122,725

Source: New York City Department of Health and Mental Hygiene, Bureau of Vital Statistics, *Summary of Vital Statistics 2005.*

Live Births by Mother's Birthplace and Age of Mother, 2005

	Under 20	20–24	25–29	30–34	35–39	40 and Above	Unknown	Total
Bangladesh	28	364	540	419	164	40	—	1,555
China	56	1,227	2,283	1,644	704	186	—	6,100
Colombia	58	218	291	270	212	82	—	1,131
Cuba	3	4	14	18	16	9	—	64
Dominican Republic	618	1,855	2,262	1,819	1,065	284	—	7,903
Ecuador	201	769	898	720	460	138	—	3,186
El Salvador	73	169	242	192	105	23	—	804
Germany	5	21	42	102	77	27	—	274
Guyana	79	433	673	597	375	118	—	2,275
Haiti	37	177	416	508	371	124	—	1,633
Honduras	74	195	239	161	93	32	—	794
India	9	196	605	533	221	35	—	1,599
Ireland	—	7	36	100	83	20	—	246
Israel	24	200	348	404	198	54	—	1,228
Italy	1	4	40	92	79	29	—	245
Jamaica	210	602	814	741	625	197	—	3,189
Korea	1	20	202	415	221	37	—	896
Mexico	935	2,560	2,354	1,422	553	122	—	7,946
Pakistan	20	228	386	285	174	41	—	1,134
Philippines	7	51	177	262	212	59	—	768
Poland	23	107	339	235	85	27	—	816
Puerto Rico	212	406	486	375	199	67	—	1,745
Russia	14	112	280	259	134	51	—	850
Trinidad and Tobago	130	398	465	449	280	102	—	1,824
Ukraine	3	80	232	264	113	26	—	718
United States	5,231	12,183	12,966	14,019	9,333	2,663	—	56,395
Other and not stated	527	2,467	4,467	5,420	3,461	1,063	2	17,407
Total	8,579	25,053	32,097	31,725	19,613	5,656	2	122,725

Source: New York City Department of Health and Mental Hygiene, Bureau of Vital Statistics, *Summary of Vital Statistics 2005*.

Marriages, Births, Deaths, and Infant Deaths by Month and Average per Day, 2005

	Number				Average per Day			
	Marriages	Births	Deaths	Infant Deaths	Marriages	Births	Deaths	Infant Deaths
January	4,229	10,125	5,936	65	136	327	191	2.1
February	4,755	9,315	4,720	46	170	333	169	1.6
March	5,473	10,361	5,109	61	177	334	165	2.0
April	5,541	10,110	4,714	59	185	337	157	2.0
May	6,056	10,116	4,724	56	195	326	152	1.8
June	6,454	10,320	4,508	72	215	344	150	2.4
July	6,011	10,561	4,401	66	194	341	142	2.1
August	7,077	10,872	4,393	63	228	351	142	2.0
September	6,141	10,439	4,169	59	205	348	139	2.0
October	5,244	10,474	4,683	80	169	338	151	2.6
November	4,726	9,955	4,755	53	158	332	159	1.8
December	4,641	10,077	4,956	52	150	325	160	1.7
Total	66,348	122,725	57,068	732	182	336	156	2.0

Source: New York City Department of Health and Mental Hygiene, Bureau of Vital Statistics, *Summary of Vital Statistics 2005*.

Incidence of AIDS by Sex and Year of Diagnosis, 1980–2005

	Male	Female	Total		Male	Female	Total
1980–1992	46,352	10,785	57,137	2000	4,363	2,061	6,424
1993	9,517	3,169	12,686	2001	3,740	1,797	5,537
1994	9,500	3,160	12,660	2002	3,134	1,494	4,628
1995	8,304	3,053	11,357	2003	3,551	1,704	5,255
1996	6,699	2,657	9,356	2004	2,932	1,377	4,309
1997	5,109	2,284	7,393	2005	2,795	1,294	4,089
1998	3,864	1,770	5,634	Total	113,584	38,243	151,827
1999	3,724	1,638	5,362				

Source: New York City Department of Health and Mental Hygiene, Bureau of Vital Statistics, *Summary of Vital Statistics 2005*.

Deaths from AIDS and HIV by Sex, Borough, and Race, 2002–2005

	2002	2003	2004	2005
Male	1,967	1,966	1,803	1,536
Female	878	839	860	700
Manhattan	804	760	698	613
Bronx	664	665	695	548
Brooklyn	830	809	730	666
Queens	333	326	294	262
Staten Island	53	56	55	46
Unknown and outside city	161	189	191	101
Black	1,472	1,397	1,388	1,189
Hispanic	885	923	820	713
White	456	462	429	316
Asian and Pacific Islander	20	11	15	13
Native American	2	1	3	—
Other and unknown	10	11	8	5
Total	2,845	2,805	2,663	2,236

Source: New York City Department of Health and Mental Hygiene, New York City HIV/AIDS Annual Surveillance Statistics.

Selected Cases of Reportable Diseases, 1940–2005

	1940	1941–1945	1946–1950	1951–1955	1956–1960	1961–1965	1966–1970
Tuberculosis	9,005	8,608	7,862	7,002	5,472	4,427	3,194
Measles	10,496	24,890	17,348	20,025	18,170	12,279	3,508
Rubella	988	7,360	2,442	3,956	3,893	5,744	1,402
Pertussis	5,775	5,706	2,574	1,726	966	253	164
Meningococcal Meningitis	48	705	145	135	73	58	78
Scarlet Fever	13,569	8,111	3,579	2,253	2,125	1,442	733
Encephalitis	28	42	55	256	197	172	72
Syphilis	30,178	25,773	24,144	22,046	15,124	19,052	12,529
Gonorrhea	14,639	13,955	21,522	12,468	13,270	23,005	32,640

Selected Cases of Reportable Diseases, 1940–2005 (continued)

	1971	1972	1973	1974	1975	1976	1977
Tuberculosis	2,572	2,275	2,101	2,022	2,151	2,151	1,605
Measles	3,819	447	965	651	170	497	804
Rubella	626	271	502	173	193	163	336
Meningococcal Meningitis	60	44	37	26	32	51	64
Scarlet Fever	614	445	708	402	463	609	583
Encephalitis	19	11	26	17	14	20	20
Hepatitis A	—	—	—	—	—	—	566
Hepatitis B	—	—	—	—	—	—	670
Syphilis	11,642	10,390	7,334	7,593	7,236	6,832	4,749
Gonorrhea	38,472	48,414	45,467	42,071	39,981	40,589	39,302

	1978	1979	1980	1981	1982	1983	1984
Tuberculosis	1,307	1,530	1,514	1,582	1,594	1,651	1,629
Measles	405	859	1,210	108	49	72	113
Rubella	152	290	105	55	36	87	111
Pertussis	54	44	30	25	53	61	20
Meningococcal Meningitis	88	91	110	91	104	89	75
Scarlet Fever	271	312	319	464	583	454	427
Encephalitis	30	17	15	20	21	14	9
Hepatitis A	499	386	364	606	689	507	560
Hepatitis B	493	488	562	879	1,117	1,327	1,528
Syphilis	5,567	6,680	5,906	6,878	7,296	6,822	6,796
Gonorrhea	40,208	40,034	43,699	45,859	46,960	46,117	48,032

	1985	1986	1987	1988	1989	1990	1991
Tuberculosis	1,843	2,223	2,197	2,317	2,545	3,520	3,673
Measles	181	944	449	57	135	1,108	1,909
Rubella	184	2	3	7	16	4	2
Pertussis	26	10	15	11	19	21	22
Meningococcal Meningitis	70	81	57	66	50	79	30
Scarlet Fever	409	n/a	206	81	108	175	325
Encephalitis	18	21	8	6	9	12	5
Hepatitis A	n/a	n/a	172	368	502	791	1,283
Hepatitis B	n/a	n/a	1,213	1,307	1,418	674	440
Syphilis	6,947	6,465	10,472	11,966	13,748	16,195	14,895
Gonorrhea	58,532	69,998	84,022	52,404	40,533	35,236	28,945

Selected Cases of Reportable Diseases, 1940–2005 (continued)

	1992	1993	1994	1995	1996	1997	1998
Tuberculosis	3,811	3,235	2,995	2,445	2,053	1,730	1,558
Measles	68	19	15	5	12	13	—
Rubella	—	22	1	6	5	25	17
Pertussis	24	116	223	36	62	42	12
Meningococcal Meningitis	28	40	40	54	56	57	35
Scarlet Fever	258	267	335	211	164	218	527
Encephalitis	9	5	11	8	4	14	14
Hepatitis A	883	1,028	942	1,008	619	920	575
Hepatitis B	439	472	544	494	495	460	415
Syphilis	13,439	10,476	7,640	7,577	5,670	4,889	4,503
Gonorrhea	21,709	18,477	19,246	16,361	12,998	14,556	12,100

	1999	2000	2001	2002	2003	2004	2005
Tuberculosis	1,460	1,332	1,261	1,084	1,140	1,039	984
Measles	3	13	7	6	5	5	6
Rubella	6	8	6	2	2	2	1
West Nile Virus	46	14	9	29	30	2	11
Pertussis	7	11	6	5	28	61	40
Meningococcal Meningitis	59	46	42	31	45	31	27
Scarlet Fever	310	350	481	881	994	597	812
Encephalitis	143	178	172	211	169	183	214
Hepatitis A	412	550	454	469	448	354	277
Hepatitis B	305	571	666	721	211	163	134
Syphilis	3,682	2,661	3,267	3,444	3,767	3,674	3,182
Gonorrhea	12,207	11,669	12,614	12,811	13,468	10,860	10,596

Notes: West Nile viral disease data for 1999 include both hospitalized cases (n = 44) and milder illness cases (n = 2). Beginning in 2000 only hospitalized cases of West Nile encephalitis or aseptic meningitis are included. Accurate diagnosis of Hepatitis A and B based on laboratory testing became available in 1977. The way of counting Hepatitis B beginning in 2003 was changed so that the cases counted are newly acquired cases of Hepatitis B. The numbers are probable or definite new cases.
Source: New York City Department of Health and Mental Hygiene, Bureaus of Communicable Disease, Immunization, and Tuberculosis Control.

Obesity by Sex, Borough, and Age, 2003 (in Percent)

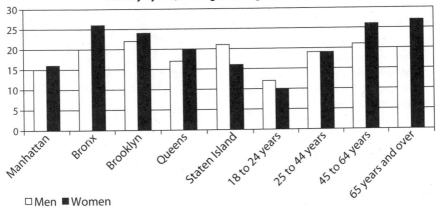

□ Men ■ Women

Source: New York City Department of Health and Mental Hygiene.

Hospitals by Borough, with Number of Beds

Manhattan

Bellevue Hospital Center	912
Beth Israel Medical Center, Petrie Campus	899
Cabrini Medical Center	474
Coler-Goldwater Specialty Hospital and Nursing Facility, Coler Hospital Site	210
Coler-Goldwater Specialty Hospital and Nursing Facility, Goldwater Hospital Site	417
Harlem Hospital Center	286
Hospital for Joint Diseases Orthopaedic Institute, Inc.	190
Hospital for Special Surgery	160
Lenox Hill Hospital	652
Manhattan Eye, Ear and Throat Hospital	150
Memorial Hospital for Cancer and Allied Diseases	514
Metropolitan Hospital Center	363
Mount Sinai Hospital	1,171
New York Downtown Hospital	254
New York Presbyterian Hospital, Allen Pavilion	212
New York Presbyterian Hospital, Columbia Presbyterian Center	973
New York Presbyterian Hospital, New York Weill Cornell Center	781
North General Hospital	200
New York Eye and Ear Infirmary	69

Manhattan (continued)

New York University Hospital Center	879
Rockefeller University Hospital	40
St. Luke's-Roosevelt Hospital, St. Luke's Hospital Division	541
St. Luke's-Roosevelt Hospital, Roosevelt Hospital Division	505
St. Vincent's Midtown Hospital	250
Saint Vincent Catholic Medical Centers, St. Vincent's Manhattan	727
Total	11,829

Bronx

Bronx-Lebanon Hospital Center, Concourse Division	401
Bronx-Lebanon Hospital Center, Fulton Division	164
Calvary Hospital, Inc.	225
Jacobi Medical Center	457
Lincoln Medical and Mental Health Center	347
Montefiore Medical Center, Jack D. Weiler Hospital of Albert Einstein College Division	396
Montefiore Medical Center, Henry and Lucy Moses Division	726
New York Westchester Square Medical Center	205
North Central Bronx Hospital	213
Our Lady of Mercy Medical Center	369
St. Barnabas Hospital	446
Total	3,949

Brooklyn

Beth Israel Medical Center, Kings Highway Division	212
Brookdale Hospital Medical Center	530
Brooklyn Hospital Center, Downtown Campus	483
Coney Island Hospital	364
Interfaith Medical Center	287
Kings County Hospital Center	700
Kingsbrook Jewish Medical Center	326
Long Island College Hospital	506
Lutheran Medical Center	476
Maimonides Medical Center	705
New York Community Hospital of Brooklyn, Inc.	134
New York Methodist Hospital	570
Saint Vincent Catholic Medical Centers, St. Mary's Hospital Brooklyn	222
University Hospital of Brooklyn	376
Victory Memorial Hospital	243

Hospitals by Borough, with Number of Beds (continued)

Brooklyn (continued)

Woodhull Medical and Mental Health Center	411
Wyckoff Heights Medical Center	324
Total	6,869

Queens

City Hospital Center at Elmhurst	545
Flushing Hospital Medical Center	293
Forest Hills Hospital	312
Jamaica Hospital Medical Center	384
Long Island Jewish Medical Center	827
Mount Sinai Hospital, Mount Sinai Hospital of Queens	235
New York Hospital Medical Center of Queens	439
Parkway Hospital	251
Peninsula Hospital Center	272
Queens Hospital Center	243
St. John's Episcopal Hospital South Shore	332
Saint Vincent Catholic Medical Centers, Mary Immaculate	265
Saint Vincent Catholic Medical Centers, St. John's Queens	346
Total	4,744

Staten Island

Staten Island University Hospital, Concord Division	71
Staten Island University Hospital, North	508
Staten Island University Hospital, South	206
Saint Vincent Catholic Medical Centers, Bayley Seton	198
Saint Vincent Catholic Medical Centers, St. Vincent's Staten Island	440
Total	1,423

Citywide total	28,814

Source: New York State Department of Health.

Fires and EMS Incidents, 2001–2006

	2001	2002	2003	2004	2005	2006
Structural fires	27,788	26,248	27,105	27,718	28,445	27,817
Non-structural fires	29,655	25,315	24,015	22,437	22,940	20,702
Non-fire emergencies	172,638	170,867	178,156	180,047	199,643	198,202
Medical emergencies	155,396	158,461	173,694	189,162	202,526	209,397
Malicious false alarms	51,544	45,651	41,018	37,732	32,138	28,836
Total	437,021	426,542	443,988	457,096	485,692	484,954
EMS incidents, segments 1–3[1]	384,253	385,748	402,652	398,976	406,757	423,223
Total EMS incidents	1,097,564	1,087,070	1,109,287	1,114,693	1,140,114	1,164,059
Response times, segments 1–3[1]	6:53	6:50	7:01	6:49	6:45	6:37

[1] Life-threatening emergencies.
Source: Fire Department of New York City.

3 Housing and Real Estate

Area of the City, Park Acreage, and Miles of Streets Laid Out

	Area in Square Miles	Area in Acres	Park Acreage	Miles of Streets
Manhattan	23.7	15,170	2,680.49	504.3
Bronx	44.0	28,165	6,940.07	803.2
Brooklyn	81.8	52,330	4,440.36	1,599.0
Queens	112.2	71,780	7,269.97	2,443.4
Staten Island	60.2	38,507	7,286.61	1,025.0
Total	321.9	205,952	28,617.5	6,374.9

Source: The Green Book.

Parks of Ten Acres or More (in Descending Order)

Manhattan

Central Park	840.10
Riverside Park and Drive	323.39
Randall's Island	273.38
Inwood Hill Park	196.40
Fort Washington Park	158.81
Ward's Island	122.36
Highbridge Park	118.75
Fort Tryon Park	66.63
East River Park	57.45
Harlem River Driveway	35.42
Morningside Park	31.23
Battery Park	22.98
St. Nicholas Park	22.74
Marcus Garvey (Mount Morris) Park	20.16
Isham Park	20.09
Theodore Roosevelt Park	17.57
Thomas Jefferson Park	15.52
Carl Schurz Park	14.94
Jackie Robinson (Colonial) Park	12.77
Tompkins Square Park	10.50

Bronx

Pelham Bay Park	2,764.00
Van Cortlandt Park	1,146.43
Bronx Park	721.00
Ferry Point Park	413.80
Hutchinson River Parkway	229.14
Bronx River Parkway	202.36
Sound View Park	163.532
Crotona Park	127.50
Bronx and Pelham Parkway	108.91
Riverdale Park	97.19
Mosholu Parkway (2 miles)	80.94
Pugsley's Creek Park	73.37
Henry Hudson Parkway (3 miles)	54.10
Claremont Park	38.23
Seton Falls Park	35.77
St. Mary's Park	34.43
North Brother Island	30.40
Macombs Dam Park	28.42
South Brother Island	22.16
Wave Hill	20.86

Parks of Ten Acres or More (in Descending Order) (continued)

Bronx (continued)

Williamsbridge Playground	19.75
John Mullaly Park	18.52
Franz Sigel Park	15.99
Harris Park	15.32
Crotona Park (Old Borough Hall)	15.00
Playground, East 172nd to East 174th Streets, Bronx River Expressway, Bronx River	12.69
Seton Park	11.54
St. James Park	11.39

Brooklyn

Marine Park	798.00
Leif Ericson Drive (Shore Parkway)	760.43
Prospect Park	526.25
Dyker Beach Park	216.65
Ocean Parkway	140.00
Canarsie Beach	132.20
Coney Island Beach and Boardwalk	107.124
Joseph T. McGuire Park	77.20
Dreier-Offerman Park	76.92
Fresh Creek Park	74.30
Eastern Parkway	60.12
Four Sparrows Marsh	68.50
Spring Creek Park	67.80
Red Hook Recreation Area	58.50
Shore Road Park	58.00
Brooklyn Botanic Garden	47.57
Manhattan Beach Park	40.40
Parade Ground, Parade Place	39.50
Coney Island Boat Basin	36.81
McCarren Park	35.71
Fort Greene Park	30.16
Owls Head Park	27.10
Leon S. Kaiser Playground	26.25
Sunset Park	24.49
Seaside–Asser Levy Park and Aquarium	22.34
Lincoln Terrace Park	20.64

Brooklyn (continued)

Bensonhurst Park	17.50
Leif Ericson Park and Square	16.80
PS 260, Breukelen Houses Playground	16.16
Brooklyn Museum	12.66
Steeplechase Park	11.70
Grand Army Plaza	11.04
Betsy Head Playground	10.56
Commodore John Barry Park and Playground	10.39
Cadman Plaza Park	10.39

Queens

Flushing Meadows–Corona Park	1,255.42
Alley Pond Park	655.29
Forest Park	538.00
Grand Central Parkway Extension	370.00
Cunningham Park	350.00
Cross Island Parkway	326.12
Rockaway Community Park	253.72
Kissena Park	234.76
Idlewild Park	224.79
Southern Parkway	202.65
Grand Central Parkway	180.00
Jamaica Bay Park	146.00
Highland Park	141.28
Baisley Pond Park	109.61
Douglaston Golf Course	104.60
Clearview Park and Golf Course	103.87
Public Place, Huxley Street, Hook Creek, and Rockaway Boulevard	100.00
Rockaway Beach and Boardwalk	96.92
Kissena Corridor Park West	92.93
Brookville Parkway	89.94
Jackie Robinson Parkway	72.75
Former Long Island Motor Parkway	72.00
Rockaway Beach Boardwalk	68.21
Astoria Park	61.24
Laurelton Parkway	59.56
Juniper Valley Park	55.24

Parts of Ten Acres or More (in Descending Order) (continued)

Queens (continued)

Roy Wilkins–Southern Queens Park	53.00
Shore Parkway	50.90
Clearview Beach	50.00
Creedmoor Farm Park	47.65
Crocheron Park	45.79
Dubos Point Wildlife Sanctuary	44.823
Spring Creek Park	37.17
Broad Channel Wetlands	35.00
Kissena Corridor Park East	33.53
Rockaway Park	31.50
Alley Park (Athletic)	30.50
Udalls Cove and Ravine Wildlife Refuge	29.83
Hermon A. MacNeil (College Point) Park	28.87
College Point Park	25.39
Michaelis-Bayswater Park	25.00
Brant Point Wildlife Sanctuary	24.19
Springfield Park	23.54
Queensbridge Park	20.34
Francis Lewis Park	16.83
Park, LIRR, 129th Avenue, 176th Street	16.44
Edward Byrne Park	14.83
Rockaway Beach	14.00
Park, Beach 17th Street and Seagirt Boulevard	13.75
Marine Park	12.00
John Bowne Park	11.79
Rufus King Park	11.50
Frank Golden Park	11.48
Southern Parkway Ballfields	11.15
St. Albans Park	10.79
Flushing Memorial Field	10.22
Fort Totten Park	10.00

Staten Island

Richmond Parkway (9.3 miles)	979.00
Fresh Kills Park	813.97
Franklin D. Roosevelt Boardwalk and Beach	638.50

Staten Island (continued)

LaTourette Park and Golf Course	511.05
Wolfe's Pond Park	318.58
Willowbrook Parkway (4.5 miles)	306.81
Great Kills Park	306.783
Conference House Park	267.465
Blue Heron Park	222.138
Silver Lake Park	209.35
Clove Lakes Park	198.05
Arden Heights Woods Park	183.00
South Shore Country Club	174.86
Willowbrook Park	164.13
Staten Island Corporate Park	156.00
Bloomingdale Park	115.30
Blood Root Valley (Greenbelt) Rockland Manor	113.20
Saw Mill Creek Marsh	111.72
Ocean Breeze	110.40
Mariner's Marsh Park	107.20
Lemon Creek Park	105.77
Isle of Meadows	103.00
Long Pond Park	94.617
Sailors' Snug Harbor	83.30
Prall's Island Bird Sanctuary	80.30
High Rock Park	77.90
Shooters Island	44.80
Crescent Beach	38.67
Staten Island Community College	35.00
Basket Willow Swamp	34.67
Islington Pond Park	23.01
Evergreen Park	22.60
Neck Creek Marsh Park	17.365
Alice Austen Park	14.63
Arthur Von Briesen Park	13.27
Park, south side of Staten Island Expressway, Fahy Avenue, Lamberts Lane	12.40
Lawrence C. Thompson Park	10.50

Source: The Green Book.

One Hundred Tallest Buildings

	Height in Feet	Number of Stories	Year Completed
1. Empire State Building	1,250	102	1931
2. Chrysler Building	1,046	77	1930
3. New York Times Tower	1,046	52	2007
4. American International	952	66	1932
5. The Trump Building	927	70	1930
6. Citigroup Center	915	59	1977
7. Trump World Tower	861	72	2001
8. GE Building (Rockefeller Center)	850	69	1933
9. CitySpire Center	814	75	1987
10. One Chase Manhattan Plaza	813	60	1961
11. Condé Nast Building	809	48	1999
12. MetLife Building	808	60	1963
13. Bloomberg Tower	806	54	2005
14. Woolworth Building	792	57	1913
15. One Worldwide Plaza	778	50	1989
16. Carnegie Hall Tower	757	60	1991
17. Bear Stearns World Headquarters	755	47	2001
18. AXA Center	752	54	1986
19. One Penn Plaza	750	57	1972
20. 1251 Avenue of the Americas	750	54	1971
21. Time Warner Center South	750	55	2004
22. Time Warner Center North	750	55	2004
23. 60 Wall Street	745	55	1989
24. One Astor Plaza	745	54	1972
25. One Liberty Plaza	743	54	1973
26. 20 Exchange Place	741	57	1931
27. Seven World Trade Center	741	49	2006
28. Three World Financial Center	739	51	1986
29. Bertelsmann Building	733	42	1990
30. Times Square Tower	726	47	2004
31. Metropolitan Tower	716	68	1987
32. JP Morgan Chase World Headquarters	707	52	1960
33. General Motors Building	705	50	1968
34. Metropolitan Life Insurance Company Tower	700	50	1909
35. 500 Fifth Avenue	697	60	1931
36. Americas Tower	692	50	1992

One Hundred Tallest Buildings (continued)

	Height in Feet	Number of Stories	Year Completed
37. Solow Building	689	50	1974
38. HSBC Bank Building	688	52	1967
39. 55 Water Street	687	53	1972
40. 277 Park Avenue	687	50	1962
41. 1585 Broadway	685	42	1989
42. Random House Tower	684	52	2003
43. Four Seasons Hotel	682	52	1993
44. McGraw-Hill Building	674	51	1969
45. Lincoln Building	673	55	1930
46. Paramount Plaza	670	48	1971
47. Trump Tower	664	58	1983
48. Citicorp Building	658	50	1990
49. Bank of New York Building	654	50	1931
50. 599 Lexington Avenue	653	50	1986
51. 712 Fifth Avenue	650	52	1990
52. Chanin Building	649	56	1930
53. 245 Park Avenue	648	44	1966
54. Sony Tower	647	37	1984
55. Two World Financial Center	645	44	1987
56. One New York Plaza	640	50	1969
57. 570 Lexington Avenue	640	50	1931
58. 345 Park Avenue	634	44	1969
59. W. R. Grace Building	630	50	1971
60. Home Insurance Plaza	630	45	1966
61. 101 Park Avenue	629	49	1982
62. One Dag Hammarskjold Plaza	628	49	1972
63. Central Park Place	628	56	1988
64. 888 Seventh Avenue	628	46	1971
65. Waldorf-Astoria	625	47	1931
66. Burlington House	625	50	1969
67. Trump Palace Condominiums	623	54	1991
68. Olympic Tower	620	51	1976
69. Mercantile Building	620	48	1929
70. 425 Fifth Avenue	618	55	2003
71. 919 Third Avenue	615	47	1971
72. New York Life Building	615	40	1928

	Height in Feet	Number of Stories	Year Completed
73. 750 Seventh Avenue	615	35	1989
74. Tower 49	614	45	1985
75. Credit Lyonnais Building	609	45	1964
76. The Orion	604	58	2006
77. 590 Madison Avenue	603	41	1983
78. Marsh & McLennan Headquarters	600	44	1974
79. Hearst Magazine Tower	596	42	2006
80. Three Lincoln Center Condominiums	595	60	1993
81. Celanese Building (Rockefeller Center)	592	45	1973
82. RIHGA Royal	590	54	1990
83. Thurgood Marshall United States Courthouse	590	37	1936
84. Millenium Hilton	588	59	1992
85. Museum Tower	588	52	1985
86. Jacob K. Javits Federal Building	587	42	1967
87. Time-Life Building	587	48	1958
88. W Times Square	583	53	2001
89. Trump International Hotel & Tower	583	44	1971
90. J. P. Stevens Company Tower	580	40	1971
91. Manhattan Municipal Building	580	34	1914
92. 520 Madison Avenue	577	43	1982
93. One World Financial Center	577	40	1985
94. Merchandise Mart Building	576	42	1974
95. 300 Madison Avenue	575	38	2003
96. Lehman Brothers Building	575	38	2001
97. One Financial Square	575	37	1987
98. 5 Times Square	575	40	2002
99. Park Avenue Plaza Building	574	45	1981
100. New York Marriott Marquis	574	56	1985

Source: Emporis Buildings.

Historic Districts on the National Register of Historic Places

Manhattan

Audubon Terrace Historic District (1980)
Building at 19 Rector Street (2002)
Central Park (1966)
Central Park West Historic District (1982)
Charlton-King–Van Dam Historic District (1973)
Chelsea Historic District (1977)
Chelsea Historic District (1982)
City and Suburban Homes Company's First Avenue Estate
Historic District (1986)
City and Suburban Homes Company's York Avenue Estate
and Shively Sanitary Tenements Historic District
(1994)
East 73rd Street Historic District (1982)
Fort Tryon Park and the Cloisters (1978)
Fraunces Tavern Block (1977)
Governors Island National Monument (1985)
Gramercy Park Historic District (1980)
Greenwich Village Historic District (1979)
Hamilton Heights Historic District (1983)
Henderson Place Historic District (1974)
Houses at 1026–28 Fifth Avenue (1999)
Jumel Terrace Historic District (1973)
Lower East Side Historic District (2000)
MacDougal–Sullivan Gardens Historic District (1983)
Manhattan Avenue–West 120th–123rd Streets Historic
District (1992)
Metropolitan Life Home Office Complex (1996)
Mount Morris Park Historic District (1973)
Old St. Patrick's Cathedral Complex (1977)
Plaza Hotel (1978)
Pomander Walk District (1983)
Residence at 5–15 West 54th Street (1990)
Riverside Drive–West 80th–81st Streets Historic District
(1984)
Riverside–West 105th Street Historic District (1980)
Rowhouses at 322–344 East 69th Street (1984)
Saint Mark's Historic District (Boundary Increase) (1985)
Schermerhorn Row Block (1971)

Manhattan (continued)

Sniffen Court Historic District (1973)
SoHo Historic District (1978)
South Street Seaport (1972)
South Street Seaport Historic District (1978)
Saint Mark's Historic District (1974)
Saint Nicholas Historic District (1975)
Statue of Liberty National Monument, Ellis Island, and
Liberty Island (1966)
Stone Street Historic District (1999)
Stuyvesant Square Historic District (1980)
Sugar Hill Historic District (2002)
Sutton Place Historic District (1985)
Tudor City Historic District (1986)
Turtle Bay Gardens (1983)
Upper East Side Historic District (1984)
West 67th Street Artists' Colony Historic District (1985)
West 73rd–74th Streets Historic District (1983)
West 76th Street Historic District (1980)

Bronx

Fort Schuyler (1976)
Grand Concourse Historic District (1987)
Jerome Park Reservoir (2000)
Longwood Historic District (1983)
Morris High School Historic District (1983)
Mott Haven Historic District (1980)
New York Botanical Gardens (1967)

Brooklyn

Albemarle-Kenmore Terraces Historic District (1983)
Boerum Hill Historic District (1983)
Brooklyn Heights Historic District (1966)
Carroll Gardens Historic District (1983)
Clinton Hill Historic District (1985)
Clinton Hill South Historic District (1986)
Cobble Hill Historic District (1976)
Cypress Avenue West Historic District (1983)
DUMBO Industrial District (2000)
Ditmas Park Historic District (1983)

Brooklyn (continued)

Floyd Bennett Field Historic District (1980)

Fort Greene Historic District (1983)

Fort Greene Historic District (Boundary Increase) (1984)

Fulton Ferry District (1974)

Greenpoint Historic District (1983)

Houses on Hunterfly Road District (1972)

Lefferts Manor Historic District (1992)

Park Slope Historic District (1980)

Pratt Institute Historic District (1990)

Prospect Heights Historic District (1983)

Prospect Park (1980)

Prospect Park South Historic District (1983)

Rockwood Chocolate Factory Historic District (1983)

Senator Street Historic District (2002)

State Street Houses (1980)

Stuyvesant Heights Historic District (1975)

Stuyvesant Heights Historic District (Boundary Increase) (1996)

Sunset Park Historic District (1988)

Willoughby-Suydam Historic District (1983)

Queens

68th Avenue–64th Place Historic District (1983)

75th Avenue–61st Street Historic District (1983)

Central Avenue Historic District (1983)

Central Ridgewood Historic District (1983)

Queens (continued)

Cornelia-Putnam Historic District (1983)

Cypress Avenue East Historic District (1983)

Cypress Avenue West Historic District (1983)

Douglaston Hill Historic District (2000)

Forest-Norman Historic District (1983)

Fort Tilden Historic District (1984)

Fresh Pond–Traffic Historic District (1983)

Grove-Linden–St. John's Historic District (1983)

Hunters Point Historic District (1973)

Jackson Heights Historic District (1999)

Jacob Riis Park Historic District (1981)

Long Island Motor Parkway Historic District (2002)

Paramount Studios Complex (1978)

Seneca Avenue East Historic District (1983)

Seneca-Onderdonk-Woodward Historic District (1983)

Stockholm-DeKalb-Hart Historic District (1983)

Sunnyside Gardens Historic District (1984)

Woodbine-Palmetto-Gates Historic District (1983)

Staten Island

Fort Wadsworth (1999)

Miller Army Air Field Historic District (1980)

Our Lady of Mount Carmel Grotto (2000)

Sailors' Snug Harbor National Register District (1972)

Sandy Ground Historic Archeological District (1982)

Ward's Point Conservation Area (1982)

Source: U.S. Department of the Interior, National Park Service.

Full Market and Assessed Actual Value of Real Property, Fiscal Year 2008
(Tentative Figures, in Millions)

	One-, Two-, and Three- Family Residential (Class 1)	All Other Residential (Class 2)	Utility (Class 3)	All Other Real Property (Class 4)	Total
Manhattan					
Full market value	$20,104.0	$105,114.3	$7,230.7	$124,670.0	$257,119.1
Assessed actual value	566.8	35,358.8	3,253.5	52,909.1	92,088.3
Bronx					
Full market value	33,408.4	11,467.1	2,241.0	8,431.9	55,548.4
Assessed actual value	1,117.3	3,602.7	1,008.4	3,182.2	8,910.8
Brooklyn					
Full market value	141,568.3	37,834.0	4,379.4	17,841.9	201,623.5
Assessed actual value	3,934.7	6,788.1	1,877.7	6,888.4	19,488.9
Queens					
Full market value	173,041.3	22,366.7	3,975.4	23,122.9	222,506.3
Assessed actual value	5,632.3	6,316.8	1,782.0	9,066.5	22,797.5
Staten Island					
Full market value	58,903.1	1,227.1	1,166.7	4,319.1	65,615.9
Assessed actual value	2,105.0	315.8	524.9	1,711.3	4,656.9
Total					
Full market value	427,025.1	178,009.3	18,993.2	178,385.8	802,413.3
Assessed actual value	13,356.1	52,382.3	8,446.6	73,757.4	147,942.4

Source: New York City Department of Finance, *Tentative Assessment Roll, Fiscal Year 2008.*

Housing Inventory, 2002 and 2005

	2002	2005	Percent Change
Total housing units	3,208,587	3,260,856	1.6
Total rental units	2,084,769	2,092,363	0.4
Occupied	2,023,504	2,027,626	0.2
Vacant, available for rent	61,265	64,737	5.7
Total owner units	997,003	1,031,780	3.5
Occupied	981,814	1,010,370	2.9
Vacant, available for sale	15,189	21,410	41.0
Vacant units, not available for sale or rent	126,816	136,712	7.8

Sources: U.S. Bureau of the Census; New York City Housing and Vacancy Surveys.

Rental Housing Inventory by Rent Regulation Status, 2002 and 2005

	2002	2005	Percent Change
Rent controlled	59,324	43,317	−27.0
Rent-stabilized[1]	1,042,397	1,043,677	0.1
Pre-1947 stabilized	775,460	747,332	−3.6
Post-1947 stabilized	266,937	296,345	11.0
Private non-regulated[2]	672,368	697,363	3.7
All other renter units[3]	310,680	308,007	−0.9
Total rental units (occupied and vacant available)	2,084,769	2,092,363	0.4

[1] All rent-stabilized units, including those whose rents were regulated by the U.S. Department of Housing and Urban Development (HUD) since they received HUD assistance.
[2] Units which were never rent-controlled or rent-stabilized; units which were decontrolled, including those in buildings with five or fewer units; and unregulated rentals in cooperative or condominium buildings.
[3] Includes Public Housing, Mitchell-Lama, *In Rem*, HUD regulated, Article 4, Loft Board.
Sources: U.S. Bureau of the Census, 2002 and 2005 New York City Housing and Vacancy Surveys.

Number of Owner-Occupied Units and Ownership Rate by Borough, 2002 and 2005

	2002 Number of Owner-Occupied Units	Ownership Rate	2005 Number of Owner-Occupied Units	Ownership Rate
Manhattan	162,580	22.6	174,179	23.6
Bronx	103,993	22.5	104,400	22.1
Brooklyn	252,021	28.7	255,955	29.2
Queens	360,529	46.0	365,040	46.4
Staten Island	102,692	64.6	110,795	67.7
Total	981,814[a]	32.7	1,010,370[b]	33.3

[a] So in original; individual figures for boroughs sum to 981,815.
[b] So in original; individual figures for boroughs sum to 1,010,369.
Note: Figures for Bronx include Marble Hill.
Sources: U.S. Bureau of the Census, 2002 and 2005 and New York City Housing and Vacancy Surveys.

Vacant Units Available for Rent by Borough, 2002 and 2005

	2002 Number of Units	Net Vacancy Rate	2005 Number of Units	Net Vacancy Rate
Manhattan	22,389	3.86	22,198	3.79
Bronx	12,200	3.29	9,952	2.63
Brooklyn	17,612	2.73	17,759	2.78
Queens	7,658	1.78	12,239	2.82
Staten Island	n/a	n/a	n/a	n/a
Total	61,265	2.94	64,737	3.09

Notes: Vacancy rate is calculated by dividing vacant, nondilapidated units available for rent by the sum of vacant, nondilapidated units available for rent and renter-occupied units. The standard error of the vacancy rate for all renter units was +/− 0.17 in 2002 and +/− 0.19 in 2005. Figures for Bronx include Marble Hill.
Sources: U.S. Bureau of the Census, 2002 and 2005 New York City Housing and Vacancy Surveys.

Rental Prices for Apartments in Manhattan, December 2005

	Median Monthly Rental	Average Monthly Rental	Average Annual Rental per Square Foot		Median Monthly Rental	Average Monthly Rental	Average Annual Rental per Square Foot
Battery Park City / Financial District				Murray Hill			
				Studio	1,850	1,932	51.52
Studio	$1,928	$2,008	$48.20	One-bedroom	2,850	2,766	53.54
One-bedroom	2,650	2,637	51.03	Two-bedroom	4,368	4,267	48.77
Two-bedroom	3,798	3,786	43.27	Three-bedroom	4,798	4,668	44.11
Three-bedroom	5,255	5,058	47.79				
				Midtown East			
SoHo / Tribeca				Studio	1,750	1,839	44.13
Studio	1,773	1,796	47.90	One-bedroom	2,450	2,673	47.17
One-bedroom	2,700	2,901	56.14	Two-bedroom	3,600	3,759	42.96
Two-bedroom	4,000	4,165	47.60	Three-bedroom	6,500	6,517	61.57
Three-bedroom	5,000	9,150	86.46				
				Midtown West			
West Village				Studio	1,738	1,785	42.84
Studio	1,950	2,081	55.49	One-bedroom	2,450	2,446	43.16
One-bedroom	2,538	2,737	52.98	Two-bedroom	3,000	3,326	38.01
Two-bedroom	3,500	3,682	42.08	Three-bedroom	3,895	3,960	37.42
Three-bedroom	5,388	5,528	52.24				
				Upper East Side			
East Village				Studio	1,525	1,632	39.17
Studio	1,750	1,823	48.60	One-bedroom	2,150	2,232	39.38
One-bedroom	2,300	2,417	46.78	Two-bedroom	2,500	3,256	37.21
Two-bedroom	2,788	2,885	32.97	Three-bedroom	4,930	5,308	50.15
Three-bedroom	3,575	3,783	35.75				
				Upper West Side			
Chelsea				Studio	1,650	1,728	46.07
Studio	1,950	1,986	52.97	One-bedroom	2,250	2,351	41.48
One-bedroom	2,585	2,648	51.25	Two-bedroom	3,200	3,217	36.76
Two-bedroom	4,300	4,638	53.00	Three-bedroom	4,575	4,711	44.51
Three-bedroom	4,200	4,471	4,225				
				Manahattan Overall			
Gramercy / Flatiron				Studio	1,750	1,830	46.90
Studio	1,850	1,930	51.48	One-bedroom	2,450	2,486	46.49
One-bedroom	2,300	2,469	47.78	Two-bedroom	3,250	3,461	39.55
Two-bedroom	2,875	3,224	36.84	Three-bedroom	4,205	4,793	45.29
Three-bedroom	4,548	4,342	41.03				

Source: Citi Habitats, *The Black and White Report*, update 8 (July–December 2005).

Average Monthly Gross Apartment Rent for New York and Selected International Cities, 2006

Source: UBS Wealth Management Research, *Prices and Earnings: A Comparison of Purchasing Power around the Globe* (2006).

Apartment Rents in New York and Selected International Cities, 2006

	Furnished Four-Room Apartment			Unfurnished Three-Room Apartment			Normal Local Rent
	Expensive	Medium	Cheap	Expensive	Medium	Cheap	
New York	$11,100	$7,380	$4,370	$5,870	$3,660	$2,530	$2,500
Amsterdam	4,520	2,470	1,030	2,770	1,570	660	1,210
Bangkok	880	740	590	620	520	410	270
Beijing	3,850	1,360	870	2,980	950	540	400
Buenos Aires	1,530	1,020	710	660	500	330	230
Chicago	4,950	3,450	1,900	3,100	1,750	1,120	1,930
Delhi	1,700	990	700	1,570	540	170	540
Dubai	4,370	2,900	1,420	2,100	1,640	1,200	1,480
Frankfurt	2,570	1,910	1,530	2,000	1,360	970	900
Geneva	3,910	2,680	2,370	1,930	1,360	1,090	1,620
Hong Kong	7,480	4,350	2,870	5,740	3,930	2,260	770
London	9,960	6,240	2,390	6,180	4,170	1,710	2,390
Los Angeles	5,740	4,200	3,290	3,420	2,400	1,690	1,390
Mexico City	2,340	1,190	620	1,560	860	380	810
Miami	2,700	2,200	1,000	2,000	1,200	690	1,050
Montreal	1,880	1,560	1,300	1,660	1,440	1,020	1,200
Moscow	3,740	2,090	1,300	2,800	1,380	810	1,150
Mumbai	4,500	4,070	1,870	2,740	1,980	1,270	1,000
Nairobi	3,070	1,960	1,330	1,400	730	490	450
Paris	3,510	2,450	1,890	2,200	1,800	1,200	1,120
Rio de Janeiro	5,080	2,700	1,500	2,410	1,640	1,150	750
Rome	3,130	1,750	1,420	2,200	1,450	1,010	1,250
Seoul	7,000	4,330	2,580	4,120	3,510	2,520	620
Sydney	6,640	3,870	2,210	3,170	2,100	1,360	880
Tokyo	10,260	7,270	5,130	4,270	1,710	850	1,200
Toronto	2,080	1,730	1,440	1,730	1,300	970	1,120

Notes: Prices based on surveys conducted in February–April and include all incidental costs. Four-room apartments are built after 1980, include garage, and have a level of comfort conforming to the expectations of salaried midmanagement employees in areas favored by them. Three-room apartments are built after 1980, do not include garage, and have an average level of comfort customary in the locality and near the city center.
Source: UBS Wealth Management, *Prices and Earnings: A Comparison of Purchasing Power around the Globe* (2006).

Prices of Cooperatives and Condominiums Citywide, July–December 2005

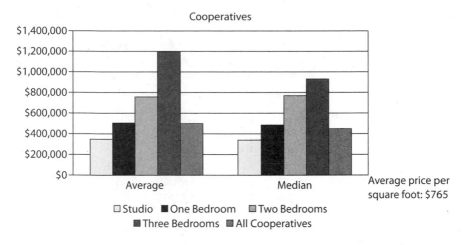

Cooperatives

Average price per square foot: $765

☐ Studio ■ One Bedroom ☐ Two Bedrooms
■ Three Bedrooms ■ All Cooperatives

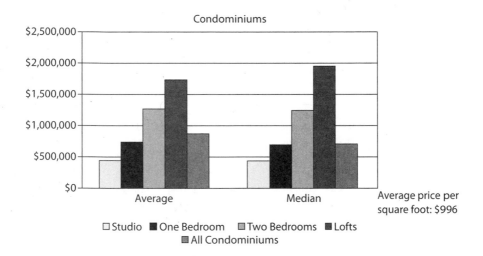

Condominiums

Average price per square foot: $996

☐ Studio ■ One Bedroom ☐ Two Bedrooms ■ Lofts
■ All Condominiums

Source: Citi Habitats, *The Black and White Report*, update 8 (July–December).

Prices of Cooperatives and Condominiums in Manhattan, 1997–2006

Average Sales Price

	Studio	One Bedroom	Two Bedrooms	Three Bedrooms	Four or More Bedrooms	All Cooperatives and Condominiums
1997	$133,542	$225,041	$488,246	$1,352,892	$2,572,343	$430,927
1998	137,218	271,739	628,356	1,534,560	3,250,131	506,934
1999	164,717	271,800	674,779	1,467,277	3,162,892	518,137
2000	254,036	343,523	865,189	1,776,326	4,639,761	710,778
2001	373,915	427,885	842,271	2,000,928	5,307,905	778,575
2002	281,373	386,851	988,010	2,451,429	4,401,987	795,079
2003	281,854	451,632	1,034,286	2,482,126	5,230,774	850,340
2004	308,366	521,967	1,244,488	2,868,754	5,825,253	1,004,232
2005	389,435	648,423	1,495,109	3,412,859	7,734,909	1,221,265
2006	445,607	705,439	1,571,807	3,559,657	7,153,295	1,295,445

Median Sales Price

	Studio	One Bedroom	Two Bedrooms	Three Bedrooms	Four or More Bedrooms	All Cooperatives and Condominiums
1997	$95,000	$180,000	$420,000	$1,200,000	$2,250,000	$239,000
1998	119,000	220,000	520,000	1,200,000	2,700,000	265,000
1999	134,000	250,000	575,000	1,450,000	3,300,000	310,000
2000	170,000	318,000	710,000	1,975,000	3,900,000	399,000
2001	210,000	360,000	750,000	2,000,000	3,850,000	430,000
2002	227,000	380,000	795,000	1,996,000	3,800,000	450,000
2003	246,188	415,000	855,000	2,050,000	3,700,000	495,000
2004	288,000	484,000	990,000	2,345,000	5,535,000	605,859
2005	365,000	610,000	1,272,000	2,995,000	5,850,000	750,000
2006	410,000	650,000	1,355,000	3,150,000	5,800,000	830,000

Prices of Cooperatives and Condominiums in Manhattan, 1997–2006 (continued)

Average Price per Square Foot

	Studio	One Bedroom	Two Bedrooms	Three Bedrooms	Four or More Bedrooms	All Cooperatives and Condominiums
1997	$256	$292	$343	$520	$631	$328
1998	273	356	442	629	837	397
1999	287	352	456	582	823	400
2000	425	450	573	678	1,061	522
2001	560	558	580	762	1,324	592
2002	552	496	682	951	1,190	617
2003	545	598	717	986	1,356	672
2004	632	689	819	1,057	1,481	767
2005	800	855	1,043	1,309	1,909	956
2006	859	922	1,103	1,409	1,900	1,031

Source: Prudential Douglas Elliman Real Estate, *Manhattan Market Report, 1997–2006: 10-Year Sales Trend Analysis*, prepared by Miller Samuel Inc.

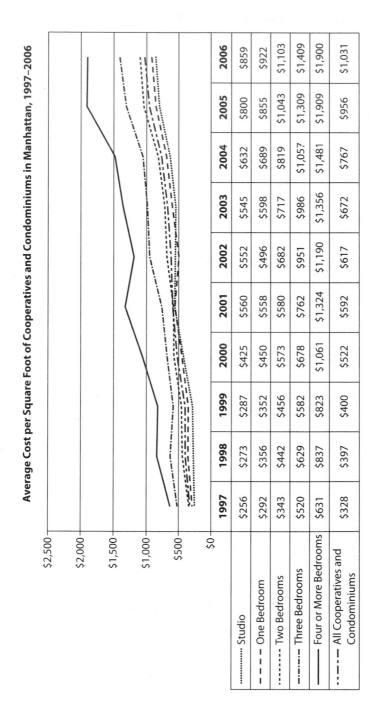

Average Cost per Square Foot of Cooperatives and Condominiums in Manhattan, 1997–2006

	1997	1998	1999	2000	2001	2002	2003	2004	2005	2006
Studio	$256	$273	$287	$425	$560	$552	$545	$632	$800	$859
One Bedroom	$292	$356	$352	$450	$558	$496	$598	$689	$855	$922
Two Bedrooms	$343	$442	$456	$573	$580	$682	$717	$819	$1,043	$1,103
Three Bedrooms	$520	$629	$582	$678	$762	$951	$986	$1,057	$1,309	$1,409
Four or More Bedrooms	$631	$837	$823	$1,061	$1,324	$1,190	$1,356	$1,481	$1,909	$1,900
All Cooperatives and Condominiums	$328	$397	$400	$522	$592	$617	$672	$767	$956	$1,031

Source: Prudential Douglas Elliman Real Estate, *Manhattan Market Report, 1997–2006: 10-Year Sales Trend Analysis*, prepared by Miller Samuel Inc.

Highest Sale Prices for Residential Properties in Each Borough, 2006 (in Millions)

Manhattan
1. 4 East 75th Street	$53.0
2. 25 East 78th Street	45.0
3. 1009 Fifth Avenue	40.0
4. 810 Fifth Avenue	31.5
5. 1040 Fifth Avenue	30.0
6. 80 Columbus Circle	28.7
7. 10 East 67th Street	28.5
8. 25 Columbus Circle	27.606
9. 998 Fifth Avenue	27.5
10. 740 Park Avenue	27.5

Bronx
1. 407 West 247th Street, Riverdale	$3.2
2. 620 West 238th Street, Kingsbridge	3.1
3. 4595 Fieldston Road, Riverdale	2.6
4. 4926 Goodridge Avenue, Riverdale	2.32
5. 4641 Grosvenor Avenue, Riverdale	2.1
6. 5051 Iselin Avenue, Riverdale	2.1
7. 4530 Waldo Avenue, Riverdale	1.98
8. 27 Sigma Avenue, Riverdale	1.96
9. 722 West 232nd Street, Kingsbridge	1.95
10. 4720 Delafield Avenue, Riverdale	1.8

Brooklyn
1. 140 Columbia Heights, Brooklyn Heights	$10.75
2. 318 94th Street, Bay Ridge	6.9
3. 45 Montgomery Place, Park Slope	6.05
4. 1946 Ocean Parkway, Gravesend	5.679
5. 125 Remsen Street, Brooklyn Heights	5.5
6. 1986 East 3rd Street, Gravesend	5.0
7. 459 Avenue S, Gravesend	5.0
8. 464 Avenue S, Gravesend	5.0
9. 273 Willow Street, Brooklyn Heights	4.65
10. 22 Willow Street, Brooklyn Heights	4.495

Queens
1. 146-10 35th Avenue, Flushing	$2.75
2. 37-05 233rd Place, Douglaston	2.6
3. 29 Center Drive. Douglaston	2.6
4. 52-27 Browvale Lane, Little Neck	2.575
5. 69-16 66th Drive, Middle Village	2.4
6. 22 Cherry Street, Douglaston	2.18
7. 226 Bay Street, Douglaston	1.85
8. 64-46 211th Street, Bayside	1.8
9. 216-28 31st Street, Bayside	1.75
10. 211 Forest Road, Douglaston	1.3

Staten Island
1. 15 Tricia Way, Tottenville	$3.5
2. 74 Buttonwood Road, Todt Hill	3.5
3. 483 Holridge Avenue, Annadale	2.5
4. 5 Tricia Way, Tottenville	2.2
5. 43 Howard Circle, Grymes Hill	2.1
6. 76 Westminster Court, Todt Hill	2.05
7. 39 Callan Avenue, Todt Hill	1.9
8. 336 Melba Street, Manor Heights	1.85
9. 63 Flagg Court, Todt Hill	1.825
10. 34 Wetmore Road, Grymes Hill	1.8

Note: Data for Manhattan and Brooklyn are for January 2006 to February 2007, for the Bronx and Staten Island for February 2006 to February 2007.
Source: Automated City Register Information System.

Vacancy Rates and Asking Rental Rates for Commercial Office Space in Manhattan, September 2005 to February 2007

	Vacancy Rates			Asking Rental Rates, per Square Foot		
	Midtown	Downtown	Total	Midtown	Downtown	Total
September 2005	9.4	10.9	9.7	$52.17	$34.13	$48.18
October 2005	8.9	10.6	9.2	52.31	33.48	48.06
November 2005	8.2	10.3	8.6	51.65	33.43	47.39
December 2005	7.6	10.1	8.1	51.92	33.58	47.42
January 2006	7.3	12.5	8.4	52.70	38.98	48.61
February 2006	7.4	12.9	8.5	52.84	38.75	48.59
March 2006	7.5	12.5	8.5	54.38	39.48	50.02
April 2006	7.5	12.0	8.4	54.58	39.93	50.41
May 2006	7.8	12.1	8.6	55.16	40.23	50.99
June 2006	6.7	11.9	7.8	54.93	40.23	50.44
July 2006	6.4	11.2	7.4	56.13	40.06	51.27
August 2006	6.3	10.3	7.1	56.96	41.78	52.55
September 2006	6.3	8.0	6.6	58.09	41.76	54.15
October 2006	6.1	8.2	6.5	62.43	43.00	57.53
November 2006	6.1	7.9	6.5	64.59	46.03	60.08
December 2006	6.1	6.9	6.3	65.66	45.02	61.13
January 2007	5.0	6.9	5.3	64.76	45.74	59.91
February 2007	5.3	6.6	5.6	67.38	47.53	62.74

Source: New York City Office of Management and Budget, *Monthly Report on Current Economic Conditions, March 2007*.

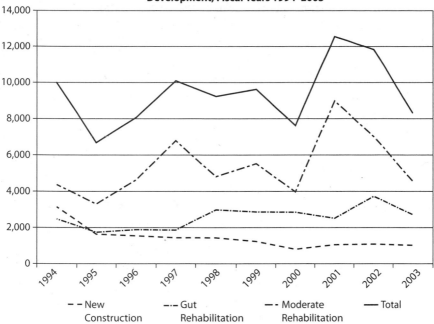

Housing Starts by Department of Housing and Preservation Development, Fiscal Years 1994–2003

- – New Construction   – ·· Gut Rehabilitation   – · Moderate Rehabilitation   — Total

Source: New York City Department of Housing and Preservation Development.

Number of Units, New Privately Owned Residential Building Permits, 2000–2006

	2000	2001	2002	2003	2004	2005	2006
Manhattan							
Single-family	0	4	3	1	1	3	2
Two-family	30	10	6	14	6	2	8
Three- and four-family	143	241	54	7	51	24	21
Five-family or more	4,937	5,854	5,344	5,210	4,497	8,464	8,759
Total	5,110	6,109	5,407	5,232	4,555	8,493	8,790
Bronx							
Single-family	36	20	18	55	33	29	74
Two-family	632	648	776	600	654	494	644
Three- and four-family	317	520	719	565	1,145	1,376	1,484
Five-family or more	661	1,028	1,113	1,715	3,092	3,038	2,456
Total	1,646	2,216	2,626	2,935	4,924	4,937	4,658
Brooklyn							
Single-family	133	229	189	118	113	105	113
Two-family	848	916	1,004	1,334	880	926	644
Three- and four-family	609	771	1,011	1,392	1,882	2,268	1,939
Five-family or more	1,314	1,057	3,043	3,210	3,950	5,729	6,495
Total	2,904	2,973	5,247	6,054	6,825	9,028	9,191
Queens							
Single-family	87	142	214	161	265	334	288
Two-family	936	1,184	1,302	1,446	2,206	1,818	2,000
Three- and four-family	620	726	884	1,194	1,627	1,595	1,798
Five-family or more	1,080	1,212	1,064	1,598	2,755	3,522	3,166
Total	2,723	3,264	3,464	4,399	6,853	7,269	7,252
Staten Island							
Single-family	1,361	1,306	913	1,222	604	829	437
Two-family	1,056	984	774	1,306	1,394	898	504
Three- and four-family	0	4	45	32	11	39	0
Five-family or more	250	0	24	38	42	106	95
Total	2,667	2,294	1,756	2,598	2,051	1,872	1,036
Total							
Single-family	1,617	1,701	1,337	1,557	1,016	1,300	914
Two-family	3,502	3,742	3,862	4,700	5,140	4,138	3,800
Three- and four-family	1,689	2,262	2,713	3,190	4,716	5,302	5,242
Five-family or more	8,242	9,151	10,588	11,771	14,336	20,859	20,971
Total	15,050	16,856	18,500	21,218	25,208	31,599	30,927

Source: U.S. Bureau of the Census.

Public Housing Developments in Full Operation

	Number of Apartments Built	Population	Date of Completion
Manhattan			
Amsterdam (West 64th Street, West 61st Street, Amsterdam Avenue, West End Avenue)	1,084	2,402	17 December 1948
Amsterdam Addition (West 64th Street, West 65th Street, Amsterdam Avenue, West End Avenue)	175	341	31 January 1974
Audubon (West 154th Street, West 155th Street, Amsterdam Avenue)	168	413	30 April 1962
Baruch (East Houston Street, FDR Drive, Delancey Street, Columbia Street)	2,194	5,396	6 August 1959
Baruch Houses Addition (Columbia Street, Delancey Street, East Houston Street, FDR Drive)	197	225	30 April 1977
Bethune Gardens (West 156th Street, Saint Nicholas Avenue, Amsterdam Avenue)	210	242	31 March 1967
Bracetti Plaza (East 3rd Street, Avenue C, East 4th Street, Avenue B)	108	288	31 May 1974
Campos Plaza I (Avenue B, East 12th Street, Avenue C, East 13th Street)	269	677	30 September 1979
Campos Plaza II (Avenue B, East 14th Street, Avenue C, East 13th Street)	224	535	30 April 1983
Carver (East 99th Street, Park Avenue, Madison Avenue, East 106th Street)	1,246	2,813	14 February 1958
Chelsea (West 25th Street, West 26th Street, Ninth Avenue)	425	964	31 May 1964
Chelsea Addition (Chelsea Park, West 26th Street, Tenth Avenue)	96	106	30 April 1968
Clinton (Park & Lexington Avenues, East 104th & 106th Streets, East 108th Street, East 110th Street)	749	1,774	31 October 1965
Corsi Houses (East 116th Street, East 117th Street, First Avenue, Second Avenue)	171	175	30 November 1973
De Hostos Apartments (Amsterdam Avenue, West 93rd Street, Broadway, West 94th Street)	223	469	28 March 1969
Douglass (West 104th Street, Manhattan Avenue, West 100th Street, Amsterdam Avenue)	2,058	4,467	25 September 1958
Douglass Addition (West 102nd Street, West 103rd Street, Amsterdam Avenue)	135	351	30 June 1965
Drew Hamilton (West 141st Street, West 144th Street, Powell Boulevard, Douglass Boulevard)	1,217	2,910	30 September 1965

Public Housing Developments in Full Operation (continued)

	Number of Apartments Built	Population	Date of Completion
Manhattan (continued)			
Dyckman (Dyckman Street, Nagle Avenue, West 204th Street, Tenth Avenue)	1,167	2,506	25 April 1951
East 120th Street Rehab (East 120th Street, First Avenue, Pleasant Avenue)	42	91	1 November 1985
East 4th Street Rehab (East 4th Street, Avenue B, Avenue C)	25	77	1 August 1988
East River (First Avenue, FDR Drive, East 102nd Street, East 105th Street)	1,170	2,531	20 May 1941
830 Amsterdam Avenue (West 101st Street, Amsterdam Avenue, West 100th Street)	159	370	31 August 1965
Elliott (West 25th Street, Chelsea Park, Ninth Avenue, Tenth Avenue)	608	1,433	15 July 1947
First Houses (East 2nd Street, East 3rd Street, Avenue A, First Avenue)	126	200	31 May 1936
Fort Washington Avenue Rehab (Riverside Drive, West 163rd Street, Fort Washington Avenue, West 165th Street)	226	261	1 October 1985
45 Allen Street (Grand Street, Allen Street, Hester Street, Eldridge Street)	107	255	31 July 1974
Fulton (West 16th Street, West 19th Street, Ninth Avenue)	944	2,243	31 March 1965
Gompers (Delancey Street, Pitt Street, Stanton Street)	474	1,168	30 April 1968
Grampion (West 119th Street, Saint Nicholas Avenue)	35	54	13 May 1977
Grant (West 125th Street, Morningside Avenue, West 123rd Street, Broadway)	1,940	4,592	31 October 1957
Harborview Terrace (West 54th Street, West 56th Street, Tenth Avenue, Eleventh Avenue)	377	699	30 June 1977
Harlem River (Macombs Place, Harlem River Drive, West 151st Street, West 153rd Street)	577	1,011	1 October 1937
Harlem River II (Douglass Boulevard, West 152nd Street, Macombs Place, West 151st Street)	116	248	31 October 1955
Hernandez (Allen Street, Stanton Street, Eldridge Street, East Houston Street)	149	285	31 August 1971
Holmes Towers (First Avenue, Isaacs Houses, FDR Drive, East 92nd Street)	537	946	30 April 1969
Isaacs (East 93rd Street, First Avenue, FDR Drive)	636	1,291	31 July 1965

Public Housing Developments in Full Operation (continued)

	Number of Apartments Built	Population	Date of Completion
Manhattan (continued)			
Jefferson (East 112th Street, Third Avenue, East 115th Street, First Avenue)	1,493	3,652	28 August 1959
Johnson (East 112th Street, East 115th Street, Third Avenue, Park Avenue)	1,310	2,368	27 December 1948
King Towers (West 112th Street, Lenox Avenue, West 115th Street, Fifth Avenue)	1,379	3,205	1 November 1954
La Guardia (Rutgers Street, Madison Street, Montgomery Street, Cherry Street)	1,094	2,626	8 August 1957
La Guardia Addition (Cherry Street, Madison Street, Rutgers Street, Montgomery Street)	160	178	31 August 1975
Lehman (Madison Avenue, Park Avenue, East 106th Street, East 110th Street)	622	1,398	30 November 1963
Lexington (East 98th Street, Third Avenue, East 99th Street, Park Avenue)	448	911	16 March 1951
Lincoln (East 132nd Street, East 135th Street, Fifth Avenue, Park Avenue)	1,286	3,099	29 December 1948
Lower East Side Infill (Delancey Street, Rivington Street, Forsythe Street, Eldridge Street)	189	411	1 June 1988
Lower East Side II (East 4th & 5th Streets, East 6th Street, Avenues B & C, Avenue D)	188	538	1 November 1988
Lower East Side III (East 9th Street, Avenue D, East 8th Street, Avenue C)	56	200	30 April 1997
Lower East Side Rehab (Group 5) (Avenue C, East 6th Street, East 7th Street)	55	115	1 December 1986
Manhattanville (West 133rd Street, Broadway, Amsterdam Avenue, West 129th Street)	1,272	2,973	30 June 1961
Manhattanville Rehab (Group 2) (Broadway, West 134th Street, Amsterdam Avenue, West 135th Street)	46	91	1 November 1988
Manhattanville Rehab (Group 3) (Broadway, West 134th Street, Amsterdam Avenue, West 135th Street)	51	116	30 September 1983
Marshall Plaza (Broadway, 158th Street, Amsterdam Avenue, 157th Street)	180	193	30 June 1986
Meltzer Tower (East 1st Street, First Avenue, East 2nd Street, Avenue A)	231	258	31 August 1971

Public Housing Developments in Full Operation (continued)

	Number of Apartments Built	Population	Date of Completion
Manhattan (continued)			
Metro North Plaza (East 101st Street, First Avenue, East 102nd Street, Second Avenue)	275	696	31 August 1971
Metro North Rehab (East 100th Street, East 102nd & 103rd Streets, First Avenue, Second Avenue)	321	308	1 January 1990
Milbank-Frawley (East 117th Street, Fifth Avenue, Madison Avenue)	80	270	1 October 1988
Morris Park Senior Citizens Home (East 124th Street, Madison Avenue, Fifth Avenue)	97	96	30 April 1977
154 West 84th Street (Amsterdam Avenue, West 84th Street, Columbus Avenue)	35	92	31 March 1996
131 Saint Nicholas Avenue (Saint Nicholas Avenue, West 116th Street, West 117th Street)	100	181	31 March 1965
Park Avenue—East 122nd & 123rd Streets (East 122nd Street, Park Avenue, East 123rd Street, Lexington Avenue)	90	196	31 March 1970
Polo Grounds Tower (Douglass Boulevard, West 155th Street, Harlem River Drive)	1,614	4,214	30 June 1968
Public School 139 (Conversion) (West 139th & 140th Streets, Powell Boulevard, Lenox Avenue)	125	126	8 October 1986
Randolph (West 114th Street, Powell Boulevard, Douglass Boulevard)	458	353	30 April 1977
Rangel (Harlem River Drive, Polo Grounds Towers, Harlem River Driveway)	984	2,332	8 October 1951
Rehab Program (Douglass Rehabs) (West 104th Street, West End Avenue, West 101st Street)	112	171	31 January 1964
Rehab Program (Taft Rehabs) (Saint Nicholas Avenue, West 119th Street, Lenox Avenue, West 112th Street)	156	297	31 January 1964
Rehab Program (Wise Rehabs) (Columbus Avenue, West 94th Street, Central Park West, West 93rd Street)	40	64	31 January 1964
Riis (FDR Drive, Avenue D, East 8th Street, East 13th Street)	1,191	2,801	17 January 1949
Riis II (FDR Drive, Avenue, East 6th Street, East 8th Street)	578	1,329	31 January 1949
Robbins Plaza (East 70th Street, First Avenue, East 71st Street, Second Avenue)	150	159	28 February 1975
Robinson (East 128th Street, East 129th Street, Lexington Avenue, Park Avenue)	189	438	31 May 1973

Public Housing Developments in Full Operation (continued)

	Number of Apartments Built	Population	Date of Completion
Manhattan (continued)			
Rutgers (Cherry Street, Pike Street, Madison Street, Rutgers Street)	721	1,625	31 March 1965
Saint Nicholas (West 127th Street, Douglass Boulevard, Powell Boulevard, West 131st Street)	1,526	3,534	30 September 1954
Samuel (City) (Lenox Avenue, 139th Street, 147th Street, Powell Boulevard)	664	1,540	31 August 1994
Seward Park Extension (Broome Street, Norfolk Street, Grand Street, Essex Street)	360	836	31 October 1973
Smith (Madison Street, Catherine Street, South Street, Saint James Place)	1,935	4,301	27 April 1953
Stanton Street (Attorney Street, Stanton Street, Ridge Street)	13	44	1 December 2003
Straus (Third Avenue, East 28th Street, Second Avenue, East 27th Street)	267	549	31 January 1965
Taft (East 112th Street, East 115th Street, Park Avenue, Fifth Avenue)	1,470	3,259	31 December 1962
Thomas Apartments (West 90th Street, Amsterdam Avenue, West 91st Street, Columbus Avenue)	87	88	31 August 1994
344 East 28th Street (East 27th Street, New Street, East 28th Street, First Avenue)	225	470	31 March 1971
335 East 111th Street (Second Avenue, East 111th Street, First Avenue, East 112th Street)	66	120	30 June 1969
Two Bridges URA (Site 7) (Clinton Street, South Street, Cherry Street, Montgomery Street)	250	637	30 April 1975
Upaca (Site 5) (East 121st Street, Lexington Avenue, East 120th Street, Park Avenue)	200	202	3 July 1986
Upaca (Site 6) (East 119th Street, Park Avenue, East 122nd Street, Lexington Avenue)	150	155	30 November 1987
Vladeck (Henry Street, Water Street, Gouverneur Street, Jackson Street)	1,531	2,403	25 November 1940
Vladeck II (Madison Street, Cherry Street, Jackson Street)	240	455	25 October 1940
Wagner (East 120th Street, Second Avenue, East 124th Street, FDR Drive)	2,162	5,169	12 June 1958
Wald (FDR Drive, Avenue D, East 6th Street, East Houston Street)	1,861	4,217	14 October 1949

Public Housing Developments in Full Operation (continued)

	Number of Apartments Built	Population	Date of Completion
Manhattan (continued)			
Washington (East 104th Street, Second Avenue, East 97th Street, Third Avenue)	1,515	3,604	20 September 1957
Washington Heights Rehab (Groups 1 &2) (West 176th Street, Amsterdam Avenue, West 177th Street, Audubon Avenue)	216	494	1 May 1988
Washington Heights Rehab Phase III (West 156th Street, Broadway, Amsterdam Avenue, West 164th & 165th Streets)	102	251	30 November 1987
Washington Heights Rehab Phase IV (C) (West 176th Street, Amsterdam Avenue, West 177th Street, Audubon Avenue)	32	174	1 October 1990
Washington Heights Rehab Phase IV (D) (West 176th Street, Amsterdam Avenue, Audubon Avenue)	32	78	1 July 1990
White (East 104th Street, Second Avenue)	248	263	30 September 1964
Wilson (FDR Drive, East 105th Street, First Avenue, East 106th Street)	398	1,293	30 June 1961
Wise Towers (West 90th Street, West 91st Street, Columbus Avenue, Amsterdam Avenue)	399	760	31 January 1965
WSUR (Brownstones) (West 89 & 90th Streets, West 91st & 93rd Streets, Columbus Avenue, Central Park West)	236	344	30 June 1968
WSUR (Site A) 120 West 94th Street (120 West 94th Street, Amsterdam Avenue)	70	156	30 September 1965
WSUR (Site B) 74 West 92nd Street (74 West 92nd Street, Columbus Avenue)	168	318	30 September 1965
WSUR (Site C) 589 Amsterdam Avenue (589 Amsterdam Avenue, West 88th Street, West 89th Street)	158	337	30 September 1965
Totals, Manhattan	54,321	118,940	
Bronx			
Adams (Westchester Avenue, Union Avenue, East 152nd Street)	925	2,384	21 August 1964
Bailey Avenue—West 193rd Street (Bailey Avenue, West 193rd Street, Heath Avenue)	233	481	31 May 1973

Public Housing Developments in Full Operation (continued)

	Number of Apartments Built	Population	Date of Completion
Bronx (continued)			
Baychester (Schieffelin Avenue, East 225th Street, East 229th Street)	441	969	31 October 1963
Betances I (Brook Avenue, East 144th Street, Saint Ann's Avenue, East 143rd Street)	309	725	31 May 1973
Betances II (East 136th Street, East 140th & 144th Streets, Jackson Avenue, Willis Avenue)	175	491	31 July 1973
Betances III (East 136th Street, East 140th & 144th Streets, Jackson Avenue, Willis Avenue)	132	128	31 July 1973
Betances IV (East 143rd Street, East 147th Street, Willis Avenue, Saint Ann's Avenue)	382	399	31 December 1973
Betances V (East 143rd Street, East 147th Street, Willis Avenue, Saint Ann's Avenue)	156	317	28 February 1974
Betances VI (East 147th Street, East 146th Street, Saint Ann's Avenue, Willis Avenue)	155	368	31 October 1982
Boston Road Plaza (Mace Avenue, Holland Avenue, Waring Avenue, Boston Road)	235	251	31 August 1972
Boston Secor (IRT Dyre Avenue line, Boston Road, Steenwick Avenue)	538	1,381	30 April 1969
Boynton Avenue Rehab (Watson Avenue, Ward Avenue, Bruckner Boulevard, Elder Avenue)	82	213	22 August 1985
Bronxchester (East 156th Street, Saint Ann's Avenue, Public School 38)	208	573	30 June 1978
Bronxdale (Watson Avenue, Bruckner Boulevard, Soundview Avenue, Leland Avenue)	1,497	3,549	28 February 1955
Bronx River (Bronx River Avenue, Harrod Avenue, East 174th Street)	1,246	3,055	28 February 1951
Bronx River Addition (East 172nd Street, East 174th Street, Manor Avenue, Harrod Avenue)	226	233	28 February 1966
Bryant Avenue—East 174th Street (East 174th Street, Bryant Avenue, East 173rd Street, Vyse Avenue)	32	106	16 April 1948
Butler (East 169th Street, East 171st Street, Webster Avenue, Park Avenue)	1,492	4,129	31 December 1964
Castle Hill (Olmstead Avenue, Havemeyer Avenue, Lacombe Avenue, Cincinnatus Avenue)	2,025	5,426	15 December 1960

Public Housing Developments in Full Operation (continued)

	Number of Apartments Built	Population	Date of Completion
Bronx (continued)			
Claremont Parkway–Franklin Avenue (Claremont Parkway, Fulton Avenue, East 171st Street, Third Avenue)	188	304	16 December 1986
Claremont Rehab (Group 2) (Clay Avenue, East 169th Street, Webster Avenue, East 166th Street)	107	250	31 December 1987
Claremont Rehab (Group 3) (East 167th Street, Teller Avenue, East 165th Street, Findlay Avenue)	115	250	28 February 1985
Claremont Rehab (Group 4) (East 169th Street, Clay Avenue, East 165th Street, Findlay Avenue)	150	355	23 October 1986
Claremont Rehab (Group 5) (College Avenue, East 167th Street, Findlay Avenue, East 165th Street)	135	311	30 November 1985
Clason Point Gardens (Story Avenue, Seward Avenue, Noble Avenue, Metcalf Avenue)	401	887	20 December 1941
College Avenue–East 165th Street (East 166th Street, Findlay Avenue, East 165th Street, College Avenue)	95	87	31 July 1972
Davidson (Prospect Avenue, Home Street, 167th Street, Union Avenue)	175	414	31 August 1973
Eagle Avenue–East 163rd Street (Eagle Avenue, East 163rd Street, Third Avenue, East 161st Street)	66	130	31 May 1971
East 152nd Street–Cortlandt Avenue (East 151st Street, East 153rd Street, Cortlandt Avenue, Melrose Avenue)	221	412	31 August 1973
East 165th Street–Bryant Avenue (Westchester Avenue, Longfellow Avenue, Aldus Street, Hoe Avenue)	111	304	31 October 1987
East 173rd Street–Vyse Avenue (Southern Boulevard, East 173rd Street, Vyse Avenue, Jennings Street)	168	411	31 October 1987
East 180th Street–Monterey Avenue (East 180th Street, East 181st Street, LaFontaine Avenue, Quarry Road)	239	557	30 September 1973
Eastchester Gardens (Burke Avenue, Bouck Avenue, Adee Avenue, Yates Avenue)	877	2,178	1 June 1950
Edenwald (Grenada Place, Baychester Avenue, East 225th Street, Laconia Avenue)	2,039	5,380	30 October 1953
Forest (Tinton Avenue, East 163rd Street, Trinity Avenue, East 166th Street)	1,350	3,240	12 November 1956

Public Housing Developments in Full Operation (continued)

	Number of Apartments Built	Population	Date of Completion
Bronx (continued)			
Fort Independence Street–Heath Avenue (Fort Independence Street, Heath Avenue, Bailey Avenue, Summit Place)	344	803	30 November 1974
1471 Watson Avenue (Watson Avenue, Colgate Avenue, Evergreen Avenue)	96	167	31 December 1970
Franklin Avenue I Conventional (East 169th Street, Franklin Avenue, East 170th Street)	61	153	31 August 1994
Franklin Avenue II Conventional (East 169th Street, Franklin Avenue, East 170th Street)	45	119	31 August 1994
Franklin Avenue III Conventional (East 170th Street, Clinton Avenue, Jefferson Place)	15	34	31 August 1994
Glebe Avenue–Westchester Avenue (Glebe Avenue, Westchester Avenue, Castle Hill Avenue, Lyon Avenue)	132	143	31 December 1971
Gun Hill (Holland Avenue, White Plains Road, Gun Hill Road, Magenta Street)	733	1,438	30 November 1950
Harrison Avenue Rehab (Group A) (Harrison Avenue, West Burnside Avenue, Grand Avenue, Kingsland Place)	34	67	1 September 1986
Harrison Avenue Rehab (Group B) (University Place, West Burnside Avenue, Grand Avenue, Kingsland Place)	150	259	1 December 1986
Highbridge Gardens (Sedgwick Avenue, West 167th Street, University Avenue)	700	1,699	18 June 1954
Highbridge Rehabs (Anderson Avenue) (Anderson Avenue, West 166th Street, Nelson Avenue, West 167th Street)	135	452	30 April 1997
Highbridge Rehabs (Nelson Avenue) (West 166th Street, Nelson Avenue, West 168th Street)	80	248	31 October 1996
Hoe Avenue–East 173rd Street (Hoe Avenue, East 173rd Street, East 174th Street, Vyse Avenue)	65	118	31 December 1970
Hunts Point Avenue Rehab (Lafayette Avenue, Hunts Point Avenue, Seneca Avenue, Irvine Street)	131	338	30 November 1991
Jackson (Park Avenue, Cortlandt Avenue, East 158th Street, East 156th Street)	868	2,471	31 July 1963
Longfellow Avenue Rehab (Westchester Avenue, Whitlock Avenue, East 165th Street, Bryant Avenue)	75	241	31 October 1990

Public Housing Developments in Full Operation (continued)

	Number of Apartments Built	Population	Date of Completion
Bronx (continued)			
Macombs Road (Featherbed Lane, Macombs Road, Nelson Avenue, West 174th Street)	156	114	1 December 1986
Marble Hill (Exterior Street, West 225th Street, Broadway, West 230th Street)	1,682	3,500	6 March 1952
McKinley (East 161st Street, East 163rd Street, Tinton Avenue, Kingsland Place)	619	1,577	31 July 1962
Melrose (Morris Avenue, East 153rd Street, Courtlandt Avenue, East 156th Street)	1,023	2,581	20 June 1952
Middletown Plaza (Roberts Avenue, Jarvis Avenue, Middletown Road, Hobart Avenue)	179	191	31 August 1973
Mill Brook (East 135th Street, Brook Avenue, East 137th Street, Cypress Avenue)	1,255	2,988	26 May 1959
Mill Brook Extension (Cypress Avenue, East 135th Street, East 137th Street)	125	364	31 January 1962
Mitchel (Lincoln Avenue, East 138th Street, Willis Avenue, East 135th Street)	1,732	3,913	28 February 1966
Monroe (Soundview Avenue, Story Avenue, Taylor Avenue, Lafayette Avenue)	1,102	2,893	2 November 1961
Moore (East 147th Street, East 149th Street, Jackson Avenue, Trinity Avenue)	463	1,155	31 March 1964
Morris Heights Rehab (West 174th Street, Unity Avenue, West Tremont Avenue, Undercliff Avenue)	315	205	1 April 1986
Morris I (Park Avenue, East 170th Street, Third Avenue, East 169th Street)	1,085	2,998	31 August 1965
Morris II (Park Avenue, East 171st Street, Third Avenue, East 170th Street)	802	2,150	31 August 1965
Morrisania (East 169th Street, Washington Avenue, Park Avenue)	206	508	31 May 1963
Morrisania Air Rights (Park Avenue, 158th Street, 161st Street, 163rd Street)	843	1,860	1 January 1981
Mott Haven (East 140th Street, East 144th Street, Alexander Avenue, Willis Avenue)	993	2,460	31 March 1965
Murphy (Crotona Avenue, Crotona Park North, Cross-Bronx Expressway)	281	737	31 March 1964

	Number of Apartments Built	Population	Date of Completion
Bronx (continued)			
Parkside (Adee Avenue, White Plains Road, Arrow Avenue, Bronx Park East)	879	1,808	12 June 1951
Patterson (Morris Avenue, Third Avenue, East 145th Street, East 139th Street)	1,791	4,491	31 December 1950
Pelham Parkway (Pelham Parkway, Wallace Avenue, Williamsbridge Road, Mace Avenue)	1,266	2,587	30 June 1950
Randall Avenue–Balcom Avenue (Randall Avenue, Balcom Avenue, Schley Avenue, Buttrick Avenue)	252	264	31 October 1978
Sack Wern (Beach Avenue, Taylor Avenue, Noble Avenue, Rosedale Avenue)	413	899	12 May 1977
Saint Mary's Park (Cauldwell Avenue, East 156th Street, Westchester Avenue, Trinity Avenue)	1,007	2,252	30 April 1959
Sedgwick (Undercliff Avenue, West 174th Street, University Avenue)	786	1,596	23 March 1951
Soundview (Rosedale Avenue, Lacombe Avenue, Bronx River Avenue, Soundview Park)	1,259	3,183	29 October 1954
South Bronx Area (Site 402) (East 158th Street, East 161st Street, Cauldwell Avenue, Eagle Avenue)	114	379	1 May 1988
Stebbins Avenue–Hewitt Place (Hewitt Place, Westchester Avenue, Rev. James Polite Avenue, Dawson Street)	120	310	17 April 1987
Teller Avenue–East 166th Street (Teller Avenue, East 167th Street, Clay Avenue, East 166th Street)	90	176	30 September 1971
1010 East 178th Street (East Tremont Avenue, Bryant Avenue, East 178th Street, Boston Road)	220	471	31 March 1971
Throggs Neck (Randall Avenue, Calhoun Avenue, Sampson Avenue, Balcom Avenue)	1,185	2,786	27 November 1953
Throggs Neck Addition (Dewey Avenue, Balcom Avenue, Randall Avenue, Throggs Neck Houses)	287	725	30 September 1971
Twin Parks East (Site 9) (Clinton Avenue, East 180th Street, Prospect Avenue, Oakland Place)	219	232	30 April 1982
Twin Parks West (Sites 1 & 2) (Webster Avenue, East 182nd Street, Tiebout Avenue, East 184th Street)	312	861	30 September 1974
Union Avenue–East 163rd Street (East 165th Street, Prospect Avenue, East 163rd Street, Union Avenue)	200	206	11 March 1985

	Number of Apartments Built	Population	Date of Completion
Bronx (continued)			
Union Avenue–East 166th Street (East 166th Street, Prospect Avenue, Home Street, Union Avenue)	120	315	1 September 1988
University Avenue Rehab (West Burnside Avenue, University Avenue, West Tremont Avenue, Andrews Avenue)	230	354	31 January 1985
Webster (East 169th Street, Park Avenue, East 168th Street, Webster Avenue)	606	1,538	30 September 1965
West Farms Road Rehab (Freeman Street, Jennings Street, West Farms Road, Longfellow Avenue)	208	429	13 August 1986
West Farms Square Conventional (East 167th Street, Longfellow Avenue, West Farms Road)	20	49	30 June 1994
West Tremont Avenue–Sedgwick Avenue Area (West Tremont Avenue, Montgomery Avenue, Palisade Place, Sedgwick Avenue)	148	155	31 July 1973
West Tremont Rehab (Group 1) (West 175th Street, Montgomery Avenue, West 176th Street, Andrews Avenue)	97	110	30 September 1983
West Tremont Rehab (Group 2) (West 175th Street, Popham Avenue, West 176th Street, University Avenue)	98	130	1 November 1989
West Tremont Rehab (Group 3) (West 174th Street, Montgomery Avenue, West 175th Street, University Avenue)	88	55	1 November 1989
Washington Avenue (East 167th Street, East 168th Street, Third Avenue, Washington Avenue)	66	175	31 December 1975
Totals, Bronx	45,532	106,128	
Brooklyn			
Albany (Albany Avenue, Saint Marks Avenue, Troy Avenue, Park Place)	829	1,927	14 October 1950
Albany II (Bergen Street, Troy Avenue, Albany Houses, Albany Avenue)	400	1,004	7 February 1957
Armstrong I (Clifton Place, Marcy Avenue, Gates Avenue, Bedford Avenue)	371	1,134	31 May 1973
Armstrong II (Greene Avenue, Gates Avenue, Tompkins Avenue, Marcy Avenue)	248	787	31 October 1974

	Number of Apartments Built	Population	Date of Completion
Brooklyn (continued)			
Atlantic Terminal Site 4B (Clermont Avenue, Atlantic Avenue, Carlton Avenue, Fulton Street)	300	662	30 April 1976
Bay View (Seaview Avenue, East 102nd Street, Rockaway Parkway, Shore Parkway)	1,610	3,678	7 June 1956
Bedford-Stuyvesant Rehab (Throop Avenue, Vernon Avenue, Marcus Garvey Boulevard, Hart Street)	85	210	31 May 1983
Belmont-Sutter Area (Belmont Avenue, Jerome Street, Sutter Avenue, Barbey Street)	72	224	28 February 1986
Berry Street–South 9th Street (South 9th Street, Bedford & Division Avenues, South 11th Street, Wythe Avenue)	150	466	30 September 1995
Borinquen Plaza I (Manhattan Avenue, Boerum Street, Bushwick Avenue, Varet Street)	509	1,198	28 February 1975
Borinquen Plaza II (Boerum Street, Humboldt Street, Seigel Street, Bushwick Avenue)	425	1,330	31 December 1975
Boulevard (Linden Boulevard, Ashford Street, Wortman Avenue, Schenck Avenue)	1,441	3,008	22 March 1951
Breukelen (Stanley Avenue, Flatlands Avenue, East 103rd Street, Williams Avenue)	1,595	3,965	6 November 1952
Brevoort (Bainbridge Street, Ralph Avenue, Fulton Street, Patchen Avenue)	896	2,035	10 August 1955
Brown (Eastern Parkway, Prospect Place, Hopkinson Avenue, Saint Marks Avenue)	200	216	23 July 1985
Brownsville (Sutter Avenue, Dumont Avenue, Mother Gaston Boulevard, Rockaway Avenue)	1,338	3,638	16 April 1948
Bushwick (Humboldt Street, Moore Street, Bushwick Avenue, Flushing Avenue)	1,220	3,128	1 April 1960
Bushwick II (Groups A & C) (Central Avenue, Harman Avenue, Green Avenue, Halsey Street)	300	814	19 July 1984
Bushwick II (Groups B & D) (Gates Avenue, Wilson Avenue, Madison Avenue, Evergreen Avenue)	300	811	5 July 1984
Bushwick II CDA (Group E) (Knickerbocker Avenue, Wilson Avenue, Gates Avenue, Menehan Street)	276	591	10 December 1986
Carey Gardens (West 24th Street, Neptune Avenue, West 22nd Street, Surf Avenue)	683	1,711	30 November 1970

Public Housing Developments in Full Operation (continued)

	Number of Apartments Built	Population	Date of Completion
Brooklyn (continued)			
Coney Island (Surf Avenue, West 32nd Street, Riegelmann Boardwalk, West 29th Street)	534	1,324	25 February 1957
Coney Island I (Site 1B) (West 20th Street, West 21st Street, Surf Avenue, Mermaid Avenue)	193	560	31 May 1973
Coney Island I (Site 8) (West 35th Street, West 36th Street, Surf Avenue, Mermaid Avenue)	125	397	31 December 1973
Coney Island (Sites 4 & 5) (Mermaid Avenue, West 25th Street, Surf Avenue, West 26th Street)	325	1,123	31 July 1974
Cooper Park (Frost Street, Morgan Avenue, Kingsland Avenue, Maspeth Avenue)	700	1,606	25 June 1953
Crown Heights (Buffalo Avenue, Bergen Street, Ralph Avenue, Saint John's Place)	121	280	4 September 1986
Cypress Hills (Sutter Avenue, Euclid Avenue, Linden Boulevard, Fountain Avenue)	1,444	3,526	25 May 1955
East New York City Line (Fountain Avenue, Hegeman Avenue, Logan Street)	66	287	31 March 1976
Farragut (York Street, Nassau Street, Navy Street, Bridge Street)	1,390	3,503	7 May 1952
Fenimore-Lefferts (Fenimore Street, Troy Avenue, Lefferts Avenue, Nostrand Avenue)	36	111	30 September 1969
Fiorentino Plaza (Glenmore Avenue, Van Siclen Avenue, Pitkin Avenue, Wyona Street)	160	474	31 October 1971
572 Warren Street (Warren Street, Baltic Street, Fourth Avenue, Third Avenue)	200	385	31 August 1974
Garvey Group A (East New York Avenue, Amboy Street, Pitkin Avenue)	321	841	28 February 1975
Glenmore Plaza (Pitkin Avenue, Glenmore Avenue, Watkins Street, Powell Street)	440	812	30 April 1968
Glenwood (East 56th Street, Farragut Road, Ralph Avenue, Avenue H)	1,188	2,765	14 July 1950
Gowanus (Wyckoff Street, Douglass Street, Bond Street, Hoyt Street)	1,139	2,889	24 June 1949
Gravesend (Neptune Avenue, Bayview Avenue, West 33rd Street)	634	1,574	28 June 1954

Public Housing Developments in Full Operation (continued)

	Number of Apartments Built	Population	Date of Completion
Brooklyn (continued)			
Haber (West 24th Street, Surf Avenue, Riegelmann Boardwalk, West 25th Street)	380	456	30 June 1965
Hope Gardens (Linden Street, Wilson Avenue, Grove Street)	324	679	31 August 1981
Howard (East New York Avenue, Mother Gaston Boulevard, Pitkin Avenue, Rockaway Avenue)	815	1,961	30 December 1955
Howard Avenue (East New York Avenue, Grafton Street, Sutter Avenue, Tapscott Street)	150	398	1 August 1988
Howard Avenue–Park Place (Howard Avenue, Sterling Place, Eastern Parkway, Saint John's Place)	156	517	31 August 1994
Hughes Apartments (Rockaway Boulevard, Mother Gaston Boulevard, Sutter Avenue, Belmont Avenue)	513	1,385	30 June 1968
Hylan (Moore Street, Humboldt Street, Seigel Street, Bushwick Avenue)	209	475	30 June 1960
Independence (Clymer Street, Wilson Street, Wythe Avenue, Bedford Avenue)	744	1,868	31 October 1965
Ingersoll (Park Avenue, Saint Edwards Street, Myrtle Avenue, Prince Street)	1,840	3,053	24 February 1944
Kingsborough (Ralph Avenue, Pacific Street, Bergen Street, Rochester Avenue)	1,163	2,429	31 October 1941
Kingsborough Extension (Bergen Street, Pacific Street, Rochester Avenue, Ralph Avenue)	184	198	31 May 1966
Lafayette (Lafayette Avenue, Classon Avenue, DeKalb Avenue, Franklin Avenue)	882	2,460	31 July 1962
Lenox Road–Rockaway Parkway (Kings Highway, East 98th Street, Wilmohr Street, East 97th Street)	74	194	1 September 1985
Linden (Vermont Street, Stanley Avenue, Schenk Avenue, Cozine Avenue)	1,586	3,979	17 July 1958
Long Island Baptist Houses (Sheffield Avenue, Sutter Avenue, Dumont Avenue, Hinsdale Street)	232	573	30 June 1981
Low Houses (Sackman Street, Powell Street, Christopher Street, Pitkin Avenue)	536	1,469	31 December 1967
Marcy (Flushing Avenue, Marcy Avenue, Nostrand Avenue, Myrtle Avenue)	1,717	4,356	19 January 1949

Public Housing Developments in Full Operation (continued)

	Number of Apartments Built	Population	Date of Completion
Brooklyn (continued)			
Marcy Avenue–Greene Avenue (Site A) (Greene Avenue, Marcy Avenue, Nostrand Avenue, Lexington Avenue)	48	166	30 June 1997
Marcy Avenue–Greene Avenue (Site B) (Greene Avenue, Marcy Avenue, Nostrand Avenue, Lexington Avenue)	30	89	30 June 1997
Marlboro (Stillwell Avenue, Avenue V, 86th Street, Avenue X)	1,765	4,086	27 February 1958
Nostrand (Avenue V, Bragg Street, Avenue X, Batchelder Street)	1,148	2,468	14 December 1950
Ocean Hill Apartments (Broadway, Macdougal Street, Mother Gaston Boulevard, Cherry Street)	238	585	31 March 1968
Ocean Hill–Brownsville (Ralph Avenue, Atlantic Avenue, Saratoga Avenue, Dean Street)	125	335	10 November 1986
O'Dwyer Gardens (West 32nd Street, Surf Avenue, West 35th Street, Mermaid Avenue)	573	1,032	31 December 1969
104–14 Tapscott Street (Tapscott Street, Union Street, Sutter Avenue, Blake Avenue)	30	73	31 October 1972
Palmetto Gardens (Palmetto Street, Gates Avenue, Evergreen Avenue, Bushwick Avenue)	115	119	31 March 1977
Park Rock Rehab (Belmont Avenue, Jerome Street, Sutter Avenue, Barbey Street)	134	331	1 September 1986
Pennsylvania Avenue–Wortman Avenue (Pennsylvania Avenue, Wortman Avenue, Stanley Avenue, Vermont Street)	336	656	30 September 1972
Pink (Crescent Street, Linden Boulevard, Elderts Lane, Stanley Avenue)	1,500	3,841	30 September 1959
Ralph Avenue Rehab (East New York Avenue, Ralph Avenue, Sutter Avenue, East 98th Street)	118	294	23 December 1986
Red Hook I (Dwight Street, Clinton Street, West 9th Street, Lorraine Street)	2,545	5,444	20 November 1939
Red Hook II (Richards Street, Dwight Street, Wolcott Street, Red Hook Park)	346	973	27 May 1955
Reid Apartments (Troy Avenue, Albany Avenue, East New York Avenue, Maple Street)	230	229	30 November 1969
Roosevelt I (Kosciusko Street, Pulaski Street, Marcus Garvey Boulevard, Stuyvesant Avenue)	763	1,921	30 September 1964

Public Housing Developments in Full Operation (continued)

	Number of Apartments Built	Population	Date of Completion
Brooklyn (continued)			
Roosevelt II (Lewis Avenue, Stuyvesant Avenue, Hart Street, Pulaski Street)	342	753	31 December 1966
Rutland Towers (East New York Avenue, East 91st Street, East 92nd Street, Rutland Road)	61	92	17 May 1977
Saratoga Square (Halsey Street, Macon Street, Broadway, Saratoga Avenue)	251	268	30 November 1980
Saratoga Village (Saratoga Avenue, Hancock Street, Halsey Street)	125	287	31 December 1966
Sheepshead Bay (Avenue X, Batchelder Street, Avenue V, Nostrand Avenue)	1,056	2,566	8 August 1950
Sterling Place Rehabs (Saint Johns–Sterling) (Saint Johns & Park Places, Sterling Place, Buffalo & Utica Avenues, Ralph Avenue)	83	320	11 May 1991
Sterling Place Rehabs (Sterling-Buffalo) (Saint Johns & Park Places, Sterling Place, Buffalo & Utica Avenues, Ralph Avenue)	125	387	11 May 1991
Stuyvesant Gardens I (Quincy Street, Malcolm X Boulevard, Monroe Street, Lewis Avenue)	331	935	31 August 1972
Stuyvesant Gardens II (Quincy Street, Malcolm X Boulevard, Stuyvesant Avenue)	150	153	28 February 1986
Sumner (Park Avenue, Lewis Avenue, Myrtle Avenue, Throop Avenue)	1,099	2,510	14 May 1958
Surfside Gardens (West 31st Street, Neptune Avenue, West 33rd Street, Surf Avenue)	600	1,272	30 June 1969
Sutter Avenue–Union Street (Sutter Avenue, Union Street, East New York Avenue)	100	292	31 August 1995
Tapscott Street Rehab (Sutter Avenue, Grafton Street, Dumont Avenue, Union Street)	155	396	24 January 1986
Taylor Street–Wythe Avenue (Wythe Avenue, Clymer Street, Ross Street)	525	1,519	30 June 1974
303 Vernon Avenue (Vernon Avenue, Marcus Garvey Boulevard, Vernon Avenue)	234	597	31 May 1967
Tilden (Dumont Avenue, Mother Gaston Boulevard, Livonia Avenue, Rockaway Avenue)	998	2,688	30 June 1961

	Number of Apartments Built	Population	Date of Completion
Brooklyn (continued)			
Tompkins (Park Avenue, Throop Avenue, Myrtle Avenue, Tompkins Avenue)	1,046	3,092	31 July 1964
Unity Plaza (Sites 17, 24 & 25A) (Sutter Avenue, Blake Avenue, Sheffield Avenue, Alabama Avenue)	167	465	30 November 1973
Unity Plaza (Sites 4–27) (Blake Street, Sheffield Avenue, Dumont Avenue, Hinsdale Street)	462	1,229	30 September 1973
Van Dyke I (Sutter Avenue, Powell Street, Livonia Avenue, Mother Gaston Boulevard)	1,603	4,291	27 May 1955
Van Dyke II (Dumont Avenue, Powell Street)	112	127	30 April 1964
Vandalia Avenue (Louisiana Avenue, Vandalia Avenue, Georgia Avenue, Flatlands Avenue)	293	326	31 May 1983
Weeksville Gardens (Pacific Street, Schenectady Avenue, Dean Street, Troy Avenue)	257	783	30 April 1974
Whitman (Park Avenue, Carlton Avenue, Myrtle Avenue, Saint Edwards Street)	1,659	2,806	24 February 1944
Williams Plaza (Roebling Street, Broadway, Division Avenue, Marcy Avenue)	577	1,435	30 April 1964
Williamsburg (Leonard Street, Bushwick Avenue, Maujer Street, Scholes Street)	1,630	3,186	10 April 1938
Woodson (Blake Avenue, Livonia Avenue, Powell Street, Junius Street)	407	420	31 August 1970
Wyckoff Gardens (Third Avenue, Nevins Street, Wyckoff Street, Baltic Street)	529	1,137	31 December 1966
Totals, Brooklyn	58,790	138,418	
Queens			
Astoria (27th Avenue, 8th Street, Hallet's Cove, East River)	1,104	3,191	9 November 1954
Baisley Park (Long Island Rail Road, Foch Boulevard, 116th Avenue, Guy Brewer Boulevard)	386	970	30 April 1961
Beach 41st Street–Beach Channel Drive (Beach 38th Street, Beach 41st Street, Norton Avenue, Beach Channel Drive)	712	1,682	30 November 1973
Bland (Roosevelt Avenue, Prince Street, College Point Boulevard, Long Island Rail Road)	400	955	8 May 1952
Carleton Manor (Rockaway Freeway, Beach Channel Drive)	174	392	31 March 1967

Public Housing Developments in Full Operation (continued)

	Number of Apartments Built	Population	Date of Completion
Queens (continued)			
Conlon LIHFE Towers (170th Street, 172nd Street, Jamaica Avenue, 93rd Avenue)	216	234	31 March 1973
Forest Hills Coop (108th Street–62nd Drive) (108th Street, 62nd Drive, Colonial Avenue, Horace Harding Expressway)	430	859	30 November 1975
Hammel (Beach 86th Street, Hammels Boulevard, Beach 81st Street, Rockaway Beach Boulevard)	712	1,962	20 April 1955
International Tower (170th Street, 69th Avenue, 169th Street, Jamaica Avenue)	159	171	31 May 1983
Latimer Gardens (34th & 35th Avenues, Linden Place, Leavitt Street, 137th Street)	423	807	30 September 1970
Leavitt Street–34th Avenue (Leavitt Street, Union Street, 34th Avenue, 34th Road)	83	91	31 October 1974
Ocean Bay Apartments (Bayside) (Beach 58th Street, Alameda Avenue, Beach 51st Street, Beach Channel Drive)	1,395	3,417	25 September 1961
Ocean Bay Apartments (Oceanside) (Arverne Boulevard, Beach 56th Street, Beach Channel Drive, Beach 54th Street)	418	838	28 February 1951
Pomonok (71st Avenue, Parsons Boulevard, Kissena Boulevard, 65th Avenue)	2,071	4,331	30 June 1952
Queensbridge North (41st Avenue, Vernon Boulevard, 40th Avenue, 21st Street)	1,543	3,483	15 March 1940
Queensbridge South (41st Avenue, Vernon Boulevard, 41st Road, 21st Street)	1,604	3,502	15 March 1940
Ravenswood (12th Street, 34th Avenue, 24th Street, 36th Avenue)	2,166	4,525	19 July 1951
Redfern (Redfern Avenue, Hassock Street, Beach Channel Drive, Beach 12th Street)	604	1,643	28 August 1959
Rehab Program (College Point) (125th Street, 22nd Avenue, 126th Street)	13	12	31 January 1964
Shelton House (162nd Street, 89th Avenue, 163rd Street, Jamaica Avenue)	155	167	31 October 1978

Public Housing Developments in Full Operation (continued)

	Number of Apartments Built	Population	Date of Completion
Queens (continued)			
South Jamaica I (158th Street, South Road, 160th Street, 109th Avenue)	448	916	1 August 1940
South Jamaica II (South Road, 160th Street, Brinkerhoff Avenue, 158th Street)	600	1,624	25 October 1954
Woodside (49th Street, 51st Street, 31st Avenue, Newton Road)	1,357	3,286	30 December 1949
Totals, Queens	17,173	39,058	
Staten Island			
Berry (Richmond Road, Dongan Hills Avenue, Seaver Avenue, Jefferson Street)	506	950	27 October 1950
Cassidy-Lafayette (Cassidy Place, Fillmore Street, Lafayette Avenue, Clinton Avenue)	380	367	30 September 1971
Mariner's Harbor (Grand View Avenue, Roxbury Street, Lockman Avenue, Continental Place)	607	1,645	3 September 1954
Markham Gardens (Richmond Terrace, Wayne Street, Broadway, North Burgher Avenue)	39	54	30 June 1943
New Lane Area (Linden Place, New Lane, Waterfront Tract)	277	315	12 July 1984
Richmond Terrace (Jersey Street, Richmond Terrace, Crescent Avenue)	487	1,292	30 April 1964
South Beach (Kramer Street, Lamport Boulevard, Reid Avenue, Parkinson Avenue)	422	966	20 March 1950
Stapleton (Broad & Hill Streets, Tompkins Avenue, Warren Street, Gordon Street)	693	1,921	31 May 1962
Todt Hill (Manor Road, Schmidts Lane, La Guardia Avenue, Westwood Avenue)	502	1,060	1 June 1950
West Brighton I (Castleton Avenue, Henderson Avenue, Alaska Street, Broadway)	490	1,342	31 December 1962
West Brighton II (Castleton Avenue, Alaska Street, Broadway)	144	72	31 December 1965
Totals, Staten Island	4,547	9,984	
Totals, Citywide	180,363	412,528	

Source: New York City Housing Authority, *Development Data Book 2006.*

4 Crime and Justice

Police Commissioners of the City of New York

Michael C. Murphy
22 February 1901 to 1 January 1902
John N. Partridge
1 January 1902 to 1 January 1903
Francis V. Greene
1 January 1903 to 1 January 1904
William McAdoo
1 January 1904 to 1 January 1906
Theodore A. Bingham
1 January 1906 to 1 July 1909
William F. Baker
1 July 1909 to 20 October 1910
James C. Cropsey
20 October 1910 to 23 May 1911
Rhinelander Waldo
23 May 1911 to December 1913
Douglas I. McKay
31 December 1913 to 8 April 1914
Arthur Woods
8 April 1914 to 1 January 1918
Frederick H. Bugher
1 January 1918 to 23 January 1918
Richard E. Enright
23 January 1918 to 30 December 1925
George V. McLaughlin
1 January 1926 to 2 April 1927
Joseph A. Warren
12 April 1927 to 18 December 1928
Grover A. Whalen
18 December 1928 to 21 May 1930
Edward P. Mulrooney
21 May 1930 to 12 April 1933
James S. Bolan
15 April 1933 to 31 December 1933
John F. O'Ryan
1 January 1934 to 24 September 1934
Lewis J. Valentine
25 September 1934 to 14 September 1945

Arthur W. Wallander
23 September 1945 to 28 February 1949
William P. O'Brien
1 March 1949 to 25 September 1950
Thomas F. Murphy
26 September 1945 to 5 July 1951
George P. Monaghan
9 July 1951 to 31 December 1953
Francis W. H. Adams
1 January 1954 to 1 August 1955
Stephan P. Kennedy
2 August 1955 to 22 February 1961
Michael J. Murphy
23 February 1961 to 6 June 1965
Vincent L. Broderick
7 June 1965 to 21 February 1966
Howard R. Leary
22 February 1966 to 8 October 1970
Patrick V. Murphy
9 October 1970 to 12 May 1973
Donald F. Cawley
13 May 1973 to 11 January 1974
Michael Codd
12 January 1974 to 31 December 1977
Robert J. McGuire
1 January 1978 to 29 December 1983
William Devine
30 December 1983 to 31 December 1983
Benjamin Ward
1 January 1984 to 22 October 1989
Richard J. Condon
23 October 1989 to 21 January 1990
Lee P. Brown
22 January 1990 to 1 September 1992
Raymond W. Kelly
1 September 1992 to 9 January 1994
William J. Bratton
10 January 1994 to 14 April 1996

Howard Safir
     15 April 1996 to 20 August 2000
Bernard B. Kerik
     21 August 2000 to 31 December 2001
Raymond W. Kelly
     1 January 2002 to present

Source: New York Police Department.

District Attorneys of the Five Counties

Manhattan (jurisdiction includes
     the Bronx until 1914)
Hugh Maxwell
     28 January 1817 to 31 May 1818
Pierre C. VanWyck
     1 June 1818 to 31 December 1820
Hugh Maxwell
     13 February 1821 to 24 May 1829
Ogden Hoffman
     26 May 1829 to 21 May 1835
James R. Whiting
     4 June 1838 to 9 June 1844
John McKeon
     6 February 1846 to 31 December 1850
Abraham Oakey Hall
     1 January 1855 to 31 December 1857
Peter B. Sweeney
     1 January 1858 to 2 October 1858
Nelson T. Waterbury
     1 January 1859 to 31 December 1861
Abraham Oakey Hall
     1 January 1862 to 31 December 1868
Samuel B. Garvin
     2 January 1869 to 31 December 1972
Benjamin K. Phelps
     1 January 1873 to 30 December 1880
Daniel G. Rollins
     1 January 1881 to 1 December 1881

John McKeon
     1 January 1882 to 22 November 1883
Wheeler H. Peckham
     1 December 1883 to 10 December 1883
Peter B. Olney
     11 December 1883 to 31 December 1884
Randolph B. Martine
     1 January 1885 to 31 December 1887
John R. Fellows
     1 January 1888 to 31 December 1890
DeLancey Nicoll
     1 January 1891 to 31 December 1893
John R. Fellows
     1 January 1894 to 10 December 1896
Vernon M. Davis
     10 December 1896 to 18 December 1896
William M. K. Olcott
     18 December 1896 to 31 December 1897
Asa Bird Gardiner
     1 January 1898 to 24 December 1900
Eugene A. Philbin
     26 December 1900 to 31 December 1901
William Travers Jerome
     1 January 1902 to 31 December 1909
Charles S. Whitman
     1 January 1910 to 31 December 1914
Edward Swann
     1 January 1916 to 31 December 1921

District Attorneys of the Five Counties (continued)

Manhattan (continued)

Joab H. Banton
1 January 1922 to 31 December 1929

Thomas C. T. Crain
1 January 1930 to 31 December 1933

William Copeland Dodge
1 January 1934 to 31 December 1937

Thomas E. Dewey
1 January 1938 to 31 December 1941

Frank Hogan
1 January 1942 to 3 February 1974

Richard H. Kuh
13 February 1974 to 31 December 1974

Robert Morgenthau
1 January 1975 to present

Bronx

Francis Martin
1914–1921

Edward J. Glennon
1922–1923

John E. McGeehan
1924–1929

Charles B. McLaughlin
1930–1932

Samuel J. Foley
1933–1949

George B. DeLuca
1950–1954

Daniel V. Sullivan
1955–1960

Isadore Dollinger
1961–1970

Burton B. Roberts
1971–1974

Mario Merola
1975–1988

Robert Johnson
1989–

Brooklyn

James B. Clarke
1819–1830

Nathan B. Morse
1830–1833

William Rockwell
1833–1839

Nathan B. Morse
1839–1847

Harmanus B. Duryea
1847–1853

Richard C. Underhill
1853–1856

John G. Schumaker
1856–1859

John Winslow
1859–1862

Samuel D. Morris
1862–1871

Winchester Britton
1871–1874

Thomas H. Rodman
1874

John Winslow
1874

Winchester Britton
1874–1877

Isaac S. Catlin
1877–1883

James W. Ridgeway
1883–1895

Foster L. Backus
1896–1897

Josiah T. Marean
1898

Hiram R. Steele
1898–1899

John F. Clarke
1900–1911

Brooklyn (continued)

James C. Cropsey
1912–1916

Harry E. Lewis
1917–1921

Henry E. Ruston
1922

Charles S. Dodd
1923–1929

George E. Brower
1930

William F. X. Geoghan
1931–1939

William O'Dwyer
1940–1945

Miles F. McDonald
1946–1953

Edward S. Silver
1954–1965

Aaron E. Koota
1966–1974

Eugene Gold
1975–1982

Elizabeth Holtzman
1983–1988

Charles J. Hynes
1989–

Queens

Eliphalet Wickes
1818–1821

William T. McConn
1821–1826

Benjamin F. Thompson
1826–1836

William H. Barroll
1836–1842

Alexander Hadden
1842–1846

John G. Lamberson
1847–1853

William H. Onderdonk
1853–1859

John J. Amrstrong
1859–1865

Benjamin W. Downing
1865–1883

John Fleming
1883–1887

Thomas F. McGowan
1887

John Fleming
1888–1893

David A. Noble
1894–1895

William J. Youngs
1896–1898

George W. Davison
1899

John B. Merrill
1900–1902

George A. Gregg
1903–1905

Ira G. Darrin
1906–1908

Frederick DeWitt
1909–1911

Matthew J. Smith
1912–1914

Denis O'Leary
1915–1920

Dana Wallace
1921–1923

Richard Saville Newcombe
1924–1929

James J. Hallinan
1930–1932

Queens (continued)

Charles S. Colden
1933–1935
Charles P. Sullivan
1935–1951
T. Vincent Quinn
1951–1955
Frank D. O'Connor
1956–1965
Nat H. Hentel
1966
Thomas J. Mackell
1967–1973
Michael F. Armstrong
1973
Nicholas Ferraro
1974–1976
John J. Santucci
1977–1991
Richard A. Brown
1991–

Staten Island

George M. Pinney
1880–1898
Edward S. Rawson
1899–1904
John J. Kenny
1905–1907

Samuel H. Evins
1908–1910
Albert Fach
1911–1919
Joseph Maloy
1920–1923
Albert Fach
1924–1931
Thomas J. Walsh
1932–1937
Frank H. Innes
1938–1941
Farrel M. Kane
1942–1947
Robert E. Johnson
1947
Herman Methfessel
1948–1951
Sidney O. Simonson
1952–1955
John M. Braisted Jr.
1956–1975
Thomas R. Sullivan
1976–1982
William L. Murphy
1983–2003
Daniel M. Donovan Jr.
2003–

Sources: Offices of the District Attorneys; Manual of the Corporation of the City of New York; Annual Legislative Manuals, New York State, 1880–1910; New York Red Books, 1911–2005.

Incidence of Major Crimes, 2001–2005

	2001	2002	2003	2004	2005	Percent Change, 2001–2005
Murder and non-negligent manslaughter	649[1]	587	597	570	539	−16.9
Forcible rape	1,530	1,689	1,609	1,428	1,412	7.7
Robbery	28,202	27,229	25,989	24,373	24,722	−12.3
Aggravated assault	37,893	34,334	31,253	29,317	27,950	−26.2
All crimes against persons	68,274	63,839	59,448	55,688	54,623	−20.0
Burglary	31,563	30,102	28,293	26,100	23,210	−26.5
Larceny theft	133,938	129,655	124,846	124,016	120,918	−9.7
Motor vehicle theft	29,989	27,034	23,628	21,072	18,381	−38.7
All crimes against property	195,490	186,791	176,767	171,188	162,509	−16.9
All crimes	263,764	250,630	236,215	226,876	217,132	−17.7

[1] Excludes World Trade Center deaths.
Note: Forcible rape excludes statutory rape and other sex offenses.
Source: Federal Bureau of Investigation, Uniform Crime Reports.

Crime Complaints by Borough, Selected Years, 1990–2006

	Manhattan	Bronx	Brooklyn	Queens	Staten Island	Total
1990						
Murder	503	653	765	312	29	2,262
Rape	689	644	1,154	559	80	3,126
Robbery	26,907	17,862	36,341	18,135	1,035	100,280
Felonious assault	10,089	9,538	16,337	6,933	1,225	44,122
Burglary	30,357	19,326	39,301	29,430	3,641	122,055
Grand larceny	58,610	8,856	19,476	19,470	2,075	108,487
Grand larceny auto	21,474	22,946	45,014	50,267	7,224	146,925
Total	148,629	79,825	158,388	125,106	15,309	527,257
1995						
Murder	241	304	387	223	26	1,181
Rape	600	763	1,078	503	74	3,018
Robbery	13,558	11,687	20,811	12,566	1,111	59,733
Felonious assault	7,990	7,979	12,581	5,927	1,051	35,528
Burglary	17,409	14,234	22,290	19,329	2,387	75,649
Grand larceny	32,793	6,251	12,259	12,780	1,342	65,425
Grand larceny auto	9,638	10,875	21,399	26,586	3,300	71,798
Total	82,229	52,093	90,805	77,914	9,291	312,332
1998						
Murder	104	166	239	108	12	629
Rape	429	633	889	470	55	2,476
Robbery	8,796	7,571	13,969	8,132	535	39,003
Felonious assault	6,105	6,474	10,254	5,270	745	28,848
Burglary	10,205	8,247	15,083	12,351	1,295	47,181
Grand larceny	25,955	4,661	10,385	9,496	964	51,461
Grand larceny auto	5,669	7,169	12,653	16,095	1,729	43,315
Total	57,263	34,921	63,472	51,922	5,335	212,913
2001						
Murder	102	190	256	88	13	649
Rape	319	502	718	353	38	1,930
Robbery	6,044	5,178	10,440	5,830	381	27,873
Felonious assault	4,625	5,335	8,287	4,136	637	23,020
Burglary	6,538	5,813	10,954	8,401	988	32,694
Grand larceny	22,103	4,373	9,827	9,025	963	46,291
Grand larceny auto	3,454	5,522	9,186	10,422	1,023	29,607
Total	43,185	26,913	49,668	38,255	4,043	162,064

Crime Complaints by Borough, Selected Years, 1990–2006 (continued)

	Manhattan	Bronx	Brooklyn	Queens	Staten Island	Total
2006						
Murder	111	155	225	86	20	597
Rape	284	332	433	400	51	1,500
Robbery	5,077	4,891	8,196	4,945	450	23,559
Felonious assault	3,353	4,362	5,996	3,004	414	17,129
Burglary	4,897	3,908	7,633	5,834	688	22,960
Grand larceny	19,289	5,275	11,850	8,987	1,133	46,534
Grand larceny auto	1,684	3,375	5,131	4,921	619	15,730
Total	34,695	22,298	39,464	28,177	3,375	128,009

Source: New York Police Department.

Crime Rates per 100,000 People, New York City and United States, 2002–2005

	2002 New York City	United States	2003 New York City	United States	2004 New York City	United States	2005 New York City	United States
Murder and non-negligent manslaughter	7.3	5.6	7.4	5.7	7.0	5.5	6.6	5.6
Forcible rape	20.9	33.1	19.9	32.3	17.6	32.4	17.4	31.7
Robbery	336.8	146.1	320.9	142.5	300.9	136.7	304.6	140.7
Aggravated assault	424.7	309.5	385.9	295.4	361.9	288.6	344.4	291.1
All violent crime	789.6	494.4	734.1	475.8	687.4	463.2	673.1	469.2
Burglary	372.3	747.0	349.4	741.0	322.2	730.3	286.0	726.7
Larceny/theft	1,603.7	2,450.7	1,541.7	2,416.5	1,530.8	2,362.3	1,489.9	2,286.3
Motor vehicle theft	334.4	432.9	291.8	433.7	260.1	421.5	226.5	416.7
All property crime	2,310.4	3,630.6	2,182.8	3,591.2	2,113.1	3,514.1	2,002.4	3,429.8

Note: Forcible rape excludes statutory rape and other sex offenses.
Source: Federal Bureau of Investigation, Uniform Crime Reports.

Incidence of Crimes per 100,000 People, New York City and United States, 2002–2005

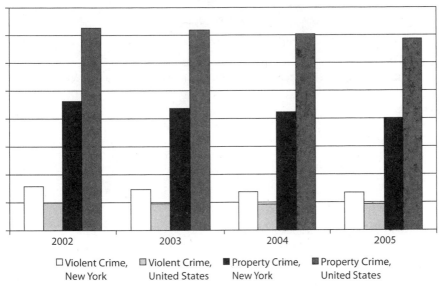

Source: Federal Bureau of Investigation, Uniform Crime Reports.

Selected Inmate Statistics, Fiscal Years 2003–2006

	2003	2004	2005	2006
Average daily inmate population	14,533	13,751	13,576	13,497
Annual inmate admissions	109,445	107,571	102,772	103,813
Average length of stay in days (detainees)	45.5	44.1	47.7	46.7
Average length of stay in days (sentenced)	40.7	39.5	38.1	37.0
Inmate arrests	671	628	684	654
Visitor arrests	341	360	367	295
Inmates delivered to court	332,510	319,885	309,608	316,023

Source: New York City Department of Correction.

Supreme Court Civil, Filings and Dispositions, 2005

	Manhattan	Bronx	Brooklyn	Queens	Staten Island	Total
Filings						
New cases	21,398	13,426	22,771	18,805	3,089	79,489
Note of issue	7,042	5,125	10,724	7,583	1,372	31,846
Dispositions						
Pre-note settlements	3,775	1,731	2,166	1,682	324	9,678
Other pre-note	14,479	8,687	17,370	11,848	1,785	54,169
Post-note settlements	4,864	3,654	7,468	5,646	676	22,308
Jury verdicts, decisions	786	367	1,143	852	217	3,365
Other note	1,689	902	3,572	3,379	323	9,865
Total dispositions	25,593	15,341	31,719	23,407	3,325	99,385

Note: Excludes ex parte applications and uncontested matrimonials.
Source: New York State Office of Court Administration, Annual Report for Calendar Year 2005.

Supreme Criminal and County Court, Felony Cases, 2005

	Manhattan	Bronx	Brooklyn	Queens	Staten Island	Total
Filings						
Indictments	6,782	4,531	4,975	1,845	473	18,606
Superior Court Information	1,117	1,235	789	2,562	215	5,918
Total	7,899	5,766	5,764	4,407	688	24,524
Dispositions						
Guilty pleas	6,842	4,682	4,382	4,083	609	20,598
Convictions	328	92	218	138	14	790
Acquittals	107	116	79	67	4	373
Nonjury verdicts	45	34	25	42	1	147
Dismissals	1,050	579	580	342	74	2,625
Other	162	148	239	53	10	612
Total dispositions	8,534	5,651	5,523	4,725	712	25,145

Source: New York State Office of Court Administration, Annual Report for Calendar Year 2005.

Family Court and Supreme Integrated Domestic Violence Court Filings and Dispositions by Type of Petition, 2005

	Filings	Dispositions		Filings	Dispositions
Termination of parental			Custody, visitation	43,319	40,520
rights	8,342	9,249	Foster care review	1,327	1,331
Surrender of child	2,083	2,174	Foster care placement	633	645
Child protective (neglect			Family offense	21,670	21,018
and abuse)	16,080	17,088	Paternity	20,432	21,151
Juvenile delinquency	9,004	8,563	Support	75,513	75,970
Designated felony	366	218	Uniform Interstate Family		
Persons in need of			Support Act	5,777	6,131
supervision	1,583	1,643	Consent to marry	2	3
Adoption	2,324	2,386	Other	89	88
Adoption certification	126	102	Total	210,927	210,670
Guardianship	2,257	2,390			

Source: New York State Office of Court Administration, Annual Report for Calendar Year 2005.

Civil Court Filings and Dispositions by Case Type and County, 2005

	Manhattan	Bronx	Brooklyn	Queens	Staten Island	Total
Civil actions						
Filings	70,544	80,363	166,582	141,753	18,683	477,925
Dispositions	37,935	46,908	75,271	74,924	11,722	246,760
Housing						
Filings	78,580	93,253	80,673	46,198	5,835	304,539
Dispositions	54,631	100,605	68,426	30,860	3,920	258,442
Small claims						
Filings	5,372	5,406	9,376	6,744	2,153	29,051
Dispositions	8,354	4,473	9,922	10,190	2,204	35,143
Commercial claims						
Filings	2,548	1,053	1,858	2,531	850	8,840
Dispositions	2,870	1,031	2,260	3,396	946	10,503
Total						
Filings	157,044	180,075	258,489	197,226	27,521	820,355
Dispositions	103,790	153,017	155,879	119,370	18,792	550,848

Notes: Filings include both answered and unanswered cases. Dispositions include courtroom dispositions and default judgments.
Source: New York State Office of Court Administration, Annual Report for Calendar Year 2005.

Criminal Court Filings and Dispositions by Case Type and County, 2005

	Arrest Cases		Summons Cases	
	Filings	Dispositions	Filings[1]	Dispositions
Manhattan	95,040	96,263	123,283	85,097
Bronx	66,705	67,866	142,458	95,346
Brooklyn	83,530	85,335	175,442	144,207
Queens	61,808	61,023	97,815	74,517
Staten Island	9,251	9,063	17,595	14,062
Total	316,334	319,550	556,593	413,229

[1] Includes both answered and unanswered cases.
Source: New York State Office of Court Administration, Annual Report for Calendar Year 2005.

Executions within the Present Boundaries of New York City, 1639–1890

Sex					
Male	268	1770–1779	15	Grand larceny	5
Female	17	1780–1789	40	Horse stealing	5
		1790–1799	20	Armed robbery	4
Race		1800–1809	5	Assault	4
White	151	1810–1819	13	Attempted rape	4
Black	95	1820–1829	6	Coining	2
Native American	2	1830–1839	8	Counterfeiting	2
Hispanic	1	1840–1849	5	High treason	2
Unknown	36	1850–1859	13	Infanticide	2
		1860–1869	9	Pederasty	2
Year		1870–1879	9	Pickpocketing	2
1639	1	1880–1889	16	Rape	2
1640–1649	4			Sodomy	1
1650–1659	0	Offense		Bestiality	1
1660–1669	4	Murder	96	Buggery	1
1670–1679	0	Robbery	31	Cowardice	1
1680–1689	1	Burglary	30	Dereliction of duty	1
1690–1699	6	Conspiracy and sedition	30	Espionage	1
1700–1709	8	Accessory to murder	16	Parole violation	1
1710–1719	29	Arson	15	Poisoning	1
1720–1729	6	Forgery	15	Privately stealing	1
1730–1739	4	Piracy	15	Slave revolt	1
1740–1749	38	Desertion	9	Theft	1
1750–1759	8	Highway robbery	8	Total	285
1760–1769	17	Mutiny	7		

Notes: Because some persons were executed for more than one offense, sum of offenses is greater than number of persons executed. Executions were carried out under the jurisdiction of local and county officials until 1890, then under the jurisdiction of the State of New York.

Sources: Daniel Allen Hearn, *Legal Executions in New York State: A Comprehensive Reference, 1639–1963* (Jefferson, N.C.: McFarland, 1997); M. Watt Espy and John Ortiz Smykla: *Executions in the United States, 1608–2002: The Espy File* (Ann Arbor, Mich.: Consortium for Political and Social Research, 2004).

5 Business, Economy, and Labor

Largest Employers by Number of Employees in New York City, 2005

1. New York–Presbyterian Healthcare System	28,909	13. Consolidated Edison Inc.	11,743
2. Citigroup Inc.	26,809	14. Saint Vincent Catholic Medical Centers	10,764
3. J. P. Morgan Chase & Co.	20,883	15. Montefiore Medical Center	10,682
4. Verizon Communications Inc.	17,622	16. Morgan Stanley	10,047
5. Federated Department Stores Inc.	17,000	17. Medisys Health Network Inc.	8,974
6. Continuum Health Partners Inc.	15,592	18. Memorial Sloan-Kettering Cancer Center	8,791
7. Columbia University	13,151	19. Bank of New York Co.	8,750
8. Time Warner Inc.	12,890	20. Merrill Lynch & Co.	8,400
9. North Shore–Long Island Jewish Health System	12,857	21. Goldman Sachs Group Inc.	8,382
		22. United Parcel Service Inc.	7,212
10. New York University	12,621	23. Bear Stearns Companies	6,800
11. Mount Sinai Medical Center	12,279	24. Pfizer Inc.	6,385
12. Personal-Touch Home Care Inc.	12,000	25. American International Group Inc.	6,213

Source: *Crain's New York Business.*

Top Ten Industrial Firms in the Fortune 500 Based in New York City
(Number in parentheses following the year indicates the total number of firms in the Fortune 500 based in New York City. Number in parentheses following the name of the firm indicates the rank of the firm in the Fortune 500.)

1955 (131)
1. Standard Oil of New Jersey (2)
2. U.S. Steel (4)
3. General Electric (6)
4. Western Electric (12)
5. Socony Mobil Oil (13)
6. Texaco (15)
7. Shell Oil (16)
8. National Dairy Products (20)
9. Union Carbide (22)
10. Sinclair Oil (25)

1960 (127)
1. Standard Oil (2)
2. General Electric (4)
3. U.S. Steel (5)
4. Socony Mobil Oil (6)
5. Texaco (8)
6. Western Electric (10)
7. General Dynamics (15)
8. Shell Oil (17)
9. National Dairy Products (20)
10. Union Carbide (24)

Top Ten Industrial Firms in the Fortune 500 Based in New York City (Number in parentheses following the year indicates the total number of firms in the Fortune 500 based in New York City. Number in parentheses following the name of the firm indicates the rank of the firm in the Fortune 500.) (continued)

1965 (128)
1. Standard Oil (2)
2. General Electric (4)
3. Socony Mobil Oil (6)
4. U.S. Steel (7)
5. Texaco (8)
6. Western Electric (10)
7. Shell Oil (15)
8. Union Carbide (21)
9. RCA (24)
10. General Telephone and Electronics (25)

1970 (117)
1. Standard Oil (2)
2. General Electric (4)
3. Mobil Oil (6)
4. International Telephone & Telegraph (8)
5. Texaco (9)
6. Western Electric (10)
7. U.S. Steel (12)
8. Shell Oil (19)
9. General Telephone and Electronics (20)
10. RCA (21)

1975 (90)
1. Exxon (formerly Standard Oil of New Jersey) (1)
2. Texaco (3)
3. Mobil Oil (5)
4. International Telephone & Telegraph (11)
5. Western Electric (18)
6. Union Carbide (21)
7. RCA (34)
8. W. R. Grace (47)
9. Borden (51)
10. Amerada Hess (54)

1980 (81)
1. Exxon (1)
2. Texaco (3)
3. International Telephone & Telegraph (13)
4. Western Electric (22)
5. Union Carbide (27)
6. RCA (41)
7. Amerada Hess (43)
8. Philip Morris (45)
9. W. R. Grace (51)
10. Gulf and Western Industries (57)

1985 (62)
1. Exxon (1)
2. Texaco (3)
3. American Telephone & Telegraph (8)
4. International Telephone & Telegraph (25)
5. Philip Morris (27)
6. Amerada Hess (48)
7. W. R. Grace (49)
8. Sperry Corporation (63)
9. Colgate-Palmolive (73)
10. Borden (77)

1990 (41)
1. Philip Morris (7)
2. RJR Nabisco Holdings (24)
3. Bristol-Myers Squibb (50)
4. Unilever U.S. (55)
5. Borden (64)
6. Amerada Hess (68)
7. American Home Products (70)
8. W. R. Grace (71)
9. Pfizer (73)
10. Hanson Industries (75)

Top Ten Industrial Firms in the Fortune 500 Based in New York City
(Number in parentheses following the year indicates the total number of firms
in the Fortune 500 based in New York City. Number in parentheses following
the name of the firm indicates the rank of the firm in the Fortune 500.) (continued)

1995 (49)
1. AT&T (5)
2. Philip Morris (10)
3. Citicorp (17)
4. ITT (23)
5. American International Group (26)
6. Metropolitan Life Insurance (27)
7. Travelers Inc. (37)
8. Merrill Lynch (40)
9. American Express (55)
10. RJR Nabisco Holdings (57)

2000 (42)
1. Citigroup (7)
2. AT&T (8)
3. Philip Morris (9)
4. American International Group (17)
5. TIAA-CREF (19)

2000 (42) (continued)
6. Merrill Lynch (29)
7. Morgan Stanley Dean Witter (30)
8. Chase Manhattan Corporation (31)
9. Bell Atlantic (33)
10. Time Warner (45)

2005 (50)
1. AT&T (5)
2. Philip Morris (10)
3. Citicorp (17)
4. ITT (23)
5. American International Group (26)
6. Metropolitan Life Insurance (27)
7. Travelers Inc. (37)
8. Merrill Lynch (40)
9. American Express (55)
10. RJR Nabisco Holdings (57)

Source: *Fortune*.

Largest Law Firms by Number of Lawyers in Metropolitan Area, 2006

1. Skadden Arps Slate Meagher & Flom and Affiliates	737	13. White & Case	434
2. Paul Weiss Rifkind Wharton & Garrison	634	14. Cadwalader Wickersham & Taft	415
2. Simpson Thacher & Bartlett	634	15. Willkie Farr & Gallagher	398
4. Weil Gotshal & Manges	604	16. Wilson Elser Moskowitz Edelman & Dicker	395
5. Davis Polk & Wardwell	537	17. Fried Frank Harris Shriver & Jacobson	381
6. Debevoise & Plimpton	503	18. Kaye Scholer	374
7. Proskauer Rose	484	19. Shearman & Sterling	371
8. Cravath Swaine & Moore	476	20. Latham & Watkins	365
9. Sidley Austin	459	21. Milbank Tweed Hadley & McCoy	329
10. Sullivan & Cromwell	458	22. Greenberg Truarig	328
11. Schulte Roth & Zabel	440	23. Kramer Levin Naftalis & Frankel	317
12. Cleary Gottlieb Steen & Hamilton	435	24. Jones Day	308
		25. Clifford Chance U.S.	303

Source: *Crain's New York Business.*

Largest Architectural Firms by Number of Architects in New York Area, 2006

	Number of Architects	Worldwide Construction Volume, 2006 (in Millions)
1. Perkins Eastman	169	$6,250.0
2. Kohn Pedersen Fox Associates	139	3,000.0
3. Gensler Architecture, Design & Planning	101	8,100.0
4. Hellmuth Obata & Kassabum Inc.	98	n/a
5. Skidmore Owings & Merrill	88	n/a
6. Cooper Robertson & Partners	72	395.0
7. Mancini Duffy	65	810.0
8. Polshek Partnership Architects	65	350.0
9. Cetra/Ruddy Inc.	56	601.0
10. HLW	56	650.0
11. Stephen B. Jacobs Group	56	500.0
12. Beyer Blinder Belle Architects & Planners	55	269.3
13. Fxfowle Architects	55	n/a
14. Costas Kondylis and Partners	51	1,700.0

Largest Architectural Firms by Number of Architects in New York Area, 2006 (continued)

	Number of Architects	Worldwide Construction Volume, 2006 (in Millions)
15. Ehrenkrantz Eckstut & Kuhn Architects	51	127.0
16. Hillier Architecture	50	877.0
17. Robert A. M. Stern Architects	50	104.4
18. Swanke Hayden Connell Architects	50	n/a
19. Spector Group	49	420.0
20. SLCE Architects	48	910.0
21. Urbahn Architects	46	312.0
22. STV Architects Inc.	42	748.0
23. Davis Brody Bond Aedas	40	140.0
24. Gruzen Samton Architects Planners & Interior Designers	39	350.0
25. Pei Cobb Freed & Partners Architects	38	88.0

Source: *Crain's New York Business.*

Largest Foundations by Market Value of Assets, 2007

1. Ford Foundation	$11,615,906,693	11. Open Society Institute	858,935,162
2. Andrew W. Mellon Foundation	5,586,112,000	12. Rockefeller Brothers Fund	815,561,407
3. Rockefeller Foundation	3,417,557,613	13. Edna McConnell Clark Foundation	808,121,944
4. Starr Foundation	3,344,801,753	14. Henry Luce Foundation	792,961,471
5. Carnegie Corporation of New York	2,244,208,247	15. Horace W. Goldsmith Foundation	788,615,258
6. Doris Duke Charitable Foundation	1,920,145,122	16. Surdna Foundation	769,100,511
7. New York Community Trust	1,897,604,374	17. Commonwealth Fund	701,275,427
8. Alfred P. Sloan Foundation	1,581,350,875	18. AVI CHAI Foundation	653,609,340
9. Wallace Foundation	1,447,299,661	19. William Randolph Foundation	624,489,259
10. Freeman Foundation	1,105,466,120	20. John A. Hartford Foundation	614,197,200

Source: The Foundation Center.

Total Pay of Most Highly Compensated Chief Executives in New York Area, 2005 (in Millions)

1. Lew Frankfort	Coach Inc.	$62.0
2. Barry Diller	ICA/InterActiveCorp	$60.5
3. Martin E. Franklin	Jarden Corp	$49.0
4. Henry M. Paulson Jr.	Goldman Sachs Group Inc.	$41.9
5. Richard S. Fuld Jr.	Lehman Brothers Holdings Inc.	$41.7
6. John J. Mack	Morgan Stanley	$38.6
7. Nelson Peltz	Triarc Companies	$37.9
8. E. Stanley O'Neal	Merrill Lynch & Co.	$35.0
9. John W. Jackson	Celgene Corp.	$27.4
10. Kenneth I. Chenault	American Express Co.	$25.8
11. James E. Cayne	Bear Stearns Companies	$25.7
12. K. Rupert Murdoch	News Corp.	$23.4
13. Charles O. Prince III	Citigroup	$22.7
14. Thomas E. Freston	Viacom Inc.	$22.6
14. Leslie Moonves	CBS Corp.	$22.6
16. Robert H. Benmosche	MetLife Inc.	$22.2
17. William B. Harrison Jr.	J. P. Morgan Chase & Co.	$22.0
18. Samuel J. Palmisano	International Business Machines Corp.	$20.7
19. Ralph Lauren	Polo Ralph Lauren Corp.	$20.3
20. Harold W. McGraw III	McGraw-Hill Companies	$20.2
21. Arthur F. Ryan	Prudential Financial Inc.	$20.1
22. Fred Hassan	Schering-Plough Corp.	$19.9
23. Richard D. Parsons	Time Warner Inc.	$19.3
24. Henry A. McKinnell	Pfizer Inc.	$18.7
25. Reuben Mark	Colgate-Palmolive Co.	$18.3
26. Ivan G. Seidenberg	Verizon Communications Inc.	$17.6
27. Steven S. Reinemund	PepsiCo. Inc.	$17.0
28. John T. Cahill	Pepsi Bottling Group Inc.	$16.2
29. Michael I. Roth	Interpublic Group of Companies Inc.	$15.9
30. Henry R. Silverman	Cendant Corp.	$15.6
31. John Adam Kanas	North Fork Bancorporation Inc.	$15.6
32. Patricia F. Russo	Lucent Technologies Inc.	$14.8
33. John A. Swainson	CA Inc.	$14.7
34. Laurence D. Fink	BlackRock Inc.	$14.4
35. Louis C. Camilleri	Altria Group Inc.	$13.6
36. James L. Dolan	Cablevision Systems Corp.	$13.3
37. John B. Hess	Hess Corp.	$12.8
38. Katherine L. Krill	Ann Taylor Stores Corp.	$11.7

Total Pay of Most Highly Compensated Chief Executives in New York Area, 2005
(in Millions) (continued)

39. Andrea Jung	Avon Products Inc.	$11.5
40. Michael G. Cherkasky	Marsh & McLennan Companies	$11.4
41. Martin J. Sullivan	American International Group Inc.	$11.4
42. Richard B. Handler	Jefferies Group Inc.	$10.9
43. Mitchell H. Caplan	E*Trade Financial Corp.	$10.5
44. J. Kerry Clayton	Assurant Inc.	$10.4
45. Peter C. Georgiopoulos	General Maritime Corp.	$10.3
46. Peter R. Dolan	Bristol-Myers Squibb Co.	$10.3
47. Keith A. Meister	American Real Estate Partners	$10.2
48. John C. Siciliano	BFK Capital Group Inc.	$9.8
49. David B. Snow Jr.	Medco Health Solutions Inc.	$9.3
50. Mark Weber	Phillips–Van Heusen Corp.	$9.3

Source: *Crain's New York Business.*

Busiest Trading Days, Weeks, Months, and Years by Volume of Shares Traded, New York Stock Exchange

Days		Months	
23 January 2008	6,040,343,165 shares	January 2008	83,147,430,859
16 August 2007	5,799,792,281	August 2007	81,355,184,104
9 August 2007	5,377,155,973	November 2007	69,691,379,125
22 January 2008	5,285,357,077	February 2008	64,995,717,778
22 June 2007	5,194,963,971	July 2007	62,896,274,814
26 July 2007	5,107,411,489	October 2007	61,653,753,408
8 August 2007	4,971,535,527	June 2007	60,681,949,883
10 August 2007	4,864,699,476	March 2007	58,751,958,662
18 January 2008	4,806,606,588	May 2007	57,714,938,200
8 January 2007	4,663,993,254	June 2006	56,806,424,762

Weeks (ending dates)		Years	
10 August 2007	24,023,200,586	2007	698,658,000,000
17 August 2007	20,536,484,912	2006	588,132,000,000
18 January 2008	20,234,385,292	2005	516,743,000,000
3 August 2007	20,090,622,048	2004	471,580,000,000
25 January 2008	19,797,367,842	2003	415,804,000,000
27 July 2007	19,581,733,398	2002	365,027,000,000
11 January 2008	19,207,499,513	2001	309,829,000,000
1 February 2008	18,948,144,953	2000	262,478,000,000
7 March 2008	18,102,594,510	1999	203,914,000,000
9 November 2007	18,058,316,196	1998	169,745,000,000

Source: New York Stock Exchange.

Range of Prices of a Seat on the New York Stock Exchange, 1869–2005

1869	$3,000	$7,500	1981	$220,000	$285,000
1870–1879	$2,750	$16,000	1982	$190,000	$340,000
1880–1889	$14,000	$34,000	1983	$310,000	$425,000
1890–1894	$15,250	$24,000	1984	$290,000	$400,000
1895–1899	$14,000	$40,000	1985	$310,000	$480,000
1900–1904	$37,500	$82,000	1986	$455,000	$600,000
1905–1909	$51,000	$95,000	1987	$605,000	$1,150,000
1910–1914	$34,000	$94,000	1988	$580,000	$820,000
1915–1919	$38,000	$110,000	1989	$420,000	$675,000
1920–1924	$76,000	$115,000	1990	$250,000	$430,000
1925–1929	$99,000	$625,000	1991	$345,000	$440,000
1930–1934	$68,000	$480,000	1992	$410,000	$600,000
1935–1939	$51,000	$174,000	1993	$500,000	$775,000
1940–1944	$17,000	$75,000	1994	$760,000	$830,000
1945–1949	$35,000	$97,000	1995	$785,000	$1,050,000
1950–1954	$38,000	$88,000	1996	$1,050,000	$1,450,000
1955–1959	$65,000	$157,000	1997	$1,175,000	$1,750,000
1960–1964	$135,000	$230,000	1998	$1,175,000	$2,000,000
1965–1969	$190,000	$515,000	1999	$2,000,000	$2,650,000
1970–1974	$65,000	$320,000	2000	$1,650,000	$2,000,000
1975	$55,000	$138,000	2001	$2,000,000	$2,300,000
1976	$40,000	$104,000	2002	$2,000,000	$2,550,000
1977	$35,000	$95,000	2003	$1,500,000	$2,000,000
1978	$46,000	$105,000	2004	$1,030,000	$1,515,000
1979	$82,000	$210,000	2005	$975,000	$4,000,000
1980	$175,000	$275,000			

Source: New York Stock Exchange.

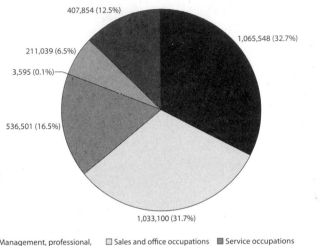

**Occupation of Employed Civilians, Citywide
1990**

407,854 (12.5%)

1,065,548 (32.7%)

211,039 (6.5%)

3,595 (0.1%)

536,501 (16.5%)

1,033,100 (31.7%)

■ Management, professional,   □ Sales and office occupations   ■ Service occupations
and related occupations

■ Farming, fishing, and forestry   ▨ Construction, extraction, and   ■ Production, transportation, and
maintenance   material moving

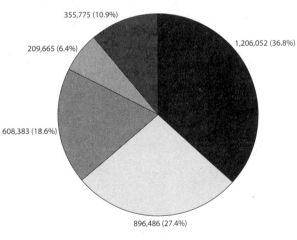

**Occupation of Employed Civilians, Citywide
2000**

355,775 (10.9%)

1,206,052 (36.8%)

209,665 (6.4%)

608,383 (18.6%)

896,486 (27.4%)

■ Management, professional,   □ Sales and office occupations   ■ Service occupations
and related occupations

                                 ▨ Construction, extraction, and   ■ Production, transportation, and
                                 maintenance   material moving

Note: Employment in farming, fishing, and forestry (1,464) is less than 0.05 percent.
Source: U.S. Bureau of the Census.

Occupation of Employed Civilians, by Borough, 2000

	Manhattan	Bronx	Brooklyn	Queens	Staten Island	Total
Management, professional, and related occupations	429,905	114,023	301,569	292,252	68,303	1,206,052
Sales and office occupations	180,692	123,693	256,891	276,015	59,195	896,486
Service occupations	95,778	105,015	187,461	186,613	33,516	608,383
Farming, fishing, and forestry	186	336	501	355	86	1,464
Construction, extraction, and maintenance	17,609	33,054	67,024	75,220	16,758	209,665
Production, transportation, and material moving	46,113	52,533	113,584	126,329	17,216	355,775
Total employed civilians 16 years and over	770,283	428,654	927,030	956,784	195,074	3,277,825

Source: U.S. Bureau of the Census.

Employees on Nonfarm Payrolls, September 2006 (in Thousands)

	Number	Percent
Natural resources, mining, and construction	119.9	3.3
Manufacturing	112.4	3.1
Trade, transportation, and utilities	555.7	15.2
Information	165.4	4.5
Financial activities	457.0	12.5
Professional and business services	566.8	15.5
Education and health services	688.6	18.8
Leisure and hospitality	290.1	7.9
Other services	155.3	4.2
Government	543.5	14.9
Total	3,654.7	100.0

Note: Figures are preliminary and not seasonally adjusted.
Source: U.S. Bureau of Labor Statistics.

Industry of Employed Civilians, Citywide

	1990 Number	Percent	2000 Number	Percent
Agriculture, forestry, fishing and hunting, and mining	9,130	0.3	2,101	0.1
Construction	136,030	4.2	139,385	4.3
Manufacturing	354,833	10.9	217,602	6.6
Wholesale trade	129,896	4.0	101,812	3.1
Retail trade	298,118	9.2	295,803	9.0
Transportation and warehousing, and utilities	239,609	7.4	211,506	6.5
Information	100,616	3.1	173,594	5.3
Finance, insurance, real estate, and rental and leasing	402,024	12.3	372,809	11.4
Professional, scientific, management, administrative, and waste management services	322,001	9.9	390,956	11.9
Educational, health, and social services	687,710	21.1	765,905	23.4
Arts, entertainment, recreation, accommodation, and food services	229,297	7.0	272,210	8.3
Public administration	163,972	5.0	146,807	4.5
Other services (except public administration)	184,401	5.7	187,335	5.7
Total employed civilians 16 years and over	3,257,637	100.0	3,277,825	100.0

Source: U.S. Bureau of the Census.

Industry of Employed Civilians, by Borough, 2000

	Manhattan	Bronx	Brooklyn	Queens	Staten Island	Total
Agriculture, forestry, fishing and hunting, and mining	445	457	571	552	76	2,101
Construction	13,097	19,102	44,696	51,610	10,880	139,385
Manufacturing	40,218	26,750	68,428	75,346	6,860	217,602
Wholesale trade	20,803	12,329	29,023	34,670	4,987	101,812
Retail trade	54,244	42,648	83,926	96,859	18,126	295,803
Transportation and warehousing, and utilities	21,139	29,070	66,453	79,700	15,144	211,506
Information	71,725	15,350	41,639	37,281	7,599	173,594
Finance, insurance, real estate, and rental and leasing	114,957	37,212	94,825	97,854	27,961	372,809
Professional, scientific, management, administrative, and waste management	140,154	36,799	96,829	96,231	20,943	390,956
Educational, health, and social services	152,003	129,509	239,467	197,065	47,861	765,905
Arts, entertainment, recreation, accommodation, and food services	81,328	31,134	64,807	84,407	10,534	272,210
Public administration	24,422	22,161	43,443	41,372	15,409	146,807
Other services	35,748	26,133	52,923	63,837	8,694	187,335
Total employed civilians 16 years and over	770,283	428,654	927,030	956,784	195,074	3,277,825

Source: U.S. Bureau of the Census.

Employment and Wages in Selected Sectors, by Borough, 2002

	Average Monthly Employment	Percent of Total Borough Employment	Wages	Percent of Total Borough Wages	Average Annual Wage
Manhattan					
Finance and insurance	293,635	13.06	$51,925,575,579	32.25	$176,837
Professional, scientific, and technical	250,109	11.12	21,955,051,846	13.63	87,782
Information	138,985	6.18	11,622,421,137	7.22	83,624
Arts, entertainment, and recreation	43,437	1.93	2,268,773,282	1.41	52,231
Management of companies	50,354	2.24	7,091,329,910	4.40	140,830
Real estate, and rental and leasing	71,891	3.20	3,983,975,512	2.47	55,417
Manufacturing	52,823	2.35	2,776,784,793	1.72	52,568
Administrative and support, and waste	134,026	5.96	5,308,308,206	3.30	39,607
Construction	31,974	1.42	2,202,635,368	1.37	68,888
Wholesale trade	82,566	3.67	6,287,160,465	3.90	76,147
Retail trade	123,477	5.49	4,534,139,745	2.82	36,721
Transportation and warehousing	25,678	1.14	1,028,589,129	0.64	40,057
Educational services	72,799	3.24	3,129,007,254	1.94	42,981
Health care and social assistance	192,262	8.55	8,118,447,888	5.04	42,226
Accommodation and food services	132,797	5.90	3,658,016,266	2.27	27,546
Other services	81,393	3.62	3,190,752,753	1.98	39,202
Government	457,926	20.36	21,062,145,527	13.08	45,995
Unclassified	7,267	0.32	384,699,699	0.24	52,938
Total Manhattan	2,249,140	100.00	161,029,255,538	100.00	71,596
Bronx					
Finance and insurance	2,881	1.33	101,206,081	1.31	35,134
Professional, scientific, and technical	3,180	1.47	110,656,135	1.43	34,794
Information	4,351	2.01	213,373,411	2.76	49,035
Arts, entertainment, and recreation	3,172	1.47	233,253,713	3.02	73,531
Management of companies	923	0.43	44,939,406	0.58	48,693

Employment and Wages in Selected Sectors, by Borough, 2002 (continued)

	Average Monthly Employment	Percent of Total Borough Employment	Wages	Percent of Total Borough Wages	Average Annual Wage
Bronx (continued)					
Real estate, and rental and leasing	10,107	4.68	285,202,168	3.69	28,217
Manufacturing	9,621	4.45	328,434,629	4.25	34,138
Administrative and support, and waste	8,113	3.76	195,221,576	2.53	24,064
Construction	9,762	4.52	480,536,174	6.22	49,228
Wholesale trade	9,956	4.61	445,121,055	5.76	44,708
Retail trade	22,653	10.49	523,325,794	6.78	23,101
Transportation and warehousing	6,773	3.14	258,200,958	3.34	38,124
Educational services	16,240	7.52	555,230,746	7.19	34,189
Health care and social assistance	80,573	37.31	3,055,312,035	39.56	37,920
Accommodation and food services	10,195	4.72	144,053,003	1.87	14,130
Other services	7,620	3.53	167,555,092	2.17	21,988
Government	6,867	3.18	430,899,955	5.58	62,749
Unclassified	1,299	0.60	24,868,134	0.32	19,143
Total Bronx	215,964	100.00	7,723,770,707	100.00	35,764
Brooklyn					
Finance and insurance	14,179	3.24	833,158,569	5.79	58,760
Professional, scientific, and technical	11,570	2.64	479,085,151	3.33	41,407
Information	7,776	1.78	372,352,812	2.59	47,886
Arts, entertainment, and recreation	3,546	0.81	94,322,774	0.66	26,600
Management of companies	1,088	0.25	49,836,824	0.35	45,799
Real estate, and rental and leasing	13,457	3.08	391,182,563	2.72	29,069
Manufacturing	35,546	8.12	1,058,185,258	7.35	29,770
Administrative and support, and waste	18,244	4.17	413,072,408	2.87	22,642
Construction	21,876	5.00	964,668,126	6.70	44,098
Wholesale trade	21,498	4.91	770,452,261	5.35	35,839

Employment and Wages in Selected Sectors, by Borough, 2002 (continued)

	Average Monthly Employment	Percent of Total Borough Employment	Wages	Percent of Total Borough Wages	Average Annual Wage
Brooklyn (continued)					
Retail trade	52,525	12.01	1,236,452,071	8.59	23,540
Transportation and warehousing	18,036	4.12	621,729,059	4.32	34,471
Educational services	26,243	6.00	964,637,832	6.70	36,758
Health care and social assistance	142,570	32.59	4,878,306,296	33.89	34,217
Accommodation and food					
services	17,464	3.99	268,251,315	1.86	15,361
Other services	20,005	4.57	423,744,669	2.94	21,182
Government	3,505	0.80	191,122,197	1.33	54,531
Unclassified	4,388	1.00	91,760,284	0.64	20,910
Total Brooklyn	437,503	100.00	14,395,292,151	100.00	32,903
Queens					
Finance and insurance	13,037	2.77	868,029,750	4.89	66,583
Professional, scientific, and					
technical	10,338	2.19	406,879,776	2.29	39,358
Information	10,233	2.17	495,871,983	2.80	48,459
Arts, entertainment, and					
recreation	4,381	0.93	194,480,208	1.10	44,388
Management of companies	1,767	0.37	106,447,472	0.60	60,245
Real estate, and rental and					
leasing	14,773	3.13	511,118,040	2.88	34,598
Manufacturing	39,277	8.33	1,376,590,867	7.76	35,049
Administrative and support, and					
waste	24,340	5.16	631,393,369	3.56	25,940
Construction	41,906	8.89	2,316,260,977	13.06	55,273
Wholesale trade	23,906	5.07	1,067,495,199	6.02	44,653
Retail trade	49,019	10.40	1,139,265,616	6.42	23,241
Transportation and warehousing	61,273	13.00	2,867,920,008	16.17	46,806
Educational services	18,379	3.90	629,567,893	3.55	34,255
Health care and social assistance	95,213	20.20	3,440,285,442	19.39	36,133
Accommodation and food					
services	28,523	6.05	478,329,315	2.70	16,770
Other services	20,695	4.39	484,821,444	2.73	23,427

Employment and Wages in Selected Sectors, by Borough, 2002 (continued)

	Average Monthly Employment	Percent of Total Borough Employment	Wages	Percent of Total Borough Wages	Average Annual Wage
Queens (continued)					
Government	7,600	1.61	450,379,581	2.54	59,257
Unclassified	4,125	0.88	82,016,747	0.46	19,885
Total Queens	471,300	100.00	17,738,593,994	100.00	37,638
Staten Island					
Finance and insurance	2,583	2.95	106,848,963	3.60	41,364
Professional, scientific, and					
technical	3,386	3.87	125,948,493	4.24	37,199
Information	2,907	3.32	148,436,878	4.99	51,059
Arts, entertainment, and					
recreation	1,246	1.42	28,373,564	0.95	22,764
Management of companies	796	0.91	47,685,627	1.60	59,919
Real estate, and rental and					
leasing	1,442	1.65	39,735,557	1.34	27,564
Manufacturing	1,328	1.52	49,718,759	1.67	37,427
Administrative and support, and					
waste	3,489	3.99	76,140,341	2.56	21,826
Construction	6,357	7.27	305,008,212	10.26	47,979
Wholesale trade	1,361	1.56	52,954,804	1.78	38,911
Retail trade	14,494	16.57	305,988,352	10.30	21,111
Transportation and warehousing	4,994	5.71	221,674,664	7.46	44,385
Educational services	4,265	4.87	150,344,791	5.06	35,251
Health care and social assistance	26,717	30.54	993,753,412	33.44	37,196
Accommodation and food					
services	5,668	6.48	75,576,702	2.54	13,334
Other services	3,454	3.95	68,959,425	2.32	19,963
Government	1,664	1.90	110,182,638	3.71	66,235
Unclassified	702	0.80	16,777,151	0.56	23,902
Total Staten Island	87,489	100.00	2,972,024,434	100.00	33,970

Note: Detailed entries do not necessarily sum to totals.
Source: U.S. Bureau of Labor Statistics, *Monthly Labor Review*, June 2004.

Employment in Selected Manufacturing Sectors, by Borough, 2002

	Number of Establishments	Number of Employees	Payroll ($1,000)	Payroll per Employee	Number of Production Workers	Production Wages ($1,000)	Wages per Production Worker	Total Value of Shipments ($1,000)
Manhattan								
Retail bakeries	95	830	$13,491	$16,254	396	$6,606	$16,682	$41,357
Fabric mills	177	4,723	151,211	32,016	700	17,198	24,569	238,951
Textile and fabric finishing mills	128	3,603	113,163	31,408	2,691	66,058	24,548	889,177
Textile furnishing mills	31	1,110	37,185	33,500	536	9,539	17,797	422,971
Men's and boys' cut and sew apparel contractors	44	669	18,203	27,209	390	8,419	21,587	127,755
Women's and girls' cut and sew blouse and shirt mfg.	38	1,162	49,494	42,594	657	17,089	26,011	562,769
Women's and girls' cut and sew suit, coat, tailored jacket, and skirt mfg.	43	921	52,187	56,663	425	10,702	25,181	430,814
Women's and girls' cut and sew other outerwear mfg.	81	2,386	64,079	26,856	1,835	32,674	17,806	501,823
Other cut and sew apparel mfg.	97	798	20,231	25,352	610	13,125	21,516	87,789
Men's and boys' neckwear mfg.	21	674	16,071	23,844	554	10,356	18,693	93,659
Other apparel accessories and other apparel mfg.	66	987	21,256	21,536	712	11,834	16,621	86,132
Commercial lithographic printing	260	3,652	169,678	46,462	2,541	98,393	38,722	548,559
Quick printing	97	739	25,144	34,024	492	15,721	31,953	85,155
Digital printing	37	1,008	43,809	43,461	678	26,174	38,605	134,410
Prepress services	91	1,769	97,392	55,055	1,048	49,117	46,867	286,379

Employment in Selected Manufacturing Sectors, by Borough, 2002 (continued)

	Number of Establish-ments	Number of Em-ployees	Payroll ($1,000)	Payroll per Em-ployee	Number of Pro-duction Workers	Produc-tion Wages ($1,000)	Wages per Pro-duction Worker	Total Value of Ship-ments ($1,000)
Manhattan (continued)								
Chemical mfg.	36	1,106	55,769	50,424	568	26,898	47,356	284,752
Fabricated metal product mfg.	61	732	24,451	33,403	550	15,113	27,478	93,163
Mfg. and reproducing magnetic and optical media	38	899	37,815	42,063	580	19,981	34,450	164,229
Electrical equipment, appliance, and component mfg.	17	657	20,268	30,849	495	11,995	24,232	204,129
Household and insti-tutional furniture mfg.	74	1,455	37,738	25,937	1,245	28,715	23,064	158,980
Jewelry (except costume) mfg.	395	6,454	227,199	35,203	4,276	113,311	26,499	1,520,154
Sign mfg.	38	533	23,214	43,553	303	10,319	34,056	68,854
Total mfg.	3,523	58,920	1,888,294	32,048	48,689	980,041	20,129	10,950,335
Bronx								
Bakeries and tortilla mfg.	83	1,082	35,374	32,693	611	17,167	28,097	137,044
Paperboard container mfg.	5	545	16,365	30,028	415	9,343	22,513	49,584
Plastics and rubber products mfg.	19	667	13,257	19,876	622	11,048	17,762	55,261
Fabricated metal product mfg.	72	2,362	78,613	33,282	1,763	49,595	28,131	242,119
Sheet metal work mfg.	9	635	19,903	31,343	510	13,759	26,978	49,379
Machinery mfg.	18	593	22,979	38,750	435	13,173	30,283	79,383
Furniture and related product mfg.	41	914	35,391	38,721	667	22,387	33,564	102,201
Total mfg.	465	10,504	342,956	32,650	7,789	209,538	26,902	1,356,541

	Number of Establish- ments	Number of Em- ployees	Payroll ($1,000)	Payroll per Em- ployee	Number of Pro- duction Workers	Produc- tion Wages ($1,000)	Wages per Pro- duction Worker	Total Value of Ship- ments ($1,000)
Brooklyn								
Sugar and confection- ery product mfg.	17	500	22,039	44,078	366	11,902	32,519	390,121
Animal slaughtering and processing	28	644	12,248	19,019	517	11,910	23,037	201,421
Commercial bakeries	68	801	25,702	32,087	538	14,594	27,126	85,419
Textile product mills	67	642	14,922	23,243	521	8,988	17,251	67,288
Women's, girls', and infants' cut and sew apparel contractors	325	3,077	44,765	14,548	2,852	37,393	13,111	79,864
Women's and girls' cut and sew apparel mfg.	78	1,228	32,656	26,593	832	16,625	19,982	317,898
Converted paper product mfg.	31	661	25,336	661	38,330	491	15,008	30,566
Commercial litho- graphic printing	59	874	34,231	39,166	635	21,448	33,776	104,047
Chemical mfg.	44	2,363	121,406	51,378	1,583	64,342	40,646	2,087,475
Plastics bag mfg.	21	623	22,621	36,310	468	13,311	28,442	105,549
Ornamental and ar- chitectural metal products mfg.	79	1,073	37,381	34,838	737	23,481	31,860	119,404
Machinery mfg.	49	546	20,805	38,104	363	12,197	33,601	73,527
Semiconductor and other electronic component mfg.	8	605	24,520	40,529	258	6,397	24,795	80,849
Household and insti- tutional furniture mfg.	98	1,025	25,742	25,114	817	19,219	23,524	108,120
Office furniture (in- cluding fixtures) mfg.	45	529	19,501	36,864	364	10,380	28,516	67,263

Employment in Selected Manufacturing Sectors, by Borough, 2002 (continued)

	Number of Establish-ments	Number of Em-ployees	Payroll ($1,000)	Payroll per Em-ployee	Number of Pro-duction Workers	Produc-tion Wages ($1,000)	Wages per Pro-duction Worker	Total Value of Ship-ments ($1,000)
Brooklyn (continued)								
Sign mfg.	37	609	17,569	28,849	459	10,174	22,166	64,370
Total mfg.	2,327	32,402	1,011,935	31,231	24,167	605,059	25,037	6,353,555
Queens								
Bread and bakery product mfg.	189	2,392	80,677	33,728	978	27,232	27,845	258,591
Commercial bakeries	49	1,745	69,963	40,093	620	21,841	35,227	219,328
Beverage mfg.	7	676	21,421	31,688	292	8,953	30,661	277,641
Textile product mills	45	998	31,247	31,310	598	14,328	23,960	124,445
Cut and sew apparel contractors	225	2,422	36,770	15,182	2,207	30,100	13,638	80,796
Apparel accessories and other apparel mfg.	25	1,483	37,797	25,487	1,096	20,632	18,825	158,467
Converted paper product mfg.	24	1,670	71,970	43,096	1,151	20,632	17,925	236,764
Stationery product mfg.	7	706	27,627	39,132	503	16,177	32,161	83,766
Commercial litho-graphic printing	74	1,874	92,805	49,522	1,485	72,524	48,838	509,887
Support activities for printing	20	576	20,559	35,6939	421	11,709	27,812	38,972
Chemical mfg.	26	1,274	51,148	40,148	860	25,624	29,795	358,725
Plastics and rubber products mfg.	42	1,157	41,681	36,025	853	24,295	28,482	215,565
Nonmetallic mineral product mfg.	39	869	30,238	34,796	676	20,621	30,504	156,499
Metal window and door mfg.	17	711	22,429	31,546	467	13,591	29,103	90,665
Sheet metal work mfg.	21	528	13,938	26,398	393	9,732	24,763	65,584
Machinery mfg.	70	1,470	62,969	42,836	995	31,087	31,243	234,455

	Number of Establishments	Number of Employees	Payroll ($1,000)	Payroll per Employee	Number of Production Workers	Production Wages ($1,000)	Wages per Production Worker	Total Value of Shipments ($1,000)
Queens (continued)								
Computer and electronic product mfg.	34	857	34,279	39,999	450	10,531	23,402	120,965
Electric lighting equipment mfg.	18	776	28,555	36,798	542	15,402	28,417	108,334
Transportation equipment mfg.	33	1,486	68,893	46,361	827	26,676	32,356	211,253
Nonupholstered wood household furniture mfg.	33	544	13,470	24,761	463	10,575	22,840	54,304
Office furniture (including fixtures) mfg.	32	790	31,007	39,249	576	17,640	30,625	104,417
Total mfg.	1,755	40,019	1,341,576	33,523	27,782	748,390	26,938	6,092,932
Staten Island								
Total mfg.	158	1,366	54,611	39,979	944	34,383	36,423	289,816
Citywide								
Confectionery mfg. from purchased chocolate	18	692	14,135	20,426	638	10,992	17,229	56,815
Fruit and vegetable preserving and specialty food mfg.	26	501	14,536	29,014	410	10,285	25,085	101,799
Dairy product (except frozen) mfg.	16	519	26,690	51,426	292	17,912	61,342	272,025
Meat processed from carcasses	36	815	26,445	32,448	628	17,020	27,102	253,237
Retail bakeries	458	2,683	44,412	16,553	1,368	22,305	16,305	138,296
Commercial bakeries	181	3,104	114,850	37,001	1,401	44,347	31,654	378,004

	Number of Establishments	Number of Employees	Payroll ($1,000)	Payroll per Employee	Number of Production Workers	Production Wages ($1,000)	Wages per Production Worker	Total Value of Shipments ($1,000)
Citywide (continued)								
Cookie and cracker mfg.	19	757	31,490	41,598	518	17,499	33,782	143,872
Seasoning and dressing mfg.	17	501	24,050	48,004	319	11,177	35,038	135,186
Soft drink mfg.	11	943	34,343	36,419	475	17,720	42,699	382,370
Knit fabric mills	42	699	18,321	26,210	556	11,561	20,793	120,454
Broadwoven fabric finishing mills	132	3,295	103,240	31,332	2,459	59,951	24,380	826,735
Textile and fabric finishing (except broadwoven fabric) mills	38	817	23,861	29,206	650	15,961	24,555	139,166
Curtain and drapery mills	46	1,132	28,295	24,996	620	9,527	15,366	125,013
Outerwear knitting mills	117	2,143	50,625	23,623	1,738	34,355	19,767	292,265
Men's and boys' cut and sew apparel contractors	99	1,289	18,890	14,655	1,104	14,747	13,358	45,400
Women's, girls', and infants' cut and sew apparel contractors	1,166	13,506	205,000	15,178	12,191	163,080	13,377	484,520
Men's and boys' cut and sew suit, coat, and overcoat mfg.	39	817	23,346	28,575	637	15,078	23,670	88,719
Women's and girls' cut and sew lingerie, loungewear, and nightwear mfg.	23	657	14,177	21,578	480	7,797	16,244	108,165
Women's and girls' cut and sew blouse and shirt mfg.	59	1,470	56,812	38,648	860	21,190	24,640	636,974
Women's and girls' cut and sew dress mfg.	172	5,787	190,985	33,002	3,047	71,740	23,544	1,536,403

Employment in Selected Manufacturing Sectors, by Borough, 2002 (continued)

	Number of Establish- ments	Number of Em- ployees	Payroll ($1,000)	Payroll per Em- ployee	Number of Pro- duction Workers	Produc- tion Wages ($1,000)	Wages per Pro- duction Worker	Total Value of Ship- ments ($1,000)
Citywide (continued)								
Women's and girls' cut and sew suit, coat, tailored jacket, and skirt mfg.	53	1,224	65,846	53,796	540	13,240	24,519	532,243
Women's and girls' cut and sew other outerwear mfg.	135	3,367	85,708	25,455	2,666	48,449	18,173	676,000
Fur and leather apparel mfg.	75	618	13,393	21,672	497	9,189	18,489	85,032
Men's and boys' neck- wear mfg.	33	1,126	29,325	26,044	850	16,073	18,909	179,197
Leather and allied product mfg.	104	949	25,073	26,420	732	14,436	19,721	92,834
Millwork	52	628	20,860	33,217	489	13,458	27,521	75,537
Corrugated and solid fiber box mfg.	13	563	25,032	44,462	414	14,037	33,906	102,690
Envelope mfg.	10	774	32,031	41,384	563	18,741	33,288	99,934
Commercial lithographic printing	423	6,558	301,793	46,019	4,762	195,096	40,969	1,177,284
Commercial screen printing	63	734	19,481	26,541	564	11,856	21,021	93,307
Quick printing	171	1,134	39,349	34,699	751	23,985	31,937	140,815
Digital printing	50	1,153	49,890	43,270	799	31,275	39,143	152,523
Tradebinding and related work	47	1,140	29,149	25,569	978	20,567	21,030	56,981
Prepress services	108	1,979	108,732	54,943	1,152	54,535	47,339	309,332
Basic chemical mfg.	9	606	33,661	55,546	380	15,500	40,789	208,232
Pharmaceutical and medicine mfg.	10	2,019	102,549	50,792	1,442	59,296	41,121	2.104,750
Toilet preparation mfg.	29	1,220	45,548	37,334	868	24,661	28,411	239,420
Plastic bag mfg.	28	714	24,630	34,496	545	14,924	27,383	117,016

	Number of Establishments	Number of Employees	Payroll ($1,000)	Payroll per Employee	Number of Production Workers	Production Wages ($1,000)	Wages per Production Worker	Total Value of Shipments ($1,000)
Citywide (continued)								
Glass product mfg. made of purchased glass	29	554	16,960	30,614	424	10,651	25,120	59,279
Ready-mix concrete mfg.	30	612	27,980	45,719	473	22,389	47,334	184,286
Forging and stamping	24	586	21,004	35,843	458	12,926	28,223	75,053
Metal window and door mfg.	48	1,535	49,190	32,046	1,090	33,149	30,412	182,652
Sheet metal work mfg.	52	1,318	38,547	29,247	1,017	26,626	26,181	131,592
Ornamental and architectural metal work mfg.	75	1,227	46,474	37,876	776	26,902	34,668	151,977
Spring and wire product mfg.	30	615	18,485	30,057	428	10,517	24,572	61,752
Machine shops, turned product, and screw, nut, and bolt mfg.	84	646	24,056	37,238	509	15,428	30,310	75,687
Electroplating, plating, polishing, anodizing, and coloring	44	518	14,272	27,552	418	9,873	23,620	34,973
Industrial machinery mfg.	47	564	22,882	40,571	360	10,887	30,242	77,639
Elevator and moving stairway mfg.	12	599	27,629	46,125	442	14,841	33,577	97,759
Semiconductor and other electronic component mfg.	24	1,129	44,663	39,560	535	12,210	22,882	149,755
Prerecorded compact disc (except software), tape, and record reproducing	43	876	36,262	41,395	538	17,754	33,000	130,747
Residential electric lighting fixture mfg.	31	637	27,112	42,562	368	12,053	32,753	130,809
Motor vehicle parts mfg.	42	1,127	52,086	46,217	601	18,317	30,478	179,478

	Number of Establishments	Number of Employees	Payroll ($1,000)	Payroll per Employee	Number of Production Workers	Production Wages ($1,000)	Wages per Production Worker	Total Value of Shipments ($1,000)
Citywide (continued)								
Aerospace products and parts mfg.	9	846	37,189	43,959	593	17,211	29,024	131,593
Wood kitchen cabinet and countertop mfg.	144	1,048	28,973	27,646	812	19,281	23,745	92,216
Upholstered household furniture mfg.	62	1,065	29,126	27,348	877	21,052	24,005	146,431
Nonupholstered wood household furniture mfg.	136	1,869	44,344	23,726	1,578	35,016	22,190	159,448
Custom architectural woodwook and millwork mfg.	40	729	35,923	49,277	471	20,512	43,550	99,550
Showcase, partition, shelving, and locker mfg.	56	1,052	35,130	33,394	743	19,339	26,028	129,294
Blind and shade mfg.	29	735	21,367	29,071	502	12,051	24,006	104,939
Dental laboratories	161	851	25,001	29,378	624	17,681	28,335	60,167
Jewelry (except costume) mfg.	444	7,998	278,829	34,862	5,282	136,910	25,920	1,957,182
Jewelers' material and lapidary work mfg.	78	1,616	39,862	24,667	994	20,580	20,704	445,047
Costume jewelry and novelty mfg.	74	800	23,448	29,310	518	9,095	17,558	110,954
Sign mfg.	130	2,625	87,667	33,397	1,793	46,482	25,924	284,472
Musical instrument mfg.	22	829	32,579	39,299	666	22,359	33,572	90,261
Total mfg.	8,228	143,211	4,639,372	32,395	101,371	2,577,411	25,426	25,043,179

Source: U.S. Bureau of the Census.

Employment in Selected Wholesale Trade Sectors, by Borough, 2002

	Number of Establishments	Sales ($1,000)	Annual Payroll ($1,000)	Number of Employees	Payroll per Employee
Manhattan					
Furniture merchant wholesalers	165	$1,483,772	$139,244	1,997	$69,727
Home furnishing merchant wholesalers	431	3,437,857	241,476	4,541	53,177
Linens, domestics, draperies, and curtains merchant wholesalers	121	2,139 368	109,947	2,104	52,256
Floor coverings merchant wholesalers	144	624,588	74,659	1,257	59,359
Brick, block, tile, clay, and cement sewer pipe merchant wholesalers	11	62,192	6,859	102	67,245
Office equipment merchant wholesalers	65	945,306	180,882	3,730	48,494
Computer and computer peripheral equipment and software merchant wholesalers	180	2,943,110	507,477	6,635	76,480
Restaurant and hotel equipment and supplies merchant wholesalers	57	123,484	12,727	422	30,159
Medical, dental, and hospital equipment and supplies merchant wholesalers	36	172,948	23,451	359	65,323
Ophthalmic goods merchant wholesalers	42	185,586	23,608	503	46,934
Metal service centers and other metal merchant wholesalers	86	5,971,056	120,091	1,031	116,480
Electrical apparatus and equipment, wiring supplies, and related equipment merchant wholesalers	84	348,327	37,912	653	58,058
Communications equipment and supplies merchant wholesalers	101	847,027	256,317	3,206	79,949
Hardware, and plumbing and heating equipment and supplies merchant wholesalers	91	330,386	39,322	831	47,319

Employment in Selected Wholesale Trade Sectors, by Borough, 2002 (continued)

	Number of Establishments	Sales ($1,000)	Annual Payroll ($1,000)	Number of Employees	Payroll per Employee
Manhattan (continued)					
Industrial supplies merchant wholesalers	45	422,199	67,102	1,358	49,412
Transportation equipment and supplies (except motor vehicle) merchant wholesalers	16	413,506	10,809	140	77,207
Toy and hobby goods and supplies merchant wholesalers	82	592,662	34,498	650	53,074
Jewelry, watch, precious stone, and silverware merchant wholesalers	2,294	12,011,399	542,618	12,777	42,468
Precious metal (except ore) merchant wholesalers	96	1,011,146	14,083	380	37,061
Stationery and office supplies merchant wholesalers	116	449,461	52,306	1,061	49,299
Drugs and druggists' sundries merchant wholesalers	198	26,062,111	947,955	11,146	85,049
Piece goods merchant wholesalers and jobbers	588	3,665,185	243,737	4,755	51,259
Notions and other dry goods merchant wholesalers	212	437,299	62,465	1,620	38,559
Men's and boys' clothing and furnishings merchant wholesalers	567	5,696,478	381,295	7,148	53,343
Women's, children's, and infants' clothing and accessories merchant wholesalers	1,720	22,679,837	1,647,873	26,285	62,693
Footwear merchant wholesalers	156	1,096,092	99,741	1,962	50,836
Poultry and poultry products (except live) merchant wholesalers	11	164,935	2,991	80	37,388
Fish and seafood merchant wholesalers	79	467,890	30,102	651	46,240
Meat and meat products merchant wholesalers	69	357,570	22,773	612	37,211

	Number of Establishments	Sales ($1,000)	Annual Payroll ($1,000)	Number of Employees	Payroll per Employee
Manhattan (continued)					
Coffee, tea, and spice merchant wholesalers	23	760,309	11,311	127	89,063
Canned goods merchant wholesalers	17	337,893	14,694	355	41,392
Farm product raw material merchant wholesalers	57	1,115,545	31,180	419	74,415
Chemical and allied products merchant wholesalers	123	6,242,173	133,483	1,403	95,141
Petroleum and petroleum products merchant wholesalers (except bulk stations and terminals)	21	1,151,885	14,767	250	59,068
Wine and distilled alcoholic beverage merchant wholesalers	59	3,168,470	131,416	1,641	80,083
Book, periodical, and newspaper merchant wholesalers	135	2,645,729	147,186	2,297	64,077
Flower, nursery stock, and florists' supplies merchant wholesalers	51	82,880	13,320	331	40,242
Art goods merchant wholesalers	201	575,342	67,414	1,237	54,498
Textile bags, bagging, and burlap merchant wholesalers	27	79,642	6,149	146	42,116
Wholesale electronic markets agents and brokers	549	14,150,193	240,220	4,007	59,950
Paper and paper products agents and brokers	13	91,648	3,062	70	43,743
Motor vehicle and motor vehicle parts and supplies merchant wholesalers	59	106,223	8,329	230	36,213
Prerecorded media merchant wholesalers	80	643,608	84,588	1,781	47,495
All wholesale trade	10,579	140,669,286	7,217,475	118,828	60,739

Employment in Selected Wholesale Trade Sectors, by Borough, 2002 (continued)

	Number of Establishments	Sales ($1,000)	Annual Payroll ($1,000)	Number of Employees	Payroll per Employee
Bronx					
Motor vehicle supplies and new parts merchant wholesalers	28	61,248	8,496	340	24,988
Lumber and other construction materials merchant wholesalers	22	96,694	12,544	315	39,822
Grocery and related product merchant wholesalers	295	4,018,597	257,022	6,193	41,502
Poultry and poultry products merchant wholesalers	10	175,523	6,193	162	38,228
Confectionery merchant wholesalers	8	156,653	8,161	279	29,251
Meat and meat products merchant wholesalers	49	1,038,569	48,888	1,159	42,181
Fresh fruit and vegetable merchant wholesalers	90	1,741,142	123,275	2,379	51,818
Petroleum and petroleum products merchant wholesalers	10	416,755	18,870	391	48,261
Brooklyn					
Automobile and other motor vehicle merchant wholesalers	28	121,235	8,835	252	35,060
Motor vehicle supplies and new parts merchant wholesalers	79	146,333	17,760	638	27,837
Furniture and home furnishing merchant wholesalers	177	557,792	49,170	1,571	31,299
Plywood, veneer, millwork, and wood panel merchant wholesalers	27	216,472	23,302	444	52,484
Brick, stone, and related construction material merchant wholesalers	25	93,763	7,293	203	35,926
Photographic equipment and supplies merchant wholesalers	18	151,044	6,418	187	34,321
Restaurant and hotel equipment and supplies merchant wholesalers	28	50,207	3,301	110	30,009
Medical, dental, and hospital equipment and supplies merchant wholesalers	84	120,133	13,406	383	35,003

	Number of Establishments	Sales ($1,000)	Annual Payroll ($1,000)	Number of Employees	Payroll per Employee
Brooklyn (continued)					
Communications equipment and supplies merchant wholesalers	46	198,843	17,158	451	38,044
Plumbing and heating equipment and supplies (hydronics) merchant wholesalers	36	100,555	14,781	314	47,073
Industrial machinery and equipment merchant wholesalers	59	74,850	10,123	292	34,668
Recyclable material merchant wholesalers	53	150,671	20,998	695	30,213
Paper and paper products merchant wholesalers	162	427,042	32,105	1,071	29,977
Apparel, piece goods, and notions merchant wholesalers	341	766,833	70,985	2,584	27,471
Dairy products (except dried or canned) merchant wholesalers	40	367,422	29,744	744	39,978
Poultry and poultry products merchant wholesalers	13	51,674	2,553	115	22,200
Confectionery merchant wholesalers	38	120,821	7,592	288	26,361
Fish and seafood merchant wholesalers	55	218,722	15,734	497	31,658
Meat and meat products merchant wholesalers	65	733,565	28,593	704	40,615
Fresh fruit and vegetable merchant wholesalers	78	265,189	14,368	492	29,203
Soft drinks and bottled water merchant wholesalers	78	333,241	23,154	689	33,605
Petroleum bulk terminals (except LP)	9	906,459	7,601	148	51,358
Beer, wine, and distilled alcoholic beverage merchant wholesalers	34	613,549	68,388	1,244	54,974
Tobacco and tobacco products merchant wholesalers	26	308,361	4,950	178	27,809
Paint, varnish, and supplies merchant wholesalers	19	48,354	5,994	195	30,738

Employment in Selected Wholesale Trade Sectors, by Borough, 2002 (continued)

	Number of Establishments	Sales ($1,000)	Annual Payroll ($1,000)	Number of Employees	Payroll per Employee
Brooklyn (continued)					
Textile bags, bagging, and burlap merchant wholesalers	12	23,923	2,134	78	27,359
Automobile and other motor vehicle merchant wholesalers	28	121,235	8,835	252	35,060
All wholesale trade	3,288	11,579,249	845,677	25,097	33,696
Queens					
Automobile and other motor vehicle merchant wholesalers	27	161,162	10,632	211	50,389
Motor vehicle supplies and new parts merchant wholesalers and jobbers	40	130,340	24,058	757	31,781
Household china, glassware, and crockery merchant wholesalers	12	88,241	4,970	216	23,009
Lumber, plywood, millwork, and wood panel merchant wholesalers	36	122,819	13,622	296	46,020
Lumber with yard merchant wholesalers	5	28,417	2,641	42	62,881
Brick, block, tile, clay, and cement sewer pipe merchant wholesalers	11	64,839	4,960	123	40,325
Roofing, siding, and insulation material merchant wholesalers	15	109,595	10,690	185	57,784
Medical, dental, and hospital equipment and supplies merchant wholesalers	46	204,544	23,764	594	40,007
Plumbing and heating equipment and supplies (hydronics) merchant wholesalers	32	80,622	12,626	258	48,938
Refrigeration equipment and supplies merchant wholesalers	11	153,035	9,925	206	48,180
Industrial machinery and equipment merchant wholesalers	85	169,072	21,730	488	44,529

Employment in Selected Wholesale Trade Sectors, by Borough, 2002 (continued)

	Number of Establishments	Sales ($1,000)	Annual Payroll ($1,000)	Number of Employees	Payroll per Employee
Queens (continued)					
Industrial supplies merchant wholesalers	45	213,822	46,924	1,067	43,978
Custodial and janitors' equipment and supplies merchant wholesalers	13	52,821	9,585	202	47,450
Laundry and dry-cleaning equipment and supplies merchant wholesalers	5	30,603	5,011	75	66,813
Recyclable material merchant wholesalers	39	204,451	47,050	1,604	29,333
Jewelry, watch, precious stone, and silverware merchant wholesalers	102	954,790	86,041	2,227	38,635
Precious metal (except ore) merchant wholesalers	12	30,703	3,529	118	29,907
Piece goods merchant wholesalers and jobbers	39	62,561	7,495	208	36,034
Men's and boys' clothing and furnishings merchant wholesalers	61	283,587	20,754	463	44,825
Women's, children's, and infants' clothing and accessories merchant wholesalers	146	735,626	59,970	1,804	33,243
Footwear merchant wholesalers	32	267,757	20,484	527	38,869
Bread and baked goods merchant wholesalers	43	110,442	14,763	478	30,885
Soft drinks and bottled water merchant wholesalers	55	310,205	35,822	989	36,220
Chemical and allied products merchant wholesalers	60	148,331	16,192	387	41,840
Beer, wine, and distilled alcoholic beverage merchant wholesalers	42	1,016,545	83,100	1,759	47,243
Paint, varnish, and supplies merchant wholesalers	12	73,114	10,665	271	39,354
Wholesale electronic markets agents and brokers	66	262,879	11,002	197	55,848

Employment in Selected Wholesale Trade Sectors, by Borough, 2002 (continued)

	Number of Establishments	Sales ($1,000)	Annual Payroll ($1,000)	Number of Employees	Payroll per Employee
Queens (continued)					
Motor vehicle supplies and new parts merchant wholesalers	93	255,619	40,448	1,285	31,477
All wholesale trade	2,940	13,868,922	1,148,732	29,665	38,723
Staten Island					
Motor vehicle and motor vehicle parts and supplies merchant wholesalers	28	48,510	3,467	122	28,418
Citywide					
Automobile and other motor vehicle merchant wholesalers	88	381,185	29,685	676	43,913
Motor vehicle supplies and new parts merchant wholesalers and jobbers	119	263,204	43,244	1,416	30,540
Household and lawn furniture merchant wholesalers	176	593,035	56,307	1,347	41,802
Office and business furniture merchant wholesalers	112	1,260,619	116,822	1,681	69,496
Linens, domestics, draperies, and curtains merchant wholesalers	189	2,370,000	126,922	2,648	47,931
Floor coverings merchant wholesalers	179	680,424	84,379	1,492	56,554
Lumber, plywood, millwork, and wood panel merchant wholesalers	107	510,797	54,981	1,128	48,742
Office equipment merchant wholesalers	99	1,047,059	196,169	4,038	48,581
Computer and peripheral equipment for end use merchant wholesalers	155	2,086,812	409,850	5,398	75,926
Medical, dental, and hospital equipment and supplies merchant wholesalers	181	538,876	64,349	1,420	45,316
Ophthalmic goods merchant wholesalers	67	260,411	35,261	760	46,396

Employment in Selected Wholesale Trade Sectors, by Borough, 2002 (continued)

	Number of Establishments	Sales ($1,000)	Annual Payroll ($1,000)	Number of Employees	Payroll per Employee
Citywide (continued)					
Metal service centers and other metal merchant wholesalers	186	6,294,470	165,721	1,984	83,529
Electrical apparatus and equipment, wiring supplies, and related equipment merchant wholesalers	243	817,491	105,180	2,077	50,640
Communications equipment and supplies merchant wholesalers	201	1,207,022	298,896	4,208	71,030
Hardware merchant wholesalers	141	385,483	53,526	1,213	44,127
Plumbing and heating equipment and supplies (hydronics) merchant wholesalers	115	300,544	41,840	919	45,528
Industrial machinery and equipment merchant wholesalers	293	503,705	70,293	1,571	44,744
Industrial containers and supplies merchant wholesalers	32	524,913	104,822	2,320	45,182
Laundry and dry-cleaning equipment and supplies merchant wholesalers	13	39,580	6,364	116	54,862
Iron and steel scrap merchant wholesalers, processors, and dealers	47	136,530	13,990	366	38,224
Printing and writing paper merchant wholesalers	59	1,815,863	68,106	872	78,103
General line drugs merchant wholesalers	177	3,235,031	116,751	2,027	57,597
Specialty line drugs, pharmaceuticals, cosmetics, and toiletries merchant wholesalers	200	25,508,834	896,159	10,726	83,550
Piece goods merchant wholesalers jobbers	685	3,811,209	258,569	5,274	49,027
Men's and boys' clothing and furnishings merchant wholesalers	709	6,203,844	420,834	8,310	50,642

	Number of Establishments	Sales ($1,000)	Annual Payroll ($1,000)	Number of Employees	Payroll per Employee
Citywide (continued)					
Women's, children's, and infants' clothing and accessories merchant wholesalers	2,044	23,870,272	1,751,554	29,602	59,170
Packaged frozen food merchant wholesalers	161	973,869	46,915	1,394	33,655
Fish and seafood merchant wholesalers	185	800,849	52,546	1,465	35,868
Fresh fruit and vegetable merchant wholesalers	293	2,406,301	158,164	3,634	43,523
Coffee, tea, and spice merchant wholesalers	79	897,724	26,107	545	47,903
Petroleum bulk stations and terminals (except LP)	35	1,573,661	23,367	507	46,089
Petroleum and petroleum products merchant wholesalers (except bulk stations and terminals)	43	1,569,937	28,445	520	54,702
Beer, wine, and distilled alcoholic beverage merchant wholesalers	174	5,172,723	307,844	5,361	57,423
Farm supplies merchant wholesalers	45	2,164,106	32,739	443	73,903
Book, periodical, and newspaper merchant wholesalers	212	2,768,013	165,990	2,878	57,675
Flower, nursery stock, and florists' supplies merchant wholesalers	112	168,920	24,627	642	38,360
Tobacco and tobacco products merchant wholesalers	83	927,688	23,278	674	34,537
Art goods merchant wholesalers	333	730,313	83,026	1,828	45,419
General merchandise (nondurable goods) merchant wholesalers	208	1,459,011	52,002	943	55,145
Furniture and home furnishings agents and brokers	60	539,463	17,079	307	55,632
Electrical and electronic goods agents and brokers	25	560,208	17,240	176	97,955
Machinery, equipment, and supplies agents and brokers	22	285,068	6,725	106	63,443

	Number of Establishments	Sales ($1,000)	Annual Payroll ($1,000)	Number of Employees	Payroll per Employee
Citywide (continued)					
Paper and paper products agents and brokers	20	101,055	3,692	85	43,435
Apparel, piece goods, and notions agents and brokers	334	3,008,671	88,196	1,604	54,985
Roofing, siding, and insulation material merchant wholesalers	26	122,836	13,230	244	54,221
Electrical and electronic goods merchant wholesalers	752	3,192,638	313,736	6,542	47,957
Stationery and office supplies merchant wholesalers	222	544,845	71,953	1,745	41,234
Piece goods, notions, and other dry goods merchant wholesalers	912	3,313,179	294,273	6,584	44,695
Footwear merchant wholesalers	219	1,360,560	120,976	2,534	47,741
Lumber and other construction materials merchant wholesalers' sales branches and offices	8	44,550	1,788	38	47,053
Electrical and electronic goods merchant wholesalers' sales branches and offices	24	674,330	206,993	2,198	94,173
Book, periodical, and newspaper merchant wholesalers' sales branches and offices	15	1,745,608	52,652	566	93,025
All wholesale trade	17,870	173,539,688	9,737,824	186,600	52,186

Source: U.S. Bureau of the Census.

Employment in Selected Retail Trade Sectors, by Borough, 2002

	Number of Establishments	Sales ($1,000)	Annual Payroll ($1,000)	Number of Employees	Payroll per Employee
Manhattan					
New car dealers	22	$951,534	$71,701	1,308	$54,817
Used car dealers	19	30,031	1,439	35	41,114
Motorcycle, boat, and other motor vehicle dealers	12	46,835	4,184	108	38,741
Automotive parts and accessories stores	34	22,692	3,308	129	25,643
Furniture stores	260	604,711	82,849	2,188	37,865
Floor covering stores	85	152,159	31,325	785	39,904
Window treatment stores	25	21,861	4,913	166	29,596
Household appliance stores	52	125,810	11,058	354	31,237
Radio, television, and other electronics stores	370	605,412	69,932	2,385	29,321
Computer and software stores	80	249,336	23,348	712	32,792
Camera and photographic supplies stores	67	767,403	47,242	1,050	44,992
Building material and supplies dealers	332	514,629	91,259	2,503	36,460
Home centers	9	25,643	5,855	171	34,240
Paint and wallpaper stores	26	61,937	10,040	274	36,642
Hardware stores	164	118,097	23,754	816	29,110
Nursery, garden center, and farm supply stores	19	60,973	6,999	406	17,239
Supermarkets and other grocery (except convenience) stores	1,200	2,118,210	281,278	14,082	19,974
Convenience stores	136	54,962	7,018	498	14,092
Specialty food stores	593	359,222	50,904	3,001	16,962
Beer, wine, and liquor stores	265	370,678	34,487	1,293	26,672
Pharmacies and drug stores	473	2,281,473	184,014	7,278	25,284
Proprietary stores	41	43,535	6,330	322	19,658
Cosmetics, beauty supplies, and perfume stores	159	185,870	31,435	1,281	24,539
Optical goods stores	198	144,063	35,279	1,097	32,160
Food (health) supplement stores	155	129,749	17,243	956	18,037
Gasoline stations	86	162,780	6,528	342	19,088

Employment in Selected Retail Trade Sectors, by Borough, 2002 (continued)

	Number of Establishments	Sales ($1,000)	Annual Payroll ($1,000)	Number of Employees	Payroll per Employee
Manhattan (continued)					
Men's clothing stores	268	434,102	68,640	2,385	28,780
Women's clothing stores	769	1,827,299	227,255	9,711	23,402
Children's and infants' clothing stores	104	143,883	18,120	1,040	17,423
Family clothing stores	373	1,926,169	238,867	11,575	20,636
Clothing accessories stores	166	255,360	53,919	1,164	46,322
Men's shoe stores	50	55,295	8,433	259	32,560
Women's shoe stores	133	119,344	15,653	980	15,972
Children's and juveniles' shoe stores	8	8,625	1,347	71	18,972
Family shoe stores	202	326,225	43,223	1,812	23,854
Athletic footwear stores	90	162,188	20,174	1,014	19,895
Jewelry stores	744	1,061,571	113,302	3,022	37,492
Luggage and leather goods stores	85	185,944	24,008	580	41,393
General line sporting goods stores	24	114,989	9,504	605	15,709
Specialty line sporting goods stores	61	97,052	14,812	526	28,160
Hobby, toy, and game stores	64	163,615	21,519	689	31,232
Sewing, needlework, and piece goods stores	86	71,870	13,059	455	28,701
Musical instrument and supplies stores	44	85,415	8,436	337	25,033
Bookstores	127	363,004	45,759	2,547	17,966
News dealers and newsstands	285	94,688	12,356	826	14,959
Prerecorded tape, compact disc, and record stores	154	250,462	23,229	1,577	14,730
Department stores	8	1,383,342	205,466	6,772	30,341
Variety stores	77	73,370	9,779	566	17,277
Miscellaneous general merchandise stores	100	213,357	34,567	1,356	25,492
Florists	227	122,820	24,050	977	24,616
Office supplies and stationery stores	129	268,188	33,967	1,460	23,265
Gift, novelty, and souvenir stores	448	256,893	37,569	2,060	18,237
Used merchandise stores	289	335,505	50,788	1,267	40,085
Pet and pet supplies stores	69	53,426	7,592	449	16,909
Art dealers	476	1,423,154	201,377	2,619	76,891

Employment in Selected Retail Trade Sectors, by Borough, 2002 (continued)

	Number of Establishments	Sales ($1,000)	Annual Payroll ($1,000)	Number of Employees	Payroll per Employee
Manhattan (continued)					
Electronic shopping and mail order houses	282	2,372,429	248,914	6,321	39,379
Vending machine operators	16	6,582	2,311	55	42,018
Heating oil dealers	6	9,883	2,038	47	43,362
All retail trade	11,620	25,904,575	3,206,434	116,328	27,564
Bronx					
New car dealers	25	387,988	28,423	712	39,920
Used car dealers	51	33,039	2,464	111	22,198
Automotive parts and accessories stores	81	67,938	11,927	575	20,743
Tire dealers	22	20,879	2,923	111	26,333
Furniture stores	94	85,782	9,827	372	26,417
Floor covering stores	28	26,842	6,731	227	29,652
Window treatment stores	10	5,132	604	46	13,130
Household appliance stores	14	55,891	4,718	138	34,189
Radio, television, and other electronics stores	98	72,864	10,570	483	21,884
Computer and software stores	5	3,633	412	27	15,259
Building material and supplies dealers	122	252,676	33,571	1,088	30,856
Supermarkets and other grocery (except convenience) stores	762	819,104	72,699	4,655	15,617
Convenience stores	67	23,676	2,071	146	14,185
Specialty food stores	212	99,114	11,389	695	16,387
Beer, wine, and liquor stores	103	67,823	4,415	231	19,113
Pharmacies and drug stores	234	800,555	57,560	2,339	24,609
Cosmetics, beauty supplies, and perfume stores	52	14,249	1,796	117	15,350
Optical goods stores	28	14,193	4,331	151	28,682
Food (health) supplement stores	13	5,925	718	37	19,405
Gasoline stations	168	235,861	12,081	630	19,176
Men's clothing stores	73	70,519	7,303	549	13,302
Women's clothing stores	138	135,681	12,986	1,055	12,309

Employment in Selected Retail Trade Sectors, by Borough, 2002 (continued)

	Number of Establishments	Sales ($1,000)	Annual Payroll ($1,000)	Number of Employees	Payroll per Employee
Bronx (continued)					
Children's and infants' clothing stores	36	79,429	12,073	804	15,016
Family clothing stores	64	117,385	11,353	807	14,068
Clothing accessories stores	9	5,957	1,121	62	18,081
Women's shoe stores	8	3,214	236	20	11,800
Family shoe stores	48	43,147	4,374	303	14,436
Athletic footwear stores	36	33,056	3,307	219	15,100
Jewelry, luggage, and leather goods stores	96	20,584	3,058	193	15,845
Sporting goods stores	19	37,581	3,967	227	17,476
Hobby, toy, and game stores	20	57,201	3,386	192	17,635
Bookstores and news dealers	36	25,898	2,555	176	14,517
Prerecorded tape, compact disc, and record stores	23	8,695	1,095	75	14,600
Department stores	6	228,089	24,809	1,491	16,639
Variety stores	87	41,152	5,011	377	13,292
Miscellaneous general merchandise stores	67	75,143	9,566	639	14,970
Florists	32	6,753	1,314	85	15,459
Office supplies, stationery, and gift stores	72	51,967	5,975	397	15,050
Used merchandise stores	24	11,226	2,844	144	19,750
Pet and pet supplies stores	23	10,580	1,761	102	17,265
Electronic shopping and mail order houses	16	12,702	1,413	53	26,660
Vending machine operators	13	16,537	2,972	140	21,229
Heating oil dealers	26	60,255	8,845	207	42,729
All retail trade	319	4,318,169	424,939	21,811	19,482
Brooklyn					
New car dealers	51	1,159,772	85,992	1,860	46,232
Used car dealers	86	106,570	5,309	170	31,047
Automotive parts and accessories stores	104	93,657	15,484	704	21,994
Tire dealers	29	40,471	7,907	252	31,377

Employment in Selected Retail Trade Sectors, by Borough, 2002 (continued)

	Number of Establishments	Sales ($1,000)	Annual Payroll ($1,000)	Number of Employees	Payroll per Employee
Brooklyn (continued)					
Furniture stores	216	198,221	24,332	936	25,996
Floor covering stores	61	34,800	6,230	212	29,387
Window treatment stores	22	10,290	1,557	85	18,318
Household appliance stores	65	159,988	13,790	430	32,070
Radio, television, and other electronics stores	202	204,345	25,911	1,154	22,453
Computer and software stores	65	48,156	6,907	216	31,977
Camera and photographic supplies stores	22	14,227	1,495	73	20,479
Building material and supplies dealers	382	930,462	99,223	3,332	29,779
Hardware stores	129	75,819	11,387	530	21,485
Lawn and garden equipment and supplies stores	11	5,913	1,028	55	18,691
Supermarkets and other grocery (except convenience) stores	1,250	1,702,774	160,929	9,624	16,722
Convenience stores	163	44,843	4,258	300	14,193
Specialty food stores	644	325,379	34,617	2,347	14,749
Beer, wine, and liquor stores	217	157,630	10,130	560	18,089
Pharmacies and drug stores	486	1,508,929	116,420	5,319	21,888
Proprietary stores	18	16,763	2,086	156	13,372
Cosmetics, beauty supplies, and perfume stores	91	36,834	4,623	300	15,410
Optical goods stores	104	48,984	9,953	421	23,641
Food (health) supplement stores	58	44,520	5,893	298	19,775
Gasoline stations	270	429,644	18,389	1,163	15,812
Men's clothing stores	143	118,758	12,324	734	16,790
Women's clothing stores	380	320,501	34,584	2,729	12,673
Children's and infants' clothing stores	97	124,995	18,447	1,161	15,889
Family clothing stores	154	277,688	32,955	2,091	15,760
Clothing accessories stores	73	26,335	4,679	293	15,969
Men's shoe stores	19	7,455	903	56	16,125
Women's shoe stores	54	27,097	3,528	288	12,250
Children's and juveniles' shoe stores	13	8,954	869	60	14,483

Employment in Selected Retail Trade Sectors, by Borough, 2002 (continued)

	Number of Establishments	Sales ($1,000)	Annual Payroll ($1,000)	Number of Employees	Payroll per Employee
Brooklyn (continued)					
Family shoe stores	124	90,054	9,276	583	15,911
Athletic footwear stores	61	53,777	5,127	341	15,035
Jewelry stores	165	45,679	7,179	415	17,299
Luggage and leather goods stores	11	3,122	578	33	17,515
General line sporting goods stores	36	72,515	6,108	405	15,081
Specialty line sporting goods stores	30	17,120	1,857	109	17,037
Hobby, toy, and game stores	49	89,044	6,857	272	25,210
Bookstores, general	36	34,490	3,814	268	14,231
Specialty bookstores	8	6,474	630	26	24,331
College bookstores	13	18,857	1,430	108	13,241
News dealers and newsstands	43	14,177	1,472	105	14,019
Prerecorded tape, compact disc, and record stores	57	28,875	2,777	215	12,916
Department stores	8	473,751	52,928	2,968	17,833
Miscellaneous general merchandise stores	135	126,680	18,388	1,251	14,699
Florists	107	28,269	5,398	281	19,210
Office supplies, stationery, and gift stores	211	117,829	13,540	913	14,830
Used merchandise stores	66	20,717	4,995	287	17,404
Pet and pet supplies stores	47	21,228	3,320	187	17,754
Art dealers	16	2,940	454	22	20,636
Electronic shopping and mail order houses	141	368,947	22,387	783	28,591
Vending machine operators	24	10,617	1,481	85	17,423
Heating oil dealers	64	401,712	36,299	762	47,636
All retail trade	7,687	10,909,140	1,051,070	51,181	20,536
Queens					
New car dealers	71	1,890,487	147,901	2,787	53,068
Used car dealers	102	216,176	9,249	284	32,567
Automotive parts and accessories stores	122	99,146	16,600	745	22,282
Tire dealers	32	21,299	2,668	114	23,404
Furniture stores	158	181,312	23,518	827	28,438

Employment in Selected Retail Trade Sectors, by Borough, 2002 (continued)

	Number of Establishments	Sales ($1,000)	Annual Payroll ($1,000)	Number of Employees	Payroll per Employee
Queens (continued)					
Floor covering stores	71	33,002	4,456	189	23,577
Window treatment stores	9	3,675	676	36	18,778
Household appliance stores	53	142,634	11,513	297	38,764
Radio, television, and other					
electronics stores	198	269,228	25,869	1,190	21,739
Computer and software stores	53	73,310	6,178	253	24,419
Camera and photographic supplies					
stores	10	2,119	290	18	16,111
Paint and wallpaper stores	21	60,279	7,949	206	38,587
Lawn and garden equipment and					
supplies stores	14	20,515	3,771	134	28,142
Supermarkets and other grocery					
(except convenience) stores	1,009	1,822,569	170,141	10,123	16,807
Convenience stores	193	68,422	6,189	488	12,682
Specialty food stores	481	209,379	22,812	1,497	15,238
Beer, wine, and liquor stores	203	130,407	8,724	488	17,885
Pharmacies and drug stores	374	1,317,455	110,584	5,553	19,914
Proprietary stores	13	13,484	1,148	45	25,511
Cosmetics, beauty supplies, and					
perfume stores	87	48,330	5,750	362	15,884
Optical goods stores	94	41,817	12,794	496	25,794
Food (health) supplement stores	74	36,263	4,587	266	17,244
Gasoline stations	312	508,703	24,381	1,409	17,304
Men's clothing stores	87	52,485	6,735	402	16,754
Women's clothing stores	238	179,304	19,863	1,518	13,085
Children's and infants' clothing stores	54	88,342	10,980	697	15,753
Family clothing stores	124	310,680	31,471	2,243	14,031
Clothing accessories stores	41	15,927	2,741	144	19,035
Men's shoe stores	11	3,103	351	21	16,714
Women's shoe stores	28	15,740	1,711	154	11,110
Children's and juveniles' shoe stores	5	3,964	427	28	15,250
Family shoe stores	99	82,992	8,726	591	14,765
Athletic footwear stores	34	42,773	3,908	188	20,787
Jewelry stores	178	84,247	11,650	530	21,981

Employment in Selected Retail Trade Sectors, by Borough, 2002 (continued)

	Number of Establishments	Sales ($1,000)	Annual Payroll ($1,000)	Number of Employees	Payroll per Employee
Queens (continued)					
Luggage and leather goods stores	13	8,228	718	39	18,410
General line sporting goods stores	31	76,569	7,987	465	17,176
Specialty line sporting goods stores	19	8,209	918	41	22,390
Hobby, toy, and game stores	37	99,922	8,294	553	14,998
Sewing, needlework, and piece goods stores	26	10,584	1,658	107	15,495
Musical instrument and supplies stores	15	21,393	1,967	93	21,151
Bookstores, general	19	28,218	2,706	207	13,072
Specialty bookstores	8	2,695	334	34	9,824
College bookstores	8	19,411	1,343	99	13,566
News dealers and newsstands	90	55,613	5,621	401	14,017
Prerecorded tape, compact disc, and record stores	51	25,237	2,884	192	15,021
Department stores	12	578,359	60,129	3,442	17,469
Florists	112	24,219	4,528	293	15,454
Office supplies and stationery stores	59	92,769	9,032	492	18,358
Gift, novelty, and souvenir stores	162	84,086	9,876	645	15,312
Used merchandise stores	37	9,034	2,221	130	17,085
Pet and pet supplies stores	49	25,915	3,449	217	15,894
Art dealers	13	1,298	239	20	11,950
Electronic shopping and mail order houses	75	84,707	8,889	440	20,202
Vending machine operators	22	19,799	3,474	127	19,480
Fuel dealers	35	158,643	24,808	592	41,905
All retail trade	6,395	11,226,779	1,071,425	50,252	21,321
Staten Island					
New car dealers	18	548,494	31,292	732	42,749
Motorcycle, boat, and other motor vehicle dealers	9	71,339	5,281	99	53,343
Automotive parts and accessories stores	25	29,372	4,638	192	24,156
Tire dealers	7	7,450	986	37	26,649

Employment in Selected Retail Trade Sectors, by Borough, 2002 (continued)

	Number of Establishments	Sales ($1,000)	Annual Payroll ($1,000)	Number of Employees	Payroll per Employee
Staten Island (continued)					
Furniture stores	31	49,334	4,728	151	31,311
Floor covering stores	13	17,680	2,517	54	46,611
Window treatment stores	9	3,452	441	25	17,640
Household appliance stores	9	12,117	1,297	45	28,822
Radio, television, and other electronics stores	20	85,882	7,760	346	22,428
Computer and software stores	7	7,992	531	33	16,091
Camera and photographic supplies stores	6	1,977	153	6	25,500
Paint and wallpaper stores	5	3,810	386	11	35,091
Nursery, garden center, and farm supply stores	10	8,703	1,385	74	18,716
Supermarkets and other grocery (except convenience) stores	139	590,753	73,368	3,600	20,380
Convenience stores	64	35,073	2,338	204	11,461
Specialty food stores	61	28,669	3,635	261	13,927
Beer, wine, and liquor stores	35	23,743	1,828	100	18,280
Pharmacies and drug stores	64	298,302	18,597	1,333	13,951
Cosmetics, beauty supplies, and perfume stores	12	10,350	1,420	102	13,922
Optical goods stores	23	12,908	3,721	132	28,189
Food (health) supplement stores	7	7,061	662	51	12,980
Gasoline stations	60	113,701	4,809	256	18,785
Men's clothing stores	10	13,835	1,700	78	21,795
Women's clothing stores	46	69,146	7,287	559	13,036
Children's and infants' clothing stores	16	33,237	3,437	259	13,270
Family clothing stores	23	77,904	7,079	587	12,060
Clothing accessories stores	8	3,040	499	31	16,097
Women's shoe stores	7	5,013	689	80	8,613
Family shoe stores	20	15,375	1,556	108	14,407
Athletic footwear stores	7	15,562	1,349	140	9,636
Jewelry, luggage, and leather goods stores	40	22,604	3,350	131	25,573

Employment in Selected Retail Trade Sectors, by Borough, 2002 (continued)

	Number of Establishments	Sales ($1,000)	Annual Payroll ($1,000)	Number of Employees	Payroll per Employee
Staten Island (continued)					
Sporting goods stores	14	18,894	1,571	106	14,821
General line sporting goods stores	7	16,596	1,303	89	14,640
Hobby, toy, and game stores	11	48,257	3,494	248	14,089
Specialty bookstores	3	810	106	5	21,200
Prerecorded tape, compact disc, and record stores	13	11,101	1,110	91	12,198
Department stores	5	241,989	27,100	1,517	17,864
Florists	33	13,888	2,701	176	15,347
Office supplies, stationery, and gift stores	38	46,390	5,180	349	14,842
Used merchandise stores	9	1,566	571	48	11,896
Pet and pet supplies stores	13	12,725	1,431	104	13,760
Art dealers	4	1,182	284	16	17,750
Electronic shopping and mail order houses	16	10,902	1,528	48	31,833
Vending machine operators	7	3,299	528	16	33,000
Fuel dealers	12	17,411	2,849	72	39,569
All retail trade	1,231	3,159,828	296,687	14,611	20,306
Citywide					
New car dealers	187	4,938,275	365,309	7,399	49,373
Used car dealers	275	395,504	18,839	625	30,142
Motorcycle dealers	24	67,463	4,485	165	27,182
Boat dealers	19	100,988	8,653	205	42,210
Automotive parts and accessories stores	366	312,805	51,957	2,345	22,157
Tire dealers	103	95,791	15,878	563	28,202
Furniture stores	759	1,119,360	145,254	4,474	32,466
Floor covering stores	258	264,483	51,259	1,467	34,941
Window treatment stores	75	44,410	8,191	358	22,880
Household appliance stores	193	496,440	42,376	1,264	33,525
Radio, television, and other electronics stores	888	1,237,731	140,042	5,558	25,196
Computer and software stores	210	382,427	37,376	1,241	30,118

	Number of Establishments	Sales ($1,000)	Annual Payroll ($1,000)	Number of Employees	Payroll per Employee
Citywide (continued)					
Camera and photographic supplies stores	109	786,038	49,237	1,151	42,778
Building material and supplies dealers	1,189	2,916,370	361,191	11,467	31,498
Outdoor power equipment stores	4	5,194	638	37	17,243
Nursery, garden center, and farm supply stores	54	92,389	12,912	644	20,050
Supermarkets and other grocery (except convenience) stores	4,360	7,053,410	758,415	42,084	18,021
Convenience stores	623	226,976	21,874	1,636	13,370
Specialty food stores	1,991	1,021,763	123,357	7,801	15,813
Beer, wine, and liquor stores	823	750,281	59,584	2,672	22,299
Pharmacies and drug stores	1,614	6,186,415	485,541	21,727	22,347
Proprietary stores	89	94,081	11,198	618	18,120
Cosmetics, beauty supplies, and perfume stores	401	295,633	45,024	2,162	20,825
Optical goods stores	447	261,965	66,078	2,297	28,767
Food (health) supplement stores	307	223,518	29,103	1,608	18,099
Gasoline stations	896	1,450,689	66,188	3,800	17,418
Men's clothing stores	581	689,699	96,702	4,148	23,313
Women's clothing stores	1,571	2,531,931	301,975	15,572	19,392
Children's and infants' clothing stores	307	469,886	63,057	3,961	15,919
Family clothing stores	738	2,709,826	321,725	17,303	18,594
Clothing accessories stores	297	306,619	62,959	1,694	37,166
Men's shoe stores	85	68,243	10,011	356	28,121
Women's shoe stores	230	170,408	21,817	1,522	14,334
Children's and juveniles' shoe stores	34	29,236	3,345	204	16,397
Family shoe stores	493	557,793	67,155	3,397	19,769
Athletic footwear stores	228	307,356	33,865	1,902	17,805
Jewelry stores	1,218	1,232,091	138,276	4,276	32,338
Luggage and leather goods stores	114	199,888	25,567	667	38,331
General line sporting goods stores	108	314,491	28,372	1,770	16,029
Specialty line sporting goods stores	126	128,438	18,352	714	25,703
Hobby, toy, and game stores	181	458,039	43,550	1,954	22,288

Employment in Selected Retail Trade Sectors, by Borough, 2002 (continued)

	Number of Establishments	Sales ($1,000)	Annual Payroll ($1,000)	Number of Employees	Payroll per Employee
Citywide (continued)					
Sewing, needlework, and piece goods stores	161	95,535	16,576	699	23,714
Musical instrument and supplies stores	68	121,140	12,282	503	24,417
Bookstores	240	511,113	59,790	3,544	16,871
News dealers and newsstands	451	172,655	20,437	1,397	14,629
Prerecorded tape, compact disc, and record stores	298	324,370	31,095	2,150	14,463
Department stores	39	2,905,530	370,432	16,190	22,880
Florists	511	195,949	37,991	1,812	20,966
Office supplies and stationery stores	243	487,576	52,992	2,507	21,138
Gift, novelty, and souvenir stores	876	430,546	62,147	3,809	16,316
Used merchandise stores	425	378,048	61,419	1,903	32,275
Pet and pet supplies stores	201	123,874	17,553	1,059	16,575
Art dealers	512	1,428,896	202,416	2,680	75,528
Electronic shopping and mail order houses	530	2,849,687	283,131	7,645	37,035
Vending machine operators	82	56,834	10,766	423	25,452
Heating oil dealers	139	643,514	74,181	1,661	44,660
Liquefied petroleum gas (bottled gas) dealers	4	4,390	658	19	34,632
All retail trade	30,252	55,518,491	6,050,555	254,183	23,804

Source: U.S. Bureau of the Census.

Employment in Selected Information Services, by Borough, 2002

	Number of Establishments	Receipts ($1,000)	Annual Payroll ($1,000)	Number of Employees	Payroll per Employee
Manhattan					
Newspaper publishers	129	$2,365,810	$676,600	10,192	$66,385
Periodical publishers	428	14,322,309	2,373,401	26,939	88,103
Book publishers	226	5,543,907	755,073	11,437	66,020
Software publishers	225	1,689,726	588,068	7,260	81,001
Sound recording studios	136	117,757	40,620	1,062	38,249
Telecommunications resellers	72	331,702	60,265	937	64,317
Internet service providers and web search portals	110	423,513	105,483	1,674	63,013
Data processing, hosting, and related services	282	995,381	536,304	7,473	71,766
Libraries and archives	76	233,981	97,745	2,974	32,867
Brooklyn					
Publishing industries (except Internet)	96	128,412	41,037	1,050	39,083
Internet service providers, web search portals, and data processing services	60	519,898	145,601	1,980	73,536
Queens					
Newspaper publishers	41	100,634	30,713	986	31,149
Citywide					
Newspaper publishers	214	2,563,392	746,627	12,144	61,481
Periodical publishers	466	14,411,958	2,403,553	27,535	87,291
Book publishers	259	5,601,001	772,701	11,887	65,004
Software publishers	255	1,729,790	606,882	7,483	81,101
Postproduction and other motion picture and video industries	271	519,014	194,871	3,612	53,951
Sound recording studios	160	121,082	41,679	1,123	37,114
Broadcasting (except Internet)	242	20,028,337	2,697,510	29,710	90,795
Data processing, hosting, and related services	401	1,630,948	746,891	11,006	67,862

Source: U.S. Bureau of the Census.

Employment in Selected Real Estate Sectors and Rental and Leasing Sectors, by Borough, 2002

	Number of Establishments	Revenue ($1,000)	Annual Payroll ($1,000)	Number of Employees	Payroll per Employee
Manhattan					
Lessors of apartment buildings	3,571	$5,030,350	$511,930	16,292	$31,422
Lessors of dwellings other than apartment buildings	279	176,925	22,615	772	29,294
Lessors of professional and other office buildings	1,078	6,418,589	408,275	9,001	45,359
Lessors of manufacturing and industrial buildings	118	150,605	19,212	416	46,183
Lessors of shopping centers and retail stores	227	506,735	57,420	1,222	46,989
Lessors of other nonresidential buildings and facilities	142	298,728	35,521	1,180	30,103
Lessors of miniwarehouses and self-storage units	32	86,141	9,439	313	30,157
Lessors of manufactured (mobile) home sites	71	37,267	5,650	172	32,849
Offices of residential real estate agents and brokers	607	927,464	152,032	3,710	40,979
Offices of nonresidential real estate agents and brokers	316	865,943	379,657	3,896	97,448
Residential property managers	925	956,813	412,973	9,358	44,130
Nonresidential property managers	422	1,070,508	551,826	9,303	59,317
Offices of real estate appraisers	41	40,118	19,722	308	64,032
Passenger car rental and leasing	25	85,813	18,814	648	29,034
Truck, utility trailer, and RV (recreational vehicle) rental and leasing	13	27,412	4,836	144	33,583
Consumer electronics and appliances rental	24	15,707	4,967	118	42,093
Formal wear and costume rental	14	7,886	2,345	92	25,489
Video tape and disc rental	90	48,764	10,501	631	16,642
Office machinery and equipment rental and leasing	21	34,174	7,067	132	53,538
All real estate and rental and leasing	8,698	18,208,302	2,990,227	62,411	47,912

Employment in Selected Real Estate Sectors and Rental
and Leasing Sectors, by Borough, 2002 (continued)

	Number of Establishments	Revenue ($1,000)	Annual Payroll ($1,000)	Number of Employees	Payroll per Employee
Bronx					
Lessors of apartment buildings	1,413	933,071	99,397	4,349	22,855
Lessors of dwellings other than apartment buildings	67	23,632	2,363	131	18,038
Lessors of professional and other office buildings	68	34,201	4,674	161	29,031
Lessors of manufacturing and industrial buildings	18	5,736	792	26	30,462
Lessors of miniwarehouses and self-storage units	11	11,655	1,110	40	27,750
Offices of residential real estate agents and brokers	148	54,076	7,018	314	22,350
Offices of nonresidential real estate agents and brokers	14	4,809	1,724	41	42,049
Residential property managers	249	267,702	83,267	3,083	27,008
Nonresidential property managers	25	11,953	2,995	103	29,078
Consumer goods rental	48	42,829	11,562	585	19,764
All real estate and rental and leasing	2,267	1,528,997	239,937	9,612	24,962
Brooklyn					
Lessors of apartment buildings	1,884	1,110,298	107,487	4,948	21,723
Lessors of dwellings other than apartment buildings	146	42,031	4,257	251	16,960
Lessors of nonresidential buildings (except miniwarehouses)	370	329,041	31,944	1,058	30,193
Lessors of professional and other office buildings	153	218,752	18,007	544	33,101
Lessors of manufacturing and industrial buildings	72	27,982	4,656	178	26,157
Lessors of shopping centers and retail stores	101	67,280	6,919	223	31,027
Lessors of other nonresidential buildings and facilities	44	15,027	2,362	113	20,903
Lessors of miniwarehouses and self-storage units	27	21,548	2,572	115	22,365

Employment in Selected Real Estate Sectors and Rental
and Leasing Sectors, by Borough, 2002 (continued)

	Number of Establishments	Revenue ($1,000)	Annual Payroll ($1,000)	Number of Employees	Payroll per Employee
Brooklyn (continued)					
Lessors of manufactured (mobile) home sites	36	8,601	959	58	16,534
Offices of residential real estate agents and brokers	351	152,565	21,197	884	23,979
Offices of nonresidential real estate agents and brokers	60	32,150	4,891	262	18,668
Residential property managers	412	184,180	62,767	2,092	30,003
Nonresidential property managers	73	70,590	24,063	608	29,577
Offices of real estate appraisers	40	13,129	2,706	106	25,528
Truck leasing	12	46,967	7,349	162	45,364
Video tape and disc rental	80	32,875	5,546	398	13,935
All real estate and rental and leasing	3,396	2,232,078	322,185	12,447	25,885
Queens					
Lessors of apartment buildings	1,087	951,300	110,841	3,891	28,487
Lessors of dwellings other than apartment buildings	99	54,909	6,952	283	24,565
Lessors of professional and other office buildings	154	136,772	20,760	447	46,443
Lessors of manufacturing and industrial buildings	52	41,940	3,998	139	28,763
Lessors of shopping centers and retail stores	124	79,808	10,724	372	28,828
Lessors of other nonresidential buildings and facilities	31	11,996	1,533	60	25,550
Lessors of miniwarehouses and self-storage units	15	19,831	3,204	86	37,256
Lessors of manufactured (mobile) home sites	19	5,661	549	38	14,447
Offices of residential real estate agents and brokers	300	239,849	25,211	739	34,115
Offices of nonresidential real estate agents and brokers	55	50,865	8,202	247	33,206

Employment in Selected Real Estate Sectors and Rental and Leasing Sectors, by Borough, 2002 (continued)

	Number of Establishments	Revenue ($1,000)	Annual Payroll ($1,000)	Number of Employees	Payroll per Employee
Queens (continued)					
Residential property managers	234	164,085	49,409	1,668	29,622
Nonresidential property managers	88	64,817	22,675	535	42,383
Offices of real estate appraisers	22	5,072	1,721	46	37,413
Passenger car rental	26	189,373	24,958	974	25,624
Truck rental without drivers	11	17,889	3,905	117	33,376
Truck leasing	11	75,655	11,635	234	49,722
Consumer electronics and appliances rental	16	11,389	2,417	83	29,120
Video tape and disc rental	82	39,579	6,569	460	14,280
Rental and leasing of heavy construction equipment without operators	25	99,438	20,658	331	62,411
All real estate and rental and leasing	2,671	2,520,496	416,250	13,100	31,775
Staten Island					
Lessors of apartment buildings	59	59,348	7,287	236	30,877
Lessors of professional and other office buildings	25	22,378	1,517	76	19,961
Offices of residential real estate agents and brokers	62	42,136	5,348	185	28,908
Residential property managers	26	9,596	2,370	81	29,259
Offices of real estate appraisers	12	4,966	1,206	35	34,457
Rental and leasing services	38	26,753	4,653	240	19,388
All real estate and rental and leasing	316	256,037	31,676	1,153	27,473
Citywide					
Lessors of apartment buildings	8,014	8,084,367	836,942	29,716	28,165
Lessors of dwellings other than apartment buildings	597	298,620	36,371	1,453	25,032
Lessors of professional and other office buildings	1,478	6,830,692	453,233	10,229	44,309
Lessors of manufacturing and industrial buildings	264	227,575	29,038	765	37,958

Employment in Selected Real Estate Sectors and Rental
and Leasing Sectors, by Borough, 2002 (continued)

	Number of Establishments	Revenue ($1,000)	Annual Payroll ($1,000)	Number of Employees	Payroll per Employee
Citywide (continued)					
Lessors of shopping centers and retail stores	529	747,083	83,115	2,098	39,616
Lessors of other nonresidential buildings and facilities	240	344,054	42,876	1,468	29,207
Lessors of miniwarehouses and self storage units	94	146,517	17,283	599	28,853
Lessors of manufactured (mobile) home sites	147	60,315	8,571	321	26,701
Offices of residential real estate agents and brokers	1,468	1,416,090	210,806	5,832	36,146
Offices of nonresidential real estate agents and brokers	450	955,085	394,884	4,459	88,559
Residential property managers	1,846	1,582,376	610,786	16,282	37,513
Nonresidential property managers	613	1,221,985	602,622	10,584	56,937
Offices of real estate appraisers	122	66,428	26,484	519	51,029
Automotive equipment rental and leasing	172	563,741	85,310	2,776	45,233
Video tape and disc rental	296	152,581	27,876	1,886	14,780
Commercial and industrial machinery and equipment rental and leasing	215	521,072	124,166	2,948	42,119
All real estate and rental and leasing	17,748	24,745,910	4,000,275	98,723	40,520

Source: U.S. Bureau of the Census.

Employment in Selected Professional, Scientific, and Technical Services, by Borough, 2002

	Number of Establishments	Receipts/ Revenue ($1,000)	Annual Payroll ($1,000)	Number of Employees	Payroll per Employee
Manhattan					
Offices of lawyers	3,939	$20,137,103	$6,959,470	74,531	$93,377
Title abstract and settlement offices	30	69,591	23,575	294	80,187
Offices of certified public accountants	916	4,225,430	1,535,348	20,972	73,209
Tax preparation services	102	35,391	11,200	944	11,864
Payroll services	100	737,415	478,678	15,531	30,821
Architectural services	925	1,594,946	596,033	9,970	59,783
Landscape architectural services	49	54,501	20,551	409	50,247
Engineering services	393	2,247,655	934,824	13,905	67,229
Surveying and mapping (except geophysical) services	8	11,378	6,079	68	89,397
Testing laboratories	18	46,995	15,816	318	49,736
Interior design services	571	638,279	145,918	2,472	59,028
Industrial design services	72	71,860	32,790	537	61,061
Graphic design services	927	1,245,369	490,743	6,614	74,198
Custom computer programming services	1,001	2,341,918	1,198,002	13,596	88,114
Computer systems integrators	297	826,386	264,456	3,667	72,118
Computer systems consultants (except systems integrators)	512	914,697	377,659	4,755	79,424
Computer facilities management services	90	319,178	109,329	1,537	71,131
Administrative management and general management consulting services	1,166	3,215,447	1,501,330	14,907	100,713
Actuarial consulting	22	210,743	133,605	1,176	113,610
Executive placement services	485	605,991	324,590	4,204	77,210
Human resources and personnel management consulting	153	344,993	165,502	2,549	64,928
Marketing consulting services	590	798,388	284,124	4,456	63,762
Process, physical distribution, and logistics consulting services	55	72,239	25,520	360	70,889

Employment in Selected Professional, Scientific, and Technical Services, by Borough, 2002 (continued)

	Number of Establishments	Receipts/ Revenue ($1,000)	Annual Payroll ($1,000)	Number of Employees	Payroll per Employee
Manhattan (continued)					
Environmental consulting services	56	78,712	42,848	588	72,871
Economic and related consulting services	160	181,514	72,648	912	79,658
Research and development in the physical, engineering, and life sciences	182	759,929	351,340	7,183	48,913
Advertising agencies	717	5,121,011	2,407,977	28,344	84,955
Public relations agencies	651	1,188,450	583,946	7,349	79,459
Radio and television advertising representatives	71	280,780	123,191	1,659	74,256
Publishers' advertising representatives	59	121,383	48,683	733	66,416
Display advertising	68	338,559	78,382	1,272	61,621
Direct mail advertising	91	476,971	156,408	2,682	58,318
Advertising specialties goods distributor	77	173,270	23,851	452	52,768
Sign painting and lettering shop	20	8,250	2,304	65	35,446
Marketing research and public opinion polling	255	916,795	250,307	4,825	51,877
Photography studios, portrait	230	107,924	22,917	663	34,566
Commercial photography	447	368,447	106,260	2,076	51,185
Translation and interpretation services	66	82,317	28,725	832	34,525
Veterinary services	69	91,090	39,509	1,024	38,583
All professional, scientific, and technical services	17,417	53,123,054	20,764,317	271,882	76,373
Bronx					
Tax preparation services	60	15,836	4,320	1,047	4,126
Architectural, engineering, and related services	28	13,362	5,784	151	38,305
Graphic design services	11	5,272	1,409	43	32,767
Computer systems design and related services	49	7,861	3,384	70	48,343

Employment in Selected Professional, Scientific, and Technical Services, by Borough, 2002 (continued)

	Number of Establishments	Receipts/ Revenue ($1,000)	Annual Payroll ($1,000)	Number of Employees	Payroll per Employee
Bronx (continued)					
Administrative management and general management consulting services	44	58,123	32,646	1,111	29,384
Advertising and related services	26	16,940	6,171	158	39,057
Photography studios, portrait	18	3,862	925	51	18,137
Commercial photography	4	3,909	1,395	32	43,594
Veterinary services	14	7,190	2,668	84	31,762
All professional, scientific, and technical services	589	350,054	142,836	5,150	27,735
Brooklyn					
Offices of lawyers	583	358,531	127,579	2,710	47,077
Title abstract and settlement offices	24	44,357	18,290	309	59,191
Offices of certified public accountants	145	44,327	17,749	483	36,747
Tax preparation services	75	18,881	5,594	990	5,651
Payroll services	25	38,018	26,885	1,168	23,018
Architectural services	75	30,614	11,344	289	39,253
Engineering services	52	23,071	9,661	220	43,914
Building inspection services	8	2,651	874	22	39,727
Surveying and mapping (except geophysical) services	5	3,705	2,033	32	63,531
Interior design services	54	21,846	3,754	130	28,877
Graphic design services	104	21,074	5,772	179	32,246
Custom computer programming services	334	79,275	28,656	596	48,081
Computer systems integrators	55	37,522	7,742	158	49,000
Computer systems consultants (except systems integrators)	174	39,433	14,697	257	57,187
Administrative management and general management consulting services	226	102,914	32,909	778	42,299

Employment in Selected Professional, Scientific, and Technical Services, by Borough, 2002 (continued)

	Number of Establishments	Receipts/ Revenue ($1,000)	Annual Payroll ($1,000)	Number of Employees	Payroll per Employee
Brooklyn (continued)					
Executive placement services	16	16,365	2,914	77	37,844
Marketing consulting services	61	16,985	4,404	108	40,778
Process, physical distribution, and logistics consulting services	18	8,732	4,716	109	44,491
Environmental consulting services	18	7,571	3,438	67	51,313
Economic and related consulting services	35	7,483	2,265	85	26,647
Research and development in the physical, engineering, and life sciences	14	92,914	42,395	1,406	30,153
Advertising agencies	32	11,696	4,352	96	45,333
Public relations agencies	21	7,121	2,724	77	35,377
Direct mail advertising	9	37,273	5,825	175	33,286
Photography studios, portrait	46	11,034	1,920	112	17,143
Commercial photography	15	3,037	670	19	35,263
Veterinary services	43	24,630	9,452	439	21,531
All professional, scientific, and technical services	2,845	1,369,503	461,180	13,324	34,613
Queens					
Offices of lawyers	566	261,724	83,588	2,045	40,874
Title abstract and settlement offices	27	37,846	13,534	283	47,823
Offices of certified public accountants	143	33,451	12,253	424	28,899
Tax preparation services	80	18,854	4,969	837	5,937
Payroll services	12	43,463	35,536	1,990	17,857
Architectural services	82	31,117	12,427	288	43,149
Engineering services	88	58,363	25,093	558	44,969
Building inspection services	12	5,930	2,527	63	40,111
Surveying and mapping (except geophysical) services	9	10,793	3,829	128	29,914
Testing laboratories	18	18,927	8,858	234	37,855

Employment in Selected Professional, Scientific, and Technical Services, by Borough, 2002 (continued)

	Number of Establishments	Receipts/ Revenue ($1,000)	Annual Payroll ($1,000)	Number of Employees	Payroll per Employee
Queens (continued)					
Industrial design services	8	10,385	5,550	119	46,639
Graphic design services	51	15,539	4,387	113	38,823
Custom computer programming services	240	46,869	21,395	444	48,187
Computer systems integrators	56	53,969	18,797	345	54,484
Computer systems consultants (except systems integrators)	126	55,872	20,891	357	58,518
Administrative management and general management consulting services	138	72,233	25,228	528	47,780
Human resources and executive search consulting services	33	5,248	2,907	74	39,284
Marketing consulting services	59	15,219	4,449	138	32,239
Process, physical distribution, and logistics consulting services	22	9,770	3,524	105	33,562
Environmental consulting services	15	6,952	2,556	52	49,154
Economic and related consulting services	22	10,141	1,460	38	38,421
Display advertising	8	55,600	8,584	178	48,225
Advertising specialties goods distributor	16	13,395	2,479	71	34,915
Sign painting and lettering shop	14	4,039	1,368	37	36,973
Photography studios, portrait	47	15,016	3,286	224	14,670
Commercial photography	18	7,694	2,390	57	41,930
Veterinary services	47	28,445	10,567	433	24,404
All professional, scientific, and technical services	2,508	1,200,968	444,916	13,713	32,445
Staten Island					
Offices of certified public accountants	45	18,581	5,578	218	25,587
Tax preparation services	16	3,617	1,358	152	8,934
Architectural services	31	9,852	3,108	97	32,041

Employment in Selected Professional, Scientific, and Technical Services, by Borough, 2002 (continued)

	Number of Establishments	Receipts/ Revenue ($1,000)	Annual Payroll ($1,000)	Number of Employees	Payroll per Employee
Staten Island (continued)					
Engineering services	28	17,219	6,022	145	41,531
Surveying and mapping (except geophysical) services	7	4,445	2,135	65	32,846
Graphic design services	13	1,712	717	27	26,556
Custom computer programming services	84	22,762	8,108	159	50,994
Computer systems consultants (except systems integrators)	38	11,993	4,221	82	51,476
Administrative management and general management consulting services	41	18,335	6,179	119	53,267
Marketing consulting services	14	5,214	1,217	33	36,879
Sign painting and lettering shop	5	1,735	429	25	17,160
Photography studios, portrait	16	3,835	897	61	14,705
Veterinary services	19	16,227	6,467	259	24,969
All professional, scientific, and technical services	804	371,012	124,340	3,892	31,948
Citywide					
Offices of lawyers	5,479	20,996,204	7,247,928	81,172	89,291
Title abstract and settlement offices	105	170,608	62,013	1,029	60,265
Offices of certified public accountants	1,265	4,324,003	1,571,606	22,126	71,030
Tax preparation services	333	92,579	27,441	3,970	6,912
Payroll services	148	836,126	552,181	19,042	28,998
Architectural services	1,122	1,668,461	623,395	10,658	58,491
Landscape architectural services	70	60,783	22,157	460	48,167
Engineering services	570	2,352,614	978,464	14,904	65,651
Building inspection services	42	22,991	10,682	266	40,158
Surveying and mapping (except geophysical) services	29	30,321	14,076	293	48,041
Testing laboratories	48	71,252	27,478	626	43,895

Employment in Selected Professional, Scientific, and Technical Services, by Borough, 2002 (continued)

	Number of Establishments	Receipts/ Revenue ($1,000)	Annual Payroll ($1,000)	Number of Employees	Payroll per Employee
Citywide (continued)					
Interior design services	685	681,336	154,670	2,730	56,656
Industrial design services	92	85,843	39,127	680	57,540
Graphic design services	1,106	1,288,966	503,028	6,976	72,108
Custom computer programming services	1,682	2,494,113	1,257,795	14,826	84,837
Computer systems integrators	428	929,233	293,789	4,222	69,585
Computer systems consultants (except systems integrators)	859	1,023,555	418,164	5,458	76,615
Computer facilities management services	168	354,819	120,803	1,772	68,173
Administrative management and general management consulting services	1,615	3,467,052	1,598,292	17,443	91,629
Actuarial consulting	27	211,342	133,790	1,183	113,094
Executive placement services	521	624,450	328,253	4,297	76,391
Human resources and personnel management consulting	193	358,052	169,819	2,647	64,155
Marketing consulting services	734	837,465	294,404	4,744	62,058
Process, physical distribution, and logistics consulting services	103	98,045	36,666	642	57,112
Environmental consulting services	101	96,751	50,065	752	66,576
Economic and related consulting services	237	203,752	77,383	1,063	72,797
Research and development in the physical and engineering sciences	92	197,493	60,687	955	63,547
Research and development in biotechnology	66	353,328	199,130	6,452	30,863
Research and development in other life sciences	66	406,873	188,163	3,496	53,822
Advertising agencies	789	5,140,044	2,414,817	28,510	84,701
Public relations agencies	690	1,199,279	587,961	7,480	78,604
Media representatives	146	412,594	174,851	2,460	71,078

Employment in Selected Professional, Scientific, and Technical Services, by Borough, 2002 (continued)

	Number of Establishments	Receipts/ Revenue ($1,000)	Annual Payroll ($1,000)	Number of Employees	Payroll per Employee
Citywide (continued)					
Display advertising	90	404,661	88,635	1,545	57,369
Direct mail advertising	121	546,447	175,760	3,296	53,325
Advertising specialties goods distributor	107	192,076	27,230	575	47,357
Sign painting and lettering shop	49	15,392	4,407	144	30,604
Marketing research and public opinion polling	288	935,730	260,121	5,318	48,913
Photography studios, portrait	357	141,671	29,945	1,111	26,953
Commercial photography	491	384,402	111,118	2,195	50,623
Veterinary services	192	167,582	68,663	2,239	30,667
All professional, scientific, and technical services	24,163	56,414,591	21,937,589	307,961	71,235

Source: U.S. Bureau of the Census.

Employment in Selected Administrative and Support Services and Waste Management and Remediation Services, by Borough, 2002

	Number of Establishments	Receipts ($1,000)	Annual Payroll ($1,000)	Number of Employees	Payroll per Employee
Manhattan					
Office administrative services	515	$1,318,164	$603,043	10,611	$56,832
Facilities support services	70	282,396	152,936	4,887	31,294
Employment placement agencies	438	460,330	228,956	4,668	49,048
Temporary help services	410	2,264,027	1,458,212	56,592	25,767
Professional employer organizations	56	790,893	645,900	9,386	68,815
Telephone answering services	31	34,010	11,694	452	25,872
Telemarketing bureaus	30	69,250	27,909	1,531	18,229
Private mail centers	42	34,671	5,132	175	29,326
Collection agencies	37	80,832	31,765	643	49,401
Court reporting and stenotype services	42	80,959	32,685	576	56,745
Travel agencies	792	516,423	254,446	6,530	38,966
Tour operators	155	265,787	67,089	1,585	42,327
Security guards and patrol services	123	697,678	502,955	26,098	19,272
Security systems services (except locksmiths)	35	117,304	41,442	981	42,245
Locksmiths	65	28,409	8,296	261	31,785
Exterminating and pest control services	37	30,940	17,445	417	41,835
Janitorial services	279	1,042,580	580,979	21,770	26,687
Landscaping services	32	29,669	10,481	257	40,782
Carpet and upholstery cleaning services	22	10,782	3,916	156	25,103
Ventilation duct, chimney, and gutter cleaning	7	3,124	1,100	47	23,404
Packaging and labeling services	11	15,870	3,440	84	40,952
Convention and trade show organizers	177	425,464	106,108	2,445	43,398
Economic or industrial planning or development organization	45	303,818	56,233	1,031	54,542
Waste collection	9	6,639	1,635	48	34,063
All administrative and support and waste management and remediation services	4,329	11,049,612	5,472,424	165,099	33,146

Employment in Selected Administrative and Support Services and Waste Management and Remediation Services, by Borough, 2002 (continued)

	Number of Establishments	Receipts ($1,000)	Annual Payroll ($1,000)	Number of Employees	Payroll per Employee
Bronx					
Office administrative services	61	63,090	19,885	588	33,818
Employment services	25	25,140	16,614	613	27,103
Business support services	28	9,760	3,809	164	23,226
Travel arrangement and reservation services	76	24,096	3,785	177	21,384
Investigation, guard, and armored car services	35	98,912	70,192	5,587	12,563
Locksmiths	25	7,139	2,085	86	24,244
Exterminating and pest control services	20	4,077	1,426	66	21,606
Janitorial services	54	29,292	16,368	999	16,384
Carpet and upholstery cleaning services	6	1,722	638	22	29,000
Economic or industrial planning or development organization	7	6,586	2,221	61	36,410
Waste collection	29	106,498	21,293	471	45,208
All administrative and support and waste management and remediation services	424	479,454	192,203	9,888	19,438
Brooklyn					
Office administrative services	254	241,747	110,940	2,542	43,643
Facilities support services	23	32,609	11,697	300	38,990
Temporary help services	46	163,037	122,515	6,542	18,727
Telephone call centers	22	13,567	7,922	651	12,169
Collection agencies	25	18,533	9,761	402	24,281
Travel agencies	174	27,926	11,237	509	22,077
Tour operators	20	7,348	2,337	80	29,213
Security guards and patrol services	41	62,531	43,653	2,536	17,213
Security systems services (except locksmiths)	32	16,310	6,023	170	35,429
Locksmiths	38	7,884	1,878	101	18,594
Exterminating and pest control services	57	16,101	7,039	260	27,073
Janitorial services	117	63,999	32,878	1,518	21,659
Carpet and upholstery cleaning services	18	11,902	4,669	151	30,921

Employment in Selected Administrative and Support Services and Waste Management and Remediation Services, by Borough, 2002 (continued)

	Number of Establishments	Receipts ($1,000)	Annual Payroll ($1,000)	Number of Employees	Payroll per Employee
Brooklyn (continued)					
Ventilation duct, chimney, and gutter cleaning	7	12,956	6,750	259	26,062
Packaging and labeling services	13	19,037	6,010	285	21,088
Economic or industrial planning or development organization	14	4,273	1,925	59	32,627
Solid waste collection	53	261,421	42,553	1,302	32,683
All administrative and support and waste management and remediation services	1,312	1,410,811	557,469	22,613	24,653
Queens					
Office administrative services	191	183,362	83,696	3,062	27,334
Employment placement agencies	40	15,169	8,112	356	22,787
Temporary help services	33	48,343	32,166	2,156	14,919
Professional employer organizations	13	64,514	52,849	1,875	28,186
Telephone answering services	12	14,890	3,311	104	31,837
Business service centers	25	51,266	9,778	295	33,146
Travel agencies	227	39,057	14,330	586	24,454
Tour operators	29	10,704	3,349	116	28,871
Security guards and patrol services	74	192,945	138,716	6,999	19,819
Security systems services (except locksmiths)	48	82,268	27,375	732	37,398
Locksmiths	28	16,703	3,644	116	31,414
Exterminating and pest control services	43	20,914	9,743	317	30,735
Janitorial services	153	99,043	42,297	2,557	16,542
Landscaping services	97	70,771	25,589	578	44,272
Carpet and upholstery cleaning services	31	6,576	1,599	86	18,593
Waste collection	44	104,216	22,517	615	36,613
Asbestos abatement and lead paint removal	19	96,733	35,748	3,170	11,277

Employment in Selected Administrative and Support Services and Waste Management and Remediation Services, by Borough, 2002 (continued)

	Number of Establishments	Receipts ($1,000)	Annual Payroll ($1,000)	Number of Employees	Payroll per Employee
Queens (continued)					
All administrative and support and waste management and remediation services	1,350	1,317,861	591,406	27,025	21,884
Staten Island					
Office administrative services	41	23,587	9,258	363	25,504
Employment services	18	17,091	11,994	315	38,076
Business support services	26	9,358	3,684	188	19,596
Travel arrangement and reservation services	38	10,243	6,011	246	24,435
Investigation, guard, and armored car services	36	28,747	16,470	1,088	15,138
Security systems services (except locksmiths)	19	17,763	3,537	128	27,633
Exterminating and pest control services	24	4,698	1,764	89	19,820
Janitorial services	39	13,480	5,563	355	15,670
Landscaping services	80	28,293	9,452	374	25,273
Carpet and upholstery cleaning services	10	4,644	1,552	91	17,055
Waste collection	12	12,614	4,273	115	37,157
Remediation and other waste management services	12	13,995	5,478	554	9,888
All administrative and support and waste management and remediation services	418	209,315	87,837	4,324	20,314
Citywide					
Office administrative services	1,062	1,829,950	826,822	17,166	48,166
Facilities support services	138	346,492	174,478	5,544	31,472
Employment placement agencies	536	514,261	252,191	5,699	44,252
Temporary help services	509	2,495,652	1,627,247	65,663	24,782
Professional employer organizations	81	883,413	720,273	12,217	58,957
Telephone call centers	119	149,519	59,174	3,480	7,004

Employment in Selected Administrative and Support Services and Waste Management and Remediation Services, by Borough, 2002 (continued)

	Number of Establishments	Receipts ($1,000)	Annual Payroll ($1,000)	Number of Employees	Payroll per Employee
Citywide (continued)					
Private mall centers	73	79,325	12,219	374	32,671
Collection agencies	87	109,392	47,261	1,207	39,454
Travel agencies	1,295	615,282	289,125	8,025	36,028
Tour operators	212	284,718	73,262	1,798	40,746
Other travel arrangement and reservation services	126	344,495	90,541	1,965	46,077
Security guards and patrol services	290	1,070,330	767,251	41,997	18,269
Security systems services (except locksmiths)	140	238,055	80,076	2,057	38,929
Locksmiths	164	61,775	16,343	583	28,033
Exterminating and pest control services	181	76,730	37,417	1,149	32,565
Janitorial services	642	1,248,394	678,085	27,199	24,931
Landscaping services	316	156,947	54,414	1,503	36,204
Carpet and upholstery cleaning services	87	35,626	12,374	506	24,455
Ventilation duct, chimney, and gutter cleaning	28	19,830	9,216	372	24,774
Swimming pool cleaning and maintenance	17	7,955	2,488	102	24,392
Cleaning building exteriors (except sandblasting)	10	10,381	4,374	95	46,042
Packaging and labeling services	34	44,284	12,039	508	23,699
Convention and trade show organizers	201	439,208	109,451	2,524	43,364
Economic or industrial planning or development organization	78	319,289	62,297	1,204	51,742
Waste collection	156	507,011	96,146	2,704	35,557
Waste treatment and disposal	16	109,420	20,002	510	39,220
Asbestos abatement and lead paint removal	36	169,561	66,696	4,353	15,322
Septic tank and related services	17	18,434	7,072	155	45,626

Employment in Selected Administrative and Support Services and Waste Management and Remediation Services, by Borough, 2002 (continued)

	Number of Establishments	Receipts ($1,000)	Annual Payroll ($1,000)	Number of Employees	Payroll per Employee
Citywide (continued)					
All administrative and support and waste management and remediation services	7,833	14,467,053	6,901,339	228,949	30,144

Source: U.S. Bureau of the Census.

Employment in Selected Educational Services, by Borough, 2002

	Number of Establishments	Sales ($1,000)	Annual Payroll ($1,000)	Number of Employees	Payroll per Employee
Manhattan					
Business schools and computer and management training	170	$414,079	$139,051	3,470	$40,072
Technical and trade schools	87	152,950	56,442	2,029	27,818
Dance schools (including children's and professionals')	78	47,556	20,119	936	21,495
Art, drama, and music schools	109	93,409	36,903	1,817	20,310
Language schools	41	73,622	26,871	1,829	14,692
Exam preparation and tutoring	63	80,621	66,060	1,444	45,748
Educational support services	113	659,337	117,125	2,286	51,236
All educational services	844	1,714,258	528,481	15,948	33,138
Bronx					
All educational services	72	35,709	13,148	599	21,950
Brooklyn					
All educational services	272	105,511	38,628	1,976	19,549
Queens					
Technical and trade schools	30	19,958	5,835	214	27,266
Fine arts schools	58	9,012	2,737	215	12,730
All educational services	286	111,868	42,177	2,261	18,654

Employment in Selected Educational Services, by Borough, 2002 (continued)

	Number of Establishments	Sales ($1,000)	Annual Payroll ($1,000)	Number of Employees	Payroll per Employee
Staten Island					
All educational services	56	22,009	6,914	481	14,374
Citywide					
Fine arts schools	301	162,628	64,522	3,310	19,493
Exam preparation and tutoring	160	113,589	76,649	2,208	34,714
All educational services	1,530	1,989,355	629,348	21,265	29,103

Source: U.S. Bureau of the Census.

Employment in Selected Health Care and Social Assistance Services, by Borough, 2002

	Number of Establishments	Receipts/ Revenue ($1,000)	Annual Payroll ($1,000)	Number of Employees	Payroll per Employee
Manhattan					
Offices of physicians (except mental health specialists)	2,649	$2,825,940	$1,057,413	15,287	$69,171
Offices of physicians, mental health specialists	305	100,534	42,584	741	57,468
Offices of dentists	1,234	826,186	266,934	5,975	44,675
Offices of chiropractors	198	66,250	18,301	493	37,122
Offices of optometrists	76	39,138	13,328	397	33,572
Offices of mental health practitioners (except physicians)	238	73,343	30,304	890	34,049
Speech therapists and audiologists	33	16,063	5,854	148	39,554
Physical and occupational therapists	147	94,499	43,626	1,112	39,232
Offices of podiatrists	126	46,794	10,845	355	30,549
Family planning centers	22	48,739	21,205	605	35,050

Employment in Selected Health Care and Social Assistance
Services, by Borough, 2002 (continued)

	Number of Establishments	Receipts/ Revenue ($1,000)	Annual Payroll ($1,000)	Number of Employees	Payroll per Employee
Manhattan (continued)					
Outpatient mental health and substance abuse centers	63	153,603	68,788	2,311	29,765
Kidney dialysis centers	7	32,995	11,631	231	50,351
Freestanding ambulatory surgical and emergency centers	16	32,078	11,533	282	40,897
Medical laboratories	32	230,608	46,517	862	53,964
Diagnostic imaging centers	59	220,573	75,888	956	79,381
Home health care services	96	1,113,343	599,951	30,761	19,504
Blood and organ banks	9	75,836	40,167	782	51,364
General medical and surgical hospitals, government	7	1,632,304	790,812	15,102	52,365
General medical and surgical hospitals, except government	14	6,805,013	3,027,575	56,687	53,409
Nursing care facilities	35	907,471	438,912	11,059	39,688
Residential mental retardation facilities	38	135,365	56,035	2,241	25,004
Residential mental health and substance abuse facilities	70	143,179	69,057	2,289	30,169
Community care facilities for the elderly	35	60,167	22,399	940	23,829
Child and youth services	175	353,923	129,607	5,472	23,685
Services for the elderly and persons with disabilities	215	493,454	276,877	12,608	21,960
Temporary shelters	80	156,526	73,988	2,744	26,964
Emergency and other relief services	26	197,272	47,289	1,090	43,384
Vocational rehabilitation services	89	329,609	159,343	6,164	25,851
Child day care services	300	256,076	133,524	6,366	20,975
All health care and social assistance services	7,062	20,836,778	8,880,032	215,913	41,128
Bronx					
Offices of physicians (except mental health specialists)	486	496,065	244,874	3,595	68,115

Employment in Selected Health Care and Social Assistance
Services, by Borough, 2002 (continued)

	Number of Establishments	Receipts/ Revenue ($1,000)	Annual Payroll ($1,000)	Number of Employees	Payroll per Employee
Bronx (continued)					
Offices of physicians, mental health specialists	21	12,533	3,260	149	21,879
Offices of dentists	268	134,504	42,509	1,233	34,476
Offices of chiropractors	43	11,913	3,606	139	25,942
Offices of optometrists	23	12,524	3,017	135	22,348
Speech therapists and audiologists	7	6,291	3,857	85	45,376
Physical and occupational therapists	18	9,699	3,415	90	37,944
Offices of podiatrists	41	9,471	2,020	91	22,198
Medical and diagnostic laboratories	25	60,803	14,107	259	54,467
Home health care services	43	283,505	176,219	9,384	18,779
General medical and surgical hospitals	9	3,066,726	1,383,886	28,632	48,334
Nursing care facilities	53	1,188,301	553,994	15,738	35,201
Individual and family services	273	343,957	168,910	7,972	21,188
Vocational rehabilitation services	22	38,166	18,746	831	22,558
Child day care services	189	148,208	75,132	3,595	20,899
All health care and social assistance services	1,868	6,648,523	3,105,058	83,700	37,097
Brooklyn					
Offices of physicians (except mental health specialists)	1,549	1,235,390	457,861	8,402	54,494
Offices of physicians, mental health specialists	49	20,607	5,921	143	41,406
Offices of dentists	828	357,703	106,525	3,542	30,075
Offices of chiropractors	157	42,492	9,446	400	23,615
Offices of optometrists	60	22,785	5,717	241	23,722
Offices of mental health practitioners (except physicians)	60	27,444	6,948	223	31,157
Speech therapists and audiologists	40	18,828	6,034	198	30,475
Physical and occupational therapists	157	75,530	25,309	882	28,695
Offices of podiatrists	123	30,801	7,802	333	23,429
Family planning centers	9	10,616	4,845	168	28,839

Employment in Selected Health Care and Social Assistance
Services, by Borough, 2002 (continued)

	Number of Establishments	Receipts/ Revenue ($1,000)	Annual Payroll ($1,000)	Number of Employees	Payroll per Employee
Brooklyn (continued)					
Outpatient mental health and substance abuse centers	63	93,810	50,686	1,671	30,333
Medical laboratories	29	74,417	26,664	734	36,327
Diagnostic imaging centers	66	79,596	22,879	633	36,144
Home health care services	92	893,388	505,699	25,659	19,708
Ambulance services	28	126,293	58,270	1,938	30,067
General medical and surgical hospitals, government	6	1,539,432	767,039	14,640	52,393
General medical and surgical hospitals, except government	13	3,217,014	1,540,615	30,280	50,879
Nursing care facilities	44	947,523	396,351	11,750	33,732
Residential mental retardation facilities	224	202,185	93,762	4,198	22,335
Residential mental health and substance abuse facilities	49	68,001	30,074	1,161	25,904
Homes for the elderly	25	41,858	15,194	689	22,052
Child and youth services	116	153,008	71,212	3,189	22,331
Services for the elderly and persons with disabilities	184	381,027	232,213	12,242	18,969
Community housing services	71	92,545	40,108	1,499	26,757
Vocational rehabilitation services	48	57,527	21,764	904	24,075
Child day care services	472	249,676	142,877	6,938	20,593
All health care and social assistance services	5,071	10,936,571	5,045,991	144,012	35,039
Queens					
Offices of physicians (except mental health specialists)	1,391	1,051,252	387,855	7,462	51,977
Offices of physicians, mental health specialists	37	16,302	8,289	200	41,445
Offices of dentists	908	368,494	105,825	3,530	29,979
Offices of chiropractors	156	38,479	11,327	448	25,283
Offices of optometrists	51	17,487	5,197	207	25,106

Employment in Selected Health Care and Social Assistance
Services, by Borough, 2002 (continued)

	Number of Establishments	Receipts/ Revenue ($1,000)	Annual Payroll ($1,000)	Number of Employees	Payroll per Employee
Queens (continued)					
Offices of mental health practitioners (except physicians)	27	25,226	8,164	309	26,421
Speech therapists and audiologists	20	6,078	2,118	48	44,125
Physical and occupational therapists	114	48,682	20,751	619	33,523
Offices of podiatrists	129	32,982	7,638	407	18,767
Outpatient care centers	120	334,017	142,529	3,565	39,980
Freestanding ambulatory surgical and emergency centers	11	28,158	13,466	252	53,437
Medical laboratories	20	36,636	13,758	292	47,116
Diagnostic imaging centers	53	133,334	47,343	921	51,404
Home health care services	84	574,823	306,352	17,087	17,939
Nursing care facilities	57	978,196	445,628	12,780	34,869
Residential mental retardation facilities	85	103,194	51,621	2,189	23,582
Residential mental health and substance abuse facilities	23	46,468	20,379	798	25,538
Services for the elderly and persons with disabilities	116	188,940	108,873	5,793	18,794
Temporary shelters	9	24,973	12,281	443	27,722
All health care and social assistance services	4,092	7,579,936	3,318,228	95,582	34,716
Staten Island					
Offices of physicians (except mental health specialists)	364	395,823	191,151	3,231	59,162
Offices of physicians, mental health specialists	11	6,612	4,214	67	62,896
Offices of dentists	184	97,402	29,357	1,135	25,865
Offices of chiropractors	51	11,717	3,375	148	22,804
Offices of optometrists	10	4,302	1,049	50	20,980
Physical and occupational therapists	28	13,889	6,623	233	28,425
Offices of podiatrists	22	7,484	2,506	99	25,313
Outpatient care centers	36	105,298	25,433	556	45,743

Employment in Selected Health Care and Social Assistance

Services, by Borough, 2002 (continued)

	Number of Establishments	Receipts/ Revenue ($1,000)	Annual Payroll ($1,000)	Number of Employees	Payroll per Employee
Staten Island (continued)					
Medical and diagnostic laboratories	16	28,631	15,619	248	62,980
Home health care services	26	135,849	70,572	3,386	20,842
Nursing care facilities	13	212,040	96,604	3,360	28,751
All health care and social assistance services	1,007	1,927,640	832,251	23,671	35,159
Citywide					
Offices of physicians (except mental health specialists)	6,439	6,004,470	2,339,154	37,977	61,594
Offices of physicians, mental health specialists	423	156,588	64,268	1,300	49,437
Offices of dentists	3,422	1,784,289	551,150	15,415	35,754
Offices of chiropractors	605	170,851	46,055	1,628	28,289
Offices of optometrists	220	96,236	28,308	1,030	27,483
Offices of mental health practitioners (except physicians)	341	132,259	49,205	1,498	32,847
Speech therapists and audiologists	105	48,977	18,405	499	36,884
Physical and occupational therapists	464	242,299	99,724	2,936	33,966
Offices of podiatrists	441	127,532	30,811	1,285	23,977
Kidney dialysis centers	36	160,698	54,429	1,233	44,144
Medical laboratories	92	350,555	89,485	1,980	45,194
Diagnostic imaging centers	208	514,043	173,290	2,925	59,244
Home health care services	341	3,000,908	1,658,793	86,277	19,226
Ambulance services	54	177,202	82,790	2,958	27,989
General medical and surgical hospitals	69	19,692,749	9,014,988	177,117	50,898
Nursing care facilities	202	4,233,531	1,931,489	54,687	35,319
Residential mental retardation facilities	445	556,135	259,277	11,165	23,222
Residential mental health and substance abuse facilities	184	311,374	142,518	5,137	27,743
Continuing care retirement communities	14	15,132	5,838	338	17,272

Employment in Selected Health Care and Social Assistance Services, by Borough, 2002 (continued)

	Number of Establishments	Receipts/ Revenue ($1,000)	Annual Payroll ($1,000)	Number of Employees	Payroll per Employee
Citywide (continued)					
Homes for the elderly	90	206,475	74,372	3,137	23,708
Child and youth services	423	669,880	276,361	11,858	23,306
Services for the elderly and persons with disabilities	648	1,250,058	710,363	35,327	20,108
Community housing services	308	435,346	188,908	6,896	27,394
Vocational rehabilitation services	183	449,259	212,160	8,391	25,284
Child day care services	1,310	810,586	435,106	21,411	20,322
All health care and social assistance services	19,100	47,929,448	21,181,560	562,878	37,631

Source: U.S. Bureau of the Census.

Employment in Selected Arts, Entertainment, and Recreation Sectors, by Borough, 2002

	Number of Establishments	Receipts/ Revenue ($1,000)	Annual Payroll ($1,000)	Number of Employees	Payroll per Employee
Manhattan					
Theater companies and dinner theaters	410	$1,632,544	$417,842	10,706	$39,029
Symphony orchestras and chamber music organizations	33	86,494	33,219	921	36,068
Promoters of performing arts, sports, and similar events with facilities	99	739,318	230,552	6,058	38,057
Promoters of performing arts, sports, and similar events without facilities	207	718,374	149,543	2,359	63,393
Agents and managers for artists, athletes, entertainers, and other public figures	597	903,477	249,535	3,776	66,084

Employment in Selected Arts, Entertainment, and Recreation Sectors, by Borough, 2002 (continued)

	Number of Establishments	Receipts/ Revenue ($1,000)	Annual Payroll ($1,000)	Number of Employees	Payroll per Employee
Manhattan (continued)					
Independent artists, writers, and performers	1,262	922,660	423,612	5,797	74,627
Museums	94	803,555	269,766	8,345	32,327
Zoos and botanical gardens	5	33,509	12,573	369	34,073
Amusement arcades	10	7,402	2,206	133	16,586
Marinas	6	3,992	863	31	27,839
Fitness and recreational sports centers	277	607,544	187,708	9,893	18,974
Bowling centers	9	17,476	5,639	250	21,476
Concession operators of amusement devices and rides	6	3,133	1,659	61	27,197
All arts, entertainment, and recreation	3,536	7,476,533	2,422,692	55,711	43,487
Bronx					
Fitness and recreational sports centers	34	28,665	11,143	546	20,408
All arts, entertainment, and recreation	137	461,827	210,134	2,629	79,929
Brooklyn					
Musical groups and artists	18	10,329	2,567	89	28,843
Independent artists, writers, and performers	92	25,616	9,416	224	42,036
Amusement parks and arcades	12	6,939	2,668	318	8,390
Fitness and recreational sports centers	82	70,546	22,804	1,615	14,120
Bowling centers	9	7,599	2,526	169	14,947
Coin-operated amusement devices (except slot machine operation)	10	6,661	2,013	53	37,981
All arts, entertainment, and recreation	389	279,387	103,960	5,019	20,713

Employment in Selected Arts, Entertainment, and
Recreation Sectors, by Borough, 2002 (continued)

	Number of Establishments	Receipts/ Revenue ($1,000)	Annual Payroll ($1,000)	Number of Employees	Payroll per Employee
Queens					
Performing arts, spectator sports, and related industries	147	341,511	153,819	2,119	72,590
Museums, historical sites, and similar institutions	28	43,069	15,614	737	21,186
Amusement, gambling, and recreation industries	196	238,813	50,315	2,558	19,670
Golf courses and country clubs	8	12,720	4,116	157	26,217
Fitness and recreational sports centers	95	124,592	25,717	1,438	17,884
Bowling centers	12	15,498	4,665	298	15,654
All arts, entertainment, and recreation	371	623,393	219,748	5,414	40,589
Staten Island					
Marinas	9	5,916	1,740	84	20,714
Fitness and recreational sports centers	25	13,892	3,174	276	11,500
All arts, entertainment, and recreation	97	68,188	19,078	988	19,310
Citywide					
Theater companies and dinner theaters	460	1,646,473	422,207	10,949	38,561
Dance companies	96	130,210	49,260	1,893	26,022
Musical groups and artists	357	398,437	108,786	3,152	34,513
Promoters of performing arts, sports, and similar events with facilities	124	789,237	252,878	7,334	34,480
Promoters of performing arts, sports, and similar events without facilities	230	726,172	151,338	2,459	61,545
Agents and managers for artists, athletes, entertainers, and other public figures	640	919,381	254,087	3,861	65,809
Independent artists, writers, and performers	1,428	977,302	443,848	6,160	72,053
Museums	139	884,157	303,676	9,724	31,230
Nature parks and other similar institutions	5	33,619	14,456	370	39,070
Amusement arcades	30	12,.360	3,296	211	15,621

Employment in Selected Arts, Entertainment, and Recreation Sectors, by Borough, 2002 (continued)

	Number of Establishments	Receipts/ Revenue ($1,000)	Annual Payroll ($1,000)	Number of Employees	Payroll per Employee
Citywide (continued)					
Golf courses and country clubs	32	40,541	12,474	463	26,942
Marinas	48	21,484	5,559	222	25,041
Fitness and recreational sports centers	513	845,239	250,546	13,768	18,198
Bowling centers	44	47,606	13,927	808	17,236
Concession operators of amusement devices and rides	22	6,686	2,592	101	25,663
Miniature golf courses	7	2,839	528	39	13,538
Coin-operated amusement devices (except slot machine operation)	36	62,278	13,552	503	26,942
All arts, entertainment, and recreation	4,530	8,909,328	2,975,612	69,761	42,654

Source: U.S. Bureau of the Census.

Employment in Selected Accommodation and Food Services, by Borough, 2002

	Number of Establishments	Receipts/ Revenue ($1,000)	Annual Payroll ($1,000)	Number of Employees	Payroll per Employee
Manhattan					
Hotels (except casino hotels) and motels	283	$4,000,108	$1,181,929	35,649	$33,155
RV (recreational vehicle) parks and recreational camps	11	16,032	3,521	59	59,678
Rooming and boarding houses	33	46,705	13,161	634	20,758
Full service restaurants	3,458	4,032,109	1,326,994	68,974	19,239
Limited service restaurants	1,915	1,015,958	240,292	18,969	12,668
Cafeterias, buffets, and grill buffets	71	19,745	6,111	340	17,974
Snack and nonalcoholic beverage bars	486	285,682	67,216	5,372	12,512

Employment in Selected Accommodation and Food Services, by Borough, 2002 (continued)

	Number of Establishments	Receipts/ Revenue ($1,000)	Annual Payroll ($1,000)	Number of Employees	Payroll per Employee
Manhattan (continued)					
Special food services	697	801,702	236,828	11,688	20,262
Drinking places (alcoholic beverages)	639	483,496	122,469	7,061	17,344
All accommodation and food services	7,612	10,714,578	3,202,748	148,922	21,506
Bronx					
Accommodation	27	26,550	6,020	308	19,545
Full service restaurants	334	127,412	35,942	2,446	14,694
Limited service restaurants	526	219,005	53,355	5,035	10,597
Cafeterias, buffets, and grill buffets	12	9,767	2,957	62	47,694
Snack and nonalcoholic beverage bars	91	26,546	6,851	514	13,329
Special food services	59	67,194	19,052	1,103	17,273
Drinking places (alcoholic beverages)	115	14,108	3,385	327	10,352
All accommodation and food services	1,164	490,582	127,562	9,795	13,023
Brooklyn					
Hotels (except casino hotels) and motels	24	59,098	18,644	697	26,749
Full service restaurants	923	342,018	101,355	6,785	14,938
Limited service restaurants	1,002	380,252	89,265	8,160	10,939
Cafeterias, buffets, and grill buffets	17	4,606	1,334	86	15,512
Snack and nonalcoholic beverage bars	249	74,924	15,571	1,379	11,292
Special food services	128	124,105	28,037	1,719	16,310
Drinking places (alcoholic beverages)	198	30,695	7,467	589	12,677
All accommodation and food services	2,553	1,020,122	262,831	19,455	13,510

Employment in Selected Accommodation and Food Services, by Borough, 2002 (continued)

	Number of Establishments	Receipts/ Revenue ($1,000)	Annual Payroll ($1,000)	Number of Employees	Payroll per Employee
Queens					
Hotels (except casino hotels) and motels	53	190,325	54,895	2,053	26,739
Full service restaurants	1,123	437,644	122,910	8,694	14,137
Limited service restaurants	1,136	455,837	106,271	9,720	10,933
Cafeterias, buffets, and grill buffets	20	3,610	1,020	110	9,273
Snack and nonalcoholic beverage bars	270	90,876	22,361	1,757	12,727
Special food services	197	505,786	135,906	5,934	22,903
Drinking places (alcoholic beverages)	343	55,270	12,779	1,032	12,383
All accommodation and food services	3,149	1,748,340	459,202	29,433	15,602
Staten Island					
Traveler accommodation	6	18,587	6,047	289	20,924
Full service restaurants	224	114,134	29,353	2,362	12,427
Limited service restaurants	198	90,461	23,451	2,312	10,143
Cafeterias, buffets, and grill buffets	6	5,471	1,314	270	4,867
Snack and nonalcoholic beverage bars	62	21,818	4,109	383	10,728
All accommodation and food services	587	306,863	75,108	6,380	11,772
Citywide					
Hotels (except casino hotels) and motels	385	4,283,688	1,264,985	38,865	32,548
Bed and breakfast inns	16	10,873	3,055	162	18,858
RV (recreational vehicle) parks and recreational camps	16	19,387	4,514	78	57,872
Rooming and boarding houses	48	62,968	17,951	857	20,946
Full service restaurants	6,062	5,053,317	1,616,554	89,261	18,110
Limited service restaurants	4,777	2,161,513	512,634	44,196	11,599
Cafeterias, buffets, and grill buffets	126	43,199	12,736	868	14,673
Snack and nonalcoholic beverage bars	1,158	499,846	116,108	9,405	12,345

Employment in Selected Accommodation and Food Services, by Borough, 2002 (continued)

	Number of Establishments	Receipts/ Revenue ($1,000)	Annual Payroll ($1,000)	Number of Employees	Payroll per Employee
Citywide (continued)					
Special food services	1,123	1,550,065	429,379	21,096	20,354
Drinking places (alcoholic beverages)	1,344	588,683	147,378	9,121	16,158
All accommodation and food services	15,065	14,280,485	4,127,451	213,985	19,289

Source: U.S. Bureau of the Census.

Employment in Selected Miscellaneous Services, by Borough, 2002

	Number of Establishments	Receipts/ Revenue ($1,000)	Annual Payroll ($1,000)	Number of Employees	Payroll per Employee
Manhattan					
General automotive repair	122	$45,094	$9,495	425	$22,341
Automotive body, paint, and interior repair and maintenance	30	13,981	3,625	157	23,089
Consumer electronics repair and maintenance	27	16,367	9,280	249	37,269
Computer repair and maintenance	49	146,568	37,851	626	60,465
Office machine repair and maintenance	16	10,241	2,549	68	37,485
Communication equipment repair and maintenance	8	5,765	2,941	82	35,866
Commercial and industrial machinery and equipment (except automotive and electronic) repair and maintenance	46	32,314	10,358	313	33,093
Appliance repair and maintenance	16	7,724	2,989	65	45,985
Reupholstery and furniture repair	64	27,274	9,361	282	33,195
Footwear and leather goods repair	94	13,098	4,361	280	15,575
Garment repair and alteration services	46	8,766	3,149	162	19,438
Barber shops	148	19,033	8,436	489	17,252

Employment in Selected Miscellaneous Services, by Borough, 2002 (continued)

	Number of Establishments	Receipts/ Revenue ($1,000)	Annual Payroll ($1,000)	Number of Employees	Payroll per Employee
Manhattan (continued)					
Beauty salons	934	405,886	186,386	6,863	27,158
Nail salons	394	53,342	15,460	1,036	14,923
Diet and weight reducing centers	15	7,990	1,821	134	13,590
Funeral homes and funeral services	51	58,064	11,847	295	40,159
Cemeteries and crematories	4	5,116	1,386	25	55,440
Coin-operated laundries and dry-cleaning stores	243	37,026	7,495	511	14,667
Dry-cleaning plants	370	85,757	20,137	1,094	18,407
Garment pressing and agents for laundries	142	33,288	7,878	416	18,938
Pet care (except veterinary) services	36	14,576	4,755	198	24,015
Photofinishing laboratories (except one hour)	111	98,121	34,725	1,089	31,887
One-hour photofinishing	84	17,747	3,858	236	16,347
Parking lots and garages	967	742,147	144,898	7,129	20,325
Bail bonding	48	14,373	3,949	159	24,836
Dating services	21	8,930	2,279	65	35,062
Pay telephone operators	24	22,093	3,930	84	46,786
All miscellaneous services	8,423	13,689,315	2,770,422	77,083	35,941
Bronx					
General automotive repair	226	40,538	10,666	552	19,322
Automotive transmission repair	22	4,456	1,460	70	20,857
Automotive body, paint, and interior repair and maintenance	81	28,574	8,256	335	24,645
Automotive glass replacement	15	4,259	946	72	13,139
Automotive oil change and lubrication	12	5,485	1,298	74	17,541
Car washes	37	9,070	3,605	242	14,897
Electronic and precision equipment repair and maintenance	22	3,322	1,208	66	18,303
Commercial and industrial machinery and equipment (except automotive and electronic) repair and maintenance	41	45,430	13,439	378	35,553

Employment in Selected Miscellaneous Services, by Borough, 2002 (continued)

	Number of Establishments	Receipts/ Revenue ($1,000)	Annual Payroll ($1,000)	Number of Employees	Payroll per Employee
Bronx (continued)					
Home and garden equipment and appliance repair and maintenance	16	7,496	986	38	25,947
Reupholstery and furniture repair	14	6,065	2,185	66	33,106
Barber shops	49	2,281	792	66	12,000
Beauty salons	190	13,105	4,757	417	11,408
Nail salons	107	6,519	1,826	175	10,434
Funeral homes	40	32,945	7,962	213	37,380
Dry-cleaning plants	116	24,789	7,317	429	17,056
Pet care (except veterinary) services	4	1,012	326	10	32,600
All miscellaneous services	1,652	534,945	148,512	6,716	22,113
Brooklyn					
General automotive repair	524	99,051	26,157	1,437	18,203
Automotive exhaust system repair	12	3,395	974	39	24,974
Automotive transmission repair	41	12,183	3,423	164	20,872
Brake, front end, and wheel alignment	12	5,577	1,770	69	25,652
Radiator repair	7	2,340	349	19	18,368
Paint or body repair	168	45,313	12,547	620	20,237
Automotive glass replacement	21	4,615	1,149	53	21,679
Automotive oil change and lubrication	13	3,916	918	51	18,000
Car washes	57	15,196	4,492	374	12,011
Consumer electronics repair and maintenance	27	5,691	2,052	104	19,731
Commercial and industrial machinery and equipment repair (except welding repair)	78	58,794	18,747	582	32,211
Home and garden equipment and appliance repair and maintenance	55	24,173	7,120	259	27,490
Reupholstery and furniture repair	46	13,411	3,814	203	18,788
Watch, clock, and jewelry repair	12	2,000	407	24	16,958
Garment repair and alteration services	18	1,709	726	49	14,816
Barber shops	82	4,372	1,620	131	12,366
Beauty salons	414	40,749	14,375	1,142	12,588
Nail salons	239	13,195	4,465	440	10,148

Employment in Selected Miscellaneous Services, by Borough, 2002 (continued)

	Number of Establishments	Receipts/ Revenue ($1,000)	Annual Payroll ($1,000)	Number of Employees	Payroll per Employee
Brooklyn (continued)					
Diet and weight reducing centers	17	6,538	1,779	113	15,743
Funeral homes	88	80,750	18,697	528	35,411
Cemeteries and crematories	8	21,328	10,122	198	51,121
Coin-operated laundries and dry-cleaning stores	270	30,658	5,689	509	11,177
Laundries, family and commercial	32	24,993	9,397	390	24,095
Dry-cleaning plants	245	33,198	9,666	602	16,056
Linen and uniform supply	18	70,950	27,060	907	29,835
Pet care (except veterinary) services	15	2,399	563	21	26,810
One-hour photofinishing	19	2,098	445	29	15,345
Parking lots and garages	83	37,691	8,087	450	17,971
Bail bonding	18	5,242	900	73	12,329
All miscellaneous services	3,584	1,179,842	329,182	15,256	21,577
Queens					
General automotive repair	614	151,828	40,638	1,767	22,998
Automotive exhaust system repair	12	2,532	709	29	24,448
Automotive transmission repair	45	13,340	4,295	157	27,357
Brake, front end, and wheel alignment	10	2,826	631	31	20,355
Electrical repair, motor vehicle	15	3,708	1,470	62	23,710
Radiator repair	7	5,809	772	30	25,733
Paint or body repair	187	59,931	17,009	731	23,268
Automotive glass replacement	24	6,574	1,748	71	24,620
Automotive oil change and lubrication	15	6,542	1,325	88	15,057
Car washes	55	18,090	6,070	444	13,671
Consumer electronics repair and maintenance	32	9,342	3,080	115	25,333
Computer and office machine repair and maintenance	27	8,304	3,044	89	34,202
Commercial and industrial machinery and equipment repair (except welding repair)	85	78,957	23,861	563	42,382
Appliance repair and maintenance	24	14,783	7,910	239	33,096
Reupholstery and furniture repair	49	16,744	5,470	206	26,553

Employment in Selected Miscellaneous Services, by Borough, 2002 (continued)

	Number of Establishments	Receipts/ Revenue ($1,000)	Annual Payroll ($1,000)	Number of Employees	Payroll per Employee
Queens (continued)					
Footwear and leather goods repair	16	1,468	487	35	13,914
Garment repair and alteration services	9	985	225	18	12,500
Barber shops	106	6,379	2,176	227	9,586
Beauty salons	487	50,414	17,140	1,327	12,916
Nail salons	209	11,802	3,529	337	10,472
Diet and weight reducing centers	12	8,765	1,727	188	9,186
Funeral homes and funeral services	91	93,091	23,519	585	40,203
Cemeteries and crematories	23	43,696	26,687	557	47,912
Coin-operated laundries and dry-cleaning stores	342	41,694	6,935	611	11,350
Laundries, family and commercial	26	27,372	9,586	404	23,728
Dry-cleaning plants	237	43,170	13,206	810	16,304
Garment pressing and agents for laundries	29	4,132	815	72	11,319
Linen supply	4	3,901	1,528	81	18,864
Industrial launderers	5	26,131	10,470	284	36,866
Pet care (except veterinary) services	7	832	222	18	12,333
Photofinishing laboratories (except one hour)	22	17,204	5,005	285	17,561
One-hour photofinishing	26	3,148	836	49	17,061
Parking lots and garages	99	65,014	18,687	1,046	17,865
Pay telephone operators	9	15,725	3,327	70	47,529
All miscellaneous services	3,937	1,606,576	460,377	18,898	24,361
Staten Island					
General automotive repair	105	31,249	7,879	298	26,440
Automotive exhaust system repair	7	2,603	730	30	24,333
Automotive transmission repair	9	2,475	631	31	20,355
Paint or body repair	39	21,632	5,722	208	27,510
Electronic and precision equipment repair and maintenance	15	3,907	1,677	72	23,292
Commercial and industrial machinery and equipment (except automotive and electronic) repair and maintenance	21	12,546	3,949	159	24,836

Employment in Selected Miscellaneous Services, by Borough, 2002 (continued)

	Number of Establishments	Receipts/ Revenue ($1,000)	Annual Payroll ($1,000)	Number of Employees	Payroll per Employee
Staten Island (continued)					
Home and garden equipment and appliance repair and maintenance	15	5,452	1,416	54	26,222
Reupholstery and furniture repair	11	3,560	1,762	215	8,195
Boat repair	5	4,373	1,406	54	26,037
Garment repair and alteration services	3	917	413	14	29,500
Barber shops	10	870	425	30	14,167
Beauty salons	127	19,298	6,682	574	11,641
Nail salons	75	4,205	1,436	122	11,770
Funeral homes and funeral services	20	28,354	5,362	144	37,236
Dry-cleaning plants	45	6,866	1,757	128	13,727
Pet care (except veterinary) services	4	549	148	9	16,444
All miscellaneous services	761	250,441	69,827	3,789	18,429
Citywide					
General automotive repair	1,591	367,760	94,835	4,479	21,173
Automotive exhaust system repair	44	11,294	3,047	129	23,620
Automotive transmission repair	122	34,159	10,427	447	23,327
Brake, front end, and wheel alignment	33	11,324	3,285	137	23,978
Paint or body repair	502	169,311	47,107	2,048	23,001
Automotive glass replacement	67	18,759	4,775	220	21,704
Car washes	189	58,263	17,126	1,263	13,560
Consumer electronics repair and maintenance	103	32,825	14,902	504	29,567
Computer repair and maintenance	94	154,063	40,082	713	56,216
Office machine repair and maintenance	36	17,400	5,281	156	33,853
Communication equipment repair and maintenance	32	15,962	7,188	224	32,089
Welding repair	23	9,438	3,165	103	30,728
Commercial and industrial machinery and equipment repair (except welding repair)	265	226,056	69,736	1,965	35,489
Home and garden equipment repair and maintenance	15	4,947	1,063	35	30,371
Appliance repair and maintenance	115	54,905	19,459	624	31,184
Reupholstery and furniture repair	184	67,054	22,592	972	23,243

Employment in Selected Miscellaneous Services, by Borough, 2002 (continued)

	Number of Establishments	Receipts/ Revenue ($1,000)	Annual Payroll ($1,000)	Number of Employees	Payroll per Employee
Citywide (continued)					
Footwear and leather goods repair	123	15,274	5,056	329	15,368
Watch, clock, and jewelry repair	66	22,434	10,917	315	34,657
Boat repair	24	9,600	2,187	90	24,300
Garment repair and alteration services	80	12,737	4,561	248	18,391
Barber shops	395	32,935	13,449	943	14,262
Beauty salons	2,152	529,452	229,340	10,323	22,216
Nail salons	1,024	89,063	26,716	2,110	12,662
Diet and weight reducing centers	53	29,410	6,561	574	11,430
Funeral homes and funeral services	294	294,318	67,550	1,772	87,500
Cemeteries and crematories	45	91,295	49,373	1,043	47,337
Coin-operated laundries and dry-cleaners	1,079	149,876	27,946	2,181	12,813
Laundries, family and commercial	117	74,609	27,317	1,203	22,707
Dry-cleaning plants	1,013	193,780	52,083	3,063	17,004
Garment pressing and agents for laundries	219	41,593	9,681	592	16,353
Linen supply	22	84,895	32,298	1,186	27,233
Industrial launderers	19	45,184	16,105	472	34,121
Pet care (except veterinary) services	66	19,368	6,014	256	23,492
Photofinishing laboratories (except one hour)	157	119,828	40,982	1,459	28,089
One-hour photofinishing	141	24,242	5,394	335	16,101
Parking lots and garages	1,245	874,268	178,198	8,987	19,828
Bail bonding	85	22,379	5,368	266	20,180
Dating services	27	9,457	2,437	71	34,324
Pay telephone operators	67	51,999	14,549	460	31,433
All miscellaneous services	18,357	17,261,119	3,778,320	121,742	31,035

Source: U.S. Bureau of the Census.

Unemployment Rate by Borough, 1994–2006

	1994	1995	1996	1997	1998	1999	2000	2001	2002	2003	2004	2005	2006
Manhattan	7.6	7.0	7.4	7.8	6.7	5.9	5.1	5.8	7.7	7.5	6.2	5.0	4.2
Bronx	10.2	9.7	10.6	11.7	9.9	8.2	7.2	7.4	9.8	10.5	9.1	7.5	6.5
Brooklyn	9.9	9.3	10.0	10.7	9.3	8.0	6.4	6.6	8.7	9.0	7.6	6.2	5.3
Queens	8.3	7.7	8.1	8.5	6.9	6.1	5.3	5.4	7.2	7.4	6.3	5.2	4.4
Staten Island	7.8	7.5	7.8	8.4	6.9	5.8	5.1	5.1	6.9	7.3	6.2	5.2	4.4
New York City	8.8	8.2	8.8	9.4	7.9	6.9	5.8	6.1	8.0	8.3	7.0	5.7	4.9
United States	6.1	5.6	5.4	4.9	4.5	4.2	4.0	4.7	5.8	6.0	5.5	5.1	4.6

Sources: U.S. Bureau of Labor Statistics; New York State Department of Labor.

Labor Union Locals with at Least One Hundred Members, 2007

Service Employees Local Union 1199	321,985
Teachers AFL-CIO Local Union 2	152,782
Service Employees Local Union 32	78,965
Transport Workers AFL-CIO Local Union 100	39,975
Actors and Artistes AFL-CIO Branch Actors Equity Association	39,969
Hotel Employees, Restaurant Employees AFL-CIO Local Union 6	21,023
TV and Radio Artists AAAA AFL-CIO Local Union	20,619
Auto Workers AFL-CIO Local Union 7902	18,651
Office and Professional Employees AFL-CIO Local Union 153	18,249
Teachers AFL-CIO Local Union 2334	15,031
State, County and Municipal Employees AFL-CIO Region 2	12,519
Postal Mail Handlers, LIUNA Local Union 300	11,468
Interns and Residents, Committee	10,349
Teamsters Local Union 210	10,145
Musicians AFL-CIO Local Union 802	9,299
State, County and Municipal Employees AFL-CIO Local Union 389	8,740
Communications Workers AFL-CIO Local Union 1101	8,410
Laborers Local Union 79	8,132
Communications Workers AFL-CIO Local Union 1180	7,965
Postal Workers, American, AFL-CIO Local Union 10	7,758
Hotel Employees, Restaurant Employees AFL-CIO Local Union 100	7,110
Carpenters Independent Local Union 608	6,991
Letter Carriers, National Association, AFL-CIO Branch 36	6,447
Engineers, Operating, AFL-CIO Local Union 94	5,840
Engineers, Operating, AFL-CIO Local Union 15	4,741
Sheet Metal Workers AFL-CIO Local Union 28	4,538
State, County and Municipal Employees AFL-CIO Local Union 215	4,100
Carpenters Independent Local Union 157	4,031
Auto Workers AFL-CIO Local Union 2179	3,940
Retail Wholesale, DC, UFCW Local Union 670	3,706
Auto Workers AFL-CIO Local Union 2320	3,660
Painters AFL-CIO Local Union 829	3,379
IUISTHE, District 6	3,300
Retail Wholesale, DC, UFCW Local Union 1	3,300
Communications Workers AFL-CIO Local Union 3	3,250

Labor Union Locals with at Least One Hundred Members (continued)

Stage and Picture Operators AFL-CIO Local Union 52	3,208	Graphic Artists Guild Inc.	1,302
		Laborers Local Union 108	1,291
Unite AFL-CIO Local Union 23	3,080	Teamsters Local Union 584	1,270
Stage and Picture Operators AFL-CIO Local Union 1	2,963	Teamsters Local Union 553	1,269
		New York Professional Nurses Union	1,250
Teamsters Local Union 810	2,809	Service Employees Local Union 693	1,250
Auto Workers AFL-CIO Local Union 2110	2,769	Painters AFL-CIO Local Union 806	1,205
Laborers Local Union 78	2,703	Security Police and Guards Union Independent Local Union 2	1,200
Unite Here Local Union 2552	2,687		
Retail Wholesale, DC, UFCW Local Union 3	2,521	Stage and Picture Operators AFL-CIO Local Union 798	1,180
State, County and Municipal Employees AFL-CIO Local Union 95	2,429	Painters AFL-CIO Local Union 1974	1,169
		Unite AFL-CIO Local Union 331	1,158
Hotel Employees, Restaurant Employees AFL-CIO Local Union 37	2,279	Carpenters Independent Local Union 1536	1,134
		Novelty and Production Workers AFL-CIO Local Union 223	1,118
Doctors Council	2,200		
Stage Directors and Choreographers	2,169	Stage and Picture Operators AFL-CIO Local Union 764	1,083
Iron Workers AFL-CIO Local Union 580	2,070		
Auto Workers AFL-CIO Local Union 259	1,923	Unite AFL-CIO Local Union 340	999
Electrical Workers IBEW AFL-CIO Local Union 1212	1,922	Amalgamated Lithographers of America Local Union 1	998
Unite AFL-CIO Local Union 13298	1,861		
Carpenters Independent Local Union 1456	1,837	Communications Workers AFL-CIO Local Union 31222	960
Communications Workers AFL-CIO Local Union 51011	1,710	Unite AFL-CIO Local Union 62	795
State, County and Municipal Employees AFL-CIO Local Union 1930	1,704	Commuter Rail Employees, Independent Local Division 1	793
Communications Workers AFL-CIO Local Union 51016	1,634	Painters AFL-CIO Local Union 1281	791
Treasury Employees Union Independent Chapter 47	1,600	State, County and Municipal Employees AFL-CIO Local Union 253	791
Major League Baseball Players Association	1,525	Government Employees AFGE AFL-CIO Local Union 1917	756
Stage and Picture Operators AFL-CIO Local Union 306	1,467	Communications Workers AFL-CIO Local Union 14170	750
Iron Workers AFL-CIO Local Union 40	1,464		
Teachers AFL-CIO Local Union 3882	1,426	Security Personnel Brotherhood	750
Unite AFL-CIO Local Union 89	1,414	State, County and Municipal Employees AFL-CIO Local Union 107	738
Iron Workers AFL-CIO Local Union 46	1,407		
Unite AFL-CIO Local Union 340	1,332	Postal and Federal Employees Alliance Independent Local Union 813	733
Carpenters Independent Local Union 2287	1,325		
Painters AFL-CIO Local Union 8	1,319	Unite AFL-CIO Local Union 189	711

Labor Union Locals with at Least One Hundred Members (continued)

State, County and Municipal Employees AFL-CIO		Unite AFL-CIO Local Union 919	295
Local Union 1503	703	Unite AFL-CIO Local Union 10	288
Benefit Fund Staff Association	698	Communications Workers AFL-CIO Local	
Unite AFL-CIO Local Union 155	697	Union 14156	282
Transport Workers AFL-CIO Local Union 241	680	Painters AFL-CIO Local Union 1422	270
Stage and Picture Operators AFL-CIO Local		Communications Workers AFL-CIO Local	
Union 18032	678	Union 1150	265
Unite AFL-CIO Local Union 300	665	United Construction Trade and Local Union 1130	265
Unite AFL-CIO Local Union 330	564	Graphic Communications, IBT Local Union 119	264
Graphic Communications, IBT Local Union 2	560	Unite AFL-CIO Local Union 1733	264
Painters AFL-CIO Local Union 1969	512	Unite AFL-CIO Local Union 246	246
Unite AFL-CIO Local Union 239	506	Government Employees AFGE AFL-CIO Local	
Food and Commercial Workers Local Union 359	492	Union 3911	242
State, County and Municipal Employees AFL-CIO		Unite AFL-CIO Local Union 63	237
Local Union 374	486	Treasury Employees Union Independent	
Transport Workers AFL-CIO Local Union 1460	475	Chapter 183	235
Unite AFL-CIO Local Union 250	467	Painters AFL-CIO Local Union 490	228
Unite AFL-CIO Local Union 169	450	TV and Radio Artists AAAA AFL-CIO Local	
Other Councils and Committees AFL-CIO Local		Union 225	227
Union 1	444	Stage and Picture Operators AFL-CIO Local	
National Basketball Players Association	435	Union 829	219
Musicians AFL-CIO Local Union 1000	431	Unite AFL-CIO Local Union 400	216
Unite AFL-CIO Local Union 25	401	Unite AFL-CIO Local Union 1932	212
Graphic Communications, IBT Local Union 51	400	Journeymen and Allied Trades Independent	
Service Employees Local Union 56	400	Local Union 400	210
Stage and Picture Operators AFL-CIO Local		Communications Workers AFL-CIO Local	
Union 751	400	Union 1190	208
Stage and Picture Operators AFL-CIO Local		Women's National Basketball Players	192
Union 161	397	Actors and Artistes AFL-CIO Branch	190
Unite AFL-CIO Local Union 800	386	Unite AFL-CIO Local Union 506	189
Painters AFL-CIO Local Union 18	363	National Basketball Coaches Association	179
Unite AFL-CIO Local Union 75	361	State, County and Municipal Employees AFL-CIO	
Stage and Picture Operators AFL-CIO Local		Local Union 1306	178
Union 794	351	Stage and Picture Operators AFL-CIO Local	
Government Employees AFGE AFL-CIO Local		Union 751	176
Union 2094	345	New York Physicians and Dentists	150
Painters AFL-CIO Local Union 19	331	Transport Workers AFL-CIO Local Union 264	143
Painters AFL-CIO Local Union 28	304	Government Employees AFGE AFL-CIO Local	
Unite AFL-CIO Local Union 158	298	Union 3432	141

Labor Union Locals with at Least One Hundred Members (continued)

Anti-Defamation League Professional Staff Association	140
Government Employees AFGE AFL-CIO Local Union 3148	140
Longshoremens Association AFL-CIO Local Union 824	138
Government Employees AFGE AFL-CIO Local Union 2431	125
State, County and Municipal Employees AFL-CIO Local Union 1559	125
Government Employees AFGE AFL-CIO Local Union 913	119
Government Employees AFGE AFL-CIO Local Union 1151	113
Unite AFL-CIO Local Union 800	109
Laborers Local Union 279	106
Professional Staff Association DC #37 Education Fund	104
Unite AFL-CIO Local Union 1528	102
Hearst International Employees Association	100
Jewish Committee Staff Organization of America	100

AAAA = Actors and Artistes, AFL-CIO
AFGE = American Federation of Government Employees
AFL-CIO = American Federation of Labor and Congress of Industrial Organizations
DC = District Council
IBEW = International Brotherhood of Electrical Workers
IBT = International Brotherhood of Teamsters
IUISTHE = International Union of Industrial, Service, Transport and Health Employees
LIUNA = Laborers' International Union of North America
UFCW = United Food and Commercial Workers International Union
Note: Figures based on most recent report submitted as of June 2007.
Source: U.S. Department of Labor, Employment Standards Administration.

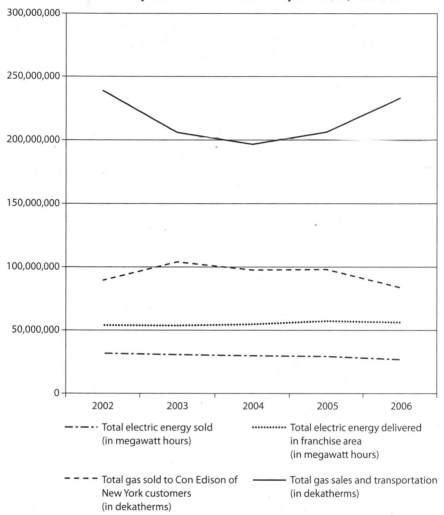

Electricity and Gas Sold and Delivered by Con Edison, 2002–2006

- – – – Total electric energy sold
(in megawatt hours)

··········· Total electric energy delivered
in franchise area
(in megawatt hours)

- - - - Total gas sold to Con Edison of
New York customers
(in dekatherms)

——— Total gas sales and transportation
(in dekatherms)

Source: Consolidated Edison of New York, 2006 Annual Report.

Gross City Product and Gross Domestic Product, 1993–2005 (in Billions of 2000 Dollars)

	Gross City Product (New York City)	Gross Domestic Product (United States)	GCP as Percentage of GDP			Gross City Product (New York City)	Gross Domestic Product (United States)	GCP as Percentage of GDP
1993	$314.6	$7,532.7	4.18		2000	437.8	9,817.0	4.46
1994	322.1	7,835.5	4.11		2001	431.8	9,890.7	4.37
1995	334.5	8,031.7	4.16		2002	415.4	10,074.8	4.12
1996	351.5	8,328.9	4.22		2003	405.3	10,381.3	3.90
1997	370.3	8,703.5	4.25		2004	415.1	10,837.2	3.83
1998	394.7	9,066.9	4.35		2005	453.6	11,134.6	4.07
1999	415.3	9,470.3	4.39					

Sources: New York City Office of the Comptroller; U.S. Department of Commerce, U.S. Bureau of Economic Analysis.

Household Income by Borough, 1999

	Manhattan	Bronx	Brooklyn	Queens	Staten Island	Total
Less than $10,000	106,521	109,177	169,849	86,268	13,491	485,306
$10,000 to $14,999	44,437	40,001	74,280	47,850	7,853	214,421
$15,000 to $24,999	71,941	63,874	114,571	90,765	13,262	354,413
$25,000 to $34,999	70,141	60,959	107,095	94,613	13,969	346,777
$35,000 to $49,999	90,586	65,028	126,402	126,663	21,618	430,297
$50,000 to $74,999	111,853	65,911	136,962	155,763	33,233	503,722
$75,000 to $99,999	66,838	30,029	68,813	85,146	22,726	273,552
$100,000 to $149,999	73,074	19,618	53,988	67,315	20,558	234,553
$150,000 to $199,999	34,555	4,351	14,663	16,365	5,692	75,626
$200,000 or more	69,221	4,294	14,383	11,898	4,014	103,810
Total households	739,167	463,242	881,006	782,646	156,416	3,022,477
Median household income	$47,030	$27,611	$32,135	$42,439	$55,039	$38,293

Source: U.S. Bureau of the Census.

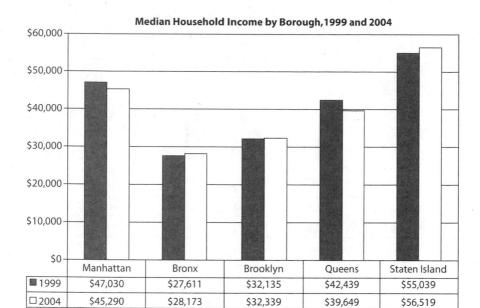

Median Household Income by Borough, 1999 and 2004

	Manhattan	Bronx	Brooklyn	Queens	Staten Island
■ 1999	$47,030	$27,611	$32,135	$42,439	$55,039
□ 2004	$45,290	$28,173	$32,339	$39,649	$56,519

Source: U.S. Bureau of the Census.

Family Income by Borough, 1999

	Manhattan	Bronx	Brooklyn	Queens	Staten Island	Total
Less than $10,000	38,486	64,989	88,633	40,847	6,071	239,026
$10,000 to $14,999	18,617	25,573	47,382	26,406	3,788	121,766
$15,000 to $24,999	32,942	43,691	77,426	57,844	7,521	219,424
$25,000 to $34,999	28,966	41,825	72,738	64,081	8,888	216,498
$35,000 to $49,999	33,551	45,478	85,883	89,190	15,315	269,417
$50,000 to $74,999	37,729	48,427	98,635	116,741	25,966	327,498
$75,000 to $99,999	25,176	23,956	52,237	69,020	19,763	190,152
$100,000 to $149,999	30,939	16,407	42,681	55,802	18,724	164,553
$150,000 to $199,999	17,176	3,547	11,798	13,422	4,994	50,937
$200,000 or more	42,638	3,355	11,457	9,451	3,637	70,538
Total families	306,220	317,248	588,870	542,804	114,667	1,869,809
Median family income	$50,229	$30,682	$36,188	$48,608	$64,333	$41,887

Source: U.S. Bureau of the Census.

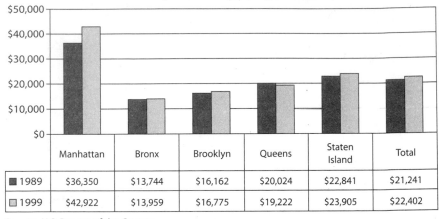

Per Capita Income by Borough, 1989 and 1999

	Manhattan	Bronx	Brooklyn	Queens	Staten Island	Total
■ 1989	$36,350	$13,744	$16,162	$20,024	$22,841	$21,241
□ 1999	$42,922	$13,959	$16,775	$19,222	$23,905	$22,402

Source: U.S. Bureau of the Census.

Poverty Status, Citywide

	1990	2000	Change Number	Percent
Below 50% of poverty level	719,008	891,266	172,258	24.0
Below poverty level	1,384,994	1,668,938	283,944	20.5
Below 125% of poverty level	1,706,855	2,062,876	356,021	20.9
Below 150% of poverty level	1,990,588	2,442,008	451,420	22.7
Below 175% of poverty level	2,295,978	2,790,840	494,862	21.6
Below 185% of poverty level	2,407,979	2,936,066	528,087	21.9
Below 200% of poverty level	2,583,698	3,124,894	541,196	20.9
Persons under 18 years below poverty level	496,999	571,756	74,757	15.0
Persons 18 to 64 below poverty level	737,673	936,905	199,232	27.0
Persons 65 years and over below poverty level	150,322	160,277	9,955	6.6
Families below poverty level	285,476	345,834	60,358	21.1
Families with related children under 18 below poverty level	224,988	266,616	41,628	18.5
Families with related children under 5 below poverty level	114,385	122,601	8,216	7.2
Families with female head of household below poverty level	179,357	194,083	14,726	8.2

Note: Poverty level for each individual or family depends on age of individual or householder, size of family unit, and number of related children in family unit under 18 years of age.
Source: U.S. Bureau of the Census.

Poverty Status by Borough, 2000

	Manhattan	Bronx	Brooklyn	Queens	Staten Island	Total
Below 50% of poverty level	159,185	225,538	322,787	160,677	23,079	891,266
Below poverty level	298,231	395,263	610,476	321,102	43,866	1,668,938
Below 125% of poverty level	364,669	470,210	752,952	418,501	56,544	2,062,876
Below 150% of poverty level	427,936	540,843	882,999	521,006	69,224	2,442,008
Below 175% of poverty level	482,698	605,045	999,140	622,955	81,002	2,790,840
Below 185% of poverty level	504,258	630,157	1,047,448	666,827	87,376	2,936,066
Below 200% of poverty level	532,938	665,924	1,110,050	720,655	95,327	3,124,894
Persons under 18 years below poverty level	79,944	160,344	221,255	95,167	15,046	571,756
Persons 18 to 64 below poverty level	183,997	208,259	330,153	190,496	24,000	936,905
Persons 65 years and over below poverty level	34,290	26,660	59,068	35,439	4,820	160,277
Families below poverty level	53,792	88,848	129,694	64,468	9,032	345,834
Families with related children under 18 below poverty level	39,756	74,405	99,005	46,593	6,857	266,616
Families with related children under 5 below poverty level	16,024	34,379	48,203	20,945	3,050	122,601
Families with female head of household below poverty level	33,157	61,791	67,730	26,648	4,757	194,083

Note: Poverty level for each individual or family depends on age of individual or householder, size of family unit, and number of related children in family unit under 18 years of age.
Source: U.S. Bureau of the Census.

Average Quarter-Hour Persons Share of Radio Stations, Listeners 12 Years Old and Above, Monday–Sunday, 6 A.M.–Midnight

	Spring 2006	Summer 2006	Fall 2006	Winter 2007
WLTW-FM Adult Contemporary	7.0	6.0	7.1	6.2
WSKQ-FM Spanish Tropical	5.2	5.7	5.2	4.8
WHTZ-FM Pop Contemporary Hit Radio	4.5	4.9	4.5	4.6
WPAT-FM Spanish Contemporary	3.9	4.4	4.8	4.1
WINS-AM All News	3.7	3.5	3.6	3.9
WBLS-FM Urban Contemporary	4.2	4.0	4.0	3.6
WABC-AM News Talk Information	3.4	3.5	3.3	3.5
WRKS-FM Urban Adult Contemporary	4.3	4.4	4.0	3.5
WQHT-FM Rhythmic Contemporary Hit Radio	3.9	4.1	3.6	3.2
WWPR-FM Urban Contemporary	4.1	3.6	3.5	3.2
WAXQ-FM Classic Rock	3.2	2.9	3.0	3.1
WKTU-FM Rhythmic Adult Contemporary	2.7	2.7	2.7	2.8
WWFS-FM Adult Contemporary	n/a	n/a	n/a	2.7
WQCD-FM New Adult Contemporary / Smooth Jazz	2.9	2.9	3.2	2.6
WCBS-AM All News	2.8	2.8	2.5	2.4
WCAA-FM Latino Urban	2.5	2.1	1.7	2.2
WCBS-FM Adult Hits	1.7	1.8	2.1	2.2
WQXR-FM Classical	2.2	2.4	2.4	2.2
WFAN-AM All Sports	2.7	2.7	2.6	2.1
WOR-AM News Talk Information	2.1	2.0	1.8	2.1
WPLJ-FM Hot Adult Contemporary	2.4	2.5	2.1	1.9
WFNY-FM Talk/Personality	1.4	1.3	1.2	1.3
WADO-AM Spanish News/Talk	1.3	1.5	1.5	1.2
WQBU-FM Mexican Regional	n/a	n/a	n/a	1.2
WALK-FM Adult Contemporary	1.0	1.1	1.1	1.0
WEPN-AM All Sports	0.7	0.6	0.8	0.9
WKXW-FM Talk/Personality	0.8	0.9	0.9	0.9
WLIB-AM Gospel	1.0	1.0	0.5	0.8
WHUD-FM Adult Contemporary	0.5	0.4	0.5	0.7
WWRL-AM News Talk Information	n/a	n/a	0.8	0.7
WBAB-FM Album-Oriented Rock	0.7	0.6	0.5	0.6
WBLI-FM Pop Contemporary Hit Radio	0.7	0.8	0.7	0.6
WAWZ-FM Contemporary Christian	0.4	0.6	0.4	0.5
WBBR-AM All News	0.3	0.4	0.5	0.5
WBZO-FM Oldies	0.4	0.4	0.4	0.5

Average Quarter-Hour Persons Share of Radio Stations, Listeners 12 Years Old and Above, Monday–Sunday, 6 A.M.–Midnight (continued)

	Spring 2006	Summer 2006	Fall 2006	Winter 2007
WHLI-AM Adult Standards	0.8	0.6	0.7	0.5
WKJY-FM Adult Contemporary	0.7	0.5	0.6	0.5
WMGQ-FM Adult Contemporary	0.4	0.3	0.3	0.4
WDHA-FM Album-Oriented Rock	n/a	0.4	0.4	0.3
WMTR-AM Oldies	n/a	0.4	n/a	0.3
WMCA-AM Religious	0.5	n/a	n/a	n/a
WNEW-FM Adult Contemporary	1.9	1.8	1.5	n/a
WZAA-FM Latino Urban	0.3	n/a	n/a	n/a

Source: Arbitron.

Top Countries for International Visitors to New York City, 2005

1. United Kingdom	1,169,000	6. France	268,000
2. Canada	815,000	7. Ireland	253,000
3. Germany	401,000	8. Australia	235,000
4. Japan	299,000	9. Spain	205,000
5. Italy	292,000	10. Netherlands	147,000

Source: NYC & Company.

Oldest Businesses and Organizations by Year of Founding (Selective List)

Collegiate School	1628	Bowne & Company	1775
Parish of Trinity Church	1697	The Bank of New York	1784
Caswell-Massey Company	1752	Society of the Friendly Sons of St. Patrick	1784
Columbia University	1754	General Society of Mechanics and Tradesmen	
Fraunces Tavern	1762	of the City of New York	1785
Brick Presbyterian Church	1767	Schieffelin & Somerset Company	1794
New York City Partnership & Chamber of		Society for the Relief of Women and Children	1797
Commerce	1768	J. P. Morgan Chase Bank	1799
Marine Society of the City of New York	1770	New York Post	1801

Oldest Businesses and Organizations by Year of Founding (Selective List) (continued)

New-York Historical Society	1804	Samuel French	1830
Emmet, Marvin & Martin	1806	New York Institute for Special Education	1831
Graham-Windham Services to Families and		New York University	1831
Children	1806	William H. Sadlier	1832
Bartlett Ludlum & Dill Associates	1809	Seamen's Church Institute of New York and	
New York City Mission Society	1812	New Jersey	1834
American Bible Society	1816	Tiffany & Company	1837
General Theological Seminary	1817	C. O. Bigelow Chemists	1838
New York Academy of Sciences	1817	United Methodist City Society	1838
Brooks Brothers	1818	Gillies Coffee Company	1840
Sheltering Arms Children's Service	1823	Atlantic Mutual Companies	1842
Henry W. T. Mali & Company	1826	Dazian	1842
Delmonico's	1827	Bendiner & Schlesinger	1843
Hunter, Walton & Company	1827	Franciscan Sisters of the Poor Foundation	1845
Journal of Commerce	1827	Fresh Air Fund	1845
Dancker Sellew & Douglas	1829	Scientific American	1845
Inwood House	1830	Knoedler & Company	1846
Kings County Hospital Center	1830	St. Luke's–Roosevelt Hospital Center	1846

Sources: 100 Year Association of New York; Kenneth T. Jackson, ed., *The Encyclopedia of New York City* (New Haven, Conn.: Yale University Press / New York: New-York Historical Society, 1995).

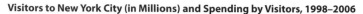

Visitors to New York City (in Millions) and Spending by Visitors, 1998–2006

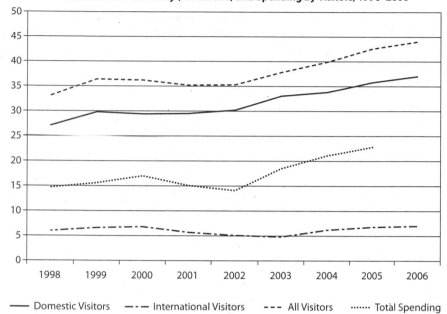

—— Domestic Visitors   —·— International Visitors   – – – All Visitors   ······· Total Spending

Note: Figures for 2006 are preliminary for number of visitors and unavailable for spending.

Source: NYC & Company.

Largest Hotels, 2006

	Number of Rooms	Number of Employees	Year Founded
1. Hilton New York	1,980	1,453	1963
2. New York Marriott Marquis	1,946	1,448	1985
3. Sheraton New York Hotel and Towers	1,750	n/a	1962
4. New York's Hotel Pennsylvania	1,700	465	1918
5. Grand Hyatt New York	1,311	959	1980
6. Milford Plaza Hotel	1,300	300	1980
7. Waldorf-Astoria	1,245	1,600	1931
8. Roosevelt Hotel New York	1,015	550	1924
9. Park Central New York	935	327	1928
10. Edison Hotel	900	275	1931
11. New York Palace Hotel	893	1,000	1980
12. Westin New York at Times Square	863	556	2002
13. New Yorker Hotel–Ramada Plaza	860	450	1930
14. Hudson	802	550	2000
15. New York Helmsley Hotel	779	430	1981
16. Crowne Plaza Times Square Manhattan	770	450	1989
17. Doubletree Metropolitan Hotel, New York City	755	303	1961
18. Millennium Broadway Hotel	750	650	1989
19. Le Parker Meridien Hotel	730	560	1981
20. Radisson Lexington Hotel New York	705	205	1929
21. Wellington Hotel	700	175	1902
22. W New York	688	650	1998
23. InterContinental The Barclay New York	686	517	1926
24. Sheraton Manhattan	665	n/a	1963
25. New York Marriott East Side	646	450	1924

Source: *Crain's New York Business.*

Oldest Restaurants in Continuous Operation

1762	Fraunces Tavern	1924	Totonno Pizza	1938	Wo Hop
1827	Delmonico's	1925	El Charro Español	1939	L & B Spumoni Gardens
1864	Pete's Tavern	1926	Frankie & Johnnie	1941	Sevilla
1868	Old Homestead	1926	Palm	1943	Burger Heaven
1885	Keens	1927	El Faro	1944	Patsy's
1887	Peter Luger	1927	Gallagher's	1945	Gino
1888	Katz's Deli	1929	John's Pizzeria	1945	V&T
1892	Ferrara	1929	"21" Club	1946	Lobster Box
1896	Rao's	1930	Carlyle	1947	Delegates Dining Room
1900	Belmonte's	1930	El Quijote	1950	Junior's
1902	Algonquin	1931	Café Pierre	1950	Paul & Jimmy's
1902	Angelo's (Mulberry)	1932	Pietro's	1953	King Yum
1904	Ferdinando's	1933	Patsy's Pizzeria	1953	Liebman's
1904	Vincent's	1934	Papaya King	1954	Mother's Bake Shop
1906	Barbetta	1934	Rainbow Room	1954	Pink Tea Cup
1908	Barney Greengrass	1936	Tom's	1954	Serendipity 3
1912	Frank's	1937	Denino's	1954	Veselka
1917	Café des Artistes	1937	Le Veau d'Or	1957	Arturo's Pizzeria
1919	Mario's	1937	Minetta Tavern	1957	Giambelli
1921	Sardi's	1938	Brennan & Carr	1957	La Taza de Oro
1922	Rocco	1938	Heidelberg	1957	Moran's Chelsea
1922	Tosca Café	1938	Stage Deli		

Source: Zagat.

Most Expensive Restaurants, 2007 (Average per Person, Including Beverage, Tax, and Tip)

1. Masa (sushi)	$446
2. Per Se (American, French)	287
3. L'Atelier de Joël Robuchon (French)	157
4. Gilt (American)	142
5. Daniel (French)	112
6. Kuruma Zushi (sushi)	109
7. Le Bernardin (French, seafood)	106
8. Jean Georges (French)	98
9. Craftsteak (steakhouse)	98
10. Megu (Japanese)	95
11. Sugiyama (Japanese)	94
12. La Grenouille (French)	94
13. Le Cirque (French)	93
14. Bouley (French)	91
15. Del Posto (Italian)	90
16. Morimoto (Japanese)	88
17. Mr. Chow Tribeca (Chinese)	87
18. Four Seasons (Continental)	86
19. Cru (Mediterranean)	86
20. Danube (Austrian)	86
21. Caviar Russe (American, caviar)	85
22. Veritas (American)	85
23. Alto (Italian)	84
24. Asiate (French, Japanese)	84
25. Aureole (American)	83

Source: Zagat.

Consumer Expenditures, United States and New York City, 1901 to 2002–2003

1901	U.S. Dollars	Percent	New York Dollars	Percent
Food	327	42.5	356	43.7
Alcoholic beverages	12	1.6	24	2.9
Housing	179	23.3	191	23.5
Apparel and services	108	14.0	106	13.0
Health care and insurance	40	5.2	49	6.1
Entertainment	12	1.6	14	1.7
Reading and education	8	1.0	9	1.1
Tobacco	11	1.4	11	1.4
Miscellaneous	62	8.1	45	5.5
Religion and charity	10	1.3	9	1.1
Total	769	100.0	814	100.0
Average income per family	$750		$675	

Consumer Expenditures, United States and New York City, 1901 to 2002–2003 (continued)

1934–1936	U.S. Dollars	Percent	New York Dollars	Percent
Food	508	33.6	670	36.4
Housing	485	32.0	589	32.0
Apparel and services	160	10.6	202	11.0
Transportation	125	8.3	93	5.1
Health care	59	3.9	64	3.5
Entertainment	82	5.4	114	6.2
Personal care products and services	30	2.0	35	1.9
Reading and education	7	0.5	6	0.3
Miscellaneous	32	2.1	37	2.0
Cash contributions	24	1.6	30	1.6
Total	1,512	100.0	1,839	100.0
Average income per family	$1,524		$1,745	

1950	U.S. Dollars	Percent	New York Dollars	Percent
Food and alcoholic beverages	1,195	28.8	1,527	30.4
Housing	1,035	24.9	1,296	25.8
Apparel and services	437	10.5	560	11.2
Transportation	510	12.3	377	7.5
Health care	197	4.7	264	5.3
Entertainment	168	4.0	223	4.4
Personal care products and services	85	2.0	94	1.9
Reading and education	58	1.4	89	1.8
Tobacco	68	1.6	76	1.5
Miscellaneous	55	1.3	68	1.4
Cash contributions	165	4.0	253	5.0
Personal insurance	177	4.3	195	3.9
Total	4,150	100.0	5,022	100.0
Average income per family	$4,237		$5,105	

Consumer Expenditures, United States and New York City, 1901 to 2002–2003 (continued)

1960	U.S. Dollars	Percent	New York Dollars	Percent
Food and alcoholic beverages	1,401	23.3	1,788	25.1
Housing	1,588	26.4	1,958	27.5
Apparel and services	558	9.3	708	9.9
Transportation	793	13.2	691	9.7
Health care	355	5.9	422	5.9
Entertainment	217	3.6	239	3.4
Personal care products and services	155	2.6	158	2.2
Reading and education	109	1.8	128	1.8
Tobacco	95	1.6	108	1.5
Miscellaneous	119	2.0	155	2.2
Cash contributions	303	5.0	402	5.6
Personal insurance	324	5.4	362	5.1
Total	6,017	100.0	7,117	100.0
Average income per family	$6,691		$7,918	

1984–1985	U.S. Dollars	Percent	New York Dollars	Percent
Food	3,290	15.0	4,091	16.4
Alcoholic beverages	275	1.3	331	1.3
Housing	6,674	30.4	7,753	31.1
Apparel and services	1,319	6.0	1,860	7.5
Transportation	4,304	19.6	3,924	15.8
Health care	1,049	4.8	1,029	4.1
Entertainment	1,055	4.8	1,121	4.5
Personal care products and services	289	1.3	315	1.3
Reading and education	435	2.0	574	2.3
Tobacco	228	1.0	240	1.0
Miscellaneous	451	2.1	503	2.0
Cash contributions	706	3.2	945	3.8
Personal insurance and pensions	1,897	8.6	2,220	8.9
Total	21,975	100.0	24,907	100.0
Average income per family	$23,464		$29,339	

Consumer Expenditures, United States and New York City, 1901 to 2002–2003 (continued)

1996–1997	U.S. Dollars	Percent	New York Dollars	Percent
Food	4,750	13.8	5,927	15.4
Alcoholic beverages	309	0.9	443	1.2
Housing	11,011	32.1	14,234	37.0
Apparel and services	1,741	5.1	2,211	5.7
Transportation	6,420	18.7	5,202	13.5
Health care	1,806	5.3	1,736	4.5
Entertainment	1,824	5.3	1,791	4.7
Personal care products and services	520	1.5	600	1.6
Reading and education	708	2.1	1,066	2.8
Tobacco	259	0.8	224	0.6
Miscellaneous	851	2.5	822	2.1
Cash contributions	971	2.8	923	2.4
Personal insurance and pensions	3,142	9.2	3,291	8.6
Total	34,312	100.0	38,470	100.0
Average income per family	$38,983		$45,877	

2002–2003	U.S. Dollars	Percent	New York Dollars	Percent
Food	5,357	13.1	7,005	13.9
Alcoholic beverages	384	0.9	469	0.9
Housing	13,359	32.8	18,919	37.6
Apparel and services	1,694	4.2	2,638	5.2
Transportation	7,770	19.1	7,729	15.4
Health care	2,384	5.9	2,235	4.4
Entertainment	2,069	5.1	2,350	4.7
Personal care products and services	526	1.3	643	1.3
Reading and education	901	2.1	1,426	2.8
Tobacco	305	0.7	266	0.5
Miscellaneous	698	1.7	771	1.5
Cash contributions	1,324	3.2	949	1.9
Personal insurance and pensions	3,978	9.8	4,918	9.8
Total	40,748	100.0	50,319	100.0
Average income per family	$50,302		$66,643	

Source: U.S. Bureau of Labor Statistics, *100 Years of U.S. Consumer Spending: Data for the Nation, New York City, and Boston* (Washington, D.C.: U.S. Government Printing Office, 2006).

Consumer Price Index for All Urban Consumers, New York–Northeastern New Jersey– Long Island Metropolitan Statistical Area and United States, 1965–2006

	New York– Northeastern New Jersey– Long Island MSA	Percent Change from Preceding Year	United States	Percent Change from Preceding Year
1965	32.6	1.6	31.5	1.6
1966	33.7	3.4	32.4	2.9
1967	34.6	2.7	33.4	3.1
1968	36.1	4.3	34.8	4.2
1969	38.3	6.1	36.7	5.5
1970	41.2	7.6	38.8	5.7
1971	43.6	5.8	40.5	4.4
1972	45.5	4.4	41.8	3.2
1973	48.3	6.2	44.4	6.2
1974	53.5	10.8	49.3	11.0
1975	57.6	7.7	53.8	9.1
1976	61.0	5.9	56.9	5.8
1977	64.2	5.2	60.6	6.5
1978	67.8	5.6	65.2	7.6
1979	73.7	8.7	72.6	11.3
1980	82.1	11.4	82.4	13.5
1981	90.1	9.7	90.9	10.3
1982	95.3	5.8	96.5	6.2
1983	99.8	4.7	99.6	3.2
1984	104.8	5.0	103.9	4.3
1985	108.7	3.7	107.6	3.6
1986	112.3	3.3	109.6	1.9
1987	118.0	5.1	113.6	3.6
1988	123.7	4.8	118.3	4.1
1989	130.6	5.6	124.0	4.8
1990	138.5	6.0	130.7	5.4
1991	144.8	4.5	136.2	4.2
1992	150.0	3.6	140.3	3.0
1993	154.5	3.0	144.5	3.0
1994	158.2	2.4	148.2	2.6
1995	162.2	2.5	152.4	2.8
1996	166.9	2.9	156.9	3.0

Consumer Price Index for All Urban Consumers, New York–Northeastern New Jersey–Long Island Metropolitan Statistical Area and United States, 1965–2006 (continued)

	New York–Northeastern New Jersey–Long Island SMA	Percent Change from Preceding Year	United States	Percent Change from Preceding Year
1997	170.8	2.3	160.5	2.3
1998	173.6	1.6	163.0	1.6
1999	177.0	2.0	166.6	2.2
2000	182.5	3.1	172.2	3.4
2001	187.1	2.5	177.1	2.8
2002	191.9	2.6	179.9	1.6
2003	197.8	3.1	184.0	2.3
2004	204.8	3.5	188.9	2.7
2005	212.7	3.9	195.3	3.4
2006	220.7	3.8	201.6	3.2

Notes: 1982–1984 = 100. Definition of metropolitan statistical area differs for earlier years.
Source: U.S. Bureau of Labor Statistics.

Detailed Consumer Price Index for All Urban Consumers, New York–Northeastern New Jersey–Long Island Metropolitan Statistical Area and United States, March 2007

	New York–Northeastern New Jersey–Long Island MSA	Percent Change from Preceding Year	United States	Percent Change from Preceding Year
All items	224.551	2.9	205.352	2.8
Food and beverages	207.674	3.0	200.869	3.3
Food	206.669	3.0	200.403	3.3
Food at home	205.142	2.5	198.766	3.4
Food away from home	214.038	3.7	204.082	3.3
Alcoholic beverages	218.554	2.9	205.663	2.8
Housing	244.042	4.6	208.080	3.4
Shelter	293.493	4.6	238.980	3.9

Detailed Consumer Price Index for All Urban Consumers, New York–Northeastern New Jersey–Long Island Metropolitan Statistical Area and United States, March 2007 (continued)

	New York–Northeastern New Jersey–Long Island MSA	Percent Change from Preceding Year	United States	Percent Change from Preceding Year
Rent of primary residence[1]	277.974	4.7	232.495	4.6
Owners' equivalent rent of primary residence[1,2]	300.334	5.4	244.602	4.1
Fuels and utilities	182.536	7.4	196.414	2.1
Household energy	184.117	7.7	177.635	1.6
Gas (piped) and electricity[1]	182.703	8.4	182.624	1.5
Household furnishings and operations	132.378	1.4	127.655	0.8
Apparel	114.281	−5.3	122.582	0.5
Transportation	185.679	1.2	180.346	1.7
Private transportation	176.063	1.2	176.468	1.7
Motor fuel	199.110	7.8	220.515	7.2
Gasoline (all types)	198.332	7.8	219.473	7.2
Medical care	357.692	5.6	347.172	4.0
Recreation[3]	114.437	−1.1	111.244	0.6
Education and communication[3]	123.451	3.6	118.231	2.3
Other goods and services	332.024	0.2	331.144	4.5
Commodity and service group				
Commodities	170.811	1.3	165,710	1.8
Services	270.606	3.9	244.671	3.4
Special aggregate indexes				
All items less shelter	197.517	1.9	194.482	2.2
Commodities less food	147.810	0.1	148.240	1.0
Energy	191.671	7.7	196.929	4.4
All items less energy	229.287	2.5	207.850	2.6
All items less food and energy	234.982	2.5	209.923	2.5

[1] Index series calculated using a Laspeyres estimator. All other item stratum index series calculated using a geometric means estimator.
[2] December 1982 = 100.
[3] December 1997 = 100.
Notes: Unless otherwise noted, 1982–1984 = 100. Index applies to month as a whole, not to any specific date.
Source: U.S. Bureau of Labor Statistics.

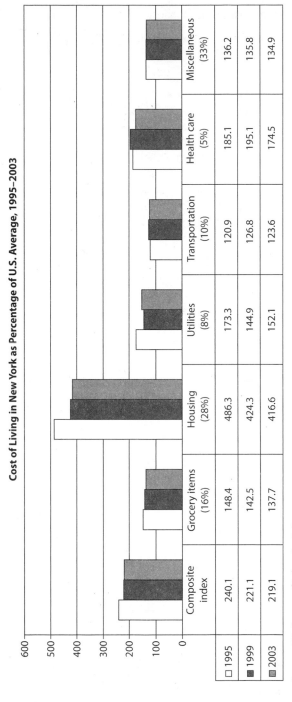

Cost of Living in New York as Percentage of U.S. Average, 1995–2003

	Composite index	Grocery items (16%)	Housing (28%)	Utilities (8%)	Transportation (10%)	Health care (5%)	Miscellaneous (33%)
1995	240.1	148.4	486.3	173.3	120.9	185.1	136.2
1999	221.1	142.5	424.3	144.9	126.8	195.1	135.8
2003	219.1	137.7	416.6	152.1	123.6	174.5	134.9

Source: U.S. Bureau of Labor Statistics.

Average Paid Circulation of Major Newspapers, 2007

	Weekday	Saturday	Sunday
American Banker	12,975	—	—
Amsterdam News	12,379	—	—
Staten Island Advance	59,461	55,481	73,203
El Diario La Prensa	50,049	45,656	37,655
Chief–Civil Service Leader	29,362	—	—
Daily News	718,174	520,708	775,543
New York Post	724,748	472,746	439,202
Daily Racing Form	23,122	60,003	40,961
New York Times	1,120,420	1,011,900	1,627,062
Wall Street Journal	2,062,312	1,968,413	—
Women's Wear Daily	47,031	—	—

Note: Figures represent averages for the six-month period ending 31 March 2007.
Source: Audit Bureau of Circulations, FAS-FAX Report.

Personal Income Tax Burden and Sales Tax Burden as Percentage of Income, Tax Year 2003

Income bracket	Mean New York Adjusted Gross Income	Mean Personal Income Tax Liability	Personal Income Tax Liability as Percentage of Income	Sales Tax Liability as Percentage of Income	Combined Tax Liability as Percentage of Income
Less than $10,000	−$260.21	−$3.10	—	4.5	4.5
$10,000–$20,000	$14,574.72	$99.77	0.7	4.1	4.8
$20,000–$30,000	$24,904.14	$391.77	1.6	3.3	4.9
$30,000–$40,000	$34,754,05	$717.28	2.1	2.7	4.8
$40,000–$50,000	$44,487.42	$1,021.82	2.3	2.4	4.7
$50,000–$60,000	$54,801.16	$1,355.41	2.5	2.2	4.7
$60,000–$75,000	$66,712,35	$1,722.62	2.6	2.1	4.7
$75,000–$100,000	$85,536.83	$2,309.02	2.7	1.6	4.3
$100,000–$150,000	$120,194.11	$3,492.30	2.9	1.6	4.5
$150,000–$200,000	$170,100.55	$5,564.88	3.3	1.2	4.5
$200,000–$500,000	$295,028.14	$11,155.90	3.8	1.1	4.9
$500,000–$1,000,000	$689,840.24	$28,281.44	4.1	0.7	4.8
$1,000,000 and above	$3,664,638.13	$152,155.48	4.2	0.6	4.8

Notes: Figures based on statistical sample of full-year, New York City resident tax returns from the Office of Tax Policy Analysis, New York State Department of Taxation and Finance. Excludes filers claimed as dependents by others. Mean values calculated using number of filers, not number of people. Using number of people yields similar results. Sales tax burden based on study by Institute on Taxation and Economic Policy of combined New York state and local burden for tax year 2002, using 2000 income levels and adjusted for city share of burden. Combined tax liability percentages were computed by summing percentages for personal income tax liability and sales tax liability, and because of rounding may differ from percentages derived from raw figures.
Source: Independent Budget Office.

Total Tax Burden for Family of Three at Selected Income Levels, New York City and United States, 2005

	$25,000	$50,000	$75,000	$100,000	$150,000
New York City	$2,917	$4,751	$7,882	$11,053	$17,911
Percentage of income	11.7	9.5	10.5	11.1	11.9
United States	$2,792	$4,379	$6,614	$8,477	$12,381
Percentage of income	11.2	8.8	8.8	8.5	8.3
New York City as Percentage of United States	104.5	108.5	119.2	130.4	144.7
Rank of New York City among 51 cities in survey	22	16	8	4	2

Notes: Total tax burden includes individual income tax, residential property tax, sales and use tax, and automobile taxes (gasoline tax, registration fees, excise tax, and personal property tax). Figures assume two wage-earning spouses and one school-age child. Figures assume that families earning $25,000 are renters, families earning $50,000 and above own a home within city confines. Housing values based on 2004 American Community Survey and adjusted by linear regression for each income level. Amount of mortgage deduction based on amortization schedule for estimated housing value for each income level. Survey includes largest city in each state and District of Columbia.
Source: Government of the District of Columbia, Office of Tax and Revenue, *Tax Rates and Tax Rate Burdens in the District of Columbia: A Nationwide Comparison* (2005).

6 Arts and Letters

Broadway Theater Box Office and Attendance, 2001–2002 to 2005–2006

	2001–2002	2002–2003	2003–2004	2004–2005	2005–2006
Attendance					
Musicals	8,465,556	9,089,914	10,022,404	9,541,666	10,090,793
Plays	2,475,761	2,292,377	1,572,175	1,971,978	1,912,355
Specials	13,551	40,388	10,901	13,705	—
Totals	10,954,868	11,422,679	11,605,480	11,527,349	12,003,148
Gross Receipts					
Musicals	$522,643,624	$606,771,565	$683,636,473	$648,102,341	$734,130,811
Plays	120,195,827	112,646,293	86,900,854	119,885,667	127,515,688
Specials	554,388	1,500,014	453,642	565,411	—
Totals	$643,393,840	$720,917,872	$770,990,969	$768,553,418	$861,646,499
New Shows					
Musicals, new	8	7	10	11	12
Musicals, revivals	2	6	3	4	3
Plays, new	14	11	14	14	14
Plays, revivals	10	9	9	9	10
Plays, return engagements	1	—	1	—	—
Specials	2	3	2	1	—
Totals	37	36	39	39	39
Average Paid Admission					
Musicals	$61.74	$66.75	$68.21	$67.92	$72.75
Plays	$48.55	$49.14	$55.27	$60.79	$66.68
Specials	$40.91	$37.14	$41.61	$41.26	—
All Shows	$58.73	$63.11	$66.43	$66.67	$71.79

Source: League of American Theatres and Producers.

Broadway Theaters, with Number of Seats and Affiliation

Al Hirschfeld (formerly Martin Beck)	302 West 45th Street	1,437	Jujamcyn Theaters
American Airlines	227 West 42nd Street	740	Roundabout Theatre Co.
Belasco	111 West 44th Street	1,018	Shubert Organization
Biltmore	261 West 47th Street	650	Manhattan Theatre Club
Broadhurst	235 West 44th Street	1,186	Shubert Organization
Brooks Atkinson	256 West 47th Street	1,044	Nederlander Organization
Circle in the Square	1633 Broadway	623	
Ethel Barrymore	243 West 47th Street	1,096	Shubert Organization
Gerald Schoenfeld (formerly Plymouth)	236 West 45th Street	1,079	Shubert Organization
Helen Hayes	240 West 44th Street	597	
Imperial	249 West 45th Street	1,421	Shubert Organization
Longacre	220 West 48th Street	1,096	Shubert Organization
Lyceum	149 West 45th Street	924	Shubert Organization
Marquis	1535 Broadway	1,604	Nederlander Organization
Music Box	239 West 45th Street	1,010	Shubert Organization and Estate of Irving Berlin
New Amsterdam	214 West 42nd Street	1,747	Disney
Palace	1564 Broadway	1,784	Nederlander Organization
Shubert	225 West 44th Street	1,521	Shubert Organization
Studio 54	254 West 54th Street	920	Roundabout Theatre Co.
Ambassador	219 West 49th Street	1,125	Shubert Organization
August Wilson (formerly Virginia)	245 West 52nd Street	1,275	Jujamcyn Theaters
Bernard B. Jacobs (formerly Royale)	242 West 45th Street	1,078	Shubert Organization
Booth	222 West 45th Street	785	Shubert Organization
Broadway	Broadway at 53rd Street	1,752	Shubert Organization
Cadillac Winter Garden	1634 Broadway	1,513	Shubert Organization
Cort	138 West 48th Street	1,084	Shubert Organization
Eugene O'Neill	230 West 49th Street	1,108	Jujamcyn Theaters
Gershwin	222 West 51st Street	1,933	Nederlander Organization
Hilton Theatre (formerly Ford Center for the Performing Arts)	213 West 42nd Street	1,813	Clear Channel
John Golden	252 West 45th Street	805	Shubert Organization
Lunt-Fontanne	205 West 46th Street	1,475	Nederlander Organization
Majestic	247 West 44th Street	1,655	Shubert Organization
Minskoff	200 West 45th Street	1,710	Nederlander Organization
Nederlander	208 West 41st Street	1,203	Nederlander Organization
Neil Simon	250 West 52nd Street	1,297	Nederlander Organization
Richard Rodgers	226 West 46th Street	1,368	Nederlander Organization

Broadway Theaters, with Number of Seats and Affiliation (continued)

St. James	246 West 44th Street	1,623	Jujamcyn Theaters
Vivian Beaumont	150 West 65th Street	1,080	Lincoln Center Theater
Walter Kerr	219 West 48th Street	947	Jujamcyn Theaters

Source: League of American Theatres and Producers.

Longest-Running Broadway Shows

The Phantom of the Opera	26 January 1988	present	8,479 performances
Cats	7 October 1982	10 September 2000	7,485
Les Misérables	12 March 1987	18 May 2003	6,680
A Chorus Line	25 July 1975	28 April 1990	6,137
Oh! Calcutta!	24 September 1976	6 August 1989	5,959
Beauty and the Beast	18 April 1994	present	5,461
Rent	29 April 1996	present	5,027
Chicago	14 November 1996	present	4,804
The Lion King	13 November 1997	present	4,389
Miss Saigon	11 April 1991	28 January 2001	4,092
42nd Street	25 August 1980	8 January 1989	3,486
Grease	14 February 1972	13 April 1980	3,388
Fiddler on the Roof	22 September 1964	2 July 1972	3,242
Life with Father	8 November 1939	12 July 1947	3,224
Tobacco Road	4 December 1933	31 May 1941	3,182
Hello, Dolly!	16 January 1964	27 December 1970	2,844
Mamma Mia!	18 October 2001	present	2,752
My Fair Lady	15 March 1956	29 September 1962	2,717
Threepenny Opera	20 September 1955	17 December 1961	2,611
The Producers	19 April 2001	22 April 2007	2,502
Hairspray	15 August 2002	present	2,410
Annie	21 April 1977	2 January 1983	2,377
Cabaret	19 March 1998	4 January 2004	2,377
Man of La Mancha	22 November 1965	26 June 1971	2,328
Abie's Irish Rose	23 May 1922	1 October 1927	2,327
Oklahoma!	31 March 1943	29 May 1948	2,212
Smokey Joe's Cafe	2 March 1995	16 January 2000	2,036
Avenue Q	31 July 2003	present	2,014
Pippin	23 October 1972	12 June 1977	1,944

Longest-Running Broadway Shows (continued)

Show	Open	Close	Performances
South Pacific	7 April 1949	16 January 1954	1,925
The Magic Show	28 May 1974	31 December 1978	1,920
Wicked	30 October 2003	present	1,910
Aida	23 March 2000	5 September 2004	1,852
Gemini	21 May 1977	6 September 1981	1,819
Deathtrap	26 February 1978	13 June 1982	1,793
Harvey	1 November 1944	15 January 1949	1,775
Dancin'	27 March 1978	27 June 1982	1,774
La Cage aux Folles	21 August 1983	15 November 1987	1,761
Hair	29 April 1968	1 July 1972	1,750
The Wiz	5 January 1975	28 January 1979	1,672
Born Yesterday	4 February 1946	31 December 1949	1,642
Crazy for You	19 February 1992	7 January 1996	1,622
Ain't Misbehavin'	9 May 1978	21 February 1982	1,604
The Best Little Whorehouse in Texas	19 June 1978	27 March 1982	1,584
Mary, Mary	8 March 1961	12 December 1964	1,572
Evita	25 September 1979	26 June 1983	1,567
The Voice of the Turtle	8 December 1943	3 January 1948	1,557
Jekyll & Hyde	28 April 1997	7 January 2001	1,543
Barefoot in the Park	23 October 1963	25 June 1967	1,530
42nd Street	2 May 2001	2 January 2005	1,524

Source: Internet Broadway Database.

Major Tony Awards, 1947–2007

	Play	Musical	Actor in a Play	Actor in a Musical	Actress in a Play	Actress in a Musical
1947	*All My Sons*[1]	not given	José Ferrer Fredric March	not given	Ingrid Bergman Helen Hayes	not given
1948	*Mister Roberts*	not given	Henry Fonda Paul Kelly Basil Rath-bone	Paul Hartman	Judith Anderson Katharine Cornell Jessica Tandy	Grace Hartman

	Play	Musical	Actor in a Play	Actor in a Musical	Actress in a Play	Actress in a Musical
1949	Death of a Salesman	Kiss Me Kate	Rex Harrison	Ray Bolger	Martita Hunt	Nanette Fabray
1950	The Cocktail Party	South Pacific	Sidney Black-mer	Ezio Pinza	Shirley Booth	Mary Martin
1951	The Rose Tattoo	Guys and Dolls	Claude Rains	Robert Alda	Uta Hagen	Ethel Merman
1952	The Fourposter	The King and I	José Ferrer	Phil Silvers	Julie Harris	Gertrude Lawrence
1953	The Crucible	Wonderful Town	Tom Ewell	Thomas Mitchell	Shirley Booth	Rosalind Russell
1954	The Teahouse of the August Moon	Kismet	David Wayne	Alfred Drake	Audrey Hepburn	Dolores Gray
1955	The Desperate Hours	The Pajama Game	Alfred Lunt	Walter Slezak	Nancy Kelly	Mary Martin
1956	The Diary of Anne Frank	Damn Yankees	Paul Muni	Ray Walston	Julie Harris	Gwen Verdon
1957	Long Day's Journey into Night	My Fair Lady	Fredric March	Rex Harrison	Margaret Leighton	Judy Holliday
1958	Sunrise at Campo-bello	The Music Man	Ralph Bellamy	Robert Preston	Helen Hayes	Thelma Ritter Gwen Verdon
1959	J.B.	Redhead	Jason Robards	Richard Kiley	Gertrude Berg	Gwen Verdon
1960	The Miracle Worker	The Sound of Music	Melvyn Douglas	Jackie Gleason	Anne Bancroft	Mary Martin
1961	Beckett	Bye, Bye Birdie	Zero Mostel	Richard Burton	Joan Plow-right	Elizabeth Seal
1962	A Man for All Seasons	How to Succeed in Business without Really Trying	Paul Scofield	Robert Morse	Margaret Leighton	Anna Maria Alber-ghetti

	Play	Musical	Actor in a Play	Actor in a Musical	Actress in a Play	Actress in a Musical
1963	Who's Afraid of Virginia Woolf?	A Funny Thing Happened on the Way to the Forum	Arthur Hill	Zero Mostel	Uta Hagen	Vivien Leigh
1964	Luther	Hello, Dolly!	Alec Guinness	Bert Lahr	Sandy Dennis	Carol Channing
1965	The Subject Was Roses	Fiddler on the Roof	Walter Matthau	Zero Mostel	Irene Worth	Liza Minnelli
1966	Marat/Sade	Man of La Mancha	Hal Holbrook	Richard Kiley	Rosemary Harris	Angela Lansbury
1967	The Home-coming	Cabaret	Paul Rogers	Robert Preston	Beryl Reed	Barbara Harris
1968	Rosencrantz and Guilden-stern Are Dead	Hallelujah, Baby!	Martin Balsam	Robert Goulet	Zoe Caldwell	Patricia Routledge Leslie Uggams
1969	The Great White Hope	1776	James Earl Jones	Jerry Orbach	Julie Harris	Angela Lansbury
1970	Borstal Boy	Applause	Fritz Weaver	Cleavon Little	Tammy Grimes	Lauren Bacall
1971	Sleuth	Company	Brian Bedford	Hal Linden	Maureen Stapleton	Helen Gallagher
1972	Sticks and Bones	Two Gentle-men of Verona	Cliff Gorman	Phil Silvers	Sada Thompson	Alexis Smith
1973	That Cham-pionship Season	A Little Night Music	Alan Bates	Ben Vereen	Julie Harris	Glynis Johns
1974	The River Niger	Raisin	Michael Moriarty	Christopher Plummer	Colleen Dewhurst	Virginia Capers
1975	Equus	The Wiz	John Kani Winston Ntshona	John Cullum	Ellen Burstyn	Angela Lansbury

Major Tony Awards, 1947–2007 (continued)

	Play	Musical	Actor in a Play	Actor in a Musical	Actress in a Play	Actress in a Musical
1976	Travesties	A Chorus Line	John Wood	George Rose	Irene Worth	Donna Mc-Kechnie
1977	The Shadow Box	Annie	Al Pacino	Barry Bostwick	Julie Harris	Dorothy Loudon
1978	Da	Ain't Mis-behavin'	Barnard Hughes	John Cullum	Jessica Tandy	Liza Minnelli
1979	The Elephant Man	Sweeney Todd	Tom Conti	Len Cariou	Constance Cummings	Angela Lansbury
1980	Children of a Lesser God	Evita	John Rubinstein	Jim Dale	Phyllis Frelich	Patti LuPone
1981	Amadeus	42nd Street	Ian McKellen	Kevin Kline	Jane Lapotaire	Lauren Bacall
1982	The Life and Adventures of Nicholas Nickleby	Nine	Roger Rees	Ben Harney	Zoe Caldwell	Jennifer Holliday
1983	Torch Song Trilogy	Cats	Harvey Fierstein	Tommy Tune	Jessica Tandy	Natalia Makarova
1984	The Real Thing	La Cage aux Folles	Jeremy Irons	George Hearn	Glenn Close	Chita Rivera
1985	Biloxi Blues	Big River	Derek Jacobi	Ron Richardson	Stockard Channing	none given
1986	I'm Not Rappaport	The Mystery of Edwin Drood	Judd Hirsch	George Rose	Lily Tomlin	Bernadette Peters
1987	Fences	Les Misérables	James Earl Jones	Michael Crawford	Linda Lavin	Maryann Plunkett
1988	M Butterfly	The Phantom of the Opera	Ron Silver	Robert Lindsay	Joan Allen	Joanna Gleason
1989	The Heidi Chronicles	Jerome Robbins' Broadway	Philip Bosco	Jason Alexander	Pauline Collins	Ruth Brown
1990	The Grapes of Wrath	City of Angels	Robert Morse	James Naughton	Maggie Smith	Tyne Daly

Major Tony Awards, 1947–2007 (continued)

	Play	Musical	Actor in a Play	Actor in a Musical	Actress in a Play	Actress in a Musical
1991	Lost in Yonkers	The Will Rogers Follies	Nigel Hawthorne	Jonathan Pryce	Mercedes Ruehl	Lea Salonga
1992	Dancing at Lughnasa	Crazy for You	Judd Hirsch	Gregory Hines	Glenn Close	Faith Prince
1993	Angels in America: Millennium Approaches	Kiss of the Spider Woman: The Musical	Ron Liebman	Brent Carver	Madeline Kahn	Chita Rivera
1994	Angels in America: Perestroika	Passion	Stephen Spinella	Boyd Gaines	Diana Rigg	Donna Murphy
1995	Love! Valour! Compassion!	Sunset Boulevard	Ralph Fiennes	Matthew Broderick	Cherry Jones	Glenn Close
1996	Master Class	Rent	George Grizzard	Nathan Lane	Zoe Caldwell	Donna Murphy
1997	The Last Night of Ballyhoo	Titanic	Christopher Plummer	James Naughton	Janet McTeer	Bebe Neuwirth
1998	Art	The Lion King	Anthony LaPaglia	Alan Cumming	Marie Mullen	Natasha Richardson
1999	Side Man	Fosse	Brian Dennehy	Martin Short	Judi Dench	Bernadette Peters
2000	Copenhagen	Contact	Stephen Dillane	Brian Stokes Mitchell	Jennifer Ehle	Heather Headley
2001	Proof	The Producers	Richard Easton	Nathan Lane	Mary-Louise Parker	Christine Ebersole
2002	The Goat, or Who Is Sylvia?	Thoroughly Modern Millie	Alan Bates	John Lithgow	Lindsay Duncan	Sutton Foster
2003	Take Me Out	Hairspray	Brian Dennehy	Harvey Fierstein	Vanessa Redgrave	Marissa Jaret Winokur
2004	I Am My Own Wife	Avenue Q	Jefferson Mays	Hugh Jackman	Phylicia Rashad	Idina Menzel

Major Tony Awards, 1947–2007 (continued)

	Play	Musical	Actor in a Play	Actor in a Musical	Actress in a Play	Actress in a Musical
2005	Doubt	Monty Python's Spamalot	Bill Irwin	Norbert Leo Butz	Cherry Jones	Victoria Clark
2006	The History Boys	Jersey Boys	Richard Griffiths	John Lloyd Young	Cynthia Nixon	LaChanze
2007	The Coast of Utopia	Spring Awakening	Frank Langella	David Hyde Pierce	Julie White	Christine Ebersole

[1] Award was for best author (Arthur Miller).
Source: American Theatre Wing.

Attendance at Cultural Institutions, Fiscal Years 2001–2003

	2001	2002	2003
Manhattan			
American Museum of Natural History	3,387,324	2,640,402	2,546,101
Carnegie Hall	646,414	679,532	637,340
City Center	358,000	365,525	297,760
Lincoln Center for the Performing Arts	394,230	446,851	409,508
Metropolitan Museum of Art	5,415,815	4,383,211	4,937,502
El Museo del Barrio	56,796	74,651	79,426
Museum of the City of New York	338,080	66,650	92,499
Museum of Jewish Heritage	106,197	98,391	52,680
New York Shakespeare Festival	184,932	183,824	195,467
New York State Theater	724,650	665,689	651,121
New York City Ballet	473,912	377,319	374,852
New York City Opera	250,738	288,370	276,269
Studio Museum in Harlem	116,159	128,297	134,250
Total Manhattan	12,453,247	10,398,712	10,684,775

Attendance at Cultural Institutions, Fiscal Years 2001–2003 (continued)

	2001	2002	2003
Bronx			
Bronx County Historical Society	8,447	6,662	6,571
Bronx Museum of Art	14,474	21,808	15,614
New York Botanical Garden	548,435	585,307	571,192
Wildlife Conservation Society / Zoo	2,144,908	2,073,287	1,707,474
Wave Hill	108,708	108,352	109,997
Total Bronx	2,824,972	2,795,416	2,410,848
Brooklyn			
Brooklyn Academy of Music	374,858	294,785	393,181
Brooklyn Botanic Garden	873,886	836,499	768,832
Brooklyn Children's Museum	119,000	118,600	163,320
Brooklyn Museum of Art	351,837	415,232	314,909
Wildlife Conservation Society / Aquarium	735,627	773,428	669,104
Total Brooklyn	2,455,208	2,438,544	2,309,346
Queens			
American Museum of the Moving Image	60,371	62,016	71,684
Flushing Town Hall	39,761	57,602	60,631
Institute for Contemporary Art / PS1	116,159	123,300	95,000
Jamaica Center for Arts and Learning	67,630	37,986	33,182
New York Hall of Science	265,543	280,620	246,686
Queens Botanical Garden	311,895	318,884	289,404
Queens Museum of the Arts	60,912	46,215	76,447
Queens Theater in the Park	113,330	106,440	108,789
Total Queens	1,035,601	1,033,063	981,823
Staten Island			
Snug Harbor Cultural Center	52,055	46,900	22,934
Staten Island Botanical Garden[1]	300,000	33,500	30,680
Staten Island Children's Museum	107,257	91,615	86,310
Staten Island Historical Society	91,790	85,336	86,783
Staten Island Institute of Arts and Sciences	43,508	15,129	18,197
Staten Island Zoological Society	211,019	221,905	180,549
Total Staten Island	805,629	494,385	425,453
Total Citywide	19,574,657	17,160,120	16,812,245

[1] Change reflects recalculation of attendance figures by Department of Cultural Affairs.
* Source: New York City Department of Cultural Affairs.

Most Frequently Performed Works at the Metropolitan Opera

	Number of Performances	First Performance	Most Recent Performance
La Bohème (Puccini)	1,178	9 November 2000	15 December 2005
Aida (Verdi)	1,093	12 November 1886	18 February 2006
Carmen (Bizet)	936	5 January 1884	17 December 2005
La Traviata (Verdi)	917	5 November 1883	22 June 2006
Tosca (Puccini)	880	4 February 1901	16 May 2006
Rigoletto (Verdi)	803	16 November 1883	9 May 2006
Madama Butterfly (Puccini)	799	11 February 1907	26 February 2005
Faust (Gounod)	722	22 October 1883	21 May 2005
Pagliacci (Leoncavallo)	695	11 December 1893	26 March 2005
Cavalleria Rusticana (Mascagni)	655	4 December 1891	26 March 2005
Lohengrin (Wagner)	618	7 November 1883	6 May 2006
Il Trovatore (Verdi)	598	26 October 1883	21 February 2003
Lucia di Lammermoor (Donizetti)	557	24 October 1883	5 January 2006
Il Barbiere di Siviglia (Rossini)	550	23 November 1883	17 March 2005
Die Walküre (Wagner)	512	30 January 1885	21 June 2006
Don Giovanni (Mozart)	500	28 November 1883	23 June 2006
Tannhäuser (Wagner)	470	17 November 1884	18 December 2004
Tristan und Isolde (Wagner)	442	1 December 1886	14 October 2003
Le Nozze di Figaro (Mozart)	429	31 January 1894	27 April 2006
Die Meistersinger von Nürnberg (Wagner)	404	4 January 1886	1 May 2003
Der Rosenkavalier (Strauss)	369	9 December 1913	2 April 2005
Die Zauberflöte (Mozart)	357	30 March 1900	3 February 2006
Roméo et Juliette (Gounod)	311	16 April 1884	9 March 2006
Otello (Verdi)	306	23 November 1891	8 January 2005
Parsifal (Wagner)	288	24 December 1903	18 May 2006
Un Ballo in Maschera (Verdi)	278	11 December 1889	3 May 2005
La Gioconda (Ponchielli)	274	20 December 1883	8 February 1990
Boris Godunov (Mussorgsky)	264	19 March 1913	14 February 2004
Turandot (Puccini)	259	16 November 1926	5 May 2005
Manon (Massenet)	257	16 January 1895	8 April 2006
L'Elisir d'Amore (Donizetti)	252	23 January 1904	20 May 2006
Siegfried (Wagner)	252	9 November 1887	6 May 2004
Les Contes d'Hoffmann (Offenbach)	240	11 January 1913	8 January 2005
Hänsel und Gretel (Humperdinck)	239	25 November 1905	5 January 2002
Fidelio (Beethoven)	230	19 November 1884	13 April 2006
La Forza del Destino (Verdi)	229	15 November 1918	23 March 2006

Most Frequently Performed Works at the Metropolitan Opera (continued)

	Number of Performances	First Performance	Most Recent Performance
Samson et Dalila (Saint-Saëns)	226	8 February 1895	2 March 2006
Götterdämmerung (Wagner)	221	25 January 1888	8 May 2004
Die Fledermaus (Strauss)	209	16 February 1905	7 January 2006
Manon Lescaut (Puccini)	207	18 January 1907	23 March 1990
Don Carlo (Verdi)	183	23 December 1920	2 April 2005
Falstaff (Verdi)	175	4 February 1895	22 October 2005
Andrea Chénier (Giordano)	171	1 March 1921	24 October 2002
Così Fan Tutte (Mozart)	171	24 March 1922	28 January 2006
Salome (Strauss)	150	22 January 1907	10 April 2004
Das Rheingold (Wagner)	149	4 January 1889	3 May 2004
Der Fliegende Holländer (Wagner)	147	27 November 1889	20 December 2000
Norma (Bellini)	139	27 February 1890	3 November 2001
Les Huguenots (Meyerbeer)	129	19 March 1884	26 April 1915
Don Pasquale (Donizetti)	124	23 December 1899	28 April 2006
Gianni Schicchi (Puccini)	123	14 December 1918	16 December 1989
Simon Boccanegra (Verdi)	122	28 January 1932	13 February 1999
Eugene Onegin (Tchaikovsky)	121	24 March 1920	23 February 2002
Martha (Flotow)	116	4 January 1884	3 February 1968
Mignon (Thomas)	110	31 October 1883	18 May 1949
Pelléas et Mélisande (Debussy)	109	21 March 1925	8 February 2005
Le Prophète (Meyerbeer)	99	12 February 1884	26 October 1979
Elektra (Strauss)	95	3 December 1932	21 December 2002
La Fanciulla del West (Puccini)	95	10 December 1910	19 March 1993
La Fille du Régiment (Donizetti)	88	6 January 1902	28 November 1995
Luisa Miller (Verdi)	86	21 December 1929	1 April 2006
Ariadne auf Naxos (Strauss)	83	29 December 1962	11 October 2005
The Bartered Bride (Smetana)	83	19 February 1909	1 November 1996
Orfeo ed Euridice (Gluck)	82	11 April 1885	27 November 1972
Ernani (Verdi)	81	28 January 1903	29 March 1985
Macbeth (Verdi)	80	5 February 1959	15 February 1988
Werther (Massenet)	73	29 March 1894	22 January 2004
L'Africaine (Meyerbeer)	71	7 December 1888	24 February 1934
L'Italiana in Algeri (Rossini)	71	5 December 1919	17 March 2004
La Juive (Halévy)	70	16 January 1885	19 December 2003
Le Coq d'Or (Rimsky-Korsakov)	68	6 March 1918	3 May 1945
Mefistofele (Boito)	67	5 December 1883	26 February 2000

Most Frequently Performed Works at the Metropolitan Opera (continued)

	Number of Performances	First Performance	Most Recent Performance
Adriana Lecouvreur (Cilea)	66	18 November 1907	26 March 1994
L'Amore dei Tre Re (Montemezzi)	66	2 January 1914	15 January 1949
Il Tabarro (Puccini)	65	14 December 1918	30 September 1994
La Sonnambula (Bellini)	65	14 November 1883	25 November 1972
Die Entführung aus dem Serail (Mozart)	64	29 November 1946	6 February 2003
Peter Grimes (Britten)	64	12 February 1948	10 January 1998
Lakmé (Delibes)	63	22 February 1892	1 May 1947
Thaïs (Massenet)	63	16 February 1917	22 May 1978
Wozzeck (Berg)	60	5 March 1959	6 January 2006
Die Frau ohne Schatten (Strauss)	59	2 October 1966	12 December 2003
Idomeneo (Mozart)	59	14 October 1982	31 January 2002
Suor Angelica (Puccini)	59	14 December 1918	16 December 1989
The Queen of Spades (Tchaikovsky)	59	5 March 1910	3 March 2004
L'Oracolo (Leoni)	55	4 February 1915	20 January 1933
Dialogues des Carmélites (Poulenc)	54	5 February 1977	4 January 2003
La Périchole (Offenbach)	54	21 December 1956	27 May 1971
Porgy and Bess (Gershwin)	54	6 February 1985	6 December 1990
Arabella (Strauss)	52	10 February 1955	15 December 2001
Louise (Charpentier)	52	15 January 1921	5 February 1949
Die Königin von Saba (Goldmark)	46	2 December 1885	16 April 1906
I Vespri Siciliani (Verdi)	45	23 August 1967	11 December 2004
Nabucco (Verdi)	45	24 October 1960	8 March 2005
Billy Budd (Britten)	44	19 September 1978	14 March 1997
I Puritani (Bellini)	42	29 October 1883	1 February 1997
Jenůfa (Janáček)	39	6 December 1924	13 February 2003
Königskinder (Humperdinck)	39	28 December 1910	18 April 1914
Rise and Fall of the City of Mahagonny (Weill)	39	16 November 1979	9 December 1995
Francesca da Rimini (Zandonai)	37	22 December 1916	20 March 1986
Les Troyens (Berlioz)	37	22 October 1973	27 March 2003
Fedora (Giordano)	35	5 December 1906	1 May 1997
La Clemenza di Tito (Mozart)	35	18 October 1984	14 May 2005
Lulu (Berg)	33	18 March 1977	20 April 2002
Khovanshchina (Mussorgsky)	32	16 February 1950	20 March 1999
L'Enfant et les Sortilèges (Ravel)	31	20 February 1981	28 March 2002
Le Rossignol (Stravinsky)	31	6 March 1926	21 February 2004
Les Mamelles de Tirésias (Poulenc)	31	20 February 1981	28 March 2002

Most Frequently Performed Works at the Metropolitan Opera (continued)

	Number of Performances	First Performance	Most Recent Performance
William Tell (Rossini)	31	28 November 1884	5 December 1931
Der Freischütz (Weber)	30	24 November 1884	19 April 1972
La Cenerentola (Rossini)	29	16 October 1997	28 October 2005
Semiramide (Rossini)	28	22 March 1892	16 January 1993
The Merry Widow (Lehar)	26	17 February 2000	17 January 2004
La Favorita (Donizetti)	25	29 November 1895	9 June 1978
Bluebeard's Castle (Bartók)	24	10 June 1974	21 May 2000
Oedipus Rex (Stravinsky)	23	3 December 1981	21 February 2004
The Rake's Progress (Stravinsky)	23	14 February 1953	3 May 2003
Zazà (Leoncavallo)	23	16 January 1920	22 April 1922
Peter Ibbetson (Taylor)	22	7 February 1931	4 April 1935
Rienzi (Wagner)	21	5 February 1886	26 February 1890
Rinaldo (Handel)	21	19 January 1984	27 June 1984
Sadko (Rimsky-Korsakov)	20	25 January 1930	16 April 1932
Kát'a Kabanová (Janáček)	19	25 February 1991	1 January 2005
Madame Sans-Gêne (Giordano)	19	25 January 1915	8 April 1918
The Siege of Corinth (Rossini)	19	7 April 1975	24 January 1976
Alceste (Gluck)	18	24 January 1941	11 February 1961
Der Barbier von Bagdad (Cornelius)	18	3 January 1980	8 January 1926
Der Zigeunerbaron (Strauss)	18	15 February 1906	31 May 1960
La Rondine (Puccini)	18	10 March 1928	21 March 1936
Vanessa (Barber)	18	15 January 1958	13 April 1965
Stiffelio (Verdi)	17	21 October 1993	10 April 1998
The King's Henchman (Taylor)	17	17 February 1927	28 March 1929
Giulio Cesare (Handel)	16	27 September 1988	6 May 2000
Iris (Mascagni)	16	6 December 1907	9 April 1931
The Last Savage (Menotti)	16	23 January 1964	24 May 1965
Death in Venice (Britten)	15	18 October 1974	26 February 1994
Lady Macbeth of Mtsensk (Shostakovich)	15	10 November 1994	30 March 2000
Mârouf (Rabaud)	15	19 December 1917	27 May 1937
Rusalka (Dvořák)	15	11 November 1993	8 May 2004
The Emperor Jones (Gruenberg)	15	7 January 1933	5 April 1934

Note: Figures are through end of 2005–2006 season; non-operatic works excluded.
Source: Metropolitan Opera.

Best-Selling Books in Metropolitan Area by Number of Copies Sold, 2006

Clothbound Fiction
1. Mitch Albom, *For One More Day* (Hyperion)	162,000
2. James Patterson *Cross* (Little, Brown)	102,000
3. James Patterson, *Beach Road* (Little, Brown)	75,000
4. Nelson DeMille, *Wild Fire* (Warner)	64,000
5. Nicholas Sparks, *Dear John* (Warner)	61,000
6. James Patterson, *The Fifth Horseman* (Little, Brown)	58,000
7. James Patterson, *Judge and Jury* (Little, Brown)	54,000
8. Michael Crichton, *Next* (HarperCollins)	50,000
9. Dan Brown, *The Da Vinci Code* (Doubleday)	49,000
10. Stephen King, *Cell* (Scribner)	48,000

Paperbound Fiction
1. Kim Edwards, *The Memory Keeper's Daughter* (Penguin Books)	190,000
2. Khaled Hosseini, *The Kite Runner* (Riverhead Books)	97,000
3. Dan Brown, *The Da Vinci Code* (Anchor Books)	75,000
4. Mitch Albom, *The Five People You Meet in Heaven* (Hyperion Books)	63,000
5. Jodi Picoult, *My Sister's Keeper* (Washington Square Press)	57,000
6. Paulo Coelho, *The Alchemist* (HarperSan Francisco)	57,000
7. Sue Monk Kidd, *The Mermaid Chair* (Penguin Books)	56,000
8. Gregory Maguire, *Wicked* (Reganbooks)	55,000
9. Sue Monk Kidd, *The Secret Life of Bees* (Penguin Books)	50,000
10. Anita Shreve, *A Wedding in December* (Back Bay Books)	48,000

Clothbound Nonfiction
1. John Grogan, *Marley and Me* (William Morrow)	160,000
2. John Grisham, *The Innocent Man* (Doubleday)	94,000
3. Barack Obama, *The Audacity of Hope* (Crown)	87,000
4. Nora Ephron, *I Feel Bad about My Neck* (Alfred A. Knopf)	75,000
5. Bob Woodward, *State of Denial* (Simon & Schuster)	72,000
6. Steven D. Levitt, *Freakonomics* (William Morrow)	66,000
7. Bill O'Reilly, *Culture Warrior* (Broadway)	64,000
8. Thomas L. Friedman, *The World Is Flat* (Farrar, Straus & Giroux)	61,000
9. Tim Russert, *Wisdom of Our Fathers* (Random House)	45,000
10. Nathaniel Philbrick, *Mayflower* (Viking)	42,000

Paperbound Nonfiction
1. Elie Wiesel, *Night* (Hill & Wang)	133,000
2. James Frey, *A Million Little Pieces* (Anchor)	104,000
3. Jeannette Walls, *The Glass Castle* (Scribner)	83,000

Paperbound Nonfiction (continued)

4. Truman Capote, *In Cold Blood* (Vintage)	71,000
5. Augusten Burroughs, *Running with Scissors* (Picador)	67,000
6. Malcolm Gladwell, *The Tipping Point* (Back Bay)	53,000
7. Erik Larson, *The Devil in the White City* (Vintage)	37,000
8. David McCullough, *1776* (Simon & Schuster)	36,000
9. Albert Gore Jr., *An Inconvenient Truth* (Rodale)	35,000
10. Mitch Albom, *Tuesdays with Morrie* (Broadway)	34,000

Advice, How-to, and Miscellaneous (All Bindings)

1. Michael F. Roizen, *You on a Diet* (Free Press)	97,000
2. Cesar Millan, *Cesar's Way* (Harmony)	63,000
3. *The Official SAT Study Guide* (College Board)	59,000
4. Heidi E. Murkoff, *What to Expect When You're Expecting* (Workman)	50,000
5. Rachael Ray, *Rachael Ray 365* (Clarkson N. Potter)	49,000
6. Robert T. Kiyosaki, *Rich Dad, Poor Dad* (Warner)	49,000
7. *Zagat New York City Restaurants 2006* (Zagat)	46,000
8. Mehmet C. Oz, *You: The Owner's Manual* (HarperCollins)	43,000
9. Giada De Laurentiis, *Giada's Family Dinners* (Clarkson N. Potter)	40,000
10. *Zagat New York City Restaurants 2005* (Zagat)	40,000

Source: Nielsen BookScan.

Library Statistics, Fiscal Years 2004–2006 (in Thousands)

	New York Public Library Research Division			New York Public Library Branch Libraries		
	2004	2005	2006	2004	2005	2006
Attendance	1,680	1,948	1,933	11,688	11,926	12,434
Circulation	—	—	—	14,598	15,546	15,859
Reference queries	613	650	622	6,359	6,825	6,923
Visits to web site	n/a	n/a	n/a	12,754	15,133	19,451

	Brooklyn Public Library			Queens Borough Public Library		
	2004	2005	2006	2004	2005	2006
Attendance	9,917	9,910	10,210	14,556	14,296	13,971
Circulation	10,409	14,000	15,923	16,821	18,899	20,224
Reference queries	4,568	5,183	3,572	3,453	3,440	3,488
Visits to web site	n/a	2,790	3,414	1,764	2,062	2,108

Source: Preliminary Mayor's Management Report, February 2007.

7 Sports

New York Yankees Season Records, 1903–2007

	Wins	Losses	Winning Percentage	Games Behind	Attendance
1903	72	62	.537	17.0	211,808
1904	92	59	.609	1.5	438,919
1905	71	78	.477	21.5	309,100
1906	90	61	.596	3.0	434,700
1907	70	78	.473	21.0	350,020
1908	51	103	.331	39.5	305,500
1909	74	77	.490	23.5	501,700
1910	88	63	.583	14.5	355,857
1911	76	76	.500	25.5	302,444
1912	50	102	.329	55.0	242,194
1913	57	94	.377	38.0	357,551
1914	70	84	.455	30.0	359,477
1915	69	83	.454	32.5	256,035
1916	80	74	.519	11.0	469,211
1917	71	82	.464	28.5	330,294
1918	60	63	.488	13.5	282,047
1919	80	59	.576	7.5	619,164
1920	95	59	.617	3.0	1,289,422
1921	98	55	.641	—	1,230,696
1922	94	60	.610	—	1,026,134
1923	98	54	.645	—	1,007,066
1924	89	63	.586	2.0	1,053,533
1925	69	85	.448	28.5	697,267
1926	91	63	.591	—	1,027,675
1927	110	44	.714	—	1,164,015
1928	101	53	.656	—	1,072,132
1929	88	66	.571	18.0	960,148
1930	86	68	.558	16.0	1,169,230
1931	94	59	.614	13.5	912,437
1932	107	47	.695	—	962,320
1933	91	59	.607	7.0	728,014
1934	94	60	.610	7.0	854,682
1935	89	60	.597	3.0	657,508
1936	102	51	.667	—	976,913
1937	102	52	.662	—	998,148
1938	99	53	.651	—	970,916

New York Yankees Season Records, 1903–2007 (continued)

	Wins	Losses	Winning Percentage	Games Behind	Attendance
1939	106	45	.702	—	859,785
1940	88	66	.571	2.0	988,975
1941	101	53	.656	—	964,722
1942	103	51	.669	—	922,011
1943	98	56	.636	—	618,330
1944	83	71	.539	6.0	789,995
1945	81	71	.533	6.5	881,845
1946	87	67	.565	17.0	2,265,512
1947	97	57	.630	—	2,178,937
1948	94	60	.610	2.5	2,373,901
1949	97	57	.630	—	2,283,676
1950	98	56	.636	—	2,081,380
1951	98	56	.636	—	1,950,107
1952	95	59	.617	—	1,629,665
1953	99	52	.656	—	1,537,811
1954	103	51	.669	8.0	1,475,171
1955	96	58	.623	—	1,490,138
1956	97	57	.630	—	1,491,784
1957	98	56	.636	—	1,497,134
1958	92	62	.597	—	1,428,438
1959	79	75	.513	15.0	1,552,030
1960	97	57	.630	—	1,627,349
1961	109	53	.673	—	1,747,725
1962	96	66	.593	—	1,493,574
1963	104	57	.646	—	1,308,920
1964	99	63	.611	—	1,305,638
1965	77	85	.475	25.0	1,213,552
1966	70	89	.440	26.5	1,124,648
1967	72	90	.444	20.0	1,259,514
1968	83	79	.512	20.0	1,185,666
1969	80	81	.497	28.5	1,067,996
1970	93	69	.574	15.0	1,136,879
1971	82	80	.506	21.0	1,070,771
1972	79	76	.510	6.5	966,328
1973	80	82	.494	17.0	1,262,103
1974	89	73	.549	2.0	1,273,075

New York Yankees Season Records, 1903–2007 (continued)

	Wins	Losses	Winning Percentage	Games Behind	Attendance
1975	83	77	.519	12.0	1,288,048
1976	97	62	.610	—	2,012,434
1977	100	62	.617	—	2,103,092
1978	100	63	.613	—	2,335,871
1979	89	71	.556	13.5	2,537,765
1980	103	59	.636	—	2,627,417
1981	59	48	.551	2.0	1,614,353
1982	79	83	.488	16.0	2,041,219
1983	91	71	.562	7.0	2,257,976
1984	87	75	.537	17.0	1,821,815
1985	97	64	.602	2.0	2,214,587
1986	90	72	.556	5.5	2,268,030
1987	89	73	.549	9.0	2,427,672
1988	85	76	.528	3.5	2,633,701
1989	74	87	.460	14.5	2,170,485
1990	67	95	.414	21.0	2,006,436
1991	71	91	.438	20.0	1,863,733
1992	76	86	.469	20.0	1,748,733
1993	88	74	.543	7.0	2,416,965
1994	70	43	.619	—	1,675,556
1995	79	65	.549	7.0	1,705,263
1996	92	70	.568	—	2,250,877
1997	96	66	.593	2.0	2,580,325
1998	114	48	.704	—	2,919,046
1999	98	64	.605	—	3,293,259
2000	87	74	.540	—	3,227,657
2001	95	65	.594	—	3,264,847
2002	103	58	.640	—	3,465,807
2003	101	61	.623	—	3,465,600
2004	101	61	.623	—	3,775,294
2005	95	67	.586	—	4,090,440
2006	97	65	.599	—	4,243,780
2007	94	68	.580	2.0	4,271,083
Totals	9,265	7,009	.569		159,808,528

Source: Major League Baseball.

Managers of the New York Yankees

		Wins	Losses	Winning Percentage
Clark Griffith	1903–1908	419	370	.531
Norm Elberfeld	1908	27	71	.276
George Stallings	1909–1910	153	138	.526
Hal Chase	1910–1911	85	78	.521
Harry Wolverton	1912	50	102	.329
Frank Chance	1913–1914	117	168	.411
Roger Peckinpaugh	1914	10	10	.500
Bill Donovan	1915–1917	220	239	.479
Miller Huggins	1918–1929	1,067	719	.597
Art Fletcher	1929	6	5	.545
Bob Shawkey	1930	86	68	.558
Joe McCarthy	1931–1946	1,460	867	.627
Bill Dickey	1946	57	48	.543
Johnny Neun	1946	8	6	.571
Bucky Harris	1947–1948	191	117	.620
Casey Stengel	1949–1960	1,149	696	.623
Ralph Houk	1961–1963, 1966–1973	944	806	.539
Yogi Berra	1964, 1984–1985	192	148	.565
Johnny Keane	1965–1966	81	101	.445
Bill Virdon	1974–1975	142	124	.534
Billy Martin	1975–1978, 1979, 1983, 1985, 1988	556	385	.591
Bob Lemon	1978–1979, 1981–1982	99	73	.576
Dick Howser	1980	103	60	.632
Gene Michael	1981, 1982	92	76	.548
Clyde King	1982	29	33	.468
Lou Piniella	1986–1987, 1988	224	193	.537
Dallas Green	1989	56	65	.463
Bucky Dent	1989–1990	36	53	.404
Stump Merrill	1990–1991	120	155	.320
Buck Showalter	1992–1995	313	268	.539
Joe Torre	1996–2007	1,173	767	.605
Joe Girardi	2008–			
Totals		9,265	7,009	569

Source: Major League Baseball.

New York Yankees Team Records

Club Records, Batting

Most runs, game, 9 innings, home	22	26 July 1931	versus Chicago
Most runs, game, 9 innings, road	25	24 May 1936	at Philadelphia
Most runs, game, both teams	33 (3 times)	3 June 1932[1]	at Philadelphia
Most runs, game, both teams, home	31	21 June 2005	versus Tampa Bay
Most runs, game, opponent, home	19	17 June 1925	versus Detroit
		10 September 1977	versus Toronto
Most runs, game, opponent, road	24	29 July 1928	at Cleveland
Most runs, shutout game	21	13 August 1939	at Philadelphia
Most runs, shutout game, opponent	15	15 July 1907	at Chicago
		4 May 1950	versus Chicago
Most runs, inning	14 (5th)	6 July 1920	at Washington
Most runs, start of game, no outs	8	24 April 1960	versus Baltimore
		25 September 1990	versus Baltimore
Most hits, game, 9 innings	30	28 September 1923	versus Boston
Most hits, game, both teams	45	29 September 1928	at Detroit
Most hits, consecutive, start of game	8	25 September 1990	versus Baltimore
Most singles	22	12 August 1953	at Washington
Most doubles	10	12 April 1988	at Toronto
		5 June 2003	at Cincinnati
Most triples	5	1 May 1934	at Washington
Most home runs, game	8	28 June 1939	versus Philadelphia
Most home runs, game, versus one pitcher	6	27 June 1936	at St. Louis
Most home runs, inning	4	30 June 1977	at Toronto
		21 June 2005	versus Tampa Bay
Most home runs, inning, with 2 outs	3	28 June 1939	versus Philadelphia
		21 June 2005	versus Tampa Bay
Most home runs, consecutive	3 (10 times)	21 June 2005[1]	versus Tampa Bay
Most home runs, start of game	2	27 April 1955	versus Chicago
		30 July 1999	at Boston
		6 April 2003	at Tampa Bay
		28 June 2003	at New York Mets
		21 June 2005	versus Tampa Bay
Most grand slams, game	2	24 May 1936	versus Philadelphia
		29 June 1987	at Toronto
		14 September 1999	at Toronto
Most bases on balls	16	23 June 1915	at Philadelphia
Most strikeouts, game	17	10 September 1999	versus Boston
Most stolen bases, game	15	28 September 1911	versus St. Louis

Club Records, Batting (continued)

Most stolen bases, game, both clubs	15 (Yankees 15, St. Louis 0)	28 September 1911	versus St. Louis
Most steals of home, game	3	17 April 1915	versus Philadelphia
Most times grounded into double play	5 (3 times)	27 September 1968[1]	at Boston
Most left on base, game, 9 innings	20	21 September 1956	at Boston
Most left on base, game, extra innings	23	5 September 1927	at Boston

Individual Records, Batting

Most at-bats	11	Bobby Richardson	24 June 1962	at Detroit
Most runs scored	5 (14 times)	Jason Giambi	24 July 2002[1]	at Cleveland
Most hits	6	Myril Hoag	6 June 1934	at Boston
				at Baltimore
		Gerald Williams	1 May 1996	(15 innings)
Most singles	6	Myril Hoag	6 June 1934	at Boston
Most doubles	4	Johnny Lindell	17 August 1944	versus Cleveland
		Jim Mason	8 July 1974	at Texas
Most triples	3	Hal Chase	30 August 1906	versus Washington
		Earle Combs	22 September 1927	versus Detroit
		Joe DiMaggio	27 August 1938	versus Cleveland
Most home runs	4	Lou Gehrig	3 June 1932	at Philadelphia
Most home runs, consecutive	4	Lou Gehrig	3 June 1932	at Philadelphia
				versus Cleveland
		Bobby Murcer	24 June 1970	(doubleheader)
Most grand slams	2	Tony Lazzeri	24 May 1936	at Philadelphia
Most total bases	16	Lou Gehrig	3 June 1932	at Philadelphia
Most runs batted in	11	Tony Lazzeri	24 May 1936	at Philadelphia
Most sacrifice flies	3	Bob Meusel	15 September 1926	at Cleveland
		Don Mattingly	3 May 1986	versus Texas
Most stolen bases	4 (18 times)	Tony Womack	15 May 2005[1]	at Oakland
Most times caught stealing	3	Fritz Maisel	26 April 1916	versus Boston
		Lee Magee	29 June 1918	at Philadelphia
Most bases on balls	5 (6 times)	Hersh Martin	1 September 1945[1]	at Washington
Most strikeouts	5	Johnny Broaca	25 June 1934	versus Chicago
		Bernie Williams	1 August 1991	versus Minnesota
		Andy Phillips	2 May 2005	versus Tampa Bay
		Eddie Robinson	30 May 1955	at Washington
Most times grounded into double play	3	Jim Leyritz	4 July 1990	at Kansas City
		Matt Nokes	3 May 1992	versus Minnesota

Club Records, Pitching

Most hits, game	28	29 September 1928	at Detroit
Most runs, game	24	29 July 1928	at Cleveland
Most runs, inning	13	17 June 1925	versus Detroit
Most runs, two consecutive games	33	28 July 1928 (9)	at Cleveland
		29 July 1928 (24)	at Cleveland
Most home runs, game	7	4 July 2003	versus Boston
Most home runs, inning	4	17 June 1977	at Boston
		2 May 1992	versus Minnesota
		21 August 2005	at Chicago
Most strikeouts, game	18	17 June 1978	versus California
Most bases on balls, game	17	11 September 1949	versus Washington
Most bases on balls, inning	11	11 September 1949	versus Washington (3rd)
Most wild pitches, game	3	many times	

Individual Records, Pitching

Most runs allowed, game	13	Jack Warhop	31 July 1911	versus Chicago
		Ray Caldwell	3 October 1913	at Philadelphia
		Carl Mays	17 July 1923	at Cleveland
Most hits allowed, game	21	Jack Quinn	29 June 1912	at Boston
Most home runs allowed, game	5	Joe Ostrowski	22 June 1950	at Cleveland
		John Cumberland	24 May 1970	at Cleveland
		Ron Guidry	17 September 1985	at Detroit
		Jeff Weaver	21 July 2002	versus Boston
		David Wells	4 July 2003	versus Boston
Most home runs allowed, inning	4	Catfish Hunter	17 June 1977 (1st)	at Boston
		Scott Sanderson	2 May 1992 (5th)	versus Minnesota
		Randy Johnson	21 August 2005 (5th)	at Chicago
		Chase Wright	22 April 2007 (3rd)	at Boston
Most strikeouts, game, lefthander	18	Ron Guidry	17 June 1978	versus California
Most strikeouts, game, righthander	16	David Cone	23 June 1997	at Detroit
Most strikeouts, inning	3	many pitchers		
Most strikeouts, relief	8	Ron Davis	4 May 1981	at Oakland
Most strikeouts, consecutive	8	Ron Davis	4 May 1981	at Oakland
Most bases on balls, game	13	Tommy Byrne	8 June 1949	at Detroit
Most balks, game	4	Vic Raschi	3 May 1950	versus Chicago

Miscellaneous Club Records

Longest game, innings	22	24 June 1962	at Detroit
Longest game, innings, home	20	29 August 1967	versus Boston
Longest game, innings, loss	19	24 May 1918	versus Cleveland
Longest game, time, 9 innings	4:45	18 August 2006	at Boston
Largest deficit overcome	9 (4 times)	17 May 2006[1]	versus Texas

Club Records, Season

Most wins, season	114	1998
Most wins, home	65	1961
Most wins, road	54	1939
Most wins, month	28	1938 (August)
Most wins, consecutive	19	1947
Most wins, consecutive, home	18	1942
Most wins, consecutive, road	15	1953
Most wins, shutout	24	1951
Most wins, 1–0	6	1908, 1968
Fewest wins, season	50	1912
Fewest wins, home	27	1913
Fewest wins, road	19	1912
Most losses, season	103	1908
Most losses, home	47	1908, 1913
Most losses, road	58	1912
Most losses, month	24	1908 (July)
Most losses, consecutive	13	1913
Most losses, consecutive, home	17	1913
Most losses, consecutive, road	12	1908
Most losses, shutout	27	1914
Most losses, 1–0	9	1914
Fewest losses, season	44	1927
Fewest losses, home	15	1932
Fewest losses, road	20	1939
Most games	164	1964, 1968
Fewest games	107	1981
Most consecutive extra-inning games	4	1992
Longest 1–0 game won	15 innings (versus Philadelphia, 4 July 1925, first game)	
Longest 1–0 game lost	14 innings (at Boston, 24 September 1969)	
Most total players used	51	2005
Fewest total players used	25	1923, 1927
Most pitchers used	28	2005
Fewest pitchers used	8	1922, 1923

Club Records, Batting, Season

Most at-bats	5,710	1997
Most runs	1,067	1931
Fewest runs	459	1908
Most hits	1,683	1930
Fewest hits	1,136	1903
Highest batting average	.309	1930
Lowest batting average	.214	1968
Most singles	1,237	1988
Most doubles	325	1997
Most triples	110	1930
Most home runs	240	1961
Most consecutive games with a home run	25	1941
Most home runs in consecutive games in which home runs were hit	40	1941
Most grand slams	10	1987
Most home runs, pinch hitters	10	1961
Most total bases	2,703	1936
Most runs batted in	995	1936
Most bases on balls	766	1932
Most times hit by pitch	81	2003
Fewest times hit by pitch	14	1969
Most stolen bases	289	1910
Fewest stolen bases	24	1948
Most times caught stealing	82	1920
Fewest times caught stealing	18	1961, 1964
Most strikeouts	1,171	2002
Fewest strikeouts	420	1924
Highest slugging percentage	.489	1927
Lowest slugging percentage	.287	1914
Most times grounded into double play	153	1996
Fewest times grounded into double play	91	1963
Most left on base	1,258	1996
Fewest left on base	1,010	1920
Most .300 hitters	9	1930
Most players with 10 or more home runs	10	1998

New York Yankees Team Records (continued)

Individual Records, Batting, Season

Record	Value	Player	Year
Most games	162	Bobby Richardson	1962
		Roy White	1970
		Chris Chambliss	1978
		Don Mattingly	1986
		Roberto Kelly	1990
Most at-bats	696	Alfonso Soriano	2002
Highest batting average, righthander	.381	Joe DiMaggio	1939
Highest batting average, lefthander	.393	Babe Ruth	1923
Highest batting average, switch hitter	.365	Mickey Mantle	1957
Most hits, righthander	219	Derek Jeter	1999
Most hits, lefthander	238	Don Mattingly	1986
Most hits, switch hitter	204	Bernie Williams	2002
Most consecutive games hitting safely	56	Joe DiMaggio	1941
Most runs scored	177	Babe Ruth	1921
Most consecutive games with run scored	18	Red Rolfe	1939
Most singles	171	Steve Sax	1989
Most doubles	53	Don Mattingly	1986
Most triples	23	Earle Combs	1927
Most home runs, righthander	48	Alex Rodriguez	2005
Most home runs, lefthander	61	Roger Maris	1961
Most home runs, switch hitter	54	Mickey Mantle	1961
Most home runs, home (Polo Grounds)	32	Babe Ruth	1921
Most home runs, home (Yankee Stadium)	30	Lou Gehrig	1934
		Roger Maris	1961
Most home runs, road	32	Babe Ruth	1927
Most home runs, month, righthander	15	Joe DiMaggio	1937 (July)
Most home runs, month, lefthander	17	Babe Ruth	1927 (September)
Most home runs, rookie	29	Joe DiMaggio	1936
Most consecutive games with home run	8	Don Mattingly	1987
Most grand slams	6	Don Mattingly	1987
Most runs batted in, righthander	167	Joe DiMaggio	1937
Most runs batted in, lefthander	184	Lou Gehrig	1931
Most runs batted in, switch hitter	130	Mickey Mantle	1956
Most consecutive games with run batted in	11	Babe Ruth	1931
Most extra-base hits	119	Babe Ruth	1921
Most total bases	457	Babe Ruth	1921
Highest slugging percentage	.847	Babe Ruth	1920

Individual Records, Batting, Season (continued)

Most strikeouts, righthander	157	Alfonso Soriano	2002
Most strikeouts, lefthander	133	Reggie Jackson	1978
Most strikeouts, switch hitter	151	Jorge Posada	2000
Most bases on balls, righthander	119	Willie Randolph	1980
Most bases on balls, lefthander	148	Babe Ruth	1923
Most bases on balls, switch hitter	146	Mickey Mantle	1957
Most sacrifice hits	42	Willie Keeler	1905
Most sacrifice flies	17	Roy White	1971
Most stolen bases	93	Rickey Henderson	1988
Most times caught stealing	23	Ben Chapman	1931
Most times hit by pitch	24	Don Baylor	1985
Most times grounded into double play	30	Dave Winfield	1983
Fewest times grounded into double play	2	Mickey Mantle	1961
		Mickey Rivers	1977

Club Records, Pitching, Season

Lowest earned run average	2.57	1904
Highest earned run average	4.88	1930
Most innings pitched	1506.2	1964
Most complete games	123	1904
Fewest complete games	3	1991
Most shutouts	24	1951
Most consecutive shutouts	4	1932
Most consecutive shutout innings	40	1932
Fewest shutouts	2	1994
Most saves (since 1969)	58	1986
Fewest hits allowed	1,143	1919
Most hits allowed	1,566	1930
Fewest home runs allowed	13	1907
Most home runs allowed	179	1987
Fewest runs allowed	507	1942
Most runs allowed	898	1930
Fewest earned runs allowed	394	1904
Most earned runs allowed	753	2000
Fewest bases on balls	245	1903
Most bases on balls	812	1949
Most strikeouts	1,266	2001
Fewest strikeouts	431	1927

Individual Records, Pitching, Season

Most wins, righthander	41	Jack Chesbro	1904
Most wins, lefthander	26	Lefty Gomez	1934
Most consecutive wins, righthander	16	Roger Clemens	2001
Most consecutive wins, lefthander	14	Whitey Ford	1961
Most shutouts	9	Ron Guidry	1978
Most shutouts lost	7	Bill Zuber	1945
Lowest earned run average, righthander	1.64	Spud Chandler	1943
Lowest earned run average, lefthander	1.74	Ron Guidry	1978
Highest winning percentage	.893	Ron Guidry	1978
Most losses, righthander	22	Joe Lake	1908
Most losses, lefthander	17	Herb Pennock	1921
Most consecutive losses, righthander	9	Bill Hogg	1908
		Thad Tillotson	1967
Most consecutive losses, lefthander	11	George Mogridge	1916
Most innings pitched, righthander	454	Jack Chesbro	1904
Most innings pitched, lefthander	286.1	Herb Pennock	1924
Most saves, righthander	50	Mariano Rivera	2001
Most saves, lefthander	46	Dave Righetti	1986
Most games, righthander	78	Steve Karsay	2002
Most games, lefthander	79	Mike Stanton	2002
Most games started	51	Jack Chesbro	1904
Most complete games	48	Jack Chesbro	1904
Most innings pitched	454	Jack Chesbro	1904
Most strikeouts, righthander	239	Jack Chesbro	1904
Most strikeouts, lefthander	248	Ron Guidry	1978
Most bases on balls, righthander	177	Bob Turley	1955
Most bases on balls, lefthander	179	Tommy Byrne	1949
Most hits allowed	337	Jack Chesbro	1904
Most runs allowed	165	Russ Ford	1912
Most earned runs allowed	127	Sam Jones	1925
Most home runs allowed	40	Ralph Terry	1962
Most hit batsmen	26	Jack Warhop	1909
Most wild pitches	23	Tim Leary	1990

New York Yankees Team Records (continued)

Club Records, Fielding, Season

Highest fielding percentage	.986	1995
Lowest fielding percentage	.939	1912
Fewest errors	91	1996
Most errors	386	1912
Most errorless games	91	1964
Most consecutive errorless games	10	1977, 1993, 1995
Most putouts	4,520	1964
Fewest putouts	3,993	1935
Most assists	2,086	1904
Fewest assists	1,487	2000
Most double plays	214	1956
Fewest double plays	81	1912
Most consecutive games with double play turned	19 (27 double plays)	1992
Most passed balls	32	1913
Fewest passed balls	0	1931
Most chances accepted	6,584	1916
Fewest chances accepted	5,551	1935

[1] Most recent.
Note: Records in "fewest" categories are based on full seasons and do not include 1918, 1981, and 1994.
Source: Major League Baseball.

New York Mets Season Records, 1962–2007

	Wins	Losses	Winning Percentage	Games Behind	Attendance
1962	40	120	.250	60.5	922,530
1963	51	111	.315	48.0	1,080,108
1964	53	109	.327	40.0	1,732,597
1965	50	112	.309	47.0	1,768,389
1966	66	95	.410	28.5	1,932,693
1967	61	101	.377	40.5	1,565,492
1968	73	89	.451	24.0	1,781,657
1969	100	62	.617	—	2,175,373
1970	83	79	.512	6.0	2,697,479
1971	83	79	.512	14.0	2,266,680
1972	83	73	.532	13.5	2,134,185

New York Mets Season Records, 1962–2007 (continued)

	Wins	Losses	Winning Percentage	Games Behind	Attendance
1973	82	79	.509	—	1,912,390
1974	71	91	.438	17.0	1,722,209
1975	82	80	.506	10.5	1,730,566
1976	86	76	.531	15.0	1,468,754
1977	64	98	.395	37.0	1,066,825
1978	66	96	.407	24.0	1,007,328
1979	63	99	.389	35.0	788,905
1980	67	95	.414	24.0	1,192,073
1981	41	62	.398	18.5	704,244
1982	65	97	.401	27.0	1,323,036
1983	68	94	.420	22.0	1,112,774
1984	90	72	.556	6.5	1,842,695
1985	98	64	.605	3.0	2,761,601
1986	108	54	.667	—	2,767,601
1987	92	70	.568	3.0	3,034,129
1988	100	60	.625	—	3,055,445
1989	87	75	.537	6.0	2,918,710
1990	91	71	.562	4.0	2,732,745
1991	77	84	.478	20.5	2,284,484
1992	72	90	.444	24.0	1,779,534
1993	59	103	.364	38.0	1,873,183
1994	55	58	.487	18.5	1,151,471
1995	69	75	.479	21.0	1,273,183
1996	71	91	.438	25.0	1,588,323
1997	88	74	.543	13.0	1,766,174
1998	88	74	.543	18.0	2,287,942
1999	97	66	.595	6.5	2,726,008
2000	94	68	.580	1.0	2,820,530
2001	82	80	.506	6.0	2,658,330
2002	75	86	.466	26.5	2,804,838
2003	66	95	.410	34.5	2,205,323
2004	71	91	.438	25.0	2,318,322
2005	83	79	.512	7.0	2,829,930
2006	97	65	.599	—	3,340,386
2007	88	74	.543	1.0	3,853,949
Totals	3,496	3,816	.478		92,761,123

Source: Major League Baseball.

Managers of the New York Mets

		Wins	Losses	Winning Percentage
Casey Stengel	1962–1965	175	404	.302
Wes Westrum	1965–1967	142	237	.375
Salty Parker	1967	4	7	.364
Gil Hodges	1968–1971	339	309	.523
Yogi Berra	1972–1975	292	296	.497
Roy McMillan	1975	26	27	.491
Joe Frazier	1976–1977	101	106	.488
Joe Torre	1977–1981	286	420	.405
George Bamberger	1982–1983	81	127	.389
Frank Howard	1983	52	64	.448
Davey Johnson	1984–1990	595	417	.588
Bud Harrelson	1990–1991	145	129	.529
Mike Cubbage	1991	3	4	.429
Jeff Torborg	1992–1993	85	115	.425
Dallas Green	1993–1996	229	283	.447
Bobby Valentine	1996–2002	536	467	.534
Art Howe	2003–2004	137	186	.424
Willie Randolph	2005–	268	218	.551
Totals		3,496	3,816	.478

Source: Ultimate Mets Database.

New York Mets Team Records

Club Records, Batting

Most at-bats, game	89	11 September 1974	versus St. Louis (25 innings)
Most at-bats, game, 9 innings	48	17 April 1976	at Pittsburgh
Most runs, inning	10	12 June 1979	versus Cincinnati (6th)
		30 June 2000	versus Atlanta (8th)
Most runs, game	23	16 August 1987	at Chicago
Most runs, two consecutive games	34	12 June 1990	at Chicago (19)
		13 June 1990	at Chicago (15)
Most runs, doubleheader	24	13 June 1990	at Chicago
Most hits, game, 9 innings	23	26 May 1964	at Chicago
		29 April 2000	at Colorado
Most hits, extra innings	28	4 July 1985	at Atlanta (19 innings)
Most doubles	10	27 September 2001	at Montreal
Most triples	4 (2 times)	6 July 1979[1]	versus San Diego (12 innings)
Most consecutive home runs	3	28 April 1962	versus Philadelphia, 6th inning (Thomas, Neal, Hodges)
		18 May 1970	at Montreal, 8th inning (Marshall, Foy, Grote)
		20 July 1974	at San Diego, 5th inning (Theodore, Staub, Jones)
		27 July 1986	at Atlanta, 3rd inning (Carter, Strawberry, Mitchell)
		1 May 1988	at Cincinnati, 5th inning (Teufel, Hernandez, Strawberry)
		17 April 1989	versus Philadelphia, 3rd inning (Strawberry, McReynolds, Hernandez)
Most home runs	7	19 April 2005	at Philadelphia (Reyes 2, Diaz 2, Mientkiewicz, Piazza, Wright)
Most consecutive games with home run	21	16 July to 5 August 1996	
Most consecutive games without home run	17	27 August to 12 September 1980	
Most extra-base hits	13	24 August 2005	at Arizona
Most total bases	44	24 August 2005	at Arizona

Club Records, Batting (continued)

Most sacrifice hits	5 (2 times)	26 April 1995[1]	at Colorado (14 innings)
Most sacrifice hits, 9-inning game	3 (by many)	25 August 2000[1]	at Arizona
Most sacrifice flies	4	26 July 1967	at San Francisco
		23 September 1972	versus Philadelphia
		24 June 2005	at Yankees
Most times hit by pitch	3 (21 times)	15 September 2006[1]	at Pittsburgh
Most left on base	25	11 September 1974	versus St. Louis (25 innings)
Most left on base, 9-inning game	16	25 July 2001	at Florida
Most stolen bases	6	9 September 1963	at Philadelphia (Harkness 3, D. Smith 2, Sherry)
		4 August 1982	at Chicago (Brooks 2, Jorgensen, Backman, Stearns, Bailor)
		10 April 1991	versus Philadelphia (Herr, Johnson, Jeffries, Coleman 2, Boston)
Most walks	16	29 June 1962	at Los Angeles
Most strikeouts	22	31 May 1964	versus San Francisco (23 innings)
Most strikeouts, 9-inning game	19	15 September 1969	at St. Louis
Fewest runs allowed, both games of doubleheader	0	12 September 1969	at Pittsburgh
Most consecutive games without being shut out	110	12 September 1985– 17 July 1986	
Most times grounded into double play	5 (6 times)	6 August 2002[1]	at Milwaukee

Individual Records, Batting

Most at-bats	11	Dave Schneck	11 September 1974	versus St. Louis (25 innings)
Most runs scored	6	Edgardo Alfonzo	30 August 1999	at Houston
Most hits	6	Edgardo Alfonzo	30 August 1999	at Houston
Most doubles	3 (18 times)	Edgardo Alfonzo	18 April 2000[1]	versus Milwaukee
Most triples	3	Doug Flynn	5 August 1980	at Montreal
Most home runs	3	Jim Hickman	3 September 1965	at St. Louis
		Dave Kingman	4 June 1976	at Los Angeles
		Claudell Washington	22 June 1980	at Los Angeles
		Darryl Strawberry	5 August 1985	at Chicago
		Gary Carter	3 September 1985	at San Diego
		Edgardo Alfonzo	30 August 1999	at Houston

Individual Records, Batting (continued)

Most home runs, pitcher	2	Walt Terrell	6 August 1983	at Chicago
Most home runs, two consecutive games	5	Gary Carter	3–4 September 1985	
Most home runs, three consecutive games	6	Frank Thomas	1–3 August 1962	
Home run, first major league at-bat		Benny Ayala	27 August 1974	versus Houston
		Mike Fitzgerald	13 September 1983	at Philadelphia
		Kazuo Matsui	6 April 2004	at Atlanta
		Mike Jacobs	31 August 2005	versus Washington
Most home runs, month	13	Dave Kingman	1975 (July)	
		Gary Carter	1985 (September)	
Most consecutive games with home run	4	Larry Elliot	21–24 August 1964	
		Ron Swoboda	19–21 April 1968	
		Lee Mazzilli	1–4 July 1980	
		Dave Kingman	25–29 May 1981	
		Bobby Bonilla	19–23 August 1992	
		Mike Piazza	17–21 August 1999	
		Mike Piazza	13–16 August 1999	
		Edgardo Alfonzo	23–26 April 2001	
Most grand slams, pitcher	1	Carl Wiley	15 July 1963	versus Houston (off Ken Johnson)
		Jack Hamilton	20 May 1967	versus St. Louis (off Al Jackson)
Most runs batted in	8	Dave Kingman	4 June 1976	at Los Angeles
Most consecutive games with run batted in	15	Mike Piazza	14 June to 2 July 2000	
Most total bases	16	Edgardo Alfonzo	30 August 1999	versus Houston
Most stolen bases	4	Vince Coleman	26 June 1992	at St. Louis
		Vince Coleman	23 June 1993	versus St. Louis
		Roger Cedeño	14 May 1999	at Philadelphia
Most sacrifice hits	3	Sid Fernandez	24 July 1987	versus Houston (1st game)
Most sacrifice flies	2 (by many)	Jose Reyes[1]	24 June 2005	versus Yankees

Individual Records, Batting (continued)

Most strikeouts	5	Ron Swoboda	22 June 1969	versus St. Louis (1st game)
		Frank Taveras	1 May 1979	versus San Diego
		Dave Kingman	28 May 1982	versus Houston
		Ryan Thompson	29 September 1993	versus St. Louis
Most walks (16 innings)	5	Vince Coleman	10 August 1992	versus Pittsburgh
Most intentional walks	3	Todd Hundley	28 June 1997	at Pittsburgh
Most times grounded into double play	4	Joe Torre	21 July 1975	versus Houston

Club Records, Pitching

Most runs allowed, inning	11	18 July 1964	at St. Louis (8th inning)
		30 July 1969	versus Houston (9th inning, 1st game)
		1 April 1997	at San Diego (6th inning)
Most earned runs allowed	24	11 June 1985	at Philadelphia
Most hits allowed	27	11 June 1985	at Philadelphia
Most home runs allowed	7	11 June 1967	at Chicago
		8 September 1998	at Philadelphia
Most walks allowed	14	12 April 1986	at Philadelphia (13 innings)
Most walks allowed, 9-inning game	12	21 August 1998	versus St. Louis (1st game)
Most strikeouts	19	22 April 1970	versus San Diego
		6 October 1991	at Philadelphia
Most pitchers used	8	15 April 1968	at Houston (24 innings)
		7 September 1999	versus San Francisco
		28 September 1999	versus Atlanta
		8 September 2001	at Florida

Individual Records, Pitching

Most innings pitched	15	Al Jackson	14 August 1962	versus Philadelphia
		Rod Gardner	2 October 1965	versus Philadelphia
Most innings pitched without allowing a run	31.2	Jerry Koosman	19 August to 7 September 1973	
Most innings pitched without allowing a walk	47.2	Bret Saberhagen	10 May to 13 June 1994	
Most consecutive batters retired	25	Tom Seaver	9 July 1969	versus Chicago
Fewest hits allowed	1 (23 times)	Aaron Heilman	15 April 2005[1]	versus Florida
Most home runs allowed, consecutive innings	3	Pete Harnisch	1 April 1997	at San Diego

Individual Records, Pitching (continued)

Most home runs allowed, inning	4	Steve Trachsel	17 May 2001	versus San Diego
Most home runs allowed	5	Roger Craig	4 May 1963	versus San Francisco
Most strikeouts, inning	4	Derek Wallace	13 September 1996	versus Atlanta
Most strikeouts, game, righthander	19	Tom Seaver	22 April 1970	versus San Diego
		David Cone	6 October 1991	at Philadelphia
Most strikeouts, game, lefthander	16	Sid Fernandez	14 July 1989	at Atlanta
Most strikeouts, game, rookie righthander	16	Dwight Gooden	12 and 17 September 1984	versus Philadelphia
Most strikeouts, game, rookie lefthander	12	Jerry Koosman	21 July 1968	versus St. Louis
Most consecutive strikeouts	10	Tom Seaver	22 April 1970	versus San Diego
Most consecutive strikeouts to start a game	6	Pete Falcone	1 May 1980	versus Philadelphia
Most strikeouts, two consecutive games	32	Dwight Gooden	12 and 17 September 1984	
Most walks	10	Mike Torrez	21 July 1983	at Cincinnati

Club Records, Batting, Season

Most at-bats	5,618	1996
Most runs	853	1999
Fewest runs	473	1968
Most hits	1,553	1999
Fewest hits	1,168	1963
Most singles	1,087	1980
Most doubles	297	1999
Most triples	47	1996, 1978
Most home runs	198	2000
Fewest home runs	61	1980
Most grand slams	8	2000
Most runs batted in	814	1999
Most extra-base hits	513	1987
Most total bases	2,430	1987
Most sacrifice hits	108	1973
Most sacrifice flies	59	1997

Club Records, Batting, Season (continued)

Most times hit by pitch	65	2001
Most stolen bases	159	1987
Fewest stolen bases	27	1973
Most walks	717	1999
Most strikeouts	1,203	1968
Fewest strikeouts	735	1974
Most times shut out	30	1963
Most times grounded into double play	149	1999
Highest batting average	.279	1999
Lowest batting average	.219	1963
Most pinch-hit at-bats	327	1965
Most pinch hits	75	1993
Highest pinch-hitting average	.363	1999
Lowest pinch-hitting average	.153	1968

Individual Records, Batting, Season

Most at-bats	682	Lance Johnson	1996
Most at-bats, rookie	537	Lee Mazzilli	1977
Most runs scored	123	Edgardo Alfonzo	1999
Most runs scored, rookie	74	Cleon Jones	1966
Most hits	227	Lance Johnson	1996
Most hits, rookie	145	Ron Hunt	1963
Most consecutive games hitting safely, righthander	24	Hubie Brooks	1984
		Mike Piazza	1999
Most consecutive games hitting safely, lefthander	23	John Olerud	1998
Most consecutive games hitting safely, rookie	23	Mike Vail	1975
Most doubles	44	Bernard Gilkey	1996
Most doubles, rookie	28	Ron Hunt	1963
		Gregg Jeffries	1989
Most triples	21	Lance Johnson	1996
Most triples, rookie	8	Mookie Wilson	1981
Most home runs, righthander	40	Mike Piazza	1999
Most home runs, lefthander	39	Darryl Strawberry	1987, 1988
Most home runs, switch hitter	41	Todd Hundley	1996
Most home runs, rookie	26	Darryl Strawberry	1983
Most home runs at home	24	Darryl Strawberry	1990
Most home runs on the road	23	Howard Johnson	1987

Individual Records, Batting, Season (continued)

Most grand slams	3	John Milner	1976
		Robin Ventura	1999
		Mike Piazza	2000
Most runs batted in, righthander	124	Mike Piazza	1999
Most runs batted in, lefthander	120	Robin Ventura	1999
Most runs batted in, rookie	74	Darryl Strawberry	1983
Most total bases, righthander	321	Bernard Gilkey	1996
Most total bases, lefthander	327	Lance Johnson	1996
Most total bases, switch hitter	319	Howard Johnson	1989
Most stolen bases	66	Roger Cedeño	1999
Most stolen bases, rookie	24	Mookie Wilson	1981
Most time caught stealing	21	Lenny Randle	1981
Most sacrifice hits	24	Felix Millan	1974
Most sacrifice flies	15	Gary Carter	1986
		Howard Johnson	1991
Most strikeouts, righthander	156	Tommie Agee	1970
		Dave Kingman	1982
Most strikeouts, lefthander	145	Mo Vaughn	2002
Fewest strikeouts	14	Felix Millan	1974
Most walks	125	John Olerud	1999
Most times hit by pitch	13	Ron Hunt	1963
		John Olerud	1997
Most times grounded into double play	27	Mike Piazza	1999
Fewest times grounded into double play	4	Howard Johnson	1991
Highest batting average, righthander	.340	Cleon Jones	1969
Highest batting average, lefthander	.354	John Olerud	1998
Highest batting average, switch hitter	.304	Lenny Randle	1977
Highest batting average, rookie	.275	Cleon Jones	1966
Highest slugging average	.614	Mike Piazza	2000
Highest slugging average, rookie	.512	Darryl Strawberry	1983
Most extra-base hits	80	Howard Johnson	1989
Most extra-base hits, rookie	48	Darryl Strawberry	1983
Most pinch-hit at-bats	84	Lenny Harris	2001
Most pinch hits	24	Rusty Staub	1983
Most consecutive pinch hits	8	Rusty Staub	11–26 June 1983
Most pinch-hit appearances	95	Lenny Harris	2001

Individual Records, Batting, Season (continued)

Most pinch-hit home runs	4	Danny Heep	1983
		Mark Carreon	1989
Most pinch-hit runs batted in	25	Rusty Staub	1983

Club Records, Pitching, Season

Most complete games	53	1976
Fewest complete games	5	1999
Most shutouts	28	1969
Fewest shutouts	4	1962
Most consecutive shutouts	4	24–28 September 1969
Most consecutive 1–0 shutouts won	9	1969
Most consecutive shutout innings pitched	42	23–28 September 1969
Most runs allowed	948	1962
Fewest runs allowed	499	1968
Most earned runs allowed	801	1962
Fewest earned runs allowed	449	1968
Most hits allowed	1,577	1962
Fewest hits allowed	1,217	1969
Most home runs allowed	192	1962
Fewest home runs allowed	78	1968
Most walks allowed	617	1999
Fewest walks allowed	404	1988
Most strikeouts	1,217	1990
Fewest strikeouts	717	1964, 1983
Lowest earned run average	2.72	1968
Highest earned run average	5.04	1962
Most saves	51	1987
Fewest saves	14	1974
Most pitchers used	27	1967
Fewest pitchers used	13	1976, 1971
Most pitchers with 10 wins or more	6	1968

[1] Most recent.
Source: Major League Baseball.

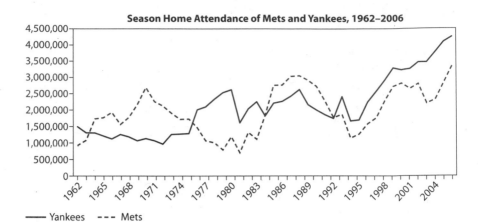

Season Home Attendance of Mets and Yankees, 1962–2006

—— Yankees --- Mets

Source: Major League Baseball.

New York (Baseball) Giants Season Records, 1883–1957

	Wins	Losses	Winning Percentage	Games Behind	Attendance
1884	62	50	.554	22.0	105,000
1885	85	27	.759	2.0	185,000
1886	75	44	.630	12.5	189,000
1887	68	55	.553	10.5	270,945
1888	84	47	.641	—	305,455
1889	83	43	.659	—	201,989
1890	63	68	.481	24.0	60,667
1891	71	61	.538	13.0	210,568
1892	71	80	.470	31.5	130,566
1893	68	64	.515	19.5	290,000
1894	88	44	.667	3.0	387,000
1895	66	65	.504	21.5	240,000
1896	64	67	.489	27.0	274,000
1897	83	48	.634	9.5	390,340
1898	77	73	.513	25.5	206,700
1899	60	90	.400	42.0	121,384
1900	60	78	.435	23.0	175,000
1901	52	85	.380	37.0	297,650

New York (Baseball) Giants Season Records, 1883–1957 (continued)

	Wins	Losses	Winning Percentage	Games Behind	Attendance
1902	48	88	.353	53.5	302,875
1903	84	55	.604	6.5	579,530
1904	106	47	.693	—	609,826
1905	105	48	.686	—	552,700
1906	96	56	.632	20.0	402,850
1907	82	71	.536	25.5	538,350
1908	98	56	.636	1.0	910,000
1909	92	61	.601	18.5	783,700
1910	91	63	.591	13.0	511,785
1911	99	54	.647	—	675,000
1912	103	48	.682	—	638,000
1913	101	51	.664	—	630,000
1914	84	70	.545	10.5	364,313
1915	69	83	.454	21.0	391,850
1916	86	66	.566	7.0	552,056
1917	98	56	.636	—	500,264
1918	71	53	.573	10.5	256,618
1919	87	53	.621	9.0	708,857
1920	86	68	.558	7.0	929,609
1921	94	59	.614	—	973,477
1922	93	61	.604	—	945,809
1923	95	58	.621	—	820,780
1924	93	60	.608	—	844,068
1925	86	66	.566	8.5	778,993
1926	74	77	.490	13.5	700,362
1927	92	62	.597	2.0	858,190
1928	93	61	.604	2.0	916,191
1929	84	67	.556	13.5	868,806
1930	87	67	.565	5.0	868,714
1931	87	65	.572	13.0	812,163
1932	72	82	.468	18.0	484,868
1933	91	61	.599	—	604,471
1934	93	60	.608	2.0	730,851
1935	91	62	.595	8.5	748,748
1936	92	62	.597	—	837,952
1937	95	57	.625	—	926,887

New York (Baseball) Giants Season Records, 1883–1957 (continued)

	Wins	Losses	Winning Percentage	Games Behind	Attendance
1938	83	67	.553	5.0	799,633
1939	77	74	.510	18.5	702,457
1940	72	80	.474	27.5	747,852
1941	74	79	.484	25.5	763,098
1942	85	67	.559	20.0	779,621
1943	55	98	.359	49.5	466,095
1944	67	87	.435	38.0	674,483
1945	78	74	.513	19.0	1,016,468
1946	61	93	.396	36.0	1,219,873
1947	81	73	.526	13.0	1,600,793
1948	78	76	.506	13.5	1,459,269
1949	73	81	.474	24.0	1,218,446
1950	86	68	.558	5.0	1,008,878
1951	98	59	.624	—	1,059,539
1952	92	62	.597	4.5	984,940
1953	70	84	.455	35.0	811,518
1954	97	57	.630	—	1,155,067
1955	80	74	.519	18.5	824,112
1956	67	87	.435	26.0	629,179
1957	69	85	.448	26.0	653,923
Totals	6,021	4,848	.554		47,176,021

Note: Team was known as New York Gothams, 1883–1885.
Source: Major League Baseball.

Brooklyn Dodgers Season Records, 1884–1957

	Wins	Losses	Winning Percentage	Games Behind	Attendance
1884	40	64	.385	33.5	65,000
1885	53	59	.473	26.0	85,000
1886	76	61	.555	16.0	185,000
1887	60	74	.448	34.5	273,000
1888	88	52	.629	6.5	245,000
1889	93	44	.679	—	353,690
1890	86	43	.667	—	121,412
1891	61	76	.445	25.5	181,477
1892	95	59	.617	9.0	183,727
1893	65	63	.508	20.5	235,000
1894	70	61	.534	20.5	214,000
1895	71	60	.542	16.5	230,000
1896	58	73	.443	33.0	201,000
1897	61	71	.462	32.0	220,831
1898	54	91	.372	46.0	122,514
1899	101	47	.682	—	269,641
1900	82	54	.603	—	170,000
1901	79	57	.581	9.5	198,200
1902	75	63	.543	27.5	199,868
1903	70	66	.515	19.0	224,670
1904	56	97	.366	50.0	214,600
1905	48	104	.316	56.5	227,924
1906	66	86	.434	50.0	277,400
1907	65	83	.439	40.0	312,500
1908	53	101	.344	46.0	275,600
1909	55	98	.359	55.5	321,300
1910	64	90	.416	40.0	279,321
1911	64	86	.427	33.5	269,000
1912	58	95	.379	46.0	243,000
1913	65	84	.436	34.5	347,000
1914	75	79	.487	19.5	122,671
1915	80	72	.526	10.0	297,766
1916	94	60	.610	—	447,747
1917	70	81	.464	26.5	221,619
1918	57	69	.452	25.5	83,831
1919	69	71	.493	27.0	360,721

Brooklyn Dodgers Season Records, 1884–1957 (continued)

	Wins	Losses	Winning Percentage	Games Behind	Attendance
1920	93	61	.604	—	808,722
1921	77	75	.507	16.5	613,245
1922	76	78	.494	17.0	498,865
1923	76	78	.494	19.5	564,666
1924	92	62	.597	1.5	818,883
1925	68	85	.444	27.0	659,435
1926	71	82	.464	17.5	650,819
1927	65	88	.425	28.5	637,230
1928	77	76	.503	17.5	664,863
1929	70	83	.458	28.5	731,886
1930	86	68	.558	6.0	1,097,329
1931	79	73	.520	21.0	753,133
1932	81	73	.526	9.0	681,827
1933	65	88	.425	26.5	526,815
1934	71	81	.467	23.5	434,188
1935	70	83	.458	29.5	470,517
1936	67	87	.435	25.0	489,618
1937	62	91	.405	33.5	482,481
1938	69	80	.463	18.5	663,087
1939	84	69	.549	12.5	955,668
1940	88	65	.575	12.0	975,978
1941	100	54	.649	—	1,214,910
1942	104	50	.675	2.0	1,037,765
1943	81	72	.529	23.5	661,739
1944	63	91	.409	42.0	605,905
1945	87	67	.565	11.0	1,059,220
1946	96	60	.615	2.0	1,796,824
1947	94	60	.610	—	1,807,526
1948	84	70	.545	7.5	1,398,967
1949	97	57	.630	—	1,633,747

Brooklyn Dodgers Season Records, 1884–1957 (continued)

	Wins	Losses	Winning Percentage	Games Behind	Attendance
1950	89	65	.578	2.0	1,185,896
1951	97	60	.618	1.0	1,282,628
1952	96	57	.627	—	1,088,704
1953	105	49	.682	—	1,163,419
1954	92	62	.597	5.0	1,020,531
1955	98	55	.641	—	1,033,589
1956	93	61	.604	—	1,213,562
1957	84	70	.545	11.0	1,028,258
Totals	5,624	5,280	.516		42,693,475

Note: Team played in American Association 1884–1889, in National League 1890–1957.
Source: Major League Baseball.

Postseason Records of New York Baseball Teams

Yankees

1921	World Series	New York Giants	Lost, 5–3
1922	World Series	New York Giants	Lost, 4–0–1
1923	World Series	New York Giants	Won, 4–2
1926	World Series	St. Louis Cardinals	Lost, 4–3
1927	World Series	Pittsburgh Pirates	Won, 4–0
1928	World Series	St. Louis Cardinals	Won, 4–0
1932	World Series	Chicago Cubs	Won, 4–0
1936	World Series	New York Giants	Won, 4–2
1937	World Series	New York Giants	Won, 4–1
1938	World Series	Chicago Cubs	Won, 4–0
1939	World Series	Cincinnati Reds	Won, 4–0
1941	World Series	Brooklyn Dodgers	Won, 4–1

Yankees (continued)

1942	World Series	St. Louis Cardinals	Lost, 4–1
1943	World Series	St. Louis Cardinals	Won, 4–1
1947	World Series	Brooklyn Dodgers	Won, 4–3
1949	World Series	Brooklyn Dodgers	Won, 4–1
1950	World Series	Philadelphia Phillies	Won, 4–0
1951	World Series	New York Giants	Won, 4–2
1952	World Series	Brooklyn Dodgers	Won, 4–3
1953	World Series	Brooklyn Dodgers	Won, 4–2
1955	World Series	Brooklyn Dodgers	Lost, 4–3
1956	World Series	Brooklyn Dodgers	Won, 4–3
1957	World Series	Milwaukee Braves	Lost, 4–3
1958	World Series	Milwaukee Braves	Won, 4–3
1960	World Series	Pittsburgh Pirates	Lost, 4–3
1961	World Series	Cincinnati Reds	Won, 4–1
1962	World Series	San Francisco Giants	Won, 4–3
1963	World Series	Los Angeles Dodgers	Lost, 0–4
1964	World Series	St. Louis Cardinals	Lost, 4–3
1976	AL Championship Series	Kansas City Royals	Won, 3–2
	World Series	Cincinnati Reds	Lost, 4–0
1977	AL Championship Series	Kansas City Royals	Won, 3–2
	World Series	Los Angeles Dodgers	Won, 4–2
1978	AL Championship Series	Kansas City Royals	Won, 3–1
	World Series	Los Angeles Dodgers	Won, 4–2
1980	AL Championship Series	Kansas City Royals	Lost, 3–0
1981	Eastern Division Series	Milwaukee Brewers	Won, 3–2
	AL Championship Series	Oakland Athletics	Won, 3–0
	World Series	Los Angeles Dodgers	Lost, 4–2
1995	AL Division Series	Seattle Mariners	Lost, 3–2
1996	AL Division Series	Texas Rangers	Won, 3–1
	AL Championship Series	Baltimore Orioles	Won, 4–1
	World Series	Atlanta Braves	Won, 4–2
1997	AL Division Series	Cleveland Indians	Lost, 3–2
1998	AL Division Series	Texas Rangers	Won, 3–0
	AL Championship Series	Cleveland Indians	Won, 4–2
	World Series	San Diego Padres	Won, 4–0
1999	AL Division Series	Texas Rangers	Won, 3–0
	AL Championship Series	Boston Red Sox	Won, 4–1
	World Series	Atlanta Braves	Won, 4–0

Postseason Records of New York Baseball Teams (continued)

Yankees (continued)

Year	Series	Opponent	Result
2000	AL Division Series	Oakland A's	Won, 3–2
	AL Championship Series	Seattle Mariners	Won, 4–2
	World Series	New York Mets	Won, 4–1
2001	AL Division Series	Oakland A's	Won, 3–2
	AL Championship Series	Seattle Mariners	Won, 4–1
	World Series	Arizona Diamondbacks	Lost, 4–3
2002	AL Division Series	Anaheim Angels	Lost, 3–1
2003	AL Division Series	Minnesota Twins	Won, 3–1
	AL Championship Series	Boston Red Sox	Won, 4–3
	World Series	Florida Marlins	Lost, 4–2
2004	AL Division Series	Minnesota Twins	Won, 3–1
	AL Championship Series	Boston Red Sox	Lost, 3–4
2005	AL Division Series	Los Angeles Angels of Anaheim	Lost, 3–2
2006	AL Division Series	Detroit Tigers	Lost, 3–1

Dodgers

Year	Series	Opponent	Result
1916	World Series	Boston Red Sox	Lost, 4–1
1920	World Series	Cleveland Indians	Lost, 5–2
1941	World Series	New York Yankees	Lost, 4–1
1947	World Series	New York Yankees	Lost, 4–3
1949	World Series	New York Yankees	Lost, 4–1
1952	World Series	New York Yankees	Lost, 4–3
1953	World Series	New York Yankees	Lost, 4–2
1955	World Series	New York Yankees	Won, 4–3
1956	World Series	New York Yankees	Lost, 4–3

Note: Brooklyn also won championships in 1858, 1864, and 1866 before becoming a professional franchise. Brooklyn was the American Association champion in 1889 and the National League champion in 1890, 1899, and 1900, before there was a World Series.

Giants

Year	Series	Opponent	Result
1905	World Series	Philadelphia Phillies	Won, 4–1
1911	World Series	Philadelphia Phillies	Lost, 4–2
1912	World Series	Boston Red Sox	Lost, 4–3–1
1913	World Series	Philadelphia Phillies	Lost, 4–1
1917	World Series	Chicago Cubs	Lost, 4–2
1921	World Series	New York Yankees	Won, 5–3
1922	World Series	New York Yankees	Won, 4–0–1
1923	World Series	New York Yankees	Lost, 4–2

Postseason Records of New York Baseball Teams (continued)

Giants (continued)

Year	Series	Opponent	Result
1924	World Series	Washington Senators	Lost, 4–3
1933	World Series	Washington Senators	Won, 4–1
1936	World Series	New York Yankees	Lost, 4–2
1937	World Series	New York Yankees	Lost, 4–1
1951	World Series	New York Yankees	Lost, 4–2
1954	World Series	Cleveland Indians	Won, 4–0

Mets

Year	Series	Opponent	Result
1969	NL Championship Series	Atlanta Braves	Won, 3–0
	World Series	Baltimore Orioles	Won, 4–1
1973	NL Championship Series	Cincinnati Reds	Won, 3–2
	World Series	Oakland A's	Lost, 4–3
1986	NL Championship Series	Houston Astros	Won, 4–2
	World Series	Boston Red Sox	Won, 4–3
1988	NL Championship Series	Los Angeles Dodgers	Lost, 4–3
1999	NL Division Series	Arizona Diamondbacks	Won, 3–1
	NL Championship Series	Atlanta Braves	Lost, 4–2
2000	NL Division Series	San Francisco Giants	Won, 3–1
	NL Championship Series	St. Louis Cardinals	Won, 4–1
	World Series	New York Yankees	Lost, 4–1
2006	NL Division Series	Los Angeles Dodgers	Won, 3–0
	NL Championship Series	St. Louis Cardinals	Lost, 4–3

Source: Major League Baseball.

New York (Football) Giants Season Records, 1925–2007

	Wins	Losses	Ties	Finish		Wins	Losses	Ties	Finish
1925	8	4	0	4th	1932	4	6	2	5th
1926	8	4	1	6th	1933	11	3	0	1st
1927	11	1	1	1st	1934	8	5	0	1st
1928	4	7	2	6th	1935	9	3	0	1st
1929	13	1	1	2nd	1936	5	6	1	3rd
1930	13	4	0	2nd	1937	6	3	2	2nd
1931	7	6	1	5th	1938	8	2	1	1st

New York (Football) Giants Season Records, 1925–2007 (continued)

	Wins	Losses	Ties	Finish		Wins	Losses	Ties	Finish
1939	9	1	1	1st	1974	2	12	0	5th
1940	6	4	1	3rd	1975	5	9	0	4th
1941	8	3	0	1st	1976	3	11	0	5th
1942	5	5	1	3rd	1977	5	9	0	4th
1943	6	3	1	2nd	1978	6	10	0	4th
1944	8	1	1	1st	1979	6	10	0	4th
1945	3	6	1	3rd	1980	4	12	0	5th
1946	7	3	1	1st	1981	9	7	0	3rd
1947	2	8	2	5th	1982	4	5	0	8th
1948	4	8	0	3rd	1983	3	12	1	5th
1949	6	6	0	3rd	1984	9	7	0	2nd
1950	10	2	0	2nd	1985	10	6	0	2nd
1951	9	2	1	2nd	1986	14	2	0	1st
1952	7	5	0	2nd	1987	6	9	0	5th
1953	3	9	0	5th	1988	10	6	0	2nd
1954	7	5	0	3rd	1989	12	4	0	1st
1955	6	5	1	3rd	1990	13	3	0	1st
1956	8	3	1	1st	1991	8	8	0	4th
1957	7	5	0	2nd	1992	6	10	0	4th
1958	9	3	0	1st	1993	11	5	0	2nd
1959	10	2	0	1st	1994	9	7	0	2nd
1960	6	4	2	3rd	1995	5	11	0	4th
1961	10	3	1	1st	1996	6	10	0	5th
1962	12	2	0	1st	1997	10	5	1	1st
1963	11	3	0	1st	1998	8	8	0	3rd
1964	2	10	2	7th	1999	7	9	0	3rd
1965	7	7	0	2nd	2000	12	4	0	1st
1966	1	12	1	8th	2001	7	9	0	3rd
1967	7	7	0	2nd	2002	10	6	0	2nd
1968	7	7	0	2nd	2003	4	12	0	4th
1969	6	8	0	2nd	2004	6	10	0	2nd
1970	9	5	0	2nd	2005	11	5	0	1st
1971	4	10	0	5th	2006	8	8	0	3rd
1972	8	6	0	3rd	2007	10	6	0	2nd
1973	2	11	1	5th	Totals	606	506	33	

Super Bowl Record

1987	W, Denver Broncos, 39–20
1991	W, Buffalo Bills, 20–19
2001	L, Baltimore Ravens, 34–7
2008	W, New England Patriots, 17–14

Source: CBS Sportsline.

Head Coaches of the New York (Football) Giants

		Wins	Losses	Ties	Winning Percentage
Robert Folwell	1925	8	4	0	.667
Joe Alexander	1926	8	4	1	.667
Earl Potteiger	1927–1928	15	8	3	.635
LeRoy Andrews	1929–1930[1]	24	5	1	.817
Benny Friedman and Steve Owen	1930	2	0	0	1.000
Steve Owen	1930–1953	151	100	17	.602
Jim Lee Howell	1954–1960	53	27	4	.655
Allie Sherman	1961–1968	57	51	4	.527
Alex Webster	1969–1973	29	40	1	.421
Bill Arnsparger	1974–1976[2]	7	28	0	.200
John McVay	1976–1978	14	23	0	.378
Ray Perkins	1979–1982	23	34	0	.404
Bill Parcells	1983–1990	77	49	1	.610
Ray Handley	1991–1992	14	18	0	.438
Dan Reeves	1993–1996	31	33	0	.484
Jim Fassel	1997–2003	58	53	1	.513
Tom Coughlin	2004–	35	29	0	.547
Totals		606	506	33	.545

[1] Replaced after fifteen games in 1930.
[2] Replaced after seven games in 1976.
Source: New York Giants 2006 Information Guide.

New York (Football) Giants Team Records

Individual Records, Single Play

Longest field goal	56 yards	Ali Haji-Sheikh	7 November 1983	at Detroit
Longest run from scrimmage	95 yards	Tiki Barber	31 December 2005	at Oakland
Longest punt	90 yards	Rodney Williams	10 September 2001	at Denver
Longest punt return	87 yards	Amani Toomer	1 September 1996	versus Buffalo
Longest kickoff return	100 yards	Clarence Childs	6 December 1964	versus Minnesota
Longest fumble return	87 yards	Keith Hamilton	10 September 1995	at Kansas City
Longest gain by interception	102 yards	Erich Barnes	15 October 1961	at Dallas
Longest kickoff return	100 yards	Clarence Childs	6 December 1964	versus Minnesota

Individual Records, Game

Most points	24	Rodney Hampton	24 September 1995	versus New Orleans
Most touchdowns	4	Ron Johnson	2 October 1972	at Philadelphia
		Earnest Gray	7 September 1980	at St. Louis
		Rodney Hampton	24 September 1995	versus New Orleans
Most points after touchdown	8	Pete Gogolak	26 November 1972	versus Philadelphia
Most field goals	6	Joe Danelo	18 October 1981	at Seattle
Most rushing attempts	43	Butch Woolfolk	20 November 1983	at Philadelphia
Most yards gained, rushing	220	Tiki Barber	17 December 2005	versus Kansas City
Highest average gain, rushing (at least 10 attempts)	13.3 yards	Frank Reagan	1 December 1946	versus Rams
Most rushing touchdowns	4	Rodney Hampton	24 September 1995	versus New Orleans
Most all-purpose yards	279	Joe Scott	14 November 1948	versus L.A. Rams
Most passes attempted	62	Phil Simms	13 October 1985	at Cincinnati
Most passes completed	40	Phil Simms	13 October 1985	at Cincinnati
Highest completion percentage (at least 20 attempts)	84.62 (22 of 26)	Kerry Collins	15 September 2002	at St. Louis
Most passing yards	513	Phil Simms	13 October 1985	at Cincinnati
Most touchdown passes	7	Y. A. Tittle	28 October 1962	versus Washington
Most pass attempts without interception	51	Scott Brunner	26 December 1982	versus St. Louis
Most passes had intercepted	5	Jeff Rutledge	22 November 1987	at New Orleans
Most pass receptions	13	Tiki Barber	2 January 2000	at Dallas
Most yards gained, passing	269	Del Shafner	28 October 1962	versus Washington

Individual Records, Game (continued)

Highest average gain, passing (at least 4 attempts)	50.3	Gene Roberts	23 October 1949	versus Chicago Bears
Most interceptions by	3	18 times, last by Terry Kinard	20 September 1987	versus Dallas
Most yards gained by interception	109	Ward Cuff	13 September 1941	at Philadelphia
Most punts	14	Carl Kinscherf	7 November 1943	at Detroit
Most punting yards	583	Carl Kinscherf	7 November 1943	at Detroit
Highest average, punting (minimum 4 punts)	55.4 yards	Brad Maynard	1 October 2000	at Tennessee
Most punt returns	9	Phil McConkey	6 December 1987	versus Philadelphia
Most fair catches	5	Amani Toomer	8 September 1996	at Dallas
Most punt return yards	147	Emlen Tunnell	14 October 1951	versus Chicago Cardinals
Highest average punt return (minimum 3 returns)	36.8 yards	Emlen Tunnell	14 October 1951	versus Chicago Cardinals
Most kickoff returns	8	Willie Ponder	18 December 2004	versus Pittsburgh
Most kickoff return yards	259	Willie Ponder	18 December 2004	versus Pittsburgh
Highest average kickoff return (minimum 3 returns)	51.8	Joe Scott	14 November 1948	versus Rams
Most fumbles	5	Charlie Conerly	1 December 1957	versus San Francisco
Most own fumbles recovered	3	Tiki Barber	29 October 2000	versus Philadelphia
Most opponents' fumbles recovered	2	Often, last by Michael Strahan	26 September 2004	versus Cleveland
Most sacks	4.5	Pepper Johnson	24 November 1991	at Tampa Bay

Individual Records, Season

Most points	148 (43 points after touchdown, 35 field goals)	Jay Feely	2005
Most touchdowns	21	Joe Morris	1985
Most points after touchdown	52	Don Chandler	1963
Most points after touchdown with no misses	46	Pat Summerall	1961
Most points after touchdown attempted	56	Don Chandler	1963

New York (Football) Giants Team Records (continued)

Individual Records, Season (continued)

Most field goals	35	Jay Feely	2005
Most field goals attempted	42	Jay Feely	2005
Highest field-goal percentage (minimum 14 attempts)	88.9 (24 of 27)	Brad Daluiso	1996
Most field goals, 50 or more yards	3	Jay Feely	2005
Most rushing attempts	357	Tiki Barber	2005
Most rushing yards gained	1,860	Tiki Barber	2005
Most games 100 yards or more rushing	9	Tiki Barber	2004
Highest average gain, rushing (qualifiers)	5.21 yards (1,860 yards, 357 attempts)	Tiki Barber	2005
	5.21 yards (865 yards, 166 attempts)	Tiki Barber	2001
Most rushing touchdowns	21	Joe Morris	1985
Most all-purpose yards	2,390	Tiki Barber	2005
Most passes attempted	568	Kerry Collins	2001
Most passes completed	335	Kerry Collins	2002
Highest completion percentage (qualifiers)	62.82 (174 of 277)	Kurt Warner	2004
Most passing yards	4,073	Kerry Collins	2002
Most games, 300 yards or more passing	5	Kerry Collins	2001
Most touchdown passes	36	Y. A. Tittle	1963
Lowest percentage passes had intercepted	1.3 (4 in 311 attempts)	Phil Simms	1990
Most passes had intercepted	25	Charlie Connerly	1953
Most pass receptions	82	Amani Toomer	2002
Most yards gained, passing	1,343	Amani Toomer	2002
Highest average gain (qualifiers)	24.7 yards (1,209 yards, 49 receptions)	Homer Jones	1967
Most passing touchdowns	13	Homer Jones	1967
Most interceptions by	11	Jimmy Patton	1958
Most yards gained by interception	251	Dick Lynch	1963
Most touchdowns by interception	3	Dick Lynch	1963
Most punts	111	Brad Maynard	1997
Most punting yards	4,566	Brad Maynard	1998
Highest average, punting (minimum 35 punts)	46.6	Don Chandler	1959
Most punt returns	53	Phil McConkey	1985
Most fair catches	25	Phil McConkey	1988
Most punt return yards	582	David Meggett	1989
Highest average return (qualifiers)	16.6	Amani Toomer	1996

Individual Records, Season (continued)

Most touchdowns, punt returns	3	Emlen Tunnell	1951
Most kickoff returns	55	Brian Mitchell	2003
Most kickoff return yards	1,117	Brian Mitchell	2003
Highest average kickoff return (qualifiers)	31.6	John Salscheider	1949
Most fumbles	23	Kerry Collins	2003
Most own fumbles recovered	7	Kerry Collins	2001
Most opponents' fumbles recovered	5	Ernie Jones	1978
Most sacks	22.5	Michael Strahan	2001

Individual Records, Career

Most seasons played	15	Phil Simms
Most games played	207	Howard Cross
Most points	646	Pete Gogolak
Most touchdowns	78	Frank Gifford
Most points after touchdown attempted	277	Pete Gogolak
Most points after touchdown	268	Pete Gogolak
Most field goals attempted	219	Pete Gogolak
Most field goals	126	Pete Gogolak
Highest field-goal percentage (minimum 50 attempts)	76.9	Brad Daluiso
Most field goals, 50 or more yards	9	Joe Danelo
Most safeties	3	Jim Katcavage
Most rushing attempts	1,890	Tiki Barber
Most rushing yards gained	8,787	Tiki Barber
Most games 100 yards or more rushing	30	Tiki Barber
Most rushing touchdowns	50	Tiki Barber
Most all-purpose yards	15,232	Tiki Barber
Most passes attempted	4,647	Phil Simms
Most passes completed	2,576	Phil Simms
Highest completion percentage (minimum 1,000 attempts)	58.51 (1,447 of 2,473)	Kerry Collins
Most passing yards	33,462	Phil Simms
Most games, 300 yards or more passing	21	Phil Simms
Most touchdown passes	199	Phil Simms
Lowest percentage passes had intercepted (minimum 100 attempts)	2.8 (70 interceptions, 2,473 attempts)	Kerry Collins
Most passes had intercepted	25	Charlie Conerly
Most pass receptions	529	Amani Toomer
Most passing yards gained	7,797	Amani Toomer

New York (Football) Giants Team Records (continued)

Individual Records, Career (continued)

Highest average gain, passing (minimum 200)	22.6 yards	Homer Jones
Most touchdowns, pass receptions	48	Kyle Rote
Most interceptions by	74	Emlen Tunnell
Most yards gained by interception	1,240	Emlen Tunnell
Most touchdowns, interceptions	4	Emlen Tunnell
		Dick Lynch
		Jason Sehorn
Most punts	931	Dave Jennings
Most punting yards	38,792	Dave Jennings
Highest punting average (minimum 150 punts)	43.8	Don Chandler
Most punt returns	261	Emlen Tunnell
Most fair catches	84	Phil McConkey
Most punt return yards	2,230	David Meggett
Highest average punt return (minimum 30 returns)	12.1	Ward Cuff
Most touchdowns, punt returns	6	David Meggett
Most kickoff returns	146	David Meggett
Most kickoff return yards	3,163	Clarence Childs
Highest average kickoff return (minimum 40 returns)	27.2	Rocky Thompson
Most fumbles	18	Phil Simms
Most own fumbles recovered	28	Phil Simms
Most opponents' fumbles recovered	19	Jim Katcavage
Most sacks	132.5	Lawrence Taylor

Individual Records, Streaks

Most consecutive games scoring	61	Pete Gogolak
Most consecutive games scoring touchdowns	10	Frank Gifford
Most consecutive points after touchdown	133	Pete Gogolak
Most consecutive games kicking field goals	18	Joe Danelo
Most consecutive games rushing for touchdowns	7	Bill Paschal
Most consecutive passes completed	13	Kerry Collins
Most consecutive games with touchdown passes	15	Y. A. Tittle
Most consecutive games with pass receptions	98	Amani Toomer
Most consecutive games with touchdown reception	7	Kyle Rote
Most consecutive games with interceptions by	7	Tom Landry

Team Records, Game

Most points	62	26 November 1972	versus Philadelphia
Most touchdowns	8	26 November 1972	versus Philadelphia
Most points after touchdown	8	26 November 1972	versus Philadelphia
Most field goals	6	18 October 1981	at Seattle
Most field goals attempted	6	30 October 2005	versus Washington
Most safeties	2	17 September 1950	at Pittsburgh
		5 November 1961	versus Washington
Most first downs	34	13 October 1985	at Cincinnati
Fewest first downs	0	1 October 1933	at Green Bay
		27 September 1942	at Washington
Most first downs rushing	19	19 November 1950	at Baltimore
Most first downs passing	29	13 October 1985	at Cincinnati
Most first downs by penalty	6	5 October 1957	at Philadelphia
		27 November 1966	at Washington
		11 November 1979	versus Atlanta
		14 September 1997	versus Baltimore
		26 October 1997	versus Cincinnati
Most rushing attempts	61	3 October 1937	at Philadelphia
Most rushing yards	423	19 November 1950	at Baltimore
Most touchdowns rushing	6	19 November 1950	at Baltimore
Most passes completed	40	13 October 1985	at Cincinnati
Most passes attempted	62	13 October 1985	at Cincinnati
Most net passing yards gained	505	28 October 1962	versus Washington
Most touchdowns passing	7	28 October 1962	versus Washington
Most passes had intercepted	7	30 November 1952	versus Washington
Most punts	15	17 November 1935	at Chicago Bears
Most yards punting	607	23 September 1934	at Detroit
Most punt returns	9	6 December 1987	at Philadelphia
Most fair catches	6	31 October 1971	versus Minnesota
Most yards gained, punt returns	149	14 October 1951	versus Chicago Cardinals
Most kickoff returns	12	27 November 1966	at Washington
Most yards gained, kickoff returns	274	27 November 1966	at Washington
Most fumbles	9	20 October 1975	at Buffalo
Most own fumbles recovered	6	20 October 1975	at Buffalo
Most opponents' fumbles recovered	6	17 September 1950	at Pittsburgh
Most penalties	17	28 November 1948	versus Boston Yankees
		9 October 1949	at Washington

Team Records, Game (continued)

Most yards penalized	177	9 October 1949	at Washington
Most points allowed	72	27 November 1966	at Washington
Most touchdowns allowed	10	27 November 1966	at Washington
Most points after touchdown allowed	9	27 November 1966	at Washington
Most field goals allowed	7	15 September 2003	versus Dallas
Most first downs allowed	38	13 November 1966	at Rams
Fewest first downs allowed	1	20 September 1933	at Pittsburgh
Most first downs allowed, rushing	19	26 November 1978	at Buffalo
Most first downs allowed, passing	23	19 October 1980	at San Diego
Most net yards allowed	682	14 November 1943	versus Chicago Bears
Fewest net yards allowed	48	17 October 1943	at Brooklyn Dodgers
Most rushing attempts by opponent	60	9 December 1945	at Washington
Fewest rushing attempts by opponent	7	8 December 1985	at Houston
Most rushing yards allowed	420	8 October 1933	at Boston (Redskins)
Fewest rushing yards allowed	−24	17 October 1943	at Brooklyn Dodgers
Most rushing touchdowns allowed	5	26 November 1978	at Buffalo
Most passing attempts by opponent	62	2 October 2005	versus St. Louis
Fewest passing attempts by opponent	3	23 December 1934	at Detroit
Most completions allowed	40	2 October 2005	versus St. Louis
Fewest completions allowed	0	11 December 1960	at Washington
Most net yards allowed, passing	488	14 November 1943	versus Chicago Bears
Fewest net yards allowed, passing	−13	11 December 1977	at Philadelphia
Most passing touchdowns allowed	7	14 November 1943	versus Chicago Bears
Most interceptions	8	21 November 1948	at Green Bay
		16 December 1951	at New York Yankees
Most yards on interception returns	144	13 September 1941	at Philadelphia
Most touchdowns on interception returns	2	4 December 1938	versus Washington
		8 December 1963	versus Washington
		27 October 1996	at Detroit

Team Records, Season

Most points	448	1963
Fewest points	79	1928
Most touchdowns	57	1963
Fewest touchdowns	12	1928
Most touchdowns rushing	27	1930
Fewest touchdowns rushing	3	1932
Most touchdowns passing	39	1963
Fewest touchdowns passing	0	1928
Most touchdowns on interception returns	10	1951
Most points after touchdown	52	1963
Fewest points after touchdown	4	1928
Most field goals	35	2005
Most field-goal attempts	42	2005
Fewest field goals	0	1932
Highest field-goal percentage	88.9	1996
Most safeties	3	1927
Most first downs	356	1985
Most first downs rushing	138	1985
Most first downs passing	198	1984
Most first downs by penalty	36	1997
Most net yards gained	5,884	1985
Most rushing attempts	581	1985
Fewest rushing attempts	244	1982
Most rushing yards	2,451	1985
Fewest rushing yards	769	1945
Most touchdowns rushing	27	1930
Most passes completed	350	1999
Most passes attempted	616	2003
Fewest passes completed	47	1944
Fewest passes attempted	125	1944
Highest completion percentage	61.6	2002
Most net passing yards gained	3,951	2002
Most touchdown passes	39	1963
Most passes had intercepted	34	1953
Fewest passes had intercepted	5	1990
Most punts	112	1997
Fewest punts	47	1972
Most punting yards	4,566	1998

Team Records, Season (continued)

Highest punting average	46.6	1959
Most punt returns	64	1981
Most yards gained, punt returns	717	1941
Highest punt-return average	15.3	1941
Most kickoff returns	80	1966
Most yards gained, kickoff returns	1,688	1964
Highest kickoff-return average	27.4	1944
Most fumbles	49	1960
Most own fumbles recovered	23	1960
Most opponents' fumbles recovered	27	1950
Most penalties	143	2005
Most yards penalized	1,115	2005
Most points allowed	501	1966
Fewest points allowed	20	1927
Most touchdowns allowed	66	1966
Fewest touchdowns allowed	3	1927
Most points after touchdown allowed	63	1966
Most field goals allowed	29	1994
Most safeties by opponent	3	1984
Most first downs allowed	336	1980
Fewest first downs allowed	104	1938
Most first downs rushing allowed	156	1980
Fewest first downs rushing allowed	55	1982
Most first downs passing allowed	195	1997
Fewest first downs passing allowed	41	1937
Most net yards allowed	5,752	1980
Fewest net yards allowed	2,029	1938
Most rushing attempts by opponent	640	1978
Fewest rushing attempts by opponent	301	1982
Most rushing yards allowed	2,656	1978
Fewest rushing yards allowed	913	1951
Most rushing touchdowns allowed	31	1980
Fewest rushing touchdowns allowed	1	1927
Most completions by opponent	334	1986
Fewest completions by opponent	54	1934
Most passing attempts by opponent	596	1997
Fewest passing attempts by opponent	149	1963
Most net passing yards allowed	3,616	1997

New York (Football) Giants Team Records (continued)

Team Records, Season (continued)

Fewest net passing yards allowed	744	1934
Most passing touchdowns allowed	36	1966
Fewest passing touchdowns allowed	2	1927
Most interceptions	41	1951
Fewest interceptions	10	2003
Most yards on Interception returns	569	1941
Fewest yards on interception returns	62	1976
Most touchdowns on interception returns	5	1963
Most sacks	68	1985

Source: New York Giants 2006 Information Guide.

New York Jets Season Records, 1960–2007

	Wins	Losses	Ties	Finish	Points For	Points Against	Attendance
1960	7	7	0	2nd	382	399	114,628
1961	7	7	0	3rd	301	390	107,119
1962	5	9	0	4th	278	423	26,162
1963	5	8	1	4th	249	399	111,906
1964	5	8	1	3rd	278	315	320,596
1965	5	8	1	2nd	285	303	396,851
1966	6	6	2	3rd	322	312	415,768
1967	8	5	1	2nd	371	329	437,036
1968	11	3	0	1st	419	280	433,760
1969	10	4	0	1st	353	269	440,422
1970	4	10	0	3rd	255	286	439,688
1971	6	8	0	4th	212	299	441,099
1972	7	7	0	2nd	367	324	440,311
1973	4	10	0	5th	240	306	323,867
1974	7	7	0	4th	279	300	346,933
1975	3	11	0	5th	258	433	361,102
1976	3	11	0	4th	169	383	329,643
1977	3	11	0	4th	191	300	312,269
1978	8	8	0	3rd	359	364	400,704
1979	8	8	0	3rd	337	383	403,383
1980	4	12	0	5th	302	395	396,642

New York Jets Season Records, 1960–2007 (continued)

	Wins	Losses	Ties	Finish	Points For	Points Against	Attendance
1981	10	5	1	2nd	355	287	428,766
1982	6	3	0	6th	245	166	182,349
1983	7	9	0	5th	313	331	416,987
1984	7	9	0	3rd	332	364	514,591
1985	11	5	0	2nd	393	264	541,832
1986	10	6	0	2nd	364	386	542,669
1987	6	9	0	5th	334	360	352,895
1988	8	7	1	4th	372	354	483,037
1989	4	12	0	5th	253	411	429,465
1990	6	10	0	4th	295	345	482,910
1991	8	8	0	2nd	314	293	495,562
1992	4	12	0	4th	220	315	465,563
1993	8	8	0	3rd	270	247	531,702
1994	6	10	0	5th	264	320	527,147
1995	3	13	0	5th	233	384	488,079
1996	1	15	0	5th	279	454	395,154
1997	9	7	0	3rd	348	287	543,181
1998	12	4	0	1st	416	266	589,768
1999	8	8	0	4th	308	309	626,258
2000	9	7	0	3rd	321	321	623,711
2001	10	6	0	3rd	308	295	627,808
2002	9	7	0	1st	359	336	628,812
2003	6	10	0	4th	283	299	622,255
2004	10	6	0	2nd	333	261	623,181
2005	4	12	0	4th	240	355	619,958
2006	10	6	0	2nd	316	295	618,575
2007	4	12	0	3rd	268	355	616,855
Totals	322	394	8		14,543	15,852	21,018,959

Super Bowl Record
1969   W, Baltimore Colts, 16–7

Note: Team was known as New York Titans, 1960–1962.
Source: Theganggreen.com.

Head Coaches of the New York Jets

		Wins	Losses	Ties	Winning Percentage
Sammy Baugh	1960–1961	14	14	0	.500
Clyde "Bulldog" Turner	1962	5	9	0	.357
Weeb Ewbank	1963–1973	71	77	6	.480
Charley Winner	1974–1975	9	14	0	.391
Ken Shipp	1975	1	4	0	.200
Lou Holtz	1976	3	10	0	.231
Mike Holovak (interim)	1976	0	1	0	.000
Walt Michaels	1977–1982	39	47	1	.453
Joe Walton	1983–1989	53	57	1	.482
Bruce Coslet	1990–1993	26	38	0	.406
Pete Carroll	1994	6	10	0	.375
Rich Kotite	1995–1996	4	28	0	.125
Bill Parcells	1997–1999	29	19	0	.604
Al Groh	2000	9	7	0	.563
Herman Edwards	2001–2005	39	41	0	.488
Eric Mangini	2006–	14	18	0	.438
Totals:		322	394	8	.450

Source: New York Jets.

New York Jets Team Records

Individual Records, Single Play

Longest field goal	55 yards	Pat Leahy	14 December 1985	versus Chicago
		John Hall	31 August 1997	at Seattle
Longest run from scrimmage	90 yards	Johnny Johnson	25 September 1994	versus Chicago
Longest punt	98+ yards	Steve O'Neal	21 September 1969	at Denver
Longest punt return	98 yards	Terance Mathis	4 November 1990	versus Dallas
Longest kickoff return	101 yards	Leon Burton	28 October 1960	versus Oakland
		Leon Johnson	14 December 1997	versus Tampa Bay
Longest gain by interception	100 yards	Aaron Glenn	15 September 1996	at Miami
Longest passing play	96 yards	Ken O'Brien to Wesley Walker	8 December 1985	at Buffalo

New York Jets Team Records (continued)

Individual Records, Game

Most points	24	Wesley Walker	21 September 1986	versus Miami
Most touchdowns	4	Wesley Walker	21 September 1986	versus Miami
Most points after touchdown	8	Pat Leahy	17 November 1985	versus Tampa Bay
Most field goals	6	Jim Turner	3 November 1968	versus Buffalo
		Bobby Howfield	3 December 1972	versus New Orleans
Most rushing attempts	40	Johnny Hector	12 October 1986	at New England
Most rushing touchdowns	3	9 times, last by Curtis Martin	11 November 2001	versus Kansas City
Most yards gained, rushing	203	Curtis Martin	3 December 2000	versus Indianapolis
Most passes attempted	69	Vinny Testaverde	24 December 2000	at Baltimore
Most passes completed	42	Richard Todd	21 September 1980	versus San Francisco
		Vinny Testaverde	6 December 1998	versus Seattle
Most passing yards	496	Joe Namath	24 September 1972	at Baltimore
Most touchdown passes	6	Joe Namath	24 September 1972	at Baltimore
		Vinny Testaverde	23 October 2000	versus Miami
Most passes had intercepted	6	Joe Namath (3 times)		
Most pass receptions	17	Clark Gaines	21 September 1980	versus San Francisco
Most interceptions by	3	7 times, last by Ty Law	1 January 2006	versus Buffalo
Most yards gained by interception	116	Marcus Turner	20 November 1994	at Minnesota
Most punts	11	Steve O'Neal	19 September 1971	at Baltimore
Most punt returns	7	JoJo Townsell	2 October 1988	versus Kansas City
Most punt return yards	137	Dick Christy	24 September 1961	versus Denver
Most kickoff returns	8	Bruce Harper	29 October 1978	at New England
		Bruce Harper	9 September 1979	at New England
		Bobby Humphery	21 December 1986	at Cincinnati
Most kickoff return yards	278	Chad Morton	8 September 2002	at Buffalo

Individual Records, Season

Most points	145	Jim Turner	1968
Most touchdowns	14	Art Powell	1960
Most points after touchdown	47	Bill Shockley	1960
Most field goals	34	Jim Turner	1968
Most rushing attempts	371	Curtis Martin	2004
Most rushing touchdowns	12	Curtis Martin	2004
Most passes attempted	590	Vinny Testaverde	2000
Most passes completed	328	Vinny Testaverde	2000
Most passing yards	4,007	Joe Namath	1967
Most touchdown passes	29	Vinny Testaverde	1998

Individual Records, Season (continued)

Most passes had intercepted	30	Al Dorow	1961
Most pass receptions	93	Al Toon	1988
Most interceptions by	12	Dainard Paulson	1964
Most yards gained by interception	227	Darrol Ray	1981
Most punts	99	Brian Hansen	1995
Most punt returns	38	Roscoe Word	1974
		Clifford Hicks	1994
		Dedric Ward	1998
Most punt return yards	616	Leon Johnson	1997
Most kickoff returns	60	Justin Miller	2005
Most kickoff return yards	1,577	Justin Miller	2005
Most sacks	22	Mark Gastineau	1984

Individual Records, Career

Most games played	250	Pat Leahy
Most points	1,470	Pat Leahy
Most touchdowns	88	Don Maynard
Most points after touchdown	558	Pat Leahy
Most points after touchdown attempted	584	Pat Leahy
Most field goals	304	Pat Leahy
Most field goals attempted	426	Pat Leahy
Most rushing attempts	2,560	Curtis Martin
Most rushing yards gained	10,302	Curtis Martin
Most rushing touchdowns	58	Curtis Martin
Most passes attempted	3,655	Joe Namath
Most passes completed	2,039	Ken O'Brien
Most passing yards	27,057	Joe Namath
Most touchdown passes	170	Joe Namath
Most pass receptions	627	Don Maynard
Most interceptions by	34	Bill Baird
Most punts	553	Chuck Ramsey
Highest punting average (minimum 70 punts)	43.7	Ben Graham
Most punt returns	183	Bruce Harper
Most punt return yards	1,784	Bruce Harper
Highest average punt return	16.2 yards	Dick Christy
Most kickoff returns	243	Bruce Harper
Most kickoff return yards	5,407	Bruce Harper
Highest average kickoff return	28.7 yards	Leon Burton
Most sacks	107.5	Mark Gastineau

New York Jets Team Records (continued)

Individual Records, Streaks

Most consecutive games in regular season	204	Kyle Clifton
Most consecutive games with pass receptions	101	Al Toon

Team Records, Game

Most points	62	17 November 1985	versus Tampa Bay
Most points in a quarter	30	23 October 2000	versus Miami (4th)
Most points in a half	41	17 November 1985	versus Tampa Bay (1st)
Greatest margin of victory	42	18 September 1988	versus Houston (45–3)
Greatest margin of loss	53	9 September 1979	at New England (56–3)
Most first downs	35	17 November 1985	versus Tampa Bay
Fewest first downs	6	12 December 1976	versus Cincinnati
Most first downs rushing	20	19 September 1982	at New England
Most first downs passing	25	21 September 1980	versus San Francisco
Most rushing attempts	58	14 October 1973	at New England
Most rushing yards	333	15 October 1972	at New England
Most passes completed	42	21 September 1980	versus San Francisco
		6 December 1998	versus Seattle
Most passes attempted	69	23 December 2000	at Baltimore
Most net passing yards gained	490	24 September 1972	at Baltimore
Most punt returns	8	9 September 1966	at Miami
Most yards gained, punt returns	142	24 September 1961	versus Denver
Most kickoff returns	10	18 December 1960	at L.A. Chargers
Most yards gained, kickoff returns	290	8 September 2002	at Buffalo
Most penalties	17	18 October 1987	versus Miami
Most yards penalized	161	21 September 1970	at Cleveland
Most points by opponent	56	14 October 1962	at Houston
		9 September 1979	at New England
Most first downs allowed	39	27 November 1988	versus Miami
Fewest first downs allowed	5	22 November 1970	versus Boston
		19 September 1982	at New England
		24 December 2000	at Baltimore
Most first downs allowed, rushing	20	20 September 1981	at Pittsburgh
Most first downs allowed, passing	24	21 September 1986	versus Miami (OT)
		24 September 1989	at Miami
Most net yards allowed	621	21 September 1986	versus Cincinnati
Fewest net yards allowed	57	19 September 1982	versus New England
Most rushing attempts by opponent	64	21 September 1975	at Buffalo
Fewest rushing attempts by opponent	10	12 October 1986	at New England

Team Records, Game (continued)

Most rushing yards allowed	343	20 September 1981	at Pittsburgh
Fewest rushing yards allowed	17	10 October 1964	versus Oakland
		12 October 1986	at New England
Most passing attempts by opponent	60	23 October 1988	at Miami
		23 November 1997	at Chicago
Fewest passing attempts by opponent	2	29 September 1974	at Buffalo
Most completions allowed	36	15 December 1974	at Baltimore
Fewest completions allowed	0	29 September 1974	at Buffalo
Most net passing yards allowed	521	23 October 1988	at Miami
Fewest net passing yards allowed	−4	19 September 1982	at New England
Most interceptions	8	23 September 1973	at Baltimore
Most yards on interception returns	163	11 October 1981	versus New England
Most sacks	10	23 November 1961	versus Buffalo
Most sacks by opponent	11	4 October 1987	versus Dallas

Team Records, Season

Most points	419	1968
Fewest points	169	1976
Most first downs	344	1976
Most first downs rushing	153	1979
Most first downs passing	207	1998
Most first downs by penalty	34	1996
Most net yards gained	5,896	1985
Most rushing attempts	634	1979
Fewest rushing attempts	304	1982
Most rushing yards	2,646	1979
Fewest rushing yards	969	1963
Most passes completed	352	2000
Most passes attempted	637	2000
Fewest passes completed	119	1971
Fewest passes attempted	278	1971
Most net passing yards gained	4,023	2000
Most yards gained, punt returns	674	1997
Most yards gained, kickoff returns	1,728	2005
Most fumbles	44	1976
Fewest fumbles	15	1964, 1967
Most penalties	135	1987
Fewest penalties	53	1960, 1964

Team Records, Season (continued)

Most yards penalized	1,078	1995
Most points allowed	454	1996
Fewest points allowed	166	1982
Most first downs allowed	349	1986
Fewest first downs allowed	161	1982
Most first downs rushing allowed	157	1978
Fewest first downs rushing allowed	54	1982
Most first downs passing allowed	216	1986
Fewest first downs passing allowed	89	1982
Most net yards allowed	6,050	1986
Fewest net yards allowed	2,629	1982
Most rushing attempts by opponent	600	1978
Fewest rushing attempts by opponent	269	1982
Most rushing yards allowed	2,737	1975
Fewest rushing yards allowed	983	1982
Most completions by opponent	359	2002
Fewest completions by opponent	150	1973
Most passing attempts by opponent	603	1986
Fewest passing attempts by opponent	296	1973
Most net passing yards allowed	6,050	1986
Fewest net passing yards allowed	2,629	1982
Most interceptions	34	1964
Fewest interceptions	11	1976, 1977, 1996, 2003
Most yards on interception returns	477	1964
Fewest yards on interception returns	98	1975
Most sacks	66	1981
Fewest sacks	16	1976

Source: New York Jets 2006 Media Guide.

New York Knicks Season Records, 1946–1947 to 2007–2008

	Wins	Losses	Winning Percentage	Finish	Games Behind	Attendance
1946–1947	33	27	.550	3rd	16	82,001
1947–1948	26	22	.542	2nd	1	167,787
1948–1949	32	28	.533	2nd	6	211,284
1949–1950	40	28	.588	2nd	13	186,882
1950–1951[1]	36	30	.545	3rd	4	151,742
1951–1952[1]	37	29	.561	3rd	3	140,746
1952–1953[1]	47	23	.671	1st	—	195,240
1953–1954	44	28	.611	1st	—	221,079
1954–1955	38	34	.528	2nd	5	214,125
1955–1956	35	37	.486	3rd	10	246,756
1956–1957	36	36	.500	4th	8	266,998
1957–1958	35	37	.486	4th	14	247,632
1958–1959	40	32	.556	2nd	12	317,924
1959–1960	27	48	.360	4th	32	335,578
1960–1961	21	58	.266	4th	36	326,895
1961–1962	29	51	.363	4th	31	265,153
1962–1963	21	59	.263	4th	37	302,775
1963–1964	22	58	.275	4th	37	293,704
1964–1965	31	49	.388	4th	31	322,870
1965–1966	30	50	.375	4th	25	369,812
1966–1967	36	45	.444	4th	32	410,057
1967–1968	43	39	.524	3rd	19	534,568
1968–1969	54	28	.659	3rd	3	569,153
1969–1970[2]	60	22	.732	1st	—	761,226
1970–1971	52	30	.634	1st	—	763,487
1971–1972[1]	48	34	.585	2nd	8	785,298
1972–1973[2]	57	25	.695	2nd	11	790,031
1973–1974	49	33	.598	2nd	7	784,433
1974–1975	40	42	.488	3rd	20	760,786
1975–1976	38	44	.463	4th	16	672,745
1976–1977	40	42	.488	3rd	10	644,811
1977–1978	43	39	.524	2nd	12	626,815
1978–1979	31	51	.378	4th	23	545,715
1979–1980	39	43	.476	3rd	22	508,597
1980–1981	50	32	.610	3rd	12	546,441
1981–1982	33	49	.402	5th	30	444,189

New York Knicks Season Records, 1946–1947 to 2007–2008 (continued)

	Wins	Losses	Winning Percentage	Finish	Games Behind	Attendance
1982–1983	44	38	.537	4th	21	438,823
1983–1984	47	35	.573	3rd	15	495,944
1984–1985	24	58	.293	5th	39	457,317
1985–1986	23	59	.280	5th	44	592,486
1986–1987	24	58	.293	4th	35	538,058
1987–1988	38	44	.463	2nd	19	586,752
1988–1989	52	30	.634	1st	—	746,851
1989–1990	45	37	.549	3rd	8	730,432
1990–1991	39	43	.476	3rd	17	654,962
1991–1992	51	31	.622	1st	—	731,371
1992–1993	60	22	.732	1st	—	804,840
1993–1994[1]	57	25	.695	1st	—	810,283
1994–1995	55	27	.671	2nd	2	810,283
1995–1996	47	35	.573	2nd	13	810,283
1996–1997	57	25	.695	2nd	4	810,283
1997–1998	43	39	.524	2nd	12	810,283
1998–1999[1]	27	23	.540	4th	6	494,075
1999–2000	50	32	.610	2nd	2	810,283
2000–2001	48	34	.585	3rd	8	810,283
2001–2002	30	52	.366	7th	22	810,283
2002–2003	37	45	.451	5th	12	779,389
2003–2004	39	43	.476	3rd	8	785,739
2004–2005	33	49	.402	5th	12	800,144
2005–2006	23	59	.280	5th	26	776,176
2006–2007	33	49	.402	4th	14	735,621
2007–2008	23	59	.280	5th	43	783,739
Totals	2,422	2,413	.501			33,430,318

[1] Lost NBA finals.
[2] NBA champions.
Sources: National Basketball Association; New York Knicks Media Guide.

Head Coaches of the New York Knicks

		Wins	Losses	Winning Percentage
Neil Cohalan	1946–1947	33	27	.550
Joe Lapchick	1947–1948 to 1955–1956	326	247	.569
Vince Boryla	1955–1956 to 1957–1958	80	85	.485
Fuzzy Levane	1958–1959 to 1959–1960	48	51	.485
Carl Braun	1959–1960 to 1960–1961	40	87	.315
Eddie Donovan	1961–1962 to 1964–1965	84	194	.302
Harry Gallatin	1964–1965 to 1965–1966	25	38	.397
Dick McGuire	1965–1966 to 1967–1968	75	103	.421
Red Holzman	1967–1968 to 1976–1977,			
	1978–1979 to 1981–1982	613	483	.559
Willis Reed	1977–1978 to 1978–1979	49	47	.510
Hubie Brown	1982–1983 to 1986–1987	142	202	.413
Bob Hill	1986–1987	20	46	.303
Rick Pitino	1987–1988 to 1988–1989	90	74	.549
Stu Jackson	1989–1990 to 1990–1991	52	45	.536
John MacLeod	1990–1991	32	35	.478
Pat Riley	1991–1992 to 1994–1995	223	105	.680
Don Nelson	1995–1996	34	25	.576
Jeff Van Gundy	1995–1996 to 2001–2002	248	172	.590
Don Chaney	2001–2002 to 2003–2004	72	112	.391
Herb Williams	2003–2004, 2004–2005	17	27	.387
Lenny Wilkens	2003–2004 to 2004–2005	40	41	.494
Larry Brown	2005–2006	23	59	.280
Isiah Thomas	2006–2007 to 2007–2008	56	108	.341
Totals		2,422	2,413	.501

Source: New York Knicks Media Guide.

New York Knicks Team Records

Individual Records, Single Game

Most points, game	60	Bernard King	25 December 1984	versus New Jersey
Most points, quarter	24	Willis Reed	1 November 1967	at Los Angeles Lakers (1st)
		Allan Houston	12 January 2002	versus Milwaukee (4th)
Most rebounds	33	Willis Reed	2 February 1971	versus Cincinnati
Most assists	21	Richie Guerin	12 December 1958	versus St. Louis
Most blocked shots	10	Dikembe Mutombo	4 January 2004	versus New Jersey
Most minutes	62	Jim Baechtold	25 February 1955	at Philadelphia (3 OT)
Most field goals made	23	Willie Nauls	7 February 1961	versus Detroit
		Richie Guerin	14 February 1962	versus Boston
Most field goals attempted	37	Patrick Ewing	26 March 1991	at San Antonio
Most field goals made, no misses	11	Bernard King	19 January 1984	versus Chicago
		Johnny Newman	6 January 1988	at Boston
Most field goals missed, none made	15	Charlie Tyra	7 November 1957	at Philadelphia
Most three-point field goals made, game	9	John Starks	29 January 1998	versus Milwaukee (OT)
		Latrell Sprewell	26 January 2002	at Milwaukee (2 OT)
		Latrell Sprewell	4 February 2003	versus Los Angeles Clippers
Most three-point field goals made, quarter	6	John Starks	29 January 1998	at Milwaukee (2nd)
Most three-point field goals attempted	16	John Starks	6 April 1996	at Toronto
Most three-point field goals made, no misses	9	Latrell Sprewell	4 February 2003	versus Los Angeles Clippers
Most three-point field goals missed, none made	9	John Starks	23 February 1995	versus Sacramento
		Charlie Ward	24 November 2003	at Boston
Most free throws made, game	22	Richie Guerin	11 February 1961	at Boston
		Bernard King	25 December 1984	versus New Jersey
Most free throws made, quarter	13	Kenny Sears	3 November 1956	at Boston
Most free throws attempted	26	Carl Braun	22 February 1950	versus Washington
		Richie Guerin	11 December 1959	versus Syracuse
		Bernard King	25 December 1984	versus New Jersey
Most free throws made, no misses	19	Bill Cartwright	17 November 1981	versus Kansas City
Most free throws missed, none made	6	Johnny Green	26 November 1963	versus Los Angeles Lakers
		Dave DeBusschere	10 March 1970	versus Seattle
Most rebounds	33	Harry Gallatin	15 March 1953	at Fort Wayne
		Willis Reed	2 February 1971	2 February 1971

Individual Records, Single Game (continued)

Most offensive rebounds	14	Charles Oakley	3 January 1989	versus Boston (OT)
Most defensive rebounds	22	Patrick Ewing	19 December 1992	versus Miami
Most assists	21	Richie Guerin	12 December 1958	versus St. Louis
Most assists, no turnovers	14	Jim Cleamons	29 January 1979	versus Golden State
		Mark Jackson	19 April 1988	versus Chicago
		Doc Rivers	4 March 1993	versus Utah
		Mark Jackson	4 December 2001	at Milwaukee
Most steals	9	Micheal Ray Richardson	23 December 1980	at Chicago
Most turnovers	11	Micheal Ray Richardson	13 November 1981	at Milwaukee
Most blocked shots	10	Joe C. Meriweather	12 December 1979	at Atlanta
		Dikembe Mutombo	4 January 2004	versus New Jersey
Quickest disqualification, in minutes	6	Len Elmore	14 February 1984	at Kansas City

Individual Records, Season

Most minutes	3,457	Anthony Mason	1995–1996
Most points	2,347	Patrick Ewing	1989–1990
Highest scoring average	32.9	Bernard King	1984–1985
Most field goals made	922	Patrick Ewing	1989–1990
Most field goals attempted	1,897	Richie Guerin	1961–1962
Highest field-goal percentage (at least 100 made)	.572	Bernard King	1983–1984
Most three-point field goals made	217	John Starks	1994–1995
Most three-point field goals attempted	611	John Starks	1994–1995
Highest three-point field-goal percentage (at least 50 made)	.476	Hubert Davis	1995–1996
Most free throws made	625	Richie Guerin	1961–1962
Most free throws attempted	762	Richie Guerin	1961–1962
Highest free-throw percentage (at least 50 made)	.919	Allan Houston	2002–2003
Most rebounds	1,191	Willis Reed	1968–1969
Most assists	868	Mark Jackson	1987–1988
Most steals	265	Micheal Ray Richardson	1979–1980
Most blocked shots	327	Patrick Ewing	1989–1990
Most personal fouls	363	Lonnie Shelton	1976–1977
Most disqualifications	16	Ken Bannister	1984–1985

Individual Records, Career

Most games	1,039	Patrick Ewing
Most minutes	37,586	Patrick Ewing
Highest scoring average (at least 100 games)	26.7	Bob McAdoo
Most field goals made	9,260	Patrick Ewing
Most field goals attempted	18,224	Patrick Ewing
Highest field-goal percentage (at least 500 made)	.552	Bill Cartwright
Most three-point field goals made	982	John Starks
Most three-point field goals attempted	2,848	John Starks
Highest three-point field-goal percentage (at least 50 made)	.449	Hubert Davis
Most free throws made	5,126	Patrick Ewing
Most free throws attempted	6,904	Patrick Ewing
Highest free-throw percentage (at least 200 made)	.886	Mike Glenn
Most rebounds	10,759	Patrick Ewing
Most assists	4,791	Walt Frazier
Most steals	1,061	Patrick Ewing
Most blocked shots	2,758	Patrick Ewing
Most personal fouls	3,676	Patrick Ewing
Most disqualifications	58	Willis Reed
Most consecutive games played	610	Harry Gallatin	20 November 1948 to 13 March 1957
Most consecutive field goals made	19	Johnny Newman	1–8 January 1988
Most consecutive three-point field goals made	10	Trent Tucker	28 December to 15 January 1985
		Allan Houston	18–21 February 1999
Most consecutive free throws made	41	Latrell Sprewell	16 December 2001 to 16 January 2002

Team Records

Most points scored, game	152	11 December 1959	versus Syracuse
Most points scored by opponent, game	169	2 March 1962	versus Philadelphia
Fewest points scored, game (since 1954–1955 season)	58	15 December 2000	versus Utah
Fewest points scored by opponent, game (since 1954–1955 season)	63	21 February 1999	versus Chicago

Team Records (continued)

Most points scored, half	88	19 December 1963	versus Boston at Providence (2nd)
Fewest points scored, half	22	12 March 1999	at Chicago (1st)
Most points scored, quarter	53	26 December 1967	versus Seattle at Philadelphia (4th)
Fewest points scored, quarter	5	21 November 1956	versus Fort Wayne at Boston (1st)
		26 February 1997	at Portland (3rd)
		12 March 1999	at Chicago (2nd)
Most points scored, single overtime period	19	22 February 1964	at Detroit
Fewest points scored, single overtime period	2	26 December 1992	at Milwaukee
		14 February 1993	at Orlando (3rd OT)
		5 February 1995	at Orlando
		28 November 1995	versus Atlanta
		10 December 1995	versus San Antonio (1st OT)
		12 March 2004	at Philadelphia (2nd OT)
Most consecutive points scored	24	15 November 2003	versus Indiana (3rd quarter)
Highest combined score	316	2 March 1962	versus Philadelphia (Philadelphia 169, Knicks 147)
Lowest combined score (since (1954–1955 season)	133	12 April 1992	at Detroit (Detroit 72, Knicks 61)
Largest winning margin	48	21 April 1994	versus Philadelphia (Knicks 130, Philadelphia 82)
Largest losing margin	62	25 December 1960	at Syracuse (Syracuse 162, Knicks 100)
Most overtime periods	4	23 January 1951	at Rochester (Rochester 102, Knicks 92)
Most field goals made	63	16 December 1977	at Milwaukee (3 OT)
Fewest field goals made	19	12 March 1999	at Chicago
Most field goals attempted	140	16 December 1977	at Milwaukee (3 OT)
Fewest field goals attempted	56	13 December 2002	at Miami
Highest field-goal percentage	.685	4 March 1986	versus Washington
Lowest field-goal percentage	.235	31 December 1954	versus Milwaukee at Providence
Most three-point field goals made	17	17 April 2005	versus Atlanta
Fewest three-point field goals made	0	Often, last on 14 April 2000	at Toronto
Most three-point field goals attempted	36	6 April 1996	at Toronto

Team Records (continued)

Fewest three-point field goals attempted	0	Often, last on 22 December 1990	versus New Jersey
Most three-point field goals, no misses	5	10 January 1987	versus Sacramento
Most three-point field goals missed, none made	13	20 November 1993	versus Utah
Most free throws made	50	9 January 1958	versus Boston at Syracuse
Fewest free throws made	2	25 January 1977	versus Chicago
Most free throws attempted	66	3 December 1957	versus Cincinnati
Fewest free throws attempted	4	6 March 1974	at Atlanta
		11 March 2003	versus Memphis
Highest free-throw percentage	1.000	Often	
Lowest free-throw percentage	.333	25 January 1977	versus Chicago
Most free throws made, no misses	26	20 April 2005	versus Washington
Most rebounds	96	22 January 1958	at Detroit
Fewest rebounds	20	14 February 1955	versus Fort Wayne
Most offensive rebounds	29	1 December 1983	versus Washington
Fewest offensive rebounds	1	4 March 1978	versus Boston
Most defensive rebounds	52	7 March 1992	versus Charlotte
Fewest defensive rebounds	13	18 February 1975	versus Golden State
		20 November 1982	versus Boston
Most assists	45	24 November 1979	versus Cleveland
Fewest assists	3	28 March 1976	at Boston
Most personal fouls	48	26 March 1950	at Syracuse
Fewest personal fouls	10	18 February 1997	versus Phoenix
		21 March 2002	at Atlanta
Most steals	22	7 March 1987	versus Los Angeles Clippers
Fewest steals	0	27 February 2001	versus Seattle
Most turnovers	40	3 December 1977	versus Milwaukee
Fewest turnovers	4	3 January 1972	versus Milwaukee
Most blocked shots	15	28 January 1988	at Washington
Fewest blocked shots	0	Often, last on 16 April 2005	at Charlotte
Largest deficit overcome in victory (since 1991–1992 season)	26	14 March 2004	at Milwaukee
Largest lead lost in defeat (since 1991–1992 season)	20	8 January 1994	at Charlotte
		28 February 2000	at Miami
		9 November 2001	at Indiana
		12 March 2002	versus Philadelphia
Most consecutive wins	18	24 October to 28 November 1969	
Most consecutive losses	12	23 March to 13 April 1985	

Source: New York Knicks Media Guide.

New York Rangers Season Records, 1926–1927 to 2007–2008

	Games	Wins	Losses	Ties	Overtime Losses	Points	Goals For	Goals Against	Finish
1926–1927	44	25	13	6	—	56	95	72	1st
1927–1928[1]	44	19	16	9	—	47	94	79	2nd
1928–1929[2]	44	21	13	10	—	52	72	65	2nd
1929–1930	44	17	17	10	—	44	136	143	3rd
1930–1931	44	19	16	9	—	47	106	87	3rd
1931–1932[2,3]	48	23	17	8	—	54	134	112	1st
1932–1933[1]	48	23	17	8	—	54	135	107	3rd
1933–1934	48	21	19	8	—	50	120	113	3rd
1934–1935	48	22	20	6	—	50	137	139	3rd
1935–1936	48	19	17	12	—	50	91	96	4th
1936–1937[2]	48	19	20	9	—	47	117	106	3rd
1937–1938	48	27	15	6	—	60	149	96	2nd
1938–1939	48	26	16	6	—	58	149	105	2nd
1939–1940[1]	48	27	11	10	—	64	136	77	2nd
1940–1941	48	21	19	8	—	50	143	125	4th
1941–1942[3]	48	29	17	2	—	60	177	143	1st
1942–1943	50	11	31	8	—	30	161	253	6th
1943–1944	50	6	39	5	—	17	162	310	6th
1944–1945	50	11	29	10	—	32	154	247	6th
1945–1946	50	13	28	9	—	35	144	191	6th
1946–1947	60	22	32	6	—	50	167	186	5th
1947–1948	60	21	26	13	—	55	176	201	4th
1948–1949	60	18	31	11	—	47	133	172	6th
1949–1950[2]	70	28	31	11	—	67	170	189	4th
1950–1951	70	20	29	21	—	61	169	201	5th
1951–1952	70	23	34	13	—	59	192	219	5th
1952–1953	70	17	37	16	—	50	152	211	6th
1953–1954	70	29	31	10	—	68	161	182	5th
1954–1955	70	17	35	18	—	52	150	210	5th
1955–1956	70	32	28	10	—	74	204	203	3rd
1956–1957	70	26	30	14	—	66	184	227	3rd
1957–1958	70	32	25	13	—	77	195	188	2nd
1958–1959	70	26	32	12	—	64	201	217	5th
1959–1960	70	17	38	15	—	49	187	247	6th
1960–1961	70	22	38	10	—	54	204	248	5th
1961–1962	70	26	32	12	—	64	195	207	4th

New York Rangers Season Records, 1926–1927 to 2007–2008 (continued)

	Games	Wins	Losses	Ties	Overtime Losses	Points	Goals For	Goals Against	Finish
1962–1963	70	22	36	12	—	56	211	233	5th
1963–1964	70	22	38	10	—	54	186	242	5th
1964–1965	70	20	38	12	—	52	179	246	5th
1965–1966	70	18	41	11	—	47	195	261	6th
1966–1967	70	30	28	12	—	72	188	189	4th
1967–1968	74	39	23	12	—	90	226	183	2nd
1968–1969	76	41	26	9	—	91	231	196	3rd
1969–1970	76	38	22	16	—	92	246	189	4th
1970–1971	78	49	18	11	—	109	259	177	2nd
1971–1972[2]	78	48	17	13	—	109	317	192	2nd
1972–1973	78	47	23	8	—	102	297	208	3rd
1973–1974	78	40	24	14	—	94	300	251	3rd
1974–1975	80	37	29	14	—	88	319	276	2nd
1975–1976	80	29	42	9	—	67	262	333	4th
1976–1977	80	29	37	14	—	72	272	310	4th
1977–1978	80	30	37	13	—	73	279	280	4th
1978–1979[2]	80	40	29	11	—	91	316	292	3rd
1979–1980	80	38	32	10	—	86	308	284	3rd
1980–1981	80	30	36	14	—	74	312	317	4th
1981–1982	80	39	27	14	—	92	316	306	2nd
1982–1983	80	35	35	10	—	80	306	287	4th
1983–1984	80	42	29	9	—	93	314	304	4th
1984–1985	80	26	44	10	—	62	295	345	4th
1985–1986	80	36	38	6	—	78	280	276	4th
1986–1987	80	34	38	8	—	76	307	323	4th
1987–1988	80	36	34	10	—	82	300	283	5th
1988–1989	80	37	35	8	—	82	310	307	3rd
1989–1990	80	36	31	13	—	85	279	267	1st
1990–1991	80	36	31	13	—	85	297	265	2nd
1991–1992[3]	80	50	25	5	—	105	321	246	1st
1992–1993	84	34	39	11	—	79	304	308	6th
1993–1994[1, 3]	84	52	24	8	—	112	299	231	1st
1994–1995	48	22	23	3	—	47	139	134	4th
1995–1996	82	41	27	14	—	96	272	237	2nd
1996–1997	82	38	34	10	—	86	258	231	4th
1997–1998	82	25	39	18	—	68	197	231	5th

New York Rangers Season Records, 1926–1927 to 2007–2008 (continued)

	Games	Wins	Losses	Ties	Overtime Losses	Points	Goals For	Goals Against	Finish
1998–1999	82	33	38	11	—	77	217	227	4th
1999–2000	82	29	38	12	3	73	218	246	4th
2000–2001	82	33	43	5	1	72	250	290	4th
2001–2002	82	36	38	4	4	80	227	258	5th
2002–2003	82	32	36	10	4	78	210	231	4th
2003–2004	82	27	40	7	8	69	206	250	4th
2005–2006	82	44	26	0	12	100	257	215	3rd
2006–2007	82	42	30	0	10	94	242	216	3rd
2007–2008	82	42	27	0	13	97	213	199	3rd
Totals	5,566	2,359	2,344	808	55	5,581	17,189	17,346	

From 1926–1927 to 1937–1938 listing refers to American Division only. From 1967–1968 to 1973–1974 listing refers to East Division only. From 1974–1975 listing refers to Lester Patrick Division of Clarence Campbell Conference. From 1981–1982 listing refers to Patrick Division of Prince of Wales Conference. From 1993–1994 on listing refers to Atlantic Division of Eastern Conference.
[1] Stanley Cup champion.
[2] Stanley Cup finalist.
[3] Finished 1st overall in the league.
Source: National Hockey League.

Head Coaches of the New York Rangers

		Wins	Losses	Ties	Overtime Losses	Winning Percentage
Lester Patrick	1926–1927 to 1938–1939	281	216	107		.554
Frank Boucher	1939–1940 to 21 December 1948	166	243	77		.421
Lynn Patrick	21 December 1948 to 1949–1950	40	51	16		.449
Neil Colville	1950–1951 to 6 December 1951	26	41	26		.419
Bill Cook	6 December 1951 to 1952–1953	34	59	24		.393
Frank Boucher	1953–1954 to 6 January 1954	13	20	6		.410
Muzz Patrick	6 January 1954 to 1954–1955	35	47	23		.443
Phil Watson	1955–1956 to 12 November 1959	118	124	52		.490
Alf Pike	18 November 1959 to 1960–1961	36	66	21		.378
Doug Harvey	30 May 1961 to 1961–1962	26	32	12		.457
Muzz Patrick	7 September 1962 to 28 December 1962	11	19	4		.382

Head Coaches of the New York Rangers (continued)

		Wins	Losses	Ties	Over-time Losses	Winning Percentage
Red Sullivan	28 December 1962 to 5 December 1965	58	103	35		.385
Emile Francis	5 December 1965 to 4 June 1968	81	82	30		.497
Bernie Geoffrion	4 June 1968 to 17 January 1969	22	18	3		.547
Emile Francis	17 January 1969 to 4 June 1973	202	88	54		.666
Larry Popein	4 June 1973 to 11 January 1974	18	14	9		.549
Emile Francis	11 January 1974 to 19 May 1975	59	39	19		.585
Ron Stewart	19 May 1975 to 7 January 1976	15	20	4		.436
John Ferguson	7 January 1976 to 22 August 1977	43	59	19		.434
Jean-Guy Talbot	22 August 1977 to 2 June 1978	30	37	13		.456
Fred Shero	2 June 1978 to 22 November 1980	82	74	24		.522
Craig Patrick	22 November 1980 to 4 June 1981	26	23	11		.525
Herb Brooks	4 June 1981 to 21 January 1985	131	113	41		.532
Craig Patrick	21 January 1985 to 19 June 1985	11	22	2		.343
Ted Sator	19 June 1985 to 21 November 1986	41	48	10		.465
Phil Esposito	1986–1987	24	19	0		.558
Tom Webster	1986–1987	5	7	4		.438
Wayne Cashman / Ed Giacomin	1986–1987	0	2	0		.000
Michel Bergeron	18 June 1987 to 1 April 1989	73	67	18		.519
Phil Esposito	1 April 1989 to 24 May 1989	0	2	0		.000
Roger Neilson	15 August 1989 to 4 January 1993	141	104	35		.566
Ron Smith	4 January 1993 to 16 April 1993	15	22	7		.420
Mike Keenan	17 April 1993 to 24 July 1994	52	24	8		.667
Colin Campbell	10 August 1994 to 18 February 1998	118	108	43		.519
John Muckler	19 February 1998 to 28 March 2000	70	88	24	3	.451
John Tortorella (interim)	28 March 2000 to 9 April 2000	0	3	1	0	.125
Ron Low	12 July 2000 to 15 April 2002	69	81	9	5	.463
Bryan Trottier	6 June 2002 to 29 January 2003	21	26	6	1	.454
Glen Sather	30 January 2003 to 25 February 2004	33	39	11	7	.467
Tom Renney	25 February 2004 to present	133	98	0	35	.566
Totals		2,359	2,344	808	55	.501

Source: New York Rangers Media Guide.

New York Rangers Team Records

Individual Records, Period

Most goals	3	Often, last by		
		Adam Graves	25 November 1992	at Pittsburgh (3rd)
Most assists	4	Phil Goyette	20 October 1963	versus Boston (1st)
		Wayne Gretzky	4 January 1997	versus Ottawa (2nd)
Most points	5 (3 goals, 2 assists)	Bill Cook	12 March 1933	versus New York Americans

Individual Records, Game

Most goals	5	Don Murdoch	12 October 1976	at Minnesota
		Mark Pavelich	23 February 1983	versus Hartford
Most assists	5	Walt Tkaczuk	12 February 1972	at Pittsburgh
		Rod Gilbert	2 March 1975	versus Pittsburgh
			30 March 1975	versus Kansas City
			8 October 1976	at Colorado
		Don Maloney	3 January 1987	at Quebec
		Brian Leetch	18 April 1995	at Pittsburgh
Most points	7 (3 goals, 4 assists)	Steve Vickers	18 February 1976	versus Washington
Most penalty minutes	36	Chris Simon	2 December 2003	at Toronto
Most power play goals	4	Camille Henry	13 March 1954	at Detroit
Most shorthanded goals	2	Greg Polis	4 November 1977	at Vancouver
		Ron Duguay	22 January 1980	at Los Angeles
		Don Maloney	21 February 1981	versus Washington
			5 October 1983	versus New Jersey
			14 January 1987	at Calgary

Individual Records, Season

Most goals	52	Adam Graves	1993–1994
Most assists	80	Brian Leetch	1991–1992
Most points	109	Jean Ratelle	1971–1972
Most penalties	86	Michel Petit	1987–1988
Most penalty minutes	305	Troy Mallette	1989–1990
Most power play goals	23	Vic Hadfield	1971–1972
Most shorthanded goals	7	Theoren Fleury	2000–2001
Most shots on goal	344	Phil Esposito	1976–1977
Highest shooting percentage	29.6 (29 goals on 98 shots)	Steve Vickers	1979–1980

New York Rangers Team Records (continued)

Individual Records, Season (continued)

Most game-winning goals	9	Don Maloney	1980–1981	
		Mark Messier	1996–1997	
Most hat tricks	4	Tomas Sandstrom	1986–1987	
Longest consecutive-goal scoring streak	10	Andy Bathgate	15 December 1962 to 5 January 1963 (11 goals during streak)	
Longest consecutive-assist scoring streak	15	Brian Leetch	29 November 1991 to 31 December 1991 (23 assists during streak)	
Longest consecutive-point scoring streak	17	Brian Leetch	23 November 1991 to 31 December 1991 (5 goals, 24 assists during streak)	
Fastest goal at start of game	9 seconds	Ron Duguay	6 April 1980	at Philadelphia
		Jim Wiemer	27 March 1985	at Buffalo
Most goals by a rookie	36	Tony Granato	1988–1989	
Most points by a rookie	76	Mark Pavelich	1981–1982	
Most goals by a defenseman	25	Brad Park	1973–1974	
Most points by a defenseman	102	Brian Leetch	1991–1992	
Most wins	42	Mike Richter	1993–1994	
Most shutouts	13	Johns Ross Roach	1928–1929	
Most appearances by a goaltender	72	Mike Richter	1997–1998	

Individual Records, Career

Most games	1,160	Harry Howell	
Most goals	406	Rod Gilbert	
Most assists	741	Brian Leetch	
Most penalty minutes	1,226	Ron Greschner	
Most hat tricks	8	Bill Cook	
Most goals by a defenseman	240	Brian Leetch	
Most assists by a defenseman	741	Brian Leetch	
Most points by a defenseman	981	Brian Leetch	
Most wins	301	Mike Richter	
Most shutouts	49	Ed Giacomin	
Most appearances by a goaltender	666	Mike Richter	
Most consecutive games	560	Amdy Hebenton	1955–1956 to 1962–1963

Team Records, Period

Most goals	8	21 November 1971	versus California (3rd)
Most goals, both teams	10	16 March 1939	versus New York Americans (3rd; Rangers 7, Americans 3)
Most assists	15	21 November 1971	versus California (3rd)
Most points	23	21 November 1971	versus California (3rd; 8 goals, 15 assists)
Most penalty minutes	126	30 October 1988	versus Pittsburgh (3rd)
Most penalty minutes, both teams	272	30 October 1988	versus Pittsburgh (3rd)

Team Records, Game

Greatest winning margin	11	21 November 1971	versus California (12–1)
Greatest losing margin	15	23 January 1944	at Detroit (15–0)
Highest tie score	7–7	19 March 1978	at Minnesota
Most goals	12	21 November 1971	versus California
Most assists	23	21 November 1971	versus California
Most points	35	21 November 1971	versus California (12 goals, 23 assists)
Most points, both teams	46	4 March 1944	at Boston (Boston 10 goals, 15 assists; Rangers 9 goals, 12 assists)
Most penalty minutes	292	30 October 1988	versus Pittsburgh (Pittsburgh 158, Rangers 134)
Most power play goals	6	13 October 1993	versus Quebec
Most shorthanded goals	3	5 October 1983	versus New Jersey
Most shots on goal	65	5 April 1970	versus Detroit
Fewest shots on goal	9	11 December 1995	at Detroit

Team Records, Season

Most goals	321	1992–1992
Fewest goals (minimum 70-game schedule)	150	1954–1955
Most assists	540	1988–1989
Fewest assists	45	1925–1926 (44-game schedule)
Most scoring points	854	1978–1979
Fewest scoring points	120	1926–1927 (44-game schedule)
Most penalty minutes	2,018	1989–1990
Fewest penalty minutes	253	1943–1944 (44-game schedule)
Most power play goals	111	1987–1988
Most shorthanded goals	20	1993–1994
Most goals allowed	345	1984–1985
Fewest goals allowed (minimum 70-game schedule)	177	1970–1971
Most power play goals allowed	. 89	1995–1996
Most shorthanded goals allowed	18	1992–1993
Most shutouts	13	1928–1929

New York Rangers Team Records (continued)

Team Records, Season (continued)

Fewest shutouts	0	Often, last in 2000–2001
Most hat tricks	10	1986–1987
Most times shut out	10	1928–1929
Fewest times shut out	0	Often, last in 1993–1994

Team Records, Streaks

Longest winning streak	10	Twice, last 19 January 1973 to 11 February 1973
Longest winning streak at start of season	5	5 October 1983 to 15 October 1983
Longest undefeated streak	19	23 November 1939 to 14 January 1940
Longest losing streak	11	30 October 1943 to 28 November 1943

Source: New York Rangers Media Guide.

Venues in New York City of Professional Sports Teams

Ebbets Field
Cost: $750,000
Opening day: 9 April 1913
First night game: 15 June 1938
Last game: 24 September 1957
Demolished: 23 February 1960
Capacity: 25,000 (1913), 32,000 (1932)

Polo Grounds (first)
Years extant: 1883–1888
Abandoned when city confiscated property

Polo Grounds (second)
Years extant: 1889–1890
Abandoned by Players League, Giants moved to larger field to the north

Polo Grounds (third)
Years extant: 1891–1911
Destroyed by fire

Polo Grounds (fourth)
Opening day: 28 June 1911
Last game: 18 September 1963
First night game: 24 May 1940
Demolished: 10 April 1964
Capacity: 34,000 (1911), 55,000 (1923)

Yankee Stadium
Cost: Construction $2.5 million, renovation $48 million to more than $160 million (estimates vary based on method
    used to account for debt service)
Opening day: 18 April 1923
Last game before renovation: 30 September 1973
Reopened: 15 April 1976
First night game: 28 May 1946
Capacity: 58,000 (1923), 62,000 (1926), 82,000 (1927), 67,113 (1928), 62,000 (1929), 71,699 (1937), 70,000 (1942),
    67,000 (1948), 67,205 (1958), 67,337 (1961), 67,000 (1965), 65,010 (1971), 54,028 (1976), 57,145 (1977), 57,545
    (1980)

Hilltop Park
Opening day: 30 April 1903
Last game: 5 October 1912
Demolished: 1914
Capacity: 16,000, standing room for an additional 15,000

Shea Stadium
Cost: $28.5 million
Opening day: 17 April 1964
Capacity: 55,601

Madison Square Garden (first)
Location: 26th Street and Madison Avenue
Constructed: 1874 (as P. T. Barnum's Great Roman Hippodrome)
Opened: 31 May 1879
Demolished: July 1889
Capacity: 10,000

Venues in New York City of Professional Sports Teams (continued)

Madison Square Garden (second)
Location: 26th Street and Madison Avenue
Cost: $3 million
Opened: 16 June 1890
Demolished: 1924
Capacity: Permanent seating for 8,000, floor space for an additional 10,000

Madison Square Garden (third)
Location: 50th Street and 8th Avenue
Cost: $4.75 million
Opened: 24 November 1925
Demolished: 1968
Capacity: 18,500 (22,000 for rally for Franklin D. Roosevelt in 1932; 23,190 for title bout between Fritzie Zivic and Henry
   Armstrong on 17 January 1941)

Madison Square Garden (fourth)
Location: 32nd Street and 7th Avenue
Cost: Construction unknown, renovation (1991) $200 million
Opened: 11 February 1968
Capacity: 19,763

Source: ballparks.com.

Payrolls of Professional Teams, 1988–2007

	Mets	Yankees	Giants	Jets	Knicks	Rangers
1988	$15,502,714	$18,909,152				
1989	20,013,212	20,562,985				
1990	22,418,834	20,991,318				
1991	32,590,002	27,815,835				
1992	44,352,002	35,966,834				
1993	38,350,167	41,305,000				
1994	29,890,324	44,785,334				
1995	24,301,440	46,657,016				
1996	23,456,500	52,189,370				
1997	38,474,567	59,148,877				
1998	49,559,665	63,159,898				

Payrolls of Professional Teams, 1988–2007 (continued)

	Mets	Yankees	Giants	Jets	Knicks	Rangers
1999	71,331,425	88,130,709				
2000	79,759,762	92,938,260	$51,348,900	$53,250,400		
2001	93,674,428	112,287,143	77,617,916	69,980,467	$56,887,037	
2002	94,633,593	125,928,583	77,833,196	84,739,364	$85,253,575	64,793,530
2003	117,176,429	152,749,814	78,125,309	69,209,828	93,014,165	76,477,085
2004	96,660,970	184,193,950	81,657,826	93,866,236	84,523,891	76,488,716
2005	101,305,821	208,306,817	82,422,436	79,346,324	94,067,539	41,474,800
2006	101,084,963	194,663,079	108,196,454	86,145,839	92,904,104	45,050,760
2007	115,231,663	189,639,045	81,672,615			

Note: For Knicks and Rangers, 2002 figures are for 2001–2002 season, 2003 figures are for 2002–2003 season, etc.
Source: USA Today Salaries Database.

World Heavyweight Boxing Title Fights

9 June 1899	James J. Jeffries KO-11 Bob Fitzsimmons
3 November 1899	James J. Jeffries W-25 Tom Sharkey
11 May 1900	James J. Jeffries KO-23 James J. Corbett
25 March 1916	Jess Willard ND-10 Frank Moran
14 December 1920	Jack Dempsey KO-12 Bill Brennan
14 September 1923	Jack Dempsey KO-2 Luis Firpo
26 July 1928	Gene Tunney TKO-11 Tom Heeney
12 June 1930	Max Schmeling DSQ-4 Jack Sharkey
21 June 1932	Jack Sharkey W-15 Max Schmeling
29 June 1933	Primo Carnera KO-6 Jack Sharkey
13 June 1935	James J. Braddock W-15 Max Baer
30 August 1937	Joe Louis W-15 Tommy Farr
23 February 1938	Joe Louis KO-3 Nathan Mann
22 June 1938	Joe Louis KO-1 Max Schmeling
25 January 1939	Joe Louis TKO-1 John Henry Lewis
28 June 1939	Joe Louis TKO-4 Tony Galento
9 February 1940	Joe Louis W-15 Arturo Godoy
29 March 1940	Joe Louis KO-2 Johnny Paycheck
20 June 1940	Joe Louis TKO-8 Arturo Godoy
31 January 1941	Joe Louis KO-5 Red Burman
18 June 1941	Joe Louis KO-13 Billy Conn

World Heavyweight Boxing Title Fights (continued)

Date	Fight
29 September 1941	Joe Louis TKO-6 Lou Nova
9 January 1942	Joe Louis KO-1 Buddy Baer
27 March 1942	Joe Louis KO-6 Abe Simon
19 June 1946	Joe Louis KO-8 Billy Conn
18 September 1946	Joe Louis KO-1 Tami Mauriello
5 December 1947	Joe Louis W-15 Jersey Joe Walcott
25 June 1948	Joe Louis KO-11 Jersey Joe Walcott
10 August 1949	Ezzard Charles TKO-7 Gus Lesnevich
27 September 1950	Ezzard Charles W-15 Joe Louis
12 January 1951	Ezzard Charles TKO-10 Lee Oma
24 September 1953	Rocky Marciano TKO-11 Roland LaStarza
17 June 1954	Rocky Marciano W-15 Ezzard Charles
17 September 1954	Rocky Marciano KO-8 Ezzard Charles
21 September 1955	Rocky Marciano KO-9 Archie Moore
29 July 1957	Floyd Patterson TKO-10 Tommy Jackson
26 June 1959	Ingemar Johansson TKO-3 Floyd Patterson
20 June 1960	Floyd Patterson KO-5 Ingemar Johansson
22 March 1967	Muhammad Ali KO-7 Zora Folley
4 March 1968	Joe Frazier TKO-11 Buster Mathis (WBC title)
24 June 1968	Joe Frazier KO-2 Manuel Ramos (WBC title)
23 June 1969	Joe Frazier TKO-7 Jerry Quarry (WBC title)
16 February 1970	Joe Frazier TKO-4 Jimmy Ellis
8 March 1971	Joe Frazier W-15 Muhammad Ali
28 September 1976	Muhammad Ali W-15 Ken Norton
29 September 1977	Muhammad Ali W-15 Earnie Shavers
22 June 1979	Larry Holmes TKO-12 Mike Weaver (WBC title)
12 December 1986	James Smith TKO-1 Tim Witherspoon (WBA title)
6 February 1993	Riddick Bowe TKO-1 Michael Dokes (WBA, IBF titles)
13 March 1999	Lennox Lewis W-12 Evander Holyfield (WBC, WBA, IBF titles)
30 April 2005	James Toney W-12 John Ruiz (WBA title)[1]

W = win by decision
KO = knockout
TKO - technical knockout
DSQ = win by disqualification
ND = no decision
WBC = World Boxing Council
WBA = World Boxing Association
IBF = International Boxing Federation
[1] Fight ruled a no-contest on 10 May 2005 when Toney tested positive for a prohibited substance.

Source: Heavyweight News.

Men's and Women's Singles Winners of the U.S. Tennis Open

1881	Richard D. Sears	—
1882	Richard D. Sears	—
1883	Richard D. Sears	—
1884	Richard D. Sears	—
1885	Richard D. Sears	—
1886	Richard D. Sears	—
1887	Richard D. Sears	Ellen Hansell
1888	Henry W. Slocum Jr.	Bertha L. Townsend
1889	Henry W. Slocum Jr.	Bertha L. Townsend
1890	Oliver S. Campbell	Ellen C. Roosevelt
1891	Oliver S. Campbell	Mabel Cahill
1892	Oliver S. Campbell	Mabel Cahill
1893	Robert D. Wrenn	Aline Terry
1894	Robert D. Wrenn	Helen Hellwig
1895	Fred H. Hovey	Juliette Atkinson
1896	Robert D. Wrenn	Elisabeth Moore
1897	Robert D. Wrenn	Juliette Atkinson
1898	Malcolm D. Whitman	Juliette Atkinson
1899	Malcolm D. Whitman	Marion Jones
1900	Malcolm D. Whitman	Myrtle McAteer
1901	William A. Larned	Elisabeth Moore
1902	William A. Larned	Marion Jones
1903	Hugh L. Doherty	Elisabeth Moore
1904	Holcombe Ward	May Sutton
1905	Beals C. Wright	Elisabeth Moore
1906	William A. Larned	Helen Homans
1907	William A. Larned	Evelyn Sears
1908	William A. Larned	Maud Barger-Wallach
1909	William A. Larned	Hazel Hotchkiss
1910	William A. Larned	Hazel Hotchkiss
1911	William A. Larned	Hazel Hotchkiss
1912	Maurice E. McLoughlin	Mary Browne
1913	Maurice E. McLoughlin	Mary Browne
1914	Richard N. Williams	Mary Browne
1915	William M. Johnston	Molla Bjurstedt
1916	Richard N. Williams	Molla Bjurstedt
1917	R. Lindley Murray	Molla Bjurstedt
1918	R. Lindley Murray	Molla Bjurstedt
1919	William M. Johnston	Hazel Hotchkiss Wightman

Men's and Women's Singles Winners of the U.S. Tennis Open (continued)

1920	William T. Tilden	Molla B. Mallory
1921	William T. Tilden	Molla B. Mallory
1922	William T. Tilden	Molla B. Mallory
1923	William T. Tilden	Helen Wills
1924	William T. Tilden	Helen Wills
1925	William T. Tilden	Helen Wills
1926	Rene Lacoste	Molla B. Mallory
1927	Rene Lacoste	Helen Wills
1928	Henri Cochet	Helen Wills
1929	William T. Tilden	Helen Wills
1930	John H. Doeg	Betty Nuthall
1931	H. Ellsworth Vines	Helen Wills Moody
1932	H. Ellsworth Vines	Helen H. Jacobs
1933	Fred Perry	Helen H. Jacobs
1934	Fred Perry	Helen H. Jacobs
1935	Wilmer L. Allison	Helen H. Jacobs
1936	Fred Perry	Alice Marble
1937	J. Donald Budge	Anita Lizana
1938	J. Donald Budge	Alice Marble
1939	Robert Riggs	Alice Marble
1940	Donald McNeill	Alice Marble
1941	Robert Riggs	Sarah Palfrey Cooke
1942	Frederick R. Schroeder Jr.	Pauline Betz
1943	Lt. Joseph R. Hunt	Pauline Betz
1944	Sgt. Frank Parker	Pauline Betz
1945	Sgt. Frank Parker	Sarah Palfrey Cooke
1946	Jack Kramer	Pauline Betz
1947	Jack Kramer	A. Louise Brough
1948	Richard A. Gonzales	Margaret Osborne duPont
1949	Richard A. Gonzales	Margaret Osborne duPont
1950	Arthur Larsen	Margaret Osborne duPont
1951	Frank Sedgman	Maureen Connolly
1952	Frank Sedgman	Maureen Connolly
1953	Tony Trabert	Maureen Connolly
1954	E. Victor Seixas Jr.	Doris Hart
1955	Tony Trabert	Doris Hart
1956	Ken Rosewall	Shirley J. Fry
1957	Malcolm J. Anderson	Althea Gibson
1958	Ashley J. Cooper	Althea Gibson

Men's and Women's Singles Winners of the U.S. Tennis Open (continued)

1959	Neale Fraser	Maria Bueno
1960	Neale Fraser	Darlene R. Hard
1961	Roy Emerson	Darlene R. Hard
1962	Rodney Laver	Margaret Smith
1963	Rafael Osuna	Maria Bueno
1964	Roy Emerson	Maria Bueno
1965	Manuel Santana	Margaret Smith
1966	Fred Stolle	Maria Bueno
1967	John Newcombe	Billie Jean Moffitt King
1968	Arthur Ashe	Virginia Wade
1969	Rodney Laver	Margaret Smith Court
1970	Ken Rosewall	Margaret Smith Court
1971	Stan Smith	Billie Jean King
1972	Ilie Nastase	Billie Jean King
1973	John Newcombe	Margaret Smith Court
1974	Jimmy Connors	Billie Jean King
1975	Manuel Orantes	Christine Marie Evert
1976	Jimmy Connors	Christine Marie Evert
1977	Guillermo Vilas	Christine Marie Evert
1978	Jimmy Connors	Christine Marie Evert
1979	John McEnroe	Tracy Austin
1980	John McEnroe	Chris Evert Lloyd
1981	John McEnroe	Tracy Austin
1982	Jimmy Connors	Chris Evert Lloyd
1983	Jimmy Connors	Martina Navratilova
1984	John McEnroe	Martina Navratilova
1985	Ivan Lendl	Hana Mandlikova
1986	Ivan Lendl	Martina Navratilova
1987	Ivan Lendl	Martina Navratilova
1988	Mats Wilander	Steffi Graf
1989	Boris Becker	Steffi Graf
1990	Pete Sampras	Gabriela Sabatini
1991	Stefan Edberg	Monica Seles
1992	Stefan Edberg	Monica Seles
1993	Pete Sampras	Steffi Graf
1994	Andre Agassi	Arantxa Sanchez Vicario
1995	Pete Sampras	Steffi Graf
1996	Pete Sampras	Steffi Graf
1997	Patrick Rafter	Martina Hingis

Men's and Women's Singles Winners of the U.S. Tennis Open (continued)

1998	Patrick Rafter	Lindsay Davenport
1999	Andre Agassi	Serena Williams
2000	Marat Safin	Venus Williams
2001	Lleyton Hewitt	Venus Williams
2002	Pete Sampras	Serena Williams
2003	Andy Roddick	Justine Henin-Hardenne
2004	Roger Federer	Svetlana Kuznetsova
2005	Roger Federer	Kim Clijsters
2006	Roger Federer	Maria Sharapova

Source: United States Tennis Association.

Winners of the New York Marathon, 1970–2007

	Men's Winner	Country	Time
1970	Gary Muhrcke	United States	2:31:38
1971	Norman Higgins	United States	2:22:54
1972	Sheldon Karlin	United States	2:27:52
1973	Tom Fleming	United States	2:21:54
1974	Norbert Sander	United States	2:26:30
1975	Tom Fleming	United States	2:19:27
1976	Bill Rodgers	United States	2:10:10
1977	Bill Rodgers	United States	2:11:28
1978	Bill Rodgers	United States	2:12:12
1979	Bill Rodgers	United States	2:11:42
1980	Alberto Salazar	United States	2:09:41
1981	Alberto Salazar	United States	2:08:13
1982	Alberto Salazar	United States	2:09:29
1983	Rod Dixon	New Zealand	2:08:59
1984	Orlando Pizzolato	Italy	2:14:53
1985	Orlando Pizzolato	Italy	2:11:34
1986	Gianni Poli	Italy	2:11:06
1987	Ibrahim Hussein	Kenya	2:11:01
1988	Steve Jones	Great Britain	2:08:20
1989	Juma Ikangaa	Tanzania	2:08:01
1990	Douglas Wakiihuri	Kenya	2:12:39

Winners of the New York Marathon, 1970–2007 (continued)

	Men's Winner	Country	Time
1991	Salvador Garcia	Mexico	2:09:28
1992	Willie Mtolo	South Africa	2:09:29
1993	Andres Espinosa	Mexico	2:10:04
1994	German Silva	Mexico	2:11:21
1995	German Silva	Mexico	2:11:00
1996	Giacomo Leone	Italy	2:09:54
1997	John Kagwe	Kenya	2:08:12
1998	John Kagwe	Kenya	2:08:45
1999	Joseph Chebet	Kenya	2:09:14
2000	Abdelkhader El Mouaziz	Morocco	2:10:09
2001	Tesfaye Jifar	Ethiopia	2:07:43
2002	Rodgers Rop	Kenya	2:08:07
2003	Martin Lel	Kenya	2:10:30
2004	Hendrik Ramaala	South Africa	2:09:28
2005	Paul Tergat	Kenya	2:09:30
2006	Marilson Gomes dos Santos	Brazil	2:09:58
2007	Martin Lel	Kenya	2:09:04

	Women's Winner	Country	Time
1971	Beth Bonner	United States	2:55:22
1972	Nina Kuscsik	United States	3:08:41
1973	Nina Kuscsik	United States	2:57:07
1974	Kathrine Switzer	United States	3:07:29
1975	Kim Merritt	United States	2:46:14
1976	Miki Gorman	United States	2:39:11
1977	Miki Gorman	United States	2:43:10
1978	Grete Waitz	Norway	2:32:30
1979	Grete Waitz	Norway	2:27:33
1980	Grete Waitz	Norway	2:25:42
1981	Allison Roe	New Zealand	2:25:29
1982	Grete Waitz	Norway	2:27:14
1983	Grete Waitz	Norway	2:27:00
1984	Grete Waitz	Norway	2:29:30
1985	Grete Waitz	Norway	2:28:34
1986	Grete Waitz	Norway	2:28:06

Winners of the New York Marathon, 1970–2007 (continued)

	Women's Winner	Country	Time
1987	Priscilla Welch	England	2:30:17
1988	Grete Waitz	Norway	2:28:07
1989	Ingrid Kristiansen	Norway	2:25:30
1990	Wanda Panfil	Mexico	2:30:45
1991	Liz McColgan	Great Britain	2:27:32
1992	Lisa Ondieki	Great Britain	2:24:40
1993	Uta Pippig	Germany	2:26:24
1994	Tegla Loroupe	Kenya	2:27:37
1995	Tegla Loroupe	Kenya	2:28:06
1996	Anuta Catuna	Romania	2:28:18
1997	Franziska Rochat-Moser	Switzerland	2:28:43
1998	Franca Fiacconi	Italy	2:25:17
1999	Adriana Fernandez	Mexico	2:25:06
2000	Ludmila Petrova	Russia	2:25:45
2001	Margaret Okayo	Kenya	2:24:21
2002	Joyce Chepchumba	Kenya	2:25:56
2003	Margaret Okayo	Kenya	2:22:31
2004	Paula Radcliffe	Great Britain	2:23:10
2005	Jelena Prokopcuka	Latvia	2:24:41
2006	Jelena Prokopcuka	Latvia	2:25:05
2007	Paula Radcliffe	Great Britain	2:23:09

Source: New York Road Runners Club.

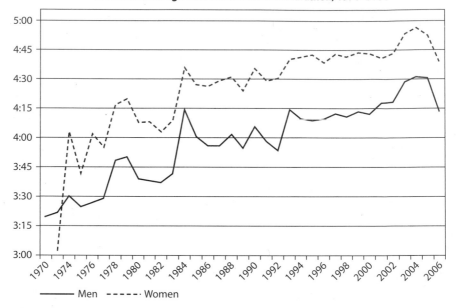

Median Finishing Times in the New York Marathon, 1970–2006

Men ——— Women - - - - -

Source: New York Road Runners Club.

Winners of the Wanamaker Mile, Millrose Games

1926	James J. Connolly	4:17.2	1954	Josy Barthel	4:07.5	1981	Eamonn Coghlan	3:53.0
1927	Lloyd Hahn	4:15.6	1955	Gunnar Nielsen	4:03.6	1982	Steve Scott	3:55.37
1928	Lloyd Hahn	4:18.6	1956	Ron Delany	4:09.5	1983	Eamonn Coghlan	3:54.40
1929	Ray Conger	4:17.4	1957	Ron Delany	4:06.7	1984	Steve Scott	3:59.38
1930	Ray Conger	4:21.8	1958	Ron Delany	4:04.6	1985	Eamonn Coghlan	3:53.82
1931	Ray Conger	4:13.6	1959	Ron Delany	4:06.5	1986	Marcus O'Sullivan	3:56.05
1932	Gene Venzke	4:11.2	1960	James Grelle	4:06.4	1987	Eamonn Coghlan	3:55.91
1933	Glenn Cunningham	4:13.0	1961	Istvan Rozsavolgyi	4:06.0	1988	Marcus O'Sullivan	3:56.89
1934	Glenn Cunningham	4:11.2	1962	Peter Close	4:08.6	1989	Marcus O'Sullivan	3:54.27
1935	Glenn Cunningham	4:11.0	1963	Tom O'Hara	4:01.5	1990	Marcus O'Sullivan	3:59.35
1936	Joseph R. Mangan	4:11.0	1964	Tom O'Hara	4:00.6	1991	Noureddine Morceli	3:53.50
1937	Glenn Cunningham	4:14.4	1965	John Whelton	4:05.4	1992	Marcus O'Sullivan	4:00.65
1938	Glenn Cunningham	4:11.0	1966	Kipchoge Keino	4:03.9	1993	Noureddine Morceli	3:55.06
1939	Glenn Cunningham	4:13.0	1967	Dave Patrick	4:03.7	1994	Niall Bruton	3:58.71
1940	Charles H. Fenske	4:07.4	1968	Preston Davis	4:03.9	1995	Graham Hood	3:57.08
1941	Walter J. Mehl	4:13.6	1969	Martin Liquori	4:00.8	1996	Niall Bruton	4:00.58
1942	Leslie MacMitchell	4:11.3	1970	Martin Liquori	4:02.6	1997	Isaac Viciosa	3:59.34
1943	Earl Mitchell	4:08.6	1971	Martin Liquori	4:00.6	1998	Laban Rotich	3:55.69
1944	Gilbert Dodds	4:10.6	1972	John Mason	4:03.2	1999	William Tanui	3:59.24
1945	James Rafferty	4:13.1	1973	Henryk Szordykowski	4:04.4	2000	Mark Carroll	3:58.19
1946	Leslie MacMitchell	4:19.0	1974	Tony Waldrop	3:59.7	2001	Bernard Lagat	3:58.26
1947	Gilbert Dodds	4:09.2	1975	Filbert Bayi	3:59.3	2002	Laban Rotich	3:57.04
1948	Gilbert Dodds	4:05.3	1976	Paul Cummings	3:57.6	2003	Bernard Lagat	4:00.36
1949	Don A. Gehrmann	4:09.5	1977	Eamonn Coghlan	4:00.2	2004	Hudson de Souza	4:02.93
1950	Don A. Gehrmann	4:09.3	1978	Dick Buerkle	3:58.4	2005	Bernard Lagat	3:52.87
1951	Don A. Gehrmann	4:07.5	1979	Eamonn Coghlan	3:55.0	2006	Bernard Lagat	3:56.85
1952	Don A. Gehrmann	4:11.2	1980	Eamonn Coghlan	3:58.2	2007	Bernard Lagat	3:54.26
1953	Fred Dwyer	4:08.2						

Source: USA Track & Field.

Meet Records at the Millrose Games

Men

60 meters	Maurice Greene	United States	6.45	2000
400 meters	Tyrone Kemp	United States	46.85	1990
500 meters	Mark Everett	United States	1:01.19	1994
600 yards	Mark Everett	United States	1:07.53	1992
800 meters	Johnny Gray	United States	1:47.17	1986
1000 meters	Sammy Koskei	Kenya	2:19.3	1985
1500 meters	Bernard Lagat	United States	3:36.1	2005
Mile	Bernard Lagat	United States	3:52.87	2005
3000 meters	Paul Bitok	Kenya	7:43.81	1999
5000 meters	Suleiman Nyambui	Tanzania	13:20.4	1981
60 meters hurdles	Allen Johnson	United States	7.43	2004
Mile walk	Tim Lewis	United States	5:33.53	1988
4 × 400 meter relay	Atlantic Coast Club		3:11.53	1988
4 × 800 meter relay	University of Richmond		7:23.08	1982
Pole vault	Jeff Hartwig	United States	19' 3" / 5.87m	2002
High jump	Jimmy Howard	United States	7' 8" / 2.34m	1985, 1986
Long jump	Carl Lewis	United States	28' 10.25" / 8.79m	1984
Shot put	Randy Barnes[1]	United States	72' 7" / 22.12m	1989
	Reese Hoffa	United States	71' 0.5" / 21.65m	2006
Weight throw	Lance Deal	United States	81' 5.25" / 24.82m	1993
College mile	Charles Cheruiyot	Kenya	3:57.9	1988
High school mile	Kevin Byrne	United States	4:08.0	1977
Masters mile	Eamonn Coghlan	Ireland	4:04.55	1994
High school 4 × 400 meter relay	Boys and Girls High School		3:21.7	1980
High School 4 × 800 meter relay	Bishop Ford High School		7:53.36	1992

Women

60 meters	Gail Devers	United States	7.00	1994
400 meters	Diane Dixon	United States	52.20	1986
800 meters	Jolanda Ceplak	Slovenia	1:59.98	2002
1500 meters	Mary Decker	United States	4:00.8	1980
Mile	Doina Melinte	Romania	4:21.45	1988
60 meter hurdles	Gail Devers	United States	7.76	2004
4 × 400 meter relay	Atoms Track Club		3:40.51	1984
4 × 800 meter relay	Villanova University		8:33.94	1989
Pole vault	Stacy Dragila	United States	15' 5.75" / 4.72m	2003
High jump	Louise Ritter	United States	6' 5.5" / 1.97m	1989

Meet Records at the Millrose Games (continued)

Women

Long jump	Jackie Joyner-Kersee	United States	22' 11.75" / 7.00m	1992
Shot put	Connie Price-Smith	United States	61' 7.75" / 18.59m	1999
Weight throw	Erin Gilreath	United States	78' 6.25" / 23.93m	2005
College mile	Vicki Huber	United States	4:28.31	1988
High school mile	Sarah Schwald	United States	4:49.94	1989
High school 4 × 400m relay	Boys and Girls High School		3:54.98	2002

[1] At Manhattan College.
Source: USA Track & Field.

8 Government and Politics

Mayors of the City of New York

#	Name	Years	#	Name	Years
1.	Thomas Willett	1665[1]	39.	Stephen Bayard	1744–1747
2.	Thomas Delavall	1666	40.	Edward Holland	1747–1757
3.	Thomas Willett	1667	41.	John Cruger Jr.	1757–1766
4.	Cornelius Steenwyck	1668–1670	42.	Whitehead Hicks	1766–1776
5.	Thomas Delavall	1671	43.	David Mathews	1776–1784
6.	Matthias Nicolls	1672	44.	James Duane	1784–1789
7.	John Lawrence	1673	45.	Richard Varick	1789–1801
8.	William Dervall	1675	46.	Edward Livingston	1801–1803
9.	Nicholas De Meyer	1676	47.	De Witt Clinton	1803–1807
10.	Stephanus Van Cortlandt	1677	48.	Marinus Willett	1807–1088
11.	Thomas Delavall	1678	49.	De Witt Clinton	1808–1810
12.	Francis Rombouts	1679	50.	Jacob Radcliff	1810–1811
13.	William Dyre	1680–1681	51.	De Witt Clinton	1811–1815
14.	Cornelius Steenwyck	1682–1683	52.	John Ferguson	1815
15.	Gabriel Minvielle	1684	53.	Jacob Radcliff	1815–1818
16.	Nicholas Bayard	1685	54.	Cadwallader D. Colden	1818–1821
17.	S. Van Cortlandt	1686–1688	55.	Stephen Allen	1821–1824
18.	Peter Delanoy	1689–1690	56.	William Paulding	1825–1826
19.	John Lawrence	1691	57.	Philip Hone	1826–1827
20.	Abraham De Peyster	1692–1694	58.	William Paulding	1827–1829
21.	Charles Lodwik	1694–1695	59.	Walter Bowne	1829–1833
22.	William Merrett	1695–1698	60.	Gideon Lee	1833–1834
23.	Johannes De Peyster	1698–1699	61.	Cornelius W. Lawrence	1834–1837
24.	David Provost	1699–1700	62.	Aaron Clark	1837–1839
25.	Isaac de Reimer	1700–1701	63.	Isaac L. Varian	1839–1841
26.	Thomas Noell	1701–1702	64.	Robert H. Morris	1841–1844
27.	Philip French	1702–1703	65.	James Harper	1844–1845
28.	William Peartree	1703–1707	66.	William F. Havemeyer	1845–1846
29.	Ebenezer Wilson	1707–1710	67.	Andrew H. Mickle	1846–1847
30.	Jacobus Van Cortlandt	1710–1711	68.	William V. Brady	1847–1848
31.	Caleb Heathcote	1711–1714	69.	William F. Havemeyer	1848–1849
32.	John Johnson	1714–1719	70.	Caleb S. Woodhull	1849–1851
33.	Jacobus Van Cortlandt	1719–1720	71.	Ambrose C. Kingsland	1851–1853
34.	Robert Walters	1720–1725	72.	Jacob A. Westervelt	1853–1855
35.	Johannes Jansen	1725–1726	73.	Fernando Wood	1855–1858
36.	Robert Lurting	1726–1735	74.	Daniel F. Tiemann	1858–1860
37.	Paul Richard	1735–1739	75.	Fernando Wood	1860–1862
38.	John Cruger	1739–1744	76.	George Opdyke	1862–1864

77. C. Godfrey Gunther	1864–1866	93. George B. McClellan	1904–1909
78. John T. Hoffman	1866–1868	94. William J. Gaynor	1910–1913
T. Coman	1868[2]	Ardolph L. Kline	1913[2]
79. A. Oakey Hall	1869–1872	95. John Purroy Mitchel	1914–1917
80. William F. Havemeyer	1873–1874	96. John F. Hylan	1918–1925
S. B. H. Vance	1874[2]	97. James J. Walker	1926–1932[3]
81. William H. Wickham	1875–1876	Joseph V. McKee	1932[2]
82. Smith Ely	1877–1878	98. John P. O'Brien	1933
83. Edward Cooper	1879–1880	99. Fiorello H. La Guardia	1934–1945
84. William R. Grace	1881–1882	100. William O'Dwyer	1946–1950[4]
85. Franklin Edson	1883–1884	101. Vincent R. Impellitteri	1950–1953[5]
86. William R. Grace	1885–1886	102. Robert F. Wagner	1954–1965
87. Abram S. Hewitt	1887–1888	103. John V. Lindsay	1966–1973
88. Hugh J. Grant	1889–1892	104. Abraham D. Beame	1974–1977
89. Thomas F. Gilroy	1893–1894	105. Edward I. Koch	1978–1989
90. William L. Strong	1895–1897	106. David N. Dinkins	1990–1993
91. Robert A. Van Wyck	1898–1901	107. Rudolph W. Giuliani	1994–2001
92. Seth Low	1902–1903	108. Michael R. Bloomberg	2002–

[1] Before 15 June 1665 (when New Amsterdam was captured by the British), the city was headed by burgomasters.
[2] Acting mayor.
[3] Resigned 1 September 1932.
[4] Resigned 2 September 1950.
[5] Acting mayor from 2 September 1950 to 14 November 1950. Elected mayor 7 November 1950.
Source: The Green Book.

Mayors of the City of Brooklyn

George Hall	1834	Martin Kalbfleisch	1861–1863
Jonathan Trotter	1835–1836	Alfred M. Wood	1864–1865
Jeremiah Johnson	1837–1838	Samuel Booth	1866–1867
Cyrus P. Smith	1839–1841	Martin Kalbfleisch	1868–1871
Henry C. Murphy	1842	Samuel S. Powell	1872–1873
Joseph Sprague	1843–1844	John W. Hunter	1874–1875
Thomas G. Talmage	1845	Frederick A. Schroeder	1876–1877
Francis B. Stryker	1846–1848	James Howell	1878–1881
Edward Copeland	1849	Seth Low	1882–1885
Samuel Smith	1850	Daniel D. Whitney	1886–1887
Conklin Brush	1851–1852	Alfred C. Chapin	1888–1891
Edward A. Lambert	1853–1854	David A. Boody	1892–1893
George Hall	1855–1856	Charles A. Schiern	1894–1895
Samuel S. Powell	1857–1860	Frederick W. Wurster	1896–1898

Note: No mayors elected after consolidation of New York City in 1898.
Source: Kenneth T. Jackson, ed., *The Encyclopedia of New York City* (New Haven, Conn.: Yale University Press / New York: New-York Historical Society, 1995).

Presidents of the Board of Aldermen (1898–1937) and City Council (1938–1993)

Randolph Guggenheimer	1898–1901	Timothy J. Sullivan	1936
Charles V. Fornes	1902–1905	William F. Brunner	1937
Patrick McGowan	1906–1909	Newbold Morris	1938–1945
John Purroy Mitchel	1910–1913	Vincent R. Impellitteri	1946–1949
George McAneny	1914–1916	Joseph T. Sharkey	1950
Frank L. Dowling	1917	Rudolph Halley	1951–1953
Alfred E. Smith	1918	Abe Stark	1954–1961
Robert L. Moran	1919	Paul R. Screvane	1962–1965
Fiorello H. La Guardia	1920–1921	Frank D. O'Connor	1966–1970
Murray Hulbert	1922–1924	Sanford D. Garelik	1971–1973
William T. Collins	1925	Paul O'Dwyer	1974–1977
Joseph V. McKee	1926–1933	Carol Bellamy	1978–1985
Bernard S. Deutsch	1934–1935	Andrew J. Stein	1986–1993

Source: Kenneth T. Jackson, ed., *The Encyclopedia of New York City* (New Haven, Conn.: Yale University Press / New York: New-York Historical Society, 1995).

Comptrollers of the City of New York

Selah Strong	1801–1805	Edward V. Loew	1885–1887
Benjamin Romaine	January 1805–December 1806	Theo. W. Myers	1888–1893
Isaac Stoutenberg	December 1806–January 1807	Ashbel P. Fitch	1894–1897
Jacob Morton	1807	M. T. Daily	1898
Garret N. Bleecker	1808–1813	Bird S. Coler	1899–1901
Thomas R. Mercein	1813–1816	Edward M. Grout	1902–1905
Garret N. Bleecker	1816–1831	Herman Metz	1906–1908
Talman J. Waters	1831–1836	W. A. Pendergast	1910–1917
Douw D. Williamson	1842	Charles L. Craig	1918–1925
Alfred A. Smith	1843, 1844	Charles W. Berry	1926–1932
Douw D. Williamson	1844, 1845	George McAneny	1933
John Ewen	1845–1848	Arthur Cunningham	1934
Talman J. Waters	1848, 1849	Joseph D. McGoldrick	1935
John L. Lawrence	1849	Frank J. Taylor	1936–1937
Joseph R. Taylor	1850–1853	Joseph D. McGoldrick	1938–1945
Azariah C. Flagg	1853–1859	Lazarus Joseph	1946–1953
Robert T. Haws	1859–1863	Lawrence E. Gerosa	1954–1961
Mathew T. Brennan	1863–1867	Abraham D. Beame	1962–1965
Richard B. Connolly	1868–1872	Mario Procaccino	1966–1969
W. F. Havemeyer	1873	Abraham D. Beame	1970–1973
Andrew Haswell Green	1874–1876	Harrison J. Goldin	1974–1989
John Kelly	1877–1880	Elizabeth Holtzman	1990–1993
Allan Campbell	1881–1883	Alan G. Hevesi	1994–2002
S. Hastings Grant	1884	William C. Thompson Jr.	2002–

Sources: Edgar A. Werner, *Civil List and Constitutional History of the County and State of New York* (Albany: Weed, Parsons, 1886); Proceedings of the Board of Aldermen, 1873–1899; Kenneth T. Jackson, ed., *The Encyclopedia of New York City* (New Haven, Conn.: Yale University Press / New York: New-York Historical Society, 1995).

Public Advocates of the City of New York

Mark J. Green	1 January 1994 to 31 December 2001
Betsy Gotbaum	1 January 2002 to present

Source: Office of the Public Advocate.

Salaries of Elected and Appointed City Officials, 2007

Mayor	$225,000
Public advocate	165,000
Members, City Council	112,500
Borough presidents	160,000
Comptroller	185,000
District attorneys	190,000
Deputy mayor for operations	204,866
Deputy mayor for policy	177,236
Deputy mayor for economic development and rebuilding	177,236
Deputy mayor for administration	177,236
Deputy mayor for legal affairs and counsel to the mayor	177,236
Chief of staff to the mayor	171,038
Director of communications and press secretary to the mayor	171,038
Senior advisor to the mayor	125,246
Special advisor to the mayor for governance and strategic planning	126,072
Director of research, Office of the Mayor	147,000
Executive director, Commission to Combat Police Corruption	124,019
City clerk and clerk of the City Council	159,368
Commissioner, Department for the Aging	151,181
Commissioner, Department of Buildings	162,800
Chair, City Planning Commission	162,800
Vice-chair, City Planning Commission	51,900
Members, City Planning Commission	45,131
Chancellor, City University of New York	350,000
President, Hunter College	175,000
President, New York City College of Technology	155,000
President, Sophie Davis School of Biomedical Education / City University of New York Medical School	192,000
Dean, City University School of Law at Queens College	189,740
President, Queens College	196,000
President, College of Staten Island	183,113
President, Bronx Community College	153,000
President, Borough of Manhattan Community College	155,000
President, Queensborough Community College	176,580
Commissioner, Department of Citywide Administrative Services	171,038
Commissioner of Correction	162,800
Commissioner, Department of Cultural Affairs	151,181
Commissioner, Department of Design and Construction	162,800
Chancellor, Department of Education	250,000
Commissioners of Elections	12,500

Commissioner, Office of Emergency Management	171,038
Commissioner, Department of Environmental Protection	171,038
Commissioner, Department of Finance	162,800
Executive Director, Financial Information Services Agency	171,038
Fire Commissioner	162,800
Commissioner of Health and Mental Hygiene	171,038
Commissioner, Department of Homeless Services	162,800
Chair, Housing Authority	177,038
Members, Housing Authority	162,183
Administrator, Human Resources Administration / Commissioner, Department of Social Services	171,038
Commissioner, Department of Information Technology and Communications	162,800
Commissioner, Department of Investigation	162,800
Commissioner, Department of Juvenile Justice	143,900
Commissioner, Office of Labor Relations	171,038
Corporation Counsel	171,038
Director, Office of Management and Budget	171,038
President, Off-Track Betting Corporation	171,017
Commissioner, Department of Parks and Recreation	171,038
Executive Director, Office of Payroll Administration	171,038
Police Commissioner	171,038
Commissioner of Probation	171,038
Commissioner, Department of Records and Information Services	119,348
Sanitation Commissioner	162,800
Commissioner, Department of Small Business Services	152,506
Chair, Board of Standards and Appeals	160,217
President, Tax Appeals Tribunal	125,600
Commissioners, Tax Appeals Tribunal	125,600
Commissioners, Tax Commission	24,168
Commissioner, Department of Transportation	171,038
Commissioner, Department of Youth and Community Development	143,900
County clerk, New York County	136,000
County clerk, Bronx County	108,128
County clerk, Kings County	108,128
County, clerk, Queens County	108,128
County clerk, Richmond County	136,500
Public administrators	91,134
Judges, Criminal Court	125,600
Judges, Civil Court	125,600
Judges, Housing Part	115,400

Salaries of Elected and Appointed City Officials, 2007 (continued)

Judges, Family Court	136,700
Support magistrates	92,214
Surrogates	136,700

Sources: *New York Times*, 6 December 2006; The Green Book.

Presidents of the Five Boroughs

Manhattan

Augustus Peters	1898–1899
James Coogan	1899–1901
Jacob Cantor	1902–1903
John F. Ahearn	1904 to December 1909
John Cloughen	December 1909 (4 days)
George McAneny	January 1910 to 1913
Marcus Marks	1914–1917
Frank Dowling	1918–1919
Edward Boyle	1919
Michael Loughman	1919
Henry H. Curran	1920–1921
Julius Miller	1922–1930
Samuel Levy	1931–1937
Stanley Isaacs	1938–1941
Edgar Nathan	1942–1945
Hugo E. Rogers	1946–1949
Robert F. Wagner	1 January 1950 to 31 December 1953
Hulan E. Jack	1 January 1954 to 16 January 1961
Edward R. Dudley	31 January 1961 to 31 December 1964
Constance Baker Motley	24 February 1965 to 13 September 1966
Percy Ellis Sutton	13 September 1966 to 31 December 1977
Andrew J. Stein	1 January 1978 to 31 December 1985
David Norman Dinkins	1 January 1986 to 31 December 1989
Ruth W. Messinger	1 January 1990 to 31 December 1997
C. Virginia Fields	1 January 1998 to 31 December 2005
Scott M. Stringer	1 January 2006 to present

Bronx

Louis F. Haffen	1898 to 30 August 1909
John F. Murray	30 August 1909 to 1910 (acting to 9 September 1909)
Cyrus C. Miller	1910–1914
Douglas Mathewson	1914–1918
Henry Bruckner	1918–1934
James Joseph Lyons	1934 to January 1962
Joseph F. Periconi	January 1962 to January 1966
Herman Badillo	January 1966 to 7 January 1970
Robert Abrams	7 January 1970 to 28 January 1979
Stanley Simon	28 January 1979 to 15 April 1987
Fernando Ferrer	15 April 1987 to 6 January 2002
Adolfo Carrión Jr.	6 January 2002 to present

Brooklyn

Edward Marshall Grout	January 1898 to December 1901
Edward J. Swanstrom	January 1902 to December 1903
Martin Wiley Littleton	January 1904 to December 1905
Bird Sim Coler	January 1906 to December 1909
Alfred E. Steers	January 1910 to June 1913
Lewis Humphrey Pounds	June 1913 to December 1917
Edward J. Riegelmann	January 1918 to December 1924
Joseph A. Guider	January 1925 to September 1926
James J. Byrne	September 1926 to March 1930
Henry Hersterberg	March 1930 to December 1933
Raymond Vail Ingersoll	January 1934 to February 1940
John Cashmore	February 1940 to 7 May 1961
John F. Hayes	7 May 1961 to 31 December 1961 (acting to 10 July 1961)
Abe Stark	1 January 1962 to 9 September 1970
Sebastian Leone	9 September 1970 to 31 December 1976
Howard Golden	3 January 1977 to 31 December 2001
Marty Markowitz	13 January 2002 to present

Queens

Frederick Bowley	1 January 1898 to 31 December 1901
Joseph Cassidy	1 January 1902 to 31 December 1905
Joseph Bermel	1 January 1906 to 29 April 1908
Lawrence Gresser	30 April 1908 to 28 September 1911
Maurice E. Connolly	4 October 1911 to 3 April 1928
Bernard M. Patten	18 April 1928 to 31 December 1928

Presidents of the Five Boroughs (continued)

Queens (continued)

George Upton Harvey	1 January 1929 to 31 December 1941
James A. Burke	1 January 1942 to 31 December 1949
Maurice A. Fitzgerald	1 January 1950 to 25 August 1951
Joseph F. Mafera	26 August 1951 to 31 December 1951
James A. Lundy	1 January 1952 to 31 December 1957
James J. Crisona	1 January 1958 to 31 December 1958
John T. Clancy	5 January 1959 to 31 December 1962
Mario J. Cariello	2 January 1963 to 31 December 1968
Sidney Leviss	3 January 1969 to 17 September 1971
Donald R. Manes	22 September 1971 to 11 February 1986
Claire Shulman	11 February 1986 to 31 December 2001 (acting to 12 March 1986)
Helen M. Marshall	3 January 2002 to present

Staten Island

George Cromwell	1898–1913
Charles J. McCormack	1914–1915
Calvin Van Name	1915–1921
Matthew J. Cahill	1922
John A. Lynch	1922–1933
Joseph A. Palma	1934–1945
Cornelius A. Hall	1946–1953
Edward G. Baker	1953–1954
Albert V. Maniscalco	1955–1965
Robert T. Connor	1966–1977
Anthony R. Gaeta	1977–1984
Ralph J. Lamberti	1984–1989
Guy V. Molinari	1990 to 31 December 2001
James P. Molinaro	6 January 2002 to present

Source: worldstatesmen.org.

Results of Mayoral Elections, 1834–1894

Candidate	Party	Number of Votes	Candidate	Party	Number of Votes
1834			**1840**		
Cornelius W. Lawrence	Democrat	17,576	Isaac L. Varian	Democrat	21,243
Gulian C. Verplanck	Whig	17,395	J. P. Phoenix	Whig	19,622
Others		18	Others		36
Total		34,989	Total		40,901
1835			**1841**		
Cornelius W. Lawrence	Democrat	17,696	Robert H. Morris	Democrat	18,605
Others		2,500	J. P. Phoenix	Whig	18,206
Total		20,196	Samuel F. B. Morse	Native American	77
			Others		45
1836			Total		36,933
Cornelius W. Lawrence	Democrat	15,754			
Seth Geer	Whig	6,136	**1842**		
Alexander Ming Jr.	Locofoco	2,712	Robert H. Morris	Democrat	20,633
Samuel F. B. Morse	Native American	1,497	J. P. Phoenix	Whig	18,755
Others		75	Thomas F. Field	Abolition	136
Total		26,174	Others		63
			Total		39,587
1837					
Aaron Clark	Whig	16,140	**1843**		
John I. Morgan	Democrat	12,974	Robert H. Morris	Democrat	24,395
Moses Jacques	Locofoco	3,911	Robert Smith	Whig	19,516
Others		28	Others		73
Total		33,053	Total		43,984
1838			**1844**		
Aaron Clark	Whig	19,723	James Harper	Native	24,606
Isaac L. Varian	Democrat	19,204	Jonathan I. Coddington	Locofoco	20,726
Richard Riker	Conservative	395	Morris Franklin	Whig	5,207
Others		19	Others		22
Total		39,341	Total		50,561
1839					
Isaac L. Varian	Democrat	21,072			
Aaron Clark	Whig	20,005			
Others		36			
Total		41,113			

Results of Mayoral Elections, 1834–1894 (continued)

Candidate	Party	Number of Votes	Candidate	Party	Number of Votes
1845			**1852**		
William F. Havemeyer	Democrat	24,183	Jacob A. Westervelt	Democrat	33,251
James Harper	Native	17,472	Morgan Morgans	Whig	23,719
Dudley Selden	Whig	7,082	Others		1,088
Others		226	Total		58,058
Total		48,963			
			1854		
1846			Fernando Wood	Soft Shells–Hard Shells	19,993
Andrew H. Mickle	Democrat	21,675			
Robert Taylor	Whig	15,111	James W. Barker	Know Nothing	18,553
William B. Cozzens	Native	8,301	Wilson G. Hunt	Reform	15,386
Others		757	Others		5,828
Total		45,844	Total		59,760
1847			**1856**		
William V. Brady	Whig	21,310	Fernando Wood	Democrat	34,860
J. Sherman Brownell	Democrat	19,877	Isaac O. Backer	American	25,209
E. G. Drake	Native	2,078	Anthony J. Bleecker	Republican	9,654
Others		433	James S. Libby	Bog Democrat	4,764
Total		43,698	James R. Whiting	Municipal Reform	3,646
			Others		84
1848			Total		78,217
William F. Havemeyer	Democrat	23,155			
William V. Brady	Whig	22,227	**1857**		
Others		848	Daniel F. Tiemann	Independent	43,216
Total		46,230	Fernando Wood	Democrat	40,889
			Others		103
1849			Total		84,208
Caleb S. Woodhull	Whig	21,656			
Myndert Van Schaick	Democrat	17,535	**1859**		
Others		103	Fernando Wood	Mozart Democrat	29,940
Total		39,294	William F. Havemeyer	Tammany Democrat	26,913
			George Opdyke	Republican	21,417
1850			Others		106
Ambrose C. Kingsland	Whig	22,546	Total		78,376
Fernando Wood	Democrat	17,973			
Others		335			
Total		40,854			

Results of Mayoral Elections, 1834–1894 (continued)

Candidate	Party	Number of Votes	Candidate	Party	Number of Votes
1861			**1869**		
George Opdyke	Republican	25,380	A. Oakey Hall	Democrat	65,568
C. Godfrey Gunther	Tammany Democrat	24,767	Others		1,051
Fernando Wood	Mozart Democrat	24,167	Total		66,619
Others		81			
Total		74,395	**1870**		
			A. Oakey Hall	Tammany Democrat	71,037
1863					
C. Godfrey Gunther	Independent Democrat	29,121	Thomas A. Ledwith	Anti-Tammany Democrat	46,392
Francis I. A. Boyle	Tammany Democrat	22,597	Others		1,989
Orison Blount	Republican	19,383	Total		119,418
Others		65			
Total		71,166	**1872**		
			William F. Havemeyer	Republican	53,806
1865			A. R. Lawrence	Liberal-Republican	45,398
John T. Hoffman	Tammany Democrat	32,820			
Marshall O. Roberts	Republican	31,657	James O'Brien	Apollo Hall Democrat	31,121
John Hecker	Mozart Democrat	10,390	Total		130,325
C. Godfrey Gunther	Independent Democrat	6,758			
Others		77	**1874**		
Total		81,702	William H. Wickham	Democrat	70,071
			Salem H. Wales	Republican	36,953
1867			Oswald Ottendorfer	Independent	24,226
John T. Hoffman	Tammany Democrat	63,061	Others		443
Fernando Wood	Mozart Democrat	22,837	Total		131,693
William A. Darling	Republican	18,483			
Others		100	**1876**		
Total		104,481	Smith Ely Jr.	Democrat	111,880
			John Dix	Republican	57,811
1868			Others		552
A. Oakey Hall	Democrat	75,109	Total		170,243
Frederick A. Conkling	Republican	20,835			
Others		321			
Total		96,265			

Results of Mayoral Elections, 1834–1894 (continued)

Candidate	Party	Number of Votes	Candidate	Party	Number of Votes
1878			**1888**		
Edward Cooper	Republican	79,986	Hugh J. Grant	Democrat	114,111
August Schell	Democrat	60,485	Joel B. Erhardt	Republican	73,037
Others		2,793	Abram S. Hewitt	Citizens Democrat	71,979
Total		143,264	Others		13,643
1880			Total		272,770
William R. Grace	Democrat	101,760	**1890**		
William Dowd	Republican	98,715	Hugh J. Grant	Democrat	116,581
Others		1,827	Francis M. Scott	Republican	93,382
Total		202,302	Others		7,846
1882			Total		217,809
Franklin Edson	Democrat	97,802	**1892**		
Allan Campbell	Republican	76,385	Thomas F. Gilroy	Democrat	173,510
Others		4,124	Edwin Einstein	Republican	97,923
Total		178,311	Henry Hicks	People's	2,466
1884			Others		12,250
William R. Grace	Independent	96,288	Total		286,149
Hugh J. Grant	Tammany Hall Democrat	85,361	**1894**		
Frederick S. Gibbs	Republican	44,386	William L. Strong	Republican	154,094
Others		1,300	Hugh J. Grant	Democrat	108,907
Total		227,335	Others		11,315
1886			Total		274,316
Abram S. Hewitt	Democrat	90,552			
Henry George	Labor Union	68,110			
Theodore Roosevelt	Republican	60,435			
Others		895			
Total		219,992			

Sources: *Manual of the Corporation of the City of New York*, 1870 [for years 1834–1870]; *The City Record* [for years 1872–1894].

Results of Mayoral Elections by Borough, 1897–2005

1897	Robert A. Van Wyck (Democrat)	Seth Low (Citizens Union)	Benjamin Tracy (Republican)
Manhattan and Bronx	143,666	77,210	55,834
Brooklyn	76,185	65,656	37,611
Queens	9,275	5,876	5,639
Staten Island	4,871	2,798	2,779
Total	233,997	151,540	101,863

Other candidates: 44,230
Total vote: 531,630

1901	Seth Low (Fusion)	Edward M. Shephard (Democrat)
Manhattan and Bronx	114,625	88,858
Brooklyn	162,298	156,631
Queens	12,757	13,321
Staten Island	7,133	6,367
Total	296,813	265,177

Total vote: 561,990

1903	George B. McClellan (Democrat)	Seth Low (Fusion)
Manhattan and Bronx	188,681	132,178
Brooklyn	102,569	101,251
Queens	17,074	11,960
Staten Island	6,458	6,697
Total	314,782	252,086

Other candidates: 28,417
Total vote: 595,285

Results of Mayoral Elections by Borough, 1897–2005 (continued)

1905	George B. McClellan (Democrat)	William R. Hearst (Independent)	William M. Ivins (Republican)
Manhattan and Bronx	140,264	123,292	64,289
Brooklyn	68,778	84,835	61,192
Queens	13,228	13,706	7,213
Staten Island	6,127	3,096	4,499
Total	228,397	224,929	137,193

Other candidates: 15,676
Total vote: 606,195

1909	William J. Gaynor (Democrat)	Otto T. Bannard (Fusion)	William R. Hearst (Independent)
Manhattan and Bronx	134,075	86,497	87,155
Brooklyn	91,666	73,860	49,040
Queens	17,570	11,907	15,186
Staten Island	7,067	5,040	2,806
Total	250,378	177,304	154,187

Other candidates: 22,198
Total vote: 604,067

1913	John Purroy Mitchel (Fusion)	Edward E. McCall (Democrat)
Manhattan	131,280	103,429
Bronx	46,944	25,684
Brooklyn	137,074	77,826
Queens	34,279	20,097
Staten Island	8,640	6,883
Total	358,217	233,919

Other candidates: 34,991
Total vote: 627,127

Results of Mayoral Elections by Borough, 1897–2005 (continued)

1917	John F. Hylan (Democrat)	John Purroy Mitchel (Fusion)	Morris Hillquit (Socialist)
Manhattan	113,728	66,748	51,176
Bronx	41,492	19,247	30,374
Brooklyn	114,487	52,921	48,880
Queens	35,399	13,641	13,477
Staten Island	8,850	2,940	1,425
Total	313,956	155,497	145,332

John Bennett (Republican): 56,438; Other candidates: 20,586
Total vote: 691,809

1921	John F. Hylan (Democrat)	Henry H. Curran (Republican)	Jacob Panken (Socialist)
Manhattan	261,452	124,253	28,756
Bronx	118,235	34,919	21,255
Brooklyn	260,143	128,259	29,580
Queens	87,676	36,415	2,741
Staten Island	22,741	9,000	275
Total	750,247	332,846	82,607

Other candidates: 31,242
Total vote: 1,196,942

1925
Democratic Primary

	James J. Walker	John F. Hylan
Manhattan	102,835	27,802
Bronx	45,308	21,228
Brooklyn	65,671	60,814
Queens	28,203	32,163
Staten Island	6,321	12,197
Total	248,338	154,204

Results of Mayoral Elections by Borough, 1897–2005 (continued)

1925 (continued)
General Election

	James J. Walker (Democrat)	Frank D. Waterman (Republican)	Norman Thomas (Socialist)
Manhattan	247,079	98,617	9,482
Bronx	131,226	39,615	11,133
Brooklyn	244,029	139,060	16,809
Queens	103,629	58,478	1,943
Staten Island	22,724	10,794	207
Total	748,687	346,564	39,574

Other candidates: 26,272
Total vote: 1,161,097

1929

	James J. Walker (Democrat)	Fiorello H. La Guardia (Republican)	Norman Thomas (Socialist)
Manhattan	232,370	91,944	37,316
Bronx	159,948	52,646	39,181
Brooklyn	283,432	132,095	71,145
Queens	166,188	75,911	24,807
Staten Island	25,584	15,079	3,248
Total	867,522	367,675	175,697

Other candidates: 53,795
Total vote: 1,464,689

1932

	John O'Brien (Democrat)	Lewis H. Pounds (Republican)	Morris Hillquit (Socialist)	Joseph McKee (write-in)
Manhattan	308,944	116,729	40,011	42,299
Bronx	181,639	48,366	68,980	50,212
Brooklyn	358,945	157,152	113,622	73,431
Queens	176,070	105,068	24,981	61,648
Staten Island	30,517	16,586	2,293	6,782
Total	1,056,115	443,901	249,887	234,372

Other candidates: 269,585
Total vote: 2,253,860

Results of Mayoral Elections by Borough, 1897–2005 (continued)

1933	Fiorello H. La Guardia (Republican–City Fusion)	Joseph McKee (Recovery)	John O'Brien (Democrat)
Manhattan	203,479	123,707	192,649
Bronx	151,669	131,280	93,403
Brooklyn	331,920	194,558	194,335
Queens	154,369	141,296	90,501
Staten Island	27,085	18,212	15,784
Total	868,522	609,053	586,672

Charles Solomon (Socialist): 59,846; Other candidates: 81,309
Total vote: 2,205,402

1937	Fiorello H. La Guardia (City Fusion–Progressive–American Labor–Republican)	Jeremiah T. Mahoney (Democrat–Trades Union–Anti-Communist)
Manhattan	328,995	237,006
Bronx	272,322	166,805
Brooklyn	494,516	286,647
Queens	213,939	172,973
Staten Island	34,858	27,325
Total	1,344,630	890,756

Other candidates: 64,834
Total vote: 2,300,220

1941	Fiorello H. La Guardia (City Fusion–United City–American Labor–Republican)	William O'Dwyer (Democrat)
Manhattan	298,225	227,717
Bronx	259,607	185,295
Brooklyn	439,856	348,048
Queens	166,364	259,239
Staten Island	22,249	33,876
Total	1,186,301	1,054,175

Other candidates: 53,250
Total vote: 2,293,726

Results of Mayoral Elections by Borough, 1897–2005 (continued)

1945	William O'Dwyer (Democrat–American Labor)	Jonah J. Goldstein (Republican-Liberal-Fusion)	Newbold Morris (No Deal)
Manhattan	253,371	100,591	100,064
Bronx	227,818	95,582	88,404
Brooklyn	386,335	161,119	136,262
Queens	228,275	65,240	77,687
Staten Island	29,558	9,069	5,931
Total	1,125,357	431,601	408,348

Other candidates: 71,385
Total vote: 2,036,691

1949	William O'Dwyer (Democrat)	Newbold Morris (Republican-Liberal-Fusion)	Vito Marcantonio (American Labor)
Manhattan	278,343	219,430	123,128
Bronx	254,014	185,248	82,386
Brooklyn	425,225	332,433	113,478
Queens	270,062	200,552	34,677
Staten Island	38,868	18,406	2,957
Total	1,266,512	956,069	356,626

Other candidates: 83,710
Total vote: 2,662,917

1950	Vincent Impellitteri (Experience)	Ferdinand Pecora (Democrat-Liberal)	Edward Corsi (Republican)
Manhattan	246,608	214,610	102,575
Bronx	215,913	217,254	54,796
Brooklyn	357,322	362,246	113,392
Queens	303,448	129,223	99,225
Staten Island	37,884	12,018	12,384
Total	1,161,175	935,351	382,372

Paul L. Ross (American Labor): 147,578; Other candidates: 70,429
Total vote: 2,696,905

Results of Mayoral Elections by Borough, 1897–2005 (continued)

1953	Robert F. Wagner (Democrat)	Harold Riegelmann (Republican)	Rudolph Halley (Liberal-Independent)
Manhattan	236,960	147,876	84,532
Bronx	206,771	97,224	122,678
Brooklyn	339,970	183,968	175,537
Queens	207,918	208,829	80,548
Staten Island	31,007	23,694	3,809
Total	1,022,626	661,591	467,104

Clifford T. McAvor (American Labor): 53,045; Other candidates: 39,780
Total vote: 2,244,146

1957	Robert F. Wagner (Democrat-Liberal-Fusion)	Robert K. Christenberry (Republican)
Manhattan	316,203	112,173
Bronx	316,299	96,726
Brooklyn	494,078	163,427
Queens	341,212	191,061
Staten Island	40,983	22,381
Total	1,508,775	585,768

Other candidates: 129,511
Total vote: 2,224,054

1961
Democratic Primary

	Robert F. Wagner	Arthur Levitt
Manhattan	122,607	66,917
Bronx	78,626	47,885
Brooklyn	136,440	103,296
Queens	102,845	64,157
Staten Island	15,498	10,471
Total	456,016	292,726

1961 (continued)
General Election

	Robert F. Wagner (Democrat-Liberal-Brotherhood)	Louis J. Lefkowitz (Republican–Civic Action–Non-Partisan)	Lawrence E. Gerosa (Independent– Citizens Party)
Manhattan	265,015	174,471	36,893
Bronx	255,528	134,964	67,213
Brooklyn	396,539	251,258	105,232
Queens	290,194	243,836	99,987
Staten Island	30,145	31,162	12,279
Total	1,237,421	835,691	321,604

Other candidates: 72,830
Total vote: 2,467,546

1965
Democratic Primary

	Abraham D. Beame	Paul R. Screvane	William F. Ryan	Paul O'Dwyer
Manhattan	53,386	66,444	48,744	6,775
Bronx	66,064	54,260	16,632	5,976
Brooklyn	128,146	79,485	24,588	8,332
Queens	82,601	63,680	22,570	6,895
Staten Island	6,148	7,512	1,204	697
Total	336,345	271,381	113,738	28,675

1965 (continued)
General Election

	John V. Lindsay (Republican– Liberal– Independent Citizen)	Abraham D. Beame (Democrat– Civil Service– Fusion)	William F. Buckley (Conservative)
Manhattan	291,326	193,230	37,694
Bronx	181,072	213,980	63,858
Brooklyn	308,398	365,360	97,679
Queens	331,162	250,662	121,544
Staten Island	37,148	23,467	20,451
Total	1,149,106	1,046,699	341,226

Other candidates: 115,420
Total vote: 2,652,451

1969
Democratic Primary

	Mario Procaccino	Robert F. Wagner	Herman Badillo	Norman Mailer	James H. Scheuer
Manhattan	26,804	40,978	74,809	17,372	7,117
Bronx	50,465	33,442	48,841	4,214	10,788
Brooklyn	87,630	81,833	52,866	10,299	11,942
Queens	79,002	61,244	37,880	8,700	8,994
Staten Island	11,628	6,967	2,769	703	509
Total	255,529	224,464	217,165	41,288	39,350

Results of Mayoral Elections by Borough, 1897–2005 (continued)

1969 (continued)
Republican Primary

	John J. Marchi	John V. Lindsay
Manhattan	12,457	44,236
Bronx	16,132	12,222
Brooklyn	33,694	20,575
Queens	40,469	26,658
Staten Island	10,946	3,675
Total	113,698	107,366

General Election

	John V. Lindsay (Liberal-Independent)	Mario Procaccino (Democrat–Non-Partisan–Civil Service Independent)	John J. Marchi (Republican-Conservative)
Manhattan	328,564	99,460	61,539
Bronx	161,953	165,647	76,711
Brooklyn	256,046	301,324	152,933
Queens	249,330	245,783	192,008
Staten Island	16,740	19,558	59,220
Total	1,012,633	831,772	542,411

Other candidates: 71,387
Total vote: 2,458,203

1973
Democratic Primary

	Abraham D. Beame	Herman Badillo	Mario Biaggi	Albert H. Blumenthal
Manhattan	45,901	73,676	17,830	41,906
Bronx	41,508	55,432	39,462	18,400
Brooklyn	96,621	57,836	48,352	31,913
Queens	73,520	33,990	45,992	28,960
Staten Island	8,912	2,902	7,524	2,062
Total	266,462	223,836	159,160	123,241

1973 (continued)
Democratic Primary Runoff

	Abraham D. Beame	Herman Badillo
Manhattan	77,928	112,482
Bronx	97,415	86,482
Brooklyn	201,866	93,140
Queens	153,415	57,658
Staten Island	17,999	4,819
Total	548,623	354,581

General Election

	Abraham D. Beame (Democrat)	John J. Marchi (Republican)	Albert H. Blumenthal (Liberal)	Mario Biaggi (Conservative)
Manhattan	158,050	45,803	101,117	17,882
Bronx	160,774	37,609	32,661	50,805
Brooklyn	321,477	73,776	60,340	51,713
Queens	283,474	90,942	66,059	60,490
Staten Island	37,355	28,445	5,120	9,096
Total	961,130	276,575	265,297	189,986

Other candidates: 7,883
Total vote: 1,700,871

1977
Democratic Primary

	Edward I. Koch	Mario M. Cuomo	Abraham D. Beame	Bella Abzug	Percy Sutton	Herman Badillo
Manhattan	49,855	25,056	23,507	54,591	34,742	26,895
Bronx	23,237	22,939	25,534	20,429	24,588	34,246
Brooklyn	49,894	55,439	62,921	37,790	42,215	28,838
Queens	51,515	56,719	44,342	33,623	28,286	8,961
Staten Island	5,747	10,335	7,306	4,286	1,366	868
Total	180,248	170,488	163,610	150,719	131,197	99,808

Results of Mayoral Elections by Borough, 1897–2005 (continued)

1977 (continued)
Democratic Primary Runoff

	Edward I. Koch	Mario M. Cuomo
Manhattan	114,084	61,555
Bronx	69,230	55,017
Brooklyn	131,583	112,862
Queens	107,182	105,149
Staten Island	9,770	19,639
Total	431,849	354,222

General Election

	Edward I. Koch (Democrat)	Mario M. Cuomo (Liberal)	Roy M. Goodman (Republican)
Manhattan	184,842	70,717	19,324
Bronx	116,436	75,754	6,102
Brooklyn	204,934	153,134	11,491
Queens	191,894	186,590	18,460
Staten Island	19,270	36,747	3,229
Total	717,376	522,942	58,606

Barry Farber (Conservative): 57,437; Other candidates: 13,781
Total vote: 1,370,142

1981

	Edward I. Koch (Democrat-Republican)	Frank J. Barbaro (Unity)
Manhattan	189,631	56,702
Bronx	132,421	22,074
Brooklyn	261,292	48,812
Queens	275,812	31,225
Staten Island	53,466	3,906
Total	912,622	162,719

Other candidates: 147,303
Total vote: 1,222,644

Results of Mayoral Elections by Borough, 1897–2005 (continued)

1985	Edward I. Koch (Democrat-Independent)	Carol Bellamy (Liberal)	Diane McGrath (Republican-Conservative)
Manhattan	179,198	41,190	17,491
Bronx	136,263	14,092	12,358
Brooklyn	246,748	29,256	25,738
Queens	246,854	25,098	36,032
Staten Island	62,163	3,835	10,049
Total	862,226	113,471	101,668

Other candidates: 29,397
Total vote: 1,106,762

1989
Democratic Primary

	David N. Dinkins	Edward I. Koch	Harrison J. Goldin	Richard Ravitch
Manhattan	151,113	96,923	6,889	17,499
Bronx	101,274	66,600	4,951	5,946
Brooklyn	170,440	139,268	9,619	13,214
Queens	113,952	129,262	5,857	9,443
Staten Island	11,122	24,260	1,493	1,432
Total	547,901	456,313	28,809	47,534

General Election

	David N. Dinkins (Democrat)	Rudolph W. Giuliani (Republican-Liberal–Independent Fusion)
Manhattan	255,286	157,686
Bronx	172,271	99,800
Brooklyn	276,903	237,832
Queens	190,096	284,766
Staten Island	22,988	90,380
Total	917,544	870,464

Henry Hewes (Right-to-Life): 17,460; Ronald S. Lauder (Conservative): 9,271; Other candidates: 85,106
Total vote: 1,899,845

Results of Mayoral Elections by Borough, 1897–2005 (continued)

1993	Rudolph W. Giuliani (Republican-Liberal)	David N. Dinkins (Democrat)
Manhattan	166,357	242,524
Bronx	98,780	162,995
Brooklyn	258,058	269,343
Queens	291,625	180,527
Staten Island	115,416	21,507
Total	930,236	876,896

George J. Marlin (Conservative–Right-to-Life): 15,926; Other candidates: 65,945
Total vote: 1,889,003

1997	Rudolph W. Giuliani (Republican)	Ruth Messinger (Democrat)
Manhattan	138,718	128,478
Bronx	81,897	102,979
Brooklyn	173,343	145,349
Queens	176,751	92,194
Staten Island	45,120	10,288
Total	615,829	479,288

Other candidates: 21,241
Total vote: 1,116,358

2001
Democratic Primary

	Fernando Ferrer	Mark Green	Alan G. Hevesi	Peter F. Vallone
Manhattan	60,839	83,856	32,925	25,296
Bronx	86,571	26,125	6,066	18,268
Brooklyn	77,516	77,805	25,110	51,210
Queens	49,441	49,692	27,163	48,576
Staten Island	5,084	5,704	3,504	11,842
Total	279,451	243,182	94,768	155,192

2001 (continued)
Republican Primary

	Michael Bloomberg	Herman Badillo
Manhattan	10,959	4,161
Bronx	3,230	1,838
Brooklyn	10,168	4.153
Queens	14,543	5,700
Staten Island	9,155	2,624
Total	48,055	18,476

Democratic Primary Runoff

	Mark Green	Fernando Ferrer
Manhattan	131,438	86,579
Bronx	38,256	106,086
Brooklyn	120,781	109,831
Queens	94,342	77,330
Staten Island	18,183 ·	7,193
Total	403,000	387,019

General Election

	Michael Bloomberg (Republican-Independence)	Mark Green (Democrat–Working Families)	Alan G. Hevesi (Liberal–Better Schools)
Manhattan	179,797	202,574	3,100
Bronx	80,597	102,280	1,619
Brooklyn	189,040	217,222	2,752
Queens	210,432	163,528	2,293
Staten Island	84,891	23,664	567
Total	744,757	709,268	10,331

Other candidates: 56,087
Total vote: 1,520,443

2005
Democratic Primary

	Fernando Ferrer	Anthony Weiner	C. Virginia Fields	Gifford Miller
Manhattan	56,579	46,668	24,856	22,075
Bronx	50,088	11,422	10,381	3,491
Brooklyn	50,068	41,358	25,612	14,324
Queens	32,506	34,028	13,918	7,956
Staten Island	3,021	5,441	1,059	1,669
Total	192,262	138,917	75,826	49,515

General Election

	Michael Bloomberg (Republican-Liberal-Independence)	Fernando Ferrer (Democrat)
Manhattan	197,009	120,813
Bronx	76,417	117,734
Brooklyn	209,722	140,282
Queens	202,115	107,086
Staten Island	67,826	17,304
Total	753,089	503,219

Other candidates: 59,052
Total vote: 1,315,360

Sources: Kenneth T. Jackson, ed., *The Encyclopedia of New York City* (New Haven, Conn.: Yale University Press / New York: New-York Historical Society, 1995); New York City Board of Elections.

Presidential Election Results for New York City, 1836–2004 (by County 1836–1896, Including Kings, Queens, Richmond, and Westchester; by Borough 1900–2004)
(Excludes some minor-party candidates; name and party of winning candidate in boldface)

1836	**Martin Van Buren (Democrat)**	William H. Harrison (Whig)
New York	17,469	16,348
Kings	2,321	1,868
Queens	1,654	1,399
Richmond	649	649
Westchester	3,009	1,749
Totals	25,102	22,013

1840	Martin Van Buren (Democrat)	**William H. Harrison (Whig)**
New York	21,936	20,959
Kings	3,157	3,293
Queens	2,550	2,522
Richmond	861	903
Westchester	4,354	4,083
Totals	32,858	31,760

1844	**James K. Polk (Democrat)**	Henry Clay (Whig)
New York	28,296	26,385
Kings	4,648	5,107
Queens	2,751	2,547
Richmond	1,063	1,049
Westchester	4,412	4,258
Totals	41,170	39,346

Presidential Election Results for New York City, 1836–2004 (by County 1836–1896, Including Kings, Queens, Richmond, and Westchester; by Borough 1900–2004) (Excludes some minor-party candidates; name and party of winning candidate in boldface) (continued)

1848	Lewis Cass (Democrat)	Zachary Taylor (Whig)	
New York	18,975	29,070	
Kings	4,881	7,511	
Queens	1,310	2,444	
Richmond	860	1,099	
Westchester	2,146	4,112	
Totals	28,172	44,236	

1852	**Franklin Pierce (Democrat)**	Winfield Scott (Whig)	
New York	34,280	23,122	
Kings	10,624	8,491	
Queens	2,903	2,209	
Richmond	1,324	1,147	
Westchester	5,283	4,033	
Totals	54,414	39,002	

1856	**James Buchanan (Democrat)**	John C. Frémont (Republican)	Millard Fillmore (American)
New York	41,913	17,771	19,924
Kings	14,174	7,846	8,651
Queens	2,394	1,886	2,523
Richmond	1,550	736	947
Westchester	4,600	4,450	3,641
Totals	64,631	32,689	35,686

Presidential Election Results for New York City, 1836–2004 (by County 1836–1896, Including Kings, Queens, Richmond, and Westchester; by Borough 1900–2004)
(Excludes some minor-party candidates; name and party of winning candidate in boldface) (continued)

1860	Stephen Douglas (Democrat)	Abraham Lincoln (Republican)
New York	62,482	33,290
Kings	20,599	15,883
Queens	4,391	3,749
Richmond	2,370	1,408
Westchester	8,126	6,771
Totals	97,968	61,101

1864	George B. McClellan (Democrat)	Abraham Lincoln (Republican)
New York	73,709	36,681
Kings	25,726	20,838
Queens	5,400	4,284
Richmond	2,874	1,564
Westchester	9,355	7,607
Totals	117,064	70,974

1868	Horatio Seymour (Democrat)	Ulysses S. Grant (Republican)
New York	108,316	47,748
Kings	39,838	27,711
Queens	6,388	4,973
Richmond	3,019	2,221
Westchester	11,667	9,642
Totals	169,228	92,295

Presidential Election Results for New York City, 1836–2004 (by County 1836–1896, Including Kings, Queens, Richmond, and Westchester; by Borough 1900–2004)
(Excludes some minor-party candidates; name and party of winning candidate in boldface) (continued)

1872	Horace Greeley (Democrat)	Ulysses S. Grant (Republican)
New York	77,814	54,676
Kings	38,108	39,125
Queens	5,655	6,082
Richmond	2,541	2,728
Westchester	11,112	10,233
Totals	135,230	107,087

1876	Samuel J. Tilden (Democrat)	Rutherford B. Hayes (Republican)
New York	112,621	58,776
Kings	57,557	39,125
Queens	9,994	6,971
Richmond	4,338	2,884
Westchester	12,054	9,574
Totals	196,564	117,330

1880	Winfield Hancock (Democrat)	James A. Garfield (Republican)
New York	123,015	58,776
Kings	61,062	51,751
Queens	10,391	8,151
Richmond	4,815	3,291
Westchester	11,858	11,367
Totals	211,151	133,336

Presidential Election Results for New York City, 1836–2004 (by County 1836–1896, Including Kings, Queens, Richmond, and Westchester; by Borough 1900–2004) (Excludes some minor-party candidates; name and party of winning candidate in boldface) (continued)

1884	**Grover Cleveland (Democrat)**	James G. Blaine (Republican)
New York	133,222	90,095
Kings	69,264	53,516
Queens	10,367	8,445
Richmond	5,135	3,164
Westchester	12,525	11,286
Totals	230,513	166,506

1888	Grover Cleveland (Democrat)	**Benjamin Harrison (Republican)**
New York	162,735	106,922
Kings	82,507	70,052
Queens	12,683	11,017
Richmond	5,764	4,100
Westchester	14,948	13,799
Totals	278,637	105,890

1892	**Grover Cleveland (Democrat)**	Benjamin Harrison (Republican)
New York	175,267	98,967
Kings	100,160	70,505
Queens	15,195	11,704
Richmond	6,122	4,091
Westchester	16,088	13,436
Totals	312,832	198,703

Presidential Election Results for New York City, 1836–2004 (by County 1836–1896, Including Kings, Queens, Richmond, and Westchester; by Borough 1900–2004)
(Excludes some minor-party candidates; name and party of winning candidate in boldface) (continued)

1896	Williams Jennings Bryan (Democrat)	**William McKinley (Republican)**
New York (including present Bronx)	135,624	156,359
Kings	76,882	109,135
Queens	11,980	18,694
Richmond	4,452	6,170
Totals	228,938	290,358

1900	Williams Jennings Bryan (Democrat)	**William McKinley (Republican)**
Manhattan and Bronx	181,786	153,001
Brooklyn	106,232	108,977
Queens	14,747	12,323
Staten Island	6,759	6,042
Totals	309,524	280,343

1904	Alton B. Parker (Democrat)	**Theodore Roosevelt (Republican)**
Manhattan and Bronx	189,712	155,003
Brooklyn	111,855	113,246
Queens	18,151	14,096
Staten Island	7,182	7,000
Totals	326,900	289,345

1908	William Jennings Bryan (Democrat)	**William H. Taft (Republican)**
Manhattan and Bronx	160,261	154,958
Brooklyn	96,756	119,789
Queens	20,342	19,420
Staten Island	6,831	7,401
Totals	284,190	301,568

Presidential Election Results for New York City, 1836–2004 (by County 1836–1896, Including Kings, Queens, Richmond, and Westchester; by Borough 1900–2004) (Excludes some minor-party candidates; name and party of winning candidate in boldface) (continued)

1912	Woodrow Wilson (Democrat)	William H. Taft (Republican)	Theodore Roosevelt (Progressive)
Manhattan and Bronx	166,157	63,107	98,985
Brooklyn	108,748	51,239	71,167
Queens	28,044	9,201	14,951
Staten Island	8,437	3,035	3,771
Totals	312,386	126,582	188,874

1916	Woodrow Wilson (Democrat)	Charles E. Hughes (Republican)	
Manhattan	139,547	111,926	
Bronx	47,870	40,338	
Brooklyn	125,625	119,657	
Queens	31,350	34,670	
Staten Island	8,843	7,204	
Totals	353,235	313,813	

1920	James Cox (Democrat)	Warren G. Harding (Republican)	Eugene V. Debs (Socialist)
Manhattan	135,249	275,013	46,049
Bronx	45,471	106,038	32,823
Brooklyn	119,612	292,692	45,100
Queens	35,296	94,630	6,143
Staten Island	9,373	17,844	712
Totals	345,001	785,947	130,827

Presidential Election Results for New York City, 1836–2004 (by County 1836–1896, Including Kings, Queens, Richmond, and Westchester; by Borough 1900–2004)
(Excludes some minor-party candidates; name and party of winning candidate in boldface) (continued)

1924	John W. Davis (Democrat)	**Calvin Coolidge (Republican)**	Robert LaFollette (Progressive)
Manhattan	183,249	190,871	86,625
Bronx	72,840	79,583	62,212
Brooklyn	158,907	236,877	100,721
Queens	58,402	100,793	28,210
Staten Island	15,801	18,007	3,702
Totals	489,199	626,131	281,470

1928	**Alfred E. Smith (Democrat)**	Herbert Hoover (Republican)
Manhattan	317,227	186,396
Bronx	404,393	245,622
Brooklyn	232,766	98,636
Queens	184,640	158,505
Staten Island	28,945	24,985
Totals	1,167,971	714,144

1932	**Franklin D. Roosevelt (Democrat)**	Herbert Hoover (Republican)	Norman Thomas (Socialist)
Manhattan	378,077	157,014	23,946
Bronx	281,330	76,587	31,247
Brooklyn	514,172	192,536	50,509
Queens	244,740	136,641	14,854
Staten Island	36,857	21,278	2,009
Totals	1,455,176	584,056	122,565

Presidential Election Results for New York City, 1836–2004 (by County 1836–1896, Including Kings, Queens, Richmond, and Westchester; by Borough 1900–2004) (Excludes some minor-party candidates; name and party of winning candidate in boldface) (continued)

1936	**Franklin D. Roosevelt (Democrat)**	Alfred M. Landon (Republican)
Manhattan	517,134	174,299
Bronx	419,625	93,151
Brooklyn	738,306	212,852
Queens	320,053	162,797
Staten Island	46,229	22,852
Totals	2,041,347	665,951

1940	**Franklin D. Roosevelt (Democrat)**	Wendell Willkie (Republican)
Manhattan	478,153	292,480
Bronx	418,931	198,293
Brooklyn	742,668	394,534
Queens	288,024	323,406
Staten Island	38,307	38,911
Totals	1,966,083	1,247,624

1944	**Franklin D. Roosevelt (Democrat)**	Thomas E. Dewey (Republican)
Manhattan	509,263	258,650
Bronx	450,525	211,158
Brooklyn	758,270	393,926
Queens	292,940	365,365
Staten Island	31,502	42,188
Totals	1,042,500	1,271,287

Presidential Election Results for New York City, 1836–2004 (by County 1836–1896, Including Kings, Queens, Richmond, and Westchester; by Borough 1900–2004)
(Excludes some minor-party candidates; name and party of winning candidate in boldface) (continued)

1948	**Harry S. Truman (Democrat)**	Thomas E. Dewey (Republican)	Henry A. Wallace (Progressive)
Manhattan	380,310	241,752	106,509
Bronx	337,129	173,044	106,762
Brooklyn	579,922	330,494	163,896
Queens	268,742	323,459	42,409
Staten Island	30,442	39,539	2,779
Totals	1,596,545	1,108,288	422,355

1952	Adlai Stevenson (Democrat)	**Dwight D. Eisenhower (Republican)**
Manhattan	446,727	300,284
Bronx	399,477	241,898
Brooklyn	656,229	446,708
Queens	331,217	450,610
Staten Island	28,280	55,993
Totals	1,861,930	1,495,493

1956	Adlai Stevenson (Democrat)	**Dwight D. Eisenhower (Republican)**
Manhattan	377,856	300,004
Bronx	343,823	257,382
Brooklyn	557,655	460,456
Queens	318,723	466,057
Staten Island	19,644	64,233
Totals	1,617,701	1,548,132

Presidential Election Results for New York City, 1836–2004 (by County 1836–1896, Including Kings, Queens, Richmond, and Westchester; by Borough 1900–2004)
(Excludes some minor-party candidates; name and party of winning candidate in boldface) (continued)

1960	**John F. Kennedy** **(Democrat)**	Richard M. Nixon (Republican)	
Manhattan	414,902	217,271	
Bronx	389,818	182,393	
Brooklyn	646,582	327,497	
Queens	446,348	367,688	
Staten Island	38,673	50,356	
Totals	1,936,323	1,145,205	

1964	**Lyndon B. Johnson** **(Democrat)**	Barry Goldwater (Republican)	
Manhattan	503,848	120,125	
Bronx	403,014	135,780	
Brooklyn	684,839	229,291	
Queens	541,418	274,351	
Staten Island	50,524	42,330	
Totals	2,183,643	801,877	

1968	Hubert H. Humphrey (Democrat)	**Richard M. Nixon** **(Republican)**	George Wallace (American Independent)
Manhattan	370,806	135,458	12,958
Bronx	277,385	142,314	21,950
Brooklyn	489,174	247,936	33,563
Queens	410,546	306,620	44,198
Staten Island	34,770	54,631	9,112
Totals	1,582,681	886,959	121,781

Presidential Election Results for New York City, 1836–2004 (by County 1836–1896, Including Kings, Queens, Richmond, and Westchester; by Borough 1900–2004)
(Excludes some minor-party candidates; name and party of winning candidate
in boldface) (continued)

1972	George McGovern (Democrat)	**Richard M. Nixon (Republican)**	
Manhattan	354,326	178,515	
Bronx	243,345	196,754	
Brooklyn	387,768	373,903	
Queens	328,316	426,015	
Staten Island	29,241	84,686	
Totals	1,342,996	1,259,873	

1976	**Jimmy Carter (Democrat)**	Gerald R. Ford (Republican)	
Manhattan	337,438	117,702	
Bronx	238,786	96,842	
Brooklyn	419,382	190,728	
Queens	379,907	244,396	
Staten Island	47,867	56,995	
Totals	1,423,380	706,663	

1980	Jimmy Carter (Democrat)	**Ronald Reagan (Republican)**	John Anderson (Independent)
Manhattan	275,742	115,911	38,597
Bronx	181,090	86,843	11,286
Brooklyn	288,893	200,298	24,341
Queens	269,147	251,333	32,566
Staten Island	37,306	64,885	7,055
Totals	1,052,178	719,270	113,845

Presidential Election Results for New York City, 1836–2004 (by County 1836–1896, Including Kings, Queens, Richmond, and Westchester; by Borough 1900–2004)
(Excludes some minor-party candidates; name and party of winning candidate in boldface) (continued)

1984	Walter F. Mondale (Democrat)	Ronald Reagan (Republican)	
Manhattan	379,521	144,281	
Bronx	223,112	109,308	
Brooklyn	368,518	230,064	
Queens	328,379	285,477	
Staten Island	44,345	83,187	
Totals	1,343,875	852,317	

1988	Michael S. Dukakis (Democrat)	George H. W. Bush (Republican)	
Manhattan	385,675	115,927	
Bronx	218,245	76,043	
Brooklyn	363,916	178,961	
Queens	325,147	217,049	
Staten Island	47,812	77,427	
Totals	1,340,795	665,407	

1992	Bill Clinton (Democrat)	George H. W. Bush (Republican)	H. Ross Perot (Independent)
Manhattan	416,142	84,501	27,689
Bronx	225,038	63,310	15,115
Brooklyn	411,183	133,344	33,014
Queens	349,520	157,651	46,014
Staten Island	56,901	70,707	19,678
Totals	1,458,784	509,423	141,510

Presidential Election Results for New York City, 1836–2004 (by County 1836–1896, Including Kings, Queens, Richmond, and Westchester; by Borough 1900–2004)
(Excludes some minor-party candidates; name and party of winning candidate in boldface) (continued)

1996	Bill Clinton (Democrat)	Robert Dole (Republican)	H. Ross Perot (Independent)
Manhattan	394,131	67,839	11,144
Bronx	248,276	30,435	7,186
Brooklyn	432,232	81,406	15,031
Queens	372,925	107,650	22,288
Staten Island	64,684	52,207	8,968
Totals	1,512,248	339,537	64,617

2000	Al Gore (Democrat)	George W. Bush (Republican)	Ralph Nader (Green)
Manhattan	449,300	79,921	30,923
Bronx	265,801	36,245	4,265
Brooklyn	497,468	96,605	19,977
Queens	416,967	122,052	13,720
Staten Island	73,828	63,903	3,550
Totals	1,703,364	398,726	72,435

2004	John Kerry (Democrat)	George W. Bush (Republican)
Manhattan	526,765	107,405
Bronx	283,994	56,701
Brooklyn	514,973	167,149
Queens	433,835	165,954
Staten Island	68,448	90,325
Totals	1,828,015	587,534

Sources: Kenneth T. Jackson, ed., *The Encyclopedia of New York City* (New Haven, Conn.: Yale University Press / New York: New-York Historical Society, 1995); New York State Board of Elections.

Number of Authorized Positions in Major City Agencies, 30 June 2004

	Full-time	Part-time (full-time equivalent)
City employees		
Education	117,759	15,949
Police	43,891	5,532
Fire	15,424	44
Social services	14,875	—
Corrections	10,921	52
Sanitation	9,798	57
Children's services	6,408	280
Environmental protection	5,991	287
City University	3,922	2,173
Health and mental hygiene	3,762	2,016
Parks and recreation	1,899	3,419
Transportation	3,983	195
Housing preservation and development	2,924	120
Finance	2,260	153
Citywide administrative services	1,834	440
Homeless services	2,259	—
All other agencies	15,718	1,465
Total, city employees	263,628	32,182
Non-city employees paid in part by city subsidies		
Health and Hospitals Corporation	35,056	2,252
Housing Authority	14,374	241
Libraries	3,459	585
Cultural institutions	1,815	6
School Construction Authority	453	—
All other	1,369	31
Total, non-city employees	56,526	3,115
Total	320,154	35,297

Source: The Green Book.

Party Enrollment by Borough, 2007

	Manhattan	Bronx	Brooklyn	Queens	Staten Island	Total	Percentage of City Enrollment
Republican	114,756	49,263	123,695	140,684	77,544	505,942	12.2
Democratic	693,014	485,077	884,291	620,565	112,657	2,795,604	67.2
Independence	26,293	12,404	24,034	19,923	6,512	89,166	2.1
Conservative	2,069	3,489	4,782	6,235	4,191	20,766	0.5
Working Families	1,764	2,452	4,183	2,573	908	11,880	0.3
Green	3,197	478	3,446	1,527	339	8,987	0.2
Libertarian	72	7	57	14	7	157	*
Blank	184,780	93,040	210,416	188,013	50,142	726,391	17.5
Total	1,025,945	646,210	1,254,904	979,534	252,300	4,158,893	100.0

* = less than 0.05 percent
Notes: Figures are as of 1 April.
Source: New York State Board of Elections.

Participation Rate by Borough of Registered Voters in General Elections, 1996–2006

	Manhattan	Bronx	Brooklyn	Queens	Staten Island	Total
1996						
Number of Registered Voters	963,126	602,790	1,146,414	926,904	231,133	3,870,367
Number of Votes Cast	507,648	301,383	563,124	525,471	130,387	2,028,013
Voter Turnout (in percent)	52.7	50.0	49.1	56.7	56.4	52.4
1997						
Number of Registered Voters	989,250	647,813	1,193,299	967,807	250,904	4,049,073
Number of Votes Cast	338,693	201,386	395,115	367,733	106,420	1,409,347
Voter Turnout (in percent)	34.2	31.1	33.1	38.0	42.4	34.8
1998						
Number of Registered Voters	998,105	640,279	1,207,419	987,557	234,496	4,067,856
Number of Votes Cast	391,912	216,489	437,488	391,875	96,997	1,534,761
Voter Turnout (in percent)	39.3	33.8	36.2	39.7	41.4	37.7

Participation Rate by Borough of Registered Voters in General Elections, 1996–2006 (continued)

	Manhattan	Bronx	Brooklyn	Queens	Staten Island	Total
1999						
Number of Registered Voters	1,018,957	654,272	1,247,099	1,004,797	249,745	4,174,870
Number of Votes Cast	143,266	66,705	132,392	117,527	38,340	498,230
Voter Turnout (in percent)	14.1	10.2	10.6	11.7	15.4	11.9
2000						
Number of Registered Voters	1,029,059	668,458	1,289,955	1,018,159	249,768	4,255,399
Number of Votes Cast	581,991	323,291	642,563	576,132	144,525	2,268,502
Voter Turnout (in percent)	56.6	48.4	49.8	56.6	57.9	53.3
2001						
Number of Registered Voters	975,218	641,090	1,241,060	1,001,625	245,930	4,104,923
Number of Votes Cast	398,659	192,529	425,951	390,500	111,879	1,519,518
Voter Turnout (in percent)	40.9	30.0	34.3	39.0	45.5	37.0
2002						
Number of Registered Voters	1,010,007	663,867	1,271,743	1,038,926	252,560	4,237,103
Number of Votes Cast	362,277	198,195	409,909	355,756	88,958	1,415,095
Voter Turnout (in percent)	35.9	29.9	32.2	34.2	35.2	33.4
2003						
Number of Registered Voters	970,302	637,864	1,220,751	1,012,298	246,689	4,087,904
Number of Votes Cast	169,935	80,464	174,784	146,091	48,888	620,162
Voter Turnout (in percent)	17.5	12.6	14.3	14.4	19.8	15.2
2004						
Number of Registered Voters	1,110,217	695,932	1,329,900	1,092,384	265,988	4,494,421
Number of Votes Cast	647,430	347,132	693,704	610,581	160,806	2,459,653
Voter Turnout (in percent)	58.3	49.9	52.2	55.9	60.5	54.7
2005						
Number of Registered Voters	1,083,330	680,661	1,297,665	1,059,371	262,249	4,383,276
Number of Votes Cast	332,853	201,393	367,671	323,691	89,752	1,315,360
Voter Turnout (in percent)	30.7	29.6	28.3	30.6	34.2	30.0
2006						
Number of Registered Voters	1,099,027	690,491	1,317,470	1,045,684	265,050	4,417,722
Number of Votes Cast	378,328	186,383	368,512	330,641	85,627	1,349,491
Voter Turnout (in percent)	34.4	27.0	28.0	31.6	32.3	30.5

Note: Numbers of registered voters are as of 1 November of each year.
Source: New York State Board of Elections.

City Revenues, Fiscal Year 2007

	Amount (in Millions)	Percentage of Total Revenues
Taxes		
Real property	$13,140	24.6
Personal income tax	7,395	13.9
General corporation tax	2,408	4.5
Banking corporation tax	525	1.0
Unincorporated business tax	1,209	2.3
Sale and use	4,508	8.4
Commercial rent	502	0.9
Real property transfer	863	1.6
Mortgage recording tax	882	1.7
Utility	359	0.7
Cigarette	118	0.2
Hotel	309	0.6
All other	385	0.7
Tax audit revenue	509	1.0
Total taxes	$33,112	62.0
Miscellaneous revenue		
Licenses, franchises, etc.	$403	0.8
Interest income	245	0.5
Charges for services	551	1.0
Water and sewer charges	1,080	2.0
Rental income	181	0.3
Fines and forfeitures	723	1.4
Miscellaneous	317	0.6
Intra-city revenue	1,307	2.4
Total miscellaneous	$4,807	9.0
Unrestricted intergovernmental aid		
New York State per capita aid	$327	0.6
Other federal and state aid	13	*
Total unrestricted intergovernmental aid	$340	0.6
Anticipated state and federal aid		
Anticipated state aid	$0	0.0
Anticipated federal aid	50	0.1
Total anticipated aid	$50	0.1

	Amount (in Millions)	Percentage of Total Revenues
Other categorical grants	$1,111	2.1
Inter fund agreements	395	0.7
Reserve for disallowance of categorical grants	(15)	(*)
Less: intra-city revenue	(1,307)	(2.4)
Total city funds	$38,493	72.1
Federal categorical grants		
Community development	$249	0.5
Welfare	2,264	4.2
Education	1,748	3.3
Other	834	1.6
Total federal grants	$5,095	9.5
State categorical grants		
Welfare	$1,757	3.3
Education	7,106	13.3
Higher education	188	0.4
Department of Health and Mental Hygiene	410	0.7
Other	343	0.6
Total state grants	$9,804	18.4
Total revenues	$53,392	100.0

* = less than 0.05 percent
Source: New York City Office of the Comptroller.

City Expenditures, Fiscal Year 2007

	Amount (in Millions)	Percentage of Total Expenditures
Mayoralty	$79,749	0.1
Board of Elections	80,119	0.2
Campaign Finance Board	13,889	*
Office of the Actuary	5,323	*
President, Borough of Manhattan	3,657	*
President, Borough of Bronx	5,332	*
President, Borough of Brooklyn	4,961	*
President, Borough of Queens	4,567	*
President, Borough of Staten Island	3,497	*
Office of the Comptroller	62,026	0.1
Dept. of Emergency Management	7,892	*
Tax Commission	2,543	*
Law Department	118,016	0.2
Department of City Planning	24,808	*
Department of Investigation	17,356	*
New York Public Library: Research	16,193	*
New York Public Library	84,048	0.2
Brooklyn Public Library	62,363	0.1
Queens Borough Public Library	60,392	0.1
Department of Education	15,314,359	28.7
City University	533,410	1.0
Civilian Complaint Review Board	9,192	*
Police Department	3,629,741	6.8
Fire Department	1,339,470	0.3
Administration for Children's Services	2,444,599	4.6
Department of Social Services	6,987,627	13.1
Department of Homeless Services	664,677	1.2
Department of Correction	867,930	1.6
Board of Correction	868	*
Department of Employment	0	0
Citywide pension contribution	4,754,616	8.9
Miscellaneous	6,656,185	12.5
Debt service	650,094	1.2
Municipal Assistance Corporation debt service	10,000	*
NYCTFA debt service	904,000	1.7

	Amount (in Millions)	Percentage of Total Expenditures
Transfer for NYCTFA debt service	(200,000)	(0.4)
Defeasance of NYCTFA debt service	(16,000)	*
Public Advocate	1,833	*
City Council	50,799	0.1
City Clerk	3,677	*
Department for the Aging	235,759	0.4
Department of Cultural Affairs	114,659	0.2
Financial Information Services Agency	53,840	0.1
Department of Juvenile Justice	106,791	0.2
Office of Payroll Administration	12,142	*
Independent Budget Office	3,005	*
Equal Employment Practices Commission	737	*
Civil Service Commission	569	*
Landmarks Preservation Commission	3,769	*
Districting Commission	0	0
Taxi & Limousine Commission	28,382	0.1
Commission on Human Rights	6,917	*
Department of Youth & Community Development	226,239	0.4
Conflicts of Interest Board	1,764	*
Office of Collective Bargaining	1,749	*
Community Boards (all)	13,222	*
Department of Probation	76,101	0.1
Department of Small Business Services	114,636	0.2
Housing Preservation & Development	480,315	0.9
Department of Buildings	82,921	0.2
Department of Health & Mental Hygiene	1,490,273	2.8
Health and Hospitals Corporation	849,044	1.6
Department of Environmental Protection	880,667	1.6
Department of Sanitation	1,193,897	2.2
Business Integrity Commission	5,370	*
Department of Finance	201,589	0.4
Department of Transportation	535,586	1.0
Department of Parks and Recreation	241,935	0.5
Department of Design & Construction	99,766	0.2
Department of Citywide Administrative Services	309,452	0.6

City Expenditures, Fiscal Year 2007 (continued)

	Amount (in Millions)	Percentage of Total Expenditures
Department of Information Technology & Communications	194,153	0.4
Department of Record & Information Services	4,521	*
Department of Consumer Affairs	14,599	*
District Attorney, Manhattan	70,737	0.1
District Attorney, Bronx	41,608	0.1
District Attorney, Brooklyn	70,703	0.1
District Attorney, Queens	37,301	0.1
District Attorney, Staten Island	6,607	*
Office of the Special Narcotics Prosecutor	14,692	*
Public Administrator, Manhattan	1,107	*
Public Administrator, Bronx	345	*
Public Administrator, Brooklyn	473	*
Public Administrator, Queens	371	*
Public Administrator, Staten Island	292	*
Prior payable adjustment	0	0
General reserve	300,000	0.6
Energy adjustment	0	0
Lease adjustment	0	0
OTPS inflation adjustment	0	0
Total	$53,392,413	100.0

NYCTFA = New York City Transitional Finance Authority
OTPS = other than personnel services
* = less than 0.05 percent
Source: New York City Office of the Comptroller.

Salaries of Police Officers, Firefighters, and Teachers

Police Officers

Police Academy (first six months): $25,100 (annualized)

On completion of training: $32,700

On completion of 1½ years: $34,000

On completion of 2½ years: $38,000

On completion of 3½ years: $41,500

On completion of 4½ years: $44,100

On completion of 5½ years: $59,588

Firefighters

Fire Academy (first thirteen weeks): $25,100

On completion of training: $32,700

On completion of 1½ years: $36,123

On completion of 2½ years: $40,373

On completion of 3½ years: $44,091

On completion of 4½ years: $46,854

On completion of 5½ years: $63,309

After promotion to lieutenant: $76,569

After promotion to captain: $87,631

After promotion to battalion chief: $121,320

Teachers

	New Hires	Ten Years of Seniority	Fifteen Years of Seniority	Twenty Years of Seniority
Base	$41,172	$60,673	$66,587	$75,427
BA plus 30 credits	42,613	62,114	68,028	76,868
BA plus 60 credits	45,279	64,780	70,694	79,534
Approved MA, or BA plus 30 credits with 36 credits in area of specialization	46,503	66,004	71,918	80,758
BA plus 60 credits including MA, or 36 credits in area of specialization	49,168	68,669	74,583	83,423
Work experience for trade licenses, or BA plus 60 credits for other stipulated licenses	47,944	67,445	73,359	82,199
Bachelor's, master's, and 30 additional credits	51,834	71,335	77,249	86,089

Notes: Salaries for police officers are for hires during January 2006 and after; salaries for teachers effective November 2005.
Sources: New York Police Department; New York Fire Department; New York City Department of Education.

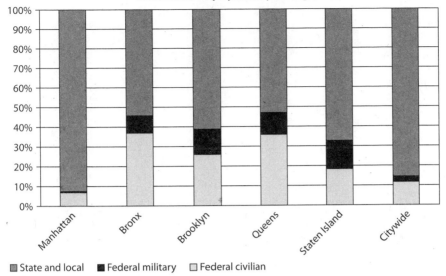

Government Employment by Borough, 2000

■ State and local   ■ Federal military   ☐ Federal civilian

Source: U.S. Bureau of the Census.

9 Transportation

Principal Bridges over Water

High Bridge (1848)	Harlem River	Manhattan-Bronx
Brooklyn (1883)	East River	Manhattan-Brooklyn
Washington (1888)	Harlem River	Manhattan-Bronx
Carroll Street (1889)	Gowanus Canal	Brooklyn
Macombs Dam (1895)	Harlem River	Manhattan-Bronx
Third Avenue (1899)	Harlem River	Manhattan-Bronx
City Island (1901)	Pelham Bay Narrows	Bronx
Willis Avenue (1901)	Harlem River	Manhattan-Bronx
Grand Street (1903)	Newtown Creek	Queens-Brooklyn
Williamsburg (1903)	Newtown Creek	Queens-Brooklyn
Ninth Street (1905)	Gowanus Canal	Brooklyn
145th Street (1905)	Harlem River	Manhattan-Bronx
Third Street (1905)	Gowanus Canal	Brooklyn
Union Street (1905)	Gowanus Canal	Brooklyn
Borden Avenue (1908)	Dutch Kills	Queens
Pelham (1908)	Eastchester Bay	Bronx
University Heights (1908)	Harlem River	Manhattan-Bronx
Manhattan (1909)	East River	Manhattan-Brooklyn
Queensboro (1909)	East River	Manhattan-Queens
Hunters Point Avenue (1910)	Dutch Kills	Queens
Hell Gate (1917)	East River	Queens–Wards Island
Ocean Avenue (pedestrian) (1917)	Sheepshead Bay	Brooklyn
Eastchester (1922)	Eastchester Creek	Bronx
North Channel (1925)	North Channel	Queens
Roosevelt Avenue (1925)	Flushing River	Queens
B&O Railroad (1928)	Arthur Kill	Staten Island–New Jersey
East 174th Street (1928)	Bronx River	Bronx
Goethals (1928)	Arthur Kill	Staten Island–New Jersey
Outerbridge Crossing (1928)	Arthur Kill	Staten Island–New Jersey
Greenpoint Avenue (1929)	Newtown Avenue	Queens-Brooklyn
Stillwell Avenue (1929)	Coney Island Creek	Brooklyn
George Washington (1931)	Hudson River	Manhattan–New Jersey
Bayonne (1931)	Kill van Kull	Staten Island–New Jersey
Cropsey Avenue (1931)	Coney Island Creek	Brooklyn
Fresh Kills (1931)	Richmond Creek	Staten Island
Hook Creek (1931)	Hook Creek	Queens–Nassau County
Little Neck (1931)	Alley Creek	Queens
Metropolitan Avenue (1933)	English Kills	Brooklyn
Henry Hudson (1936)	Harlem River	Manhattan-Bronx

Triborough (1936)	East River, Harlem River, Bronx Kills	Queens–Wards Island, Manhattan–Randalls Island
Marine Parkway–Gil Hodges (1937)	Rockaway Inlet	Brooklyn-Queens
Westchester Avenue (1938)	Bronx River	Bronx
Bronx-Whitestone (1939)	East River	Bronx-Queens
Cross Bay–Veterans' Memorial (1939)	Jamaica Bay	Queens
Flushing (Northern Boulevard) (1939)	Flushing River	Queens
Kosciuszko (1939)	Newtown Creek	Queens-Brooklyn
Whitestone Expressway (1939)	Flushing River	Queens
Midtown Highway (1940)	Dutch Kills	Queens
Mill Basin (1940)	Mill Basin	Brooklyn
Hutchinson River Park Extension (1941)	Eastchester Creek	Bronx
Hamilton Avenue (1942)	Gowanus Canal	Queens
Wards Island (pedestrian) (1951)	East River	Manhattan–Wards Island
Bruckner Boulevard (1953)	Bronx River	Bronx
Unionport (1953)	Westchester Creek	Bronx
Pulaski (1954)	Newtown Creek	Queens-Brooklyn
Roosevelt Island (1955)	East River	Queens–Roosevelt Island
Lemon Creek (1958)	Lemon Creek	Staten Island
Throgs Neck (1961)	East River	Bronx-Queens
Broadway (1962)	Harlem River	Manhattan-Bronx
Alexander Hamilton (1963)	Harlem River	Manhattan-Bronx
Hawtree Basin (pedestrian) (1963)	Hawtree Basin	Queens
Verrazano Narrows (1964)	Narrows	Brooklyn–Staten Island
Rikers Island (1966)	Bowery Basin	Queens–Staten Island

Source: Kenneth T. Jackson, ed., *The Encyclopedia of New York City* (New Haven, Conn.: Yale University Press / New York: New-York Historical Society, 1995).

Means of Commuting to Work by Borough, 2000

	Manhattan	Bronx	Brooklyn	Queens	Staten Island	Total
Drove alone	57,150	112,159	202,070	319,187	103,856	794,422
Carpooled	25,604	38,726	72,231	95,329	23,084	254,974
Bus, trolley, streetcar	76,860	65,587	95,566	94,729	36,767	369,509
Subway	328,246	143,534	403,327	319,225	4,894	1,199,226
Railroad	8,309	8,113	12,169	20,845	1,705	51,141
Ferryboat	411	106	424	143	10,109	11,193
Taxicab	35,187	5,495	6,149	6,235	715	53,781
Walked	164,934	30,076	78,933	52,776	5,545	332,264
Bicycle, motorcycle, or other means	12,560	3,523	9,495	6,567	1,264	33,409
Worked at home	43,853	7,756	20,663	16,673	3,206	92,151
Total workers 16 years and over	753,114	415,075	901,027	931,709	191,145	3,192,070
Mean travel time to work (minutes)	30.5	43.0	43.2	42.2	43.9	40.0

Source: U.S. Bureau of the Census.

New York City Transit Statistics, 2001–2005

	2001	2002	2003	2004	2005
Subways					
Annual ridership (in millions)	1,405.3	1,413.2	1,384.1	1,426.0	1,449.1
Mean distance between failures	109,914	114,619	139,960	164,152	158,953
Weekday on-time performance (in percent)	95.3	96.3	97.1	96.6	96
Customer injuries per million customer rides	3.04	2.94	2.85	3.15	3.1
Buses					
Annual ridership (in millions)	739.5	762.1	727.6	740.6	736.41
Mean distance between failures	3,242	3,478	3,554	3,564	3,618
Scheduled trips completed (in percent)	98.34	98.75	98.71	98.81	98.8
Customer injuries per million customer rides	1.67	1.58	1.47	1.53	1.49

Note: Mean distance between failures is the number of miles traveled by a subway car or bus before breaking down.
Source: Metropolitan Transportation Authority.

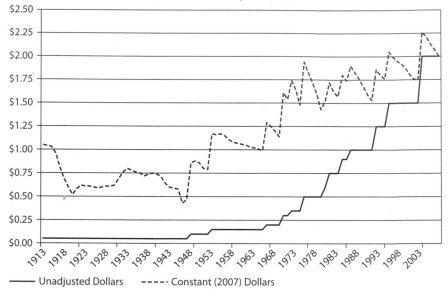

Transit Fare, 1913–2007

——— Unadjusted Dollars   - - - - Constant (2007) Dollars

Note: Constant-dollar figures derived from Consumer Price Index. Transit fare was first imposed when system opened in 1904; 1913 is first year for which Consumer Price Index is available. Sources: Metropolitan Transportation Authority; U.S. Bureau of Labor Statistics.

Average Weekday Ridership on Public Transportation, 2001–2005 (in Thousands)

	2001	2002	2003	2004	2005
MTA/NYC Transit buses	2,954.6	3,491.8	3,260.0	3,196.0	3,407.9
Private buses	n/a	370.5	340.7	332.3	365.0
MTA/NYC Transit subways	5,664.5	6,050.1	6,076.6	6,288.5	6,443.0
Metro-North Railroad	251.6	246.0	242.0	242.0	288.5
Long Island Rail Road	311.3	299.0	288.0	280.0	327.0
Staten Island Ferry	57.4	74.2	61.5	61.1	63.0
Staten Island Railway	14.8	13.2	12.3	12.1	12.7
New Jersey Transit buses	498.6	528.9	486.3	602.5	628.7
New Jersey independent buses	217.6	177.9	176.4	191.3	148.6
PATH trains	266.8	174.0	160.0	194.0	240.6

MTA = Metropolitan Transportation Authority
PATH = Port Authority Trans-Hudson
Source: New York Metropolitan Transportation Council; *2005 Regional Transportation Statistical Report.*

Average Weekday Traffic Volume, Bridges and Tunnels, 2000–2005

	2000	2001	2002	2003	2004	2005
George Washington Bridge	317,618	309,310	310,771	319,029	315,066	304,302
Holland Tunnel	101,137	43,377	92,557	101,097	96,171	96,960
Lincoln Tunnel	129,710	106,257	129,511	127,323	125,159	126,455
Bayonne Bridge	18,493	23,631	21,327	20,208	22,510	21,755
Goethals Bridge	72,791	78,196	81,384	75,724	71,532	68,790
Outerbridge Crossing	73,384	75,424	76,429	78,650	80,226	81,108
Brooklyn Battery Tunnel	63,242	13,762	56,976	56,271	54,488	49,043
Henry Hudson Bridge	66,304	69,087	70,731	72,209	73,114	70,407
Queens-Midtown Tunnel	80,879	72,864	82,834	85,377	86,599	86,063
Triborough Bridge–Manhattan Plaza	103,079	102,224	94,759	93,177	97,958	91,898
Bronx-Whitestone	117,583	111,764	123,258	113,441	117,591	105,059
Cross Bay	17,962	19,626	20,010	20,233	20,460	19,852
Marine Parkway	21,609	19,527	21,684	21,745	21,556	19,456
Throgs Neck	98,357	104,429	104,535	111,092	112,001	114,973
Triborough Bridge–Bronx Plaza	79,243	77,631	72,259	74,113	82,810	77,257
Verrazano-Narrows	202,580	218,971	212,491	206,444	205,544	193,687
Brooklyn Bridge	147,767	95,586	121,145	134,444	137,563	132,210
Manhattan Bridge	75,684	73,064	66,152	73,767	79,129	80,363
Queensboro Bridge	182,940	176,469	176,419	184,964	180,369	178,610
Williamsburg Bridge	108,376	82,202	103,364	100,243	110,528	107,030

Note: Declines in traffic through Brooklyn-Battery Tunnel and Queens-Midtown Tunnel in 2001 reflect traffic restrictions arising from events of September 11.
Source: New York City Department of Transportation, *New York City Bridge Traffic Volumes 2005*.

Number of Licensed Drivers and Registered Motor Vehicles, 2005

	Manhattan	Bronx	Brooklyn	Queens	Staten Island	Total
Licensed drivers	692,067	405,180	802,103	1,010,102	291,330	3,200,782
Registered vehicles						
Standard series	217,094	214,812	363,450	638,948	238,454	1,672,758
Commercial	10,950	8,176	17,502	30,093	5,567	77,288
Trailer	881	1,277	1,939	5,009	2,704	11,810
Motorcycle	6,548	2,712	5,870	9,042	4,525	28,697
Moped	652	156	482	529	121	1,940
Bus	219	325	2,483	1,011	3,020	7,058
Taxi	5,294	4,596	8,883	16,814	1,292	36,879
Ambulance	178	65	790	249	86	1,368
Rental	382	70	1,407	21,838	25	23,722
Farm	2	0	1	1	0	4
Total registrations	242,200	232,189	402,807	723,534	255,794	1,856,524
Estimated population	1,590,911	1,362,523	2,497,859	2,250,718	462,695	8,164,706
Licensed drivers per 1,000 inhabitants	435.0	297.4	321.1	448.8	629.6	392.0
Registered vehicles per 1,000 inhabitants	152.2	170.4	161.3	321.5	552.8	227.4
Registered vehicles per 1,000 licensed drivers	350.0	573.1	502.2	716.3	878.0	580.0

Sources: New York State Department of Motor Vehicles; U.S. Bureau of the Census.

Vehicular Accidents, 2005

	All Accidents	Police Reported
Fatal accidents	314	314
Nonfatal personal injury accidents	54,650	45,058
Reportable property damage accidents	16,203	224
Total	71,167	45,596
Vehicles involved	134,671	83,105
Drivers involved	125,231	77,861
Vehicle occupants	182,626	125,156
Pedestrian–motor vehicle accidents	10,880	10,388
Bicycle–motor vehicle accidents	3,017	2,901
Motorcycle accidents	1,259	1,097
Persons killed[1]	328	328
Drivers killed	101	101
Passengers killed	46	46
Pedestrians killed	159	159
Bicyclists killed	21	21
Other fatalities	1	1
Persons injured[1]	78,341	65,967
Drivers injured	39,641	31,004
Passengers injured	24,576	21,573
Pedestrians injured	10,692	10,197
Bicyclists injured	2,924	2,814
Other injuries	508	379

[1] Includes pedestrians, bicyclists, and all other involved persons not in vehicle as well as vehicle occupants regardless of seating position.
Notes: Reportable property damage is damage of $1,000 or more. The term "vehicle" always excludes bicycles. The term "driver" always excludes bicyclists.
Source: New York State Department of Motor Vehicles.

Factors Contributing to Vehicular Accidents, 2005

	Total Number	Percentage of All Accidents	Number with One or More Fatalities	Number with Personal Injury	Number with Property Damage
Human factors					
Aggressive driving, road rage	670	1.5	3	666	1
Alcohol involvement	873	1.9	25	845	3
Backing unsafely	753	1.7	3	747	3
Cell phone (handheld)	66	0.1	0	66	0
Cell phone (hands free)	9	*	0	9	0
Other electronic device	8	*	0	8	0
Driver asleep	241	0.5	2	224	15
Driver fatigued, drowsy	169	0.4	0	160	9
Driver inattentive, distracted	8,818	19.3	44	8,735	39
Driver inexperienced	1,128	2.5	14	1,110	4
Driver lost consciousness	148	0.3	0	143	5
Error or confusion by pedestrian, bicyclist, or other	2,336	5.1	54	2,282	0
Failure to keep right	199	0.4	2	196	1
Failure to yield right of way	4,530	9.9	25	4,488	17
Following too closely	3,481	7.6	2	3,466	13
Illegal drugs	62	0.1	2	58	2
Illness	107	0.2	0	107	0
Improper passing or lane use	881	1.9	5	870	6
Improper turning	1,418	3.1	4	1,402	12
Outside car distraction	229	0.5	2	225	2
Passenger distraction	180	0.4	0	180	0
Physical disability	57	0.1	3	52	2
Prescription medication	41	0.1	0	40	1
Reaction to other uninvolved vehicle	1,161	2.5	7	1,149	5
Traffic control disregarded	2,156	4.7	21	2,126	9
Unsafe lane changing	1,044	2.3	4	1,032	8
Unsafe speed	2,332	5.1	73	2,252	7
Other human factors	104	0.2	0	104	0
Total, human factors reported	24,755	54.3	213	24,422	120

Factors Contributing to Vehicular Accidents, 2005 (continued)

	Total Number	Percentage of All Accidents	Number with One or More Fatalities	Number with Personal Injury	Number with Property Damage
Vehicular factors					
Defective accelerator	70	0.2	0	70	0
Defective brakes	459	1.0	1	458	0
Defective headlights	9	*	0	9	0
Defective two hitch	5	*	1	4	0
Driverless or runaway vehicle	28	0.1	0	28	0
Lighting defects other than headlights	9	*	0	9	0
Oversized vehicle	116	0.3	1	114	1
Steering failure	117	0.3	2	114	1
Tire failed or inadequate	112	0.2	0	112	0
Windshield inadequate	5	*	0	5	0
Other vehicular factors	1,918	4.2	13	1,898	7
Total, vehicular factors reported	2,759	6.1	16	2,734	9
Environmental factors					
Animal's action	30	0.1	0	30	0
Defective or improper shoulder	9	*	0	9	0
Defective pavement	147	0.3	1	146	0
Glare	418	0.9	2	415	1
Improper or nonworking traffic control device	102	0.2	0	102	0
Lane marking improper or inadequate	21	*	0	21	0
Obstruction, debris	209	0.5	3	206	0
Slippery pavement	1,773	3.9	9	1,749	15
View obstructed or limited	651	1.4	5	644	2
Other environmental factors	5	*	0	4	1
Total, environmental factors reported	3,215	7.1	19	3,178	18
Total, one or more factors reported	28,359	62.2	226	27,995	138
No contributing factor reported	17,237	37.8	88	17,063	86
All accidents	45,596	100.0	314	45,058	224

* = less than 0.05 percent
Note: Many accidents have multiple factors reported.
Source: New York State Department of Motor Vehicles.

Most Dangerous Intersections for Pedestrians, 1995–2001

	Number of Fatalities	Number of Injuries
1. East 33rd Street and Park Avenue, Manhattan	0	118
2. Utica Avenue and Eastern Parkway, Brooklyn	4	88
3. West 170th Street and Grand Concourse, Bronx	0	60
4. East 183rd Street and Grand Concourse, Bronx	2	54
5. Webster Avenue and East Fordham Road, Bronx	0	56
6. East 167th Street and Grand Concourse, Bronx	2	53
7. 7th Avenue and West 34th Street, Manhattan	0	55
8. Atlantic Avenue and Nostrand Avenue, Brooklyn	3	51
9. Essex Street and Delancey Street, Manhattan	1	51
10. West 14th Street and Avenue of the Americas, Manhattan	1	51
11. 63rd Drive and Queens Boulevard, Queens	1	50
12. Eastern Parkway and Franklin Avenue, Brooklyn	3	47
13. 7th Avenue and West 145th Street, Manhattan	1	49
14. Bruckner Boulevard and Hunts Point, Bronx	2	47
15. 8th Avenue and West 42nd Street, Manhattan	2	46
16. Hillside Avenue and Parsons Boulevard, Queens	1	47
17. 3rd Avenue and East 42nd Street, Manhattan	0	47
18. 3rd Avenue and East 14th Street, Manhattan	1	45
19. 8th Avenue and West 34th Street, Manhattan	1	45
20. Fulton Street and Flatbush Avenue Extension, Brooklyn	0	46
21. 1st Avenue and East 14th Street, Manhattan	1	43
22. Eastern Parkway and Nostrand Avenue, Brooklyn	0	44
23. West 42nd Street and Avenue of the Americas, Manhattan	0	44
24. 9th Avenue and West 42nd Street, Manhattan	0	44
25. West 125th Street and Amsterdam Avenue, Manhattan	0	44
26. Main Street and Roosevelt Avenue, Queens	1	42
27. East 42nd Street and Lexington Avenue, Manhattan	0	43
28. Jamaica Avenue and Parsons Boulevard, Queens	0	43
29. East Gun Hill Road and White Plans Road, Bronx	0	42
30. Church Avenue and Flatbush Avenue, Brooklyn	0	42
31. 5th Avenue and West 34th Street, Manhattan	0	41
32. Avenue A and East Houston Street, Manhattan	3	37
33. 3rd Avenue and Melrose Avenue, Bronx	1	39
34. East 23rd Street and Park Avenue, Manhattan	1	39
35. Broadway and Union Square West, Manhattan	0	40
36. Archer Avenue and Sutphin Boulevard, Queens	0	39

Most Dangerous Intersections for Pedestrians, 1995–2001 (continued)

	Number of Fatalities	Number of Injuries
37. 9th Avenue and West 57th Street, Manhattan	3	35
38. Bowery and West Houston Street, Manhattan	2	36
39. 46th Street and Queens Boulevard, Queens	2	36
40. West 34th Street between 5th Avenue / East 34th Street and Broadway / Avenue of the Americas, Manhattan	1	37
41. West Burnside Avenue between 179th Street and University Avenue, Bronx	0	38
42. Avenue U and Flatbush Avenue, Brooklyn	0	38
43. 9th Avenue and West 23rd Street, Manhattan	0	38
44. 3rd Avenue and East 57th Street, Manhattan	0	38
45. West 57th Street and Avenue of the Americas, Manhattan	0	38
46. 71st Avenue and Queens Boulevard, Queens	1	36
47. Union Street and Northern Boulevard, Queens	1	36
48. West Fordham Road and University Avenue, Bronx	0	37
49. 7th Avenue and West 23rd Street, Manhattan	0	37
50. Archer Avenue and Parsons Boulevard, Queens	0	37

Source: Transportation Alternatives.

Average Daily Traffic Volumes into and out of New York City, Selected Years, 1963–2005

	Bronx–Westchester	Queens–Nassau	New Jersey–Manhattan	New Jersey–Staten Island	Total
1963	269,650	546,550	265,603	27,398	1,109,201
1973	361,714	670,702	397,203	81,034	1,510,653
1982	413,750	713,146	433,744	106,672	1,667,312
1986	483,252	843,538	485,751	138,436	1,950,977
1993	506,191	892,318	473,069	140,775	2,012,353
1994	515,853	897,175	473,799	143,875	2,030,702
1995	531,941	892,743	482,098	143,657	2,050,439
1996	547,972	896,144	493,194	146,565	2,083,875
1997	554,683	907,131	504,788	151,578	2,118,180
1998	565,746	919,403	522,512	156,786	2,164,447
1999	584,015	947,043	549,352	166,890	2,247,300
2000	591,022	940,147	548,465	164,668	2,244,302
2001	606,666	946,727	458,944	177,251	2,189,588
2002	619,938	944,006	532,839	179,140	2,275,923
2003	619,449	968,694	547,449	174,582	2,310,174
2004	627,294	965,605	536,396	174,268	2,303,563
2005	633,350	959,089	527,717	171,653	2,291,809

Note: Twenty-four-hour westbound volumes from Staten Island to New Jersey not available for 1973, 1982, and 1986; estimated to be the same as eastbound volumes to Staten Island obtained from toll records. Source: New York City Department of Transportation, *New York City Screenline Traffic Flow 2005*.

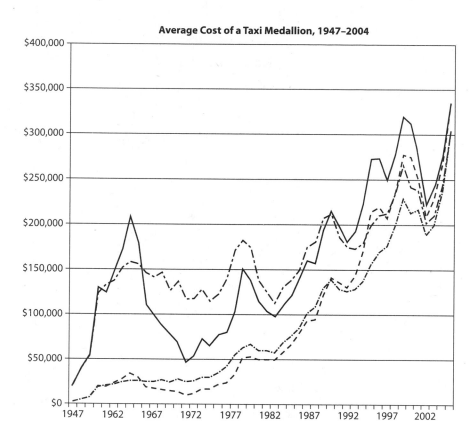

Average Cost of a Taxi Medallion, 1947–2004

Individual Medallion · —·—· In Constant Dollars · — — In Constant Dollars
Corporate Medallion · — — — In Constant Dollars

Source: New York City Taxi and Limousine Commission.

Cost of a Three-Mile Taxi Ride in New York and Selected International Cities, Including Gratuity

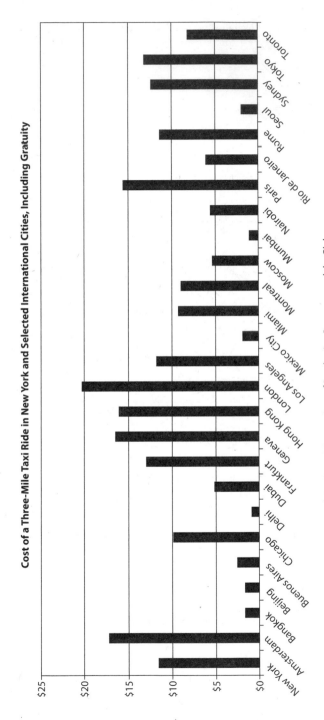

Source: UBS Wealth Management, *Prices and Earnings: A Comparison of Purchasing Power around the Globe.*

Major Airport Activity, 2001–2005

	2001	2002	2003	2004	2005
John F. Kennedy					
Commercial and Noncommercial Flights					
Domestic	180,792	180,766	174,156	205,497	231,042
International	113,234	106,891	106,162	114,517	118,364
Total	294,026	287,657	280,318	320,014	349,406
Passengers					
Domestic	13,361,480	14,602,878	16,436,858	20,088,422	22,095,542
International	15,988,572	15,336,334	15,299,631	17,487,035	18,784,955
Total	29,350,052	29,939,212	31,736,489	37,575,457	40,880,497
Cargo (short tons)					
Domestic	390,430	426,711	460,798	472,242	428,076
International	1,131,068	1,259,840	1,279,245	1,318,206	1,316,112
Total	1,521,498	1,686,551	1,740,043	1,790,448	1,744,188
La Guardia					
Commercial and Noncommercial Flights					
Domestic	348,734	343,316	355,907	377,669	381,263
International	19,137	19,123	19,054	22,106	23,590
Total	367,871	362,439	374,961	399,775	404,853
Passengers					
Domestic	21,375,263	20,869,575	21,435,246	23,191,610	24,407,472
International	1,144,611	1,117,104	1,047,524	1,261,593	1,471,129
Total	22,519,874	21,986,679	22,482,770	24,453,203	25,878,601
Cargo (short tons)					
Domestic	15,765	11,321	11,989	13,817	15,689
International	709	388	344	279	317
Total	16,474	11,709	12,333	14,096	16,006

Major Airport Activity, 2001–2005 (continued)

	2001	2002	2003	2004	2005
Newark					
Commercial and Noncommercial Flights					
Domestic	374,406	342,851	340,387	364,752	359,980
International	64,869	62,966	66,492	72,694	76,264
Total	439,275	405,817	406,879	437,446	436,244
Passengers					
Domestic	23,483,246	21,847,809	21,781,881	23,035,255	23,707,764
International	7,617,245	7,372,966	7,668,633	8,858,117	9,365,005
Total	31,100,491	29,220,775	29,450,514	31,893,372	33,072,769
Cargo (short tons)					
Domestic	705,963	728,039	738,065	739,005	718,357
International	212,741	181,733	237,530	256,251	239,108
Total	918,704	909,772	975,595	995,256	957,465
Total, All Three Airports					
Commercial and Noncommercial Flights					
Domestic	903,932	866,933	870,450	947,918	972,285
International	197,240	188,980	191,708	209,317	218,218
Total	1,101,172	1,055,913	1,062,158	1,157,235	1,190,503
Passengers					
Domestic	58,219,989	57,320,262	59,653,985	66,315,287	70,210,778
International	24,750,428	23,826,404	24,015,788	27,606,745	29,621,089
Total	82,970,417	81,146,666	83,669,773	93,922,032	99,831,867
Cargo (short tons)					
Domestic	1,112,158	1,166,071	1,210,852	1,225,064	1,162,122
International	1,344,518	1,441,961	1,517,119	1,574,736	1,555,537
Total	2,456,676	2,608,032	2,727,971	2,799,800	2,717,659

Source: Port Authority of New York and New Jersey, *2005 Airport Traffic Report*.

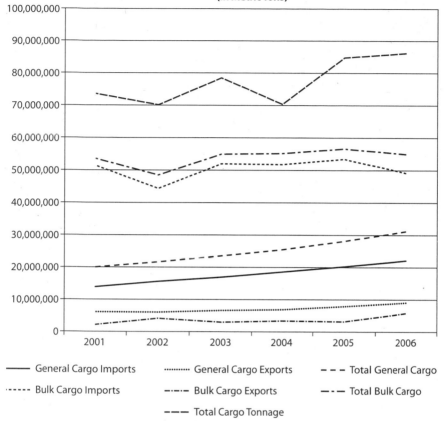

Oceanborne Cargo Tonnage, Port of New York and New Jersey, 2001–2006 (in Metric Tons)

Legend:
- General Cargo Imports
- General Cargo Exports
- Total General Cargo
- Bulk Cargo Imports
- Bulk Cargo Exports
- Total Bulk Cargo
- Total Cargo Tonnage

Source: Port Authority of New York and New Jersey.

10 Education

Superintendents of the Board of Education and Schools Chancellors since Consolidation

William H. Maxwell	1898–1918	Frank J. Macchiarola	1978–1983
William L. Ettinger	1918–1924	Richard F. Halverson	1983
William J. O'Shea	1924–1934	Anthony J. Alvarado	1983–1984
Harold G. Campbell	1934–1942	Nathan Quinones	1984–1987
John E. Wade	1942–1947	Charles I. Schonhaut	1988
William Jansen	1947–1958	Richard R. Green	1988–1989
John J. Theobald	1958–1962	Bernard Mecklowitz	1989
Bernard E. Donovan	1962–1963, 1965–1969	Joseph A. Fernandez	1990–1993
Calvin E. Gross	1963–1965	Ramon C. Cortines	1993–1995
Nathan Brown	1969–1970	Rudolph Crew	1995–1999
Irving Anker	1970, 1973–1978	Harold O. Levy	2000–2002
Harvey B. Scribner	1970–1973	Joel I. Klein	2002–

Source: Educational Priorities Panel.

Educational Attainment by Borough, 2000

	Manhattan	Bronx	Brooklyn	Queens	Staten Island	Total
Less than 9th grade	117,448	125,385	203,190	170,222	16,350	632,595
9th to 12th grade, no diploma	122,906	174,301	281,116	216,959	34,813	830,095
High school graduate (includes equivalency)	151,995	205,246	414,868	418,381	98,845	1,289,335
Some college, no degree	138,579	130,163	225,716	249,688	57,426	801,572
Associate degree	38,866	43,293	88,730	87,380	18,247	276,516
Bachelor's degree	292,665	69,854	202,103	228,419	41,517	834,558
Graduate or professional degree	263,528	46,550	137,147	138,453	26,597	612,275
Total population 25 years and over	1,125,987	794,792	1,552,870	1,509,502	293,795	5,276,946

Source: U.S. Bureau of the Census.

Educational Attainment Citywide, Population 25 Years and Over

1990

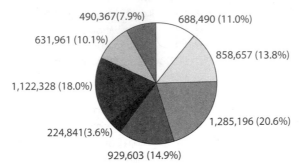

490,367(7.9%)   688,490 (11.0%)

631,961 (10.1%)   858,657 (13.8%)

1,122,328 (18.0%)

1,285,196 (20.6%)

224,841(3.6%)

929,603 (14.9%)

☐ Less than 9th grade   ☐ 9th to 12th grade, no diploma
◼ High school graduate   ◼ Some college
   (includes equivalency)
◼ Associate degree   ◼ College graduate
☐ Bachelor's degree   ◼ Graduate or professional degree

2000

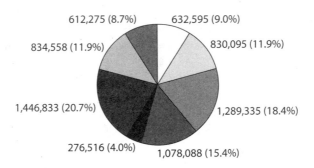

612,275 (8.7%)   632,595 (9.0%)

834,558 (11.9%)   830,095 (11.9%)

1,446,833 (20.7%)

1,289,335 (18.4%)

276,516 (4.0%)   1,078,088 (15.4%)

☐ Less than 9th grade   ☐ 9th to 12th grade, no diploma
◼ High school graduate   ◼ Some college
   (includes equivalency)
◼ Associate degree   ◼ College graduate
☐ Bachelor's degree   ◼ Graduate or professional degree

Source: U.S. Bureau of the Census.

Percentage of Public School Students at Selected Proficiency Levels, New York City, Other Large Cities, and New York State, 2003

| | New York City | | Other Large Cities[1] | | New York State | |
	Grade 4	Grade 8	Grade 4	Grade 8	Grade 4	Grade 8
English Language Arts						
Below basic	8.9	14.5	11.8	19.5	5.8	9.2
Proficient or advanced	52.5	32.6	44.3	22.5	64.3	45.3
Mathematics						
Below basic	8.7	28.2	8.3	34.3	4.8	16.7
Proficient or advanced	66.7	34.4	62.3	23.7	78.1	51.0

[1] Buffalo, Rochester, Syracuse, and Yonkers.
Source: New York City Department of Education.

Number of Eligible Immigrant Children in New York City Public Schools from Fifteen Largest National Sources, March 2000 to March 2006

	2000	2001	2002	2003	2004	2005	2006	Change, 2000–2006 Number	Percent
Bangladesh	3,667	3,437	2,795	2,633	2,236	2,072	2,105	−1,562	−42.6
China	9,067	9,029	7,967	7,610	7,557	6,914	7,205	−1,862	−20.5
Colombia	3,864	4,181	3,090	2,631	2,063	1,580	1,308	−2,556	−66.1
Dominican Republic	13,114	11,500	9,621	10,839	13,287	14,107	14,086	972	7.4
Ecuador	4,027	4,374	3,919	3,844	3,564	3,051	2,743	−1,284	−31.9
Guyana	3,475	3,351	4,241	5,526	5,716	5,074	4,274	799	23.0
Haiti	3,615	4,171	3,149	2,888	2,534	2,387	2,139	−1,476	−40.8
India	3,568	3,303	2,526	2,266	2,007	1,725	1,639	−1,929	−54.1
Jamaica	7,463	7,286	6,402	6,017	5,268	4,402	3,834	−3,629	−48.6
Korea	2,562	2,734	2,138	2,084	1,811	1,464	1,354	−1,208	−47.2
Mexico	4,066	5,051	4,793	5,086	5,070	5,015	4,843	777	19.1
Pakistan	4,687	4,872	3,619	·2,907	2,358	2,019	1,695	−2,992	−63.8
Poland	1,624	1,510	1,256	1,249	1,171	1,089	970	−654	−40.3
Russia	4,452	3,222	2,394	1,959	1,600	1,196	888	−3,564	−80.1

**Number of Eligible Immigrant Children in New York City Public Schools
from Fifteen Largest National Sources, March 2000 to March 2006** (continued)

	2000	2001	2002	2003	2004	2005	2006	Change, 2000–2006 Number	Percent
Trinidad and Tobago	3,657	3,992	3,649	3,591	3,017	2,483	2,034	−1,623	−44.4
Total, top fifteen nations	72,908	77,013	61,559	61,130	59,259	54,578	51,117	−21,791	−29.9
Total, all nations	104,618	102,867	86,974	85,320	81,946	75,046	70,313	−34,305	−32.8

Source: New York City Public Schools, *Emergency Immigrant Survey, March 2000 to 2006.*

Public School Statistics, Fiscal Years 1999–2003

	1999	2000	2001	2002	2003
Total public school enrollment	1,093,071	1,100,312	1,103,245	1,098,832	1,091,717
Total pre-kindergarten enrollment	23,982	34,043	41,069	45,028	49,876
Total kindergarten enrollment	73,019	72,385	70,015	67,196	64,660
Number of high school graduates reporting higher education plans	21,881	22,440	22,689	26,943	26,247
Percentage of high school graduates reporting higher education plans	60	63	66	66	67
Number of elementary and middle school students at performance level 1 in reading	59,619[1]	55,729[2]	60,268[2]	65,535[3]	61,172[3]
Percentage of elementary and middle school students at performance level 1 in reading	22	18	20	17	16
Number of schools with 50% or more students at performance level 1 in reading	10[1]	49[2]	60[2]	39[3]	61[3]
Number of English Language Learners (ELLs)	148,399[4]	139,695[4]	151,530	144,942	134,508
Number of special education students in related services, special education, teacher support services	64,113	64,496	64,093	65,212	65,130
Number of special education students in collaborative team teaching services	3,256	4,866	6,322	9,559	10,664

Public School Statistics, Fiscal Years 1999–2003 (continued)

	1999	2000	2001	2002	2003
Number of special education students in self-contained, home instructional, hospital/agency services	80,429	79,257	77,324	71,870	71,061
Number of initial special education referrals	30,058	34,222	29,434	30,235	32,811
Number of recommended special education decertifications	5,444	4,901	6,120	5,403	5,224
Number of pupils receiving free lunch	685,452	693,281	711,830	708,274	719,377

[1] Includes grades 3, 5, 6, and 7 only. Comparisons between 1999 and 2003 not appropriate. Before fiscal year 2000 data report numbers and percentages of students in the lowest national quartile in reading.
[2] Includes grades 3, 4, 5, and 7 only. Comparisons appropriate only for 2000 and 2001.
[3] Includes grades 3, 4, 5, 6, and 8 only. Comparisons appropriate only for 2002 and 2003.
[4] Includes general education and resource room students only.
Source: New York City Department of Education.

Selected Independent Schools

	Borough	Grades	Enrollment
Abraham Joshua Heschel School	Manhattan	pre-K–11	719
Alexander Robertson School	Manhattan	K–5	70
Allen Christian School	Queens	pre-K–8	660
Allen-Stevenson School	Manhattan	K–9	390
Anglo-American International School	Manhattan	11–12	128
Bank Street School for Children	Manhattan	pre-K–8	423
Berkeley Carroll School	Brooklyn	pre-K–12	775
Birch Wathen Lenox School	Manhattan	K–12	265
Brearley School	Manhattan	K–12	677
Brick Church School	Manhattan	pre-K–K	145
Brooklyn Friends School	Brooklyn	pre-K–2	600
Brooklyn Heights Montessori School	Brooklyn	pre-K–8	255
Browning School	Manhattan	K–12	370
Buckley School	Manhattan	K–9	356
Caedmon School	Manhattan	pre-K–5	198
Calhoun School	Manhattan	pre-K–12	670
Cathedral School	Manhattan	K–8	241

Selected Independent Schools (continued)

	Borough	Grades	Enrollment
Chapin School	Manhattan	K–12	661
Children's Storefront School	Manhattan	pre-K–8	168
Churchill School and Center	Manhattan	K–12	400
City and Country School	Manhattan	pre-K–8	285
Collegiate School	Manhattan	K–12	630
Columbia Grammar and Preparatory School	Manhattan	pre-K–12	1,065
Convent of the Sacred Heart	Manhattan	pre-K–2	667
Corlears School	Manhattan	pre-K–4	135
Dalton School	Manhattan	K–12	1,297
De La Salle Academy	Manhattan	6–8	138
Dwight School	Manhattan	K–12	439
Episcopal School	Manhattan	pre-K–K	220
Ethical Culture Fieldston School	Bronx	pre-K–2	1,609
Friends Seminary	Manhattan	K–12	655
Garden School	Queens	pre-K–12	350
Gateway School of New York	Manhattan	K–6	63
Geneva School of Manhattan	Manhattan	pre-K–8	n/a
George Jackson Academy	Manhattan	4–8	100
Grace Church School	Manhattan	pre-K–8	395
Hannah Senesh Community Day School	Brooklyn	K–8	125
Hewitt School	Manhattan	K–12	485
Kew-Forest School	Queens	K–12	375
La Scuola D'Italia Guglielmo Marconi	Manhattan	pre-K–2	190
Little Red Schoolhouse and Elisabeth Irwin High School	Manhattan	pre-K–12	560
Loyola School	Manhattan	9–12	200
Lycée Français de New York	Manhattan	pre-K–postgraduate	1,240
Madison Avenue Presbyterian School	Manhattan	pre-K–K	99
Manhattan Country School	Manhattan	pre-K–8	183
Manhattan High School for Girls	Manhattan	9–12	195
Martin Luther High School	Queens	9–12	384
Mary McDowell Center	Brooklyn	K–6	125
Marymount School	Manhattan	pre-K–2	528
Metropolitan Montessori School	Manhattan	pre-K–6	196
Nightingale-Bamford School	Manhattan	K–12	543
Packer Collegiate Institute	Brooklyn	pre-K–12	942
Parkside School	Manhattan	K–5	80
Philosophy Day School	Manhattan	pre-K–8	70

Selected Independent Schools (continued)

	Borough	Grades	Enrollment
Poly Prep Country Day School	Brooklyn	pre-K–12	975
Professional Children's School	Manhattan	4–12	195
Ramaz School	Manhattan	pre-K–12	1,105
Regis High School	Manhattan	9–12	530
Resurrection Episcopal Day School	Manhattan	pre-K–K	76
Robert Louis Stevenson School	Manhattan	7–12	75
Rodeph Sholom School	Manhattan	pre-K–8	619
Rudolf Steiner School	Manhattan	pre-K–12	349
St. Ann's School	Brooklyn	pre-K–12	1,071
St. Bernard's School	Manhattan	K–9	370
Saint David's School	Manhattan	pre-K–8	377
St. Francis Preparatory School	Queens	9–12	2,725
St. Hilda's and St. Hugh's School	Manhattan	pre-K–8	368
St. Luke's School	Manhattan	pre-K–8	194
School at Columbia University	Manhattan	K–6	335
Solomon Schechter High School of New York	Manhattan	9–12	107
Solomon Schechter School of Manhattan	Manhattan	K–8	145
Spence School	Manhattan	K–12	645
Staten Island Academy	Staten Island	pre-K–12	394
Stephen Gaynor School	Manhattan	K–7	120
Studio School	Manhattan	pre-K–8	63
Town School	Manhattan	pre-K–8	390
Trevor Day School	Manhattan	pre-K–12	795
Trinity School	Manhattan	K–12	975
United Nations International School	Manhattan	K–12	1,460
Village Community School	Manhattan	K–8	325
West End Day School	Manhattan	K–6	50
West Side Montessori School	Manhattan	pre-K–K	204
Windsor School	Queens	6–postgraduate	95
Winston Preparatory School	Manhattan	6–12	218
Xavier High School	Manhattan	9–12	922
York Preparatory School	Manhattan	6–12	320

Source: New York State Association of Independent Schools.

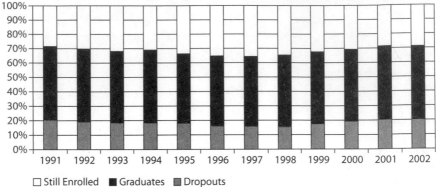

Four-Year Outcomes for the Classes of 1991–2002, Including August Graduates

☐ Still Enrolled ■ Graduates ■ Dropouts

Note: Excludes students discharged from the school system.
Source: New York City Department of Education, Division
of Assessment and Accountability.

Nonpublic School Enrollment, 1998–1999 to 2002–2003

	1998–1999	1999–2000	2000–2001	2001–2002	2002–2003
Manhattan					
Preschool	4,678	4,799	4,693	4,448	4,308
K–12	46,153	51,584	48,207	48,288	46,059
Bronx					
Preschool	2,951	2,699	2,714	2,899	2,871
K–12	42,761	45,325	43,092	43,085	42,238
Brooklyn					
Preschool	8,602	8,505	9,915	9,579	10,540
K–12	100,770	111,893	104,720	105,117	103,951
Queens					
Preschool	5,393	5,539	5,135	5,055	4,804
K–12	57,881	63,752	58,916	58,956	58,081
Staten Island					
Preschool	2,032	2,017	1,929	1,858	1,777
K–12	20,020	22,444	20,209	20,180	19,991
Total					
Preschool	23,656	23,559	24,386	23,839	24,300
K–12	267,585	294,998	275,144	275,626	270,320

Source: New York State Department of Education.

Enrollment at Institutions of Higher Education, 1999–2006

	Under-graduate	Graduate and First Professional Degree	Total		Under-graduate	Graduate and First Professional Degree	Total
1999				**2003**			
Manhattan	147,338	70,264	217,602	Manhattan	161,661	78,038	239,699
Bronx	32,964	9,764	42,728	Bronx	37,532	9,645	47,177
Brooklyn	59,234	12,221	71,455	Brooklyn	63,662	13,092	76,754
Queens	56,533	8,839	65,372	Queens	62,832	10,031	72,863
Staten Island	12,101	1,604	13,705	Staten Island	13,342	1,777	15,119
CUNY Total	170,033	26,416	196,449	CUNY Total	184,613	29,769	214,382
Grand Total	308,170	102,692	410,862	Grand Total	339,029	112,583	451,612
2000				**2004**			
Manhattan	150,124	70,979	221,103	Manhattan	179,331	69,254	248,585
Bronx	32,710	9,029	41,739	Bronx	40,939	8,150	49,089
Brooklyn	60,247	12,295	72,542	Brooklyn	66,909	10,042	76,951
Queens	56,991	8,663	65,654	Queens	66,030	8,509	74,539
Staten Island	11,820	1,749	13,569	Staten Island	13,158	1,642	14,800
CUNY Total	169,154	22,767	191,921	CUNY Total	188,923	29,213	218,136
Grand Total	311,892	102,715	414,607	Grand Total	366,367	97,597	463,964
2001				**2005**			
Manhattan	147,530	70,500	218,030	Manhattan	181,527	71,574	253,101
Bronx	33,498	9,573	43,071	Bronx	42,343	7,911	50,254
Brooklyn	58,782	12,773	71,555	Brooklyn	68,439	10,035	78,474
Queens	55,258	8,297	63,555	Queens	65,929	8,728	74,657
Staten Island	11,615	1,749	13,364	Staten Island	12,994	1,488	14,482
CUNY Total	171,006	23,175	194,181	CUNY Total	191,358	29,128	220,486
Grand Total	306,683	102,892	409,575	Grand Total	371,232	99,736	470,968
2002				**2006**			
Manhattan	159,349	75,867	235,216	Manhattan	179,877	73,006	252,883
Bronx	35,608	10,047	45,655	Bronx	43,194	7,877	51,071
Brooklyn	64,333	12,833	77,166	Brooklyn	70,083	10,492	80,575
Queens	59,758	9,440	69,198	Queens	67,618	8,453	76,071
Staten Island	12,600	1,920	14,520	Staten Island	13,319	1,389	14,708
CUNY Total	169,677	27,676	197,353	CUNY Total	197,082	28,864	225,946
Grand Total	331,648	110,107	441,755	Grand Total	374,091	101,217	475,308

CUNY = City University of New York
Source: New York State Department of Education.

College and University Campuses, with Fall 2006 Enrollment

Branches of State University of New York

SUNY Health Science Center at Brooklyn	Brooklyn	4-year, graduate	1,612
SUNY Maritime College at Fort Schuyler	Bronx	4-year, graduate	1,289
SUNY College of Optometry at New York City	Manhattan	Graduate	302
Fashion Institute of Technology	Manhattan	4-year, graduate	9,969

Branches of City University of New York

Borough of Manhattan Community College	Manhattan	2-year	18,615
Bronx Community College	Bronx	2-year	8,750
Bernard M. Baruch College	Manhattan	4-year, graduate	15,703
Brooklyn College	Brooklyn	4-year, graduate	15,442
City College of New York	Manhattan	4-year, graduate	12,998
College of Staten Island	Staten Island	4-year, graduate	12,324
Graduate School and University Center	Manhattan	4-year, graduate	4,706
Herbert H. Lehman College	Bronx	4-year, graduate	11,201
Hunter College	Manhattan	4-year, graduate	21,061
John Jay College of Criminal Justice	Manhattan	4-year, graduate	14,786
Queens College	Queens	4-year, graduate	18,002
CUNY School of Law	Queens	Graduate	431
York College	Queens	4-year, graduate	6,202
Eugenio Maria de Hostos Community College	Bronx	2-year	4,667
Fiorello H. LaGuardia Community College	Queens	2-year	13,600
Kingsborough Community College	Brooklyn	2-year	15,562
Medgar Evers College	Brooklyn	4-year, graduate	5,558
New York City College of Technology	Brooklyn	4-year, graduate	13,080
Queensborough Community College	Queens	2-year	13,519

Independent Institutions

American Academy McAllister Institute	Manhattan	2-year	110
American Academy of Dramatic Arts	Manhattan	2-year	220
Bank Street College of Education	Manhattan	Graduate	1,051
Bard Graduate Center for Studies in the Decorative Arts	Manhattan	4-year, graduate	57
Barnard College	Manhattan	4-year, graduate	2,334
Boricua College	Manhattan	4-year, graduate	1,059
Boston Graduate School of Psychoanalysis	Manhattan	Graduate	19
Bramson ORT College	Queens	2-year	542
Brooklyn Law School	Brooklyn	Graduate	1,494
College of Mount Saint Vincent	Bronx	4-year, graduate	1,618
College of New Rochelle, Brooklyn Campus	Brooklyn	4-year, graduate	n/a
College of New Rochelle, Co-op City Campus	Bronx	4-year, graduate	n/a

College and University Campuses, with Fall 2006 Enrollment (continued)

Independent Institutions (continued)

College of New Rochelle, Council 37 Campus	Manhattan	4-year, graduate	n/a
College of New Rochelle, Rosa Parks Campus	Manhattan	4-year, graduate	n/a
College of New Rochelle, John Cardinal O'Connor Campus	Bronx	4-year, graduate	n/a
Columbia University	Manhattan	4-year, graduate	24,164
Cooper Union for the Advancement of Science and Art	Manhattan	4-year, graduate	962
Cornell University Medical Campus	Manhattan	4-year, graduate	847
Fordham University	Bronx	4-year, graduate	14,155
Gamla College	Brooklyn	2-year	378
General Theological Seminary	Manhattan	Graduate	184
Hebrew Union College	Manhattan	4-year, graduate	176
Helene Fuld College of Nursing	Manhattan	2-year	330
Institute of Design and Construction	Brooklyn	2-year	175
Jewish Theological Seminary of America	Manhattan	4-year, graduate	627
Juilliard School	Manhattan	4-year, graduate	1,003
King's College	Manhattan	4-year, graduate	246
Long Island College Hospital School of Nursing	Brooklyn	2-year	141
Long Island University, Brooklyn Campus	Brooklyn	4-year, graduate	8,404
Long Island University, NYU Campus	Manhattan	4-year, graduate	128
Louis V. Gerstner Jr. Graduate School of Biomedical Sciences, Memorial Sloan-Kettering Cancer Center	Manhattan	Graduate	n/a
Manhattan College	Bronx	4-year, graduate	3,363
Manhattan School of Music	Manhattan	4-year, graduate	821
Marymount Manhattan College	Manhattan	4-year, graduate	1,954
Mercy College, Bronx Campus	Bronx	4-year, graduate	n/a
Mercy College, Manhattan Campus	Manhattan	4-year, graduate	n/a
Metropolitan College of New York	Manhattan	4-year, graduate	1,238
Mount Sinai School of Medicine of NYU	Manhattan	Graduate	755
New School University	Manhattan	4-year, graduate	9,145
New York Academy of Art	Manhattan	Graduate	111
New York College of Podiatric Medicine	Manhattan	Graduate	349
New York Institute of Technology, Manhattan Campus	Manhattan	4-year, graduate	n/a
New York Law School	Manhattan	Graduate	1,544
New York School of Interior Design	Manhattan	4-year, graduate	725
New York Theological Seminary	Manhattan	Graduate	340
New York University	Manhattan	4-year, graduate	39,225
Pace University, New York City Campus	Manhattan	4-year, graduate	13,483
Phillips Beth Israel School of Nursing	Manhattan	2-year	220
Polytechnic University	Brooklyn	4-year, graduate	2,919

Independent Institutions (continued)

Pratt Institute	Brooklyn	4-year, graduate	4,993
Pratt Manhattan Center	Manhattan	4-year, graduate	n/a
Professional Business College	Manhattan	2-year	548
Rabbi Isaac Elchanan Theological Seminary	Manhattan	4-year, graduate	308
Rockefeller University	Manhattan	Graduate	199
St. Francis College	Brooklyn	4-year, graduate	2,258
St. John's University	Queens	4-year, graduate	20,157
St. John's University, Manhattan Campus	Manhattan	4-year, graduate	n/a
St. John's University, Staten Island Campus	Staten Island	4-year, graduate	n/a
St. Joseph's College	Brooklyn	4-year, graduate	5,393
St. Vincent's Catholic Medical Centers of New York	Queens	2-year	113
St. Vincent's Catholic Medical Centers of New York, Staten Island	Staten Island	2-year	116
Teachers College	Manhattan	Graduate	4,963
Touro College	Manhattan	4-year, graduate	13,390
Touro College, Flatbush Campus	Brooklyn	4-year, graduate	n/a
Union Theological Seminary	Manhattan	Graduate	274
Vaughn College of Aeronautics and Technology	Queens	4-year, graduate	1,097
Wagner College	Staten Island	4-year, graduate	2,280
Yeshiva University	Manhattan	4-year, graduate	6,240

Proprietary Institutions

Art Institute of New York City	Manhattan	2-year	1,492
ASA Institute of Business and Computer Technology	Brooklyn	2-year	2,977
Berkeley College	Manhattan	4-year, graduate	3,061
Christie's Education, Inc.	Manhattan	Graduate	35
DeVry Institute of Technology	Queens	4-year	1,270
Globe Institute of Technology, Inc.	Manhattan	4-year	1,280
Interboro Institute	Manhattan	2-year	3,131
Katharine Gibbs School	Manhattan	2-year	1,975
Keller Graduate School of Management	Queens	Graduate	245
Laboratory Institute of Merchandising	Manhattan	4-year	970
Long Island Business Institute, Flushing	Queens	2-year	n/a
Mandl School	Manhattan	2-year	281
Monroe College	Bronx	4-year	6,313
New York Career Institute	Manhattan	2-year	706
Pacific College of Oriental Medicine	Manhattan	4-year	442
Plaza College	Queens	2-year	701

College and University Campuses, with Fall 2006 Enrollment (continued)

Proprietary Institutions (continued)

School of Visual Arts	Manhattan	4-year	3,547
Swedish Institute	Manhattan	2-year	655
Taylor Business Institute	Manhattan	2-year	n/a
Technical Career Institutes	Manhattan	2-year	3,195
Tri-State College of Acupuncture	Manhattan	4-year	154
Wood Tobé-Coburn School	Manhattan	2-year	296

Source: New York State Department of Education, Office of Higher Education.

Endowments of Colleges and Universities, Fiscal Year 2006

	Endowment	Nationwide Rank
1. Columbia University	$5,937,814,000	7
2. New York University	1,774,700,000	30
3. Rockefeller University	1,771,954,000	31
4. Yeshiva University	1,273,327,000	47
5. Juilliard School	663,886,000	94
6. Cooper Union	471,081,000	132
7. Fordham University	357,342,000	156
8. New School	199,087,000	233
9. Teachers College	182,037,000	249
10. Barnard College	173,362,000	256
11. Pace University	101,815,000	343
12. Pratt Institute	73,573,000	400
13. Brooklyn College	50,264,000	489
14. State University of New York, Health Science Center at Brooklyn, College of Medicine	47,332,000	498
15. Bank Street College of Education	24,952,000	623
16. Marymount Manhattan College	12,960,000	708
17. City University of New York Honors College	4,990,000	757

Source: National Association of College and University Business Officers, *2006 NACUBO Endowment Study*.

11 Environment, Flora and Fauna

Selected Weather Records

Highest recorded temperature, degrees Fahrenheit	107	3 July 1966
Lowest recorded temperature, degrees Fahrenheit	−15	9 February 1934
Coldest month, degrees Fahrenheit	19.6	January 1857
Coldest winter, degrees Fahrenheit	25.7	1917–1918
Warmest month, degrees Fahrenheit	81.4	July 1999
Warmest summer, degrees Fahrenheit	77.3	1966
Maximum twenty-four-hour precipitation, inches	11.17	8–9 October 1903
Maximum monthly precipitation, inches	16.85	September 1882
Minimum monthly precipitation, inches	.02	September 1949
Maximum annual precipitation, inches	67.03	1972
Minimum annual precipitation, inches	22.17	1965
Maximum twenty-four-hour snowfall, inches	26.4	26–27 December 1947
Largest single snowfall, inches	26.4	26–27 December 1947
Maximum monthly snowfall, inches	37.9	February 1894
Maximum seasonal snowfall, inches	87.2	1867–1868
Maximum depth of snowfall, inches	26.4	27 December 1947

Source: Christopher C. Burt, *Extreme Weather: A Guide and Record Book* (New York: W. W. Norton, 2004).

Monthly Weather Averages

	Jan	Feb	March	April	May	June	July	Aug	Sept	Oct	Nov	Dec	Annual
Average number of days with precipitation of 0.01 inch or more, Central Park	11	10	11	11	11	10	10	10	8	8	9	10	121
Average number of days with precipitation of 0.01 inch or more, JFK Airport	10	10	11	11	11	10	9	9	8	8	10	11	118

	Jan	Feb	March	April	May	June	July	Aug	Sept	Oct	Nov	Dec	Annual
Average number of days with precipitation of 0.01 inch or more, La Guardia Airport	11	10	11	11	11	10	9	9	8	8	10	11	118
Average relative humidity, morning, Central Park	68	68	68	67	71	74	75	78	79	76	73	69	72
Average relative humidity, afternoon, Central Park	60	57	54	51	53	56	55	57	57	55	59	60	56
Average relative humidity, morning, JFK Airport	71	71	71	70	73	75	75	78	80	78	76	72	74
Average relative humidity, afternoon, JFK Airport	60	57	56	55	59	60	59	60	60	57	59	60	58
Average relative humidity, morning, La Guardia Airport	67	65	67	67	71	72	72	75	76	74	71	68	70

	Jan	Feb	March	April	May	June	July	Aug	Sept	Oct	Nov	Dec	Annual
Average relative humidity, afternoon, La Guardia Airport	58	55	53	51	53	54	53	55	57	55	58	59	55
Mean number of clear days, Central Park	8	8	9	8	8	8	8	9	11	12	9	9	107
Mean number of partly cloudy days, Central Park	9	9	10	11	12	12	13	12	10	10	10	9	127
Mean number of cloudy days, Central Park	14	11	12	12	11	10	10	10	9	9	12	13	132
Mean number of clear days, JFK Airport	8	8	8	8	7	7	7	8	10	11	8	8	98
Mean number of partly cloudy days, JFK Airport	8	8	9	9	11	11	12	13	9	9	8	8	116
Mean number of cloudy days, JFK Airport	15	13	14	13	13	12	11	10	11	11	14	15	152
Mean number of clear days, La Guardia Airport	8	8	8	7	7	7	7	8	10	11	7	8	96

	Jan	Feb	March	April	May	June	July	Aug	Sept	Oct	Nov	Dec	Annual
Mean number of partly cloudy days, La Guardia Airport	8	7	9	9	11	11	13	12	9	9	8	9	117
Mean number of cloudy days, La Guardia Airport	15	13	14	13	13	11	11	11	11	11	14	15	153
Highest temperature on record, Central Park	72	75	86	96	99	101	106	104	102	94	84	75	106
Highest temperature on record, JFK Airport	69	71	85	90	99	99	104	100	98	88	77	75	104
Highest temperature on record, La Guardia Airport	68	73	83	94	97	99	107	104	96	87	80	75	107
Lowest temperature on record, Central Park	−6	−15	3	12	32	44	52	50	39	28	5	−13	−15
Lowest temperature on record, JFK Airport	−2	−2	7	20	34	45	55	46	40	25	19	2	−2

Monthly Weather Averages (continued)

	Jan	Feb	March	April	May	June	July	Aug	Sept	Oct	Nov	Dec	Annual
Lowest temperature on record, La Guardia Airport	−3	−2	8	22	38	46	56	51	44	30	18	−1	−3
Mean number of days with maximum temperature of 90 degrees or above, Central Park	0	0	0	*	1	3	7	5	1	*	0	0	17
Mean number of days with maximum temperature of 90 degrees or above, JFK Airport	0	0	0	*	*	2	4	3	1	0	0	0	10
Mean number of days with maximum temperature of 90 degrees or above, La Guardia Airport	0	0	0	*	1	3	6	4	1	0	0	0	16

	Jan	Feb	March	April	May	June	July	Aug	Sept	Oct	Nov	Dec	Annual
Mean number of days with minimum temperature of 32 degrees or below, Central Park	22	20	12	1	*	0	0	0	0	*	5	18	78
Mean number of days with minimum temperature of 32 degrees or below, JFK Airport	23	20	12	1	0	0	0	0	0	*	4	17	77
Mean number of days with minimum temperature of 32 degrees or below, La Guardia Airport	22	19	10	1	0	0	0	0	0	*	3	15	70
Normal precipitation	4.13	3.15	4.37	4.28	4.69	3.84	4.62	4.22	4.23	3.85	4.36	3.95	49.69
Average snowfall, Central Park	7.5	8.5	5.1	0.9	T	0	T	0	0	T	0.9	5.5	28.4

Monthly Weather Averages (continued)

	Jan	Feb	March	April	May	June	July	Aug	Sept	Oct	Nov	Dec	Annual
Average snowfall, JFK Airport	6.7	7.7	3.7	0.5	T	0	T	0	0	T	0.3	3.8	22.7
Average snowfall, La Guardia Airport	6.9	8.4	4.6	0.6	T	0	T	0	0	T	0.5	5.0	26.0
Average percentage possible sunshine	51	55	57	58	61	64	65	64	62	61	52	49	58
Average wind speed, Central Park	10.6	10.7	11.0	10.2	8.8	8.1	7.6	7.5	8.1	8.8	9.8	10.1	9.3
Average wind speed, JFK Airport	13.0	13.3	13.5	12.7	11.6	10.7	10.2	10.0	10.4	11.0	12.2	12.7	11.8
Average wind speed, La Guardia Airport	13.7	13.8	13.9	12.9	11.6	11.0	10.4	10.3	11.0	11.6	12.8	13.4	12.2

T = trace
* = Less than 0.5
Source: U.S. National Oceanic and Atmospheric Administration, *Comparative Climatic Data*; *Climatography of the United States*.

Primary Land Use by Borough (in Acres), 2002

	Manhattan	Bronx	Brooklyn	Queens	Staten Island	Total
One- and two-family houses	117	3,720	8,676	19,103	10,161	41,778
Percentage of borough	1.1	18.2	22.6	35.7	33.1	27.2
Percentage of category citywide	0.3	8.9	20.8	45.7	24.3	100.0
Multifamily residential	2,411	3,074	5,942	5,502	957	17,886
Percentage of borough	22.6	15.1	15.5	10.3	3.1	11.6
Percentage of category citywide	13.5	17.2	33.2	30.8	5.4	100.0
Mixed residential and commercial	1,272	537	1,275	790	184	4,058
Percentage of borough	11.9	2.6	3.3	1.5	0.6	2.6
Percentage of category citywide	31.1	3.2	31.4	19.5	4.5	100.0
Commercial/office	1,048	864	1,050	1,642	987	5,592
Percentage of borough	9.8	4.2	2.7	3.1	3.2	3.6
Percentage of category citywide	18.7	15.4	18.8	29.4	17.7	100.0
Industrial/manufacturing	327	826	2,001	1,959	986	6,101
Percentage of borough	3.1	4.1	5.2	3.7	3.2	4.0
Percentage of category citywide	5.4	13.5	32.8	32.1	16.2	100.0
Transportation/utility	728	580	1,741	6,255	2,301	11,605
Percentage of borough	6.8	2.9	4.5	11.7	7.5	7.5
Percentage of category citywide	6.3	5.0	15.0	53.9	19.8	100.0
Public facilities and institutions	1,240	2,006	2,228	2,790	3,113	11,378
Percentage of borough	11.6	9.8	5.8	5.2	10.1	7.4
Percentage of category citywide	10.9	17.6	19.6	24.5	27.4	100.0
Open space	2,733	6,412	13,120	10,274	6,274	38,813
Percentage of borough	25.6	31.4	34.1	19.2	20.4	25.2
Percentage of category citywide	7.0	16.5	33.8	26.5	16.2	100.0
Parking facilities	208	422	541	647	165	1,983
Percentage of borough	2.0	2.1	1.4	1.2	0.5	1.3
Percentage of category citywide	10.5	21.3	27.3	32.6	8.3	100.0
Vacant land	371	1,056	1,546	3,215	5,345	11,533
Percentage of borough	3.5	5.2	4.0	6.0	17.4	7.5
Percentage of category citywide	3.2	9.2	13.4	27.9	46.3	100.0

Primary Land Use by Borough (in Acres), 2002 (continued)

	Manhattan	Bronx	Brooklyn	Queens	Staten Island	Total
Miscellaneous lots	229	899	321	1,302	257	3,007
Percentage of borough	3.1	4.4	0.8	2.4	0.8	2.0
Percentage of category citywide	7.6	29.9	10.7	43.3	8.6	100.0
Total	10,683	20,397	38,441	53,479	30,734	153,734
Percentage of borough	100.0	100.0	100.0	100.0	100.0	100.0
Percentage of category citywide	6.9	13.3	25.0	34.8	20.0	100.0

Source: New York City Department of Planning.

Resident and Nonresident Hunting, Fishing, and Trapping Licenses, Year Ended 30 September 2000

	Manhattan	Bronx	Brooklyn	Queens	Staten Island	Total
Resident licenses						
Three-day fishing	60	26	55	116	27	284
Fishing	1,397	1,455	2,015	3,503	563	8,933
Hunting	—	100	374	994	126	1,594
Trapping	—	11	11	17	7	46
Junior trapping	—	—	—	2	—	2
Big game	—	587	1,253	2,534	1,015	5,389
Sportsman	—	1,050	2,465	4,630	1,398	9,543
Junior archery	—	13	10	16	8	47
Junior hunt	—	15	55	113	39	222
Senior	40	402	712	1,188	261	2,603
Free combination	9	2	17	56	9	93

Resident and Nonresident Hunting, Fishing, and Trapping Licenses, Year Ended 30 September 2000 (continued)

	Manhattan	Bronx	Brooklyn	Queens	Staten Island	Total
Nonresident licenses						
Fishing	190	19	30	79	42	360
Five-day fishing	49	7	8	22	5	91
Combined	—	—	12	9	22	43
Hunting	—	10	25	40	29	104
Big game	—	54	109	94	287	544
Trap	—	—	—	—	—	—
Resident and nonresident licenses						
Bow-hunting	—	564	1,326	2,038	946	4,874
Muzzle-loader	—	105	160	333	111	709
All licenses	1,745	4,420	8,637	15,784	4,895	35,481

Source: New York State Department of Environmental Conservation, Division of Fish, Wildlife, and Marine Resources.

Air Quality Measurements by Monitoring Site, 1991–2006

Sulfur Dioxide: Continuous Pulsed Fluorescence (Annual Arithmetic Means in Parts per Million; Annual Average Not to Exceed 0.03 Parts per Million)

	1996	1997	1998	1999	2000	2001	2002	2003	2004	2005	2006
Mabel Dean	(.012)	.013	.011	.013	.013	(.014)	—	—	—	—	—
PS 59	.015	.012	.012	.013	.013	.012	.012	(.014)	.010	.011	.010
Queens College	.007	.005	—	—	—	—	—	—	—	—	—
Queensboro Community College	—	—	.006	.007	.006	.007	—	—	—	—	—
Queens College	—	—	—	—	—	—	.006	.007	.005	.006	.005
IS 155	.009	.008	.009	.010	—	—	—	—	—	—	—
Morrisania	.014	.012	.011	.011	(.017)	—	—	—	—	—	—
Botanical Garden	—	—	—	—	(.009)	.010	.009	.009	.009	.009	.007
IS 52	—	—	—	(.014)	.011	(.013)	.010	.011	.010	.011	.009

	1991	1992	1993	1994	1995	1996	1997	1998	1999	2000	2001
Greenpoint	.013	.012	.010	.011	.010	(.009)	.008	.007	.007	—	—
PS 321	.013	.009	.008	.011	.008	.009	.008	.008	.009	—	—
Susan Wagner	.010	(.009)	(.009)	.008	.005	.006	.006	.006	.006	(.008)	—

Inhalable Particulates: Wedding Sampler or R&P Model 2025 Sampler (Annual Arithmetic Means in µg per m³)

	1996	1997	1998	1999	2000	2001	2002	2003	2004	2005	2006	Three-Year Expected Value
Mabel Dean (W)	25	26	24	21	22	(19)	—	—	—	—	—	—
PS 59 (R&P)	—	—	—	—	—	—	—	—	—	—	23	—
Canal Street (R&P)	—	—	—	—	—	—	—	—	24	26	23	24
Morrisania II (W)	26	24	24	—	—	—	—	—	—	—	—	—
IS 52 (W)	—	—	—	(16)	21	(21)	21	22	18	—	—	—
Greenpoint (W)	26	(26)	23	23	—	—	—	—	—	—	—	—
PS 314 (W)	27	28	26	—	—	—	—	—	—	—	—	—
JHS 126 (W)	—	—	—	—	—	20	21	20	17	—	—	—
PS 219 (R&P)	—	—	—	—	—	—	—	—	—	—	(20)	—
Susan Wagner (W)	20	19	17	16	19	16	17	16	13	—	—	—

Total Suspended Particulates: High-Volume Air Samplers (Annual Geometric Means in µg per m³)

	AAQS Geometric Means	1995	1996	1997	1998	1999	2000	2001	2002	2003	2004	2005
Mabel Dean	75	—	—	—	—	—	—	—	—	—	—	—
Midtown	75	92+	118+	117+	129+	—	—	—	—	—	—	—
Greenpoint	75	59	57	(58)	50	56	—	—	—	—	—	—
Susan Wagner	75	37	33	35	32	29	33	29	29	28	26	—
PS 26	75	47	44	(43)	—	—	—	—	—	—	—	—

Inhalable Particulates: Ambient Air Quality and Ambient Air Quality Standards for Calendar Year 2006 (Average of Last Three Years' Annual Means Not to Exceed Federal AAQS of 15 µg/ m³; and Average of 98th Percentile for Last Three Years Not to Exceed Federal AAQS of 65 µg/ m³)

Station Site	Total Observations	Maximum Values	98th Percentile				Annual Mean			
			2006	2005	2004	Three-Year Average	2006	2005	2004	Three-Year Average
JHS 45 (F)	114	44.0	37.6	36.6	38.0	37	12.8	14.3	13.1	13.4
PS 59 (F)	117	43.3	40.7	40.1	41.1	41	14.5	17.0	15.6	15.7+
IS 143 (TEOM)	350	48.3	39.8	35.3	38.7	38	15.5	16.3	15.8	15.9+
PS 64 (TEOM)	332	47.7	38.6	36.3	32.4	36	15.8	15.3	(14.1)	15.1+
Manhattanville	359	49.3	37.8	35.3	33.4	36	14.4	15.0	14.7	14.7
Park Row (TEOM) (World Trade Center)	353	46.0	36.1	39.0	37.4	38	13.8	14.4	14.5	14.2
PS 19 (F)	114	41.3	38.2	38.2	38.9	38	13.8	16.4	15.2	15.1+
Canal Street (F)	113	40.7	35.9	39.5	39.1	38	12.8	15.7	14.4	14.3
Canal Street (TEOM)	363	46.9	36.7	36.9	34.0	36	14.0	14.9	14.7	14.5

Air Quality Measurements by Monitoring Site, 1991–2006 (continued)

Carbon Monoxide: Continuous Non-dispersive Infrared (Annual Arithmetic Means in Parts per Million)

	1996	1997	1998	1999	2000	2001	2002	2003	2004	2005	2006
350 Canal Street	1.9	1.7	1.6	1.5	1.4	1.3	—	—	—	—	—
Brooklyn Transit	1.9	1.7	1.6	1.5	1.4	1.1	1.1	1.1	1.0	0.9	0.8
225 East 34th Street	1.6	1.3	1.3	1.3	1.2	1.0	1.0	1.0	0.9	—	—
Bloomingdale's	2.5	(2.4)	(2.2)	1.7	1.5	(1.3)	—	—	—	—	—
PS 59	1.1	1.0	1.0	1.0	0.9	0.8	0.7	(0.8)	0.7	0.6	0.6
Botanical Gardens	0.6	0.6	0.7	0.7	0.7	0.7	0.7	0.8	0.6	0.6	0.5
PS 321	0.8	0.8	0.8	0.8	—	—	—	—	—	—	—
Queensboro Community College	—	—	0.7	0.7	0.6	0.5	—	—	—	—	—
Queens College	—	—	—	—	—	—	0.6	0.6	0.5	0.5	0.4

Ozone: Continuous Ultraviolet Light Absorption (Annual Arithmetic Means in Parts per Million)

	1996	1997	1998	1999	2000	2001	2002	2003	2004	2005	2006
IS 155	—	.020	—	.021	—	—	—	—	—	—	—
Morrisania	.019	.021	.023	.019	—	—	—	—	—	—	—
Botanical Gardens	.018	.017	.015	.018	.016	.017	.017	.017	.017	.018	.020
IS 52	—	—	—	.007	.015	(.014)	.017	.016	.016	.016	.017
Mabel Dean High School	—	.019	.020	.013	.011	(.014)	—	—	—	—	—
Susan Wagner	.032	.035	.033	.033	.030	.032	.034	.029	.029	.030	.032
Queens College	.017	.024	—	—	—	—	—	—	—	—	—
Queensboro Community College	—	—	.021	.020	.019	.021	—	—	—	—	—
College Point Post Office	—	—	.015	.016	.015	.017	.018	.017	.016	.017	—
Queens College	—	—	—	—	—	(.017)	.019	.019	.018	.020	.021

Air Quality Measurements by Monitoring Site, 1991–2006 (continued)

**Nitric Oxide (Annual Arithmetic Means in Parts per Million; Twelve-Month Average
Not to Exceed Federal AAQS of 0.05 Parts per Million)**

	1996	1997	1998	1999	2000	2001	2002	2003	2004	2005	2006
Mabel Dean	(.036)	.038	.031	.033	.033	(.036)	—	—	—	—	—
PS 59	.052	.047	.045	.046	.045	.042	.035	(.036)	(.030)	.030	.026
Greenpoint	(.032)	—	—	—	—	—	—	—	—	—	—
Morrisania	.032	.027	.027	.031	(.039)	—	—	—	—	—	—
Botanical Gardens	.023	.023	.022	.024	.023	.026	.020	.021	.017	.015	.015
IS 52	—	—	—	(.030)	.025	(.027)	.022	.023	.022	.021	.017
Queensboro Community College	—	—	.019	.019	.018	.019	—	—	—	—	—
College Point Post Office	—	—	.030	.034	.030	.031	.026	.030	.025	.023	—
Queens College	—	—	—	—	—	(.026)	.017	.020	.015	.015	.014

Nitrogen Dioxide (Annual Arithmetic Means in Parts per Million)

	1996	1997	1998	1999	2000	2001	2002	2003	2004	2005	2006
Mabel Dean	(.035)	.035	.036	.037	.036	(.038)	—	—	—	—	—
PS 59	.042	.040	.040	.041	.038	.038	.038	(.038)	(.035)	.036	.034
Greenpoint	(.035)	—	—	—	—	—	—	—	—	—	—
Morrisania	.036	.035	.036	.033	(.033)	—	—	—	—	—	—
Botanical Gardens	.032	.030	.030	.029	.029	.031	.028	.027	.024	.027	.025
IS 52	—	—	—	(.032)	.032	(.032)	.030	.030	.030	.029	.026
Queensboro Community College	—	—	.027	.026	.026	.026	—	—	—	—	—
College Point Post Office	—	—	.028	.029	.030	.030	.028	.030	.028	.027	—
Queens College	—	—	—	—	—	(.028)	.028	.027	.025	.025	.023

Lead, High-Volume Air Samplers (Glass Fiber Filters; Annual Geometric Means in μg per m^3)

Midtown	0.05	0.05	0.08	—	—	—	—	—	—	—	—
Greenpoint	0.07	(0.08)	0.07	0.06	—	—	—	—	—	—	—
PS 314	—	—	—	—	—	—	—	—	—	—	—
JHS 126	—	—	—	—	—	—	—	0.03	0.03	(0.03)	0.02
Susan Wagner	0.02	0.02	0.02	0.03	0.02	0.02	0.01	0.01	—	—	—
PS 26	0.03	0.03	—	—	—	—	—	—	—	—	—

PS = Public School
IS = Intermediate School
W = Wedding Sampler
R&P = R&P Model 2025 Sampler
JHS = Junior High School
AAQS = Ambient Air Quality Standard
F = Federal Reference Method
TEOM = Tapered Element Oscillating Microbalance
Notes: Annual means in parentheses based on less than 75% available data. Dashes signify data not yet collected or no longer collected at site.
Source: New York State Department of Environmental Conservation.

Quality of Drinking Water, 2006 Test Results

	New York State DOH MCL	U.S. EPA MCLG	Catskill/Delaware System			Groundwater System		
			Number	Range	Average	Number	Range	Average

Conventional Physical and Chemical Parameters

Alkalinity (mg/L CaCO$_3$)	—		334	8.7–17.6	11.8	14	11.6–53.4	28.1

Sources in drinking water: Erosion of natural deposits

Aluminum (µg/L)	50–200[1]		319	7–125	34	7	ND–52	28

Sources in drinking water: Erosion of natural deposits

Barium (mg/L)	2	2	319	0.01–0.02	0.02	7	0.01–0.03	0.02

Sources in drinking water: Erosion of natural deposits

Calcium (mg/L)	—		334	4.9–8.5	5.4	14	9.2–33.4	17.1

Sources in drinking water: Erosion of natural deposits

Chloride (mg/L)	250		321	8–20	10	11	23–96	47

Sources in drinking water: Naturally occurring: road salt

Chlorine residual, free (mg/L)	4[2]		10,754	0.01–1.35	0.66	128	0.01–130	0.66

Sources in drinking water: Water additive for disinfection

Color, distribution system (color units, apparent)	—		9,661	3–42	7	82	1–12	6

Sources in drinking water: Presence of iron, manganese, and organics in water

Color, entry points (color units, apparent)	15[3]		1,095	4–13	7	46	1–9	4

Sources in drinking water: Iron and manganese, or organic sources, such as algal growth

Copper (mg/L)	1.3[4]	1.3	334	0.003–0.141	0.011	14	0.003–0.019	0.007

Sources in drinking water: Corrosion of household plumbing systems; erosion of natural deposits; leaching from wood preservatives

	New York State DOH MCL	U.S. EPA MCLG	Catskill/Delaware System			Groundwater System		
			Number	Range	Average	Number	Range	Average

Conventional Physical and Chemical Parameters (continued)

	New York State DOH MCL	U.S. EPA MCLG	Number	Range	Average	Number	Range	Average
Corrosivity (Lange-lier index)	0[1, 5]		318	−3.05 to −1.65	−2.47	6	−2.06 to −1.46	−1.69
Fluoride (mg/L)	2.2[3]	4.0	1,515	ND−1.2	0.7	128	0.3−1.3	1.0

Sources in drinking water: Erosion of natural deposits; water additive which promotes strong teeth; runoff from fertilizer

Hardness (mg/L $CaCO_3$)	—		319	17−34	18	9	38−156	80

Sources in drinking water: Erosion of natural deposits

Hardness (grains/gallon [US] $CaCO_3$)[6]			319	1.0−2.0	1.0	9	2.2−9.0	4.6

Sources in drinking water: Erosion of natural deposits

Iron (µg/L)	300[7]		336	**20−550**	50	7	ND−90	50

Sources in drinking water: Naturally occurring

Lead (µg/L)	15[4]	0	334	ND−4	0.6	14	ND−1	0.6

Sources in drinking water: Corrosion of household plumbing systems; erosion of natural deposits

Magnesium (mg/L)	—		319	1.0−3.0	1.2	9	3.6−18.0	8.6

Sources in drinking water: Erosion of natural deposits

Manganese (µg/L)	300[7]		336	6−261	9	7	11−31	21

Sources in drinking water: Naturally occurring

Nitrate (mg/L nitrogen)	10	10	321	0.13−0.84	0.22	11	0.98−5.80	2.55

Sources in drinking water: Runoff from fertilizer use; leaching from septic tanks, sewage; erosion of natural deposits

Nitrite (mg/L nitrogen)	1	1	318	ND−0.001	<0.001	9	ND	ND

Sources in drinking water: Runoff from fertilizer use; leaching from septic tanks, sewage; erosion of natural deposits

pH (pH units)[8]	6.5−8.5[1]		10,756	**6.8−8.7**	7.3	128	7.4−8.2	7.7

	New York State DOH MCL	U.S. EPA MCLG	Catskill/Delaware System Number	Range	Average	Groundwater System Number	Range	Average
Conventional Physical and Chemical Parameters (continued)								
Phosphate, Ortho- (mg/L)	—		10,750	0.6–2.8	2.0	128	1.5–2.7	2.0
Sources in drinking water: Water additive for corrosion control								
Potassium (mg/L)	—		319	0.5–0.8	0.6	6	0.8–1.0	0.9
Sources in drinking water: Erosion of natural deposits								
Silica [silicon oxide] (mg/L)	—		318	1.8–5.8	2.9	6	5.8–6.8	6.2
Sources in drinking water: Erosion of natural deposits								
Sodium (mg/L)	NDL[9]		319	6–12	8	7	13–43	18
Sources in drinking water: Naturally occurring; road salt; water softeners; animal waste								
Temperature (°F)	—		10,752	32–83	55	127	43–76	57
Total Dissolved Solids (mg/L)	500[1]		318	39–85	50	6	90–124	105
Sources in drinking water: Metals and salts naturally occurring in the soil; organic matter								
Total Organic Carbon (mg/L carbon)	—		318	1.0–3.9	1.5	6	1.0–1.4	1.3
Sources in drinking water: Organic matter naturally present in the environment								
Turbidity,[10] distribution system (NTU)	5[11]		9,661	0.8–1.5	1.0	82	0.5–1.1	0.7
Sources in drinking water: Soil runofft								

Quality of Drinking Water, 2006 Test Results (continued)

	New York State DOH MCL	U.S. EPA MCLG	Catskill/Delaware System			Groundwater System		
			Number	Range	Average	Number	Range	Average

Conventional Physical and Chemical Parameters (continued)

UV 254 Absorbency (cm⁻¹)	—		318	0.022–0.039	0.032	6	0.025–0.032	0.029

Sources in drinking water: Organic matter naturally present in the environment

Zinc (mg/L)	5		319	ND–0.065	0.004	7	ND–0.006	0.003

Sources in drinking water: Naturally occurring

Organic Contaminants

Disinfection Byproducts Detected

Bromochloroacetic acid (µg/L)	50		281	ND–3	1	2	1–2	1

Sources in drinking water: Byproduct of drinking water chlorination

Chloral hydrate (µg/L)	50		16	1.6–8.2	5	—	—	—

Sources in drinking water: Byproduct of drinking water chlorination

Chloropicrin (µg/L)	50		16	0.4–0.7	0.5	—	—	—

Sources in drinking water: Byproduct of drinking water chlorination

Haloacetonitriles (HANs) (µg/L)	50		12	1.2–3.9	2.7	—	—	—

Sources in drinking water: Byproduct of drinking water chlorination

Halogenated ketones (HKs) (µg/L)	50		16	1.7–3.2	2.3	—	—	—

Sources in drinking water: Byproduct of drinking water chlorination

Total Organic Halogen (µg/L)	—		318	101–262	171	6	106–180	148

Sources in drinking water: Byproduct of drinking water chlorination

Principal Organic Contaminants Detected

Tetrachloroethylene (µg/L)	5	0	350	ND	ND	17	ND–1.6[12]	

Sources in drinking water: Discharge from dry cleaners

Quality of Drinking Water, 2006 Test Results (continued)

	New York State DOH MCL	U.S. EPA MCLG	Catskill/Delaware System			Groundwater System		
			Number	Range	Average	Number	Range	Average

Specified Organic Contaminants Detected

Dalapon (µg/L)	50	200	237	ND–0.8[12]	ND	2	ND	ND

Sources in drinking water: Runoff from herbicide used on rights of way

Hexachlorocyclopenta-diene (µg/L)	5	50	22	ND–0.10	<0.05	1	ND	ND

Sources in drinking water: Discharge from chemical factories

Unspecified Organic Contaminants Detected

Acetone (µg/L)	50		297	ND–13	<10	14	ND	ND

Sources in drinking water: Occurs naturally and is used in the production of paints, varnishes, plastics, adhesives, organic chemicals, and alcohol. Also used to clean and dry parts of precision equipment.

Methyl tert-butyl ether (MTBE) (µg/L)	10		350	ND	ND	17	ND–1[12]	ND

Sources in drinking water: Formerly an additive to gasoline

Quality of Drinking Water, 2006 Test Results (continued)

	New York State DOH MCL	U.S. EPA MCLG	Catskill/Delaware Service Area			Croton Service Area[13]			Groundwater Service Area		
			Number	Range	RAA	Number	Range	RAA	Number	Range	RAA
Disinfection Byproducts Detected											
Haloacetic acid 5 (HAA5) (μg/L)	60[14]		245	19–69	43	18	35–54	47	20	11–50	34
Sources in drinking water: Byproduct of drinking water chlorination											
Total Trihalomethanes (μg/L)	80[14]		246	10–81	38	50	21–76	46	17	ND–50	32
Sources in drinking water: Byproduct of drinking water chlorination											

	New York State DOH MCL	U.S. EPA MCLG	Citywide Distribution Number	Range	Number of Samples Positive	Average	Highest Percentage Positive in Month
Microbial Parameters							
Total Coliform Bacteria (percentage of samples positive in month)	5	0	9,754	—	36	—	1.3
Sources in drinking water: Naturally present in the environment							
E. coli (CFU)	(15)	0	9,754	—	1	—	0.1
Sources in drinking water: Human and animal fecal waste							
Heterotrophic Plate Count (CFU/ml)	TT	—	3,262	ND–5,700	307	3	—
Sources in drinking water: Naturally present in the environment							

Quality of Drinking Water, 2006 Test Results (continued)

New York State DOH AL	U.S. EPA MCLG	Surface Water: January–December 2006					Groundwater: July–December 2006			
		Number	Range	90th Percentile Values	Number of Samples Exceeding AL		Number	Range	90th Percentile Values	Number of Samples Exceeding AL

Lead and Copper Rule Sampling at Residential Water Taps

Copper (mg/L)	1.3	1.3	120	0.022–0.661	0.239	0		99	ND–0.387	0.230	0

Sources in drinking water: Corrosion of household plumbing systems

Lead (µg/L)	15	0	120	ND–123.2	13	10	99	ND–85.3	7	3

Sources in drinking water: Corrosion of household plumbing systems

Undetected Parameters

Undetected Conventional Physical and Chemical Parameters

Antimony, Arsenic, Asbestos,[16] Beryllium, Bromide, Cadmium, Chlorate, Chromium, Cyanide, Foaming Agents, Gross Alpha,[17] Gross Beta,[17] Lithium, Mercury, Nickel, Selenium, Silver, [90]Strontium,[17] Thallium, Tritium (^{3}H)[17]

Undetected Organic Contaminants

Principal Organic Contaminants Not Detected

Benzene, Bromobenzene, Bromochloromethane, Bromomethane, n-Butylbenzene, sec-Butylbenzene, tert-Butylbenzene, Carbon Tetrachloride, Chlorobenzene, Chlorethane, Chloromethane, 2-Chlorotoluene, 4-Chlorotoluene, Dibromomethane, 1,2-Dichlorobenzene, 1,3-Dichlorobenzene, 1,4-Dichlorobenzene, Dichlorodifluoromethane, 1,1-Dichloroethane, 1,2-Dichloroethane, 1,1 Dichloroethene, cis-1,3-Dichloroethylene, 1,2-Dichloropropane, 1,3-Dichloropropane, 2,2-Dichloropropane, 1,1-Dichloropropene, cis-1,3-Dichloropropene, trans-1,3-Dichloropropene, Ethylbenzene, Hexachlorobutadiene, Isopropylbenzene, p-Isopropyltoluene, Methylene chloride, n-Propylbenzene, Styrene, 1,1,1,2-Tetrachloroethane, 1,1,2,2-Tetrachloroethane, Toluene, 1,2,3-Trichlorobenzene, 1,1,1-Trichloroethane, Trichloroethene, Trichlorofluoromethane, 1,2,3-Trichloropropane, 1,2,4-Trimethylbenzene, 1,3,5-Trimethylbenzene, m-Xylene, o-Xylene, p-Xylene

Specified Organic Contaminants Not Detected

Alachlor, Aldicarb (Temik), Aldicarb sulfone, Aldicarb sulfoxide, Aldrin, Atrazine, Benzo(a)pyrene, Butachlor, Carbaryl, Carbofuran (Furadan), Chlordane, 2,4-D, 1,2-Dibromo-3-chloropropane, Dicamba, Dieldrin, Di(2-ethylhexyl)adipate, Di(2-ethylhexyl)phthalate, Dinoseb, Diquat, Endothall, Endrin, Ethylene dibromide (EDB), Glyphosate, Heptachlor, Heptachlor epoxide, Hexachlorobenzene, 3-Hydroxycarbofuran, Lindane, Methomyl, Methoxychlor, Metolachlor, Metribuzin, Oxamyl (Vydate), Pentachlorophenol, Picloram, Polychlorinated biphenyls (PCBs), Propachlor, Simazine, Toxaphene, 2,4,5-TP (Silvex), 2,3,7,8-TCDD (Dioxin), Vinyl chloride

Unspecified Organic Chemicals Not Detected

Acanaphthene, Acenaphthylene, Acetochlor, Acifluorofen, tert-Amyl methyl ether, Anthracene, Bentazon, Benzo[a]anthracene, Benzo[b]fluoranthene, Benzo[k]fluoranthene, Benzo[g,h,i]perylene, a-BHC, b-BHC, d-BHC, Bromacil, Bromomethane, 2-Butanone (MEK), Butylbenzylphthalate, tert-butyl ethyl ether, Caffeine, a-Chlordane, g-Chlordane, Chlorobenzilate, Chloroneb, Chlorothalonil (Draconil, Bravo), Chloropyrifos (Dursban), Chrysene, 2,4-DB, DCPA (total mono and diacid degradate), p,p'DDD, p,p'DDE, p,p'DDT, Diazinon, Dibenz[a,h]anthracene, Di-n-Butylphthalate, 3,5-Dichlorobenzoic acid, Dichlorprop, Dichlorvos (DDVP), Diethylphthalate, Diisopropyl ether, Dimethoate, Dimethylphthalate, 2,4-Dinitrotoluene, 2,6-Dinitrotoluene, Di-N-octylphthalate, Endosulfan I, Endosulfan II, Endosulfan sulfate, Endrin aldehyde, EPTC, Fluoranthene, Fluorene, Heptachlor epoxide (isomer B), Indeno[1,2,3-cd] pyrene, Isophorone, Malathion, Methiocarb, 4-Methyl-2-pentanone (MIBK), Moilnate, Naphthalene, cis-Nonachlor, trans-Nonachlor, Paraquat, Parathion, Pendimethalin, Permethrin, Phenanthrene, Prometryn, Propoxur (Baygon), Pyrene, 2,4,5-T, Terbacil, Terbuthylazine, Thiobencarb, Trichlorotrifluoroethane (freon), Trifluralin

[1] U.S. EPA Secondary MCL: New York State DOH has not set an MCL for this parameter.

[2] Value represents MRDL, which is a level of disinfectant added for water treatment that may not be exceeded at the consumer's tap without an unacceptable possibility of adverse health effects. The MRDL is enforceable in the same manner as an MCL.

[3] Determination of MCL violation: if a sample exceeds the MCL, a second sample must be collected from the same location within two weeks. If the average of the two results exceeds the MCL, then an MCL violation has occurred.

[4] Action level (not an MCL) measured at the tap. The data presented in this table were collected from sampling stations at the street curb.

[5] A Langelier Index of less than zero indicates corrosive tendencies.

[6] Hardness of up to 3 grains per gallon is considered soft water; between 3 and 9 is moderately hard water.

[7] If iron and manganese are present the total concentration of both should not exceed 500 µg/L.

[8] The average for pH is the median value.

[9] Water containing more than 20 mg/L of sodium should not be used for drinking by people on severely restricted sodium diets. Water containing more than 270 mg/L of sodium should not be used for drinking by people on moderately restricted sodium diets.

[10] Turbidity is a measure of cloudiness of the water. Turbidity is monitored because it is a good indicator of water quality and can hinder the effectiveness of disinfection.

[11] This MCL for turbidity is the monthly average rounded off to the nearest whole number. Data presented are the range and average of monthly averages.

[12] The contaminant was detected in only one sample. The level found was below the MCL.

[13] Though Croton water was not put into distribution in 2006, DBP monitoring is conducted at specified locations based on the potential distribution of the different source waters to consumers. As such, each system has a defined set of monitoring sites and the data are reported by service area.

[14] U.S. EPA MCLs for HAA5 and TTHMs are the calculated quarterly running average. Data presented are the range of individual sampling results and the highest quarterly running annual average.

[15] If a sample and its repeat sample are both positive for coliform bacteria and one of the two samples is positive for E. coli, then an MCL violation has occurred.

[16] New York State DOH has issued a waiver for asbestos monitoring in the groundwater system, since no asbestos cement pipes are used anywhere in the distribution system.

[17] Radionuclide data presented were collected in 2001.

Quality of Drinking Water, 2006 Test Results (continued)

Note: Value in **boldface** indicates that a violation or exceedence occurred.

DOH = Department of Health
EPA = Environmental Protection Administration
MCL = Maximum Contaminant Level
MCLG = Maximum Contaminant Level Goal
MRDL = Maximum Residual Disinfectant Level
ND = no data
NDL = No Designated Limit
NTU = Nephelometric Turbidity Units
RAA = Running Annual Average
CFU = Colony Forming Units
TT = Treatment Technique
DBP = Disinfectant Byproducts
AL = Action Level

Source: New York City Department of Environmental Protection, *2006 Drinking Water Supply and Quality Report*.

Average Daily Demand and Supply, City and Upstate, for New York City Water Supplies, 1998–2002 (in Millions of Gallons)

| | Demand | | | New York City Supplies | |
	City	Upstate	Total	Surface Sources	Queens Groundwater
1998	1,220.0	124.7	1,344.7	1,314.0	30.7
1999	1,237.2	128.6	1,365.7	1,346.2	19.5
2000	1,240.4	124.9	1,365.3	1,353.7	11.6
2001	1,184.0	128.4	1,312.5	1,300.3	12.2
2002	1,135.6	121.1	1,256.7	1,244.6	12.1

Source: New York City Department of Environmental Protection.

Sanitation Statistics, Fiscal Years 2004–2006

	2004	2005	2006
Percentage of streets rated acceptably clean	89.8	91.5	93.1
Tons of waste disposed of	3,772,200	3,588,600	3,559,300
Tons of waste disposed per day	12,448	11,883	11,786
Tons of waste recycled	2,081,000	2,104,000	1,691,000
Tons of waste recycled per day	6,544	6,742	5,419
Refuse collection cost per ton	$154	$154	n/a
Refuse disposal cost per ton	$97	$109	n/a
Total cost per ton	$251	$263	n/a
Recycling collection cost per ton	$315	$325	n/a
Paper recycling revenue per ton	$10	$16	$10
Tons of road salt used	352,053	322,770	220,874
Department expenditures	$998,000,000	$1,034,900,000	$1,094,900,000
Uniformed personnel	7,452	7,619	7,733
Civilian personnel	1,897	1,962	2,025

Source: *Preliminary Mayor's Management Report*, February 2007.

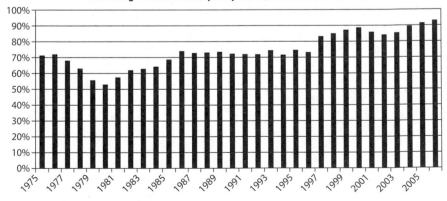

Percentage of Streets Acceptably Clean, Fiscal Years 1975–2006

Source: New York City Department of Sanitation.

Neighborhoods with Greatest Concentration of Selected Dog Breeds

Breed	Neighborhood	Number of Registered Animals
Maltese	Upper East Side	171
Shih Tzu	Upper East Side	160
Pit Bull	Spanish Harlem	140
Labrador Retriever	Upper East Side	130
Yorkshire Terrier	Upper East Side	113
Chihuahua	Spanish Harlem	106
Cocker Spaniel	Ridgewood	95
Rottweiler	Soundview	87
German Shepherd	Bergen Beach	64
Poodle	Sheepshead Bay	63
Dachshund	West Village	33
Bichon Frisé	Murray Hill	32
Pug	Greenwich Village	32
Jack Russell Terrier	Central Harlem	11

Note: Figures based on data from the New York City Department of Health and Mental Hygiene. Registered dogs represent about 20 percent of all dogs in the city.
Source: *New York Times*, 24 October 2003.

Winners of Best in Show Award, Westminster Kennel Club, 1907–2008

	Breed	Dog	Owner(s)
1907	Fox Terrier (Smooth)	Ch Warren Remedy	Winthrop Rutherfurd
1908	Fox Terrier (Smooth)	Ch Warren Remedy	Winthrop Rutherfurd
1909	Fox Terrier (Smooth)	Ch Warren Remedy	Winthrop Rutherfurd
1910	Fox Terrier (Smooth)	Ch Sabine Rarebit	Sabine Kennels
1911	Scottish Terrier	Ch Tickle Em	Jock A. Albright Jr.
1912	Airedale Terrier	Ch Kenmare Sorceress	William P Wolcott
1913	Bulldog	Ch Strathtay Prince Albert	Alex H. Stewart
1914	Old English Sheepdog	Ch Slumber	Mrs. Tyler Morse
1915	Fox Terrier (Wire)	Ch Matford Vic	George W. Quintard
1916	Fox Terrier (Wire)	Ch Matford Vic	George W. Quintard
1917	Fox Terrier (Wire)	Ch Conejo Wycollar Boy	Mrs. Roy A. Rainey
1918	Bull Terrier (White)	Ch Haymarket Faultless	R. H. Elliot
1919	Airedale Terrier	Ch Briergate Bright Beauty	G. L. Davis
1920	Fox Terrier (Wire)	Ch Conejo Wycollar Boy	Mrs. Roy A. Rainey
1921	Spaniel (Cocker) Parti	Ch Midkiff Seductive	William T. Payne
1922	Airedale Terrier	Ch Boxwood Barkentine	Frederic C. Hood
1923	[no Best in Show Award given]		
1924	Sealyham Terrier	Ch Barberryhill Bootlegger	Bayard Warren
1925	Pointer	Ch Governor Moscow	Robert F. Maloney
1926	Fox Terrier (Wire)	Ch Signal Circuit of Halleston	Halleston Kennels
1927	Sealyham Terrier	Ch Pinegrade Perfection	Frederic C. Brown
1928	Fox Terrier (Wire)	Ch Talavera Margaret	R. M. Lewis
1929	Collie (Rough)	Laund Loyalty of Bellhaven	Mrs. Florence B. Ilch
1930	Fox Terrier (Wire)	Ch Pendley Calling of Blarney	John G. Bates
1931	Fox Terrier (Wire)	Ch Pendley Calling of Blarney	John G. Bates
1932	Pointer	Ch Nancolleth Markable	Giralda Farms
1933	Airedale Terrier	Ch Warland Protector of Shelterock	S. M. Stewart
1934	Fox Terrier (Wire)	Ch Flornell Spicy Bit of Halleston	Halleston Kennels
1935	Poodle (Standard)	Ch Nunsoe Duc de la Terrace of Blakeen	Blakeen Kennels
1936	Sealyham Terrier	Ch St Margaret Mignificent of Claredale	Claredale Kennels
1937	Fox Terrier (Wire)	Ch Flornell Spicy Piece of Halleston	Halleston Kennels
1938	Setter (English)	Daro of Maridor	Maridor Kennels
1939	Doberman Pinscher	Ferry v Rauhfelsen of Giralda	Giralda Farms
1940	Spaniel (Cocker) Black	Ch My Own Brucie	H. E. Mellenthin
1941	Spaniel (Cocker) Black	Ch My Own Brucie	H. E. Mellenthin
1942	West Highland White Terrier	Ch Wolvey Pattern of Edgerstoune	Mrs J. G. Winant
1943	Poodle (Miniature)	Ch Pitter Patter of Piperscroft	Mrs P. H. B. Frelinghuysen

	Breed	Dog	Owner(s)
1944	Welsh Terrier	Ch Flornell-Rare-Bit of Twin Ponds	Mrs. Edward P. Alker
1945	Scottish Terrier	Ch Shieling's Signature	Mr. & Mrs. T. H. Snethen
1946	Fox Terrier (Wire)	Ch Heatherington Model Rhythm	Mr. & Mrs. T. H. Curruthers
1947	Boxer	Ch Warlord of Mazelaine	Mr. & Mrs. Richard C. Kettles Jr.
1948	Bedlington Terrier	Ch Rock Ridge Night Rocket	Mr. & Mrs. William A. Rockefeller
1949	Boxer	Ch Mazelaine Zazarac Brandy	Mr. & Mrs. John Phelps Wagner
1950	Scottish Terrier	Ch Walsing Winning Trick of Edgerstoune	Mrs. J. G. Winant
1951	Boxer	Ch Bang Away of Sirrah Crest	Dr. & Mrs. R. C. Harris
1952	Doberman Pinscher	Ch Rancho Dobe's Storm	Mr. & Mrs. Len Carey
1953	Doberman Pinscher	Ch Rancho Dobe's Storm	Mr. & Mrs. Len Carey
1954	Spaniel (Cocker) A.S.C.O.B.	Ch Carmor's Rise and Shine	Mrs. Carl E. Morgan
1955	Bulldog	Ch Kippax Fearnought	John A. Saylor, MD
1956	Poodle (Toy)	Ch Wilber White Swan	Bertha Smith
1957	Afghan Hound	Ch Shirkhan of Grandeur	Sunny Shay & Dorothy Chenade
1958	Poodle (Standard)	Ch Puttencove Promise	Puttencove Kennels
1959	Poodle (Miniature)	Ch Fontclair Festoon	Dunwalke Kennels
1960	Pekingese	Ch Chik T'Sun of Caversham	Mr. & Mrs. C. C. Venable
1961	Poodle (Toy)	Ch Cappoquin Little Sister	Miss Florence Michelson
1962	West Highland White Terrier	Ch Elfinbrook Simon	Wishing Well Kennels
1963	Spaniel (English Springer)	Ch Wakefield's Black Knight	Mrs. W. J. S. Borie
1964	Whippet	Ch Courtenay Fleetfoot of Pennyworth	Pennyworth Kennels
1965	Scottish Terrier	Ch Carmichaels Fanfare	Mr. & Mrs. Charles C. Stalter
1966	Fox Terrier (Wire)	Ch Zeloy Mooremaide's Magic	Marion G. Bunker
1967	Scottish Terrier	Ch Bardene Bingo	E. H. Stuart
1968	Lakeland Terrier	Ch Stingray of Derryabah	Mr. & Mrs. James A. Farrell Jr.
1969	Skye Terrier	Ch Glamoor Good News	W. Goodman & Mrs. A. Goodman
1970	Boxer	Ch Arriba's Prima Donna	Dr. & Mrs. P. Pagano & Dr. T. Fickes
1971	Spaniel (English Springer)	Ch Chinoe's Adamant James	Milton E. Prickett
1972	Spaniel (English Springer)	Ch Chinoe's Adamant James	Milton E. Prickett
1973	Poodle (Standard)	Ch Acadia Command Performance	Edward Jenner & Jo Ann Sering
1974	Pointer (German Shorthaired)	Ch Gretchenhof Columbia River	Richard P. Smith
1975	Old English Sheepdog	Ch Sir Lancelot of Barvan	Mr. & Mrs. R Vanword
1976	Lakeland Terrier	Ch Jo Ni's Red Baron of Crofton	Mrs. V. K. Dickson
1977	Sealyham Terrier	Ch Dersade Bobby's Girl	Pool Forge Kennels
1978	Yorkshire Terrier	Ch Cede Higgins	Barbara A. & Charles W. Switzer
1979	Spaniel (Irish Water)	Ch Oak Tree's Irishtocrat	Mrs. Anne E. Snelling

Winners of Best in Show Award, Westminster Kennel Club, 1907–2008 (continued)

	Breed	Dog	Owner(s)
1980	Siberian Husky	Ch Innisfree's Sierra Cinnar	Kathleen Kanzler
1981	Pug	Ch Dhandys Favorite Woodchuck	Robert A. Hauslohner
1982	Pekingese	Ch St Aubrey Dragonora of Elsdon	Mrs. Anne E. Snelling
1983	Afghan Hound	Ch Kabiks the Challenger	Chris & Marguerite Terrell
1984	Newfoundland	Ch Seaward's Blackbeard	Seaward Kennels, Reg
1985	Scottish Terrier	Ch Braeburn's Close Encounter	Sonnie & Alan Novick
1986	Pointer	Ch Marjetta's National Acclaim	Mrs. A. R. Robson & Michael Zollo
1987	German Shepherd Dog	Ch Covy Tucker Hill's Manhattan	S. Braunstein & J. Firestone
1988	Pomeranian	Ch Great Elms Prince Charming, II	Skip Piazza & Olga Baker
1989	Doberman Pinscher	Ch Royal Tudor's Wild as the Wind	R. & C. Vida, B Wilhite, A. & S. Korp
1990	Pekingese	Ch Wendessa Crown Prince	Edward B. Jenner
1991	Poodle (Standard)	Ch Whisperwind on a Carousel	Dr. & Mrs. Frederick Hartsock
1992	Fox Terrier (Wire)	Ch Registry's Lonesome Dove	Marion W. & Samuel B. Lawrence
1993	Spaniel (English Springer)	Ch Salilyn's Condor	D. & R. Herzig, MD & J. Gasow
1994	Norwich Terrier	Ch Chidley Willum the Conqueror	Ruth Cooper & Patricia Lussier
1995	Scottish Terrier	Ch Gaelforce Post Script	Dr. J. Kinnarney & Dr. V. Huber
1996	Spaniel (Clumber)	Ch Clussexx Country Sunrise	Judith & Richard Zaleski
1997	Standard Schnauzer	Ch Parsifal Di Casa Netzer	Rita Holloway & Gabrio Del Torre
1998	Norwich Terrier	Ch Fairewood Frolic	Sandina Kennels
1999	Papillon	Ch Loteki Supernatural Being	John Oulton
2000	Spaniel (English Springer)	Ch Salilyn 'N Erin's Shameless	C. Blain, F. Sunseri, J. Gasow
2001	Bichon Frisé	Ch Special Times Just Right	C. Ruggles, E. McDonald, F. Werneck
2002	Poodle (Miniature)	Ch Surrey Spice Girl	Ron L. Scott & Barbara Scott
2003	Kerry Blue Terrier	Ch Torums Scarf Michael	Marilu Hansen
2004	Newfoundland	Ch Darbydale's All Rise Pouch Cove	Peggy Helming & Carol Bernard Bergmann
2005	Pointer (German Shorthaired)	Ch Kan-Point's VJK Autumn Roses	L. & R. Stark, C. Cronk, V. Nunes-Atkinson
2006	Bull Terrier (Colored)	Ch Rocky Top's Sundance Kid	Barbara Bishop, W. F. Poole, N. Shepherd, R. P. Pool, Dorothy Cherry
2007	Spaniel (English Springer)	Ch Felicity's Diamond Jim	Teresa Patton, Allen Patton, R. Dehmel, D. Hadsall
2008	Beagle (15 Inch)	Ch K-Run's Park Me In First	Caroline Dowell, Eddie Dziuk, Jon Woodring, Kathy Weich

Source: Westminster Kennel Club.

Top 20 Species of Trees in Central Park, 2007

Species	Percentage of All Trees	Species	Percentage of All Trees
Black Cherry	21.0	Ginkgo	2.0
Pin Oak	8.0	Turkey Oak	2.0
American Elm	5.6	White Mulberry	2.0
Black Locust	5.5	Linden species	2.0
London Plane Tree	5.2	Green Ash	1.9
Norway Maple	3.5	Hawthorn species	1.9
Red Oak	2.8	Common Hackberry	1.7
Elm species	2.6	Flowering Crabapple	1.6
Ornamental Cherry	2.5	European Hornbeam	1.2
Sycamore Maple	2.3	Approximate total number of trees: 24,200	
Eastern White Pine	2.1		

Source: Central Park Conservancy.

Results of Christmas Bird Count in Central Park, 2004–2007

Common Name	Scientific Name	2004	2005	2006	2007
American Black Duck	*Anas rubripes*	4	2	4	13
American Coot	*Fulica americana*	3	9	8	6
American Crow	*Corvus brachyrhynchos*	17	21	45	2
American Goldfinch	*Carduelis tristis*	25	43	19	21
American Kestrel	*Falco sparverius*	0	2	1	0
American Robin	*Turdus migratorius*	262	62	85	84
American Tree Sparrow	*Spizella arborea*	0	2	0	0
Belted Kingfisher	*Ceryle alcyon*	0	0	1	0
Black-capped Chickadee	*Poecile atricapillus*	81	122	3	25
Blue Jay	*Cyanocitta cristata*	114	170	201	106
Boreal Owl	*Aegolius funereus*	0	0	0	1
Broad-winged Hawk	*Buteo platypterus*	1	0	0	0
Brown Creeper	*Certhia americana*	2	2	0	1
Brown Thrasher	*Toxostoma rufum*	0	2	1	2
Bufflehead	*Bucephala albeola*	24	20	13	22
Canada Goose	*Branta canadensis*	129	119	119	197

Results of Christmas Bird Count in Central Park, 2004–2007 (continued)

Common Name	Scientific Name	2004	2005	2006	2007
Carolina Wren	*Thryothorus ludovicianus*	0	1	3	4
Cedar Waxwing	*Bombycilla cedrorum*	9	33	31	219
Chipping Sparrow	*Spizella passerina*	0	1	0	0
Common Grackle	*Quiscalus quiscula*	22	323	516	1,491
Cooper's Hawk	*Accipiter cooperii*	4	3	1	2
Dark-eyed Junco	*Junco hyemalis*	14	27	14	33
Double-crested Cormorant	*Phalacrocorax auritus*	1	0	1	3
Downy Woodpecker	*Picoides pubescens*	39	43	30	18
Eastern Screech Owl	*Megascops asio*	0	1	0	1
Eastern Towhee	*Pipilo erythrophthalmus*	0	1	3	3
European Starling	*Sturnus vulgaris*	565	569	335	799
Fox Sparrow	*Passerella iliaca*	3	7	4	2
Gadwall	*Anas strepera*	6	11	5	2
Gray Catbird	*Dumetella carolinensis*	2	3	0	1
Great Black-backed Gull	*Larus marinus*	82	53	68	63
Great Horned Owl	*Bubo virginianus*	0	1	0	0
Great Blue Heron	*Ardea herodias*	0	0	2	0
Hairy Woodpecker	*Picoides villosus*	4	0	2	0
Hermit Thrush	*Catharus guttatus*	7	5	4	7
Herring Gull	*Larus argentatus*	447	368	831	663
Hooded Merganser	*Lophodytes cucullatus*	1	17	4	28
House Finch	*Carpodacus mexicanus*	9	26	94	11
House Sparrow	*Passer domesticus*	758	795	923	441
Hybrid Mallard	*Anas sp.*	4	3	5	0
Long-eared Owl	*Asio otus*	0	0	0	2
Mallard	*Anas platyrhynchos*	471	362	368	491
Merlin	*Falco columbarius*	0	1	0	0
Mourning Dove	*Zenaida macroura*	66	24	96	16
Mute Swan	*Cygnus olor*	1	2	2	2
Northern Cardinal	*Cardinalis cardinalis*	66	56	56	64
Northern Flicker	*Colaptes auratus*	3	2	13	8
Northern Harrier	*Circus cyaneus*	0	0	0	1
Northern Mockingbird	*Mimus polyglottos*	4	9	3	3
Northern Saw-whet Owl	*Aegolius acadicus*	2	1	0	0
Northern Shoveler	*Anas clypeata*	129	27	67	5
Northern Shrike	*Lanius excubitor*	0	1	0	0
Orange-crowned Warbler	*Vermivora celata*	1	0	0	0

Results of Christmas Bird Count in Central Park, 2004–2007 (continued)

Common Name	Scientific Name	2004	2005	2006	2007
Palm Warbler	*Dendroica palmarum*	0	0	1	0
Peregrine Falcon	*Falco peregrinus*	1	1	0	1
Pied-billed Grebe	*Podilymbus podiceps*	1	0	1	2
Red-bellied Woodpecker	*Melanerpes carolinus*	25	36	55	21
Red-breasted Nuthatch	*Sitta canadensis*	1	3	0	2
Red-tailed Hawk	*Buteo jamaicensis*	9	9	10	9
Red-winged Blackbird	*Agelaius phoeniceus*	1	0	4	0
Ring-billed Gull	*Larus delawarensis*	957	459	319	538
Rock Pigeon	*Columba livia*	662	899	878	603
Ruby-crowned Kinglet	*Regulus calendula*	1	0	0	0
Ruddy Duck	*Oxyura jamaicensis*	121	1,462	443	157
Rusty Blackbird	*Euphagus carolinus*	0	1	1	4
Sharp-shinned Hawk	*Accipiter striatus*	2	1	0	1
Song Sparrow	*Melospiza melodia*	21	13	3	6
Swamp Sparrow	*Melospiza georgiana*	0	1	1	1
Tufted Titmouse	*Baeolophus bicolor*	155	169	92	91
White-breasted Nuthatch	*Sitta carolinensis*	91	60	35	34
White-throated Sparrow	*Zonotrichia albicollis*	146	460	548	1,423
Wilson's Warbler	*Wilsonia pusilla*	1	0	0	0
Winter Wren	*Troglodytes troglodytes*	2	2	1	0
Wood Duck	*Aix sponsa*	0	4	1	1
Wood Thrush	*Hylocichla mustelina*	1	0	0	0
Yellow-bellied Sapsucker	*Sphyrapicus varius*	16	16	6	8
Yellow-rumped Warbler	*Dendroica coronata*	0	1	0	0
Total individuals		5,596	6,949	6,380	7,765
Total species		57	62	56	57

Source: New York City Audubon.

12 Religion

Number of Adherents of Major Religious Bodies, 2000

	Manhattan	Bronx	Brooklyn	Queens	Staten Island	Total
American Baptist Churches in the USA	28,611	11,498	57,755	14,695	1,804	114,363
American Carpatho-Russian Orthodox Greek Catholic Church	416	n/a	n/a	n/a	n/a	416
Antiochian Orthodox Christian Archdiocese of North America	n/a	n/a	2,178	n/a	n/a	2,178
Apostolic Christian Churches (Nazarean)	n/a	n/a	n/a	50	n/a	50
Armenian Apostolic Church / Catholicossate of Cilicia	1,400	n/a	n/a	840	n/a	2,240
Armenian Apostolic Church / Catholicossate of Etchmiadzin	6,272	n/a	n/a	3,000	n/a	9,272
Assemblies of God	6,019	10,968	15,600	8,983	3,443	45,013
Associate Reformed Presbyterian Church	n/a	n/a	n/a	27	n/a	27
Baháʼí	1,570	n/a	803	n/a	n/a	2,373
Baptist General Conference	418	n/a	n/a	n/a	n/a	418
Brethren in Christ Church	n/a	35	n/a	n/a	n/a	35
Bulgarian Orthodox Diocese of the USA	600	n/a	n/a	n/a	n/a	600
Catholic	564,505	581,824	912,509	644,066	264,931	2,967,835
Christian and Missionary Alliance	1,411	607	1,540	3,147	375	7,080
Christian Church (Disciples of Christ)	823	433	1,633	252	n/a	3,141
Christian Churches and Churches of Christ	318	342	635	266	54	1,615
Christian Reformed Church in North America	n/a	n/a	n/a	65	n/a	65
Church of God (Anderson, Ind.)	95	73	772	646	n/a	1,586
Church of God (Cleveland, Tenn.)	980	4,189	4,923	1,799	69	11,960
Church of God of Prophecy	154	458	1,066	386	n/a	2,064
Church of Jesus Christ of Latter-Day Saints	3,825	2,242	3,080	6,917	728	16,792
Church of the Brethren	n/a	n/a	383	n/a	n/a	383
Church of the Nazarene	432	742	2,712	1,745	5	5,636

Number of Adherents of Major Religious Bodies, 2000 (continued)

	Manhattan	Bronx	Brooklyn	Queens	Staten Island	Total
Churches of Christ	999	92	802	821	126	2,840
Churches of God, General Conference	n/a	n/a	71	n/a	n/a	71
Community of Christ	74	n/a	n/a	n/a	n/a	74
Congregational Christian churches, additional	n/a	n/a	47	n/a	n/a	47
Conservative Baptist Association of America	590	200	892	1,385	280	3,347
Conservative Congregational Christian Conference	29	64	n/a	n/a	n/a	93
Episcopal Church	23,742	8,638	15,352	12,843	2,442	63,017
Evangelical Covenant Church	28	1,525	n/a	61	n/a	1,614
Evangelical Free Church of America	n/a	n/a	846	50	287	1,183
Evangelical Lutheran Church in America	4,725	3,176	7,249	8,109	3,850	27,109
Free Methodist Church of North America	137	91	256	62	n/a	546
Friends (Quakers)	115	n/a	63	61	63	302
General Association of Regular Baptist Churches	99	n/a	63	74	88	324
Greek Orthodox Archdiocese of America	5,403	2,529	6,309	16,959	1,098	32,298
Greek Orthodox Archdiocese of Vasiloupulis	n/a	n/a	1,125	6,025	n/a	7,150
Holy Orthodox Church in North America	n/a	n/a	n/a	21	n/a	21
Independent charismatic churches	n/a	300	20,400	n/a	300	21,000
Independent non-charismatic churches	n/a	n/a	350	n/a	2,000	2,350
International Church of the Foursquare Gospel	50	26	34	195	n/a	305
International Churches of Christ	7,868	n/a	n/a	n/a	n/a	7,868
International Council of Community Churches	115	259	n/a	183	n/a	557
International Pentecostal Holiness Church	40	n/a	67	133	n/a	240
Jews	314,500	83,700	379,000	238,000	33,700	1,048,900

Number of Adherents of Major Religious Bodies, 2000 (continued)

	Manhattan	Bronx	Brooklyn	Queens	Staten Island	Total
Lutheran Church, Missouri Synod	1,588	618	1,185	3,556	906	7,853
Malankara Archdiocese of the Syrian Orthodox Church in North America	n/a	n/a	n/a	150	325	475
Malankara Orthodox Syrian Church, American Diocese	n/a	900	125	800	450	2,275
Mennonite Brethren Churches, U.S. Conference	n/a	n/a	n/a	24	n/a	24
Mennonite Church USA	152	344	343	133	45	1,017
Mennonite (other)	n/a	n/a	44	n/a	n/a	44
Missionary Church	n/a	83	288	148	n/a	519
Moravian Church in America, Northern Province	1,211	272	477	243	1,054	3,257
Muslims	37,078	12,164	57,897	52,038	8,082	167,259
National Association of Congregational Christian Churches	n/a	n/a	982	402	75	1,459
Orthodox Church in America: Albanian Orthodox Archdiocese	n/a	n/a	n/a	400	n/a	400
Orthodox Church in America: Romanian Orthodox Episcopate of America	500	n/a	n/a	580	n/a	1,080
Orthodox Church in America: Territorial Dioceses	421	n/a	580	567	n/a	1,568
Orthodox Presbyterian Church	n/a	n/a	n/a	n/a	28	28
Pentecostal Church of God	n/a	220	348	n/a	n/a	568
Presbyterian Church (U.S.A.)	10,715	2,849	3,368	6,108	749	23,789
Presbyterian Church in America	1,635	n/a	n/a	1,113	n/a	2,748
Primitive Methodist Church in the USA	n/a	n/a	61	n/a	n/a	61
Reformed Church in America	12,439	655	1,732	4,114	737	19,677
Salvation Army	751	741	3,860	978	425	6,755
Serbian Orthodox Church in the USA	4,000	n/a	n/a	n/a	n/a	4,000
Seventh-Day Adventists	6,339	7,411	22,273	11,031	587	47,641
Southern Baptist Convention	1,634	2,163	3,693	3,179	188	10,857
Syrian Orthodox Church of Antioch	n/a	n/a	150	n/a	n/a	150
Ukrainian Orthodox Church of the USA	693	n/a	750	45	n/a	1,488
Unitarian Universalist Association of Congregations	2,132	n/a	388	91	141	2,752
United Church of Christ	4,104	879	712	3,333	270	9,298

Number of Adherents of Major Religious Bodies, 2000 (continued)

	Manhattan	Bronx	Brooklyn	Queens	Staten Island	Total
United Methodist Church	12,900	6,977	12,821	10,414	3,259	46,371
Universal Fellowship of Metropolitan Community Churches	416	n/a	n/a	n/a	n/a	416
Vineyard USA	144	n/a	165	163	n/a	472
Wesleyan Church	160	124	1,579	1,185	n/a	3,048
Wisconsin Evangelical Lutheran Synod	n/a	n/a	n/a	32	n/a	32
Total Mainline Protestant	107,588	35,636	102,191	64,597	14,303	324,315
Total Evangelical Protestant	32,144	31,416	86,054	41,437	9,206	200,257
Other[1]	299,253	390,491	807,242	338,313	63,062	1,898,361
Total	1,374,628	1,140,902	2,359,578	1,411,006	396,026	6,682,140

[1] Includes estimates of traditionally African American congregations and some other groups.
Source: Association of Religion Data Archives.

Number of Congregations of Major Religious Bodies, 2000

	Manhattan	Bronx	Brooklyn	Queens	Staten Island	Total
American Baptist Churches in the USA	41	26	51	33	2	153
Antiochian Orthodox Christian Archdiocese of North America	0	0	2	0	0	2
American Carpatho-Russian Orthodox Greek Catholic Church	2	0	0	0	0	2
Apostolic Christian Churches (Nazarean)	0	0	0	1	0	1
Armenian Apostolic Church, Catholicossate of Cilicia	1	0	0	1	0	2
Armenian Apostolic Church, Catholicossate of Etchmiadzin	3	0	0	1	0	4
Assemblies of God	43	41	57	47	8	196
Associate Reformed Presbyterian Church	0	0	0	1	0	1
Bahá'í	1	0	0	0	0	1

Number of Congregations of Major Religious Bodies, 2000 (continued)

	Manhattan	Bronx	Brooklyn	Queens	Staten Island	Total
Baptist General Conference	1	0	6	0	0	7
Brethren in Christ Church	0	1	0	0	0	1
Buddhism	43	8	5	16	0	72
Bulgarian Orthodox Diocese of the USA	1	0	0	0	0	1
Calvary Chapel Fellowship Churches	1	1	1	0	0	3
Catholic Church	110	72	127	106	37	452
Christian and Missionary Alliance	7	8	10	20	1	46
Christian Church (Disciples of Christ)	4	3	11	2	0	20
Christian Churches and Churches of Christ	6	3	10	4	1	24
Christian Reformed Church in North America	0	0	0	1	0	1
Church of God (Anderson, Ind.)	2	3	6	7	0	18
Church of God of Prophecy	2	5	11	5	0	23
Church of Jesus Christ of Latter-Day Saints	10	5	7	19	2	43
Church of the Brethren	0	0	2	0	0	2
Church of the Nazarene	5	6	18	24	1	54
Churches of Christ	7	3	4	10	2	26
Churches of God, General Conference	0	0	2	0	0	2
Community of Christ	2	0	0	0	0	2
Congregational Christian churches, additional	0	0	1	0	0	1
Conservative Baptist Association of America	4	3	10	8	2	27
Conservative Congregational Christian Conference	1	2	0	0	0	3
Episcopal Church	47	23	33	32	10	145
Evangelical Covenant Church	1	1	1	1	0	4
Evangelical Free Church of America	0	0	7	1	3	11
Evangelical Lutheran Church in America	18	17	37	36	9	117
Free Methodist Church of North America	1	1	5	4	0	11
Friends (Quakers)	2	0	1	1	1	5
General Association of Regular Baptist Churches	1	0	1	1	1	4
Greek Orthodox Archdiocese of America	11	4	4	8	1	28
Greek Orthodox Archdiocese of Vasiloupulis	0	0	1	3	0	4
Hindu	10	3	8	36	0	57
Holy Orthodox Church in North America	0	0	0	1	0	1

Number of Congregations of Major Religious Bodies, 2000 (continued)

	Manhattan	Bronx	Brooklyn	Queens	Staten Island	Total
Independent charismatic churches	0	1	6	0	1	8
Independent non-charismatic churches	0	0	1	0	1	2
International Church of the Foursquare Gospel	1	1	1	2	0	5
International Churches of Christ	1	0	0	0	0	1
International Council of Community Churches	1	1	0	1	0	3
International Pentecostal Holiness Church	1	0	1	1	0	3
Jain	1	0	0	1	0	2
Jewish	102	44	256	159	18	579
Lutheran Church, Missouri Synod	4	5	8	22	3	42
Malankara Archdiocese of the Syrian Orthodox Church in North America	0	0	0	1	2	3
Malankara Orthodox Syrian Church, American Diocese	0	2	1	4	2	9
Mennonite Brethren Churches, U.S. Conference	0	0	0	1	0	1
Mennonite Church USA	4	5	6	1	1	17
Mennonite, other groups	0	0	1	0	0	1
Missionary Church	0	2	2	1	0	5
Moravian Church in America, Northern Province	2	1	2	1	4	10
Muslim	16	8	26	31	5	86
National Association of Congregational Christian Churches	0	0	5	1	1	7
Orthodox Church in America, Albanian Orthodox Archidiocese	0	0	0	1	0	1
Orthodox Church in America, Romanian Orthodox Episcopate of America	1	0	0	3	0	4
Orthodox Church in America, Territorial Dioceses	3	0	3	2	0	8
Orthodox Presbyterian Church	0	0	0	0	1	1
Patriarchal Parishes of the Orthodox Church in the USA	1	0	0	1	0	2
Pentecostal Church of God	0	1	2	0	0	3
Presbyterian Church (U.S.A.)	30	18	24	34	5	111

Number of Congregations of Major Religious Bodies, 2000 (continued)

	Manhattan	Bronx	Brooklyn	Queens	Staten Island	Total
Presbyterian Church in America	4	1	0	7	0	12
Primitive Methodist Church in the USA	0	0	1	0	0	1
Reformed Baptist Churches	1	0	0	0	1	2
Reformed Church in America	9	5	13	27	5	59
Russian Orthodox Church Outside of Russia	3	0	0	3	0	6
Salvation Army	6	2	8	5	2	23
Serbian Orthodox Church in the USA	1	0	0	0	0	1
Seventh-Day Adventist Church	15	20	48	28	5	116
Sikh	2	0	1	4	0	7
Southern Baptist Convention	15	12	24	38	3	92
Southwide Baptist Fellowship	0	0	1	1	0	2
Syrian Orthodox Church of Antioch	0	0	1	0	0	1
Tao	1	0	0	2	0	3
Ukrainian Orthodox Church of the USA	3	0	1	1	0	5
Unitarian Universalist Association of Congregations	3	0	2	2	1	8
United Church of Christ	13	12	9	19	1	54
United Methodist Church	21	20	32	28	10	111
Universal Fellowship of Metropolitan Community Churches	1	0	0	0	0	1
Vineyard USA	1	0	1	1	0	3
Wesleyan Church	1	1	4	3	0	9
Wisconsin Evangelical Lutheran Synod	0	0	0	1	0	1
Zoroastrian	1	0	0	0	0	1
Totals	665	426	959	882	154	3,086

Source: Association of Religion Data Archives.

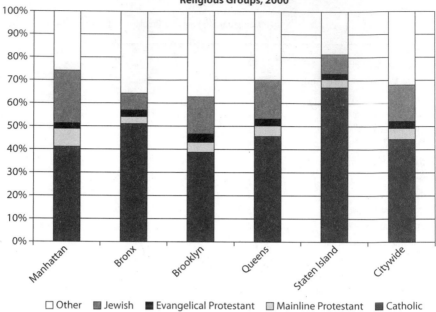

Percentage of Population in Each Borough Belonging to Major Religious Groups, 2000

□ Other ▨ Jewish ■ Evangelical Protestant ▨ Mainline Protestant ■ Catholic

Source: Association of Religion Data Archives.

13 Social Services

Public Assistance and Related Services, 2001–2006

	2001	2002	2003	2004	2005	2006
Public Assistance						
FAP (formerly AFDC)	300,532	206,924	202,626	195,996	194,431	167,722
Five-year limit[1]	81,511	127,893	132,458	127,510	106,940	88,187
SNA (formerly HR)	80,552	86,425	95,968	104,702	113,185	124,831
Total public assistance recipients	462,595	421,242	431,052	428,208	414,556	380,740
Public assistance cases	220,687	205,742	213,971	214,508	210,355	195,095
FAP (formerly AFDC)	121,351	90,802	89,095	87,387	86,027	76,324
Five-year limit[1]	24,221	39,231	41,842	40,816	34,573	28,255
SNA (formerly HR)	75,115	75,709	83,034	86,305	89,755	90,516
Public assistance children	268,787	244,394	246,782	244,696	235,626	217,119
FAP (formerly AFDC)	212,097	149,462	145,820	142,617	143,244	126,748
SNNC five-year limit[1]	54,255	87,891	91,924	87,622	72,634	61,821
SNA (formerly HR)	2,435	7,041	9,038	14,457	19,748	28,550
Social Security Income						
Aged	106,357	106,007	104,456	103,240	106,597	106,197
Disabled and blind	291,032	293,840	292,415	294,254	296,538	298,598
All recipients	397,389	399,847	396,871	397,494	403,135	404,795
Food Stamps[2]						
Public assistance recipients	439,943	418,416	451,547	465,613	450,674	412,546
Nonpublic assistance and SSI						
recipients	358,461	417,736	497,172	613,219	643,935	683,419
All Food Stamp recipients	798,404	836,152	948,719	1,078,832	1,094,609	1,095,965
Public assistance households	189,527	184,636	198,174	204,619	201,322	185,927
Nonpublic assistance households	103,224	124,271	289,109	376,297	384,630	406,295
All Food Stamp households	415,995	438,846	487,283	580,916	585,952	592,222
DAS / HASA clients	29,500	31,155	31,127	31,231	30,300	30,227
Home Care						
Total home attendant cases	46,548	46,128	45,910	46,060	43,595	45,103
Home care cases (HASA)	1,833	1,612	n/a	n/a	n/a	n/a
Housekeeper cases	7,998	8,027	7,737	7,415	6,536	7,062
Homemaker cases (HASA)	542	537	n/a	n/a	n/a	n/a
Long-term home health care cases	8,834	10,291	12,635	13,347	13,928	13,580
Total home care cases	65,755	66,595	66,282	66,675	64,059	65,745

Public Assistance and Related Services, 2001–2006 (continued)

	2001	2002	2003	2004	2005	2006
Number of cases, protective services for adults	3,492	4,238	5,075	5,575	6,132	5,607
Medicaid						
Medicaid enrollees	1,661,680	2,118,414	2,366,511	2,526,829	2,566,774	2,632,497
Medicaid users	1,414,360	1,809173	n/a	n/a	n/a	n/a
Medicaid only	667,280	1,023,401	1,539,226	1,702,284	1,782,231	1,807,613
SSI users	348,149	352,513	n/a	n/a	n/a	n/a
Managed care enrollees	479,232	927,052	1,265,522	1,408,649	1,485,428	1,499,307

[1] Cases converted to Safety Net Assistance because of five-year limit.
[2] Cyclic numbers only.

AFDC = Aid to Families with Dependent Children
DAS = Division of AIDS Services
FAP = Family Assistance Program
HASA = HIV and AIDS Services Administration
HR = Home Relief
SNA = Safety Net Assistance
SNNC = Safety Net Non-Cash
SSI = Social Security Income

Note: Figures are as of December of each year.
Source: New York City Human Resources Administration, Office of Program Reporting, Analysis and Accountability.

Public Assistance Recipients by Borough, January 2007

	Family Assistance Program (FAP)[1]		Safety Net Assistance		Five-Year Limit[2]	
	Persons	Cases	Persons	Cases	Persons	Cases
Manhattan	21,963	10,660	21,566	18,269	12,044	4,122
Bronx	62,260	27,371	40,077	26,985	35,901	11,431
Brooklyn	54,035	24,741	42,300	29,111	28,411	8,934
Queens	21,140	9,821	16,579	12,776	8,690	2,787
Staten Island	5,985	2,632	3,461	2,525	2,096	605
Other[3]	488	226	789	713	111	39
Total	165,871	75,451	124,772	90,379	87,253	27,918

[1] Formerly Aid to Families with Dependent Children (AFDC).
[2] Formerly Home Relief (HR).
[3] Nonresidents of New York City included.
Source: New York City Human Resources Administration, Office of Program Reporting, Analysis and Accountability.

Children's Services, Fiscal Years 2001–2006

	2001	2002	2003	2004	2005	2006
Protective Services						
Number of intakes	57,235	56,011	53,897	52,975	50,309	61,376
Number of consolidated investigations	57,224	55,925	53,894	51,477	47,021	57,145
Number of children in investigations	88,312	87,315	84,431	79,555	72,629	89,092
Reports to Office of Confidential Investigations						
Kinship foster care	461	382	333	264	226	268
Non-kinship foster care	1,220	1,103	1,007	963	868	952
Day care	295	282	272	261	235	305
Total	1,976	1,767	1,612	1,488	1,329	1,525
Foster Care						
Contract						
Congregate	4,172	4,137	4,134	3,894	3,473	2,951
Family foster care (FBH)	17,688	16,025	14,248	12,056	10,553	9,567
Kinship	5,384	5,351	5,212	4,763	4,032	3,724
Total contract	27,243	25,512	23,594	20,713	18,058	16,243
Direct						
Congregate	199	188	169	129	84	11
Family foster care (FBH)	712	554	365	252	190	121
Kinship	2,704	1,961	1,517	988	637	332
Total direct	3,615	2,703	2,051	1,369	910	464
Total						
Congregate	4,371	4,325	4,303	4,023	3,557	2,962
Family Foster Care (FBH)	18,399	16,579	14,614	12,308	10,743	9,688
Kinship	8,088	7,312	6,719	5,751	4,669	4,056
Grand total	30,858	28,215	25,636	22,082	18,968	16,706
Contract Agency Case Management						
Foster care cases	11,996	11,510	10,389	9,183	8,495	n/a
Number of children	21,807	19,980	17,081	14,650	13,392	n/a
Workers assigned	202	212	193	156	151	n/a
Average caseload	59.5	54.2	54.1	59.1	56.5	n/a
Preventive cases	7,422	8,684	9,161	9,741	9,465	n/a
Number of children	15,514	18,295	19,190	20,329	19,768	n/a
Workers assigned	42.7	47.3	45.8	40.0	63.0	n/a
Average caseload	174.0	183.8	201.0	251.1	150.3	n/a

Children's Services, Fiscal Years 2001–2006 (continued)

	2001	2002	2003	2004	2005	2006
Adoption Case Management						
Number of cases	4,379	4,268	4,354	4,252	3,671	n/a
Number of children	6,723	6,656	6,724	6,503	5,559	n/a
Workers assigned	71.0	74.0	71.2	57.3	59	n/a
Average caseload	61.9	57.8	61.3	74.2	62.2	n/a
Direct Foster Care Services (DFCS)						
Foster care children (kinship and non-kinship)	3,360	2,171	1,394	1,026	724	444
Workers assigned	178	114	92	60	53	28
Average caseload	18.9	19.0	15.2	17.1	13.6	16.7
Direct Care Adoption						
Foster care children	791	663	553	335	186	94
Workers assigned	48	36	31	20	15	11
Average caseload	16.6	18.5	17.9	16.5	12.5	9.0
Adoption						
Children with Adoption Goal						
Direct	2,054	1,425	937	571	360	191
Contract	9,616	9,292	8,987	8,168	7,188	6,029
Total	11,670	10,717	9,924	8,740	7,549	6,220
Children Freed						
Direct	666	487	479	306	208	109
Contract	3,570	3,707	3,716	3,304	2,874	2,696
Total	4,236	4,195	4,194	3,610	3,083	2,805
Total Children Adopted						
Direct	660	536	391	286	159	75
Contract	2,055	2,158	2,402	2,449	2,205	1,756
All	2,715	2,694	2,793	2,735	2,364	1,831
Purchased Preventive Services						
Total Cases						
Openings	10,773	12,624	12,983	12,525	11,965	10,671
Closings	9,682	11,224	12,256	12,806	10,949	9,225
Number of cases active	9,293	11,150	11,700	11,622	11,542	11,695
Cumulative cases	19,319	23,099	24,620	24,538	23,571	22,512
Pending cases	4,775	6,040	5,998	5,815	6,013	613

Children's Services, Fiscal Years 2001–2006 (continued)

	2001	2002	2003	2004	2005	2006
Total Children						
Total cases opened	26,382	30,704	29,800	28,610	27,392	22,047
Total active	23,855	28,596	29,592	29,509	28,781	27,304
Discharged from foster care	125	63	47	25	42	67
Placed in foster care	994	876	563	425	309	555
General Preventive Services						
Number of cases opened	7,500	8,059	8,235	7,502	7,416	6,299
Number referred by ACS	3,854	4,270	4,290	3,751	3,635	3,326
Percentage referred by ACS	51.4	52.8	52.2	50.2	49.1	52.3
Utilization rate	88.8	92.6	96.8	97.1	92.8	91.6
Pending cases	4,198	5,142	5,170	4,894	5,114	497
Family Rehabilitation Program						
Number of cases opened	660	893	813	815	789	823
Number of cases closed	543	715	761	844	781	624
Total active cases	679	901	1,009	1,004	971	957
Cumulative cases	1,308	1,701	1,809	1,840	1,769	n/a
Utilization rate	77.5	84.1	92.0	91.9	91.9	91.7
Pending cases	369	691	587	640	616	73
ACS Direct Preventive Services						
Opened cases	4,641	3,699	4,122	3,712	2,908	2,232
Active cases	3,541	3,207	3,051	2,795	2,379	2,081
Cumulative cases	8,086	7,214	7,072	6,679	5,603	n/a
Children placed	374	305	275	249	193	126
Court-Ordered Supervision						
Opened cases	4,371	3,431	2,922	2,773	2,424	3,177
Closed and transferred cases	4,222	4,189	3,022	2,901	2,634	2,345
Active cases	3,146	2,770	2,426	2,402	2,115	1,879
Average caseload (caseworkers, all boroughs)	15.3	13.6	11.1	11.1	10.2	n/a
Average caseload (caseworkers and supervisors, all boroughs)	14.5	12.8	10.6	10.6	9.7	n/a
Percentage of cases with two home visits	90.8	88.4	92.1	92.8	93.7	90.9

	2001	2002	2003	2004	2005	2006
Family Preservation Program						
New referrals (families)	1,296	1,302	1,446	1,213	1,374	1,296
Referrals accepted (opened cases)	882	873	1,044	952	1,110	1,033
Percentage of referrals accepted	68.1	67.1	72.2	78.5	80.8	79.7
Closed cases with complete intervention	700	663	779	794	786	747
Closed cases with incomplete intervention	154	162	380	166	256	312
Active families	178	173	210	201	224	245
Cumulative cases	1,070	1,058	1,210	1,157	1,325	1,279
Active children	566	527	623	579	637	711
Caseworkers available	108	113	132	118	91	89
Caseworkers assigned	132	140	163	150	132	125
Average caseload	2.3	2.1	2.3	2.4	3.4	3.7
Foster Care Housing Subsidy						
Opened cases	327	163	194	210	266	468
Closed cases	230	295	332	277	302	388
Active cases	593	569	415	304	260	295
Cumulative cases	862	795	694	572	561	727
Preventive Housing Subsidy						
Opened cases	302	239	357	377	595	978
Closed cases	171	222	318	387	510	678
Active cases	535	589	629	636	685	899
Cumulative cases	756	824	959	1,018	1,226	1,694
Combined Housing Subsidy						
Opened cases	629	402	537	587	861	1,446
Closed cases	401	517	619	664	812	1,066
Active cases	1,128	1,159	1,046	939	945	1,194
Cumulative cases	1,618	1,619	1,653	1,590	1,787	2,421
Homemaking						
Opened cases	559	510	314	320	343	353
Closed cases	284	254	326	168	184	125
Active cases	1,154	1,135	1,111	963	936	939
Cumulative cases	1,694	1,632	1,455	1,346	1,306	1,294

Children's Services, Fiscal Years 2001–2006 (continued)

	2001	2002	2003	2004	2005	2006
TASA Long-Term Cases						
Opened cases	1,461	1,519	1,390	1,371	1,163	1,109
Closed cases	1,096	1,202	1,033	980	1,286	1,245
Active cases	1,572	1,639	1,632	1,611	1,533	1,236
Average caseload	33	35	35	33	34	33
Cumulative cases	2,910	3,128	3,013	2,927	2,823	2,525
Child Care						
Group Child Care						
Contract	n/a	34,772	34,208	33,439	31,898	29,470
Voucher	n/a	12,404	11,525	10,580	9,956	10,607
All group child care	n/a	47,176	45,733	44,019	41,853	40,077
Family child care						
Contract	n/a	7,992	7,836	8,407	9,032	9,507
Voucher	n/a	2,541	2,529	2,539	2,618	2,848
All family child care	n/a	10,623	10,364	10,946	11,650	12,355
Informal care (voucher)	n/a	2,952	3,654	4,727	5,587	6,720
Total child care enrollment	n/a	60,751	59,751	59,693	59,090	59,152
Head Start						
Regular enrollment	14,494	14,637	14,658	14,884	16,513	15,724
Collaborative enrollment	1,820	1,833	1,714	1,750	2,333	2,465
Total enrollment	16,315	16,470	16,373	16,633	18,846	19,543
Preplacement Services						
Total PPS child care days	11,334	14,854	13,559	11,536	9,031	19,388
Number of child care days that are overnight	5,289	6,909	5,659	5,301	4,654	10,557
Percentage of child care days that are overnight	46.2	46.6	41.8	45.0	46.8	56.2
Percentage of overnight child care days by teens	69.4	67.3	66.7	68.3	73.1	63.2
Percentage of overnight child care days by PINS	20.9	20.1	24.9	21.6	26.5	15.4

ACS = Administration for Children's Services
FBH = Foster Boarding Home program
PINS = Persons in Need of Service
PPS = Preplacement Services
TASA = Teen Age Services Act
Note: Figures as in original report. Some totals differ slightly from sum of individual items.
Source: New York City Administration for Children's Services.

Number of Homeless Persons and Families, 1980–2005

	Single Men	Single Women	Families	Children	Total Persons Served by Department of Homeless Services
1980	2,026	129	n/a	n/a	n/a
1981	2,584	219	n/a	n/a	n/a
1982	3,382	404	1,005	2,507	7,584
1983	4,440	621	1,960	4,887	12,468
1984	5,447	781	2,981	7,432	17,491
1985	6,335	881	3,688	9,196	21,154
1986	7,888	1,002	4,286	10,493	24,896
1987	8,490	1,138	4,986	11,163	27,225
1988	8,411	1,264	5,091	11,401	27,646
1989	7,994	1,348	4,105	8,614	23,254
1990	7,192	1,342	3,591	6,966	20,131
1991	6,434	1,255	4,581	8,867	22,498
1992	5,713	1,209	5,270	9,607	23,494
1993	5,313	1,100	5,626	9,760	23,748
1994	5,131	1,104	5,629	9,610	23,431
1995	5,344	1,189	5,627	9,927	23,950
1996	5,755	1,266	5,692	9,945	24,554
1997	5,762	1,329	4,793	8,437	22,145
1998	5,477	1,398	4,558	8,054	21,277
1999	5,297	1,481	4,965	8,826	22,575
2000	5,361	1,573	5,192	9,290	23,712
2001	5,770	1,709	6,154	11,427	27,799
2002	5,945	1,806	8,071	14,952	34,576
2003	6,275	1,924	9,203	16,705	38,310
2004	6,569	2,043	8,922	15,705	37,319
2005	6,218	1,956	8,194	13,534	33,687

Source: New York City Department of Homeless Services.

14 Memorials and Monuments

Victims of the World Trade Center Attacks by Ethnicity, Residence, and Employer

Ethnicity		Ethnicity (continued)	
Non-Hispanic white	75.9%	Asian and Pacific Islander	6.4%
Hispanic	9.4%	Other	0.4%
Non-Hispanic Black	7.9%	Total	100.0%

Residence	Number	Percent	Residence	Number	Percent
Manhattan	330	12.6	Maryland	3	0.1
Bronx	89	3.4	Virginia	3	0.1
Brooklyn	283	10.8	Florida	2	0.1
Queens	242	9.2	Texas	2	0.1
Staten Island	183	7.0	Arizona	1	*
Other New York State	560	21.4	Colorado	1	*
New Jersey	662	25.3	Indiana	1	*
Massachusetts	81	3.1	Louisiana	1	*
Connecticut	61	2.3	Michigan	1	*
California	27	1.0	Missouri	1	*
Pennsylvania	27	1.0	New Mexico	1	*
New Hampshire	8	0.3	Ohio	1	*
Illinois	7	0.3	Tennessee	1	*
Rhode Island	5	0.2	Utah	1	*
Georgia	4	0.2	Foreign countries	25	1.0
Maine	3	0.1	Total	2,617	100.0

* = less than 0.05 percent.

Employer	Number	Percent	Employer	Number	Percent
Cantor Fitzgerald	658	25.1	Windows on the World	73	2.8
New York Fire Department	343	13.1	Carr Futures	69	2.6
Marsh & McLennan	295	11.3	Keefe, Bruyette & Woods	67	2.6
Aon	176	6.7	Sandler O'Neill and Partners	66	2.5
Fiduciary Trust International	87	3.3	New York Police Department	23	0.9
Port Authority of New York and			Other	685	26.2
New Jersey	75	2.9	Total	2,617	100.0

Note: Figures based on death certificates filed by 25 January 2002, including those for passengers on the airplanes, and represent more than 90 percent of all deaths.
Sources: New York City Department of Health; New York City Office of the Chief Medical Examiner.

107th Infantry Memorial, Perimeter Wall, Fifth Avenue and 67th Street (1926–1927, placed in park 1927)
Sculptor: Karl Illava (1896–1954)
Donated by 7th-107th Memorial Committee
Material: bronze

Alice in Wonderland, East 74th Street, north of Conservatory Water (1959)
Sculptor: José de Creeft
Architect: Hideo Sasaki
Donated by George Delacorte
Material: bronze

Angel of the Waters Fountain, mid-park on the north side of 72nd Street (1868, placed in park 1873)
Sculptor: Emma Stebbins (1815–1882)
Donated by the City of New York
Material: bronze figures, bluestone lower basin

Balto, East Drive at 67th Street (1925)
Sculptor: Frederick George Richard Roth (1872–1944)
Donated by Balto Monument Committee to the City of New York
Material: bronze statue with slate tablet over natural rock

Burnett Memorial Fountain, Conservatory Garden, south garden, 104th Street and Fifth Avenue; main entrance at 105th Street and Fifth Avenue (1926–1936, placed in park 1936)
Sculptor: Bessie Potter Vonnoh (1872–1955)
Donated by the Children's Garden Building Committee
Material: bronze

Christopher Columbus, southern end of the Mall, East Drive at 66th Street (1892, placed in park 1894)
Sculptor: Jeronimo Sunol (1839–1902)
Donated by New Yorkers under the auspices of the New York Genealogical Society
Material: bronze

Eagles and Prey, west of the Concert Ground, mid-park at 69th Street (1850, placed in park 1863)
Sculptor: Christopher Fratin (1800–1864)
Donated by Gordon Webster Burnham
Material: bronze with granite pedestal

Fitz-Greene Halleck, Literary Walk / The Mall, East Side at 66th Street (1876, placed in park 1877)
Sculptor: James Wilson Alexander MacDonald (1824–1908)
Gift by public subscription
Material: bronze

Hans Christian Andersen, west of Conservatory Water, 74th Street near Fifth Avenue (1956)
Sculptor: Georg John Lober
Donated by Danish-American Women's Association, Danish and American schoolchildren
Material: bronze on granite bench

Indian Hunter, pathway west of the Mall, east of the Sheep Meadow at 66th Street (1866, placed in park 1869)
Sculptor: John Quincy Adams Ward (1830–1910)
Donated by twenty-three American artists and art patrons
Material: bronze with granite pedestal

Johann Christoph Friedrich von Schiller, west side of the Concert Ground / Mall, mid-park at 72nd Street (1859, placed in park 1859)
Sculptor: C. L. Richter
Donated by German-Americans
Material: bronze

José Martí, Artists' Gate, entrance to the Park at 59th Street and Avenue of the Americas (1959, placed in park 1965)
Sculptor: Anna Vaughn Hyatt Huntington (1876–1959)
Donated by the artist to the Cuban government for presentation to the people of New York City
Material: bronze

King Jagiello, east side of Turtle Pond, mid-park at 79th Street (1939, placed in park 1945)
Sculptor: Stanislaw Kazimierz Ostrowski (1879–1947)
Donated by the King Jagiello Monument Committee
Material: bronze

Lehman Gates, at the entrance to the Tisch Children's Zoo, inside the Park at Fifth Avenue at 66th Street (1960–1961, placed in park 1961)
Sculptor: Paul Manship (1885–1966)
Donated by Governor and Mrs. Herbert H. Lehman
Material: bronze on a granite pedestal

Ludwig van Beethoven, west side of the Concert Ground / The Mall, mid-park at 70th Street (1884, placed in park 1884)
Sculptor: Henry Bearer (1837–1908)
Donated by the Beethoven Männerchor
Material: bronze

Maine Monument, Merchants' Gate, West 59th Street at Columbus Circle (1901–1913, placed in park 1913)
Sculptor: Attilio Picarelli (1866–1945)
Donated by the National Maine Monument Fund Committee
Material: marble, gilded bronze

Mother Goose, East 71st Street near Rumsey Playfield (1938, placed in park 1938)
Sculptor: Frederick George Richard Roth (1872–1944)
Donated by the City of New York
Material: granite

Obelisk, East Side at 81st Street (1500 BC, placed in park 1881)
Sculptor: Ancient Egyptian
Donor: Khedive of Egypt
Material: granite

Pulitzer Fountain, Grand Army Plaza at 59th Street and Fifth Avenue (1916, placed in park 1916)
Sculptor: Karl Bitter (1867–1915)
Donated by Joseph Pulitzer
Material: bronze statue, granite fountain

Sherman Monument, Grand Army Plaza, 60th Street and Fifth Avenue (1892–1903, placed in park 1903)
Sculptor: Augustus St. Gaudens (1848–1907)
Donated by the citizens of New York under the auspices of the Chamber of Commerce of New York State
Material: gilded bronze, granite pedestal

Sir Walter Scott (1871, placed in park 1872) and Robert Burns (1880, placed in park 1880), Literary Walk / The Mall, east side at 65th Street
Scott:
Sculptor: Sir John Steell (1804–1891)
Donated by Scottish-Americans
Material: bronze
Burns:
Sculptor: Sir John Steell (1804–1891)
Donated by Scottish-Americans
Material: bronze

Sophie Irene Loeb Drinking Fountain, James Michael Levin Playground, Fifth Avenue at 77th Street (1936, placed in park 1936, moved to Levin Playground 1987)
Sculptor: Frederick George Richard Roth (1872–1944)
Donated by the City of New York
Material: reinforced concrete

Sculptures and Monuments of Central Park (continued)

Still Hunt, west side of East Drive, mid-park at 76th Street
(1881–1883, placed in park 1883)
Sculptor: Edward Kemeys (1843–1907)
Material: bronze

The Falconer, mid-park on south side of 72nd Street Drive
(1875, placed in park 1875)
Sculptor: George Blackall Simonds (1844–1929)
Donated by George Kemp
Material: bronze

Tigress and Cubs, inside the Central Park Wildlife
Conservation Center, 64th Street and Fifth Avenue
(1866, placed in park 1867)
Sculptor: Auguste Cain (1821–1894)
Donated by Samuel F. B. Morse and other citizens
Material: bronze

Source: Central Park Conservancy.

Untermyer Fountain, Conservatory Garden, North Garden
entrance inside the Park at 106th Street and Fifth
Avenue; main entrance at 105th Street and Fifth
Avenue (before 1910, placed in park 1947)
Sculptor: Walter Schott (1861–1938)
Donated by the children of Samuel and Minnie
Untermyer
Material: bronze with a limestone base

William Shakespeare, south end of the Mall, East 66th
Street (1870, placed in park 1872)
Sculptor: John Quincy Adams Ward (1830–1910)
Architect: Jacob Wrey Mould (pedestal)
Donated by the Shakespeare Tricentennial Committee
Material: bronze on granite pedestal

Gravesites of Celebrated Persons

Manhattan
Brick Presbyterian Church
    Osgood, Samuel (1748–1813), postmaster general
Cathedral of St. John the Divine
    Dunne, John Gregory (1932–2003), writer
    Joffrey, Robert (1930–1988), choreographer
    Moore, Paul, Jr. (1919–2003), bishop
Episcopal Church of the Heavenly Rest
    Swanson, Gloria (1899–1983), actress
Grant's Tomb
    Grant, Julia Dent (1826–1902), first lady
    Grant, Ulysses S. (1822–85), president of the United
      States
New York Marble Cemetery
    Allen, Stephen (1767–1852), mayor
    Buck, Gurdon (1807–1877), surgeon

New York Marble Cemetery (continued)
    Clark, Aaron (1787–1861), mayor
    Jackson, David Sherwood (1813–1872), congressman
    Lenox, James (1800–1880), philanthropist
    Potter, Edward Elmer (1823–1889), brigadier general
    Reed, Luman (1787–1836), merchant, philanthropist
    Tallmadge, James (1778–1853), congressman
    Taylor, Moses (1806–1882), businessman
    Varian, Isaac (1793–1864), mayor
    Weeks, Robert Doughty (1795–1854), businessman
    Willet, Marinus (1740–1830), mayor
    Wright, Benjamin (1770–1842), civil engineer
St. Bartholomew's Episcopal Church
    Gish, Lillian (1893–1993), actress
St. Frances Cabrini Shrine Chapel
    Cabrini, Frances Xavier (1850–1917), saint

Manhattan (continued)

St. Mark's in-the-Bowery

Fish, Nicholas (1758–1833), major

Hone, Philip (1780–1851), mayor

Stuyvesant, Peter (1592–1672), governor of New
Amsterdam

Tompkins, Daniel D. (1774–1825), vice president of
the United States

St. Patrick's Cathedral

Cooke, Terence (1921–1983), archbishop

McCloskey, John (1810–1885), cardinal

O'Connor, John (1920–2000), cardinal

Sheen, Fulton (1895–1979), archbishop

Spellman, Francis (1989–1967), archbishop

St. Paul's Chapel

Cooke, George Frederick (1756–1812), actor

Emmet, Thomas Addis (1764–1827), Irish patriot

Holt, John (1721–1784), newspaperman

Montgomery, Richard (1738–1775), major general

White, Campbell P. (1787–1859), congressman

Trinity Cemetery (Riverside Drive & 155th Street)

Astor, Caroline Webster (1830–1908), society figure

Astor, John Jacob (1822–1890), merchant

Audubon, John James (1785–1851), naturalist

Chanler, John Winthrop (1826–77), congressman

Chanler, William Astor (1867–1934), congressman

Darling, William Augustus (1817–1895),
congressman

Dickens, Alfred D'Orsay Tennyson (1845–1912),
lecturer, son of Charles Dickens

Dix, John Adams (1798–1879), senator, governor,
secretary of the treasury

Ellison, Ralph Waldo (1913–1994), writer

Hall, A. Oakey (1826–1898), mayor

Jumel, Eliza Brown (1775–1865), heiress, wife of
Aaron Burr

Moore, Clement Clarke (1779–1836), writer

Monroe, James (1799–1870), congressman, nephew
of President James Monroe

Trinity Cemetery (continued)

Orbach, Jerry (1935–2004), actor

Seabury, Samuel (1873–1958), judge

Wood, Fernando (1812–1881), mayor

Trinity Churchyard (Wall Street)

Alsop, John (1724–1794), member of Continental
Congress

Astor, John Jacob (1763–1848), merchant

Bradford, William (1660–1752), printer

Cresap, Michael (1742–1775), colonel

Fellows, John R. (1832–1896), congressman

Fulton, Robert (1765–1815), inventor

Gallatin, Albert (1761–1849), secretary of the
treasury

Gates, Horatio (1726–1806), major general

Hamilton, Alexander (1755–1804), secretary of the
treasury

Hobart, John Sloss (1738–1805), senator

Hogan, William (1792–1874), congressman

Lawrence, James (1781–1813), naval officer

Lewis, Francis (1713–1802), signer of the Declaration
of Independence

Livingston, Walter (1740–1797), member of the
Continental Congress

Martin, Luther (1744–1826), member of the
Continental Congress

Morgan, John Jordan (1770–1849), congressman

Oakley, Thomas Jefferson (1783–1857), congressman

Scott, John Morin (1730–1784), member of the
Continental Congress

Shea, William (1907–1991), lawyer

Strong, George Templeton (1820–1875), diarist

Talbot, Silas (1750–1813), naval officer

Watts, John (1749–1836), congressman

Wharton, Franklin (1767–1818), lieutenant colonel

Williamson, Hugh (1735–1802), congressman,
signer of the Constitution

Zenger, John Peter (1697–1746), newspaper
publisher

Bronx

St. Anne's Episcopal Churchyard

Morris, Gouverneur (1752–1816), signer of the
Constitution

Morris, Lewis (1726–1798), signer of the Declaration
of Independence

St. Raymond's Cemetery

Allen, Henry "Red" (1908–1967), trumpeter

Coll, Vincent "Mad Dog" (1900–1932), organized-
crime figure

Duffy, Francis P. (1871–1932), chaplain

Holiday, Billie (1915–1959), singer

Lymon, Frankie (1942–1968), singer

Mallon, Mary (1870–1938), typhoid carrier

Paret, Benny "Kid" (1937–1962), boxer

Ruiz, Hilton (1952–2006), pianist, composer

Woodlawn Cemetery

Allen, Vivian Beaumont (1885–1962), philanthropist

Archipenko, Alexander (1887–1964), sculptor

Armour, H. D. (1837–1901), meatpacking executive

Armstrong, Edwin H. (1890–1954), inventor

Auchincloss, James C. (1885–1976), congressman

Bache, Jules (1861–1944), stockbroker

Bailey, James A. (1847–1906), showman

Belmont, Alva (1856–1933), society figure

Belmont, O. H. P. (1858–1908), horseman

Berlin, Irving (1888–1989), songwriter

Berlitz, Maximilian (1852–1921), language teacher

Bly, Nellie (1864–1922), journalist

Boldt, George C. (1851–1916), hotel executive

Borden, Gail, Jr. (1801–1874), businessman

Buckley, Charles W. (1835–1906), congressman

Bulova, Joseph (1851–1936), watchmaker

Bunche, Ralph (1904–1971), statesman

Busteed, Richard (1822–1898), brigadier general

Carey, Harry (1878–1947), actor

Castle, Irene (1893–1969), dancer

Castle, Vernon (1887–1918), dancer

Catt, Carrie Chapman (1859–1947), suffragist

Woodlawn Cemetery (continued)

Chapin, Alfred C. (1848–1936), mayor of Brooklyn

Clark, Horace F. (1815–1873), lawyer

Cohan, George M. (1878–1942), entertainer

Cruz, Celia (1925–2003), singer

Davis, Miles (1926–1991), trumpeter, composer

Day, Benjamin H. (1810–1889), newspaper publisher

Day, Clarence (1874–1935), writer

Deas, Zachariah (1819–1882), brigadier general

De Seversky, Alexander (1894–1974), aviator

Dodge, Charles Cleveland (1841–1910), brigadier
general

Dodge, William Earle (1805–1883), industrialist,
congressman

Durant, William C. (1861–1947), industrialist

Ederle, Gertrude (1905–2003), swimmer

Ehret, George (1836–1927), brewer

Ellington, Duke (1899–1974), composer, pianist

Farragut, David G. (1844–1916), admiral

Fitch, Clyde (1865–1909), playwright

Flagg, James Montgomery (1877–1960), artist

Fox, Richard K. (1846–1922), magazine publisher

Foy, Joe (1943–1989), baseball player

Frisch, Frankie (1898–1973), baseball player,
manager

Garvan, Francis P. (1875–1937), prosecutor

Gates, John W. "Bet-a-Million" (1855–1911),
industrialist, gambler

Gilpin, Charles (1878–1930), actor

Gould, Jay (1834–1892), financier

Graham, Charles Kinnaird (1824–1889), brigadier
general

Grinnell, George B. (1850–1938), ornithologist

Guggenheim, Simon (1867–1941), senator,
philanthropist

Hammerstein, Oscar (1845–1919), impresario

Hampton, Lionel (1908–2002), vibraphonist

Handy, W. C. (1873–1958), composer

Havemeyer, William (1804–1874), mayor

Gravesites of Celebrated Persons (continued)

Bronx (continued)

Woodlawn Cemetery (continued)

Hegeman, John R. (1844–1919), insurance executive

Henson, Matthew (1867–1955), explorer

Herbert, Victor (1859–1924), composer

Hughes, Charles Evans (1868–1948), governor, Chief
Justice

Huntington, Collis P. (1821–1900), industrialist

Hutton, Barbara (1912–1979), heiress

Hyatt, Anna (1876–1973), sculptor

Hyde, Henry B. (1834–1899), insurance executive

Jacquet, Illinois (1922–2004), saxophonist

Juilliard, Augustus D. (1836–1919), textile executive,
philanthropist

Kreisler, Fritz (1875–1962), violinist, composer

Kress, Samuel H. (1863–1955), retailer, art collector

La Guardia, Fiorello H. (1882–1947), mayor

Lamont, Daniel S. (1851–1905), secretary of war

Lee, Canada (1907–1952), actor

Leslie, Frank (1821–1880), newspaper publisher

Macy, Rowland H. (1822–1877), retailer

Marx, Louis (1896–1982), toymaker

Masterson, Bat (1837–1900), marshal

McAdoo, William Gibbs (1863–1941), secretary of
the treasury

McManus, George (1884–1954), cartoonist

Melville, Herman (1819–1891), writer

Merritt, Stephen (1834–1917), undertaker

Mills, Florence (1895–1927), singer, comedienne

Moore, John Bassett (1860–1947), jurist

Morton, Paul (1857–1911), secretary of the navy

Murphy, Johnny (1908–1970), baseball player

Nast, Thomas (1840–1902), cartoonist

Nicholas, Harold (1921–2000), tap dancer

Olcott, Chauncey (1860–1932), singer

Oliver, King (1885–1938), cornetist, bandleader

Penney, J. C. (1875–1971), retailer

Polk, William M. (1845–1918), gynecologist

Post, George B. (1837–1913), architect

Woodlawn Cemetery (continued)

Preminger, Otto (1905–1986), film director

Pulitzer, Joseph (1847–1911), newspaper publisher

Pupin, Michael I. (1858–1938), physicist

Reik, Theodor (1888–1969), psychologist

Reisinger, Hugo (1856–1914), art collector

Rice, Grantland (1880–1954), sportswriter

Richards, Vince (1903–1959), tennis player

Runyon, Damon (1884–1946), journalist

Seaman, Elizabeth Cochrane (1867–1922), journalist

Schaefer, Rudolph Jay (1863–1923), brewer

Sigel, Franz (1824–1902), major general

Snyder, Ruth Brown (1894–1928), murderess

Squier, E. G. (1821–1888), archeologist

Stanton, Elizabeth Cady (1815–1902), suffragist

Stella, Joseph (1877–1946), artist

Straus, Isidor (1845–1912), retailer

Strong, William L. (1827–1900), mayor

Taylor, Laurette (1884–1946), actress

Tilghman, Lloyd (1816–1863), brigadier general

Untermyer, Samuel (1858–1940), lawyer

Walker, Madam C. J. (1867–1919), businesswoman

Westinghouse, Henry H. (1853–1933), inventor

Whitney, William Collins (1841–1904), financier

Williams, Bert (1875–1922), minstrel

Woolworth, F. W. (1852–1919), retailer

Ziegler, William (1843–1905), industrialist

Zimmerman, Henry (1887–1969), baseball player

Brooklyn

Brooklyn Quaker Cemetery

Clift, Montgomery (1920–1964), actor

Cypress Hills Cemetery

Blake, Eubie (1887–1983), pianist, composer

Bliss, Archibald M. (1838–1922), congressman

Cardozo, Benjamin N. (1870–1938), Supreme Court
justice

Collyer, Homer (1883–1947), recluse, collector

Collyer, Langley (1886–1947), recluse, collector

Brooklyn (continued)

Cypress Hills Cemetery (continued)

Corbett, Jim (1866–1933), boxer

Duck, Mock (1879–1941), gang leader

Eastman, Monk (1873–1920), gang leader

Falk, Lee (1911–1999), cartoonist

Ferguson, Robert (1845–1994), baseball player, manager

Lee, Will (1908–1982), actor

Mondrian, Piet (1872–1944), painter

Robinson, Jackie (1919–1972), baseball player

Tucker, Richard (1914–75), singer

West, Mae (1893–1980), actress

The Evergreens Cemetery

Baker, Robert (1862–1943), congressman

Bennett, Charles Goodwin (1863–1914), congressman

Bunny, John (1863–1915), actor

Comstock, Anthony (1844–1915), reformer

Dahlen, Bill (1870–1950), baseball player

Dodge, Stephen Augustus (1822–1917), colonel

Dunwell, Charles Tappan (1852–1908), congressman

Eggleston, George Cary (1839–1911), writer

Guy, Francis (1760–1820), painter

Hall, Adelaide (1901–1993), entertainer

Hall, George (1849–1923), baseball player

Hawkins, Yusuf (1973–1989), murder victim

Heade, Martin Johnson (1819–1904), painter

Heath, Thomas K. (1853–1938), entertainer

Hegamin, Lucille (1894–1970), singer

Hickey, Bill (1928–1997), actor

Kelly, Walt (1913–1973), cartoonist

Lindsay, George H. (1837–1916), congressman

Lindsay, George W. (1865–1938), congressman

McKay, Winsor (1872–1934), cartoonist

Pastor, Tony (1837–1908), theater producer

Robinson, Bill "Bojangles" (1878–1949), dancer

Rooney, Pat (1880–1962), dancer

Rudd, Stephen Andrew (1874–1936), congressman

The Evergreens Cemetery (continued)

Schenk, Joseph (1891–1930), entertainer

Steinitz, William (1836–1900), chess player

Thiele, Bob (1922–1996), record producer

Thursby, Emma (1845–1931), singer

Vanderbilt, Amy (1908–1974), writer

Weber, Max von (1824–1901), brigadier general

Wiggins, Blind Tom (1849–1908), pianist, composer

Willett, William Forte, Jr. (1869–1938), congressman

Young, Lester (1909–1959), saxophonist

Flatlands Dutch Reformed Church Cemetery

Vanderveer, Abraham (1781–1839), congressman

Green-Wood Cemetery

Abbett, Leon (1836–1894), governor of New Jersey

Adams, James Truslow (1878–1949), historian

Adams, John Joseph (1848–1919), congressman

Anastasia, Albert (1903–1957), organized-crime figure

Aspinwall, William Henry (1807–1875), businessman

Atterbury, Grosvenor (1869–1956), architect

Barnes, Demas (1827–1888), congressman

Bartlett, Franklin (1847–1909), congressman

Basquiat, Jean-Michel (1960–1988), painter

Beach, Lewis (1835–1886), congressman

Bean, Curtis Coe (1828–1904), senator

Beecher, Henry Ward (1813–1887), minister

Bellows, George (1882–1925), painter

Benjamin, Park (1809–1864), poet

Bennett, James Gordon (1795–1872), newspaper publisher

Bergen, Teunis Garrett (1806–1881), congressman

Bergh, Henry (1811–1888), philanthropist

Bernstein, Leonard (1918–1990), conductor, composer

Blatchford, Samuel (1820–1893), Supreme Court justice

Boerum, Simon (1724–1775), member of the Continental Congress

Bogardus, James (1800–1874), architect

Gravesites of Celebrated Persons (continued)

Brooklyn (continued)

Green-Wood Cemetery (continued)

Bokee, David Alexander (1805–1860), congressman

Boody, David (1837–1930), mayor of Brooklyn

Bradstreet, John M. (1815–1863), businessman

Briggs, George (1905–1969), congressman

Bristow, Henry (1840–1906), congressman

Brooks, James (1811–1873), congressman

Brown, James (1791–1877), financier

Bryce, Lloyd Stephens (1851–1917), congressman

Calder, William Musgrave (1869–1945), senator

Cambreleng, Churchill C. (1786–1862), congressman

Carter, Luther C. (1805–1875), congressman

Cary, Alice (1820–1871), poet

Cary, Phoebe (1824–1871), poet

Catlin, George (1796–1872), painter

Cavanaugh, James Michael (1823–1879), congressman

Chadwick, Henry (1824–1908), sportswriter

Chase, Lucien Bonaparte (1817–1864), congressman

Chase, William Merritt (1849–1916), painter

Child, Thomas, Jr. (1818–1869), congressman

Chittenden, Simeon Baldwin (1814–1889), congressman

Clark, Franklin (1801–1874), congressman

Clark, Lot (1788–1862), congressman

Clinton, DeWitt (1769–1828), mayor, governor

Colgate, William (1783–1857), industrialist, philanthropist

Conkling, Frederick Augustus (1816–1891), congressman

Coombs, William J. (1833–1922), congressman

Cooper, Edward (1824–1905), mayor

Cooper, Peter (1791–1883), inventor, philanthropist

Cox, Samuel Sullivan (1824–1889), congressman

Craven, Thomas Tingly (1873–1950), vice-admiral

Crawford, Thomas W. (1813–1857), sculptor

Creamer, Thomas James (1843–1914), congressman

Creighton, James (1841–1862), baseball player

Green-Wood Cemetery (continued)

Creighton, Johnston B. (1822–1883), rear admiral

Crooke, Philip Schuyler (1810–1881), congressman

Cullum, George Washington (1809–1892), brigadier general

Cumming, Thomas William (1814–1855), congressman

Currier, Nathaniel (1813–1888), lithographer

Cutting, Bronson (1888–1935), senator

Cutting, Francis Brockholst (1804–1870), congressman

Daly, Marcus (1841–1900), industrialist

Delafield, Richard (1793–1873), major general

Delaplaine, Isaac Classon (1817–1866), congressman

Dodworth, Harvey B. (1822–1891), bandmaster

Dorn, Francis Edwin (1911–1987), congressman

Dow, Charles Henry (1851–1902), financier

Durand, Asher B. (1796–1886), painter

Duryee, Abram (1815–1890), brigadier general, police commissioner

Dwight, Theodore (1764–1846), congressman

Ebb, Fred (1928–2004), lyricist

Ebbets, Charles (1859–1925), owner of Brooklyn Dodgers

Eickhoff, Anthony (1827–1901), congressman

Feltman, Charles (1841–1910), amusement park owner

Ferrero, Edward (1831–1899), brigadier general

Finlayson, Pembroke (1888–1912), baseball player

Fleming, William Maybury (1817–1866), actor, colonel

Forbes, Edwin Austin (1839–1895), artist

Fox, Kate (1836–1892), spiritualist

Fox, Leah (1814–1890), spiritualist

Fox, Margaretta (1833–1893), spiritualist

Francis, George Blinn (1883–1967), congressman

Frazee, John (1790–1852), architect

Gallo, Joey (1929–1972), organized-crime figure

Brooklyn (continued)
Green-Wood Cemetery (continued)

Garnett, Robert Selden (1819–1861), brigadier general

Garrison, Cornelius Kingsland (1809–1885), mayor of San Francisco

Gaynor, William J. (1851–1913), mayor

George, Dudley S. (1800–1874), congressman

George, Henry (1839–1897), economist

George, Henry, Jr. (1862–1916), congressman

Gerard, James Watson, III (1867–1951), diplomat

Gottschalk, Louis Moreau (1829–1869), composer, pianist

Graham, John Hugh (1835–1895), congressman

Greeley, Horace (1811–1872), newspaper editor

Green, Robert S. (1831–1895), governor of New Jersey

Harris, Townsend (1804–1878), ambassador

Halleck, Henry W. (1815–1872), major general

Hamilton, Schuyler (1822–1903), major general

Hanbury, Harry A. (1863–1940), congressman

Hardy, John (1835–1913), congressman

Harris, Nathaniel H. (1834–1900), brigadier general

Hart, James McDougal (1828–1901), painter

Hart, William S. (1870–1946), actor

Hastings, Thomas (1784–1872), hymnodist

Havemeyer, Henry O. (1847–1907), industrialist

Haws, John Henry Hobart (1809–1858), congressman

Henderson, John Brooks (1826–1913), senator

Hendrix, Joseph Clifford (1853–1904), congressman

Herrick, Anson (1812–1868), congressman

Hewitt, Abram S. (1822–1903), mayor

Hewitt, Peter Cooper (1861–1921), inventor

Hogan, Michael J. (1871–1940), congressman

Hopkins, Stephen Tyng (1849–1892), congressman

Horman, Charles E. (1942–1973), journalist

Howe, Elias (1819–1867), inventor

Howe, James R. (1839–1914), congressman

Green-Wood Cemetery (continued)

Humphrey, James (1811–1866), congressman

Hunt, Walter (1796–1859), inventor

Hunter, John W. (1807–1900), congressman

Huntington, Daniel (1816–1906), painter

Hyer, Thomas (1819–1864), boxer

Ives, James Merritt (1824–1895), lithographer

Jacobi, Abraham (1830–1919), pediatrician

Johnson, Eastman (1824–1906), painter

Johnson, Thomas L. (1854–1911), congressman, mayor of Cleveland

Johnston, John B. (1882–1960), congressman

Jones, Morgan (1830–1894), congressman

Kalbfleisch, Martin (1804–1873), congressman, mayor of Brooklyn

Kean, Hamilton Fish (1862–1941), senator

Keene, Laura (1826–1873), actress

Kiernan, James L. (1837–1869), brigadier general

King, Gamaliel (1795–1875), architect

Kirkwood, James P. (1807–1877), civil engineer

La Badie, Florence (1888–1917), actress

LaFarge, John (1835–1910), artist

Laidlaw, Harriet Burton (1873–1949), suffragist

Lawson, John D. (1816–1896), congressman

Lee, Warren Isbell (1874–1955), congressman

Lefferts, John (1785–1829), congressman

Lewis, Dixon Hall (1802–1848), senator

Livingston, Brockholst (1757–1823), Supreme Court justice

Livingston, John W. (1804–1885), rear admiral

Livingston, William (1723–1790), signer of the Constitution, governor of New Jersey

Lorillard, Pierre (1833–1901), tobacconist

Low, Seth (1850–1916), mayor

Lyon, Caleb (1822–1875), congressman

MacKay, John William (1831–1902), businessman

Maclay, William Brown (1812–1882), congressman

McAllister, Ward (1835–1895), society figure

McClellan, Robert (1806–1860), congressman

Gravesites of Celebrated Persons (continued)

Brooklyn (continued)
Green-Wood Cemetery (continued)

McKeever, Isaac (1791–1856), commodore
McLeer, James (1839–1922), general
Miller, William S. (1793–1854), congressman
Milnor, James (1793–1844), congressman
Miner, Henry Clay (1842–1900), congressman
Mitchel, Ormsby MacKnight (1805–1862), major general
Mitchell, John Murray (1858–1905), congressman
Mitchill, Samuel Latham (1764–1831), congressman
Montez, Lola (1818–1861), dancer
Morgan, Frank (1890–1949), actor
Morse, Samuel F. B. (1791–1872), inventor, painter
Mott, Valentine (1785–1865), physician
Mould, Jacob Wrey (1825–1886), architect
Muller, Nicholas (1836–1917), congressman
Murphy, Charles (1870–1950), bicyclist
Murphy, Henry Cruse (1810–1882), mayor of Brooklyn, senator
Niblo, William (1798–1878), showman
Oakley, Violet (1874–1961), artist
Odell, Moses Fowler (1818–1866), congressman
Olcott, Jacob Van Vechten (1856–1940), congressman
Palmer, Phoebe (1807–1874), hymnodist
Parks, Gorham (1794–1877), congressman
Paulding, James Kirke (1778–1860), secretary of the navy
Persico, Alphonse (1929–1989), organized-crime figure
Pfizer, Charles (1791–1883), industrialist
Phelps, Anson Greene (1781–1853), philanthropist
Phyfe, Duncan (1768–1854), cabinetmaker
Pierson, Arthur T. (1837–1911), minister
Poole, Butcher Bill (1821–1855), gang leader
Porter, Fitz John (1822–1901), major general
Porter, James (1787–1839), congressman
Potter, Orlando Bronson (1823–1894), congressman

Green-Wood Cemetery (continued)

Raymond, Henry J. (1820–1869), newspaper publisher
Renwick, James (1818–1895), architect
Rice, Thomas D. (1806–1860), minstrel
Robinson, William Erigena (1814–1892), congressman
Roosevelt, James I. (1795–1875), congressman
Roosevelt, Robert Barnwell (1829–1906), congressman
Rowe, Frederick William (1863–1946), congressman
Sands, Joshua (1757–1835), congressman
Sands, Joshua R. (1795–1883), admiral
Sankey, Ira (1840–1908), hymnodist
Sarony, Napoleon (1821–1896), hymnodist
Schieren, Charles Adolph (1842–1915), mayor of Brooklyn
Schumaker, John Godfrey (1826–1905), congressman
Schwarz, F. A. O. (1836–1911), retailer
Scribner, Abner (1859–1932), book publisher
Seger, George Nicholas (1866–1941), congressman
Selden, Dudley (1797–1855), congressman
Singstad, Ole (1882–1969), civil engineer
Sloat, John Drake (1781–1867), rear admiral
Slocum, Henry Warner (1827–1894), major general
Smith, Cyrus P. (1800–1877), mayor of Brooklyn
Smith, John Hyatt (1824–1886), congressman
Sperry, Elmer A. (1860–1930), inventor
Spinola, Francis Baretto (1821–1891), general
Squibb, Edward R. (1819–1900), businessman
Stanton, William (1843–1927), general
Stebbins, Henry George (1811–1881), congressman
Steers, George (1820–1856), shipbuilder
Steinway, Henry Englehard (1797–1871), piano maker
Steinway, William (1835–1896), piano maker
Stevens, Ebenezer (1751–1823), major

Brooklyn (continued)

Green-Wood Cemetery (continued)

Steward, Susan Smith McKinney (1846–1918), physician

Stewart, David (1810–1891), industrialist

Stranahan, James Samuel Thomas (1808–1898), congressman

Stringham, Silas Horton (1797–1876), rear admiral

Strong, George Crockett (1832–1863), major general

Strong, William Kerley (1805–1867), brigadier general

Stryker, Francis (1811–1892), mayor of Brooklyn

Sweeney, Thomas William (1820–1892), brigadier general

Thompson, Joel (1760–1843), congressman

Tiffany, Charles Lewis (1812–1902), silversmith, jeweler

Tiffany, Louis Comfort (1848–1933), artist

Torrio, Johnny (1882–1957), organized-crime figure

Townsend, Dwight (1826–1899), congressman

Trippe, Juan T. (1900–1981), businessman

Tweed, William M. (1823–1878), political boss

Underwood, John (1857–1937), businessman

Upjohn, Richard (1802–1878), architect

Vosburgh, Abraham S. (1825–1861), colonel

Wakeman, Abram (1824–1889), congressman

Walke, Henry (1808–1886), rear admiral

Wall, William (1800–1872), congressman

Wallace, William C. (1856–1901), congressman

Walsh, Michael (1810–1859), congressman

Ward, Aaron (1851–1918), admiral

Webb, Eckford (1825–1893), shipbuilder

Webb, Isaac (1794–1840), shipbuilder

West, William H. "Billy" (1853–1902), minstrel

White, Stephen Van Cullen (1831–1913), congressman

Whitehouse, John Osborne (1817–1881), congressman

Whitney, Daniel D. (1818–1914), mayor of Brooklyn

Green-Wood Cemetery (continued)

Whitney, Stephen (1776–1860), businessman

Whitney, Thomas Richard (1807–1858), congressman

Williams, Barney (1824–1876), comedian

Williams, Gus (1848–1915), entertainer

Williams, Nelson Grosvenor (1823–1897), brigadier general

Willmott, Robert (1878–1934), captain

Wilson, Francis Henry (1944–1910), congressman

Winthrop, Grenville Lindall (1864–1943), art collector, philanthropist

Wood, John M. (1813–1864), congressman

Wright, Joseph Albert (1810–1867), senator

Wurster, Frederick (1850–1917), mayor of Brooklyn

Yerkes, Charles Tyson (1837–1905), financier

Young, Richard (1845–1935), congressman

Zabriskie, Abraham (1841–1864), colonel

Holy Cross Cemetery

Abbatemarco, Frank (1899–1959), organized-crime figure

Anastasio, Anthony (1906–1963), organized-crime figure

Brady, Diamond Jim (1856–1917), businessman

Burns, Lucy (1879–1966), reformer

Cahill, Marie (1874–1933), actress

Campbell, Felix (1829–1902), congressman

Capone, Louis (1896–1944), organized-crime figure

Cincotta, Antonino (1875–1915), organized-crime figure

Clancy, John Michael (1837–1903), congressman

Cleary, William Edward (1849–1932), congressman

Cullen, Thomas Henry (1868–1944), congressman

Delaney, John Joseph (1878–1948), congressman

Grace, William R. (1832–1904), industrialist, mayor

Griffin, Daniel Joseph (1880–1926), congressman

Harley, Bernard (1842–1886), congressman

Heffernan, James Joseph (1888–1967), congressman

Hodges, Gil (1924–1972), baseball player, manager

Gravesites of Celebrated Persons (continued)

Brooklyn (continued)

Holy Cross Cemetery (continued)

    Hurley, Dennis Michael (1843–1899), congressman

    Keeley, Patrick Charles (1816–1896), architect

    Kinsella, Thomas (1832–1884), congressman

    Kline, Ardolph L. (1858–1930), mayor, congressman

    Magner, Thomas Francis (1860–1945), congressman

    Mangano, Philip (1898–1951), organized-crime
        figure

    O'Brien, James Henry (1860–1924), congressman

    O'Malley, James Vincent (1878–1931), congressman

    O'Reilly, Daniel (1838–1911), congressman

    O'Toole, Donald Lawrence (1902–1964),
        congressman

    Reynolds, Quentin (1902–1965), journalist

    Rooney, John J. (1903–1975), congressman

    Somers, Andrew Lawrence (1895–1949),
        congressman

    Sutton, Willie (1901–1980), bank robber

    Yale, Angelo (1903–1965), organized-crime figure

    Yale, Frankie (1893–1928), organized-crime figure

Maimonides Cemetery

    Fields, Dorothy (1905–1974), lyricist

    Fisher, Israel F. (1858–1940), congressman

    Loew, Marcus (1870–1927), businessman

    Schenk, Joseph M. (1878–1961), businessman

Most Holy Trinity Cemetery

    Barry, Philip (1898–1949), playwright

Mount Hope Cemetery

    Beck, Jackson (1912–2004), voice actor

    Bernard, Sam (1823–1927), actor

Salem Fields

    Guggenheim, Harry F. (1890–1971), newspaperman

    Guggenheim, Meyer (1828–1905), industrialist

    Guggenheim, Peggy (1898–1979), art collector

    Guggenheim, Solomon R. (1861–1949), art collector

    Lewisohn, Adolph (1849–1938), financier

    Pike, Lipman (1845–1893), baseball player

    Selwyn, Edgar (1875–1944), playwright, producer

Washington Cemetery (continued)

    Shubert, Jacob (1878–1963), theater producer

    Shubert, Levi (1875–1953), theater producer

    Shubert, Samuel S. (1877–1905), theater producer

    Siegel, Isaac (1880–1947), congressman

    Warburg, Felix (1871–1937), financier,
        philanthropist

Washington Cemetery

    Axler, Abe (1901–1933), organized-crime figure

    Bernard, Barney (1877–1924), actor

    Fletcher, Eddie (1898–1933), gang leader

    Sterner, Jerry (1938–2001), playwright

    Tashman, Lilyan (1899–1934), actress

    Zelig, Jack (1888–1912), gang leader

Queens

Bayside Cemetery

    Valk, Lester D. (1884–1962), congressman

Beth El Cemetery

    Erlanger, Abraham (1860–1930), theater producer

    Robinson, Edward G. (1893–1973), actor

    Spiegel, Sam (1901–1985), film producer

    Straus, Oscar Solomon (1850–1926), secretary of
        commerce, diplomat

Beth Olom Cemetery

    Einstein, Edwin (1842–1905), congressman

    Lasker, Emanuel (1868–1941), chess player

    Lazarus, Emma (1849–1887), poet

    Levy, Uriah Phillips (1792–1862), commodore

    Magnes, Judah L. (1877–1948), religious leader

Calvary Cemetery

    Barr, Thomas Jefferson (1812–1881), congressman

    Bonventre, Vito (1875–1930), organized-crime
        figure

    Boylan, John J. (1878–1938), congressman

    Campbell, Timothy J. (1840–1904), congressman

    Carfano, Anthony (1898–1959), organized-crime
        figure

    Carley, Patrick J. (1866–1936), congressman

Queens (continued)
Calvary Cemetery (continued)
Carroll, Nancy (1903–1965), actress
Conry, Michael F. (1870–1917), congressman
Corcoran, Michael (1827–1863), brigadier general
Curto, Gandolfo (1890–1929), organized-crime figure
Delaney, James J. (1901–1987), congressman
De Sapio, Carmine (1908–2004), political boss
Dooling, Peter J. (1857–1931), congressman
Dowdney, Abraham (1841–1886), congressman
Dunphy, Edward J. (1856–1926), congressman
Evans, Marcellus H. (1884–1953), congressman
Evola, Natale (1907–1973), organized-crime figure
Farley, Michael F. (1863–1921), congressman
Ferrigno, Stefano (1900–1930), organized-crime figure
Fitzgerald, Frank T. (1857–1907), congressman
Flynn, Joseph V. (1883–1940), congressman
Fox, John (1835–1914), congressman
Gardella, Tess (1897–1950), actress
Gilmore, Patrick S. (1829–1892), bandmaster
Guinan, Texas (1884–1933), nightclub hostess
Harron, Bobby (1893–1920), actor
Herron, Francis Jay (1837–1902), major general
Higgins, Eugene (1874–1958), artist
Keeler, Wee Willie (1872–1923), baseball player
Kelly, Patsy (1910–1981), actress
Kennedy, Martin J. (1892–1955), congressman
Luchese, Thomas "Three-Finger Brown" (1903–1967), organized-crime figure
Lupo, Ignatius (1877–1947), organized-crime figure
Mahoney, Peter P. (1848–1889), congressman
Manton, Thomas J. (1932–2006), congressman
Marvin, Arthur (1857–1911), cinematographer
Masseria, Joseph (1879–1931), organized-crime figure
McCarthy, John H. (1850–1908), congressman
McKay, Claude (1889–1948), poet

Calvary Cemetery (continued)
McKiniry, Richard F. (1878–1950), congressman
Morello, Giuseppe (1870–1930), organized-crime figure
Murray, James (1901–1936), actor
Naldi, Nita (1897–1961), actress
O'Brien, James (1841–1907), congressman
O'Connell, Arthur (1908–1981), actor
O'Connor, Una (1880–1959), actress
O'Gorman, James A. (1860–1943), senator
Oliver, Daniel C. (1865–1924), congressman
Oliver, Frank (1883–1968), congressman
Petrosino, Joseph (1860–1909), detective
Pinzolo, Bonaventure (1887–1930), organized-crime figure
Quinn, John (1839–1903), congressman
Rider, Ira E. (1868–1906), congressman
Riordan, Daniel J. (1870–1923), congressman
Roberts, William R. (1830–1897), congressman
Ruggiero, Benjamino (1926–1994), organized-crime figure
Ryan, Thomas Jefferson (1890–1968), congressman
Santangelo, Alfred E. (1912–1978), congressman
Scammon, Eliakim Parker (1816–1894), general
Scoini, Joseph (1904–1925), boxer
Shaw, Wini (1901–1982), actress
Sheridan, Martin J. (1881–1918), track and field athlete
Smith, Alfred E. (1873–1944), governor
Smith, Thomas F. (1865–1923), congressman
Sullivan, Christopher D. (1870–1942), congressman
Sullivan, Timothy D. (1862–1913), congressman
Terranova, Ciro (1889–1938), organized-crime figure
Vaccarelli, Paul (1876–1936), organized-crime figure
Wagner, Robert F. (1877–1953), senator
Wagner, Robert F., Jr. (1910–1991), mayor
Walsh, James J. (1858–1909), congressman
Welch, Michael (1859–1941), baseball player

Gravesites of Celebrated Persons (continued)

Queens (continued)
Calvary Cemetery (continued)
Whalen, Grover A. (1886–1962), government
official, police commissioner
Wheeler, Bert (1895–1968), comedian
Wood, Benjamin (1820–1900), congressman
Cedar Grove Cemetery
Bitzer, G. W. (1872–1944), cinematographer
Colden Family Cemetery
Colden, Cadwallader D. (1769–1834), mayor,
congressman
Federation of French War Veterans Cemetery
Bullard, Eugene Jacques (1894–1961), combat pilot
Flushing Cemetery
Armstrong, Louis (1898–1971), trumpeter, singer
Baruch, Bernard (1870–1965), financier
Bozyk, Max (1899–1970), actor
Butler, Ellis Parker (1869–1937), writer
Fairchild, Elias (1825–1907), educator
Gillespie, Dizzy (1917–1993), trumpeter
Jackson, Thomas Birdsall (1797–1881), congressman
Lawrence, John W. (1800–1888), congressman
Ostriche, Muriel (1896–1989), actress
Powell, Adam Clayton, Sr. (1865–1953), minister
Quigg, Lemuel E. (1863–1919), congressman
Robson, May (1858–1942), actress
Sardi, Vincent (1885–1969), restaurateur
Scofield, Cyrus I. (1843–1921), theologian, editor
Scott, Hazel (1920–1981), pianist
Storm, Frederic (1844–1935), congressman
Studley, Elmer E. (1869–1942), congressman
Valk, William W. (1806–1879), congressman
Fresh Pond Crematory and Columbarium
Dale, Harry H. (1868–1935), congressman
Lardner, Ring (1885–1933), writer
Storey, Edith (1892–1967), actress
Grace Episcopal Churchyard
Duer, William (1747–1799), member of the
Continental Congress

Grace Episcopal Churchyard (continued)
King, James G. (1791–1853), congressman
King, John A. (1788–1867), governor of New York
King, Rufus (1755–1827), senator
King, Rufus (1814–1876), brigadier general
McCormick, Richard C. (1832–1901), congressman
Smith, Melancton (1744–1798), member of the
Continental Congress
Van Rensselaer, Henry Bell (1810–1864),
congressman
Ware, Nicholas (1769–1824), senator
Knollwood Park Cemetery
Berger, Phil (1942–2001), sportswriter
Linden Hill Jewish Cemetery
Javits, Jacob K. (1904–1986), senator
Linden Hill Methodist Cemetery
Belasco, David (1853–1931), playwright, producer
Bloomingdale, Joseph B. (1842–1904), retailer
Molnar, Ferenc (1878–1952), writer
Lutheran All Faiths Cemetery
Hopkins, Frank T. (1865–1951), horseman
Kissel, John (1869–1938), congressman
Kleinow, Red (1879–1929), baseball player
Reipschlager, Charlie (1854–1910), baseball player
Vehslage, John H. (1842–1904), congressman
Machpelah Cemetery
Hardeen, Theodore (1876–1945), magician
Houdini, Harry (1874–1926), magician
Maple Grove Cemetery
Baker, LaVern (1929–1997), singer
Bosch, Alfred H. (1908–2005), congressman
Branner, Martin (1888–1970), cartoonist
Cassidy, James H. (1869–1926), congressman
Marquis, Don (1878–1937), writer
Merritt, Theresa (1922–1998), actress
Rapper, Irving (1898–1999), film director
Montefiore Cemetery
Amberg, Joseph (1892–1935), organized-crime
figure

Queens (continued)

Montefiore Cemetery (continued)

Amberg, Louis (1897–1935), organized-crime figure

Davis, Al (1920–1945), boxer

Fine, Sidney A. (1903–1982), congressman

Granach, Alexander (1893–1945), actor

Halberstam, Aaron (1978–1994), murder victim

Newman, Barnett (1905–1970), artist

Schneerson, Menahem Mendel (1902–1994), religious leader

Shapiro, Joseph (1899–1947), organized-crime figure

Mount Carmel Cemetery

Abzug, Bella S. (1920–1998), congresswoman

Adler, Jacob (1855–1926), actor

Adler, Jay (1896–1978), actor

Adler, Luther (1903–1984), actor

Adler, Sarah (1898–1953), actress

Adler, Stella (1901–1992), actress, teacher

Barondess, Joseph (1863–1928), labor leader

Cahan, Abraham (1860–1951), newspaperman

Clurman, Harold (1901–1980), theater director, critic

Frank, Leo (1884–1915), murder victim

Leonard, Benny (1896–1947), boxer

London, Meyer (1871–1926), congressman, labor leader

Reles, Abraham "Kid Twist" (1907–1941), organized-crime figure

Sholom Aleichem (1859–1916), writer

Tobias, George (1901–1980), actor

Weinberg, George (1901–1939), organized-crime figure

Youngman, Henny (1906–1998), comedian

Mount Hebron Cemetery

Adler, Celia (1891–1979), actress

Bernie, Ben (1891–1943), entertainer

Bozyk, Reizl (1914–1993), actress

Buchhalter, Lepke (1897–1944), organized-crime figure

Mount Hebron Cemetery (continued)

Burstein, Lillian (1918–2005), actress

Burstein, Paul (1896–1986), actor

Dovlatov, Sergei (1941–1990), writer

Eisenstaedt, Alfred (1898–1995), photographer

Fields, Shep (1910–1981), bandleader

Gilbert, Jacob H. (1920–1981), congressman

Gilford, Jack (1907–1990), actor

Gordon, Waxey (1888–1952), bootlegger

Kalich, Bertha (1874–1939), actress

Kalich, Yankel (1891–1975), actor

Kaminska, Ida (1899–1980), actress

Kerzner, Louis (1904–1939), organized-crime figure

Kessler, Morris (1912–1935), organized-crime figure

King, Alan (1927–2004), entertainer

Landau, Abraham (1895–1935), organized-crime figure

Lebow, Fred (1932–1994), race director

Moisseiff, Leon (1872–1943), architect

Perlman, Nathan D. (1887–1952), congressman

Picon, Molly (1898–1992), actress

Schechter, Solomon (1847–1915), religious leader

Schwartz, Julius (1915–2004), editor

Schwartz, Maurice (1890–1960), actor

Sirovich, William I. (1882–1939), congressman

Thomashevsky, Boris (1868–1939), actor

Weiss, Emanuel (1906–1944), organized-crime figure

Mount Judah Cemetery

Baker, Belle (1893–1957), actress, singer

Brenner, Victor D. (1871–1924), sculptor

Goodman, Andrew (1943–1964), civil rights worker

Kohlmar, Lee (1873–1946), actor

Orgen, Jacob (1894–1927), organized-crime figure

Mount Lebanon Cemetery

Halpern, Seymour (1913–1997), congressman

Hanff, Helene (1916–1997), writer

Tucker, Richard (1913–1975), singer

Gravesites of Celebrated Persons (continued)

Queens (continued)

Mount Neboh Cemetery
Celler, Emanuel (1888–1981), congressman
Cohen, William W. (1874–1940), congressman

Mount Olivet Cemetery
Canzoneri, Tony (1908–1959), boxer
Covert, James W. (1842–1910), congressman
Diamond, Jack "Legs" (1897–1931), organized-crime figure
Gordon, Glen (1914–1977), actor
MacCrate, John (1885–1976), congressman
Matchabelli, Georges (1885–1935), diplomat, businessman
Maurice, James (1814–1884), congressman
McCarthy, Clem (1882–1962), sportscaster
Moscona, Nicola (1907–1975), singer
Polk, Oscar (1900–1949), actor
Rubinstein, Helena (1870–1965), businesswoman
Smith, Thorne (1892–1934), writer

Mount St. Mary Cemetery
Barry, William B. (1902–1946), congressman
DiBono, Louis (1927–1990), organized-crime figure
Meredith, Matthew J. (1895–1946), congressman
Nolan, Jerry (1946–1992), musician
O'Leary, Denis (1873–1943), congressman
Roe, James A. (1896–1967), congressman
Thunders, Johnny (1952–1991), musician

Mount Zion Cemetery
Hart, Lorenz (1895–1943), lyricist
Drachman, Bernard (1861–1945), religious leader, writer
Edelstein, Morris M. (1888–1941), congressman
Gersten, Berta (1894–1972), actor
West, Nathanael (1903–1940), writer

Old Mount Carmel Cemetery
Levene, Sam (1905–1980), actor

Prospect Cemetery
Benson, Egbert (1746–1833), member of the Continental Congress

St. John Cemetery
Abbundando, Frank (1910–1942), organized-crime figure
Addabbo, Joseph P. (1925–1986), congressman
Anfuso, Victor L. (1905–1966), congressman
Ardolino, Emile (1943–1993), director, choreographer
Atlas, Charles (1892–1972), bodybuilder
Barton, James (1890–1962), actor
Biondo, Joseph (1900–1973), organized-crime figure
Brunner, William F. (1887–1965), congressman
Christi, Frank (1929–1982), actor
Clemente, Louis G. (1908–1968), congressman
Colombo, Joe (1923–1978), organized-crime figure
Costello, Frank (1891–1973), organized-crime figure
D'Aquila, Salvatore (1878–1928), organized-crime figure
Dellacroce, Neill (1914–1985), organized-crime figure
DeMeo, Roy Albert (1941–1983), organized-crime figure
Dioguardi, Johnny (1914–1979), organized-crime figure
Fitzgerald, John J. (1872–1952), congressman
Galante, Carmine (1910–1979), organized-crime figure
Gambino, Carlo (1902–1976), organized-crime figure
Genovese, Vito (1897–1969), organized-crime figure
Gotti, John (1940–2002), organized-crime figure
Johnson, Wilfred (1935–1988), organized-crime figure
Hylan, John F. (1868–1936), mayor
Joplin, Scott (1868–1917), composer
Lombardozzi, Carmine (1913–1992), organized-crime figure
Luciano, Salvatore "Lucky" (1897–1962), organized-crime figure
Maione, Harry (1908–1942), organized-crime figure

Queens (continued)

St. John Cemetery (continued)

Mapplethorpe, Robert (1946–1989), photographer

Maranzano, Salvatore (1886–1931), organized-crime figure

Napoli, James (1911–1992), organized-crime figure

O'Connell, David J. (1868–1930), congressman

Parrino, Rosario (1890–1930), organized-crime figure

Pfeifer, Joseph L. (1892–1974), congressman

Phillips, Flip (1915–2001), saxophonist

Profaci, Joseph (1898–1962), organized-crime figure

Quayle, John F. (1868–1930), congressman

Rastelli, Philip (1918–1991), organized-crime figure

Tieri, Frank (1904–1981), organized-crime figure

Vario, Paul (1914–1988), organized-crime figure

St. Michael's Cemetery

Costello, Frank (1891–1973), organized-crime figure

Gallo, Joseph (1912–1975), organized-crime figure

Pereyaslavec, Valentina (1907–1997), ballerina

Welsh, Ronnie (1940–1993), actor

Woods, Granville T. (1856–1910), inventor

Union Field Cemetery

Cohn, Roy M. (1927–1986), lawyer

Dickstein, Samuel (1885–1954), congressman

Frohman, Charles (1860–1915), theater producer

Frohman, Daniel (1853–1940), theater manager

Goldfogle, Henry M. (1856–1929), congressman

Lahr, Bert (1895–1967), actor

Lansing, Robert (1928–1994), actor

Rothstein, Arnold (1882–1928), gambler

Teller, Ludwig (1911–1965), congressman

Staten Island

Baron Hirsch Cemetery

Newhouse, Samuel I. (1895–1979), newspaper publisher

Papp, Joseph (1921–1991), theater producer

Zindel, Paul (1936–2003), playwright

Cemetery of the Resurrection

Armone, Joseph (1917–1992), organized-crime figure

Day, Dorothy (1897–1980), activist

Fountain Cemetery

Duffie, Alfred Napoleon Alexander (1835–1880), brigadier general

Frederick Douglass Memorial Park

Henderson, Rosa (1896–1968), singer

Moravian Cemetery

Barton, Samuel (1785–1858), congressman

Bilotti, Thomas (1940–1985), organized-crime figure

Castellano, Paul (1915–1985), organized-crime figure

DeCicco, Frank (1945–1986), organized-crime figure

Egbert, Joseph (1807–1888), congressman

Faber, Eberhard (1822–1879), businessman

Failla, James (1919–1999), organized-crime figure

Le Fevre, Frank Jacob (1874–1941), congressman

Metcalfe, Henry Bleecker (1805–1881), congressman

Mutrie, James J. (1851–1938), baseball manager

Prall, Anning S. (1870–1937), congressman

Vanderbilt, Cornelius (1794–1877), industrialist

Vanderbilt, Cornelius, II (1843–1899), financier

Vanderbilt, George Washington (1862–1914), businessman

Vanderbilt, William Henry (1821–1885), financier

Weed, Stephen H. (1831–1863), brigadier general

Ocean View Cemetery

May, Mitchell (1870–1961), congressman

Reformed Church on Staten Island Cemetery

Tyson, Jacob (1773–1848), congressman

St. Andrews Church Cemetery

Bowne, Obadiah (1822–1874), congressman

Crocheron, Henry (1772–1819), congressman

McVean, Charles (1802–1848), congressman

St. Peters Cemetery

Benziger, August (1867–1955), artist

Gravesites of Celebrated Persons (continued)

Staten Island (continued)

St. Peters Cemetery (continued)

    Jones, Patrick Henry (1830–1900), brigadier general

    Murphy, James J. (1898–1962), congressman

    O'Leary, James A. (1889–1944), congressman

Silver Mount Cemetery

    Duer, William (1805–1879), congressman

Sources: Judi Culbertson and Tom Randall, *Permanent New Yorkers: A Biographical Guide to the Cemeteries of New York* (Chelsea, Vt.: Chelsea Green, 1987); findagrave.com.